BUSINESS ISSUES, COMPETITION AND ENTREPRENEURSHIP

OPPORTUNITY, STRATEGY AND ENTREPRENEURSHIP: A META-THEORY

VOLUME 1:
THE NATURE OF OPPORTUNITY, TIME AND SPACE, THE VISION PLATFORM, AND MAKING CONNECTIONS

BUSINESS ISSUES, COMPETITION AND ENTREPRENEURSHIP

Additional books in this series can be found on Nova's website under the Series tab.

Additional E-books in this series can be found on Nova's website under the E-book tab.

BUSINESS ISSUES, COMPETITION AND ENTREPRENEURSHIP

OPPORTUNITY, STRATEGY AND ENTREPRENEURSHIP: A META-THEORY

VOLUME 1:
THE NATURE OF OPPORTUNITY, TIME AND SPACE, THE VISION PLATFORM, AND MAKING CONNECTIONS

MURRAY HUNTER

Nova Science Publishers, Inc.
New York

For permission to use material from this book please contact us:
Telephone 631-231-7269; Fax 631-231-8175
Web Site: http://www.novapublishers.com

NOTICE TO THE READER

Library of Congress Cataloging-in-Publication Data

ISSN: 2161-8186

ISBN: 978-1-61470-822-3

Published by Nova Science Publishers, Inc. † New York

To my father
Alan

CONTENTS

PREFACE

I am shocked by the number of businesses that fail because of not taking account of the facets of opportunity. So many firms have a strategy, but it is not aligned to any identified opportunity. Most strategies are developed *'on the run'* changing as time goes on according to what works and what doesn't work. Entrepreneurs follow the advice *out in the marketplace*, however very little of it concerns anything about understanding and pursuing the elements of opportunity.

Opportunity is the centre of entrepreneurship and explaining the discovery and construction of opportunities and their subsequent development is a key part of the discipline. This book is written on the premise that opportunity is the most important factor in any firm's success and that there are many ways a strategy can be configured and companies organized to exploit an opportunity successfully. This occurs in an environment where the locus of innovation is characterized by complex and ever expanding knowledge bases, surrounded by firms that are also learning how to respond to the environment. Numerous theories about entrepreneurship have been advanced in recent years, but very few about opportunity. This book is about what makes up an opportunity, how it is composed, how it can be constructed, and how the organization and strategy can be developed in line with the components of opportunity.

In many cases strategic planning has become a ritual, a narrative, an exercise primarily aimed at reducing confusion and uncertainty in organizations. Strategy is really a scheme of doing things towards an objective that one does not really have full control of; only the direction can be guided. The time available for people to reflect is less than ever. The dysfunctional way that many companies are operated with traditional management systems keeps many organizations in a perpetual *"fire fighting mode."* It is also a fallacy that profit is the only entrepreneurial objective and as a consequence the measurement of success is subjective. Success is a socially constructed paradigm dependent upon the values of those that look at the venture.

The majority of companies are opportunistic rather than opportunity seeking. They are eager and ready to jump in with *'me-too'* products to take advantage of a developing market. Many firms are like their owners and managers where instant self gratification is sort after. Large companies tend to grow divisionally, however this growth is not so much driven by opportunity exploitation, as it is through other factors within the premises of Parkinson's Law.

Management theories that have 10 rules, habits, or points that claim to lead to success, do not prove cause and effect. The mentioned elements may exist and correlate with success, but we aren't really sure about causation. So many books mention the same companies, that it can't be possible that all these companies are utilizing all these theories at once. These positivist theories miss out on the complexities of organizations and the environments they exist within, and most often the points and issues that influence success and failure.

Implementing management theories as a checklist is potentially very dangerous. Checklists are just like putting a net into the ocean to see what can be picked up, where we assume that what is picked up is actually the essence of the ocean. As W.Edwards Deming once said *"you can only measure 3% of what matters."* Problems and opportunities arise out of imperfections and theories don't handle imperfections well.

Never has management and entrepreneurship been so keenly contested for the manager's attention as today. There is a preconception that *management gurus,* whether academic or *practademic* based know best when delivering theory. Some theories are often based on conflicting assumptions utilized from cognitive psychology to economic theories. For example, there is still no agreed definition about what constitutes a learning organization. Various learning theories exist, adding to the dilemma of managers.

In the 1970s and early 1980s we saw strategy and structure with the concepts of competitive advantage and the utilization of strategic tools. These strategic tools have become more sophisticated as time goes on. The 1990s saw focus on a company's core competencies, internal processes and organizational culture. Strategy was about strengthening a firm's capabilities and using competitive leverages within the marketplace. Firms became learning organizations and concepts of absorptive capacity became the focus. The new millennium became the age of entrepreneurship, where entrepreneurship almost broke out to become a separate discipline to business management. Thousands of pieces of research come out about the subject every year. From the business perspective, the environment, ethics, and sustainability have dominated the agenda. But from the business and entrepreneurship schools, little has been said about opportunity.

Theories are not a reflection of the world, but naïve attempts to act on the world. In addition, many management theories have been misused *(i.e., Lean manufacturing),* as excuses for doing other things like cutting jobs, which bring great insecurities to people in organizations. Sometimes theories are used as the *'great savior'* or as a *'showpiece mechanism'* to say to stakeholders that management is in control, when in reality they are not. One dimensional or univalent approaches are inadequate for providing a framework within which to comprehend the complex factors that make up the concept of opportunity. Psychology and management theories explain things using metaphors that pass concepts across to others, so one phenomenon can be explained in many different ways with emphasis one different aspects.

To understand opportunity, strategy, and entrepreneurship there is the need to develop a *meta-theory* as any single theory cannot hope to cover the situational, relational, and contextual issues of opportunity. A *meta-theory* is a set of theories that in combination offer some assistance in understanding the phenomenon we are trying to comprehend. Other existing theories, either in whole or part become part of the *meta-theory*. A *meta-theory* is like looking at a panorama with different coloured sun-glasses. Each pair of coloured sun-glasses provides a different view of the object that the others don't. To develop a *meta-theory* of opportunity at a micro level, we must undertake a macro-study of companies and also look at case histories and reasons for start-ups, growth, development, and failure. Consequently, this book is partly based on a study of the Fortune 500 companies over the last 50 years, which has been supplemented with looking for similar trends and patterns through history and the different stages of country development, utilizing raw data and other supporting materials. To theorize is to take a mental journey from the word of observed events to the world of hypothetical concepts. This requires the use of imagination in a similar way that Sir Isaac Newton and Albert Einstein gained an understanding about what they were later to theorize about respectively.

A theory should answer *what, how, why*, which can be applied in given situations. *What are the variables and factors involved?* - The constructs. *How are they related?* – The connections. *What are the underlying psychological, economic, and social dynamics involved?* And, *what are the causal relationships?* In any situational context, *who can use it? Where can it be used?*, and *When?*

However, there can be little formal proof about whether a theory is correct, or whether one theory is better than any other in explaining something. Management theorists are sometimes more concerned whether theories can be validated rather than their usefulness. In contrast, from a practitioners point of view, a theory is a roadmap to help improve the understanding of what one is seeing, and to assist them in mapping out trajectories for the future. There is no sure way of being where one wants to be in the future, but a good map helps one steer the right course, helping them prepare for any bad weather or other catastrophes that may occur along the way. Simple tests of measurements, mathematics, statistical analysis and manipulation cannot be used. Many theories are good in reconstructing the facts in hindsight, but none are effective in predicting results in the future. This is partly because of the contribution imagination, interpretation, and selections have on the process, something no theory can take any account of – the irrational. Theories cannot predict peoples' situational wisdom and consequential behaviour.

Competition and opportunity has spread to almost all sections of society, including arts, education, healthcare, philanthropy, and poverty eradication. There are growing claims upon scare resources and rising social needs and issues. The opportunity framework is relevant to both the macro and micro environments. Macro in terms of opportunities that occur during different stages of economic growth and how communities can plan and empower themselves according to the relevant opportunities available, and micro in terms of a how a firm or venture operating within a competitive environment can best identify and exploit opportunities in front of them. The uncertainty ahead will lead to great opportunities, and entrepreneurship will be at the leading edge of change. There are great win-win opportunities for both companies and societies if these opportunities are approached in ways that look to achieve *Pareto optimal solutions* and *Nash equation outcomes.*

The word *enterprise* may have been more relevant than using the word entrepreneurship, as so many definitions the term infers some form of novelty or innovation. Enterprise is common to all types of entities including sole traders, SMEs, corporations, multinationals, non-profit organizations, and even communities. They may be innovative or they may be not. The common thread is that an entity will seek opportunity to survive, earn some form of income, or seek some other objective that is viable within a certain place and time. This opportunity is found from the world in conjunction with the one's social, cognitive and psych based reference point where certain and particular facts, perceptions, events, or situations are connected with prior knowledge. To exploit the given opportunity any entity, human or enterprise must utilize what resources they have efficiently and innovatively. The entity must then utilize or create their own networks to enable the development of a process to exploit the opportunity. If it is a single person or sole trading entity, skills and competencies must be used, or in the case of a larger entity made up of more than one person, capabilities are utilized to support developed products/strategies within a competitive environment.

Individuals in organizations act as gatekeepers to filter what information comes in and also perform the role of interpreting the information. This has a distorting affect on the realities of the social world. Most organizations follow the lead by their CEO rather than adhere to any set of management theories. In effect, an organization runs on the theory believed in and practiced by the leader built up through his or her experiences. One of the greatest problems with entrepreneurial research is that it is situational with different environmental factors underlying it, making it very difficult to *roll out* any particular research into a general theory.

This book was the result of the writer's urge to try and explain the concept of opportunity, why some people see it and others don't, and why some people are successful, while others fail. It is based on almost forty years of observation as a practitioner and the last six years of the writer's own research into these questions. Venture failure appears to occur for two main reasons. Firstly, because the opportunity was not identified correctly, and secondly because something was lacking in the exploitation of the identified opportunity – networks, resources, skills, competencies, capabilities, commitment, or courage.

The companies mentioned in this book are for illustrative purposes only, not meaning to be any formal case study. The company examples are only there to extrapolate any points made in preceding text. Much of what is written in this book cannot be empirically tested for validity; it can only be observed and verified by antidote. Due to the vast nature of this project, it has been necessary to use a *broad brush approach* to fill in some of the detail to make up the *meta-theory*. This may have been at the cost of some accuracy in theories and facets presented, but hopefully this does not destroy the sentiments of the arguments put forward in this book. Some findings may be conceptual and even suggestive as it was difficult to arrive at conclusive findings in such a situational topic. Most diagrams are conceptual only, in attempts to add to understanding of the concepts discussed rather than a deliberate theory.

There is still much conjecture about entrepreneurship research as so much of it is situational and area or industry specific, if not company specific. For a success and failure standpoint, some firms succeed, while others fail and we can only suppose with other people why this is so, and one person's opinion may just be as good as another's. Hopefully this book may be considered some small incremental addition to the understanding of entrepreneurial opportunity and strategy. The exercise of writing this book would be deemed successful if it has helped to explain the issues involved in success and failure of firms.

It is the author's opinion that people can learn how to see, discover, and construct opportunity.

The book is broken up into two volumes, volume one with four chapters and volume two with seven chapters.

In the first volume, chapter one introduces the concept of opportunity, preempting some of the themes that will come later in this book. Opportunity is described as both an environmental and individual phenomenon where aspirations and imagination are just as important as changing social, economic, technological, and regulatory structures and conditions. Four basic types of opportunities exist. Imitation based opportunities occur with little innovation and value creation. Allocative opportunities occur because of mismatches in supply and demand. Discovery based opportunities occur from shifting consumer preferences, regulation, and economic conditions. Construction based opportunities don't exist until someone constructs and develops them through the process of effectuation. Opportunity is seen as a dynamic and ever shifting, where successful firms are those that match their strategy with opportunity. Opportunities begin through images which are connected with other images forming concepts which are developed, evaluated, and elaborated into ideas. The chapter concludes with a discussion about emotional sensitivity and the role it plays in seeing opportunities, the idea evaluation process, and chance and fate.

Chapter two examines opportunity from the socio-economic, economic history, economic geography, political economy, and biographical perspectives. This chapter argues that opportunity and our consequential actions occur within the realm of time and space. Due to our evolutionary accumulation of knowledge, technology advancement, and social evolution being time and spatially based, opportunity to a large degree is a product of time and space. For ideas to become valid opportunities, all the elements that enable opportunity gestation and its subsequent exploitation must be in place. The trajectories that entrepreneur/inventors take are also a product of time and space as opportunity and strategy are socially bounded. This chapter is divided into three parts. Part one examines the phases of national development through the stages of a traditional economy, under-developed economy, developing economy, developed economy, and post industrial economy. Each particular stage of national development lends itself to certain types and scope of opportunities. The second part of the chapter looks at the biographies of a number of inventor/entrepreneurs during the industrial revolution to the turn of the twentieth century. Looking directly at biographical contexts allows us to look at the flow of events in time and space in terms of innovation, invention, promotion, and effect on society at the time and into the future. This approach may provide some window into how inventor/entrepreneurs gained insight and were able to develop their inventions into commercial reality. One can also get some feeling about the motives they had, challenges they faced and see how their development of business models was crucial to the success of their ventures. Part three takes us into the twentieth century beginning in the post World War II era. A look is taken at some of the important entrepreneurial events during each decade until today. Certain entrepreneurs and their ventures are examined in the light of the social and economic conditions evident through those times.

Chapter three examines the ways we look at the world through a number of different paradigms and metaphors. The chapter is an attempt to explain how we perceive and what influences our thinking. This chapter is also broken into three parts. The first part looks at how we perceive through examining the sociological factors influencing us. These include demographic factors like family and peers, domicile outlook, the need to survive, work and life experiences, education, skills and abilities, age, and gender. The section finishes with a look at generational differences and culture. Part two explains how our cognitive system works, emphasizing its limitations and how this is compensated for. Part three takes us into the psychological domain where a number of mechanisms influence how we perceive, think, and make decisions. These include our emotions, emotional attachment, our ego, identity, and self, the unconscious, defence mechanisms, group views of reality, transference, symbolic and ritualistic delusion, groupthink, motivational bias, tiredness and complacency, cognitive traps, personality traits, entrepreneurial typologies, power and conflict, genetic inheritance, and mid life crisis and transition. Imagination, passion, enjoyment, energy, personal discipline, and what constitutes a motivational trigger are examined as processes that facilitate a person see and react to opportunity. Finally the chapter hypothesizes that opportunity is as much a product of ourselves as it is of the environment around us.

Chapter four is concerned with creativity, a concept that is not totally agreed upon as some people see creativity as a process, while others view creativity as a product. Creativity is totally interlaced with opportunity, strategy, and entrepreneurship where both its process and product are fundamental to the whole phenomenon. Creativity is necessary in idea creation, its evaluation, opportunity construction and effectuation, developing the sources of opportunity, the gathering and combining of resources, networking, and the crafting of strategy to achieve a vision and solve problems along the way. Although we know most of the cognitive processes related to creativity and can identify most of the characteristics associated with it, we still need to explore creativity through metaphors, various styles, and applications. The second half of the chapter will look at a few different approaches to applying creativity and conclude with a discussion about the barriers to creativity and how they can be overcome.

In the second volume, chapter one introduces the sources of opportunities. As opportunities can be considered gaps in the market where there is potential to do something and create value, these gaps must have a causal source. There are six basic major sources of opportunity consisting of market voids, technology infusion, structural changes, resource monopolies, regulation and non-innovative sources. Any opportunity is likely to be based on one or more of these sources, carrying multiple characteristics, but they are in fact very hard to really see and understand. Once the correct sources of opportunity have been identified, resources, capabilities, networks, can be configured to develop strategies to exploit them.

Chapter two considers the issue of resources in relation to opportunity exploitation. Resources comprise of anything that is of use to an entrepreneur, either as a tangible or intangible form. A business model can be considered a higher level resource, as it reflects how an entrepreneur combines resources to create value from those at his or her disposal. The chapter briefly discusses how needed resources for a new value chain can be identified and allocated within the venture to build the resource base. The resources base is from where enterprise capabilities and ultimately strategies are built upon. Different types of resources are needed during different stages of a firm's evolution. Eventually the entrepreneur will be able to build specialized resources that cannot easily be copied by competitors, which can form the basis of some form of competitive effectiveness. The chapter concludes with a brief discussion about how resources can be utilized as barriers to entry and outlines the resource cycle of a firm.

Chapter three considers skills, personal competencies, and enterprise capabilities. The beginning of the chapter looks at personal talents and abilities and how they can be developed into skills. Various types of skills exist along a continuum spanning between those that are domain specific and the broader cognitive and interpersonal skills. Sets of skills can be developed into personal competencies which enable a person to become an expert in a particular field and within an entrepreneurial start-up, form the basis of enterprise capabilities. Enterprise capabilities are distinctive enterprise competencies directly related to various aspects of the business. They include management capabilities, entrepreneurial capabilities, organizational culture, learning capabilities, innovative capabilities, and dynamic capabilities which assist the firm change according to the trajectory of opportunities within the environment. Enterprise capabilities form the basis of strategy that the firm employs to exploit opportunities.

Chapter four examines networks which are an entrepreneur's connection both within his or her organization and to the outside environment. Networks can be formal or informal and enable the entrepreneur to acquire resources and finance, gather market intelligence, develop new products, develop bridges where they lack capabilities, gain access to new markets, and enable the sounding out of ideas and access to emotional support. There are many formal network mechanisms including licensing agreements, sub-contracting, strategic alliances, agency and distribution agreements, and routine mechanisms like sales calls. Informal mechanisms can include social connections, family and peers. Networks are an important source of learning and have diverse influences upon decision making. The remainder of the chapter looks at network based strategies such as strategic alliances, relationship marketing, and looks briefly at network based opportunities, and network building strategies.

Chapter five outlines the composition of the competitive environment, the actual field where opportunities manifest and are exploited. The competitive environment incorporates customer and supplier influences, substitute and complementary good influences, barriers to entry, and the competitive field itself. This is continually influenced by the state of the economy, social trends, technology, and government intervention. Consequently the competitive environment is dynamic and continually changing with its own lifecycle, which influences the nature of competition. Firms are able to segment the competitive field or with radical new technology, new processes, and/or business models, create new competitive fields. The opportunity-strategy nexus is based on the sources of opportunity, the nature of the firm's resources and capabilities, which form the basis of strategy creation. The chapter concludes with a brief discussion about the steps involved in environmental analysis.

Chapter six concerns strategy, where strategy is seen as a process of finding out what works within the competitive field through effectuation and trial and error. Strategy is seen as an intuitive rather than an analytical process. Developing strategy requires prior knowledge and experience about 'what works', constrained by the firm's resources and capabilities. There are a number of basic strategies, and those listed in this chapter are not exhaustive. A firm will usually adopt and modify a particular type of strategy for specific purposes. Basic strategic typologies may be modified or merged to form new types of strategies particularly suited to the firm's situation. The chapter concludes with a discussion on the components of strategy, developing barriers to entry to prevent other firms imitating a firm's strategic position.

The final chapter synthesizes all the elements; time and space, the vision platform, making connections, resources, skills, competencies and capabilities, networks, the competitive environment, and strategy into what can be called the opportunity framework. Each element is influenced by and influenced the other elements, forming an entropic pattern, where all the elements are required to create a true opportunity. The essence of the meta-theory is that when any entrepreneur visualizes any idea, all the elements must exist for there to be any real opportunity. Likewise when the entrepreneur attempts to exploit the opportunity, strategy must be built around these interrelationships.

Not much of the meta-theory is itself new ground in entrepreneurial or strategic thinking. Everything has been hypothesized before. What is new is the way the interrelationships are structured and relate to the opportunity, the strategy, and the enterprise. The concept of opportunity is itself a metaphor for new sources of wealth, and as such any inadequacies in any of the parts of the meta-theory shouldn't detract from the conceptual framework itself.

The author hopes that this has made some small contribution towards a deeper understanding of opportunity.

Jejawi, Arau,
Perlis, Malaysia
8th February 2011

ACKNOWLEDGMENTS

Writing a book of this magnitude in a rural part of Malaysia that can be considered one of the poorest parts of the country was a great challenge due to the intellectual isolation. The only advantage of being in a place like this was the endless time available to research and write this manuscript. There would have not been the time available to think about things if the writer was in a large city campus university.

My acknowledgement and thanks first goes to my Australian history teacher back at Xavier College, Melbourne, Australia during the mid 1970s. Des King taught us how to question accounts of history and always look for the other points of view before trying to construct what could have happened. Dr. Mike Knowles and Dr. Edward Vaughan enlightened me to the different ways of seeing organizations during my classes at Monash University. Their inspiration led me to Swinburne University of Technology, the centre of organization behavior studies at the time where I met and engaged with Max Browne, Alan Brown, Dr. Barbara Cargill, Professor Chris Christodoulou, and John Batros. I especially remember the time spent with Dr. Geoff Drummond visiting Japanese automobile factories around Melbourne to *'feel'* the culture on the shop-floor under *kanban* and *JIT* work-flows. The times at Swinburne really opened my eyes to the dark side of ourselves and its influence upon what we do.

I would like to thank Professor Anis Bajrektarevic of Krems University of Applied Science in Austria for the help, discussions, exchanges and reading of my manuscript. I also like to thank Professor Howard Frederick of Deakin University, Melbourne for the like discussions and the sharing of our mutual love of entrepreneurship.

At my own university, I'm thankful to Ahmad Nazri Bin Abdullah who kept me motivated with our chats and mutual love of writing. I also cannot forget the times Professor Kamarudin bin Nor (now at University of Kuala Lumpur) and myself spent together discussing the theory and application of entrepreneurship in rural communities.

To the countless number of people in business, government, and entrepreneurship, across all the continents of the world that I have been able to met up with and spend some time with throughout my life, thank you for sharing your experiences with me.

Finally and without her this would not have been possible, thank you to my wife Kittirat who was always supportive of this project and helped me not feel too guilty about the time we missed together.

Thank you to all for assisting me on my journey.

Today, entrepreneurship is one of the most written about topics in the field of business. Books and articles exist from the theoretical, biographical, research, and educational perspectives. However the concept of opportunity, which is at the heart of entrepreneurship, has been largely ignored. This book, *Opportunity, Strategy, and Entrepreneurship* attempts to bring the concept of opportunity into mainstream discussion and consideration by presenting a meta-theory which dissects all the elements of opportunity, so this phenomenon can be better understood.

Without opportunity society cannot progress, and without opportunity, entrepreneurship cannot exist. This book considers how opportunity is closely linked with our society's development, and how innovations today will lay the foundation of further opportunities in the future. To harness the environmental streams that carry opportunities, one must have the ability to make connections and see the origins, so that resources, capabilities, and networks can be configured into strategies to exploit any seen, discovered, or constructed opportunities. A meta-theory is finally presented as a framework of opportunity where the reader can clearly see the individual elements and how they are interrelated to make up any potential opportunity. Any successful exploitation of an identified opportunity depends on satisfying all the individual elements effectively through an opportunity based strategy.

Chapter 1

INTRODUCTION: OPPORTUNITY: THE CONCEPTION OF ENTERPRISE

All human activity is directed at some perceived possible future. Our life is dominated by the channelling of our efforts towards creating the future we anticipate for ourselves. The future is a journey for which we are not certain, relying upon our imagination to picture what this future would be like, whether it is just in five minutes or five years time. We can only be certain about this future when we get there (Sarasvathy 2002). The heart of seeing opportunity is about seeing the future, a process that doesn't occur through formal analysis, forecasting or strategic planning process. Rather, opportunity is about seeing the future for what it could be through our aspirations and imagination in ways that other people don't see. There is a passionate, visionary, and exciting side to opportunity that formal systems and theory does not capture adequately. Opportunities create a path where various levels of enthusiasm, skill, resources, rigidity and commitment, and a devised strategy are pursued by individuals and firms. This journey begins with the identification of an opportunity upon which we are inspired and motivated enough to pursue, not always knowing where we will end up. Our actions test what we are anticipating, inferring that pursuing opportunities is about learning.

Opportunity cannot be explained by environmental forces or individual factors alone as they are both very much interrelated (Shane 2003). The phenomenon of opportunity spans across the disciplines of micro-economics, psychology and cognitive science, strategic management, resource based and contingency theories that are patched together, synchronized and added to form new information in the form of ideas. Opportunity is a situational phenomenon that is developed from incomplete information (Kirzner 1973, 1985, 1997). Opportunity relies on an individual recognizing, discovering or constructing patterns and concepts that can be formed into ideas. Opportunity is a poorly defined concept where theories are good at explaining creation after the event, but been very poor in predicting creation. Theories are limited in their explanations and can only point to what capabilities exist when the individual is developing opportunities. Opportunity models that have been developed by strategy and marketing researchers have difficulty in being applied to entrepreneurial start-ups. For example, in the pre-1970s it would have been totally inconceivable to predict that a group of young entrepreneurs who dropped out of university would be able to move into the computer industry and be so successful exploiting opportunities that incumbent *Fortune 500* firms like IBM couldn't (Muzyka 1997).

The central aspect of opportunity is being able to see it in the first place and acting upon it before others. This is a function of how we perceive the world and process information. The resulting intuition, vision, insight, discovery, or creation is an idea which may upon evaluation become an opportunity. This ability is not uniformly distributed throughout the community (Carland *et. al.* 1996), as people have different orientations towards time and space as depicted in Figure 1.1. Thus the opportunity *gestalt* is not a uniform or regular phenomenon that any theory can provide a general explanation[1].

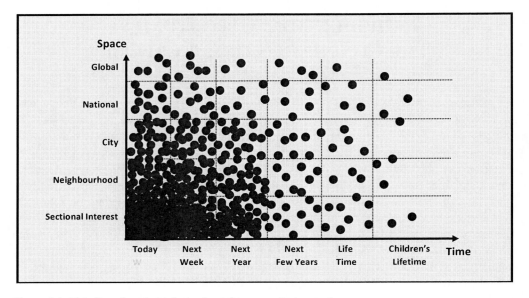

Figure 1.1. The diversity of peoples' orientation towards time and space.

Opportunity is a dynamic construct that ebbs and flows according to a continually changing environment. This also occurs in what were once called traditionally *"stable industries"* like broadcasting, entertainment, chemicals, pharmaceuticals, automotive, and aviation. Customer trends, resource costs, government regulations, changing trade conditions, competitive products, merging industries, and other types of pressures and shocks like rising petroleum prices continuously shift the panorama of the environment and thus change is the prime generator of opportunity. The financial crisis of 2008 coupled with international monetary shifts, changing exchange rates and the movement of manufacturing and jobs from Western countries to China are phenomena that change national economies and the balance of world markets, bringing massive structural shifts and potential opportunities. As we saw in 2008 this process can be extremely rapid and appear to occur with little warning just like the *'peoples' revolutions'* in Tunisia, Egypt, Jordan, Yemen, Bahrain, and Libya during 2011. Figure 1.2. depicts some of these rapid changes in relationships that are shifting the locus of opportunity in a major manner. One of the many affects of these changes has been the

---

[1] Gestalt in this situation is the formation of something whole through insight, intuition, and other forms of mental construction.

dramatic shift of firms to manufacture in China. Whole companies are being taken over turning company towns into museums where legacy exists only as a brand name like Waterford Crystal[2].

Over the last forty years we have witnessed the creation of many new multi-billion dollar industries like the modern era of biotechnology, discount retail, mutual funds, cellular telephones, personal computers, satellite television, and the internet. Industries that were important to the growth of the US during the larger part of the twentieth century like steel have massively declined, leading to the demise of giant *Fortune 500* companies like Bethlehem Steel. Companies like Intel, National Semiconductor, Microsoft, Apple, Nokia, Amazon, eBay, and Wal-Mart have risen to dominance in their industries, each in their own way transforming the way a particular industry works. The changeover of industry dominance has been so rapid that 40% of the *Fortune 500* companies that existed in 1975 were no longer operational two decades later (Griffin 1997). Today 33% of the most successful firms profits are generated from products launched within the last five years (Foster 2000). In some industries like the mobile phone, television manufacture, white goods and automobiles, etc this figure is much closer to 100%.

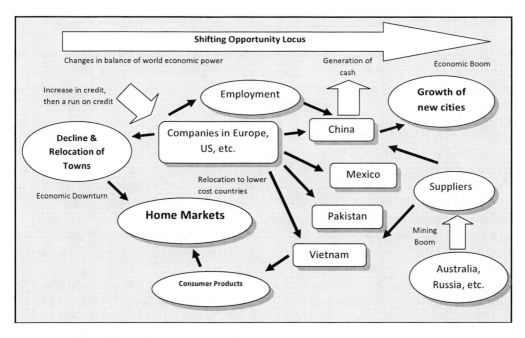

Figure 1.2. The shifting global opportunity balance.

Firms need to continually renewal themselves through taking on new opportunities by developing and launching new products, services and/or creating new business models. Companies need to shift their strategies flexibly as the characteristics of opportunities change and pursue emerging opportunities to remain successful. There however is a tendency for

---

[2] See: Workers occupy crystal factory, BBC News, http://news.bbc.co.uk/2/hi/uk_news/northern_ireland/ 7862515.stm, (accessed 29th December 2010).

successful firms to become so focused upon the internal processes of their organizations that they forgot to scan the environment and to see where the marketplace is going.

The subjective nature of opportunity makes it impossible to separate the concept from the individual. Opportunity has a deep basis in a person's prior knowledge and experience, personal aspirations, imagination, and fear of uncertainty. As opportunities are situational, so must be the practice of entrepreneurship and thus it is very difficult to agree on a common definition. What may be entrepreneurial in one context may not be entrepreneurial in another time and place, so entrepreneurship is also a relational concept. As entrepreneurship is also carried out within a social context, entrepreneurship must also be a cultural phenomenon.

For the purposes of this book, entrepreneurship is an individual or collective way of thinking, constructing an opportunity attached to a vision, which somehow precipitates the gathering, co-opting, combining and organizing of resources into enactment upon the opportunity with the goal of activating the vision, utilizing knowledge, technology, and business tools in a relatively novel way to realize results, that have the possibility of creating a sustainable organization, where there are willing followers who share the vision. The concept of novelty is also situational, relational, contextual, and cultural, and the standards of novelty – *meaning the quality of being new,* will be different in say the United States to what is novel in The Ghana, Nepal, Bangladesh, or Fiji.

Most ideas have their basis in some old idea, something seen or experienced within the past, so from this point of view most opportunities are not truly novel. For example, an old type of business can be given a new business model and professionalism like McDonalds did for burgers and Holiday Inn did for motels. New technologies can be applied to old products and processes like desktop publishing and email and domestic business models can be expanded internationally like Coca Cola and Pizza Hut.

Many people mistake their aspirations for opportunity. For example people put their money and efforts into a boutique, restaurant or spa for the wrong reasons because they like fashion and shopping, food and cooking, or aromatherapy and massage, only to close down a few months later because there was no real opportunity. In SME's the values of the founder and the firm are the same in many cases. Business opportunity is influenced to various degrees by a hierarchy of personal and family aspirations and concerns that cannot easily be separated from business goals. This can be dangerous if one is unaware of their influence upon thinking. This hierarchy of personal, family, and business aspirations are depicted in figure 1.3.

Our knowledge and personal goals are embedded within our imagination which is at the heart of our existence, a cognitive quality that we would not be human without (Kearney 1998, P.1). Imagination extends our experiences and thoughts, constructing our view of the world to lower our uncertainty of it. Just like imagination is a good way for novelists to create their stories (Jensen 1999), imagination is needed to create new value sets to consumers that separate new ideas from others. This requires originality to create innovation (Wiener 1993, P. 7). Imagination is the essence of marketing opportunity (Levitt 1986, P. 127) that conveyes image and fantasy to consumers, allowing them to imagine what it would be like to live at Sanctuary Cove in Northern Queensland, Australia, receiving a Citibank loan, driving a Mercedes 500 SLK around town, or holidaying in Bali. Imagination aids our practical reasoning (Brown & Patterson 2000, P. 7) and opens up new avenues of thinking, reflecting, organizing the world, or doing things differently. Imagination decomposes what already is, replacing it with what could be, and is the source of all our hope fear, enlightenment, and aspirations.

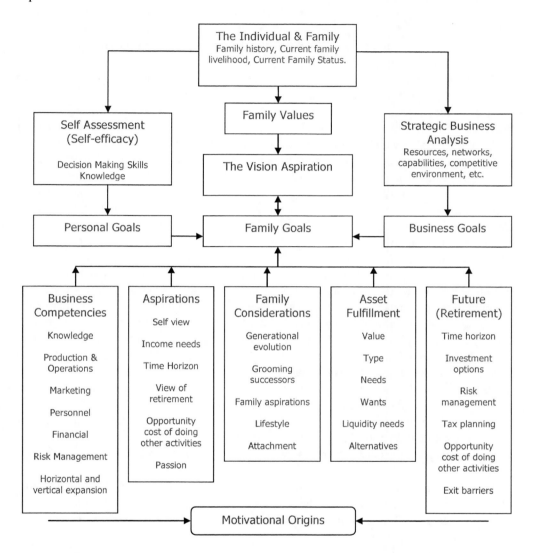

Figure 1.3. A hierarchy of family, personal and business aspirations (Adapted from Hunter 2009, P. 697).

There are really very few innovators in the business world as most firms tend to adapt, emulate, and follow other proven ideas. By emulating and matching other firm's ideas and strategies, and adopting the behaviour and actions of others, just like we did in the school playground, we reduce our personal risk and uncertainty. By far the majority of businesses follow others that successfully exploit opportunities, rather than seek their own to exploit.

Each story about a successful (or unsuccessful) entrepreneur is unique and has its own particular reasons for success (or failure) based upon the type of opportunity, skills, focus, apt timing, resource configuration, personal competencies, and a strategy for the situation, which may or may not be right for the particular opportunity and entrepreneur. Different kinds of opportunities will lead to different types of strategy and venture form, which leads to different types of enterprises, business scope, and ways organizations are run. Any individual case studies only show a limited opportunity set, resources, skills, and capabilities, source of opportunity, and strategies for a particular situation. For each and every situation all these factors will be different.

Some companies rapidly grow after start-up because they have correctly identified an opportunity, have the right capabilities, networks and resources, and devised the most appropiate strategies to exploit the opportunity effectively. Other firms may take a longer time to learn the heart of the opportunity and what is required to successfully exploit it, or may be under resourced and need to build their capabilities, so growth is much more modest.

The basis of a new entrepreneurial venture is coming up with something that others don't have. Breakthrough or revolutionary ideas may take some time for consumer acceptance where the speed of success may depend upon the extent that consumer habits must change, the convenience of the purchase process, and the familiarity with the channels of distribution. Sales revenue will be very difficult to predict, if not impossible and the only confidence an entrepreneur may be able to have in the future outcome is that their new product or service offers substantially more value than what is currently in the market. How quickly the product catches on, is really anybody's guess (Bhide 1999). New start-up firms may only be able to fulfil niche segments due to the large costs of blanket market distribution. At the other end of the continuum, products that replicate other competitive products or are only marginally better are difficult to introduce and gain any deep market penetration. These products may compete on price, value (more product for the same price), or other short term market tactics. Success in any competitive environment may just come down to the hard slog of out pacing the other competitors which drains profitability for all concerned.

Strategy is the driver of opportunity exploitation. However it must be flexible in adapting the idea, objectives, organization, product, and tactics, as they are all paramount for success. Strategy based on opportunity relies on learning, building capabilities, and making venture choices that are based upon our subjective preferences. Performance along the opportunity path will be measured against a person's own personal vision as a benchmark (Cooper 2001. P. 95).

Although entrepreneurs come from all walks of life, backgrounds, and ventures are vastly different, there is perhaps a common narrative and shared curiosity that would entail thoughts like *'why is this so?' 'Is there a better way of doing this?' 'Is there a way I can benefit?'* and *'How can I improve upon it?*

WHAT IS OPPORTUNITY

There are a number of definitions of opportunity that provide different glimpses upon its meaning. One of the most relevant definitions to this book was developed by Stevenson and Jarillo (1990) who saw opportunity as a future situation that is both desirable and feasible. Wickham (2006) saw opportunity as a gap in the market where the potential exists to do something better that creates value. From the Schumpeterian point of view an opportunity is simply a chance to meet a market need through some creative combination of resources to deliver superior value (Schumpeter 1934, Kirzner 1973, Casson 1982). Scott (2003) saw opportunity as a recombination of resources that results in new products, services, or changes within the value chain. Stevenson and Gumpert (1985) saw that for an idea to be classified as an opportunity, it must meet two criteria; Firstly the idea must represent a desirable future state involving some form of change, and secondly the individuals involved must believe that it is possible to reach that state.

The implications of the above definitions view opportunity as a perspective taken about the possible future state of the environment, a potentiality that is not yet actualized that may or may not be feasible. Opportunity is a juncture where something favourable can be realized through undertaking certain activities to realize the identified potential, based on a set of ideas and beliefs that enable the creation of goods and services that do not yet exist (Venkataraman 1997). For example a computer without an operating system is useless to most users and be of very little market potential. But the advent of an operating system adds value to the computer. There are many instances where consumers are not able to articulate their needs and wants for certain new products until they see them and are able to recognize or learn about the value the product or service may have (Von Hippel 1994). Opportunities can be exploited by fulfilling these needs, wants, or creating trends and fads with goods or services that offer value to consumers. For example, consumers may not see the need for a toothbrush sterilizer until they see one in the market and are presented with information about the bacteria build up on a toothbrush lying around in the bathroom cabinet. Therefore to see opportunity one must understand the technical aspects of the nature of the opportunity or have an intimate understanding of the value chain involved.

Opportunity implies some form of action to realize the potential, which infers entrepreneurship. It is an entrepreneur who develops an idea from some formation process, develops the goals to pursue the opportunity and has the motivation to assemble resources, and utilize networks and skills in the pursuit of exploitation.

The Global Entrepreneurship Monitor (GEM) makes a distinction between necessity based and opportunity based entrepreneurs. Necessity entrepreneurs take up self-employment out of a need to earn income as the prime motivation, where very few other viable economic alternatives exist. Opportunity entrepreneurs take advantage of perceived business opportunities. Their desire may arise out of dissatisfaction with their current life situation (Wildeman *et. al.* 1999) or out of awareness about a growing number of opportunities arising out of economic growth with new optimisms (Meredith *et. al.* 1982). It is the author's view that GEM reports have consistently overstated opportunistic entrepreneurship and understated necessity entrepreneurship in developing countries due to interview methodologies and bias as people tend to put their position in the best light during formal interviews. Personal life situations have a deep influence upon a person's willingness to look for opportunity, what they see, and how they pursue them (Reynolds *et. al.* 2004).

Many new technology innovations are pushed into the market and in some cases, products and services go on to be very successful, *i.e., iPad, iPhone, personal computer, automobile, airplane, and steam engine*[3]. Any new technology will have a number of potential applications[4], and the inventor/entrepreneur or firm must decide which area is most

---

[3] This is in contrast to a product or service being designed around unsatisfied consumer needs and wants.
[4] The steam engine could be utilized as a factory power plant, an automobile power plant, or locomotive steam engine, etc. However early steam engine inventors saw the biggest potential of the steam engine for mine pumps and factory power plants to drive machinery.

lucrative one to focus upon. Any new technologies must solve existing problems effectively and efficiently, and be able to provide consumers with benefits. Every invented device, process, or service requires an innovation period where the invention is matched with opportunity, as the new technology is not an opportunity within itself. This requires a clear understanding of what customers are looking for and why they buy. Finding this out may be a *"hit and miss"* process where mistakes can be very costly and punished very quickly (Wickham 2006, P. 189).

Consequently, the pursuit of new knowledge and technology is an endogenous phenomenon where technology must be matched to an idea. Thus an opportunity is created by an entrepreneur or team working with him or her (Griliches 1979). Opportunities are generated through the quest for new knowledge. Opportunities may then be more prevalent in industries where more new knowledge is generated, *i.e., biotechnology and ICT, etc,* than prevailing in low technology industries (Cohen & Klepper 1991,1992). In this context some opportunities can only emerge when the technology exists and has been applied as an idea to something. Thus opportunity streams into the environment through ideas to apply new technologies when they exist.

Finally it is perhaps worthwhile to distinguish opportunity from speculation. Because the future is never certain, activity that takes place overtime is to some degree speculative. Opportunities are based on the belief that value can be created which will yield future profits and any uncertainties are manageable if resources are deployed effectively within the control of the entrepreneur. The profits resulting from entrepreneurial opportunity exploitation are derived from a deliberate set of actions and the successful creation of value. Speculation however relates to a bet on an outcome, where a person may think that prices will either rise or fall in the future and base their actions upon this belief or speculation. If they believe prices will rise in the future, they will buy, if they believe prices will fall in the future, they will defer or postpone buying. This can be applied to anything that can be bought or sold and speculation tends to be successful in markets that are on a continual rise. The availability of credit tends to fan speculation. Speculators risk their capital in the expectation that the price in the market will shift to favour their position. Speculation unlike opportunity exploitation is usually paper based that does not create any new value and outcomes are usually outside the control of the investor unless large sums of capital are utilized and has influence over market price levels. In these cases speculation becomes distortive and profits are made through the distortion of the market. Speculation is usually motivated by the desire for quick gains and relies on the exogenous forces of demand, supply *(market volatility)* and speculation to achieve monetary gains, rather than acts of creation.

THE FORMS OF OPPORTUNITY

Opportunities manifest themselves in different ways and can be categorized accordingly. One of the simplest ways of mapping forms of opportunities is by the locus of change they manifest upon the environment. Less innovative forms of opportunity tend to be passive/reactive imitation or rent seeking activities, while active/imaginative forms of opportunities tend to require a proactive intervention into the environment where an entrepreneur seeks to change things. Allocative opportunities involve finding new market space through passive analysis of demand and supply and demographics, while the other sector discovery opportunities involve more active entry into the market place with products aimed at developing new market space believed to exist where incongruities and structural change may be taking place (see chapter 1, volume 2). Each form of opportunity is likely but not exclusively associated with a style of thinking as depicted in figure 1.4.

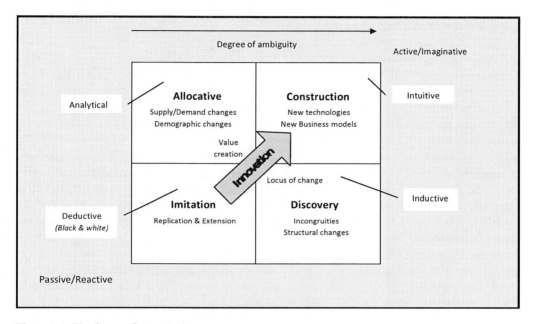

Figure 1.4. The forms of opportunity.

Imitation Based Opportunities

Imitation is the most basic form of opportunity. The imitative continuum requires little innovation and there is little value creation. Entrepreneurs see effective business models and utilize the ideas contained within them for their own benefit. There are usually few changes made to any of these observed business models and they are usually adopted in whole with minimal modification. The key for the individual is to select a suitable geographical location or customer group to target and focus upon. The thinking style and narrative would tend to be some form of arbitrary reasoning in the manner of *"people need to buy groceries and there is room for a grocery store in this area"*, *"people need to buy a cup of coffee, sandwich, and newspaper on their way to work, outside this railway station"*, and *"The residents in this apartment building could do with the convenience of a washing and ironing service"*. Imitation is reactive upon what a person sees is successful for others, probably with the prime goal of earning a living. This does not differ too much at the corporate level where most companies tend to imitate their competitors, as imitation is perhaps perceived to be a less risky option. Imitation opportunities are usually most effective in safe unambiguous environments, although also highly successful against first movers in technology based high growth markets like what is occurring to the iPad.

It is not too difficult to quantify the size of the opportunity and the key issues are how much market share a firm can obtain and how much will it cost to obtain it. The simplest form of imitation is straight out copying, spanning out into the extension of an idea, duplication in other markets which are discussed in much more detail in chapter one of volume 2.

Allocative Based Opportunities

Allocative opportunities occur when there are mismatches in supply and demand, resources are scarce in certain areas, an individual or firm has a resource monopoly, or demographic changes require specific products and services to fulfil emerging needs and wants. Allocative opportunities primarily occur out of market imperfections or changing demographics which can be identified on the most part through scanning and analysis of the competitive environment. This analysis may show where goods and services are absent, prices are inefficient, and where supply channels and value chains are not effective. Allocative opportunities represent the demand and supply issues in classical economic theory.

Allocative opportunities can be identified through market observation and information. Once identified allocative opportunities can be easily seen, *i.e., the shortage of particular goods and services in the market, or an aging population or baby boom requiring specific sectional goods and services.* The potential of allocative opportunities are greatly enhanced for firms that already serve these markets and have established supply chains and channels of distribution with strong sales networks. The key to recognising opportunities is through environmental scanning. A powerful source of ideas is through observing similar markets in other countries for new products that have not reached the entrepreneur's market yet, especially in developing markets. There is more innovation and value creation in developing allocative opportunities than with imitation opportunities, but these types of opportunities still remain within a passive/reactive strategic approach. Like imitation, allocative opportunity values are not too difficult to forecast in most cases.

Discovery Based Opportunities

Changes in technology, consumer preferences, regulation, and economic conditions most often lead to opportunity gaps within the competitive environment. Opportunities are derived from the attributes of the industry independent of an entrepreneur's action. These opportunities await discovery by an alert individual who may or may not decide to exploit them (Kirzner 1973, P. 10). If an entrepreneur can understand the attributes and structure of an industry, then he or she will be able to anticipate the type of opportunities available within the industry. These discoveries may require the recombination of old and new knowledge in novel ways to find viable opportunities (Shane 2000). However specific industry knowledge is very important and an individual through industry experience may be able to see industry opportunities that people without specific industry knowledge cannot see (Casson 1982). In addition, people with specific industry experience may discover opportunities without any systematic search (Barney 1986).

The use of discovery is suitable under conditions of risk and uncertainty where pre-existing information exists about the nature of opportunities in question. The discovery process is also good where firm and industry structure requires change like the need to create economies of scale of lower a firm/industry cost base (Porter 1990). The value of the opportunity is extremely difficult to forecast with discovery opportunities until sales actually occur within the market. Inductive reasoning is often used in the discovery process although rational, analytical, and intuitive thinking can also play an important role in the development of the opportunity.

Construction Based Opportunities

Some opportunities do not exist until they are constructed by someone (Baker & Nelson 2005, Gartner 1985, Weick 1979). Opportunity construction[5] tends to be unrelated to present information and created through an emergent process of trial and error within the competitive environment (Mintzberg & Waters 1985). The entrepreneur through experience and interaction with the environment crafts a new opportunity (Ardichvilli et. al. 2003, Chell 2000, Kruger 2000). The entrepreneur does not become aware of the opportunity by reconfiguring information and knowledge in new ways, rather new knowledge is built up through action creating new information from closely observing the results of the intervention within the competitive environment and changing the nature of action according to the results gained (Choi 1992). The final result from an entrepreneur's efforts will not be known at the beginning of the opportunity construction process as the future outcome may be totally different to what was originally conceived and irrelevant to present information (Sine et. al. 2005). A viable opportunity is the eventual result of these actions, resulting from feedback and further action (Weick 1979).

Opportunity construction is a path dependent process where an entrepreneur learns what works and what doesn't work as the process of developing a venture progresses (Arthur 1989). The entrepreneur may not immediately discover the most lucrative aspect of the opportunity first off, he or she may enter into a business which has been identified as part of an opportunity and as experience accumulates, learning occurs where the firm rolls into the full potential of the opportunity by modifying focus, strategies, target customers, etc. For example an entrepreneur may establish a boutique handmade chocolate business but find market sales don't work as well as hi-teas, so the entrepreneur changes focus and strategy away from the product towards running events. The more novel the opportunity that is ultimately constructed through this process, the more learning and new information is required through experimentation (Galbraith 1977, Schoonhoven et. al. 1990). For innovative new products and services customer information is of little use (Spinelli et. al. 2007, P. 6). It is extremely difficult to forecast the value of construction opportunities as it takes time for the entrepreneur to develop a stable income earning business model.

Construction opportunities are an exploratory process where learning through trial and error is a valuable part of developing the opportunity (Rindova & Kotha 2001). Failure to learn from action will almost certainly result in failure. Successful opportunity construction may involve many adjustments to action through reinterpreting the results which may require starting all over again or abandoning the idea all together (Cyert & march 1963, March & Simon 1958, Mosakowski 1997). As the emergence process continues entrepreneurs may be

---

[5] Often referred to as creation theory.

forced to redefine their customers, markets, or even industry they are operating within, technologies and question the original assumptions about the opportunities they are pursuing (Bhide 1992, 1999, Christensen *et. al.* 2004).

Prior industry knowledge may hinder learning (March 1991, Sine *et. al.* 2005, Weick 1979) as the individual maybe locked into pre-existing ideas and knowledge. By breaking out of this industry 'conformity', new ideas, processes, and business models can be developed and introduced into an industry (Aldrich & Ruef 2006).

Table 1.1. A comparison of the four forms of opportunity.

Aspect	Imitation	Allocative	Discovery	Construction
What is an opportunity?	The possibility of undertaking a known activity in a select geographic or customer space.	The possibility of gaining market space through finding mismatches of demand/supply and changing demographics, etc, and employing resources to exploit these mismatches.	The possibility of taking advantage of potentially identified market gaps due to technology, social issues, regulation, or economic situation.	The possibilities of creating (new) ends through new means.
What is the focus?	Operational focus.	Focus on potential market space and developing exploitive strategies (i.e., new product development)	Focus on potential market space and developing exploitive strategies (i.e., new product development)	Emergence through strategies and feedback.
How are opportunities identified?	Opportunities seen by observing other successful businesses and replicating them.	Opportunities recognized through deductive reasoning.	Opportunities discovered through inductive reasoning.	Opportunities constructed through intuitive and abductive reasoning, trial & error, experimentation.
Assumptions of entrepreneur	A selected business model and type will work in the selected market space.	A belief in information and data.	A belief that new market space exists from the incongruity and/or industry structural changes.	Wide continuum of assumptions by different entrepreneurs, but usually display strong sets of values.
Uncertainty	Uncertainty managed through imitation (what works for others will work for him or her).	Uncertainty managed through product portfolio diversification.	Uncertainty managed through control of channels, networks, adequate resources and some experimentation.	Uncertainty managed through effectuation (see cognitive styles chapter 3) and experimentation.
Desired outcomes	A viable business with a sustainable return.	Success within the selected market space.	The creation of new market space, differentiation from competitors and avoidance of failure.	A viable new product, service, business model that is differentiated from competitors and has taken new market space.

Opportunity construction primarily relies on intuitive thinking to tap a person's creativity and imagination. The process of effectuation discussed in chapter three is very common where an enterprise is built upon what is available rather than deciding what is needed before start-up. This approach results in incremental 'step by step' growth where resources are acquired as needed, *i.e., a new airline purchases aircraft as it is able to open and develop new routes*. These types of opportunity are socially constructed (Berger & Luckmann 1967), within the confines of the culture the entrepreneur is immersed within. Opportunity construction is powerful where little knowledge is available, especially where new technologies or new business models are concerned. Under conditions of uncertainty, learning is probably more useful than planning (Argote 1999). Opportunities in this form have fewer precedents to learn from other forms of opportunity and entrepreneurs will develop their own knowledge structures to give the information they generate form and meaning (Walsh 1995). Constructed opportunities are usually the most disruptive to the competitive environment.

All of these forms of opportunities exist in the real world (Daft & Weick 1984). Which form of opportunity is manifested to the entrepreneur will depend upon the information available and level of ambiguity, and it may not be uncommon for entrepreneurs to switch from using one form to another in developing the opportunities they exploit (Hannan & Freeman 1997, Rindova & Kotha 2001). As time goes on more information may exist where the discovery mode may become the most apt aid in opportunity development. A comparison between the four forms of opportunity is shown in Table 1.1.

Large firms in markets where the level of ambiguity is low will tend to rely on rational and analytical approaches to opportunity recognition, often constrained by the formal strategic planning and management processes they have in-place (Fredrickson 1983, 1986, Mintzberg 1994). A major part of management literature today focuses upon assisting corporations shed themselves of their rigidities and tunnel vision to become more innovative and entrepreneurial. To many SMEs, pursuing opportunity is the only strategy that the entrepreneur has. Opportunity is firmly implanted within the entrepreneur's mind and vision, and all efforts and initiatives focus upon exploiting it and learning through doing, trial and error, making mistakes, feedback from peers and customers, etc, copying others, solving problems, and general experimentation (Gibb 1997).

THE ENVIRONMENT OF OPPORTUNITY

When looking in retrospect opportunities may appear very simple, but they are in fact very complex phenomena which are influenced by numerous factors within the environment and through our own social interpretations.

The environment evolves because of emerging new technologies that change the nature of products, markets, and industries, consumer financial wellbeing, social attitudes, habits, values, and political and regulatory actions. New information that emerges within society may change social attitudes, or lead to the creation of new regulatory requirements. The actions of other firms may change the nature of the environment bringing new products that increase expectations and/or new business models that radically change supply and value chains. Sometimes industry boundaries merge into other industries like we are seeing within the digital camera and mobile phone industries today.

The general environment develops and closes off opportunities while opening others. For example Woolworth's retail business thrived for many years because it occupied choice locations in the centre of cities. However when the choice retail sites became outer suburban areas along highways, where people have moved due to urban sprawl, Woolworth's business suffered and Wal-Mart was able to take advantage of this and rise. Opportunities are also affected by shocks that force change. These may include events of nature like natural disasters or droughts, etc, or human initiated shocks like political upheavals, economic disasters, and wars, etc. Opportunities may just become exhausted through competition which destroys profit potential and incentive to act (Eckhardt & Shane 2003, Shane & Venkataraman 2000). This particularly occurs with imitative and allocative opportunities. The environmental factors that lead to change are depicted in figure 1.5.

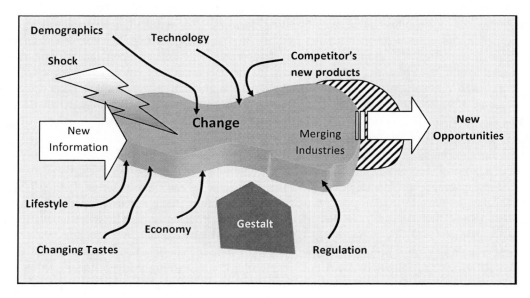

Figure 1.5. The Opportunity Environment.

What makes opportunities unique are the different ways individuals perceive the environment. Each individual will see the environment with different available information, as information is not dispersed uniformly through the society (Hayek 1945). Because situational motivation, perceptions, self-efficacy, range of social networks, available resources, and situational pressures differ in very subjective manners, each individual's product opportunity set differs from others. Individuals face biases from information overload, anxiety about uncertainty, different emotions, and ego, which influence cognition and make individuals susceptible to counterfactual thinking, affect infusion, self serving bias, planning fallacy, and self justification, etc (Baron 1998). Different types of cognitive biases are likely to emerge in different situations (Baron 1998). Different situations and contexts will affect idea generation and whether a person is reactive, proactive, or indifferent to what they see. Entrepreneurs may see that they are right while everyone else is wrong as everyone has a different perception of a situation (Casson 1982, P. 14). An entrepreneur may not see things as a given, but as something he or she can do something about (Penrose 1959, P. 86). Different firms will provide different underlying thinking environments which enhance ideas or increase bias and hinder decisions individuals make (Simon & Houghton 2002). A firm's resources, capabilities and self view will greatly affect the firm's member's images and expectations about the future (Boulding 1956). Different leader's mental models play a critical role in shaping the future direction of the firm.

Continual change and perception is what creates the potentialities of opportunity and this is what drives entrepreneurship (Drucker 1985). Individuals must perceive the concept of an opportunity through the gestalt of images to develop a concept into an idea and configure skills, resources, and networks into strategies to form a solid opportunity. This opportunity should be embedded within the market and economic, social, technological, political, and cultural interrelationships of the environment (Granovetter 1985, DiMaggio 2002, Jack & Anderson 2002, Collins 2004). The opportunity must meet the social and infrastructural conditions for it to be viable in society. It must meet the ground rules concerning exchange between different units within the environment according to how they should be carried out, where a shared trust can be established between the participants within the environment (Goss 2007). These accepted actions, rituals and arising meanings give acceptability to the opportunity if it meets all requirements of solving a problem and arousing the right emotions, enthusiasm rather than reluctance, among various groups within the environment (Smith 2004, Douglas 2005). The embeddedness of the food distribution and retail network into society is depicted in figure 1.6.

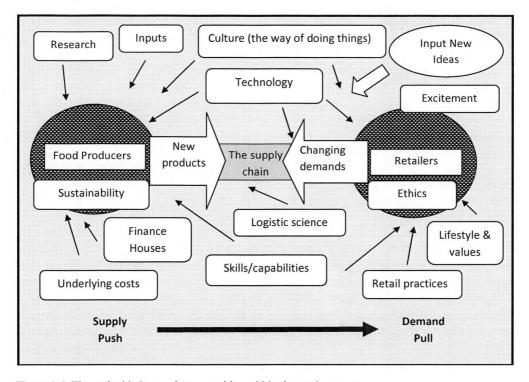

Figure 1.6. The embeddedness of opportunities within the environment.

The embeddedness set will vary according to time and space. For example consumers in the 1940s were primarily concerned about supply because of food shortages after the Second World War. Price became a major issue with consumers in the 1970s, and choice in the 1980s. Consumers required more information about the food they were eating in the 1990s and in the last decade the food market has developed multiple issues concerning buying issues like gourmet meals, food traceability, organic and ethical foods and new convivial environmentalism where farmers markets and buy local issues have been developed into alternative supply and value chains (Davis 2010). Different nations have different food preferences, methods of production, logistic supply chains, and retailing which lead to different embeddedness sets which will shape different opportunities.

A new technology brings with it a number of new opportunities in addition to the original intended purpose of the technology. For example, the railways allowed the transport of fresh milk and meat to markets much further away, just as air freight allows the quick and efficient transport of live seafood around the world. Air travel also required the invention of complementary goods and services like baggage, airport transport, and travel insurance, etc. The advent of broadcasting enabled the formation of production companies and other specialized service firms, just as the automobile industry enabled the formation and development of many satellite suppliers of car parts for production.

It is generally believed that technology development creates dynamism in industry and this is a major source of opportunity. For example the development of new building materials for construction brings more choice. Although many emerging technologies can favour small scale production through the availability of cheaper capital goods, decreasing minimum efficiency scales, and possibilities for flexible specialization (Piore & Sabel 1984, Carlsson 1989, Loveman & Sengenberger 1991), new technologies also may create barriers to entry for new firms entering specific markets and participating from regions where the technology is not available. Technology advancement can also put firms relying upon older technologies, especially traditional producers out of business. For example before refrigeration, ice supply houses flourished, now they don't exist. Polaroid processed a monopoly of instant film processing technology but lost its position in the market as consumers changed their habits as new technologies (digital) arrived. Innovation in the news and entertainment industries has completely changed the industry's nature.

Although technology evolution is increasing the potential spectrum of opportunities, the nature and complexity of opportunities is also rapidly increasing.

During periods of economic growth in the 19th and early part of the 20th centuries, major industrial changes occurred which created opportunities that allowed the formation and growth of companies including Ford, General Motors, Standard Oil, General Electric, and AT&T (Chandler 1977). This also occurred in the second half of the 20th Century and first decade of this Century in the computer and internet industries with the formation and rapid growth of companies like Microsoft, Apple, Google, eBay, and Amazon, etc. As the Chinese economy has grown rapidly over the last decade Chinese entrepreneurs have been able to exploit emerging opportunities. This has led to the establishment and growth of Chinese companies to the point that today the capitalization of the top 500 Chinese companies is higher than the top 500 US companies[6]. In growing economies the entrepreneurs and firms involved begin to perceive the emerging situation within a universal mental construct that comes into existence leading to a *'bandwagon effect'* in the actions they take in creating numerous innovations, and the start-ups of new firms (Grebel *et. al.* 2001). Size, technology and critical mass seem to enable firms to exploit many more opportunities (Boyce & Ville 2002).

---

[6] See: China's Top 500 perform better than US, China Daily, 7th September 2009, http://www.chinadaily. com.cn/china/2009-09/07/content_8660388.htm, (accessed 2nd March 2011).

As markets and economies grow, so do opportunities according to the forces at work that bring economic, socio-political, and technological change. In these times of change many successful companies struggle to survive. Many of the *'excellent'* companies IBM, NCR, Wang Laboratories, and Xerox, that Tom Peters and Robert Waterman wrote about in 1982 in their book *'In Search of Excellence'* seemed to be trapped by their success that prevented them in thinking in new ways and transforming themselves to meet the new challenges. Focusing on available opportunities seems to be a more important factor for success than the way a company is organized or plays out its strategy. If the successful identification and exploitation of opportunity is the most important factor for success, then the nature of opportunity should therefore be the major focus of the firm.

THE PROCESS OF OPPORTUNITY

Our mind is full of images stored in our memory in the form of schema. Our schema play a paramount role in our beliefs, values, and how we make sense of the world, influencing the way we think about things and make decisions (Gioia & Poole 1984). Schemata provide a cognitive structure where algorithm-like sequences assist the individual understand events and situations (Lord & Kernan 1987). Schemata also enable an individual construct scenes or vignettes in our mind (Wyer & Calston 1979) which form our desires and fantasies. Generally our schemata maintain rigidity of our belief systems (Abelson 1981, Beach and Connolly 2005) which enables the individual to maintain their inspirational and behavioural trajectories, which forms the informational basis of our thinking and decision making (Beach & Mitchell 1987, Beach 1993, Beach & Connolly 2005)[7].

Any new perceptions from the environment may not align to the information contained within our schemata and create a shock. This could a simple event like dropping a set of keys or a drastic event like the loss of a job or death in the family. Shocks such as these bring attention to a state of disequilibrium where current information is challenged. Without suppression or denial of these challenges, an individual may be able to develop solutions to these discontinuities (Tushman & Romanelli 1985) and view alternative courses of action (Lee & Mitchell 1994). These shocks will be accompanied with either positive or negative emotions which may also influence the new trajectories taken by the individual (Holtom & Inderrieden 2006).

Shock may lead to a situation where the individual doesn't know how to respond and begins to use effectuation to assess the situation, thereby making connections and constructions out of different pieces of information that the person has in their memory. Existing schemata will integrate the person's own values into the new thought vectors which brings congruency in thoughts and judgment (Huning 2009). These thoughts begin to form concepts as the individual is re-assessing the situation which may result in recognition of a unique situation.

---

[7] Mitchell *et. al.* (2000) define a number of scripts that influence individual's reasoning. Those relevant to opportunity include arrangement scripts that are knowledge structures about the specific arrangements that that support performance and expert level mastery within an organization, willingness scripts that are knowledge structures that underlie commitment to new venture creation, and ability scripts that contain knowledge about a person's skills, competencies, norms, and attitudes.

Concepts are the building blocks of ideas, very general abstract notions that can be built into specific ideas. Concepts are built upon images and perceptions and tend to have vague and descriptive meanings, rather than meanings that action can be taken upon. Concepts are descriptive views of something in the environment that exist, or something from the imagination that is non-existent or fantasy. One or more conceptualizations will usually be combined together to form an idea, which can be refined, developed, enlarged, and elaborated upon to form something that can be acted upon.

A description of a restaurant is a concept that describes the characteristics has little actionable meaning. Mexican food is another concept that is also descriptive of something, but when they are combined together they become a Mexican restaurant which is an idea that can be elaborated upon, expanded, refined, developed and action taken. Likewise the concept of a theatre company and the concept of a restaurant can be combined together to form a theatre restaurant. In Melbourne, Australia, the concept of a tram running around the city was combined with the concept of a restaurant to form the Colonial Tramway Restaurant[8]. The first airplane, the Wright Flyer 1 was invented from a number of concepts including the basic concepts of aerodynamics (thrust, drag, lift, and gravity), the box kite, a petrol engine powering a propeller to create thrust, balance, and stability.

Concepts can be formed from information where ideas can be developed by fusing the different pieces together. For example; Information (1): the population in many developed countries is aging. Information (2): As there are less people at study age, universities are developing excess capacity. Information (3): Universities are subject to funding cuts. Information (4): Many developing countries have young populations at study age who wish to gain an education. These threads of information can be developed into the idea of taking foreign fee paying students into developed country universities that have excess capacity. Similarly, Information (1): the costs of running a service department in a firm within a developed country are very high. Information (2): Operational costs in countries like India are much lower. Information (3): Countries like India have abundant and highly educated people, who speak English very well. Information (4): Voice over internet protocol (VOIP) allows direct and cheap communication around the world. Therefore this information can be developed into the concept of a customer service centre located in Mumbai to service customers over the phone in the United States.

Developing concepts into ideas is very much a learning process that creates a linkage between real world experiences and the conceptual world of how we see the world ought to be. Figuring out which conceptual ideas may be viable opportunities requires testing them in the real world.

The first step of this process is to identify concepts, test them in the real world, creating concrete experiences and then reflect upon the outcomes and make decisions about their validity against the desired outcomes. Unsatisfactory results will trigger another round of experimentation with refined concepts and further reflection of the results. In the absence of testing concepts through action, the entrepreneur may test these concepts through the socio-cognitive process of *'talking through'* the issues as a means of thinking and articulating them to create clarity (Koning & Muzyka 1999). This process may continue a number of times as concepts are refined. If after continued experimentation the results are still not satisfactory, then a complete evaluation seeking further information may be required before further testing

---

[8] See: http://www.tramrestaurant.com.au/en/

and experimentation. Eventually new divergent knowledge is created in the form of new ideas. This process of trial and is seen on the right hand side of figure 1.7. and are very common in the opportunity construction and effectuation processes.

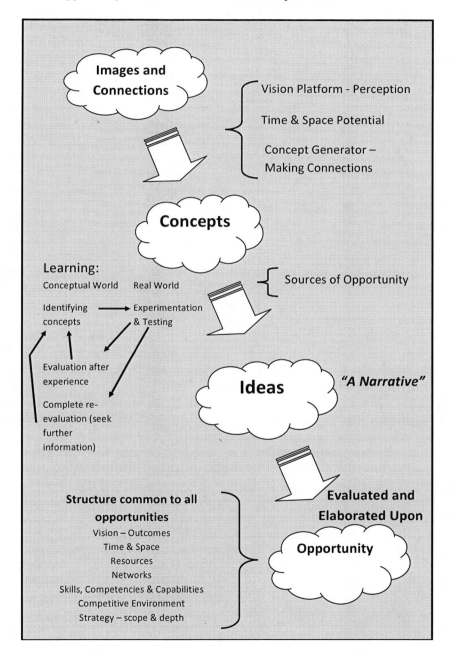

Figure 1.7. The opportunity process.

Some people will learn better through actively testing their ideas in the real world, while others through reflection upon the different attributes of their experience and ideas. In addition a person's learning style may be more suited to different stages of the venture process (Brigham & DeCastro 2003). According to Ward (2004) different cognitive approaches to creativity will process information differently and affect the constructs that are made, and people have their own preferred learning styles.

Greater knowledge and wisdom is developed through the learning process (Kolb 1984), which in this case is the generation of an idea. Some people may prefer the method of assimilation and grasp experience by thinking and theorizing and then transforming the information by watching and reflecting. Assimilators abstract conceptualize and undertake reflective observation (Kolb 1984). People with assimilative learning preferences will tend to stew over potential solutions to problems and directions to take (Gaglio & Taub 1992, Lumpkin *et. al.* 2004). Assimilators are excellent at pulling together disparate observations and building these separate information strands into coherent ideas (Grochow 1973). In their ideas, assimilators will tend to be logically precise putting more emphasis on the theory behind the concept than the practical side.

The converger grasps by thinking and theorizing and then transforms the information by doing and applying. Convergers rely on abstract conceptualization and experimentation (Kolb 1984). While convergers may not be doing something all the time, they never stop thinking about problems and their solutions (Torrealba 1972). They will build up their technical knowledge and platform, ready to utilize it on developing solution and products once they understand all the issues involved (Corbett 2002). They tend to be more technically rather than socially orientated (Hudson 1966).

The diverger grasps by feeling and doing and then transforms the information by watching and reflecting. Divergers have the opposite strengths to convergers. They have a strong imagination and ability to read people and situations through their social awareness abilities. They are able to look at situations from many perspectives and organize many interrelationships into a meaningful gestalt. They are strong at evaluating concepts through the market, financial, and operational issues, etc., through rich personal networks they build up (Bhave 1994, Gaglio & Taub 1992, Singh *et. al.* 1999).

The accommodator grasps experience by feeling and doing and then transforms the information by doing and applying. Accommodators tend to have the opposite strengths to assimilators. Accommodators prefer concrete experiences and active experimentation. They prefer to do rather than to theorize. They are opportunity seeking and like to act rather than spend a long period of time evaluating the opportunity. They are able to implement plans extremely well and their strength is towards opportunity exploitation.

Learning can be hindered or distorted by a number of cognitive mechanisms (Keh *et. al.* 2002). For example many entrepreneurs are flawed in their thinking due to the use of small samples, and display overconfidence in their abilities when evaluating opportunities. Other cognitive biases influence thought patterns that an entrepreneur could adopt, such as '*obstacle thinking*' which leads to an individual focus on the negative aspects of an opportunity, providing reasons for giving up and abandoning the opportunity (Manz 1986, Neck & Manz 1992, 1996). This will be discussed in much greater detail in chapter three.

The evolving idea becomes a personal narrative of the entrepreneur, a conceptual framework with a motivated objective. The idea is attached to excitement and a set of other emotions becoming the individual's gestalt, *'a theory of success'*, a new mantra for the future.

Narrative becomes absorbed within the person of whom the tone has some influence on momentum (Schleicher & Walker 2010). The narrative calls the present into question, replacing it with an alternative future. Through narrative, ambiguity is eliminated and replaced with a clear and guiding path of action, which become the new meaning for the entrepreneur and venture, exerting influence on those involved to accomplish it (Gioia & Chittipaddi 1995).

With a map of the future by which to navigate, the vision is set out so the idea can take on a framework where structure can be added by assembling skills, competencies, organizational capabilities, and resources together, and identifying which parts of the entrepreneur's networks are required, or what new networks need to be created, and what action is required within the competitive environment through a formulated strategy. Once an idea has structure it can be evaluated for its viability as an opportunity.

The narrative that the entrepreneur develops about the opportunity provides insight into his or her future effectiveness (Fleming 2001). How the opportunity is described, what histories, analogies, and metaphors used will provide insight into the meaning and commitment towards the opportunity.

SEEING OPPORTUNITY

The creation of a new venture is more an evolutionary process rather than an event (Spinelli *et. al.* 2007, P. 4). Conceptual and idea development comes from an alertness which is dependent upon peoples' cognitive processes and experiences (Baron 2006). Cognition research has shown that prior knowledge is paramount to the capacity to recognize opportunities (Shane 2000) and creativity is important in elaborating and developing them into something exploitable (Whiting 1988). In addition to prior knowledge and creativity, a person's managerial, technical, strategic and entrepreneurial skills and competencies have strong bearing on what a person perceives within the environment (Ucbasaran *et. al.* 2008). The small differences in perception at the beginning of the opportunity process may lead to very different ideas and subsequent strategies. How different people react depends upon individual responses to stimulus related to their knowledge and the situation.

As a consequence of the above arguments, peoples' emotional sensitivity to the environment will differ across the general population (see figure 1.8). Emotional sensitivity is a person's ability to be sensitive to the dimensions of an actual situation that can be shaped and acted upon. This requires the capacity to perceive complex aspects of any situation rather than looking for ways to simplify how to deal with what one perceives through heuristics and other cognitive biases. Everybody sees the environment according to their own assumptions, beliefs, and understandings that can get in the way of a person seeing what is actually there in front of them. This is influenced by our prior knowledge and fundamental assumptions of the world[9]. Emotional sensitivity involves unbiased perception to stimuli within the environment of any particular situation that may house potential opportunities or require decision making.

---

[9] Prior knowledge influences what we see. For example an infant visiting an agricultural show for the first time who has not seen a bull before, may identify it as a large dog that it understands as a domestic pet until he or she is corrected by a parent or other bystander as to the existence of bulls. Thus it is prior knowledge that determines what a person sees in this case. A person's decisions and behavior will be influenced by their basic assumptions. For example people may believe that they can control nature may tend to discard the potential effects of nature

Emotional sensitivity runs across a continuum from *mindlessness* to *mindfulness.* Mindlessness numbs individuals' senses to the outside environment and patterns them into seeing situations as absolutes (Corbett & McMullen 2007, P. 48). Whereas mindfulness is a state of psychological freedom without any attachment to any point of view and being attentive to what is occurring at present (Martin 1997, Brown & Ryan 2003). Many peoples' emotional sensitivity is inhibited by their past categorizations, rules and routines that cloud the ability to view any current situation with novel distinctions (Langer & Moldoveanu 2000). Therefore the more mindful a person is, the more open to the environment they will be.

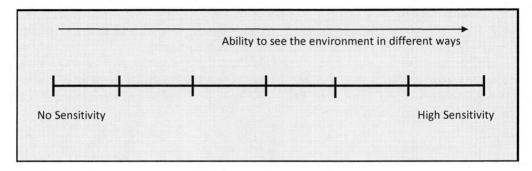

Figure 1.8. The continuum of emotional sensitivity.

Mindfulness allows a person access to environmental perceptions without schema blocking or altering the interpretation of events. The more mindfulness, the better the perception of opportunities, however other facets such as prior knowledge are still vitally important, which without any individual will not be able to perceive opportunity for new ventures, products, and services (Corbett & McMullen 2007, P. 50). Langer (1997) proposed that mindfulness may enhance the ability to perceive and shape new opportunities through five components that have been empirically tested;

- Openness to novelty – the ability to reason with relatively novel forms of stimuli,
- Alertness to distinction – the ability to distinguish minute differences in the details of an object, action, or environment,
- Sensitivity to different contexts- tasks and abilities will differ according to the situational context,
- Awareness of multiple perspectives – the ability to think dialectically, and
- Orientation in the present- paying attention to here and now.

One would assume that the degree of mindfulness an individual possesses will also influence the depth of opportunity that can be observed within the environment. Table 1.2. shows the different levels of ideas that can be observed and associated forms of thinking involved in seeing and creating them.

---

when making decisions about activities like farming, whereas people who believe that nature cannot be controlled will develop their decisions based on a respect for the power of nature and possibly try to find ways to work in harmony with nature.

Table 1.2. The Levels of Ideas

Level One	Imitation	See and belief, little thought except for viability-logical thinking
Level Two	Creative Imitation	See and enhance, maybe with some connection, logic and holistic creativity
Level Three	Creating a new business Model	Connectivity of different pieces of information, some imaginatively, or through re-engineering
Level Four	Creating something new to the world	Complete holistic, imaginative construction, building from deep and sparse pieces of prior knowledge.

Lack of mindfulness would not stop a person search deliberately for opportunities through undertaking market and industry analysis (Porter 1980), suitable for imitative and allocative forms of opportunities.

However it is sometimes advantageous to utilize heuristics that prevent a person seeing *'unrealistic'* ideas for their personal or firm situation. An individual's or firm's level of skills, competencies, capabilities, resources, networks, attitudes, values, and sense of mission will be suited best to certain opportunity magnitudes. According to Markman and Baron (2003), the closer the fit between an individual's attributes and the needs to exploit the opportunity, the more likely the opportunity will be successfully exploited. This can no better be seen in a person's desire verses scale. Certain types of opportunities best suit certain types of entrepreneurs according to the size of their business (resource sets) as figure 1.9. depicts.

In addition to scale, entrepreneurs may also have a point of anchorage from where business opportunities are perceived. For example, an automobile manufacturer would tend to look at value chain opportunities like downstream investment in car dealerships and service centres and upstream investment in auto-part manufacturing. Soft drink bottlers may consider developing wholesale distribution centres and franchise operations, as may fast-food providers. Grocery chain operators may consider diversification, moving their business model into other products like hardware, etc.

There is anecdotal evidence that opportunity and new venture creation is a deeply emotional activity (Bower 1988, 1993, Roddick 2000, Branson 2000, Kets de Vries 1996, Goss 2005a, 2005b). Although Schumpeter (1934) and Keynes alluded to the emotional side of entrepreneurship (Zafirovski 1999), there has been little exploratory or explanatory works linking the variable of emotion with opportunity.

Emotion is closely associated with cognition and is influential upon our perceptions and behaviour. Through emotion people tend to be either drawn towards or repelled from certain situations. Emotional energy is important in determining the level of effort and enthusiasm put into something, and can perform a motivation role. There is a continuum of emotional charge ranging from excitement and happiness on one side to depression and sadness on the other (Collins 2004). The cognition component acts through our memory resulting in expectations about situations.

Our emotions are also connected to the wider social world where participation in particular situations brings peer and other observer emotion that may encourage or discourage action. This could be seen in the development of the personal computer or the culture that has developed at *Palo Alto* in California where individuals are immersed in a positive inertia of enthusiasm and excitement around them that encouraged innovative practices within their domain (Cringely 2005). In this way opportunity and innovation can be seen as a collective social activity. The whole personal computer market can be seen as a movement of enthusiasts seeking fulfilment, rather than the actions of a single astute entrepreneur spotting an opportunity (Goss 2007). The personal computer, the internet, green energy, and biotechnology industries can be seen as people seeking participation within an industry as a membership symbol – a collective sense of effervescence (Goss 2007). This membership can combat any prevailing sense of scepticism from the general community concerning new concepts and ideas.

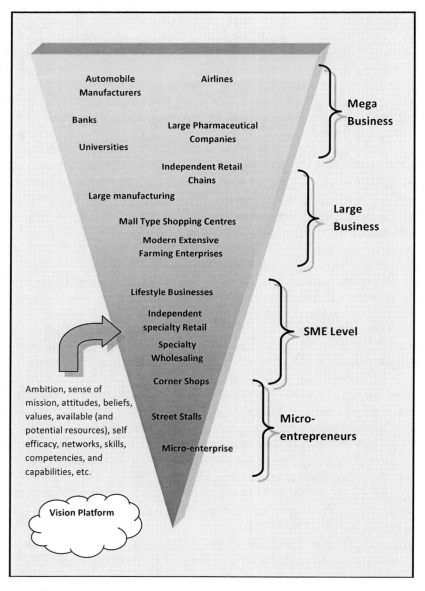

Figure 1.9. Business and Opportunity Scale.

People vary in their motivation to look for opportunity and exploit it. There are some forms of motivations that may, although research is yet inconclusive, increase the propensity of people to look for and act upon opportunity. These include the need for achievement, risk taking propensity, goal setting, independence, drive, and egotistic passion (Shane *et. al.* 2003). People with high self-efficacy may be more encouraged to act than those with lower self-efficacy and a host of other cognitive factors like overconfidence and representativeness biases may also influence their decisions. What also plays a role in motivation is a person's view of the opportunity cost of pursuing the opportunity (Amit *et. al.* 1995), their level of financial capital (Evans & Leighton 1989), creditability and relationship to investors (Aldrich & Zimmer 1986), career experience (Carroll & Mosakowski 1987, Cooper *et. al.* 1989), personal knowledge (Kor *et. al.* 2007), and even some psychological assumptions like the need to control. Differing motivations and biases will lead people to perceive and act differently to others in the same situations where the same information, skills, and resources exist.

Opportunities can be deliberately sought after through scanning the environment, or alternately through recognizing the value of information and ideas they come across, without any intention to seek new opportunities (Koller 1988). An organization may scan the environment to understand the external forces of change so that it may find ways to improve its position in the future by finding new opportunities to exploit. Environmental scanning is a mode of organizational learning, where organizations differ in their approach to scanning. Where an organization believes the environment is analyzable, where events and processes are measurable, it will tend to systematically gather and analyse information, whereas an organization that believes the environment is un-analyzable, it will tend to interpret what is going on as an explanation of past behavior (Daft & Weick 1984). Which approach used will also depend upon the amount of information available and level of turbulence within the environment. Analysis is better for identifying imitative and allocative types of opportunities and interpretation is better for discovery and construction types of opportunities. Accidental discoveries may occur because of emotional sensitivity and mindfulness described above in what could be called a *'passive search'* (Ardichvili *et. al.* 2003) where an individual is receptive but not engaged in any formal systematic search.

Most new ideas are adaptations of something already existing and most business ideas emerge from a situation or problem that the entrepreneur sees within his or her immediate environment. Hills (1985) listed prior experience as the source of 73% of new ideas, business associations 33%, a similar business 26%, a hobby or personal interest 17%, market research 11%, serendipity 11%, and other sources 7.4%.

EVALUATING OPPORTUNITY

The opportunity-entrepreneurial process is decision demanding across the whole spectrum right into the gamut of strategy and daily operations. The feasibility of the spotted opportunity will only truly be known during the implementation of strategies selected to exploit it, as only then the true nature of the opportunity can be observed. Before actual start-up the real nature of the opportunity is mysterious and the real issues involved only emerge as strategy is implemented, and we can only suppose and speculate about its nature and characteristics.

The opportunity-entrepreneurial process is shown in figure 1.10. This begins with our perceptions and personal creativity, supported by our competencies in spotting ideas. The rest of the process involves the evaluation of an idea to determine whether an opportunity actually exists. Innovation is required to evaluate and elaborate on the idea. Suitable strategies out of a number of possible options need to be selected which involves strategic thinking. Our skills, resources, networks, capabilities and strategies should then match the nature of the opportunity for exploitation to be successful, as it is our management capability that is important in effectively exploiting the opportunity. As we progress in the exploitation of the opportunity, we learn more about its nature and modify our strategies in accordance with what we learn. This together with the accuracy that we have matched our strategy with the perceived nature of the opportunity identified, and level of competitive effectiveness we have developed within the competitive environment determines performance.

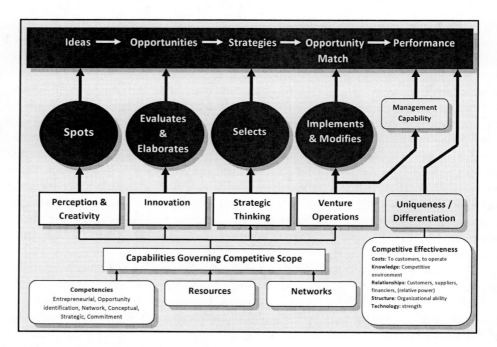

Figure 1.10. The Opportunity-Entrepreneurial Process.

The depiction of the opportunity-entrepreneurship process infers that it is a learning process where the entrepreneur/firm selects the strategies and operational processes that best serve them – becoming a unique theory applicable for the entrepreneur/firm in question. Although the opportunity-entrepreneurial process is unique for every firm, there is a common structure that defines the process of opportunity exploitation depicted in figure 1.10.

Some of the skills needed for the successful operation of a particular business maybe unique to that business and cannot be formally learnt. For example, the character Miranda Priestly in the David Frankel directed film *The Devil Wears Prada* had an uncanny ability to pick next season's fashion successes which was one of the primary reasons that the *Runway* magazine was so highly successful. These types of skills enhance the perception of opportunity in specialized domains and themselves attributes that can assist effective business performance.

In addition, because of a unique environmental position and combination of resources existing with each firm, the barriers to entry and obstacles to successful implementation will also tend to be unique to each firm. What is an insurmountable barrier to one firm may be a strength for another. This in part gives ideas various levels of attractiveness as opportunities to different firms.

Opportunity is a relative concept which can be measured by the potential return that it may provide a person perceiving it. The value of this return will vary according to individual. For an idea to qualify as an opportunity, it has to provide a viable return for the individual, which is not a static benchmark, as it differs between people. Therefore what might be an opportunity for one person may just remain an idea for another.

Another factor influencing the viability of an opportunity is the uncertainty and risk involved. There will always be uncertainty with any potential outcome of a new venture. This includes the uncertainty regarding demand and uncertainty regarding capability. Both of these forms of uncertainties create some probability of failure, but individuals see these uncertainties very differently. For example, some individuals will exhibit biases of overconfidence and high perceptions of self-efficacy which lowers their perceptions of uncertainty and risk about an idea and thus deem the idea an opportunity in their personal perception.

Uncertainty will always exist with a venture and there is no way of eliminating this (Shane 2003, P. 7). As the opportunity-entrepreneurship process is also a learning process, this infers that we start out not knowing what the future will be and where we will quite end up. The future cannot be known in advance and this is a source of uncertainty about what will occur (Knight 1921). What will potentially occur can only be calculated as a probable outcome. Forecasting is a matter of extrapolating historical data which will provide different results depending upon the methods used and in the case of new products and new ventures there is no historical data to base any forecasts on. The future cannot be forecast, only expected and there are dangers in using forecasts as imaginary maps we believe to be true (Schumacher 1974, P. 195). The environment will always change unexpectedly which requires changes in strategy to accommodate these phenomenon.

There are two aspects of entrepreneurial risk. First there is risk of firm failure. In the worst case scenario, a business failure can lead to a loss of investment, and even bankruptcy. Venture failure also carries the personal stigma of failure for the individual which is viewed differently in various countries. The second form of risk is in changing lifestyle and that mishaps in pursuing an entrepreneurial opportunity will result in a loss of current income and lifestyle.

Due to the wide and varied nature of ideas, there is no one correct way to evaluate opportunity viability. Imitative and allocative opportunities can be analysed in terms of market demand at the customer level, market size, and margin analyses based on historical data. Critical to underpinning the viability of imitative and allocative opportunities is the marketshare that the entrepreneur can potentially gain and the size of the market (Gaglio 1997). This will not just depend upon the qualities of the product, but the abilities of the firm to promote and distribute the product.

However discovery and construction opportunities rely on much more intuition and *'gut feel'* in evaluating viability. The high levels of uncertainty of these types of opportunities makes conventional forms of strategic analysis of very limited value (March 1991, Mintzberg 1994). These types of opportunities are usually best if evaluated informally or even unarticulated (Timmons 1987). Formal business plans and forecasts based on historical information do little to assist in the analysis of the viability of the idea and any large amount of time spent analysing the idea in depth will probably not shed much further understanding or reduce uncertainty about its potential success. Entrepreneurs will probably look at the opportunity cost of investing time and resources into the idea under conditions of risk and uncertainty and then compare this to a situation where he or she had pursued other actions of choice (Casson 1982). The only way to understand the viability of the opportunity is to learn about it through implementation, where the willingness to continue experimenting is a further expression of commitment by the entrepreneur (Staw 1981).

The only aspect of discovery and construction opportunities that can be evaluated is to consider the probable customer perception of the value proposition and price-value relationships – which are purely subjective. These perceptions can be further tested as to how easily this value is perceived by potential customers through focus groups. The longer it takes for individuals to perceive value, the more risk in the inherent opportunity (Spinelli *et. al.* 2007, P. 6).

The value of opportunities will vary between industries, but this does not appear to be a major factor influencing entrepreneurs in their focus upon industries that have opportunities of higher value. The average value of opportunities in one industry may be lower than another but an individual's types of experiences and aspirations will influence where their focus and attention is applied. Weight is apparently given to areas where an individual feels interested and is capable of exploiting.

There are also timing and resource costs, among other factors that influence opportunity viability. For example, Butler Lampson and Chuck Thacker, two researchers at Xerox who invented the first personal computer – the Alto, cost over USD \$10,000 to build. Steve Jobs and Steve Wornack's Apple design cost around 20% of the Lampson and Thacker design to build, making the Apple more viable as an opportunity. Although there were other factors involved like Jobs and Wornack's intention to go into business prior to designing the Apple, this example shows that other environmental and motivational factors create different scenarios of viability for potential opportunities, and that individuals make different decisions based upon these factors.

Opportunity evaluation becomes a complex interrelationship of subjective and objective issues that can be looked at with a modified SWOT analysis used in strategic planning. Strengths and weaknesses refer to internal influences on the individual or firm and affect the ability to exploit any opportunity. These would include issues that the individual perceives as strengths that can be capitalized upon and weaknesses that must be improved so that they don't inhibit potential opportunity exploitation. Threats relate to issues from the external environment which is perceived to be critical to the activities and wellbeing of the enterprise that would exploit the opportunity. Risks and uncertainties would include factors that would either make outcomes uncertain in the future or that may lead to venture failure. Strengths, Weaknesses (internal) and threats, risks and uncertainties (external) should be examined around the opportunity. The viability of the potential opportunity is a function of the surrounding strengths, weaknesses, threats, risks, and uncertainties. It must also be remembered that our perceptions of opportunities are influenced by emotions, cognitive biases and heuristics which affect of judgments about viability. This framework is shown in figure 1.11.

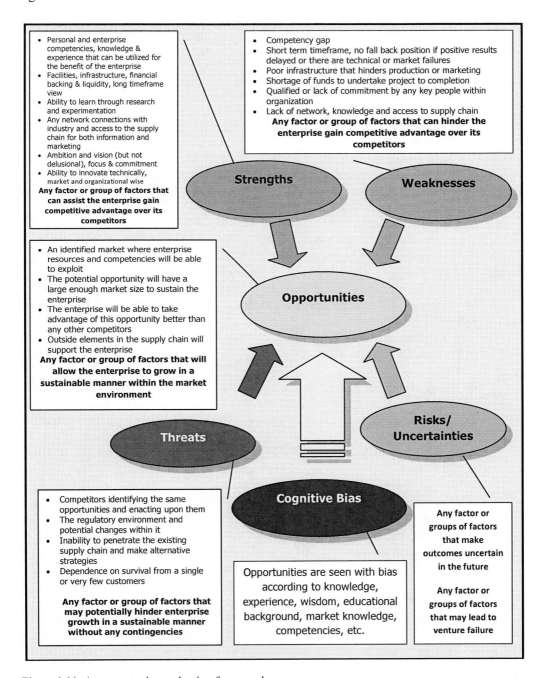

Figure 1.11. An opportunity evaluation framework.

For an idea to become an opportunity it must;

a) Represent a future desirable state that an individual has aspirations for,
b) It must be achievable, and
c) An individual or firm has the skills, resources, and networks, or can acquire them to exploit the opportunity.

The analysis will lead to a set of questions that can help determine whether the above criteria can be met.

1. What is happening in the competitive environment?
2. What changes are occurring?
3. Will these changes continue to occur?
4. What do I know that others don't know (or behave like they don't know)?
5. How can I carve out a unique or novel place within the competitive environment where others don't exist?
6. Can the idea be accepted?
7. Do I have the skills, competencies, capabilities, resources and networks (or can I build them up and/or acquire them)?
8. Will this be beneficial to the consumer and me?

But as every idea is unique, at least situationally, a different set of criteria is required to evaluate different types of ideas.

The consideration and determination of the answers to the above questions may be influenced by some higher order heuristics like;

1. *Risk-reward profile:* the valuation of relative rewards and risks, where a person will weigh up the worth of forgoing guaranteed income and health insurance, etc, against the potential benefits that could be gained by pursuing an opportunity (Parker 1996, Bosma *et. al.* 1999).
2. *The reference benchmark:* Individuals use reference points to decide on what they may do based on their pertinent aspirations at a point of time (Fiegenbaum *et. al.* 1995),
3. *Reasoning:* Every individual seeks to control the flow of events they are involved in with their own expectations, anticipations, hypothesis to test and experiments to conduct and as a consequence has different viewpoints from others (Kelly 1970).
4. *Pareto optimal solutions:* the idea maintains a level of well-being for all without causing any personal loss or psychological stress to any participant in the market space, while increasing the personal well being of the entrepreneur (Headey & Wearing 1992), and
5. For socially conscious entrepreneurs a *Nash equilibrium outcome:* a solution that has all individuals satisfied with a pattern of outcomes that improves the position of the entrepreneur, and for members of the new venture team, while also increasing the level of satisfaction with life as a whole for the society at large (Miller 2003).

As a consequence, information will be interpreted differently by individuals who may think of similar ideas, but have completely different vectors of that idea in mind.

There are many types of businesses where it is extremely difficult to identify the elements of success, e.g. restaurants, boutiques, and spas, etc. They rely on very tight (but not necessarily apparent) formulas for success, which the entrepreneur may not even understand. Also quite often what looks like a solid viable opportunity that appears very logical and may even gather favourable market research (Schindler 1992) may fail dismally in the marketplace. Some examples of spectacular market failures include Federal Express's launch of ZAP Mail facsimile service in 1984, The Coca Cola Company's launch of New Coke in 1985, and the launch of 3G video calling around 2003.

CHANCE AND FATE

Chance and fate is responsible for the creation of many firms and industries. Chance is closely associated with time and space and is not a random occurrence. Chance is reliant upon an individual possessing prior knowledge, perceptions, and cognitive thinking skills and be willing to act for chance to have a benefit. Chance is reliant upon a person having the relevant technical and/or business skills so that he or she will have the confidence to exploit the opportunity they have seen; otherwise the opportunity will take up only a short span of attention and be quickly forgotten.

Chance also has its roots in domicile outlook (see chapter 3). A person will be influenced by their parents, family, friends, social institutions like schools and culture influences the locust of control, adversity to risk taking, self esteem, sense of identity, and other attributes like creativity, innovation, and the propensity to interact socially. Culture also influences one's belief in fate and if one believes that it is important to be in the right place at the right time, with the right perceptions and right skills and some knowledge, this will to some degree predetermine fate. In addition location is very important. People living in the heart of Borneo, or the plains of Siberia, will have different outlooks and access to information, knowledge and people than people living in Palo Alto, California, London, New York, or Sydney.

On national levels, the dimension of time and space gave the United States a great advantage after the Second World War as no other country was in a position to make a challenge until the 1970s. At firm levels, Coca Cola and Caterpillar went international because both companies followed the US Army around the world. Global interconnections have tremendous effects on industries around the world. The oil shocks in the 1970s created many winners and losers. Turmoil in the Middle East in 2011 is creating great stress on price levels which are felt all around the world, particularly on food prices. Political instability in the Ivory Coast is affecting the price of chocolate all around the world forcing companies to consider reformulating their products. Chance events outside the control of firms such as new inventions, the development of new technologies, external political developments change industry structures that change the nature of opportunities (Porter 1990, P. 73). Chance changes discontinuities that change the competitive position of resources, nations, industries, and firms that can change the nature of supplier-customer relationships, raise the urgency to undertake research, and create new advantages/disadvantages for firms located in various countries (Porter 1990, P. 124).

It is easy to explain the invention of products and start-up of firms as chance events created by a visionary or inventor located in any nation. However these events don't completely occur by chance as there are usually other underlying factors that may be present or act as a precursor. What may look like chance may be a difference of factor environments across different regions.

CONCLUSION

Opportunity is as much about aspirational designs about what the future could be, coming just as much from the inside as it does from the outside environment. Start-ups depend upon the drive of someone to turn an idea into an opportunity. This requires special perspectives that permeate through entrepreneurs of the ages (Kuratko 2005). And it is this special perspective that opens up new market space (Schoohoven & Romanelli 2001). This is tied to emotion, motivation, our perspectives, creativity and courage.

Opportunity is about learning rather than planning, where ideas emerge and strategy is crafted and shaped around the opportunity, as it is seen. It is not knowledge or intelligence that is important, but how knowledge is processed through creativity and what is then done with it.

We have also seen that some people seek limited opportunities based upon their domicile outlooks, skills, and resources, while others have large ambitions and even visions of grandeur. We have also seen that there is no set of rules, no formal theory that can explain all this. Opportunity and success is situational, and it must be seen in this context, depending upon so many factors. Opportunities are not something equal to all. People have their own vision, time frames, ability to perceive, emotional sensitivity, levels of knowledge and domicile outlooks that influence their ability to see opportunity.

The continued pursuit of opportunity is something very important to the survival of a firm. The author's research into the Fortune 500 data shows that firms continue to prosper when their sectors are in growth mode and struggle when growth in their sectors slows down and declines. But what can also be seen is that over half of the formation of Fortune 500 companies occurred during times of economic recession where structural changes to industries were taking place (Strangler 2009).

Most businesses fail from not fulfilling the requirements of the identified opportunity, through misreading it, or not having the correct combination of resources to exploit it. They fail to have an adequate or appropriate appreciation for the intangible part of opportunity. Correctly acquiring opportunity requires flexibility and changes in direction from where a firm first started out.

Seeing opportunity can be inhibited by internal complacency. This is the prime cause of many enterprise failures. Opportunity on a national scale can be inhibited through a 'rent seeking' or 'corrupt' business culture prevalent in many developing countries, the creditability of law and fairness of regulatory conditions, monopolistic environments, high costs of doing business, low economic growth rates, and other general barriers to entry for firms entering the market.

The rest of this book will examine the issues brought out in this chapter in much more detail, starting with the time and space paradigm next chapter. The various paradigms of opportunity will be pieced together in the final chapter to form a meta-theory framework to assist in understanding the phenomenon of opportunity.

REFERENCES

Abelson, R.P. (1981). Psychological status of the script concept, *American Psychologist,* Vol. 36, No. 7, pp. 715-729.

Aldrich, H. & Zimmer, C. (1986). Entrepreneurship through social networks, In: Sexton, D., & Smilor, R. (Eds.), *The Art and Science of Entrepreneurship,* Cambridge, MA, Ballinger, pp. 3-23.

Aldrich, H.E. & Ruef, M. (2006). *Organizations Evolving, 2nd Edition,* Thousand Oaks, Sage.

Amit, R., Meuller, E., & Cockburn, I. (1995). Opportunity Costs and Entrepreneurial Activity, *Journal of Business Venturing,* Vol. 10, pp. 95-106.

Ardichvili, A., Cardozo, R., & Ray, S. (2003). A theory of entrepreneurial opportunity identification and development, *Journal of Business Venturing,* Vol. 18, pp. 105-123.

Argote, L. (1999). *Organizational Learning: Creating, Retaining and transferring Knowledge,* Norewell, Kluwer Academic Publishers.

Arthur, W.B. (1989). Competing technologies, increasing returns, and lock-in by historical events, *Economic Journal,* Vol. 99, No. 394, pp. 116-131.

Baker, T. & Nelson, R. (2005). Creating something from nothing: Resource construction through entrepreneurial bricolage, *Administrative Science Quarterly,* Vol. 50, pp. 329-366.

Barney, J.B. (1986). Strategic factor markets: expectations, luck, and business strategy, *Management Science,* Vol. 32, No. 10, pp. 1231-1241.

Baron, R.A. (1998). Cognitive mechanisms in entrepreneurship: why and when entrepreneurs think differently than other people, *Journal of Business Venturing,* Vol. 13, pp. 113-134.

Baron, R.A. (2006). Opportunity Recognition as pattern recognition: how entrepreneurs 'connect the dots' to identify new business opportunities, *Academy of Management Perspectives,* Vol. 20, No. 1, pp. 104-119.

Beach, L.R. & Mitchell, T.R. (1987). Image Theory: Principals, goals, and plans in decision making, *Acta Psychologica,* Vol. 66, pp. 201-220.

Beach, L.R. & Connolly, T. (2005). *The psychology of decision making: People in organizations, 2nd Edition,* Thousand Oaks, CA, Sage Publications, Inc.

Beach, L.R. (1993). Broadening the definition of decision making: The role of prochoice screening options, *Psychological Science,* Vol. 4, No. 4, pp. 215-220.

Berger, P.L. & Luckmann, T. (1967). *The Social Construction of reality: A Treatise in the Sociology of Knowledge,* New York, Anchor Books Doubleday and Company, Inc.

Bhave, M.P. (1994). A process model of entrepreneurial venture creation, *Journal of Business Venturing,* Vol. 9, pp. 223-242.

Bhide, A. (1992). Bootstrap Finance: The art of start-ups, *Harvard Business Review,* Vol. 70, No. 6, pp. 109-117.

Bhide, A. (1999). *How Entrepreneurs Craft Strategies that Work,* Boston, Harvard Business School Press.

Bosma, N.S., Zwinkels, W.S. & Carree, M.A. (1999). Determinanten voor toe- en uittreding van ondernemers: een analyse van de ontwikkelingen in Nederland over de period 1987-1997, EIM Business Policy and research, Zoetermeer.

Bower, T. (1988), *Maxwell,* Mandarin, London.

Bower, T. (1993). *Tiny Roland,* Heinemann, London.

Boyce, G. & Ville, S.P. (2002). *The Development of Modern Business,* Basingstoke, Palgrave Macmillan.

Boulding, K.E. (1959). *The Image,* Ann Arbor, MI, University of Michigan Press.

Branson, R. (2000). *Losing my Virginity,* Virgin, London.

Brigham, K.H. & DeCastro, J.O. (2003). Entrepreneurial fit: The role of cognitive misfit, In: Katz, J.A. & Shepherd, D.A. (Eds.) *Cognitive Approaches to Entrepreneurship Research,* Oxford, Elsevier, pp. 37-71.

Brown, S. & Patterson, A. (2000). Figments for sale: marketing, imagination and the artistic imperative, In: Brown, S. & Patterson, A. (Eds.), *Imagining Marketing: Art, Aesthetics and the Avant-Garde,* London, Routledge.

Brown, K.W. & Ryan, R.M. (2003), The benefits of being present: Mindfulness and its role in psychological well-being, *Journal of Personality and Social Psychology*, Vol. 84, No. 4, pp. 822-848.

Carland, J.A., Carland, J. & Stewart, W.H. (1996). Seeing what's not there: The enigma of entrepreneurship, *Journal of Small Business Strategy,* Vol. 7, No. 1, pp, 1-20.

Carlson, B. (1989). The evolution of manufacturing technology and its impact on industrial structure: an international study, *Small Business Economics,* Vol. 1, No. 1, pp. 21-38.

Carroll, G. & Mosakowski, E. (1987). The career dynamics of self-employment, *Administrative Science Quarterly,* Vol. 32, pp. 570-589.

Casson, M. (1982). *The Entrepreneur,* Totowa, NJ, Barnes & Noble Books.

Chandler, A.D. (1977). *The Visible Hand: The Management Revolution in American Business,* Cambridge Mass. Harvard University Press.

Chell, E. (2000). Towards researching the "opportunistic entrepreneur": a social construction approach and research agenda, *European Journal of Work and Organizational Psychology,* Vol. 9, No. 1, pp. 63-80.

Choi, Y.B. (1993). *Paradigms and Conventions: Uncertainty, Decision Making and Entrepreneurship,* Ann Arbor, University of Michigan Press.

Christensen, C.M., Anthony, S.D., & Roth, E.A. (2004). *Seeing What's Next,* Boston, Harvard Business School Press.

Cohen, W.M. & Klepper, S. (1991). Firm size verses diversity in the achievement of technological advance, In: Acs, Z.J. & Audretsch, D.B. (Eds.), *Innovation and Technological Change: An International Comparison,* Ann Arbor, University of Michigan Press, pp. 183-203.

Cohen, W.M. & Klepper, S. (1992). The tradeoff between firm size and diversity in the pursuit of technological progress, *Small Business Economics,* Vol. 4, No. 1, pp. 1-14.

Collins, R. (2004). *Interaction Ritual Chains,* Oxford, Princeton University Press.

Cooper, R.G. (2001). *Winning at New Products: Accelerating the Process from Idea to Launch, 3rd Edition,* New York, basic Books.

Corbett, A.C. (2002). Recognizing high-tech opportunities: A learning and cognitive approach, *Frontiers of Entrepreneurship Research,* pp. 49-61.

Corbett, A.C. (2005). Experiential learning within the process of opportunity identification, *Entrepreneurship Theory and Practice,* Vol. 29, No. 4, pp. 473-491.

Corbett, A.C. & McMullen, J.S. (2007), Perceiving and Shaping New Venture Opportunities through Mindful Practice, In: Zacharakis, A. & Spinelli, S., (Eds.). *Entrepreneurship: The Engine of Growth, Volume 2, Process,* Westport CN, Praeger Perspectives, pp. 43-64.

Cringely, R. X. (2005) *Triumph of the Nerds,* Transcript, PBS Television, *http://www.pbs.org/nerds/part1.html,* (accessed 10th March 2011).

Cyert, R.M. & March, J.G. (1963). *A Behavioral Theory of the Firm,* Englewood Cliffs, NJ. Prentice-Hall.

Daft, R. L. & Weick, K.E. (1984). Toward a model of organizations as interpretation systems, *Academy of Management Review,* Vol. 9, No. 2, pp. 284-295.

Davis, W.P. (2010). Responding to Change: Encouraging Innovation in Agri-Food Supply, Paper presented to the *1st East Asia Agri-Business Seminar 2010,* Sedang, Malaysia, 30th November.

De Koning, A. & Muzyka, D. (1999). Conceptualizing opportunity recognition as a socio-cognitive process, *Research Paper,* Centre for Advanced Studies in Leadership, Stockholm, Sweden.

DiMaggio, P. (2002). Endogenizing "Animal Spirits": Towards a Sociology of Collective Response to Uncertainty and Risk, In: Guillen, M., Collins, R., England, P., and Meyer, M. (Eds.), *The New Economic Sociology,* New York, Russell Sage.

Douglas, D. (2005). The human complexities of entrepreneurial decision making: a grounded case considered, *International Journal of Entrepreneurial Behaviour and Research,* Vol. 11, pp. 422-435.

Drucker, P. F. (1985). *Innovation & Entrepreneurship,* New York, Harper & Row.

Eckhardt, J.T. & Shane, S.A. (2003). Opportunities and Entrepreneurship, *Journal of Management,* Vol. 29, No. 3, pp. 333-349.

Evans, D. & Leighton, L. (1989). Some empirical aspects of entrepreneurship, *American Economic Review,* Vol. 79, pp. 519-535.

Fiegenbaum, A., Hart, S., & Schendel, D. (1995). Strategic Reference Point Theory, *Strategic management Journal,* Vol. 10, pp. 507-522.

Fleming, D. (2001). Narrative leadership: using the power of stories, *Strategy & Leadership,* Vol. 29, No. 4, pp. 34-36.

Foster, R., N., (2000), 'Managing Technological Innovation for the Next 25 Years', *Research-Technology Management,* 43, 1., Jan/Feb., P. 20.

Fredrickson, J.W. (1983). Strategic processes research: Questions and Recommendations, *Academy of Management Review,* Vol. 8, pp. 565-575.

Fredrickson, J.W. (1986). The strategic decision process and organizational structure, *Academy of Management Review,* Vol. 11, No. 2, pp. 280-297.

Gaglio, C.M. (1997). Opportunity identification: Review, critique, and suggested research directions, In: Katz, J.A. (Ed.), *Advances in Entrepreneurship, Firm Emergence and Growth,* 3, pp. 139-202.

Gaglio, C.M. & Taub, E. (1992). Entrepreneurs and opportunity recognition, *Frontiers of Entrepreneurial Research,* pp. 136-147.

Galbraith, J.R. (1977). *Designing Complex Organizations,* Reading, MA, Addison-Wesley.

Gartner, W.B. (1985). A conceptual framework for describing the phenomenon of new venture creation, *Academy of Management Review,* Vol. 10, pp. 696-706.

Gibb, A.A.(1997). Small Firm' Training and Competitiveness. Building Upon Small Business as a learning Organization, *International Small Business Journal,* Vol. 15, No. 3, pp. 13-29.

Gioia, D.A. & Poole, P.P. (1984). Scripts in Organizational Behavior, *The Academy of Management Review,* Vol. 9, No. 3, pp. 449-459.

Gioia, G.A.C. & Chittipeddi, K. (1995). Sensemaking and Sensegiving in Strategic Change Initiation, *Strategic Management Journal,* pp. 443-448.

Goss, D. (2005a) Schumpeter's legacy? Interaction and emotions in the sociology of Entrepreneurship, *Entrepreneurship: Theory and Practice,* Vol. 29, pp. 205-218.

Goss, D. (2005b), Entrepreneurship and the 'social': towards a deference-emotion theory, *Human Relations,* Vol. 58, No. 5, pp. 617-636.

Goss, D. (2007). Reconsidering Schumpeterian opportunities: the contribution of interaction ritual chain theory, *International Journal of Entreprenerial Behaviour and Research,* Vol. 13, No. 1, pp. 3-18.

Granovetter, M. (1985). Economic Action and Social Structure: The Problem of Embeddedness, *American Journal of Sociology,* Vol. 91, pp. 481-510.

Grebel, T., Pyka, A. & Hanusch, H. (2001). *An Evolutionary Approach to the Theory of Entrepreneurship,* Augsburg, Germany, Department of Economics, University of Augsburg.

Griffin, A. (1997). *The Drivers of NPD Success: The PDMA Report,* Chicago, Product Development & Management Association.

Griliches, Z. (1979). Issues in assessing the contribution of R&D to productivity growth, *Bell Journal of Economics,* Vol. 10, pp. 92-116.

Grochow, J. (1973). Cognitive style as a factor in the design of interactive decision-support systems, Doctoral Dissertation, Sloan School of management, MIT.

Hannan, M.T. & Freeman, J. (1977). The population ecology of organizations, *American Journal of Sociology,* Vol. 82, pp. 50-73.

Hayek, F.A. (1945), The use of knowledge in society, *The American Economic Review,* Vol. 35, pp. 519-530.

Headey, B. & Wearing, A. (1992). *Understanding Happiness: A Theory of Subjective Well-Being,* Melbourne, Longman Cheshire.

Hills, G.E. (1985), Market Analysis in the Business Plan: Venture Capitalist's Perceptions, *Journal of Small Business Management,* January, pp. 38-46.

Holtom, B.C. & Inderrieden, E.J. (2006). Integrating the unfolding model and job embeddedness model to better understand voluntary turnover, *Journal of Management Issues,* Vol. 18, No. 4, pp. 435-453.

Hudson, L. (1966). *Contrary Imaginations,* Middlesex, England, Penguin Books.

Huning, T. M. (2009). New Venture Creation: An Image Theory Perspective, *Southern Journal of Entrepreneurship,* Annual Conference Papers, pp. 130-144.

Hunter, M. (2009). *Essential Oils: Art, Agriculture, Science, Industry and Entrepreneurship: A focus on the Asia-Pacific Region,* New York, Nova Scientific Publishers.

Jack, S. & Anderson, A. (2002). The effects of embeddedness on entrepreneurial process, *Journal of Business Venturing,* Vol. 17, pp. 467-487.

Kearney, R. (1998). *Poetics of Imagining: Modern to Postmodern,* New York, Fordham University Press.

Keh, H.T., Foo, M.D. & Lim, B.C. (2002). Opportunity evaluation under risky conditions: The cognitive processes of entrepreneurs, *Entrepreneurship Theory and Practice,* Winter, pp. 125-148.

Kelly, G.A. (1970). A Brief Introduction to Personal Construct Theory, In: Bannister, D. (Ed.), *Perspectives in Personal Construct Theory,* London, Academic Press, pp. 1-29.

Kets de Vries, M. (1996). The anatomy of the entrepreneur, *Human Relations,* Vol. 49, pp. 853-884.

Kirzner, I. (1973). *Competition and Entrepreneurship,* Chicago, University of Chicago Press.

Kirzner, I. (1985). *Discovery and the Capitalist Process,* Chicago, University of Chicago Press.

Kirzner, I. (1997). Entrepreneurial discovery and the competitive market process: An Austrian Approach, *The Journal of Economic Literature,* Vol. 35, pp. 60-85.

Knight, F. (1921). *Risk, Uncertainty, and Profit,* New York, Houghton Mifflin.

Kolb, D.A. (1984). *Experimental Learning,* Englewood Cliffs, NJ. Prentice Hall.

Koller, R.H. (1988). On the source of entrepreneurial ideas*, Frontiers of Entrepreneurship Research,* Wellesley, MA, Babson College, pp. 78-85.

Kor, Y.Y., Mahoney, J.T. & Michael, S.C. (2007). Resources, Capabilities and Entrepreneurial Perceptions, *Journal of Management Studies,* Vol. 44, No. 7, pp. 1187-1212.

Kruger, N. (2000). The cognitive infrastructure of opportunity emergence, *Entrepreneurship, Theory, & Practice,* Vol. 24, No. 3, pp. 5-23.

Kuratko, D.F. (2005). The emergence of entrepreneurship education: development, trends, and challenges, *Entrepreneurship: Theory and Practice,* Vol. 29, No. 5, pp. 577-598.

Langer, E.J. (1997), *The Power of Mindful Learning,* Reading, MA, Addison Wesley.

Langer, E. J., & Moldoveanu, M. (2000). The construct of mindfulness, *Journal of Social Issues,* Vol. 56, No. 1, pp. 1-9.

Lee, T.W. & Mitchell, T.R. (1994). An alternative approach: The unfolding model of voluntary employee turnover, *Academy of Management Review,* Vol. 19, No. 1, pp. 51-89.

Levitt, T. (1986), *The Marketing Imagination, New Expanded Edition,* New York, Free Press.

Lord, R.G. & Kernan, M.C. (1987). Scripts as determinants of purposeful behavior in organizations, *The Academy of management Review,* Vol. 12, No. 2, pp. 265-277.

Loveman, G. & Sengenberger, W. (1991). The re-emergence of small-scale production: an international comparison, *Small Business Economics,* Vol. 3, No. 1, pp. 1-37.

Lumpkin, G.T., Hills, G., & Shrader, R. (2004). Opportunity recognition, In: Welsch, H.P. (Ed.), *Entrepreneurship: The Way Ahead,* New York, Routledge, pp. 73-90.

Manz, C.C. (1986). Self-leadership: Toward an expanded theory of self-influence processes in organizations, *The Academy of Management Review,* Vol. 11, No. 3, pp. 585-600.

March, J.G. & Simon, H.A. (1958), *Organizations,* New York, John Wiley.

March, J.G. (1991). Exploration and exploitation in organizational learning, *Organizational Science,* Vol. 2, No. 1, pp. 71-87.

Markman, G.D. & Baron, R.A. (2003). Person-Entrepreneurship fit: why some people are more successful as entrepreneurs than others, *Human Resources Management Review,* Vol. 13, pp. 281-301.

Martin, J.R. (1997). Mindfulness: A proposed common factor, *Journal of Psychotherapy Integration,* Vol. 7, pp. 291-312,

Meredith, G.G., Nelson, R.E., & Neck, P.A. (1982). *The Practice of Entrepreneurship,* Geneva, International Labour Office.

Miller, J.D. (2003). *Game Theory at Work,* New York, McGraw-Hill.

Mintzberg, H. (1994). *The rise and fall of strategic planning,* New York, Free Press.

Mintzberg, H. & Waters, J.A. (1985). Of Strategies, Deliberate and Emergent, *Strategic Management Journal,* Vol. 6, No. 3, pp. 257-272.

Mitchell, R., Smith, B., Seawright, K.& Morse, E. (2000). Cross-cultural cognitions and the venture creation process, *Academy Management Journal,* Vol. 43, No. 5, pp. 974-993.

Mosakowski, E. (1997). Strategy Making Under Causal Ambiguity: Conceptual issues and Empirical Evidence, *Organizational Science,* Vol. 8, No. 4, pp. 414-442.

Muzyka, D. (1997). Spotting the market opportunity, In: Birley, S. & Muzyka, D. (Eds.), *Mastering Enterprise,* London, Financial Times, Pitman Publishing, pp. 28-31.

Neck, C.P. & Manz, C.C. (1992). Thought self-leadership: The influence of self-talk and mental imagery on performance, *Journal of Organizational Behavior,* Vol. 13, No. 7, pp. 681-699.

Neck, C.P. & Manz, C.C. (1996). Thought self-leadership: The impact of mentalstrategies training on employee cognition, behaviour, and affect, *Journal of Organizational Behavior,* Vol. 17, No. 5, pp. 445-467.

Parker, S.C. (1996). A time series model of self-employment under uncertainty, *Economica,* Vol. 63, No. 251, pp. 459-475.

Penrose, E.T. (1959). *The Theory of the growth of the firm,* New York, John Wiley & Sons.

Peters, T. & Waterman, R.H. (1982). *In Search of Excellence: Lessons from Americas Best-Run Companies,* New York, Harper & Row.

Porter, M.E. (1980), *Competitive Strategy: Techniques for Analyzing Industries and Competitors,* New York, Free Press.

Porter, M.E. (1990). *The Competitive Advantage of Nations,* New York, Free Press.

Piore, M.J. & Sabel, C.F. (1984). *The Second Industrial Divide Possibilities for Prosperity,* New York, Basic Books.

Reynolds, P., Bygrave, W., Aoutio, E. (2004). *Global Entrepreneurship Monitor (GEM) 2003 Global Report,* MA., Babson College, *http://www.gemconsortium.org/about.aspx?page=global_reports_2003*, (accessed 25th August 2006).

Rindova, V. & Kotha, S. (2001). Continuous morphing: Competing through dynamic capabilities, form, and function, *Academy of Management Journal,* Vol. 44, pp. 1263-1280.

Sarasvathy, S.D. (2002). Causation and Effectuation: Toward a theoretical shift from economic inevitability to entrepreneurial contingency, *Academy of Management Review,* Vol. 26, No. 2, pp. 243-288.

Schindler, R.M. (1992). The Real lesson of New Coke: The Value of Focus Groups for Predicting the Effects of Social Influence, *Marketing Research,* December, pp. 22-27.

Schleicher, T & Walker, M. (2010). Bias in the tone of forward-looking narrative, *Accounting and Business Research,* Vol. 40, No. 3, pp. 371-390.

Schmacher, E.F. (1974). *Small is beautiful: A Study of Economics as if People Mattered,* London, Abacus.

Schoonhoven, C.B., Eisenhardt, K.M. & Lyman, K. (1990). Speeding products to market: Waiting time to first product introduction in new firms, *Administrative Science Quarterly,* Vol. 35, No. 1, pp. 177-207.

Schoonhoven, C.B. & Romanelli, E. (2001). *The Entrepreneurship Dynamic: Origins of Entrepreneurship and the Evolution of Industries,* Stanford, CA, Stanford University Press.

Schumpeter, J. (1934). *Capitalism, Socialism, and Democracy,* New York, Harper & Row.

Shane, S. (2000). Prior knowledge and the discovery of entrepreneurial opportunities, *Organizational Science,* Vol. 11, No. 4, pp. 448-469.

Shane, S. (2003). *A General Theory of Entrepreneurship,* Northampton, MA. Edward Elgar Publishing.

Shane, S. & Venkataraman, S. (2000). The promise of entrepreneurship as a field of research, *Academy of Management Review,* Vol. 26, No. 1, pp. 217-226.

Shane, S., Locke, E.A. & Collins, C.J., (2003). Entrepreneurial Motivation, *Human Resource Management Review,* Vol. 13, pp. 257-279.

Simon, M. & Houghton, S.M. (2002). The relationship among biases, misconceptions, and the introduction of pioneering products: Examining differences in venture decision contexts, *Entrepreneurship Theory & Practice,* Vol. 27, No. 2, pp. 105-124.

Sine, W.D., Haverman, H.A., & Tolbert, P.S. (2005). Risky Business? Entrepreneurship in the new independent power sector, *Administrative Science Quarterly,* Vol. 50, pp. 200-232.

Singh, R., Hills, G.E., Hybels, R.C., & Lumpkin, G.T. (1999). Opportuntiy recognition through social network characteristics of entrepreneurs, *Frontiers in Entrepreneurship Research,* pp. 228-241.

Smith, R. (2004). Rural rogues: a case story on the 'smokies' trade, *International Journal of Entrepreneurial Behaviour and Research,* Vol. 10, pp. 277-294.

Spinelli, S., Neck, H.M., & Timmons, J.A. (2007). The Timmons Model of the Entrepreneurial Process, In: Zacharakis, A. & Spinelli, S., (Eds.). *Entrepreneurship: The Engine of Growth, Volume 2, Process,* Westport CN, Praeger Perspectives, pp. 1-18.

Staw, B.M. (1981). The escalation of commitment to a course of action, *Academy of Management Review,* Vol. 6, pp. 5777-587.

Stevenson, H. H. & Gumpert (1985). The heart of entrepreneurship, *Harvard Business Review,* March-April, pp. 85-94.

Stevenson, H.H. & Jarillo, J.C. (1990). A Paradigm of Entrepreneurship: Entrepreneurial Management, *Strategic management Journal,* Vol. 11, Special issue: Corporate Entrepreneurship, pp. 17-27.

Strangler, D. (2009). *The Economic Future Just Happened,* 9th June, Ewing Marion Kauffman Foundation.

Timmons, J.A., Muzyka, D.F., Stevenson, H.H., Bygrave, W.D. (1987). Opportunity recognition: the core of entrepreneurship, In: Churchill, N.C. (Ed), *Frontiers of Entrepreneurship Research,* Wellesley, M.A., Babson College.

Torrealba, D. (1972). Convergent and divergent learning styles, *Master Thesis,* Sloan School of Management, MIT.

Tushman, M. & Romanelli, E. (1985). Organizational Evolution: A metamorphosis model of convergence and reorientation, *Research in Organizational Behavior,* Vol. 7, pp. 171-222.

Ucbasaran, D., Westhead, P., & Wright, M. (2008). Opportunity identification and Pursuit: Does an Entrepreneur's Human Capital Matter? *Small Business Economics,* Vol. 30, pp. 153-173.

Venkataraman, S. (1997). The distinctive domain of entrepreneurship research: an editor's perspective, In: Katz, J. & Brockhaus, R. (Eds.), *Advances in entrepreneurship, firm emergence and growth, Vol. 3,* Greenwich, CT, JAI Press, pp. 119-138.

Von Hippel, E. (1994). "Sticky Information" and the locus of problem solving: Implications for innovation, *Management Science,* Vol. 40, No. 4, pp. 429-439.

Walsh, J.P. (1995). Managerial and Organizational cognition: Notes from a trip down memory lane, *Organization Science,* Vol. 6, No. 3, pp. 280-321.

Ward, T.B. (2004). Cognition, creativity, and entrepreneurship, *Journal of Business Venturing,* Vol. 19, No. 2, pp. 173-188.

Weick, K.E. (1979). *The Social Psychology of Organizing,* Reading, MA, Addison-Wesley.

Whiting, B.C. (1988). Creativity and Entrepreneurship: How do they relate? *Journal of Creative Behavior,* Vol. 22, No. 3, pp. 178-183.

Wickham, P.A. (2006). *Strategic Entrepreneurship 4th Edition,* New York, Prentice Hall.

Wyer, R.S. & Carlston, D.E. (1979). *Social cognition, inference, and attribution,* New York, Lawrence Erlbaum Associates.

Wiener, N. (1993). *Invention: The Care and Feeding of Ideas,* Cambridge, MA, MIT Press.

Wildeman, R.E., Hofstede, G., Wennekers, A.R.M. (1999). *Culture's role in entrepreneurship: Self-employment out of dissatisfaction,* Rotterdam, Rotterdam Institute for Business Economic Studies.

Zafirovski, M. (1999). Probing into the social layers of entrepreneurship: outlines of the sociology of enterprise, *Entrepreneurship and Regional Studies,* Vol. 11, pp. 351-371.

Chapter 2

TIME AND SPACE:
BEING IN THE RIGHT PLACE AT THE RIGHT TIME?

INTRODUCTION

This chapter is somewhat different from the others as it takes a general look at opportunity from the socio-economic, economic-history and geography, political economy, and biographical perspectives. Our vision platform, the way we make connections, our inventory of resources, our skills, competencies, and capabilities, the competitive environment and product strategies we select are all immersed within a configuration of time and space. The element of time and space exist within all the aspects of the meta-theory argued in this book, and is paramount to the way things are seen, decisions made, and trajectories pursued in the exploitation of opportunity. To understand the importance of time and space to opportunity we must understand the history of our economic and social evolution, the way our societies spatially evolved, the way inventors, entrepreneurs and business people behaved, and how continual evolution of our incomes, values, behaviors, government, regulation, markets, and technologies change the way we live (McCraw 2006).

There are so many different interactive forces impacting upon both the individual and the environment which influences opportunity configuration. Events may occur either in a particular sequence or at the same time in a way that both influences and/or is influenced by each other leading to another event and/or a potential situation that we call an opportunity. This may be a sequence of events that are foreseen like demographical changes that take years to evolve, or unforeseen like dramatic changes in weather conditions that lead to natural disasters. Spatially, different regions within countries possess different combinations of resources, climate conditions, populations, political institutions, human capital skills and capacities, transport and communication infrastructure that links the region to the outside world, a propensity to be enterprising and trade, access to capital and technology, histories, cultures, and traditions that greatly influence the nature and scope of opportunity. The level of regional or national development and the corresponding characteristics related with the level of development are partially a product of the combined characteristics of time and space. Time and space aspects of opportunity causality are so complex that they are difficult to precisely determine.

Looking at opportunity from an socio-economic, economic-history and geography, political economy, and biographical contexts allows us to look at the flow of events in time and space such as inventions and innovations, the context in which they occurred and the impacts upon society these actions and events had. Looking directly at the biographies of historical figures can assist us in seeing the historical contexts of their efforts, innovations, or inventions. This may help us to understand how their insights occurred and opportunities were identified and exploited, showing us the reasons behind the trajectories these historical figures took with their inventions and innovations which impacted upon society's future development path (Chandler 1962). Take for example the biography of Thomas Edison we can see the importance of systematic development work, self promotion, and having a workable and viable business model in mind to exploit any subsequent invention. These were paramount elements of his success. Many of the failing entrepreneurs of the *dot.com* bust of 2000 failed to see the necessity of having a workable and viable business model to exploit their ideas and could have well learnt from the lessons Edison gave us.

Many inventions, subsequent commercialization and acceptance by society have dramatically changed our way of life over the centuries. Electricity and the electric light, the aircraft and jet engine, the automobile and combustion engine, and microchips, computers and mobile phones have all in different ways drastically changed society. These changes have led to further opportunities where entrepreneurs have been able to exploit. The transmission of electricity to homes allowed a host of other electrical devices to be invented, air travel led to air freight, travel agents, air terminal services, interstate, inter-regional and international business travel, and the building of hotels around the world, the automobile has led to automobile service stations, the invention of seat beats and other safety equipment, microchips have led to the invention of many items like digital watches, calculators, hand held GPS devices, and a host of other products, and computers and mobile phones have led to opportunities in software development and peripheral products and services. We owe the progression of our social existence to the invention of new technologies and ways of doing things, the creation of so many concepts and tangible things like alphabets, language, the wheel, farming techniques, cooking, social institutions, and the legal system, etc.

From the historical context it can be argued that innovation is governed by the period and place an entrepreneur resides (Gibb & Ritchie 1982, McGuire 1964, 1976, Newman 1981). Thus innovation is a period and regional phenomenon (Filion 1997) and the great inventors through history were products of their environment spotting, and exploiting opportunities, rather than people with brilliance in isolation (Diamond 1997). The inventors and entrepreneurs only knew what their time and place allowed them to know[1]. Innovation is thus a situational phenomenon and therefore the time and space aspect of understanding opportunity is important.

Following on from the above argument, novelty becomes a relative concept to time and space. Something that is new to one location may have long time been accepted product or service in another location. McDonalds was accepted in the United States market before it was introduced into foreign markets, were it was novel in each new market at the time of its introduction. Pizza was long accepted in Italy and Greece before it was introduced into the United States in the early 20th century and rest of the world after the Second World War. This

---

[1] Indeed management theories can also be seen as being a product of their time and place. Scientific management at the turn of the century could be seen as being reflective upon the values and needs of industry at the time, as with strategic planning in the 1960s, international management of the 1970s, the quality management movement of the 1980s, the learning organization of the 1990s, and knowledge management of the turn of this millennium. As we will see later on in this book, one's surroundings are critical to creativity.

has been an advantage for many students from developing countries studying in developed countries, where they have been able to identify novel business concepts in countries that they studied in, and went home to apply these concepts in their home countries upon their return. For example, many new manufacturing, retailing or service business concepts were started in South-East Asia by returning students. The *Econsave* supermarket group in Malaysia was inspired and foundered by Malaysian students observing independent *Foodtown* supermarkets in Melbourne, Australia[2].

The nature of opportunity is such that it is ephemeral and transitory (Shane & Venkataraman 2000) through time and space. Opportunity can be equated to periodically opening and closing doors along a corridor. True opportunities may not exist because a piece of technology is missing. For example, the idea of tourists visiting orbital hotels for holidays will remain only a concept until low cost transportation from the Earth to orbit has been developed. Thus space holidays may be an opportunity for another time, although it is an idea today. Many ideas have to wait for technology to catch up. An opportunity may exist in one place but not in another. Opportunities may exist for high end cafes and coffee shops in densely populated urban areas and high volume passenger transport terminals like railway stations and airports but there may be no opportunity for the same concept in much less populous rural areas where incomes may be much lower and the *"urban café culture"* does not exist. This shows the importance of time and space.

Geographical location is immensely important to the form and type of new venture creation which is based upon opportunity identification and exploitation influenced by the surroundings of the founder's location. Influence is based upon a multitude of factors which may include population densities, aggregate and per capita income, consumer habits of the group the new venture aims to serve, competition, the extent of variety, differentiation and other segmentation within the market, the view that the founder has towards risk which may differentiate between regions (Saxenian 1994), locational knowledge (Lawson 1999) and aptitude, the stigma attached to failure, the costs of start-ups (Landier 2006), the propensity of people to have savings, the ability to raise capital, local industries and linkages, predisposed skills and competencies, available technology available, localized learning (Maskell & Malmberg 1999), and regionalized domicile outlooks[3]. These factors influence the search channels for opportunities that local agents are most familiar with. The creation of novelty as mentioned is relative and subject to the environment to some degree. How this develops is influenced by complex interactions of the above factors, the location and interaction between people and institutions within those locations (Cooke & Morgan 1998). Why some regions are able to adapt and continually develop to a changing economic and social environment and why others become locked into their increasingly uncompetitive positions is related to these factors, although not fully understood (Grabher 1993, Martin & Sunley 2006). New technologies alone don't provide survival, other regional and institutional factors are very important in channeling the trajectories of regions and the industries within them (Essletzbichler & Rigby 2005)[4].

---

[2] Private communication.
[3] See Domicile outlook in Chapter 3 for some further explanations.
[4] Certain industries are favoured by particular national endowments and locally existing institutional arrangements and characteristics. For example, an auto-industry would grow easier in areas where a large labour pool exists and knowledge is available in the market place through a plentiful range of suppliers and research institutions. Software and biotechnology industries would tend to prosper where there is a large pool of scientific knowledge,

Time defines existence, the existence of knowledge and the existence of a market. Invention or innovation cannot occur without complete knowledge. Mechanical powered human flight could only occur after the forces of lift-gravity and thrust-drag were understood, the aerodynamics of a wing and the propeller discovered, and a light and economic power plant was developed with a very high power to weight ratio. With anyone of these pieces of knowledge missing mechanical human flight would not have been possible.

Time is required for a market to develop. There is most often a lag between invention and general consumer acceptance of a concept due to many factors which may include the general availability of a product in the market place, the costs of a product[5], the available substitutes, and general consumer usage habits. The rate of adoption of a Product tends to follow an S-curve. When the personal computer industry which began around the mid 1970s only enthusiasts would purchase a computer during the early innovation period and the rate of adoption was low. During the growth period in the late 1980s as software and applications improved more consumers purchased one leading to a much greater rate of product adoption in the United States. Increased computer power, decreasing prices, and further availability of a wide variety of applications continued to enhance the rate of adoption of the population using personal computers during the 1990s. The arrival of the internet in the early 1990s and the eventual integration of computer application and internet application added great impetus to personal computer usage where today the rate of adoption is almost saturated[6]. A depiction of the S-curve showing the rate of adoption of personal computers is shown in Figure 2.1.

Specific industries have tended to cluster at various times in different locations. During the Nineteenth century, the United Kingdom was the centre of industry and productivity, where a large number of inventor/entrepreneurs were domiciled, which resulted in the country having much higher levels of income over neighboring countries at the time. At the end of the Nineteenth Century Germany became a centre of the chemical industry and in the Twentieth Century the United States became the dominant industrial and technological nation throughout most of the century, pioneering many new industries.

What has been repeatedly observed throughout history is that innovation brings opportunity which leads to a subsequent string of innovations that supersede each other in the marketplace in what Schumpeter (1939) called *creative destruction*. However the more radical ideas require social and institutional change to become viable and exploitable opportunities, which is not always easy to achieve as society through its institutions tends to have an inbuilt institutional resistance (Veblen 1899) to change when new technologies requires structural and habitual changes in the ways things are done[7]. This was the case for the electricity industry more than a century ago, the airline industry fifty years ago, and the

---

highly defined intellectual property systems, and a financial sector or venture capitalists that are willing to fund innovative ventures.

[5] Generally costs of a product decline over time as production costs decrease assisting in making the product more affordable so that more consumers may purchase and use the product. This has been seen in the automobile industry, airline industry, telephone industry, and for computers, entertainment equipment, and televisions, etc. The speed of this happening is greatly accelerated today. It took American consumers almost 40 years before most families could afford to purchase an automobile and the use of automobiles reached saturation point. Today the prices of electrical goods like plasma or LED televisions may decrease and usage reaching saturation point within a couple of years.

[6] The ability to download songs and films, play interactive games, utilize email and now social networking media, etc.

[7] Institutions can be seen as "settled habits of thought".

ICT industry today. In some cases this may take years to overcome (Perez 1983, 1985), which has a bearing on national evolution in different countries.

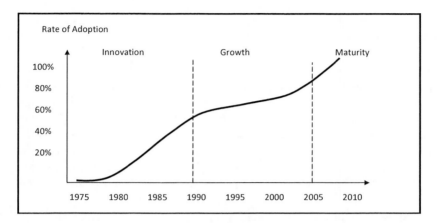

Figure 2.1. A depiction of the rate of adoption of personal computers in the United States.

PART ONE: THE STAGES OF A NATION'S DEVELOPMENT

All economies evolve and develop over time and there have been many theories developed over the years that have attempted to give both descriptive and predictive explanations. One of the more widely accepted theories was Rostow's *linear stages of growth model,* modified from Marx's *stages theory* of development, focusing upon the accumulation of capital through the utilization of both domestic savings and foreign investment as a means of creating economic growth and development (Meier 1984, P. 91). The Rostow model postulates that an economy goes through five stages of development – *the traditional society, the pre-conditions of take-off, the take-off, the drive to maturity, and the age of mass consumption* (Rostow 1960).

However other economists pointed out that that capital accumulation is not a sufficient condition one its own for development and other cultural, political, social, institutional and geographical factors are also important in creating the right conditions for development.

Michael E. Porter (1990, Chapter 10) postulated a linear stage model emphasizing a nation's type of development drivers as a source of competitive advantage. Porter postulated that a *factor driven* economy gains its competitive advantage from natural resources, favourable conditions for growing crops, and low cost labour sources, an *investment driven* economy from the willingness of firms and individuals to invest in modern plant, equipment, and technologies, an *innovation driven* economy based on firms creating novel processes, products, and business models, and a *wealth driven* economy *(also one in decline)* where investment is based on accumulated capital in low risk ventures and activities like shopping centres.

From the point of view of opportunity, the accumulation of capital, social, cultural, political, regulatory, technological, and attitudes towards risk and investment are all important factors in the creation of the opportunity landscape which is related to the stage of national development – demographically, economically, socially, regulatory, and technologically. The following paragraphs attempt to describe the stages of a nation's evolution in reference to the types of opportunities available within each stage of growth.

Traditional Economy

Traditional economies can be found in two forms, a subsistence society where its inhabitants live off the land on a daily basis using handed down generational knowledge with minimal outside interference, and an agrarian society where some crops are cultivated and livestock reared, producing some surpluses that can be sold or bartered to acquire outside items that the people feel they need or want. Within an agrarian society today, two types exist, one that relies on outside inputs and the other where people utilize their own inputs, reflecting their degree of both economic and social isolation. Traditional societies can usually be recognized by the high proportion of people involved in land based activities such as agriculture.

The type of activities a subsistence or agrarian society undertakes is shaped by the general topography and climate of the region they inhabit. For example, within an arid ecosystem some horticultural and pastoral activities can be undertaken, within a coastal ecosystem some livestock, fisheries, and horticulture can be undertaken, within a hilly ecosystem horticulture and livestock activities can be undertaken, and with a rain-fed ecosystem arable farming, forestry and livestock can be undertaken (Hunter 2009, P. 330). The general geography and resources available are important to development.

These include the physical landscape, genetic endowments, the institutions and rules people follow, and the dynamics of interactions between inhabitants and outsiders. The role of development greatly depends upon the types of institutions, culture and education of the population.

Today traditional societies are mostly socially remote from the education system and urban societies evolving around them. Most often the absence and/or high cost of transport acts as a strong disincentive to development, so there is generally very little trade. For example the cost of transporting goods from the New Guinea capital Port Moresby to the other major urban centres in the country cost more than shipping goods from other countries to those centres. The high cost of transporting goods is also a problem in many of the islands of Indonesia and the Philippines. In addition, these types of societies usually carry values and norms which allow very little room for modernization or expansion to a larger scale. The whole pre-Newtonian world once existed in this way prior to the acceptance of science for advancement.

The first step of evolution comes from subsistence farmers and hunter-gatherers moving to agriculture with the domestication of animals and plants into fixed location farming. Different locations have different advantages and disadvantages in making this step depending upon what animals and plants locally exist (without the introduction of external species). For example in our early history the Eurasian region had an abundant number of animals and plants to domesticate compared to the Americas and sub-Saharan Africa. In addition the Americas and Africa were fragmented by geo-climatic features that increased the difficulty of domesticating crops and animals over wide areas, *i.e, with the difference of growing conditions each side of the Rocky Mountains in North America and the vast differences in climates and physical separation by deserts and jungles running along Africa.*

In contrast Europe benefitted in its East-West orientation in the very first millennium BC, where the Mediterranean areas of Europe through Roman conquest were able to adopt economically useful animals and plants from the Middle East. Increased agricultural productivity allowed some of the population to move off the land into small towns and specialize in craft and other professions. Society could begin to develop through these new specializations. Once populations began to grow, great divisions of wealth occurred where some groups amassed political power and formed small nation states within the European area using natural boundaries such as rivers and mountains for defenses against external threats. Many societies within old Europe, the Middle East, Central and South Asia have emerged this way.

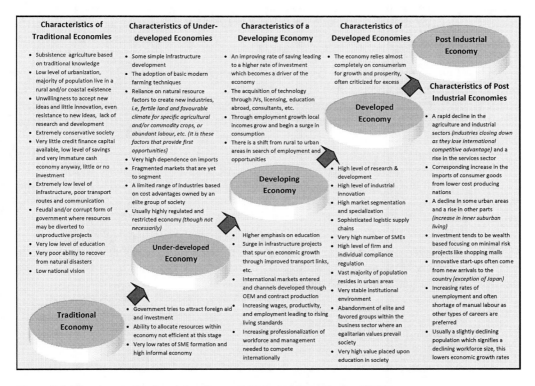

Figure 2.2. The stages of national development (Adapted from Hunter 1993).

Today there are very few whole countries that are based on traditional economies, except perhaps for Bhutan. Some traditional societies certainly exist within parts of countries within Africa, Asia and South America. Some hill tribes are still living traditional lifestyles in Northern Thailand, inland tribes exist within inland pockets of Sarawak and Sabah within the island of Borneo, within tropical Africa and the Amazon basin within South America, etc. Most of these societies remain the same until they become encroached by timber logging, infrastructure development like dams, tourism, or the settlement of immigrants from other areas[8].

---

[8] For example the residents of the Laotian town of Luang Prabang maintained a traditional lifestyle until very recently when tourism numbers rose to the extent of radically disturbing the culture of the place.

Opportunity is very limited in traditional economies due to remoteness, lack of capital, lack of travel and outside experience by the local population, lack of education, knowledge and skills, and lack of motivation to do anything different. The more backward a country the less likely to be any shift to industrialization and special institutions will most likely be required to facilitate capital to assist any potential nascent industries start up (Meier 1984, P. 101). Agriculture will not be sufficiently large enough or productive to supply raw material to any potential industry. The lack of any infrastructure is also a barrier to developing any new industry or enterprises due to the extra costs that would be involved in overcoming this lack of infrastructure. The main types of opportunities that would exist will be in the newly developing urban areas (when they begin to occur) supplying staple foods, hardware and construction materials to any development that is slowly occurring within the region. The speed and scale of these opportunities develop depend upon the rate of urban growth. It is only when education, saving through a monetary economy, and when people begin travelling outside their region that ideas and the will to pursue them develops. A general increase in agricultural production allows any urban growth to continue on a gradual basis. The general difference between the development of Asia and Africa from their traditional economic bases is that Asian agricultural productivity was able to increase dramatically where Africa didn't. Small countries with large populations have generally been able to progress out of traditional livelihoods better than small countries with small populations due to the larger potential size of their domestic markets (Beinhocker 2007, P. 80).

The very nature of subsistence agriculture is very risky and susceptible to disaster and uncertainty which breeds conservatism (Galbraith 1980). People tend to want to be safe rather than put themselves at risk and may prefer inferior outcomes to the prospect of higher than average returns with a greater degree of risk (Thirlwall 1983, P. 96). The most important aspect of transition from a traditional economy is the willingness of the people to change their customs and traditions into accepting to produce goods for consumption through the monetary economy. As well as the willingness there must also be the ability to raise capital through savings or loan to purchase inputs to do this.

Under-Developed Economies

An under-developed economy is one that has broken out of the traditional mode and is beginning to experience some development spurred on by government investment in transport, social capital, and other infrastructure. Government supported roads, railways, airports, communications services, and schools enhance the ability of society to develop and transform itself from a rural based society. At this point of time the economy may enter what Rostow called the transition stage, driving the nation into rapid development (the next stage). However with poor economic management, nepotism, misallocation of resources and corruption, the economy may plunge into a backward state of poverty.

Early development within this stage will be based upon the country's basic resource endowments which include its natural resources like timber, minerals, petroleum, gas, coal, precious metals or stones, arable land and favourable growing conditions for certain crops, fishery resources, and inexpensive labour supplies, etc. Early America relied very heavily on tobacco for the establishment of its original colonies, timber for development, and cotton that helped to develop the South. Malaysia developed on rubber, palm oil and later petroleum.

Botswana had been able to gain rapid economic development through its endowment in diamonds. Resource poor countries like Japan, Taiwan, and Korea initially utilized their low cost labour resources to produce cheap products that could be exported to the rest of the world.

The types of factor endowments a country processes severely limit the types of industries and development trajectories that can be taken. The country's resource base may be developed enough to enable the creation of other industries that spur further development[9], however a resource driven economy may be a poor foundation for sustained growth as it is subject to changing world economic conditions, exchange rate fluctuations and other countries becoming more competitive with their own resource endowments. Quite often, many industries will be temporary ones that die out as more lucrative opportunities occur and factor costs rise through higher demand for labour.

At this point there are few SME start-ups except for those that sell basic products such as food, motorcycles, cars, vans, light trucks, etc. There are opportunities for new businesses that supply need based products to consumers. As the market grows there is more room for new competitors who may apply some minor forms of innovation to their businesses[10]. A social elite may grow with some aspirations and be willing to take risks with their savings to invest in new businesses.

Many new local industries will tend at these early stages not to compete on price as there is little direct competition. Their monopoly positions enable them to avoid acting in any competitive sense focusing on profit rather than volume sales. Manufacturing companies tend to purchase technology through turnkey plants imported from other countries to enable some limited import substitution manufacturing on high volume and bulky items like detergents and paint. These companies usually imitate other companies operating in other countries as far as the products and services offered. They will grow as the economy grows but in most part remain domestic producers as they will not develop any economies of scale, superior product quality, branding or other type of international competitiveness that will enable any exports. Those companies that set up an export based business will have few direct links to customers and usually be limited to producing OEM products in the early years of operation.

Where people are attracted to the urban environment do not for some reason obtain formal employment, they most often enter the informal sector. Although the informal sector is often thought of as being made up of petty traders and other under-employed groups, it is actually an efficient and profitable small scale form of business that is limited by capital, technology, and lacks links with other sectors of the economy (Meier 1984, P. 183). These businesses may look poor but actually contribute enormous income to the economy and provide a living for a large population of many underdeveloped countries.

As mentioned, the informal sector is large in many under-developed countries *(which sometimes continue into the developing, developed and even post industrial stages of some economies)*, consisting of three main types. First are legal but may be not ethical such as people in Indonesia collecting cigarette butts off the streets to produce them into recycled cigarettes for resale. Other types of legal informal businesses may be collecting used cooking

---

[9] These may initially be direct support industries that are complementary to the resource industry but overtime may become diversified into industries that supply goods to the employees of these industries and eventually become adjunct or allied industries that may use the resource based products as raw materials, etc.

[10] In this context this may simply mean a new retailer offering a wider range of clothes, new car models, or restaurants with novel cuisines to the region.

oil for recycling into cooking oil for resale in Malaysia, producing biodiesel from used cooking oil, or doing odd jobs and home repair work on a cash basis in developed and post industrial economies. Secondly illegal, but victimless businesses may include unlicensed or unregistered taxies, selling numbers in an illegal sweepstakes *(very popular in S.E. Asia),* or prostitution. Finally illegal businesses include selling counterfeit DVDs, bags and fashion accessories, drug dealing, cultivating marijuana, human trafficking, organ harvesting and selling, and illegal casinos. Some of these often occur because there is a weak law enforcement system and a belief that the person can get away with it.

The informal sector is characterized by the ease of entry, reliance on indigenous resources, adaptive technology, family ownership, small scale of operation, labour intensiveness, skills acquired from outside of the school system, and operate primarily in unregulated and competitive markets. The illegal activities are generally actively discouraged by authorities. People in the informal sector generally operate outside the taxation system and have no access to formal credit institutions, although various microcredit schemes may accommodate them in some regions. Many informal traders operate in parallel with the formal sector producing foodstuffs and other consumer goods.

The informal sector is also a training ground for some to emerge into the formal economy at a later stage. For example, back in the 1950s Ayu Masagung without any schooling carried and sold newspapers around the Semarang area on foot, later became the founder of the *Gunung Agung* group which is one of the largest book selling and consumer goods distribution operations within the Republic of Indonesia. In this way the informal sector can be a source of future dynamism and change for an economy, being an internal source of entrepreneurship generation within the country. The informal sector is a source of future growth, developing talent, practical skills, and entrepreneurial approaches to business.

Whether an under-developed economy can make the transition to the developing stage will depend upon a number of positive factors and even chance in some cases[11]. Some positive factors that may contribute to the conditions of development include;

- Output from various resource endowments, *i.e., land, labour, capital, and technology,* are especially favourable to the country and provide it with a large advantage over other nations, *e.g., coal from Australia, palm oil from Malaysia, rubber from Thailand and Indonesia, etc.*
- Growth of the domestic market coupled with an increase in savings and loan capital,
- A sufficient level of infrastructure exists, *e.g., telecommunications, ports, roads, railways, and airports,* to enable efficient and competitive logistical chains to develop,
- Improvements in the quality of labour occur through training and education, *for example the workers in some countries are known to be more productive than others and therefore attract investment to take advantage of this factor,*
- There is a change in the value of a resource, *e.g. increasing demand for bio-fuel makes sugar cane production more valuable, the price of oil goes up making oil reserves that are more costly to extract viable,*
- New innovations are applied to agriculture enabling large productivity gains,

---

[11] For example the lemongrass oil industry could only develop within Haiti during the Second World War because stocks could not be shipped to the United States from countries like India at the time.

- The ability to exploit unused resources through either capital inflows or new knowledge,
- Access to new markets, *e.g., through improved infrastructure, foreign investment, and/or free trade agreements,*
- Immigration *(responsible for the development of America and Australia),*and
- Positive government policy, economic and social management, and implementation *(this includes lack of barriers, restrictions and regulations that distort growth).*

The last point on positive government policy, economic and social management is extremely important and if not in place can prevent a country evolving into the development stage. Tim Harford (2006) in a very colourfully written chapter in his book *The Undercover Economist* described what life is like within a failed state that does not develop any further economically. Harford lists the characteristics as follows;

- Endemic corruption through all levels of bureaucracy to the point that it ceases to function effectively,
- The informal economic sector is larger than the formal economic sector,
- Poor and inconsistent enforcement of the law,
- Poor, insufficient, poorly maintained, and decaying infrastructure,
- Feudalistic society with a privileged elite that provides them advantages in business,
- Extremely high fees and procedures for starting up a new business,
- Poor legal enforcement of commercial and intellectual property laws,
- Lack of encouragement for business and entrepreneurship leading to a low tax base,
- Dysfunctional and poorly motivated agencies and institutions within the country that supervise projects that are for prestige or self interest rather than the public interest and have large spending leakages,
- Failure to localize and adopt imported technologies and ideas to suit the local culture leading to poor performance or failure, and a
- Poor and inadequate education system.

Table 2.1. below shows some of the bottom level countries in the *Transparency International* Corrupt Perceptions Index[12] with some additional economic statistics[13] showing broad common characteristics of poor development and high perceived corruption.

Developing Economies

The impetus of a developing economy is industrialization. This may occur in a number of ways. Established primary industries whether resource or agricultural based may support the establishment of complementary industries which utilize a by-product of that industry. For example the pine plantations in Scandinavia and America enabled the production of turpentine oil which can be used as a feedstock to produce a wide range of other chemicals.

---

[12] See http://www.transparency.org/publications/gcr/gcr_2009#dnld
[13] Compiled from CIA World Factbook https://www.cia.gov/library/publications/the-world-factbook/ (accessed 11th January 2011)

Citrus plantations in both Italy and Brazil enabled the production of citrus oils from the skins of fruit, a by-product of pulped juice. Early industrialization in a developing economy may also involve the production of industrial goods that service demand from existing primary industries thus forming some of the early secondary industries within the country. This may encourage the development of engineering shops that produce specialized equipment or small factories that produce products relevant to established industries like maintenance chemicals. Alternatively there may be some special advantages in the country's resource endowment that other countries resources don't possess. The Swedish steel making industry emerged because of the low phosphorus iron ore reserves which provided an advantage over steel industries in other countries with higher phosphorus ores. Other local factors may include topographies and climates that may be particularly attractive for tourism or be especially suitable for the cultivation of specific industrial crops. Simple physical conditions, climate and activities may create demand for heaters or air conditioners, tray trucks, and fertilizers, etc. Finally pure chance may play a role where an entrepreneur may have an idea through serendipity, unconnected to existing resource endowments or related industries.

Some of these early industries may grow out of factor advantages such as low cost labour, as did the Japanese consumer product manufacturing during the 1950s and 1960s. However to maintain any industry in the long term, a new basis of competitive advantage should be developed on the production and/or market sides, *i.e., new technologies, design superiority, the development of enhanced logistical chains, or the targeting of special market segments like the Japanese did with small automobiles, etc.* Within the area that these new industries have been created, suppliers, workers, and managers will develop specific experience, expertise, skills and competencies related to that particular industry, which can be considered a cpuntry specific source of competitive advantage.

A predominant policy of the 1950s and 1960s in many countries had been the development of protection to encourage the production of consumer goods as substitutes for imports. Governments would construct a high tariff regime around a potential industry and allow the importation of raw materials, but insist on final assembly inside the country. Governments through this top-down policy hoped to attract new technologies and foster new import replacing industries by encouraging local and foreign manufacturers to set up local manufacturing to escape import controls and tariffs. Governments believed that this support would incubate new industries and expand new employment opportunities outside of agriculture. Import substitution would have little effect on attracting supply-orientated industries but play a significant role in attracting local market orientated industries where the domestic market potential was large. However this policy's long term success depends upon the ability of the new industry to create new technologies and sources of competitive advantage to survive competitively once tariffs have been retracted. However from the micro, individual or firm perspective, protection offers an opportunity to invest and operate in the marketplace without competition from imported products. In general however most import substitution era based industries failed to survive trade liberalization in the 1980s and 1990s and declined or even disappeared. But in the days of early development these industries did play a role in creating wealth through employment and developing urbanization.

Table 2.1. Some of the bottom level countries in the *Transparency International* Corrupt Perceptions Index

Country	Population	GDP[14]	GDP Per-capita[15]	Rank[16]	2008 CPI Score[17]	Confidence Range[18]	Literacy[19]	Labour force
Belarus	9,612,632	$120.7 B	$12,500	91	2.0	1.6-2.5	99.6%	Service 51.3%
Central African Republic	4,844,927	$3.295 B	$700	223	2.0	1.9-2.2	48.6%	-
Côte d'Ivoire	21,058,798	$35.94 B	$1,700	195	2.0	1.7-2.5	47.8%	Agric. 68%
Ecuador	14,790,608	$110.4 B	$7,600	128	2.0	1.8-2.2	91%	Service 70.4%
Laos	6,368,162	$14.2 B	$2,300	181	2.0	1.6-2.3	73%	Agric. 80%
Papua New Guinea	6,064,515	$13.85 B	$2,300	183	2.0	1.6-2.3	57.3%	Agric. 85%
Tajikistan	7,487,489	$13.65 B	$1,900	191	2.0	1.7-2.3	99.5%	Agric. 49.8%
Angola	13,068,161	$106.2 B	$8,300	120	1.9	1.5-2.2	67.4%	Agric. 85%
Azerbaijan	8,303,512	$85.65 B	$10,400	105	1.9	1.7-2.1	98.8%	Service 49.6%
Burundi	9,863,117	$3,241 B	$300	228	1.9	1.5-2.3	59.3%	Agric. 93.6%
Congo, Republic	4,125,916	$15.56 B	$3,900	159	1.9	1.8-2.4	83.8%	-
Gambia	1,824,158	$3.196 B	$1,800	192	1.9	1.5-2.4	40.1%	Agric. 75%
Guinea-Bissau	1,565.126	$1.712 B	$1,100	211	1.9	1.8-2.0	42.4%	Agric. 82%
Sierra Leonie	5,245,695	$4.507 B	$900	220	1.9	1.8-2.0	35.1%	-
Venezuela	27,223,228	$384.8 B	$13,000	86	1.9	1.8-2.0	93%	Services 64%
Cambodia	14,453,680	$27.88 B	$2,000	188	1.8	1.7-1.9	73.6%	Agric. 67.9%
Kyrgyzstan[20]	5,508,626	$12.09 B	2,200	185	1.8	1.7-1.9	98.7%	Agric. 48%
Turkmenistan[21]	4,940,916	$32.52 B	$6,700	131	1.8	1.5-2.2	98.9%	Agric. 48.2%
Uzbekistan	27,865,738	$78.37 B	$2,800	170	1.8	1.5-2.1	99.3%	Agric. 44%
Zimbabwe	11,651,858	$4.161 B	<$100	>229	1.8	1.5-2.1	90.7%	Agric. 66%
Congo, Democratic Republic	70,916,439	$21.75 B	$300	229	1.7	1.6-1.9	67.2%	-
Equatorial Guinea[22]	650,702	$23.82 B	$37,600	28	1.7	1.5-1.8	87%	-
Chad	10,543,464	$17.93	$1,700	194	1.6	1.5-1.7	25.7%	Agric. 80%
Guinea	10,324,025	$10.51 B	$1,000	213	1.6	1.3-1.9	29.5%	Agric. 76%
Sudan	43,939,598	$92.52 B	$2,200	186	1.6	1.5-1.6	61.1%	Agric. 80%
Afghanistan	29,121,286	$26.98 B	$900	217	1.5	1.1-1.6	28.1%	Agric. 78.6%
Haiti	9,648,924	$11.97 B	$1,200	206	1.4	1.1-1.7	52.9%	Agric. 66%
Iraq	29,671,605	$109.9 B	$3,800	160	1.3	1.0-1.5	74.1%	Service 59.8%
Myanmar	53,414,364	$57.41 B	$1,100	210	1.3	1.0-1.5	89.9%	Agric. 70%
Somalia	10,112,453	$5.665 B	$600	225	1.0	0.5-1.4	37.8%	Agric. 71%

National development during this stage is dependent upon the willingness and ability of individuals and firms to invest. The general investment climate will be influenced by the general and specific segment growth within the national market, available, access to technology, the stability of government regulation, and general national stability. The market evolves from one based on goods of need to one based on goods of value, which greatly widens the scope of market opportunities. However for firms to be able to exploit these

---

[14] GDP in US dollars at purchasing power parity.

[15] At purchasing power parity.

[16] Country comparison to the rest of the world

[17] The '2008 CPI Score' related to the degree of corruption perception as seen by businesspeople and country analysts.

[18] The 'Confidence Range' provides a range of possible values to the CPI Score as it varies according to survey taken.

[19] People age 15 and over who can read and write.

[20] A progress government is reforming the economy, tackling issues like poverty and attracting foreign investment.

[21] A largely desert economy with intensive agriculture in irrigated areas where production has declined in recent years. The major income is now oil and gas but the country is slow to privatize, has inadequate export routes, widespread poverty (30%), endemic corruption, poor educational system, government misuse of oil and gas revenues, and reluctance to introduce economic reforms.

[22] The discovery of large oil reserves have contributed to dramatic economic growth. However there is a 30% unemployment rate and most businesses are owned by government officials and their families.

emerging opportunities they must be able to acquire the best technology available through licensing or developing a joint venture with foreign companies. It was usually individuals that were able to communicate with foreign firms that could create business relationships with the foreign firms. Therefore those who had the opportunity to study in developed countries and understand the language and business culture had an advantage over those that didn't, such as was the case of many South-East Asian Chinese studying overseas between 1950s-1990s.

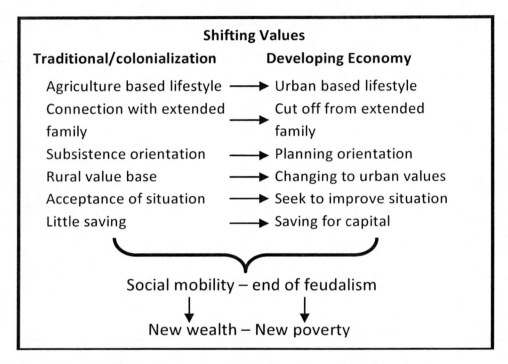

Figure 2.3. The shifting values that urban society brings to a developing economy.

At this stage urban society begins to grow rapidly. This is triggered by the much higher wages offered for factory employment than can be obtained in agricultural activities. Initially this migration is selective with the younger educated seeking urban employment but as demand for workers grows and stories about higher wages filter back to the rural areas, larger numbers of people migrate to the cities. Urban populations become consumers and increase demand for all types of food, accommodation, consumer and durable goods. They also partake in savings either voluntary or through nationally induced savings schemes developed by government through an emerging banking system. The education system is enhanced from basic systems distilling discipline to those that place more emphasis on critical and creative thinking. Growing urban development attracts new entrepreneurs who values are shifting from traditional attitudes to those more in line with an urban environment of a newly developing country (see figure 2.3.). Those with natural abilities are quick to emerge and the socio-economic structure of society begins changing away from its feudal base. They pick up new skills and competencies from education and employment and learn as they go along in their new businesses.

A developing economy experiences rapidly changing demographics leaving a deeply divided agrarian society and newly educated urban society. This can still be seen today in most South-East Asian countries which have become part of the source of political problems in countries like Thailand[23]. Developing society has some influence on agrarian society through urban residents remitting funds back to parents and families in their villages and returning to build new houses and buy consumer goods. This starts to break down traditional values and bring envy into village societies.

Although economic growth is destroying traditional culture and values, a whole range of new opportunities begin to emerge with rural based urban centres developing. These new towns commercially serve their respective hinterlands with goods, basic education and health services provided by government. Newly developed infrastructure, roads, railways, communications, schools, and health centres help provide the ability of rural society to transform itself. This brings a whole new range of opportunities to those that can see the opportunity, have the resources, networks and skills to develop them. The economy is now developed into partitioned agricultural, manufacturing and service industries with many new opportunities continually developing (Table 2.2).

Table 2.2. Emerging opportunities within a developing economy.

Construction	Processed food manufacture	Car mechanics and other service industries
Hardware goods manufacturing, window sills, doors, door frames, tiles, roof tiles, insulation, flooring, paints, cement, pipes, etc.	Fast food, restaurants, cafes, coffee shops, etc.	Engineering shops
Hardware retailing	Basic urban entertainment	Child minding nurseries
Furniture manufacturing	General healthcare	Printers
Household product manufacture	General retail	Real estate development
Market gardens and poultry farming	Logistics and transport	Banking

The United States, Europe, and Australia experienced increased birth rates from the 1950s. The high proportion of people of working age with low dependency rates dramatically increased the size of the workforce, savings, investment, and consumption, contributing to economic growth substantially in what was called the demographic dividend (Bloom & Canning 2004). This demographic bulge *the baby boom* was also seen in Ireland, East Asia and Latin America between the 1960s-90s, however Latin America did not benefit much from this because the quality of government institutions, labour legislation, macroeconomic management, education, and openness to trade was poor (Bloom & canning 2001). The processes of rural-urban migration, population growth in urban centres, and increasing education, increased consumption and saving. Rising entrepreneurship occurred through increased opportunities, fueling increased investment and rapid economic growth. These phenomenon are shown in the schematic in figure 2.4. below.

---

[23] See: Profile: Thailand's reds and yellows, BBC News, 20th April 2010, http://news.bbc.co.uk/2/hi/asia-pacific/8004306.stm, accessed 20th April, 2010).

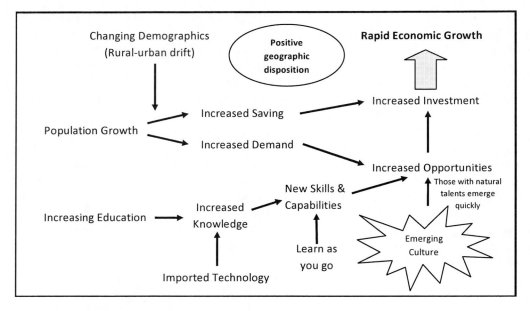

Figure 2.4. The path to rapid economic growth in a developing economy.

Rising populations create momentum, which create opportunities and begin to feed off each other creating a chain in the economy and expand as other opportunities become exploited. Real estate developments, need building contractors, which need hardware suppliers, which need hardware goods manufacturers, who need workers who are paid and spend money on food, accommodation, and consumer goods. Sales operations are needed to sell the real estate and credit facilities are needed to enable people to buy the homes and properties. The development of a textile industry needs suppliers, tool manufacturers and dye manufacturers, and the development of the automobile industry needs parts manufacturers, paint manufacturers, steel suppliers, logistic transport providers, and automobile dealers. All these interactions creates and environment with a set of opportunities. This pattern of development, growth, and creation of opportunities, as well as decline, are in a perpetual motion. The inner city and suburban areas of cities develop certain socio-economic characteristics in terms of the sets of needs and wants consumers have leading to its own set of interrelationships which determines what can happen and what cannot happen. Adjacent suburbs may have a completely different set of dynamics. The development of cities like Detroit was dominated by an industry, in this case the automobile industry. London, Melbourne, Singapore, or Bangkok will have their own trajectories, dynamics, and patterns of growth and interrelationships which create the window for certain opportunities in different places at different times. Looking at this on a global scale where growth is varied and staggered, opportunities are thus forever changing over space and time (Harvey 2010, pp. 147-150)[24].

---

[24] For examples many cities in the old East Germany are declining in favour of cities on the western side of Germany, The Pearl River Delta has seen unprecedented industrial and urban growth over the last thirty years while at the same time many industrial cities in the United States are declining. What were very recently empty desert space in the Gulf States are now the sites of modern new mega cities, Bangalore in India has become an

Rapid urbanization and developing rural regions begins to break down traditional society structure. There are pressures to adopt new more egalitarian business structures which sometimes challenge long existing orders. During the under-developed and early developing phases of economic development in many countries, businesses have been controlled by families of government officials and the military protected by restrictive regulation and practices that allow monopolies and oligopoly competition. Such situations would be similar to those under the Suharto regime in Indonesia and the Marcos regime in the Philippines, but also exists throughout Africa, the Middle East and Latin America. In some of the old Soviet Block countries, state capitalism was replaced by a small group of politically supported entrepreneurs in what could be called *'oligarch capitalism'*. To a lesser in some countries like Malaysia certain parts of industries are controlled by Government Linked Companies (GLCs) under another version of state capitalism. The effect of these business structures is to restrict opportunity and growth to small groups of people.

In most cases it takes some form of shock event like a political upheaval or even revolution to change the situation where a more egalitarian business society is created where more liberal business environments exist[25]. These reforms usually come under pressure by the people who have become educated, having the confidence to recognize opportunities and had the opportunity to travel and see other countries where the business environment is much more open. Once this change in society occurs the economy can move onto the next stage of becoming a developed economy. Figure 2.5. shows the transformation from a feudal to a more egalitarian business society.

In the transition from a developing to a developed economy competition becomes based on much wider parameters than price. Markets also become segmented as there are large and distinct groups of consumers with different demographics, needs, and wants. The economy is beginning to rely on household consumption to drive growth rather than resource endowments or investment. The continued rise in per-capita incomes and the associated savings and investment guarantees growth for years to come. The process of industrialization, urbanization, and suburbanization develops a self-driving momentum of its own. Business replication as a source of opportunity is becoming replaced with new innovations, and spin-offs often leading to new industries creating further growth for the economy. For example the rapid development of *Bollywood* in India has brought many spin-offs, support and service industries including special effects, costume design, set design, set building, pyrotechnics, protection, catering, transport, and insurance services. Further examples of industries and spin-off industries that have emerged over the last few decades are listed in table 2.2. below.

---

international IT industry centre, Shanty towns still exist in South Africa while there is still conflict in areas of Central Africa.

[25] However even in some cases this does not change even after a revolution, i.e, the fall of the Soviet Union just replaced state capitalism with 'oligarch capitalism', the peoples revolution against Marcos did not dispose of 'crony capitalism', and the revolutions in Latin America during the 1960s and 1970s did not change the situation much.

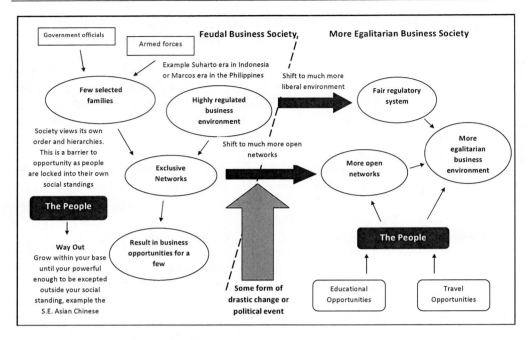

Figure 2.5. The shift from a feudal to an egalitarian business society.

Table 2.2. Industries and their spin-off industries

Industry	Spin-off Industry	Country
Industrial chemicals	Fine chemicals and Printing inks	Germany
Lighting	Furniture	Italy
Dairy products and beer brewing	Industry enzymes	Denmark
VCRs	Videotape	Korea
Port facilities	Ship repairs	Singapore
Electronic testing equipment	Medical diagnostic equipment	United States
Aircraft	Spacecraft	United States
Automobiles	Trucks and buses	Sweden
Communication equipment	Mobile phones	United states
Personal Computers	Mobile phones	United States

The leading industry sectors will differ by country due to different situational factors, however primary industries will encourage secondary industries to develop and eventually tertiary service industries to service the former. Some firms would have developed their own channels of distribution within foreign markets and begin to market their own brands in addition to the OEM brands they have been manufacturing. Research efforts begin to be supported through some basic university research which is now capable of developing new applications from existing technologies.

One of the most dramatic aspects of the advanced stage of a developing economy is the tendency for credit to become more liberal through a deregulated banking sector. This is an important key to entrepreneurs being able to exploit opportunities at an SME level. As many cities are relatively new, business networking is much easier which is important in urban opportunities[26]. Business formation is greatly enhanced by relaxed procedures and lower costs for forming business organizations. The *World Bank* has been collecting detailed data on the costs and time required to form a business throughout the world and been reporting the results in their *Doing Business* Report[27]. Virtually all of the countries where it is easy to start a business are developed countries, but where it is difficult and costly to start a new business are still developing or very poor countries.

Many large companies either foreign or nationally owned may take the lead in the prominent sectors of the economy. These firms develop a '*management logic*' and organize themselves through hierarchical systems. This is particularly efficient where there are focused investments and manufacturing operations (Williamson 1991). Many large resource based companies require equity based capital from equity markets due to their capital intensity and use of specialist assets. Family based businesses tend to fill opportunities that are too small and niche orientated for larger companies to exploit. They develop upon their own equity and extensive networks, enabling them to take quick action upon emerging opportunities.

Small businesses still tends to be more replicative than innovative at this stage but the number of people employed in SMEs may now be higher than those employed in large manufacturing firms. Business replication must give way to innovation to maintain growth in the future. The transition into becoming a developed economy depends upon industry and firm diversity and synergy within the economy that provides strength, laying ground for further opportunities that firms can begin to exploit utilizing new sources of innovation.

Developed Economies

A number of economies may reach the stage of being developed where the general population will be enjoying a reasonably high standard of living in primarily urban environments, benefitting from the decades of vertical deepening of the industrial base. The nation's markets have become large, complex, and segmented, deep international trade links have developed along with a rich service industry base. The economy is largely private sector driven where industry linkages are complex. Generally the world's coastal areas and land locked countries with good transport logistics linking the country to the outside world are the countries developing to this stage.

At the developed economy stage there has been an almost complete factor change from resources to innovation based development. Corporate advances cannot be undertaken by investment alone as innovation is usually required to gain new angles of competitive advantage within the marketplace at this time. Most markets are now highly competitive where competition helps to insure against any company single gaining *higher than average* profits through forms of monopolistic competition[28]. Inefficient manufacturers that can't satisfy consumer wants will be driven out of business. This represents a big change from the days firms competed primarily on price.

---

[26] This is very important to small enterprises where they have access to potential landlords, contractors, suppliers, credit providers, and customers.

[27] See: http://www.doingbusiness.org/reports/doing-business/doing-business-2011

[28] This doesn't mean that firms have ceased trying to distort pricing through methods like collusion and bullying. There have been over the years many high profile corporate cases about this issue with many companies being found guilty and being forced to pay large fines.

Firms during the developing stages tended to sell high volume products in a similar fashion as to how one would sell commodities focusing on sales rather than branding. Luxury goods were pushed through heavy advertising. There was really very little product differentiation of substance. This changes dramatically in a developed economy where consumers are much more varied about what they want, forming various need/want segments. Firms have to learn how to make this transition from a production and sales orientation to competition based on product quality, brand, image, and after sales service, *i.e., a full marketing orientation.*

Firms have become much more sophisticated in running their operations and no longer seek to maximize sales volumes and market-share. Gross profit orientations have become much more important. Products that are cheaper versions of well known branded products have less influence over customer decisions to purchase, except in the commodity type product segments. Retailers will develop category management and store shelf space planning systems that maximize gross profit from the shelf sales and complex pricing and rebate schemes with manufacturers. Manufacturers will focus upon building brands that have customer loyalty, developing as much influence over the distribution channels that they can seeking to differentiate their product from other companies to minimize the effects of competition.

Consequently logistical supply chains have become very integrated lowering distribution costs and providing retailers with much more control over the market. The growth of retailer concentration is an important characteristic of a developed economy, which has wide influence over how business is undertaken. Retailer concentration drastically decreases the viability of family owned independent supermarket and corner stores that cannot afford to purchase in the same quantities as major chain stores, stay open long hours, and sell items on low margins to attract customers during promotions. Growing specialization of chain retailers within supermarkets and discount stores has greatly affected the viability of small specialty enterprises like bakeries, delicatessens, milk bars, sundry shops, liquor shops, pharmacies, and poultry shops, etc. At the same time the development of centralized suburban shopping malls puts pressure on long established stores in strip shopping centres along primary roads. Consumers once in the car tend to drive to these shopping malls for the comfort of shopping in heated and air conditioned environment.

Small consumer product manufacturers begin to struggle to operate in the growing concentrated environment. The effect of category management is to rationalize shelf space so that smaller companies miss out on their products being carried in the major chain supermarkets. This forces them to service the smaller independent stores which have a much lower presence and national retail market share, often not enough for the small firm to remain viable. Some of the small companies with brands that are seen to have potential are bought out by multinational companies that specialize in selected areas. This further adds to manufacturer-retailer concentration and rationalization of consumer brands within markets[29]. Opportunities for smaller entrepreneurial firms in the consumer product manufacturing and retail industry are substantially diminished during the developed stage.

The prime form of firm competitive advantage is now innovation. However it becomes very difficult for one firm to develop advantages other the other. Firms that grow quickly tend to be those based upon some form of new technology, an important improvement upon what is already being done within the market, serving identified incongruities, and utilizing new business models that bring more value and/or convenience to consumers. In a developed economy firms now create new technologies through their own research and development where large efforts are put in to convert ideas into products that consumers highly value. Breakthrough or new to the world products where feasibility cannot be easily determined through market research are often launched on the hunches and faith of the organization (or founder) developing them. Such examples would be the *Sony Walkman* and *Apple's Macintosh* (now *iPhone* and *iPad* as well) where enormous efforts were put in to develop these products by the development teams concerned. Likewise non-technical innovation in developing new business models like fast-food and hotel chains that provide for the needs and wants of large groups of consumers have been extremely important in bringing further evolution and growth to markets.

A developed country may still have resource based industries but modern technology and consumer accepted practices may be applied to them to improve product acceptance, quality, and production efficiency to maintain the industry's desirability and competitiveness as will be discussed in a number of examples later in this chapter. As relative factor costs between countries change, many industries in developed countries start becoming uncompetitive, especially labour intensive ones. Companies within these industries will be forced to relocate, source their product offshore or fail. Changing factor costs often cause firms in developed countries to completely change their operational orientation from being a manufacturing based company to being a marketing based company. This leads to a great reduction of general factory or blue-collar workers in the economy towards white-collar workers in the growing services sector.

One of the most pronounced changes in the economy during this stage is the rapid rise of the services sector. There has always been traditional services and services linked to the resource, agricultural, and manufacturing sectors, but during the developed stage a dramatic rise in leisure, lifestyle, and high mass consumption services with a high income elasticity of demand occurs[30]. The growth progression of the the service sector size and per-capita incomes of some selected countries is shown in Table 2.3. below.

Businesses in developed countries have many more needs for specialized services than firms in developing countries. Over the last three decades there has also been a tendency for firms to outsource many services due to its apparent cost effectiveness. Firms require specialized marketing services, ICT, advertising, HR and headhunting, management training and motivation, and taxation and finance services. Also the growing increase in business regulation and compliance in occupational health and safety, food and chemical regulations, adoption of international (ISO) standards, and environmental compliance is creating new specialized and lucrative opportunities for those with specialist education and experience.

---

[29] These factors have increased global branding by manufacturers. Multinational manufacturers in efforts to seek better economies of scale will also make regional or worldwide supply agreements with their suppliers, thus also eliminating the ability of small domestic suppliers to deal with multinational companies.

[30] They can be considered to have a high income elasticity of demand because they open up choice to consumers and compete for their limited incomes.

Table 2.3. The growth progression of the service sector and GDP per-capita income for some selected countries[31]

Country	1960		1980		2000		2009	
	Service % GDP	Per-capita Income	Service % GDP	Per-capita Income	Service % GDP	Per-capita Income	Service % GDP	Per-capita Income
Ireland	52%	$684	57%	$5,230	56%	$20,300	49%	$37,600
Spain	-	$396	57%	$5,640	63.2%	$17,300	71.6%	$29,500
Italy	46%	$804	53%	$6,960	65.8%	$21,400	73.3%	$30,700
New Zealand	-	$2,368	58%	$7,700	69%	$17,400	74%	$28,000
Netherlands	45%	$1,115	63%	$11,700	69.7%	$23,100	72.4%	$40,500
United Kingdom	54%	$1,379	65%	$9,110	73%	$21,800	80.4%	$35,100
Japan	42%	$470	53%	$10,400	63%	$23,400	75.7%	$34,200
Austria	43%	$935	57%	$10,210	66.3%	$23,400	69.1%	$40,300
Finland	49%	$1,172	57%	$10,680	63%	$21,000	68.2%	$35,300
Australia	48%	-	-	$11,080	71%	$22,200	71.2%	$41,300
Canada	61%	$2,262	64%	$11,400	66%	$23,300	71.3%	$38,700
Belgium	52%	$1,278	62%	$11,920	71.6%	$23,900	77.2%	$37,900
France	51%	$1,386	61%	$12,190	70.6%	$23,300	79%	$33,000
United States	58%	$2,881	63%	$12,820	80%	$33,900	76.7%	$47,400
Germany	41%	-	49%	$13,450	68.4%	$22,700	71.3%	$34,700
Denmark	58%	$1,383	64%	$13,120	69%	$23,800	76.1%	$36,400
Norway	58%	$1,444	54%	$14,060	71.5%	$25,100	57.8%	$59,100
Sweden	53%	$1,963	66%	$14,870	67.3%	$20,700	72,2%	$39,000
Switzerland	-	$1,731	-	$17,430	66.1%	$27,100	71.2%	$42,900
Singapore	78%	$394	58%	$5,230	72%	$27,800	72.8%	$62,200
Korea	43%	$155	44%	$1,700	50%	$13,300	57.6%	$30,200

Many of the Gulf States are attempting to invest their way into the developed stage through the belief that building modern cities with the best infrastructure will spark new innovation based industries which will drive future growth. This can be seen in the tourism industry which has used investment and innovation but it is yet to be seen whether this will attract and create complementary and other innovation based industries to the Gulf.

A developed economy fosters maturity and national confidence but other dynamics like changing demographics, particularly aging populations, can drastically change economic trajectories where the nation flows into a post industrial state.

Post Industrial Economies

A fully developed economy will eventually drift into becoming a post industrial economy when the major source of employment and income for the nation is the service sector. The agricultural and industrial sectors over decades have slowly lost competitiveness where the manufacturing base has narrowed and importance to national GDP declined drastically (see

---

[31] Shown as service sector percentage of GDP and GDP per-capita (PPP) US$ extracted from the World Bank Development Report and other data.

table 2.4.). The primary type of industries that remain within a post industrial economy are those that;

1. Have been able to maintain a strong competitiveness through accumulated investment over the years, continue to generate advantaged technology for the industry, higher education and research institutions compliment the industry, a wide range of relevant skilled workforce exists, and companies are domiciled within the country *i.e., defense or highly scientific based industries like microchip processors, biotechnology, and some specialist engineering industries like jet engine production,*
2. Industries where early mover advantages still exist like the aircraft or scientific instrument industries that have strong branding and buyer loyalty,
3. Industries that still hold factor advantages because of exclusive access to particular resources, and
4. Industries that serve the wealth and consumer sophistication of the nation like real estate, financial services, health service, convenience and packaged good products, and the entertainment industries.

Table 2.4. The decline of the agricultural and industry sectors in selected countries over a 50 year period[32].

Country	1960			1980			2000			2009		
	Agri % GDP	Ind % GDP	Service % GDP	Agri % GDP	Ind % GDP	Service % GDP	Agri % GDP	Ind % GDP	Service % GDP	Agri % GDP	Ind % GDP	Service % GDP
Ireland	22%	26%	52%	-	-	57%	5%	39%	56%	5%	46%	49%
Spain	-	-	-	7%	36%	57%	3.2%	33.6%	63.2%	2.9%	25.5%	71.6%
Italy	13%	41%	46%	6%	42%	53%	2.5%	31.6%	65.8%	1.8%	24.9%	73.3%
New Zealand	-	-	-	11%	31%	58%	8%	23%	69%	4.6%	24%	74%
Netherlands	9%	46%	45%	4%	33%	63%	3.5%	26.8%	69.7%	2.6%	24.9%	72.4%
United Kingdom	3%	43%	54%	2%	33%	65%	1.7%	25.3%	73%	0.9%	22.1%	80.4%
Japan	13%	45%	42%	4%	43%	53%	2%	35%	63%	1.5%	22.8%	75.7%
Austria	11%	46%	43%	4%	39%	57%	1.3%	32.4%	66.3%	1.5%	29.4%	69.1%
Finland	17%	34%	49%	7%	36%	57%	5%	32%	63%	2.6%	29.1%	68.2%
Australia	12%	40%	48%	5%	-	-	3%	26%	71%	4%	24.8%	71.2%
Canada	5%	34%	61%	4%	32%	64%	3%	31%	66%	2.3%	26.4%	71.3%
Belgium	7%	41%	52%	2%	37%	62%	1.4%	27%	71.6%	0.7%	22.1%	77.2%
France	10%	39%	51%	4%	35%	61%	3.3%	26.1%	70.6%	1.8%	19.2%	79%
United States	4%	38%	58%	3%	34%	63%	2%	18%	80%	1.2%	22.2%	76.7%
Germany	6%	53%	41%	2%	46%	49%	1.2%	30.4%	68.4%	2.4%	29.7%	71.3%
Denmark	11%	31%	58%	4%	32%	64%	4%	27%	69%	1.1%	22.8%	76.1%
Norway	9%	33%	58%	5%	42%	54%	2.2%	26.3%	71.5%	2.1%	40.1%	57.8%
Sweden	7%	40%	53%	3%	315	66%	2.2%	30.5%	67.3%	1.7%	26.1%	72,2%
Switzerland	-	-	-	-	-	-	2.8%	31.1%	66.1%	1.3%	27.5%	71.2%
Singapore	4%	18%	78%	1%	41%	58%	>1.0%	28%	72%	0%	27.2%	72.8%
Korea	37%	20%	43%	17%	39%	44%	5%	45%	50%	3%	39.4%	57.6%

---

[32] Agriculture, industry, and service sector percentage of GDP and GDP per-capita (PPP) US$ extracted from the World Bank Development Report and other data.

The extent to which a nation's economy is service orientated depends upon the extent products that are imported from other countries have a cost advantage over local products. Due to lower production costs offshore and low tariff regimes, it is much cheaper to source products from lower cost producing countries. Durable consumer goods are now much cheaper than they were during the past stages of economic development.

However becoming a post industrial economy may not altogether be a negative process, and does not always involve de-industrialization. The economy may be going through a restructuring where lower productivity industries are being replaced by higher productivity industries in other sectors. The services sector may be growing at a much faster rate than the manufacturing sector which statistically shows a decline of the agricultural and industry sector relative to the services sector.

While some industries have declined and disappeared, other industry structures have radically changed, and/or merged together with other industries. Many industries have become extremely competitive where segmentation has become intense. Some companies practice custom mass production, *i.e., Toyota Scion targeted at Gen Y customers and Dell computer allowing customers to order computers according to their own specifications.* The personal computer, mobile phone, and even books are becoming one industry with the arrival of products like the *Apple iPhone* and *iPad*. The airline industry, once used by a privileged few has radically changed through the low cost segment growing rapidly, redefining how the industry and customers behave. Banking was just a necessary institution within an economy at one time to provide a means for savings, loans, and financial transactions. In post industrial society banks transform to become much more integrated with consumers' lives where services are almost unconsciously utilized through paying for groceries at the supermarket with debit cards and paying bills through ATMs and on the internet, where cash from transactions is disappearing. The processed and fast food industry has become corporatized focusing on presentation, convenience through replication, and sophisticated logistical systems to place product within very easy reach of consumers.

Over the last decades of economic development firms have moved from a production to a marketing orientation. In the post industrial economy firms start making a transition into developing integrated values within the whole company, reflected in strategies, and products. Consumers at the same time have become very paradoxical. Consumers live within a corporatized society and accept luxury and branding, shopping in the comfort of shopping malls and hypermarkets, yet at the same time yearn to return to the street markets and the specialty and boutique corner stores. They also have concern for local issues, the environment, and the future, and seek out farmers' markets, buy local products, seek to live with low carbon footprints, prefer organic, and Fairtrade products in increasing numbers. Today it is not unusual for people to travel on a low budget airline to an exotic holiday location and stay at a five star resort. At the same time we are becoming skeptical about government, frustratingly looking for alternatives that may not yet exist[33]. There are no existing or new political movements in sight that appear to have the answers, just an apparent

---

[33] People around the world appear to be looking for new political hopes in different ways. The US elected Barak Obama with such great hopes, yet the *Republican tea party* movement is gaining some momentum. The recent UK and Australian elections returned major parties without any preference for either one, requiring minor parties and independents to make or break the government. Although the greens vote rose slightly, there is really no political party or movement that appears to be inspiring voters. The Edelman Trust Barometer 2011 shows that

vacuum or void. The corporate world is also looking for the answers about where they stand in society through *corporate social responsibility (CSR)*. What is mostly apparent is the variety of different approaches taken. Is it civic responsibility – making a difference to society? Is it about empowerment – whose? Is it about aid to the less fortunate – some special projects? Is it about ethics, environmental responsibility, and sustainability? Is it about community development – local, national, or global citizenship? Is it about philanthropy? What are the specialized values the corporate world should adopt? Post industrial society is a somewhat more paradoxical society than those of the previous phases.

All of the above is occurring at a time where corporations are devoid of shareholder influence (Drucker 1993). The motivations of managers are moving in directions that undermine sustained investment and innovation. Investment becomes focused on financial assets rather than acquiring real assets. Mergers and acquisitions stifle innovation. Foreign investments are now purely financial rather than aimed invest in building capacity and productivity that they once were. General investment in the previous stages had been undertaken within an almost continuous growth rate which maintained a positive momentum of return that could be supported by borrowing. However capital gains are not assured within a post capitalist economy due to the many structural changes taking place and end of the high growth period that the early stages of economic development experienced. Asset values start declining with the structural changes leaving investments that are not covered by the equity within the assets.

The concept of what constitutes an investment and what is an expense is under threat. No longer can a house be looked upon as an asset that acquires value continually, as this ignores the fundamental issue that a house depreciates through wear, and upkeep costs are expensive and rarely factored into value, leaving only value in the land. Land value is only relative to demand and suburban areas that were once in demand two decades ago in American cities are the urban prairies of today. Post industrial economies will continue to experience readjustments that will change the nature of opportunities and what constitutes good investment.

Business investment tends to be more wealth based rather than innovation based, utilizing past wealth. During this stage the lower productive segments of industry drop away. Many national size firms are acquired by larger multinationals and/or shift off-shore to become based in other countries, leaving only a small subsidiary operation within the original country. Other established industries close down their manufacturing operations and source their products offshore from lower cost producers. Many established firms begin to consolidate their market positions rather than enhance it, have a declining inclination to invest, become headed by stewards rather than entrepreneurs, lose their aspirations, become complacent risk takers, and develop organizations that have a culture resistant to change. This is reflected in the high turnover of companies on the *S&P, Forbes*, and *Fortune* lists, where vibrant new entrepreneurial companies are taking the place of the complacent companies with outdated products for their market and older technologies.

A post industrial economy is one that is no longer balanced and requires new activities to rebalance it. Post industrial societies face the trauma of losing export orientated industries, increasing imports, higher public debt, and growing unemployment. This raises possibilities

the majority (over 50%) of people distrust their governments in France, Italy, India, United Kingdom, United States, Russia, and Germany. See http://www.edelman.com/trust/2011/ (Accessed 27th January 2001).

that the urban areas of many societies will become poorer and fall into relative poverty. There are even risks that a whole new generation of people may not have jobs. How this evolving scenario is countered depends upon how many new entrepreneurs can create new industries that will create new domestic and regional demand and increase employment. However this is hindered by rising taxes on wealth and income created by governments trying offset their dwindling tax bases.

Changing age structures in many post industrial economies are beginning to have a significant effect on economic performance. Populations are shifting from a high proportion of working people to non-working people to an aging population where assets must be put into aged and health care, which inhibit economic growth. This is the *'pay up'* period for the *'demographic dividend'* the country enjoyed two decades ago. Age expectancy has also increased due to better knowledge, nutrition, and healthcare resulting in declining death rates which further stress government welfare systems. The population of people aged 80 or above is projected to rise around 3.5% per annum until 2050 and will force Governments in East Asia, Europe, the United States and Australia to develop surpluses in future budgets. Meanwhile declining fertility rates in Europe will lead to massive labour shortages that must be supplemented through increased immigration.

Standards of education are declining due to less domestic demand because of demographic shifts. Many higher learning institutions seek overseas students to supplement declining enrolments and maintain revenues. Education is a growth business for students from developing countries and becomes a major growth industry in post industrial economies with a stock of high reputation universities and other colleges. Education is now Australia's third largest export earner behind coal and iron ore[34]. However Finland has shown through investment in education other industries can be developed which in her case include the forestry industry.

Post industrial societies have also neglected the rural areas which have fallen into crisis. With tightening credit, many rural families are forced off the land. Chronic shortages of labour affect harvests and production. Declining services and infrastructure lowers the quality of life for rural families. Educational pathways between urban and rural societies widen (Golding 2001), which could inhibit the ability of rural people to scan for opportunities and exploit them in the next generation (Hunter 2009, P. 22). There is a genuine social inequality between urban and rural populations. Rural population will have fewer opportunities from limited economic activity, where disadvantages include the remoteness from urban markets, the high cost and deterioration of transport services, poor access to services, and lack of private and government investment. This lack of rural investment leads to higher unemployment where a large percentage of rural youth population leave for potential work in the cities.

Post industrial societies become high compliance cultures. Value added taxation systems (VAT or GST), environmental compliances, occupational health and safety compliances, require large amounts of documentation in business. Civil society is also regulated very heavily with service fees and infringement penalties are important sources of revenue for government. This substantially increases the licenses, costs and knowledge required to start a business just like high start up costs that discourage entrepreneurial start-ups in under-

---

[34] See Export Income to Australia from Education, Research Snapshot, No. 34, March 2008, http://www.isana.org.au/files/AEI%20March%20sshot%20expt%20income.pdf, (accessed 17th January 2011).

developed economies. Opening a simple business like a café or restaurant now most likely requires a loan from a bank to enable the individual to comply with health, building, and food storage and preparation regulations. This puts the opportunity of starting many types of businesses out of the reach of many people without the ability to save or raise finance.

However, even given all the above it is likely that the environment for potential opportunities will increase in the post industrial environment due to large urban diversity, high incomes, and sophisticated market segmentation that has evolved over decades. For example, high market segmentation presents new opportunities that established channels of distribution do not cater for and new distribution channels can be created to exploit these opportunities. New alternative channels appealing to particular segment groups like *buy local, organic, Halal, Kosher, Fairtrade* create many new product and retail opportunities. Internet retailing is on a massive growth path and the discount shop[35] phenomenon throughout Europe, Japan, the United States and Australia is now a very significant worldwide industry. In a post industrial economy it will take more investigation to see potential opportunities as small niches are harder to see than the general environment. Figure 2.6. shows conceptually the level of potential opportunities in relation to the stage of economic development.

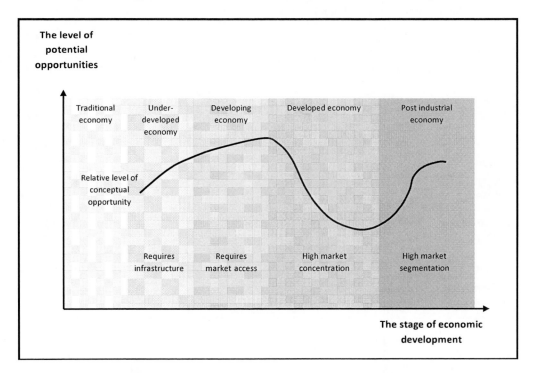

Figure 2.6. The level of potential opportunities in relation to the stage of economic development.

---

[35] Also known as dollar, $2, or One Euro or Pound Shops.

National Economic Development is Not a Linear Process

Countries do not necessarily develop directly along the path outlined previously. Resources are unevenly distributed within a country and in addition, geography, population and infrastructure will be distributed in such a way that development may occur unevenly.

The first development within a country will most likely be related to existing natural resources and the new industry would locate itself within proximity to the resource location. How quickly and large this industry may develop will depend upon the agents involved in the industry, access to markets, production or extraction costs, transport costs, and the ability of the industry to grow and sustain itself. How quickly and substantially complementary and support industries accumulate in the region depend upon the substance of the industry and potential growth. The suitability of local topography to support transport infrastructure, *i.e., potential to house a natural port, build roads and railways to the region,* support a large population, and availability of labour either currently present or willing to relocate to the new area will support further regional growth. Some areas within a country are better endowed than others promoting uneven growth within almost every economy. This can be seen in the rapid growth along the coast of China and stagnation within the interior of the country.

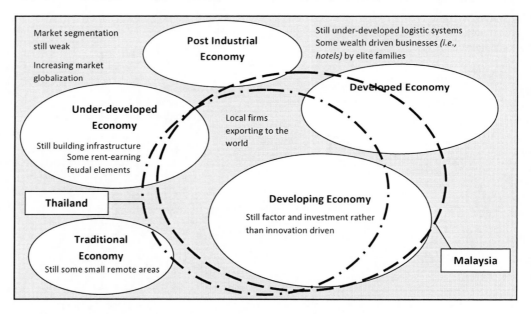

Figure 2.7. Where Thailand and Malaysia's development would be placed over the five stages of development.

Figure 2.7. shows where both Thailand and Malaysia's current development levels would be placed over the five stages of development. Both Thailand and Malaysia are predominantly developing countries relying on investment to drive their respective manufacturing sectors. However at the same time there are many aspects of both countries industries and markets that have the characteristics of a developed economy. Both Malaysia and Thailand's services sectors are rapidly growing. Malaysia could also be said to display some characteristics of a post industrial society where some of the large government linked companies (GLCs) make substantially wealth based investments in real estate and construction projects rather than investments in innovation. Outside the major cities both Thailand and Malaysia are characteristic of under developed economies still using traditional techniques in local farming and fishery enterprises, still lacking basic infrastructure in some places. Paradoxically Thailand still has hill tribes around Chiang Rai that still maintain traditional lifestyles and Malaysia still has the Iban, Dayak, and Dusun tribes in Borneo.

PART TWO: THE INDUSTRIAL REVOLUTION TO THE 20TH CENTURY: THE PRECURSOR TO TODAY

Between 1000-1820 economic growth was adequate to support a four-fold population growth (Maddison 2007). As ships and navigation improved, the opening up of trade between Europe and Asia between 1500-1800s expanded European empires, bringing a wave of globalism. This ability came from improved ship design, better accuracy from navigation, and available credit from the Netherlands and British trading corporations *(Dutch East India Company and British East India Company)*. One of the more important aspects of this new trade to European society was the new goods discovered and brought back, including spices, tea, coffee, Asian porcelain, and textiles which inspired new tastes and fashions in food, beverages, clothing, domestic utensils, decorative fabrics, and wallpapers, etc. This showed that consumer familiarity with goods in itself increases demand (O'Brien *et. al.* 1991) and opportunity. This is something which can be seen in the electronics industry where the arrival of new technology stimulates its own demand. The other lesson of the time is that improvements in technology advance society.

This early trade between 1500-1800s created employment, growth, and opportunities throughout the world, including *Africa, Asia, and the Americas.* New territories and cities were built from trade. History shows the rise and decline of regions due to ebbs and flows in trade over time.

One important influence upon the technical sophistication and social organization of our society today was the industrial revolution which began in Great Britain in the late 18th Century. Some inventions enabled the creation of industries that led nations to prosperity for many years. Other inventions were incremental improvements upon past inventions which enabled the development of breakthroughs that radically changed society.

The development of industry and utilization of new technologies slowly spread across the English Channel to Europe, Atlantic to America, and eventually Japan. By 1914 much developed British technology was obsolete and superseded with US and German inventions and technologies[36]. The industrial revolution spurred technological breakthroughs which enabled production to outpace growing population, creating economic growth and wealth, and a platform to support a massive rise in population. For this reason the results and achievements of the industrial revolution can be seen as a necessary precursor to the 20th Century.

The industrial revolution did not just occur. It unfolded through ideas, action, and determination of many people who were not just inventors, but entrepreneurs, and publicists

---

[36] This also showed that all technologies have a built in obsolescence which eventually leads to a loss of comparative advantage to a more innovative technology.

at the same time (Weightman 2007). Many inventors were uneducated, but able to think unconventionally and see opportunity by creating new visions for society, promote these ideas to seek backers and supporters to turn these ideas into realties. Many of these inventor/entrepreneurs failed a number of times before they succeeded. They worked in adversity and often had to finance themselves because of the skepticism of potential investors, at high personal cost. This is not in too different in terms of how entrepreneurs operate today. This was a time of great rivalries, copying, and improvement upon other inventions and lobbying[37]. Many European and American inventors at the time traveled between the two continents to learn, study, or spy on other developments. Some inventions actually occurred on both sides of the Atlantic at a similar time by two distinct inventor/entrepreneurs who were not working together.

We also see how important intellectual property regimes were for promoting a positive environment for inventor/entrepreneurs at the time. During the early industrial periods in Britain and the United States, courts consistently supported inventor's patent rights based on the premise that the patent system fostered economic growth (Khan 2005). Patent protection seemed to be an important factor in determining technological development and its adoption and diffusion into society. This is in contrast to countries like Mexico that had very selective enforcement of property rights which inhibited innovation (Maurer 2002).

A few entrepreneurs was not enough, there had to be a large and diverse group, with new ideas to develop society. If this condition is lacking, national development may be more difficult. South East Asia to a certain extent relied on foreign investment to compensate for lack of local innovation. Sometimes disastrous events like the American War of Independence was required to create shocks and force new trajectories like merchants in the colonies who became forced to manufacture their own stocks to sell, as it was no longer possible to import them.

Breakthroughs rarely occurred through a single invention, but rather through a collection of other previous inventions, ideas, and improvements that would create new technologies. Many inventions did not lead to instant success and took a number of years to become accepted by society. Some inventions missed a vital piece of knowledge that didn't yet exist to perfect it properly. It was often a case of chance, being in the right place, and being in the right time, with the necessary knowledge, resources, and networks with a conceptualized business model thought out. The evolution of society can be seen in terms of high entrepreneurial push and effort to commercialize ideas and inventions. It was the entrepreneurs together who propelled society to new visions about how things could be.

The industrial revolution showed that technology itself could be an opportunity, a source of innovation that enabled further society development, and this again can be seen in the development of East Asia during the second part of the 20th Century. Some of the important industries of the industrial revolution and later during the 19th Century included the steam engine, railways, steamships, automobiles, airplanes, the electric light, and refrigeration. These industries, technology inventors and some others will be looked at as examples as to how opportunities were created and developed. Figure 2.8. shows a timeline of inventions from the industrial revolution to the turn of the 20th Century.

---

[37] Entrepreneurial personalities were very different. Many were single minded in the pursuit of success and power, often with complete ruthlessness like Henry Ford and John D. Rockefeller who incidentally became a great philanthropist later in life. Many like Thomas Edison actually bribed journalists to present his inventions in a positive light, especially at exhibitions, and many like J.P. Morgan lived a grandeur lifestyle.

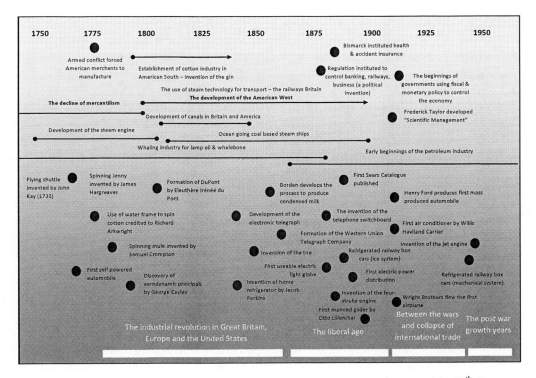

Figure 2.8. shows a timeline of inventions from the industrial revolution to the turn of the 20th Century.

The Steam Engine

The importance of the steam engine to society cannot be under-estimated as it was steam power that drove the mills, enabled much faster trans-Atlantic travel than the sailing ships of the time and allowed the development of railroads as a vital means of transport that opened up many countries during early to mid 19th Century. Perhaps most importantly the steam engine also enabled the transition from craft based home-work to mass production in centralized factories during the industrial revolution. An economic source of mechanical power was needed for society to further increase its level of productivity. Until steam, power was provided by overworked animals to drive pulleys and transport people and goods. The development of the steam engine evoked so much passion on the part of the inventors and promoters they designed and built, causing many rivalries. The steam engine is also an example of how inventors built upon the knowledge of previous inventions through incremental development over a number of years, gradually improving the efficiency of the engine.

Otto von Guericke was one of the first to show the enormous power that could be generated from a piston in a cylinder through his development of the vacuum pump in 1650 which started curiosity about steam. One of the early steam powered cylinder and piston arrangements was invented by Denis Papin in the later part of the 17th Century. In 1704 Papin constructed the first steam powered vehicle of any kind, a paddleboat. Papin's work was not acknowledged by the Royal Society in London and he failed to gain any financial, dying a pauper in 1712 (Matschoss 1939).

A military engineer Thomas Savvy spent his spare time undertaking mechanical experiments and in 1698 he patented an early steam engine. This engine had no piston or moving parts and worked by creating a vacuum in a pipe that drove water into a chamber. Savvy described the power of the engine using the term *'horsepower'* for the first time. As Savvy's patent covered any engine which raised water by fire, this forced another inventor Thomas Newcomen who had carried out his own independent research with John Calley devising a piston driven steam cylinder that was similar to the one invented earlier by Papin, to work with Savvy (Rolt & Allen 2007). After Savvy's death the patent was assigned to the company and any party who wished to build and operate a Newcomen steam engine required a license.

The Newcomen engine remained principally the same for a number of years, although a number of improvements had been made in its construction. Between 1765-1775 engineer John Smeaton made a number of precision and design improvements to steam engines without making any changes to the principals of operation. Smeaton succeeded in utilizing steam engines for pumping out water from underground mines which had previously been largely unsuccessful.

James Watt was a learned man who did a number of things to make a living, including making mathematical instruments, repairing musical instruments, and building organs. He was very methodical, studying the literature on the subject first, developing models to experiment with before building the real thing. Watt had only turned his attention to the steam engine on rare occasions, but was asked in 1763 to repair a small model of a Newcomen steam engine. During the re-commissioning Watt was amazed how much steam the engine really needed to run the piston, where the boiler only gave enough for a few strokes. He went on to think about the problem with months and months of hard methodical thinking of how to prevent condensation within the cylinder and stop the wastage of steam. Watt immediately consulted his friend Joseph Black who had made the discovery of latent heat. After further deep and obsessive thinking Watt came up with the idea that condensation could be prevented by closing the cylinder and steam jacketing the piston. Although Watt had found an idea that will provide a solution, it took him a number of years of hard work and collaboration to achieve this in practice.

Any invention is never complete with only an idea. The construction of a model will enhance it, but time is usually required to incorporate incremental innovations upon the original concepts until it is a really perfected product, rather than one immediate breakthrough. During Watt's improvements on the engine, a number of failures occurred and Watt himself started to run out of money for personal expenses a number of times. Watt turned to John Roebuck, after an introduction from a friend for help. Roebuck himself was a promoter of new ventures particularly in ironworks and mines, owning the Carron ironworks in Scotland. Roebuck immediately saw potential in the steam engine for industrial applications and financed continual work by Watt.

A wide patent which was later to be bitterly contested was taken out[38]. Both Watt and Roebuck were becoming very tired and financially drained. Watt had to take time off to

---

[38] Watt and Bolton had a very difficult fight with the patent office where great opposition was raised about the monopoly the patent would create. Watt and Bolton finally convinced the patent office that if the patent was not

undertake survey work for income, found it very difficult to continue working on the steam engine in open air due to the cold and rain, and failed to reach home in time for the death of his ill wife.

At the most desperate hour of his life a friend introduced Watt to Matthew Bolton, where a collaborative friendship was immediately formed. Bolton was an industrialist who had extended his father's interests in metal and ironware, including products like clocks, silverware, gold leaf, and gilt bronze. Bolton had also worked deeply on the minting of coins around Europe which gave him an international reputation. Bolton bought out Roebuck's share and relieved Watt of the worry about earning an income.

However troubles in development continued, particularly in the construction of the machine as no foundries to build it were in existence. Working by lathe was an art and nobody had been able to machine parts to the accuracy that the piston and cylinder required. Both Watt and Bolton had to act as consulting engineers to the machine shops that built each part. Furthermore very few users were interested in buying the engine as so many advised against it. Watt and Bolton devised a business model where users would pay a royalty based on the coal saved. Although this model was very satisfactory early on, as the Watt engine consumed only a quarter of the coal other machines required, many mines became angry at having to pay the annual royalty. The monopoly imposed by the patent was challenged resulting in long drawn out litigation over the patent, which Watt and Bolton eventually won. In the later years Watt concentrated on developing new applications in industry for the steam engine to increase its market potential; however Watt was prevented from doing so in some areas because of prior patents on certain crank devises and applications and had to find ways around the patents. James Watt continued to improve his engines adding a throttle and centrifugal governor to the machine.

The story of the steam engine shows how far sighted vision is just as important as the new technologies and the positive roll that patents play in acting as an incentive to invest. Just as important as the invention is the business model devised to commercialize it. This story also shows that most often the invention of breakthrough products and processes requires great sacrifice and very narrow focus, without becoming blinded by the mission. James Watt's obsessive style of thinking of solutions is a kind of problem solving/creative process that many other inventors have utilized over the years. This story also shows the importance of incremental development and prior knowledge that is necessary for an inventor to work upon. Thus each invention has its own time where knowledge and technology makes it possible. Finally, networking, the ability to gather knowledge, raise finance, and promote the concept was invaluable in the development of the steam engine.

The Railways

People, especially those living in near the coal mines of England and Wales have seen steam engines, but no one has imagined what transport powered by steam would look like. The concept of a steam locomotive was novel and new to the world at that time. There were

---

extended the necessary money to fully develop the machine for commercial applications would not be forthcoming due to lack of protection for the investors. Watt's wide claim was finally extended for another 20 years which aggravated many of his competitors.

still many technical problems to solve by engineers and the *modus operandi* of travel, *i.e., on roads or on tracks*, not yet conceptualized at this point of time. The gestation of the modern railway took many incremental steps initiated by so many people. The concept was not immediately accepted and took a lot of promotion on the part of various inventors.

James Watt's development of the steam engine brought the concept from an inefficient machine to the mechanized workhouse of the industrial revolution that helped to revolutionize factory work from a craft based activity to a mass production operation. This opened up the possibilities for new types of industrial opportunities due to their greatly improved viability with steam as a source of power (Prasad 2003). This attracted many people to the cities in search of work and brought immense social change.

Nicolas-Joseph Cugnot was a French inventor believed to have built the first self-propelled mechanized vehicle in 1769. Cugnot was able to convert the upright motion of the steam piston into a rotary motion utilizing a ratchet arrangement. However the vehicle was unstable, had poor weight distribution and inefficient steam boiler performance. After a number of trials the French navy withdrew funding and the project was abandoned.

William Murdoch was a Scottish engineer employed by Bolton and Watt, eventually becoming a partner. Murdoch made a number of improvements to Watt's steam engine which included the development of the *sun and planet gear*, the *D slide valve*, and the *steam wheel* which was the precursor to the steam turbine. He also made a number of applied inventions based on steam, compressed air and developed the concept of gas lighting and distribution.

Murdoch developed Britain's first steam carriage in 1784. He envisaged a steam powered vehicle that would draw carriages along a road, but James Watt his employer was against the idea[39]. However upon Bolton's suggestions, Watt added the concept of a steam powered carriage to a patent application. Murdoch did not give away the idea completely working on it in his own time.

Coincidently, Richard Trevithick moved to the town of Redruth and became Murdoch's neighbor. During their brief time as neighbors Trevithick would have heard about and seen Murdoch's steam engine. Richard Trevithick himself was a mining engineer born in the Cornwell mining region. Trevithick during his youth observed the low pressure steam engines used to pump water out of the mines. At an early age Trevithick became a consultant modifying Watt's engines to avoid paying patent royalties. As his experience and expertise grew, Trevithick realized that there were many advantages with high pressure steam which could drive a piston in a steam engine on its own account rather than using atmospheric pressure in a condensing engine. Trevithick began building models of high pressure steam engines utilizing a double action cylinder with four-way valves to make it more efficient. The exhausted steam was vented directly out via a chimney to avoid any infringement of Watt's patent. Trevithick built a full size locomotive in 1801, naming it the *Puffing Devil*. In 1802 Trevithick took out a patent for his high pressure steam engine. He built a number of other prototypes, having a number of mishaps along the way with four men dying in a boiler explosion in Greenwich. His competitors Bolton and Watt used the mishap to promote their low pressure engine. Trevithick incorporated a number of safety valves into the boiler to solve this problem.

---

[39] James Watt was very much against high pressure steam which he considered dangerous because at the time it would not have been possible to build boilers strong enough to withstand the pressure.

In 1802 Trevithick built a steam locomotive on wheels in South Wales. Samuel Homfray was so impressed with the concept he purchased the patent from Trevithick. In 1803 Homfray went on to make a bet with Richard Crawshay that that Trevithick's steam engine could haul 10 tons of iron along the Merthyr Tydfil Tramroad from Penydarren, a distance of almost ten miles[40]. The locomotive did this successfully in 1804 and the bet was won by Homfray, showing that steam locomotives were a potentially viable transport option. The fact that the locomotive carried 10 tons of iron and 70 men showed that the engine had the power to become a real workhorse.

Trevithick built a couple more locomotives and then in 1808 built a small circular railway system in London as a tourist attraction where people would pay one shilling per ride. This turned into a financial disaster and Trevithick abandoned his interest in steam locomotives to work on other projects.

Meanwhile quite independently across the Atlantic, Oliver Evans had developed a high pressure steam engine. Evans had built an automated flour mill powered by paddles in the adjunct river to the factory. Evans was interested in steam as a source of power and apparently read about Newcomen engines, pondering about the limitations without the power high pressure steam could provide. Evans found technicians who could build a high pressure boiler, building the boiler out of wood and iron ring reinforced copper. Evans engine was just as compact as Trevithick's and he patented the engine in 1787.

William James, a lawyer from Warwickshire, England was involved in the search for coal deposits and became an enthusiast for the railways. He envisaged the Liverpool-Manchester line and the belief that one day a whole railway network would exist around Britain. Many collieries had been using horse driven railroads to haul their coal, as well as the canals. However the upkeep of horses was becoming very expensive. Christopher Blackett, the owner of the Wylam Colliery on the Tyne in Northumberland was concerned about the rise in upkeep costs of horses and commissioned John Steel in 1804 to build a Trevithick style steam engine for a locomotive. John Steel worked with Trevithick on the Menthyr Tydfil – Penydarren venture. However because of the problem of the Wylam rails being too soft and brittle to carry the weight of the locomotive, Blackett did not buy the concept and the steam engine ended up being used as a stationary engine.

With improving perfection of the steam engine and locomotive, the issue of tracks was emerging as another problem to solve. The locomotive and carriages were potentially too heavy for any tracks manufactured to date and if railways were going to be the transport of the future, this problem had to be solved. Tracks at this stage were wooden laid upon a rock and gravel base with oak sleepers. Canals were also becoming too expensive to build and operate with investors wanting high dividends and users resenting the tolls. There was a drastic need for a more economic form of power to transport people and goods around Britain.

The first improvement was made by John Blenkinsop who was asked to produce a working steam engine running on rails at the Middleton Colliery in Yorkshire, near Leeds. Blenkinsop developed smooth engine wheels which had a cog interlinked with sockets on the

---

[40] Homfray was an iron founder and Iron was transported to Cardiff using a canal which was now congested. A horse drawn railway was built by some of the iron founders beside the canal where the carriages were pulled by horses. The upkeep of horses in stables was expensive and Homfray hoped that Trevithick's steam engine could haul the carriages.

side of the rail. The Middleton railway was opening in 1812 and was the first functioning steam railway in the world, attracting a lot of international attention.

Back at Wylam Colliery, one of the workmen William Hedley experimented with different kinds of smooth rails. In 1811 Hedley built a locomotive called the *Wylam Dilly* which solved the weight problem by distributing the weight over eight wheels rather than four wheels used on previous locomotives. The weight of the locomotive in its own right gave the smooth wheels and rails grip.

George Stephenson was born in Wylam, Northumberland and was the son of a fireman. George's parents could not afford to send him to schooling so at the age of 18 he could neither read nor write, but had an intimate knowledge of the collieries. Stephenson got a job at the Black Callerton Colliery and at the same time learnt how to read and write at night. He also took up jobs to repair shoes and clocks to supplement his income.

Stephenson was one of the people to see the Trevithick locomotive in action which truly inspired him. With the support of the colliery owners Sir Thomas Liddell, Stuart Wortley, and the Earl of Strathmore he designed his first locomotive in 1814 for hauling coal on the Killingworth Wagonway. The locomotive used flanged wheels upon iron tracks depending upon its own weight for traction and could haul 30 ton of coal at 4 mph up a hill. This was the first time that iron tracks were ever used. However cast iron was too brittle to be used as rails with heavy engines. An eventual solution came for this from an ironmonger in Norpeth, Northumberland John Birkinshaw who produced wrought-iron rails which were rolled out in convenient lengths for track laying[41].

William James had been commissioned by a consortium of Liverpool and Manchester merchants, manufacturers, and traders to survey the possibility of a railway line between the two cities. The alternative was to build a canal where the legal processes were straight forward, but the building the canal with a series of locks would be very expensive and the profitability of the project was questionable. On the other hand, getting a railway started required getting permission from parliament which was a drawn out process where any resistance by land owners would get the petition thrown out. This happened during the first attempt to petition for the Darlington to Stockton railway line. James was looking for the best locomotives available and went to Stephenson who agreed to assist with his partner William Losh who produced cast iron rails.

James introduced Stephenson to Edward Pease who both immediately got on extremely well together. They ended up forming a company to produce locomotives together with Stephenson's son Robert as managing director. George Stephenson had a fall out with William Losh over James wish to use wrought-iron rails from John Birkinshaw due to the superiority of wrought-iron over the brittle iron rails. This caused a permanent rift between the two men that was never reconciled. The company built four locomotives for the project and laid 4ft 8 ½ inch gauge line which became almost internationally accepted as a standard gauge. The official opening was an outstanding success with the arrival at Stockton with a crowd of 40,000 people to greet them with a six-gun salute.

While the Stockton to Darlington railway was being built Stephenson was invited to look at the potential of a Liverpool to Manchester Railway. William James was in deep financial trouble and Stephenson replaced him. James felt that he had been poorly treated by

---

[41] Wrought iron is malleable and has much more tensile strength than cast iron.

Stephenson and that all his work on promoting railways and getting the best engineers together had all gone without recognition.

Stephenson had learnt a lot from the Stockton to Darlington railway. Even small inclines greatly hinder the progress of a locomotive and brakes are to the large part almost totally ineffective on downward gradients. Another technical difficulty was that the line had to travel through approximately four miles of beat bog, which is very spongy and anything of weight would tend to sink down into it. Stephenson solved the problem by laying brushwood and heather with a layer of stones and this would float over the peat bog (Davies 2004). Many other engineers were also after the project and contracts to build the locomotives and other rolling stock, so it was decided that a competition be held to determine which engineer had the superior locomotive. Out of five entries Stephenson's *Rocket* was successful. The *Rocket* was primarily designed by George Stephenson's son Robert who returned from South America. The *Rocket* utilized a new type of fire-tube boiler designed by French engineer Marc Seguin that improved heat exchange dramatically increasing the speed of the locomotive many fold. The line opened on 15th September 1830 with much fanfare, marred by the death of the MP for Liverpool William Huskisson who was struck and killed by the *Rocket*.

The success of the Liverpool-Manchester railway line forced the lowering of canal tolls and stagecoach traffic on the road dropped substantially. This led to a railway boom in Britain with more than eighty new railway companies being formed to promote new railroads. The railway boom also spread to Europe and Russia opening up new areas within those respective countries for trade and development. The railway was conceptualized as a means to transport coal to ports and markets but stimulated the whole momentum of the industrial revolution enabling the transport of raw materials to factories and products to markets. Towns along the railway lines boomed.

The development of the railways also showed the importance of prior knowledge and collaboration of ideas into the creation of new technologies. Without these collaborations, ideas would take much longer to develop and perfect. Intensive activities in an industry seem to attract talent and lead to clusters of expertise in certain areas as is seen in the development of many industries during latter periods, *i.e., the porcelain, automobiles, and even computer industries*. The development of the railway industry also showed that there may often be streaks of ruthlessness on the part of single minded entrepreneurs, which we will see more of in the petroleum industry later. What can also be seen is that brilliant and creative engineers are not always the successful ones and that failure is a common occurrence.

The development of the railways and related technologies has enabled both technology spin-offs into new inventions, *in these cases new forms of transport based on railway concepts and technologies,* and created opportunities for other industries to develop that could not have existed before railway infrastructure was built (see figure 2.9). The railways were initially promoted as a means to transport coal to market for the British collieries and local merchants. However the railways quickly took on a much larger role that helped to transform the regions that the lines served, enabling the growth of new towns and provide access to markets for potential new industries. The railways were initially hindered by the *immature technology* of the steam engine until it was developed satisfactorily enough to run practically and efficiently. This took many incremental innovations by many people. Some of the early attempts to develop steam locomotives did not incorporate *mature* technology and thus failed to develop any momentum. Further enhancement and introductions of new technologies such as electricity enables the basic *railway technologies* to be adapted to trams and other commuter transport systems. The advent of diesel and diesel electric enabled efficient long distance travel at much faster speeds making train travel even more convenient. Never before could people travel so quickly across land. The basic infrastructure of the railway itself allowed for the complementary application of other inventions like the telegraph to be incorporated into the railway system.

The railways enabled the creation of many new opportunities and industries. The very existence of railway infrastructure created a demand for maintenance, repair, and carriage building industries to develop to serve the railways directly. Towns were able to develop with their own *micro-economies,* complete with general stores, bakeries, hotels, and cafes, etc. Primary and farm based enterprises could use the railways to sent their produce to the large cities and other industries could develop anywhere along the railway with ready access to markets. This enabled interior economic development in Britain, Europe, America, and Australia that was never seen before from the 1830s. The railways also allowed the enhancement of the postal services which created the conditions for new creative business models like the mail order business. The incorporation of cold technologies allowed the transport of perishable produce and meat thus allowing for the expansion of grazing and cattle into multi-million dollar industries. When full networks of railways existed modern manufacturing could centralize their production in one place and use the railway system to distribute products to wholesalers and distributors all over the country. The railway had an impact on the world in the 19th Century that air travel and transport would have in the next century.

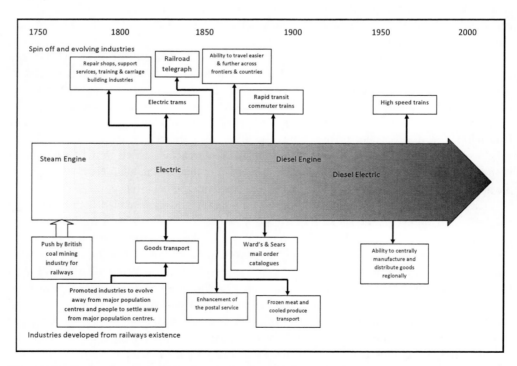

Figure 2.9. The development of the railways showing spin-off industries and industries that developed from the existence of the railway.

The American Mail Order Business

American engineers crossed the Atlantic to Britain to learn how to build steam locomotives and lay down railway tracks. No fewer than fifteen American engineers visited Britain between 1825 and 1838 to improve their understanding of building railroads (Stapleton 1987). However American industry was far behind Britain at the time and rail tracks and locomotives had to be shipped across the Atlantic. Like Britain, canals in the North-East of America were important means of transportation. Once Napoleon sold Louisiana to America in 1803, the network of rivers in the south with the Mississippi as the hub could be utilized for transportation in the South. The steamboat became the symbol of prosperity of the South and helped establish the cotton industry and settlement along the river states. But it was the railroads that were going to an instrumental role in developing the Western United States from the 1830s onwards, taking settlers with it all the way across the time zones of the United States. Railroads settled and developed the Western United States bringing with it immense opportunities for entrepreneurs to exploit.

As people settle in the West they needed goods but retail stores at that time were very limited and expensive. The development of the railroads and postal system made a mail order business feasible. The concept of mail order was not new in America as it is believed Benjamin Franklin developed the concept of selling science and academic books in 1744[42]. The earliest known surviving business in America is Hammacher Schlemmer which began as a hardware store in New York City in 1848. In 1881 the company printed and distributed their first mail order catalogue selling tools and other hardware products. Over the years the company expanded the catalogue to include pianos, radios, and other electrical goods. In 1863 Washington Atlee Burpee used to post office to deliver catalogues and dispatch the resulting orders of seeds to homes, extending the concept to rural areas in 1896.

In 1872 Aaron Montgomery Ward published the first general merchandise mail order catalogue specifically aimed at rural communities through the post office. Ward had been in retailing for many years and worked for the Marshall Field department store which produced a single page catalogue featuring low prices and an emphasis on customer satisfaction (Schweikart & Doti 2010). Ward saw the potential of the market and the railroads had built the logistics needed to enable extension of the postal system. Ward's business grew steadily benefitting from the guarantee that the company would accept returned goods. Wards customer base grew out of merchant wary farmers of the Midwest and over 20 years the catalogue expanded to include over 24,000 items in more than 500 pages. By 1913 the company had had annual revenue of over USD $40 million and built a tower in Chicago and (Sobel & Sicilia 1986).

It was not long before Ward's concept caught the attention of Richard Warren Sears who was a railroad station agent in North Redwood, Minnesota. Sears received a shipment of watches from a Chicago jeweler that the local jeweler didn't want, so he purchased them and sold the watches to other station agents along the railroad line. This encouraged him to purchase more and start a watch sales business which led him to Chicago where he met Alvah C. Roebuck and together they started a company that was going to be known as Sears, Roebuck & Co.

---

[42] This is reported by a number of websites but not verified by any historian's accounts to the author's knowledge.

Sears being an ex-station agent knew the farmers brought their crops to town where they could be sold and shipped. While in the town the farmers generally bought their supplies from local general stores at very high prices. Sears published his catalogue with bold pricing so that customers knew what they were buying and at what price, and be able to order conveniently. The range initially was based on watches, chains, and jewelry, but soon household items, bicycles, sporting goods, and sewing machines and the like were added. The first catalogue appeared in 1888 and by 1895 the catalogue was in excess of 500 pages and a firm competitor to Ward's catalogue. Sears, Roebuck & Co. developed a good reputation for quality customer satisfaction. By 1895 the company had annual sales of USD $400,000 and by 1907 USD $38 million (Schweikart & Doti 2010, P. 255).

Sears and Ward relied on rural consumers, competing primarily with local merchants in small towns. Consumers accepted the mail order business well and lobbied the US Congress to expand the postal service so it was easier to obtain a mail order catalogue (Bryant & Dethloff 1990). However, overtime the demographics changed with people moving to cities which were serviced by the rise in departmental stores, another new phenomenon in the 20th Century. Both Sears and Ward's companies were seriously hurt during the great depression of 1929.

There are a number of parallels between the mail order companies of the turn of the 20th Century and the Dot.Com companies of the turn of the 21st Century. Mail order companies utilized the growing railroads and improved postage services to send out catalogues and ship out orders, while the Dot.Com companies utilize the internet. To succeed then and now, customer wants and needs must be satisfied, as the novelty of the method of doing business is not enough. There appears to only be a limited window of opportunity for any idea before the structure of the environment changes through demographic shifts, and/or new appealing business models appear that are a more convenient or beneficial business model than the existing one. The lifespan of any opportunity is limited.

Perishable Goods, Refrigeration and New Production and Logistical Models

Before the advent of refrigeration, livestock raised on the great plains of the United States had to be transported live to the Eastern markets in specialized stock cars. The 1,200 mile journey took its toll on the livestock causing tremendous weight loss with usually a number of cattle dying along the way. This meant that livestock had to be slaughtered by the wholesalers themselves and meat delivered fresh to butcher shops for retail sales. This was very inefficient and expensive as 60% of the cow is inedible, yet the whole cow is transported with great losses. There were also similar problems with other agricultural products that were perishable.

There were a number of early attempts to develop 'cold' boxcars for railway transport beginning as early as 1851. The first attempts were basically developed as an 'icebox on wheels' only being functional in cold weather. Another attempt was made in 1857 with a boxcar fitted with bins of ice but this resulted in discoloration and affected the taste of the meat. William Davis patented a refrigerator car that employed suspended metal racks to hang the carcasses above a frozen mixture of ice and salt. He sold the design to George H. Hammond, a Detroit meat-packer in 1868 who built a number of boxcars to transport carcasses to Boston using ice from the great lakes for cooling (White 1995). However with suspended carcasses swinging from the metal racks the centre of gravity of the boxcars was too high which resulted in a number of derailments.

Gustavus Swift worked at his brother's butcher shop where he saw the advantage of developing logistics that improved the process of purchasing cattle, slaughtering them, and carving them up into saleable cuts, selling them for a higher price than the original purchase of the animal (Swift & Van Vlissington 1928). Swift soon opened his own butcher shops, purchased local cattle and extended his sales to Albany and Buffalo, New York. Swift saw the waste within the current supply chain and realized that if cattle were slaughtered in Chicago and only processed meat shipped eastward then this would make meat cheaper. Swift moved to Chicago in 1875 and purchased a local slaughterhouse and started shipping hung meat in boxcars only relying on the cold winter to keep it fresh.

In 1877 Swift hired an engineer Andrew Chase to develop a completely insulated refrigeration car that had ice packed in the roof so the chilled air would naturally flow downward onto the meat. The meat was packed compactly at the bottom of the boxcar to keep the centre of gravity low so there would not be any rail mishaps. This method proved very practical but relied on finding a source of ice along the route and the need to sell all the meat immediately upon arriving at the destination, or quickly refreezing it (Kujovich 1970).

The concept was initially resisted by the railroad companies due to their investments in stock cars and holding pens. Swift eventually found a railroad that would support him through Michigan and Canada. Once the concept was proven his competitors including Philip Armour and the Cudahy Brothers quickly followed suit (Gras & Larsen 1939).

In further moves to improve efficiency and eliminate wastage, Swift introduced overhead conveyors to transport animal carcasses to each processing stage within the meat processing plant. Swift also extracted the fat out of the waste water to recycle the lost fat and also developed a series of by-products including glue, soap, fertilizers, margarine, beef extract, bone based products like knives and combs, baseball covers, gloves, canned pet foods, and even red paint from the blood. The meat processing plants in Chicago were among the first to utilize production line techniques that inspired Henry Ford to develop mass production in the automobile industry some 30 years later (Ford 2008). Swift took the meat trade from a craft to a mass production operation. Swift's attempts to develop *sustainable* and *zero waste* production more than a century ago are two important principals today in industry. The meat processing industry was also one of the first industries to understand and practice economies of scale. Swift also utilized the concept of vertical integration controlling the whole supply chain from slaughter to retail.

The Arrival of Petroleum

Before the arrival of petroleum there were a number of different fuels that could be used for light and power. Coal became an important fuel in industry for steam engines, but houses still cooked with wood and lit their houses with candles or whale oil. A large whaling industry existed in many parts of the world primarily to secure oil for lighting (Creighton 1995). However whale oil was expensive and only affordable by the well to do of society, particularly in 1850 where stocks dwindled due to being hunted almost to the point of extinction, the price went up dramatically (Chernow 1998) – *a hint and forerunner into the future petroleum oil scenario.* This created an impetus to find another source of fuel for lighting.

In the late 1840s and early 1850s there were a number of people working on extracting oils from naturally occurring bituminous tars, coal, oil shale, and crude oil. In 1846 a Canadian geologist Abraham Gesner announced and demonstrated that he could distill a clear thin fluid from coal which made an excellent lamp oil he called kerosene. As the cost of dry distillation proved too high, Gesner looked at extracting kerosene from albertite that occurs in natural bituminous tar. After some difficulties in finding a place to mine the material due to coal mining companies having the mining rights, Gesner moved to Long Island in 1854. With the backing of a group of businessmen they formed the North American Gas Light Company. Gesner later commenced distilling kerosene from bituminous coal and oil shale around the Boston area (Loris 2003).

In 1848 a Scottish chemist James Young experimented with oil seeping from a coal mine as a source of lubricating and illuminating oil. Young expanded production to extracting what he called paraffin oil from locally mined torbanite, shale, and bituminous coal. In 1851 Samuel Martin Kier distilled oil from crude oil which he called carbon oil, selling it as lamp oil. Across in Europe Ignacy Lukasiewicz, a Polish pharmacist in Lvov and used local seep oil to experiment with different kerosene distillation techniques, trying to improve upon Gesner's techniques. Doctors at his hospital needed a strong light for an emergency operation and called him to assist with the lighting. The lamps performed extremely well and Lukasiewicz seeing the potential of this product moved to the Gorlice region of Poland in 1854 sinking a number of wells over the following decade. He set up a refinery near Jasto in 1859.

A Professor Benjamin Silliman Jr. was commissioned by George Bissell and Jonathan Eveleth who where mining oil in Pennsylvania and selling it for medicinal purposes. They were able to extract kerosene from crude oil in 1855 with much higher yields than coal or bituminous tar. With the news that crude oil could make a number of high value products, Bissell and Eveleth formed the Pennsylvania Rock Company (later known as Seneca Oil) and commissioned Edward Drake to investigate the possibility of oil deposits in Titusville, Pennsylvania. In 1859 Drake with the help of a salt driller constructed a 30 ft high derrick and drilled seventy feet into the ground and stuck oil (Pusateri 1988). This spurred an oil rush with many speculators coming to the region to prospect for oil. There were so many speculators drilling for oil that no one could make a profit with Drake himself dying in poverty. It was an unexpected event, the American Civil War that eventually drove prices up making it worthwhile to go into the crude oil drilling business. Within a decade the oil business had expanded to more than 5 million barrels with the majority of oil being converted to kerosene for homes and later industry, paraffin for candles, and tar for paving, displacing the use of whale oil which declined rapidly as an industry (Starbuck 1989).

John D. Rockefeller was born in Richmond, New York in 1810 to a meager family. In his teens, Rockefeller took great interest in bookkeeping and was a thrifty and devout Baptist who devoted part of his salary each month to the church. His first job was at a produce company where he worked long hours. In 1859 Rockefeller set a his own produce company with Maurice B. Clark and the business steadily grew and returned a profit each year (Segall 2001). In 1863 during the American Civil War, Clark and Rockefeller ventured into the oil refining business with Samuel Andrews, a chemist and inventor[43]. During the Civil War Rockefeller bought out Maurice Clark and his brother's shares in the company by auction and renamed the company Rockefeller & Andrews. This enabled Rockefeller to position himself to take advantage of the growing demand for fuel with the westward push of the railroads. Rockefeller borrowed heavily, and obtained $100,000 from Stephen V. Harkness on the condition that Henry Morrison Flagler[44] is made a partner. The company was renamed Rockefeller, Andrews & Flagler. With Flagler on board Rockefeller was able to quickly adapt to changing markets (Segall 2001, P. 32). Flagler introduced rebates to customers in order to strengthen the company's position against competitors, while Rockefeller looked at ways to become more production efficient. One of these schemes was to vertically integrate into the barrel production business (Schweikart & Doti 2010). As this business grew Rockefeller brought in his brother William and renamed the company, the Standard Oil Company.

Rockefeller focused on finding as many potential uses for crude oil by-products as possible by bringing in outside chemists and eliminating waste during the refining process. This had the effect of pushing prices for kerosene so low that coal and other crude oil extractors had problems surviving. The whaling industry floundered and the concept of electricity for lighting was ignored during this time. Standard oil became one of the most efficient refineries in the industry.

Early on Rockefeller had become one of the largest shippers of product on the railroads. The railroads were fiercely competing for business. In an attempt to form a cartel, Standard Oil with a few other refiners formed the Southern Improvement Company. The scheme involved the railroad companies raising freight rates and paying back rebates to Southern Investment Company, both on their own and competitors' shipments. Independent competitors and consumers found out about the scheme which led to protests, boycotts and even vandalism of company property. The Pennsylvania Legislature revoked the company's charter. Rockefeller admitted his mistake and abandoned efforts to create a freight cartel.

Rockefeller turned his attention to expanding the company and went about acquiring competing refiners, taking on their managers and employees, improving the efficiencies of the firm's operations, and passing on discounts to their customers. Where possible, Rockefeller exchanged shares for the purchase of his competitors preferring to save the cash for further expansion. By the late 1870s Standard oil controlled between 80-90% of the kerosene market and owned the majority of refiners. This gave Rockefeller an enormous bargaining chip over the railroads and he insisted on rebates at a time when the railroads were already within a round of price wars.

Rockefeller planned for the use of pipelines to transport oil and began to acquire land to do this. The Pennsylvania Railroad seeing the potential threat of Standard's incursion into the transport business began buying up refiners. Rockefeller retaliated by holding back shipments and using alternative railroads with the effect of dramatically reducing freight charges. The Pennsylvania Railroad Company eventually gave in and sold all its oil interests to Standard Oil. In 1879 the Commonwealth of Pennsylvania indicted Rockefeller on charges of

---

[43] Samuel Andrews immigrated to the United States from England and had experience in shale oil production in the newly discovered fields of Western Pennsylvania. Andrews was the person who approached Rockefeller about the oil business. Andrews was a good creative engineer who was able to develop the chemical processes of fractional distillation required for isolating the different fractions or chemicals from crude oil.

[44] Henry Flagler is credited for his marketing strategies and schemes that could capitalize on Andrew's technical knowledge.

monopoly, starting a number of court proceedings against the company for monopolistic practices.

Standard oil had a number of oil fields, its own tankers, was constructing pipelines, and building networks of dealers and overseas subsidiaries. Standard used this infrastructure to keep oil prices low enough to prevent potential competitors entering the market[45], and be affordable to the average household, with the price of kerosene dropping more than 75% during the life of Standard Oil.

Standard Oil faced a number of challenges. New oil finds in other countries were diluting Standard Oil's international dominance. The Russians discovered oil in Baku, Central Asia that was of higher quality and cheaper to extract. As Russian production increased Standard Oil's market share declined to just over 50% of the world market. The Russian fields were also more centrally located for the European and Asian markets. Robert Nobel, brother of Alfred Nobel decided to try the oil industry and went to Baku to develop oil wells and refining operations financed by the Rothschilds. Additional fields were discovered in Burma and Java and the electric light bulb was finding interest as an alternative to kerosene for lighting. Nevertheless Rockefeller retaliated building more tankers and sold oil cheaper than what was coming out of Baku. Standard Oil was able to win back some of its international market share.

Back in the United States Standard Oil was operating across a number of states with a myriad of companies which was unruly to manage and control. Rockefeller's lawyers devised a trust which could take ownership of the equities of all the companies. This came into being by 1882 where all assets were under the control of the trust with Rockefeller as one of the nine trustees. As the largest business entity in the world Standard Oil came under criticism of competitors, politicians, and the public and under the scrutiny of anti-trust laws. Standard oil in 1899 restructured again under a holding company in New Jersey capitalized at USD $110 Million.

During the 1890s the company expanded into natural gas production and bought fields in Ohio, Indiana, and West Virginia as the Pennsylvania fields began to dry out. Standard also began selling gasoline for automobiles which until then was considered a waste product. Rockefeller also moved into other industries buying out iron ore interests. Rockefeller formally retired in 1902, but remained president of the corporation. Rockefeller became very weary of all the criticisms of himself and Standard Oil and consequently made himself more accessible to the public. In 1911 the Supreme Court of the United States found Standard Oil in violation of the Sherman Anti-Trust Act and ruled that the company originated in illegal monopoly practices and ordered it to be broken up into 34 separate companies. Today some of these companies have developed into very successful corporations in their own right which included Conoco, ConocoPhillips, Amoco (now part of BP), Mobil (now ExxonMobil), Sohio (now part of BP), Chevron, and Pennzoil. Rockefeller kept his stock in all the companies at the time of breakup with increased his personal wealth to almost USD $1 Billion.

Rockefeller was criticized by competitors, the public and the media all throughout his career for being cruel, ruthless, pitiless, and engaging in unfair, heavy handed and monopolistic practices to get his own way and had plenty of enemies. This is paradoxical to the espoused philosophies of Rockefeller who claimed it was never about the money, but

---

[45] Standard Oil's major weapons against its competitors were low pricing through economies of scale, freight rebates and differential pricing to customers.

giving a fair deal to the poor working man by providing them with the best quality and cheapest product (Nevins 1953). Although critics claim he sanitized his memoirs published in 1908 as being contrary to his real business methods (Segall 2001, P. 91), it must not be forgotten that he contributed 10% of his income to the church and became one of the greatest philanthropists of all time.

There are a number of lessons that can be learnt from the history of Standard Oil. Opportunities often come from a person one knows within or outside their business network as was the case with Rockefeller's church friend Samuel Andrews. The start-up of a business is extremely vital to the future trajectory of the business. This is a critical time. The decisions made and directions taken in the early stages will usually influence the formation of future strategies. It is also important that the early formation activities be led in total competence and with skill. Rockefeller's assistance came from Andrews on the technical aspects and Flagler on marketing and strategy were vital to success. A company needs to be well managed in the growth stage. Company success is influenced strongly by a founder's drive, passion, vision and far sighted planning. The culture of the company is also heavily influenced by the founder and even reflected in the companies chosen strategies. Rockefeller was considered to be ruthless and many of the strategies and actions he took reflected this.

In the Standard Oil case, controlling a limited resource and developing a supply chain that gave an advantage over other producers was the key to their position within the competitive environment. Standard Oil sought to control a resource through owning as many wells as possible, being as efficient as possible, and gaining advantage over the supply chain to the point where the price of kerosene was low enough to act as a barrier to entry to potential competitors. Rockefeller also realized the link between research and development and gaining more products that would increase revenues.

The start-up of Standard Oil was at a time where the main product substitute was whale oil which was much more expensive than kerosene. Standard oil also started before electrical lighting was able to gain a foothold in the market. During the growth stage of Standard Oil the automobile industry began to emerge providing a new market for the company. Finally at the time of start-up the technology required existed to make the venture viable. There is one final lesson for firms of the future that the Standard Oil story can provide. Just because a firm gives money away to charity or works on community projects doesn't always go into support the company's image if it is not seen to be ethical in its business dealings.

One Man, Multiple Inventions

Thomas Edison was born in Milan, Ohio in 1837, the Seventh child of Samuel Ogden Edison and Nancy Matthews Elliot. His parents were actually Canadian but his father had to flee Canada due to the role he played in the Mackenzie rebellion of 1837[46]. Edison only spent a very short time in formal schooling and was taught at home by his mother who was a school teacher, for the rest of his early years. There are numerous stories about Edison's youth which cannot be accurately verified[47]. However it can be verified from a number of sources are that Edison had the tendency to daydream and one of his first entrepreneurial activities was to sell

---

[46] A series of uprisings in Canada in the name of seeking political reform.
[47] There are many versions of Edison's early life with different dates related to events.

newspapers and snacks on the train from Port Huron to Detroit (Weightman 2007, P. 328). It is also reported from Edison's early years that he preferred reading literature, which he did at the Detroit library while waiting for the return train to Port Huron and had distaste for physics and mathematics (Israel 1998). Edison tended to be weak at mathematics and draughting, preferring to think up things that needed to be invented and getting financiers to support while he worked out how things could be done, most often hiring someone who would be most likely to find the solution to the particular problem (Weightman 2007, P. 328).

Edison saved a station master's three year old son from falling in front of an oncoming train for which the father was grateful and rewarded him with an intensive course of training as a Morse code operator (Baldwin 1995). This was a great career opportunity at the time and after the course, Edison got a job at Stratford Junction, Ontario. Shortly after Edison decided to return home to Port Huron and found that the military had acquired the family home, his father did not have a steady job and his mother was on the verge of a breakdown. Around 1866 Edison took a job with Western Union where he worked on the Associated Press news wire. He requested the night shift so he could read and do his experiments. However this caused him dismissal when sulfuric acid from a battery he was working on split onto the floor and dripped through to his boss's office below (Baldwin 1995, pp. 40-41).

Edison moved to New Jersey where he stayed as a lodger with a friend Franklin Leonard Pope who was also a telegrapher. During this time Edison experimented with the telegraph and also invented a voting machine which failed to work when he demonstrated it. Edison and Pope formed a partnership Pope, Edison & Company Electrical Engineers in 1869. Pope had been working on a stock ticker, which was accepted and employed in a number of stock exchanges around the country. The company was bought out for the sum of USD $15,000, a small fortune at the time, where Edison was now able to financially assist his parents.

Edison had established a name for himself as an inventor and was commissioned by *Western Union* to undertake some invention on their behalf. Edison solved the problem of share-price printing machines going haywire and this impressed many within the firm. Edison was made a payment of somewhere in between USD $30-40,000, which was a staggering sum for the time (Weightman 2007, P. 330). Edison was then allowed to head his own division and hire his own staff to build stock-price ticker machines. It was during this time that Edison recruited a number of men that were to stay with him for a number of years. These included Charles Batchelor an engineer and draughtsman, John Kruesi a Swiss clockmaker, and Sigmund Bergmann a German mechanic. During this period Edison often worked day and night, not worrying about his own personal appearance but produced a number of inventions and improvements to inventions.

Edison made his first trip abroad to England in 1873 to see if the British Post Office might be interested in buying some of his patents. He proved his telegraph worked well between Liverpool and London, but upon being asked to demonstrate how his telegraph would work over a 2,200 mile cable that was to be laid between Britain and Brazil, his telegraph failed.

Edison returned from Britain empty handed. Back in the United States Edison became involved in so many jobs for competing companies but was losing money. A financier Jay Gould from Atlantic and Pacific Telegraph company appeared with a check for USD $30,000 to buy out Edison and get him away from Western Union. Even though Edison now had funding, he was very tired of the maneuverings between Gould and his rival Vanderbilt at Western Union.

In 1876 Edison left what he was doing and with the money he received from Jay Gould set up what could be called the first industrial research laboratories at Menlo Park, New Jersey. Now Edison was free to take work from anybody he wanted and brought over many of his colleagues in to carry out the development work under his direction. Again Edison showed his determination by working day and night, motivated by the possibility of fame and fortune from his inventions. Edison was the first inventor to see that the business aspects were more important than the invention itself (Weightman 2007, P. 333). There was no point inventing something that nobody wanted.

One of Edison's first jobs was for Western Union to improve the telephone devised by Alexander Graham Bell and Elisha Gray. While working on improvement of the telephone Edison and his team found that they could record and play back the spoken word. Edison originally conceived of a device that would be like an answering machine. Although his phonograph recorded on tinfoil around a ground cylinder, it had poor quality, and could only be used a few times. However this invention seemed so amazing to the public that Edison himself became dubbed the *'wizard of Menlo Park'.* Such a device had numerous potential applications and a company was set up to commercialize it, but the technology was too crude for commercial use.

During 1878, a professor at the University of Pennsylvania George Barker invited Edison to accompany a group to observe the total eclipse of the sun in the Rockies. Edison went along and both of them discussed the potential operations of electricity, including its use for lighting. Barker upon their return arranged for Edison to visit a company called Wallace and Sons in Connecticut that operated a brass and copper foundry and had developed a powerful electrical generator or telemachon[48]. They were experimenting with carbon arc lighting systems and trying to send electrical currents over long distances.

According to a report, Edison was totally enraptured by the concept and gloated over the demonstration, immediately sitting down trying to calculate the power of the instrument, the lights and the probable loss of power during the transmission. Edison saw the technology in terms of how much coal it could save over a week, a month, and a year, and the effect it would have on manufacturing (Friedel *et. al.* 1988).

Edison immediately ordered one of Wallace's telemachons and envisaged a world lit by an electrical lighting system modeled on the existing gas supply system which was fed through the streets and into individual homes. Carbon arc lights were too bright and uneconomical for home use, so Edison had to devise a new version of the incandescent light bulb which had been the subject of experimentation by other inventors for many years. Edison also considered the numerous other requirements that an electrical distribution system would require including generators, sockets, switches, meters, etc., to produce the equivalent to a gas network.

Electric light was not a new idea, especially in Europe. There had been a number of attempts by people including Humphry Davy, James Bowman Lindsay, Moses G. Farmer, William E. Savage, and Heinrich Göbel to perfect the concept. Most of the electric lights produced had a very short lifespan, used a lot of electricity and were expensive to make. Paul Jablochkoff developed arc lamps which were very successful for street and lighthouse lighting. By 1877 Jablochkoff's were used all over Paris streets. A year later electric street

---

[48] http://paperspast.natlib.govt.nz/cgi-bin/paperspast?a=d&d=NOT18781225.2.14&e=-------10--1----2-- (Accessed 27th January 2011)

lights were tested along the Thames Embankment. However they didn't last long because they were more expensive to run than gas.

Joseph Swan in the United Kingdom had been developing the light independently of Edison. By the 1860s Swan had a working model and obtained a British patent for a carbon filament incandescent lamp in partial vacuum. However due to the poor vacuum, the light was inefficient and had only a very short life span. By 1875 Swan was able to improve the light bulb with a better vacuum. Swan obtained another patent for the lamp in 1878 about a year before Edison and then obtained another patent in 1880, where he started into commercial production.

Meanwhile Edison at Menlo Park was frantically undertaking experiments on the light globe and other devices required to build an electrical distribution system. William J. Hammer was assisting Edison on perfecting the incandescent lamp, testing each version as it was developed. By 1879 Edison had been able to produce a high resistance lamp in a very high vacuum that would burn hundreds of hours. Edison was ready to show his inventions to the public.

The Paris exhibition was chosen by Edison as the stage to show off his invention and outshine his rivals. The judges were asked to compare four different incandescent light bulbs from Swan, Edison, a British inventor St George Lane Fox-Pitt, and an American Hiram Maxim[49]. The four light globes appeared much the same but it was the good public relations of Edison and alleged bribing of some influential journalists to give Edison a favorable write up that won the day for him (Weightman 2007, P. 339).

Edison continued to improve upon the light globe and had a number of disputes over intellectual property that took a number of years to sort out. Some of Edison's financiers managed to sort out a dispute with Swan's patent claims by forming a joint venture company which became known as Ediswan in 1883, where Swan also agreed to Edison having the American rights to the light bulb.

In the United States Edison had filed a patent for an electricity distribution system in 1880 and formed the Edison illuminating Company in New York City. The system went live soon after with a generating plant in Lower Manhattan producing a 110 volt DC current supplying 59 homes in the area.

There were a lot of obstacles to electricity being accepted universally. Gas in Europe was much cheaper and the price of kerosene made lighting by lamps much cheaper than electricity. Edison and George Westinghouse were locked in a battle over using direct verses alternating current (AC) which led to many theatrics such as the public execution of animals by Edison's people to show that AC was more dangerous than DC.

Although Edison didn't invent the first electric light bulb, it can be argued he developed the first commercially practical light bulb. However through his good public relations he convinced most that he was the actual inventor. Edison's Menlo Park laboratory had expanded to occupy almost two city blocks, showcasing the first commercially orientation new product development laboratory in modern industrial history, with an objective of systematic invention and development. Edison's laboratories went on to invent and develop carbon microphones, the fluoroscope, the kinescope, and the development of electric trains. General Electric was formed in 1890 to bring together all of Edison's interests and stands as a legacy to his work. Edison had more than 1,000 patents to his name and became an industrial leader based on invention, innovation, ability to attract financiers and scientists, and public relations.

The Automobile

Even though the railways now existed in Britain, Europe and America most road transport was still undertaken by house and carriage. There were over three million horses in Britain and ten times that many in America which had to be breed, fed, cared for, and housed. A large amount of farmland was devoted to producing hay and oats for horse feed and it was becoming an expensive exercise to maintain a house and carriage. The industry was reaching the limits to its potential growth by 1900. The automobile was not invented by any one individual and was developed from a combination of other inventions and incremental innovations over time to create what we know as the automobile today.

One of the first forms of self-propelled automobiles was Cugnot's steam wagon in 1771 discussed earlier in the steam engine section. This was followed in Britain by William Murdoch's steam carriage in 1784 and Richard Trevithick's full size steam vehicle in 1801. However the British Parliament passed the *Locomotive Act (1865)* that required any self-propelled vehicles on roads to be preceded by a man on foot with a red flag and blowing a horn, effectively discouraging much more development of the automobile in Britain, where attention was shifted back to the steam engine.

Outside Britain there were a number of various vehicles built, some having useful features that would be incorporated into later versions of the automobile. For example Ivan Kulibin in Russia developed a steam carriage in 1791 that incorporated a flywheel, brake, gearbox, and bearings. In 1805 Oliver Evens, an American developed a self-propelled vehicle that was also an amphibious vehicle. In 1815 Josef Buzek from Prague, from what is now known as the Czech Republic built an oil fired steam car that could run further than other steam vehicles developed until that date due to its more efficient fuel. In 1830s there were also a number of electric cars developed including Anyos Jedlik's model car powered by his electric motor in 1928, Thomas Davenport's model electric car in 1834, Stratingh and Becker's small electric car in 1835, Robert Davidson's electric car in 1838 that ran on tracks, a forerunner to an electric tram, and Robert Anderson's electric carriage in 1839.

However steam and electricity were not practical power sources for an automobile, and the absence of a suitable power source hindered commercial development. Likewise the ride on these early vehicles was very rough due to the wheels being fabricated out of wood or iron. A softer material that could take some shock out of the road was necessary. These problems had to be solved before any commercial vehicle could be invented.

One of the very early concepts of a combustion engine was a water pump driven by gunpowder in the 17th Century to pump water for the Versailles Palace gardens developed by Christiaan Huygens. Shortly after, a number of piston engines utilizing gas were developed. In 1807 a Swiss engineer François Isaac de Rivaz developed an internal combustion engine

---

[49] Hiram Maxim was ahead of Edison in the United States. He started his career as a carriage maker at the age of fourteen on to engineering works, gas lighting, and then to pioneer the electric light. He sold out to Edison in 1881 and moved to London where he invented the Maxim machine-gun.

driven by a hydrogen and oxygen mixture, ignited by an induced spark based on Alessandro Volta's concept of propulsion using air and hydrogen in a pistol to propel a cork from the end of the barrel from 1790s. Over the years a number of improvements to the combustion engine were made by Sadi Carnot, Samuel Morey, William Bernett, Eugenio Barsanti and Felice Matteucci, and Pietro Benini. The development of an efficient combustion engine was hindered by the absence of petroleum as a fuel which was just appearing in the later part of the 19th century.

Around 1860 the Belgian Etienne Lenoir developed a gas fueled electrically ignited internal combustion engine that utilized cylinders, pistons connected to rods and a flywheel where the gas basically took the place of steam, as in the Watt steam engines. The engine was commercially produced and used extensively to drive stationary machinery. Although the Lenoir engine attracted much publicity, it was not suitable for a moving vehicle but inspired others to refine and develop upon the basic design.

One of these people was Nikolaus August Otto who thought that running the engine on gas was impractical and imagined an engine running on the vapour of petrol mixed with air. Together with a friend Michael Zons who had a workshop, they built a small engine that ran on alcohol and applied for a patent that stipulated an engine that would propel vehicles serviceably along a country road (Diesel *et. al.* 1960). The patent application was turned down on the basis that the engine was too close to others, so Otto and Zons continued to development until they created a four-stroke cycle engine. That year Otto formally joined Zons in his machine shop and went across to London to see if anybody else was offering any similar types of engines. He found that nobody else had anything like it.

Otto had a number of ideas to make the engine more efficient but was starting to run out of money. He eventually met up with a young engineer Eugene Langen from a wealthy family who became a partner and bankrolled Otto, forming N.A. Otto & Company, engine builders. After selling a few engines they found that in their present form the engine was not too saleable and spent the next three years experimenting until they created an engine with a vertical cylinder and piston connected to a cog wheel that went up and down. They presented it at the Great Exhibition in Paris during 1867. It just so happened that one of Otto's old acquaintances Professor Franz Reuleaux of Berlin University was on the judging committee and insisted Otto's engine be directly compared to the Lenoir engines on display. The judges found that the Otto engine used only one third the fuel used by the Lenoir engine and Otto and Langen won the gold medal personally presented to them by Napoleon III. After the exhibition sales increased dramatically and by 1871 they had licensed production of the engine to Crossley Brothers of Manchester and were making profits. The company continued to grow and took on some new partners and was renamed Deutz-AG-Gasmotorenfabrik.

Gottlieb Daimler was interested in building an automobile from an early age. He showed himself to be a very skilled craftsman during his apprenticeship at a gunsmith workshop and was awarded a place at the School for Advanced Training in Stuttgart where he studied at night while working during the day. Daimler later moved to Strasbourg where he worked on steam locomotives and built railway cars, becoming foreman at the age of 22. He was given leave to study at the Stuttgart Polytechnic Institute and completed the four year course in two years. Daimler then spent some time in Paris and Britain where he toured and worked at a number of engineering works. He also attended the 1862 Great Exhibition in London. Upon his return to Germany Daimler spent a few years working at the Bruderhaus Factory producing machines for paper mills, farms, and weighbridges. During his time at Bruderhaus,

Daimler met Wilhelm Mayback with whom he developed a very close relationship. Maybach was a very creative draughtsman who was later to follow Daimler from job to job.

Daimler was approached by Langen in 1872 to work for Deutz which was expanding their production of the Otto engine. Daimler persuaded Langen to also take on Mayback as chief designer for the company. They both spent about ten years at Deutz, with Daimler leaving to set up his own company in Cannstatt from the compensation he got from Otto for his work on the patents. Maybach soon joined him and they set out to produce a petrol engine that had an efficient and quick starting ignition and a power-to-weight ratio that would be suited for an automobile. By 1885 they had produced a one horsepower engine with some improvements over the Otto engine including a carburetor to mix fuel with the air for better combustion. Daimler fixed an engine to a bicycle and created the first powered motorcycle. Daimler also bought a carriage he bought from Stuttgart and mounted the engine onto it as a *"present to his wife"*.

Quite independently Karl Friedrich Benz was also working on a petrol engine. Benz was born into a relatively poor family but was able to get a good education where he studied locomotive engineering at university. During these years Benz had a dream of building a self-propelled horseless carriage. Benz started his first business a machine shop and supplier of construction materials in 1871 with a partner August Ritter. The company ran into financial trouble and Benz fiancée Bertha Ringer bought out Ritter with money from her dowry. After further poor business performance the firm got into further financial trouble where Benz admitted a new partner and lost control of the company. In 1883 Benz left the company and bought into a bicycle repair shop in Mannheim with Max Rose and Friedrich Wilhelm Eβlinger.

Benz soon left and went into the engine building business and formed Benz & Cie Rheinsche Gasmotoren-Fabrik. The business went well producing engines for a growing market and this gave Benz the opportunity to focus his attention on building an automobile. Benz developed an automobile primarily based on bicycle technology. It was powered by a four-stroke engine Benz had designed, sitting between the rear wheels with the power being transmitted through chains to the rear axle. Benz patented his automobile in 1886 calling it the Benz Patented Motorwagen. This first model had plenty of room for improvement and Benz over successive years created new versions that ironed out faults in the previous model. Although his invention had plenty of attention, there was actually little interest in purchasing the vehicle. Most of the sales were in France through Benz's agent Emile Roger, who was already building Benz engines under license there.

There were still a number of problems. Gasoline at the time was only sold by pharmacies as a cleaning fluid, and the automobile still lacked power to climb small hills and the brakes were rough. The automobile could not go in reverse. An important event in the history of Benz was the story of Bertha Benz in 1888 using the car to travel from Mannheim to Pforzheim to visit her mother, a round trip of some 212 km. During the trip she apparently made some technical improvements to the automobile which included putting leather brake linings on the brakes to help with downhill braking and recommended to her husband to add another gear to the engine so it could go up hills better.

By 1895 the Benz factory had sold more than 135 cars and was known as one of the most important manufacturer of automobiles (Weightman 2007, P. 320). Now Germany had three manufacturers of petrol engines.

The early bicycles and automobiles used wooden or iron rims for tyres which had no shock absorbing properties. However for the tyre to be invented, a pliable material that could be used in its construction was required. Charles Goodyear heard about the properties of gum elastic[50] and went to see J. Haskins, the manager of Roxbury Rubber Company in New York. Goodyear found that the rubber used to make products disintegrated over time rendering them useless. He started working with Indian rubber by heating it and adding different materials in attempts to get the stickiness out of the material. Goodyear thought that he found the solution using an acidic material to cure the latex and built up a business manufacturing life preservers, rubber shoes, and other rubber based products. Due to the crash of 1837, Goodyear became penniless and it was only the financial support given to him by J. Haskins who he knew at Roxbury Rubber Company that saved him. Goodyear continued to experiment to improve the curing process. In 1838 Goodyear met with Nathaniel Hayward who had been using sulphur to dry rubber. Goodyear found that when rubber was heated with sulphur, the rubber cured perfectly–heating sulphur with rubber created vulcanized rubber, named after the Greek god of fire. It is debated today whether Goodyear found the solution by pure luck or through careful application and observation. Goodyear made the discovery in 1839 but only patented it in 1844 after he enhanced and fine tuned the process. Vulcanized rubber could be utilized to make many products of which automobile tyres was one of them.

Robert William Thomson was born in Stonehaven, Scotland and moved to America at the age of 14 where he was apprenticed to a merchant. Two years later he returned to Scotland teaching himself chemistry, electricity, and astronomy. Robert's father built him a workshop where he improved upon his mother's washing mangle so wet linen could be passed through, designed a ribbon saw, made a working model of an elliptic steam engine, and a number of other inventions. He set up his own railway consulting company, while he designed and built a pneumatic tyre for horse carriages. The tyre consisted of a hollow India rubber and canvas tube inflated with air enclosed in a strong leather casing of leather and bolted to the wheel. The wheels formed a cushion of air upon the road or track they ran on which greatly improved the comfort of travel and reducing the noise. One set of tyres lasted for more than 1,200 miles. Thomson patented the tyre in France in 1846 and in America in 1847.

Thomson's invention basically went unnoticed and forty years and forgotten. A Scottish veterinary surgeon John Boyd Dunlop came up with the idea again as a way to improve the suspension of carriages. Dunlop had worked with sheets of rubber at his surgery and first made a pneumatic tyre for his son's tricycle from wrapping the sheet into a hollow lined with linen that he blew up with his son's football pump. After finding that bicycles with pneumatic tyres were much faster than existing tyres at the time, the bicycle fraternity in Ireland switched over to them and in 1889 Dunlop formed a company with Harvey du Cros, President of the Irish Cyclists Association. On filing a patent application, Dunlop's claim to novelty was invalidated by Thomson's prior patent. Other aspects of the tyre were patented and Dunlop assigned his patent over to Harvey du Cros and du Cros formed the Dunlop Rubber Company of which Dunlop had no interest. Dunlop had reinvented the pneumatic tyre, unlike in Thomson's time, at a crucial time in the development of road transport.

At about the same time Dunlop was producing tyres in Ireland, Edouard and André Michelin in France were running a rubber factory in France. The company produced rubber balls and invented rubber brake pads for horse-drawn carriages. There are a number of stories

---

[50] Natural rubber derived from latex.

about how the Michelin brothers started making tyres but one story tells of how the Grand Pierre asked for help at the Michelin workshop to repair one of his pneumatic tyres on the bicycle (Lottman 2003). According to this story the tyre was glued to the wheel rim and it took hours to remove it and all night for the glue to dry after it was repaired. Edouard saw the need to have pneumatic tyres that could be easily removed from wheel rims for repairs. From 1891 the Michelin brothers began manufacturing tyres where France became the number one tyre maker in the world until the end of the century.

A number of companies ventured into automobile manufacturing in Europe and the automobile started replacing the bicycle and horse and carriage. After lobbying British restrictions on automobiles were lifted and the industry flourished. Motor buses and trucks began appearing changing public and goods transport. With the petroleum industry established in the United States and large distances to travel the automobile very quickly became popular with the likes of Charles and Frank Duryea forming the Duryea Motor Company, Ransom E Olds forming the Olds Motor Vehicle Company, and the eventual formation of the Ford Motor Company that was going to take automobiles onto a new plain in the new Millennium.

The Beginning of the Aviation Era

No other concept had been dreamed about more than the ability of man to undertake powered flight. Ever since the Greek Mythology of *Icarus* and *Daedalus,* man has been on a great quest to discover the secret of flight and when man finally managed to fly, this discovery was to change the way he lived upon this Earth. Like the advent of the automobile, powered manned flight was not a single invention but a gathering together of necessary knowledge to allow flight to be possible. This knowledge began being collected by the Chinese who flew kites for the first time somewhere around 500 BC.

The kite was an important step in achieving powered manned flight because it showed that something heavier than air could stay aloft. The kite may have been the invention of the Chinese philosophers *Mozi* and *Lu Ban* during the 5th Century BC. Although not fully understood at the time, the kite showed the basic laws of aerodynamics at work. Air flowing over a kite's wing will have a high pressure below the wing and a low pressure above the wing, giving the kite lift. This lift also produces drag at the bottom of the kite opposite to the oncoming wind. When the kite is tethered to a guide-wire the forces of the wind against the the tension from the guide-wire forces the kite into the air along a vector opposed to the tension of the guide-wire and wind. Some kites have tails to stabilize the direction of the kite adding the force of drag to the equation pulling on the tail, thus keeping the kite stable and upright.

A box kite design provides relatively high amounts of lift and most of the early aircraft of the Twentieth Century were inspired by this design. The box kite was invented by the Australian inventor Lawrence Hargrave in 1893 in his attempts to develop his own manned flying machine. Series of tandem box kites were able to lift Hargrave 16 feet off the ground (Hudson & Ruhen 1977).

In 1738 a Dutch-Swiss mathematician published an important aerodynamic principal in his book *Hydrodynamica,* which stated that any air (or fluid) flow as speed increases will result in a simultaneous decrease in pressure over a solid surface, which became known as

Bernoulli's principal. Air running over the top of an airfoil will run faster than the air running under the bottom of the airfoil thus creating a decrease of temperature and pressure which provides lift. The significance of this to flight is that *Bernoulli's principal* explains the concept of lift and allows lift to be calculated on airfoils.

In 1799 Sir George Cayley was credited with formally identifying the four aerodynamic forces acting upon flight – lift, gravity, thrust and drag. Cayley believed that that any drag created by a flying machine must be countered by thrust in order for level flight to occur, which led to a better understanding that any design of a flying machine must minimize drag. These discoveries led to the development of cambered wings, which enabled them to create the force of lift for an aircraft. According to a recent discovery of Cayley's school notebooks, he pondered over the problems like the angle of attack much earlier than previously thought in his early years (Dee 2007). Cayley designed an efficient cambered wing with the correct dihedral angle that provided lateral stability in flight, where he deliberately set the centre of gravity below the wings for that purpose (Ackroyd 2002). Cayley's model gliders incorporated all these features, monoplane wings with back horizontal stabilizers, looking similar to modern aircraft of today. There was possibly a glider built by Cayley in 1853 that was piloted by his grandson George John Cayley (Dee 2007).

The propeller has a long history of development for nautical use which had to be applied to flight. One of the major challenges to the Wright Brothers in developing an airplane for their first flight at Kitty Hawk was that there was no aircraft propeller readily developed, so had to develop one on their own. They found that a propeller is essentially a wing and therefore they utilized early wind tunnel data on their wing experiments. They found that the relative angle of attack of the propeller had to be different along the propeller blade and therefore had to be twisted slightly.

The Wright brothers believed that the ability to fly depended upon balance and control, rather than the power of an engine to propel the airplane forward. This perhaps came from their background as bicycle makers where balance was essential. Control in the air was an important issue as there had been many deaths of aeronauts in gliding and balloon accidents over a number of years.

The Wright brothers believed they had enough knowledge about wings and engines and decided it was important to practice control in gliding before powered flight so the needs of control could be understood (Crouch 2003). They believed that previous practice used by Lilienthal of balancing and controlling a glider through redistributing body weight was fatally flawed (Tobin 2004, P. 53). Many before them including Langley and Chanute considered changing direction in midflight would be like moving a ship's rudder for steering while the aircraft remained in straight and level flight[51] (Crouch 2003). Wilbur Wright observed that birds change direction in flight by changing their angle at the end of the wings to make their body's roll to the left or right and he thought that this would also be a good way for an aircraft to change direction by banking left or right by changing the wing tilt through the use of a moveable airfoil on the sides of the wing. Again this was something similar to a bicycle going at high speed where a rider would distribute his or her weight to the side of a turn (Tobin 2004).

---

[51] This was a very different attitude to other pioneers at the time like Ader, Maxim, and Langley who believed that after attaching an engine to an airframe they could just go out and fly it without any experience.

In 1900 the Wright brothers went to Kitty hawk, North Carolina after researching the best place to do glide tests and taking advice from Octave Chanute. The area had a good breeze coming onshore from the Atlantic, a soft sandy ground to land on, and was relatively remote for privacy. The first glider was based more on the work of previous pioneers and resembled the Chanute-Herring glider which flew well near Chicago back in 1896 and some aeronautical data that Lilienthal had published. The wings were cambered according to the theories of Sir George Cayley. The Wrights placed a horizontal elevator in front of the wings as they believed this would help them stop any nose dives that killed Lilienthal (Jakab 1997) and did not build a tail for the glider as at this stage as they thought it unnecessary. Most of the glider tests were unmanned with the glider held by ropes so glide characteristics could be studied.

The second glider in 1901 had its wings greatly enlarged in an attempt to increase lift. Approximately 100 flights were made at varying distances from 50 to 400 feet. The glider stalled a number of times but *"pancaked"* out and landed flat due to the forward elevator. This changed the brothers thinking towards the canard design[52], which they used until 1910. In general the second glider was very disappointing as it failed to yaw adequately to the wing ailerons, where the nose of the glider pointed away from the turn as the wings produced differential drag and didn't have the lift that they had expected. This left the Wright brothers feeling very down about the prospects of manned flight.

The Wright brothers discovered that the equation that Lilienthal had been using to calculate lift was incorrect. Lilienthal and the Wright brothers both used the *"Smeaton coefficient"* in the lift equation which had a constant of 0.0054, overstating lift. The Wright brothers believed and determined through some bicycle tests that the coefficient was more like 0.0033 and adjusted their designing accordingly. Knowing that building gliders was expensive and trial and error was very time consuming they built their own wind tunnel so they could test models to speed up their experimentation and learning. These experiments proved to be very fruitful and they made an important discovery that longer and narrower wings *(i.e., larger aspect ratio)* would provide a better lift to drag ratio than broader wings. They also reduced the camber of airfoils which made them more efficient for banking. They totally discarded Lilienthal's calculations and relied solely on their own data.

The third glider had some other design changes including a rear fixed vertical rudder which would assist in turning. The brothers flew the third glider unmanned like the first two trials. The glider gave the expected lift and allowed tighter turns without the amount of differential wing drag that occurred on the earlier gliders. However the rudder caused a new problem. When in a tight turn and trying to level back out again the glider failed to respond to the airfoil corrections and persisted in a tighter turn where the glider would slide towards the lower wing. The brothers found that by making the rudder movable this problem did not reoccur so with a movable rudder and wing airfoils the pilot had to control both the airfoils and rudder when maneuvering the glider. This enabled the brothers to make very controlled turns.

The three-axis control for the glider was a major breakthrough for controlled flight. It made the aircraft very controllable in flight and was the result of almost 1,000 test glides at Kitty Hawk. Some aeronautical historians believe that this is where the airplane was really invented (Langewiesche 1944).

---

[52] Canard is French for duck and in aeronautic refers to a wing configuration where the forward wings have a smaller area than the back wings, which adds to lift.

The powered Wright Flyer I constructed of spruce and covered with muslin. The engine was built with an aluminum block by the brothers. The Wrights decided on twin pusher counter rotating propellers to cancel out the torque. They suffered many delays at Kitty Hawk with broken propeller shafts. After a number of attempts the brothers finally got the airplane off the ground on 17th December 1903 with a flight distance of 120 feet. The first flights received little publicity. Over the following year the second aircraft the Wright Flyer II made many flights at Dayton with many hard landings and minor mishaps. Much progress was made in 1904 with some longer flights lasting a few minutes but the airplane was still very difficult to control.

In 1905 the brothers made all the controls independent of each other so pitch, roll, and yaw could be controlled separately of each other. After a nearly fatal crash the brothers rebuilt the flyer with a much larger rudder and forward elevator placed further away from the wings. This made control much easier and led to a number of much longer flights. Ironically the media had ignored this story that Wilbur and Orville Wright made the first flights with a powered flying machine and later would become national heroes at their own doorstep (Tobin 2004, P. 211)[53].

The brothers believed that they now had a flying machine with practical utility that they could sell. They were finally granted a patent in 1906 and in 1907 went to Europe to sell their airplane. In early 1908 the Wright brothers finally signed contracts with a French company and the US Army. Wilbur made a number of demonstration flights showing advanced maneuvers during 1908 which captured the attention and admiration of the world.

The Wright brothers' patent was challenged vigorously in the law courts for a number of years and Wilbur Wright also challenged any other flyer who infringed them. This took up a lot of time and it prevented the brothers from developing new aircraft designs. By 1911 the Wright airplanes were considered inferior to many of the new European designs. Wilbur passed away in 1912 and the brothers won their court case against Curtiss which had been going on for a few years. With the arrival of the First World War, the US Government found that American technology was behind the European builders and encouraged companies to cross license their technologies.

Businesswise the invention of the airplane did not lead to a great number of aircraft sales and the brothers formed an exhibition team which was later disbanded due to a number of team member deaths. Between 1910 and 1916 the Wright Company operated a flying school at Huffman Prairie, Dayton, training more than 100 pilots. In addition with the large number of airplane accidents and deaths the safety of the plane came into question by the US Army. Orville Wright sold the Wright Company in 1915 and took on public service as an elder aviation statesman becoming director of the National Advisory Committee for Aeronautics (NACA), which he served for 28 years. It was only after the First World War when airplanes made a contribution to field warfare as a reconnaissance, fighter and bomber, and larger airplanes could carry passengers and cargo with much better safety that the aviation industry started to boom from the 1920s onwards.

What we see with the inventions of the automobile and airplane is that an invention cannot occur until all relevant knowledge that makes it possible exists. The inventor may go the final step and either synthesize all previous knowledge or incrementally enhance upon

---

[53] However the Wright Brothers themselves can be part of the blame for this as they discouraged media attention in fear of competitors stealing their ideas and they would not be able to get a patent.

existing knowledge to complete the invention. What we also see is that any invention that does not fulfill the present needs of an opportunity will not be commercially acceptable. In the cases of the early automobiles and aircraft, they were not at an advanced enough state for potential users to accept them because of the state of the invention and social situation surrounding it, *i.e., early automobiles not practical due to faults and UK laws had to be amended to make the invention acceptable an means of transport.* The other option that may make an invention commercially successful is if a new use is found for it, *i.e., early aircraft could be utilized in a war situation during the First World War.* Both the stories about the automobile and airplane development show how essential trial and error or learning by doing is to the successful development of an invention.

The opportunities that we looked at above show the importance of the right timing for an invention to be successful, be that existing knowledge is sufficient to create the invention in the first place and that there is a use for the invention in some part of the society. The examples also show the importance of location on available knowledge and potential uses of the invention. An invention should be relevant to the current level of society. In these cases Britain, Europe and America were still developing regions. Most breakthroughs were achieved through incremental innovation brought about through trial and error. Networks and financiers *(now called venture capitalists or business angels)* were also very important, giving us an insight into the very structure of opportunity; vision, a connection in time and space, a source of opportunity, resources required, networks, the competitive environment that the opportunity resides within, and a strategy. Many opportunities are similar to others throughout history, *i.e., those that have a similar source of opportunity (see chapter 1, volume 2).* For example the way *McDonalds* expanded in the second half of the 20th Century is very similar to how *Coca Cola* expanded in the first half of the 20th Century. However it is time, space, the environment, and the mode of technology that differs, although the structure is the same. Chance meetings or events also played some role in opportunity.

Although personality characteristics have been widely discarded as a predictor of an entrepreneur, within the previous examples there were a number of common experiences and behavioral traits shared by inventor/entrepreneurs. None were inspired by patriotism or altruistic motives but by the desire for fame and fortune (Weightman 2007, P. 383). Most had experienced failure at some time before becoming successful. Most were engaged in competition with other inventor/entrepreneurs to bring their invention to the world. Most showed a single minded commitment, dedication, or persistence in chasing after their particular vision. Most had some form of courage to keep them going even in the most adverse conditions. Most possessed patience to think out what they should do according to the conditions and situations they found themselves in and finally most showed some form of ruthlessness that prevented anybody getting in the way of their objectives.

PART THREE: INTO THE TWENTIETH CENTURY

The inventors of the 18th and 19th Centuries made great contribution to the development of Britain, Europe, and America, laying the foundation for these regions to grow at unprecedented rates over the next century. The American South was developed through the steam boats and the cotton industry established with the aid of inventions by Kay,

Hargreaves, Arkwright, and Crompton. The American West was settled through the assistance of the railroads and innovation with refrigeration which allowed the cattle industries to supply the East with meat. Some of the most well known American brand names were created during this time from entrepreneurial start-ups aimed at exploiting an opportunity, with similar stories to those outlined in the last section (see Table 2.5). Mercantilism declined in at the end of the 18th Century and the whale industry around the middle of the 19th Century when petroleum became a substitute for whale oil, showing that opportunity is characterized with a limited lifespan.

Table 2.5. Some major companies founded during the 19th Century

Year Founded	Company	Founder	Major Products/Activities
1857	Bethlehem Steel Corporation	First organized by Augustus Wolle. Charles M. Schwab and Joseph Wharton assumed name in 1904	Iron mining, coal mining, steel production, ship building, and railroad car production. Suffered from more competitive foreign competition, domestic mini mill production and change to lighter construction materials and went into bankruptcy in 2001.
1887	The Coca Cola Company	Asa Griggs Candler purchased exclusive rights to John Pemberton's formula.	Originally developed as a non-alcoholic drink during prohibition in Atlanta in 1886. Became Americas No. 1 selling soft drink by the early 1990s. Coca Cola followed the American war effort around the world and established franchising operations in numerous countries. The Coca Cola company has acquired many brands and is now a leading beverage brands company around the world.
1802	E.I. du Pont de Nemours and Company	Eleuthère Irénée du Pont	Originated as a gunpowder manufacturer, expended into dynamite, divested some assets due to Sherman Antitrust Act in 1912. Invested in Ford Motor Company in 1914, focused on materials science making a number of discoveries and commercializations. 1981 acquired Conoco and expanded into fibre and plastic manufacture. Now a major science based R&D company.
1901	Gillette Safety Razor Company	King Camp Gillette	Developed a safety razor in an era where people had to go to the barber or use a blade prior to this invention. The company developed a brand synonymous with shaving and personal care. The company was purchased by Proctor & gamble in 2007.
1907	Harley-Davidson	William Harley and Arthur Davidson	Started experimenting and making small motorcycles. First offered engines to do-it-yourself trade, then began selling motorcycles. Supplied motorcycles for US war effort, survived the depression. Motorcycles developed outlaw image during 1950s, almost went bankrupt. Revived in the 1980s with a retro-image and Harley motorcycles became sought after, in the *"heavy bike"* bracket.
1851	I.M. Singer & Co. (The Singer Company).	Isaac Merrit Singer & Edward Clark	Started as a manufacturer of sewing machines. In the 1960s diversified into navigation equipment through acquisition, but sold off in 1990. Sold off sewing machine division in 1989. Singer now produces a wide range of consumer products, including electronic sewing machines. Now owned by SVP Worldwide that also owns Pfaff and Husqvarna Viking Brands.
1873	Levi Strauss & Co.	Levi Strauss and Jacob Davis	Started a work pants manufacturing business with patented copper rivets, which grew to become an internationally fashionable denim leisurewear brand.
1857	New York Condensed Milk Company (Now known as Borden)	Gail Borden	Initially a publisher Gail Borden invented and patented a method of producing condensed milk. The business grew during the American Civil War. Still a dairy based company that diversified into fruit juices, flavored milk, cultured milk, and organic products.

1837	Proctor & Gamble	William Proctor and James Gamble	Started as a candle and soap maker, expanded into cleaning and personal care. Now the holding company of numerous household and personal care consumer brands.

By the end of the 19th Century and beginning of the 20th Century governments had begun creating regulations and laws governing the railways, roads, banking, and business, establishing a stable business environment. Governments also began to realize their own fiscal and monetary abilities and began to manage their economies from a macro viewpoint. However the continued use of tariffs and protection was to hinder trade in the early 20th Century partly contributing to war and depression. Many entrepreneurs of the 19th Century set the tone of how invention and innovation would occur later in the 20th Century as individuals and corporations, *i.e., industrial laboratories, skunk works, etc.* Many of the industries started at the turn of the 20th Century were going to grow within massive industries as the century progressed, *i.e., automobiles, aviation, steel, petroleum, electric power, communications, media entertainment, and processed products, etc.* Entrepreneurship and innovation along the lines of the Schumpeter concept of *creative destruction* is what made society progress and this was best achieved when encouraged. Figure 2.10 shows a timeline for the second half of the 20th Century.

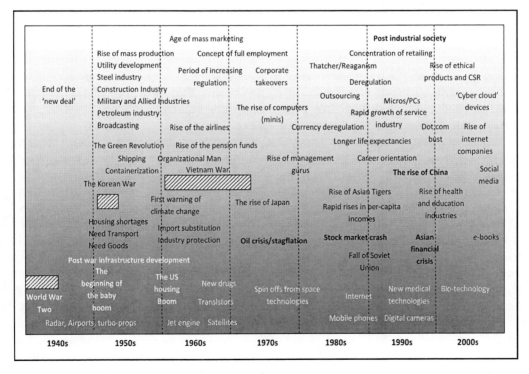

Figure 2.10. Timeline for the second half of the 20th century.

The first part of the 20th Century was chaotic for growth and development due to protectionism and national self interest. There were two world wars within a space of less than thirty years. Britain was still a colonial power; Japan was rapidly becoming the power of the East, South-East Asia still underdeveloped and entrepreneurship in America stifled by

Roosevelt's quasi-socialist *new deal* programs (Schweikart & Doti, 2010, P. 309). Although the Second World War had a positive influence on new technology development, it was only in the post war years that entrepreneurs began to reemerge in perhaps the fastest thirty years of growth the world had ever experienced. A barrage of new industries based upon newly developed technologies was created and grew, rapidly changing society.

The United States played a major role in victories in both the European and Pacific theatres of war. Most countries within Europe were devastated along with Germany and Japan. China was still locked in civil war and was then to undergo more than 30 years of isolation under Mao's communist rule. The United States was intact and still had occupation troops in both Germany and Japan. The United States under the Marshall Plan took some responsibility for the restoration of Europe and focused on preventing loss of what had been gained in the battlefield to the communist movement. The US war effort had mobilized the steel/shipbuilding, aviation, automobile, and created a host of new technologies with post war civilian applications, where no other country was in this favored position.

After the Second World War, peace and the likelihood of better times ahead, birthrates dramatically increased across the United States, Europe, and Australia. This lead to a boom in housing with millions of new homes built in the United States alone within the first decade after the war. Automobile sales soared giving Americans the mobility they had never had before. Great demographic changes were occurring in the United States where people in the north were migrating to the south and west. Cities like Phoenix, Los Angeles, Tampa, Orlando, Dallas, and Houston grew dramatically. Women who worked in the factories during the war to support the war effort now had their own incomes and drastically increased purchases of clothes, ladies fashion items, cosmetics, and other consumer items leading to a great growth in consumption that led to many new opportunities in the personal consumption and household products sectors. This drove an emerging banking and financial sector which grew on mortgage and business borrowings.

These changed conditions gave way to many creative opportunities for those who could see them. For example, after the Second World War there were plenty of experienced women that had idle time after their children had grown up. Many mothers wanted part time work and many businesses wanted temporary skilled workers. Russell Kelly saw this connection in 1946 and started finding temporary jobs for part-time workers on a temporary basis. In his first year of business Kelly had 3 employees, 12 customers, and USD $848 in sales (Eaton 1998). Today Kelly Services has more than USD 5.3 Billion sales[54] and operates across 30 countries. It can be claimed that Russell Kelly created the temporary employee industry that is worth more than USD 40 Billion worldwide covering engineering, education, nursing, and other industries with many 1000s of large and small businesses following the Kelly business model.

The example of Amway also shows how innovation can also come from a new business model that is constructed to take advantage of the increasing affluence and spending power of a growing American middle class and recognition that personal relationships have a great influence upon consumer buying decisions. Jay Van Andel and Richard DeVos were close friends and participated in a number of ventures together as partners in the 1940s that included a hamburger stall, air charter service, and sailing business. In 1949 they were

---

[54] CNN Money Fortune 500 information (2006) http://money.cnn.com/magazines/fortune/fortune500/snapshots/735.html (accessed 29th January 20110

introduced to *Nutrilite* Products, a direct selling company founded by Dr. Carl Rhenborg. *Nutrilite* had the first multivitamin tablet ever sold in the United States and Van Andel and DeVos seeing the potential of this product signed up as distributors. After attending a *Nutrilite* conference in Chicago a few months later Van Andel and DeVos decided to go into distributing *Nutrilife* on a full time basis (Conn 1977). Later that year Van Andel and DeVos set up Ja-Ri Corporation in an attempt to add more products to the *Nutrilite* range they were selling by importing wooden products from South America (Van Andel 1998). They introduced what is called the *multi level* concept of marketing where distributors would be given an extra commission on sales made by people they recruit in addition to the margins they make from their own sales, plus another commission based on the sales volume they and their recruited sellers achieve (Xardel 1993). By 1958 they had over 5,000 distributors.

Van Andel and DeVos with some other top distributors looked into how they could get more products to sell through their *multi level* marketing networks in addition to *Nutrilite* and formed the *The American Way Association* to represent distributors (Robinson 1977). Van Andel and DeVos bought the rights to manufacture and market a product called *Liquid Organic Cleaner (LOC)* and subsequently formed Amway Sales Corporation. In 1960 they purchased a 50% interest in the manufacturer of *LOC,* ATCO Manufacturing Company in Detroit and renamed it Amway manufacturing Company. In 1964 all the companies under the AMWAY banner were consolidated into Amway Corporation. Amway expanded into Canada (1962), Australia (1971), United Kingdom (1973), Hong Kong (1974), Germany (1975), Malaysia (1976), Netherlands (1978), Japan (1979), and to another 45 countries over the last 30 years. Amway is one of the largest privately owned companies in the world today with sales of USD 8.9 Billion in 2009[55].

The Post World War II Period

Within the first decade of the Second World War more than half American households owned cars, where Ford, General Motors, and Chrysler dominated the market. The automobile very quickly became a concentrated industry based at Detroit. This promoted the growth of specialist manufacturers like A.O. Smith, Bendix, Bosch, Electric Autolite, American Axle & Manufacturing Holdings, and Johnson Controls, etc. which carved out extremely narrow specialist niches. The automobile manufacturers also developed networks of dealers and service centres. The future role of the automobile as a means of travel was greatly enhanced when the US Congress passed the National Highway Act in 1956 to build four lane interstate highways across the United States. Just what the railroads did in the 19th Century, the automobile was going to do in the 20th century opening up the way for passenger and freight travel by road.

As the highways opened up travel between towns and cities, restaurants were needed for people to eat while travelling. Ray Kroc just quit his job at 53 as a paper cup salesman to sell a multiple milkshake mixer to restaurants around the United States. One of the restaurants he called upon was the McDonald's brothers' store in San Bernardino California in 1954. Mac and Dick McDonald's drive-in store had an assembly line arrangement that handled fries, hamburgers, and beverages on a mass production basis which was very efficient and allowed

---

[55] Reuters http://www.reuters.com/article/2009/02/05/idUS173002+05-Feb-2009+PRN20090205

the brothers to monitor quality. Kroc also saw that the restaurant was much cleaner than others around America at the time and had a family, rather than *'hang-out'* type atmosphere that *burger joints* were notorious for. Kroc envisaged that this model could work successfully all over the United States and negotiated a franchise agreement with the McDonald brothers[56]. Within a year Kroc opened a test store in Des Plaines, Illinois developing procedures and checklists right down to how and when to clean rubbish in the carpark. From the first store in 1955, Kroc opened more than 200 stores in the first five years and by the mid 1960s was opening more than 100 stores per year. Kroc opened the Hamburger University to train employees to the procedures of making burgers to operating a store. Today McDonalds Corporation is the World's largest chain of fast food restaurants.

The automobile also changed the way cities developed, now families could live further away from their place of work in newly sprawling suburbs which drove the home construction industry. New suburbs would also create new opportunities for local businesses that supplied groceries and other staples and services to residents, greatly decentralizing retailing in the United States. The new suburbs encouraged the establishment of hardware, furnishing, plumbing, kitchen, white and electrical goods industries to grow. This saw the rise of General Electric consumer products, RCA radios, and Zenith televisions that rapidly expanded to supply increasing consumer demand. Utility companies supplying telephone and electricity became large corporations during this period with rapid increases in demand for basic services.

By the 1950s ordinary people in the United States could afford to travel and the emerging airlines around the world were picking up increased business. Aircraft could fly further in much less time. Aircraft navigation and safety had greatly improved. The Douglas DC 4 and later the much faster Lockheed Constellation were both capable of travelling across the American continent and across the Atlantic directly from New York to London. The development of tracking and weather radar allowed airports to control traffic much more efficiently. Flight was now becoming a common occurrence. This not only led to a growing aviation industry but also led to opportunities to create new tourist industries where locations had suitable vistas and spurred the growth of the hotel industry in major cities.

One entrepreneur at that time Kemmons Wilson saw that hotels around America tended to be dirty, had few conveniences and facilities and didn't have enough space for children who they charged at the same rate as adults (Wilson & Kerr 1996). Wilson travelled around the United States with his wife and children staying in many hotels to see what they had to offer. He concluded that people should expect familiar surroundings in the different cities that they stay in, thus a Holiday Inn should be standardized but at the same time have a local theme, clean, predictable, family friendly, and readily accessible to road travelers. He designed what he believed should be a good hotel, opening the first Holiday Inn in Memphis, Tennessee in 1952. By 1968 there were over 1,000 Holiday inns around the United States alone. The Holiday Inn chain set the benchmark and standards for hotels linking them with an international reservation system that later rivals Best Western, Quality Inns, and Ramada Inns had to match.

By the 1950s radio and television was becoming an important part of American culture. Radio during the war had kept everybody up to date with what was happening and radio took

---

[56] Kroc later purchased the McDonalds brothers' equity in the business in 1961 which lead to a protracted dispute over the terms.

the mantle from newspapers as the most important source of news. Radio broadcast stations increased from 900 in 1945 to over 3,000 by 1948. The National broadcasting Company (NBC) and Columbia Broadcasting System (CBS) dominated the airwaves through their own and affiliate stations. Both networks fought to get the best personalities for their various children's, drama, comedy, mystery, and news programs. Radio advertising became a powerful means to promote products and both networks competed strongly for the advertising dollars. Although experimental television broadcasts began in 1928, regular broadcasting only commenced in 1946 with DuMont Television Network, with NBC following in 1947, and CBS and ABC in 1948. By 1948 more than one million households owned television sets with about 30 broadcasting stations operating in 20 cities around the United States. NBC dominated the early television programming producing similar types of programs to what had been popular on radio. Ownership of television sets grew as they got larger, programming improved and color came in 1954. By the mid 1950s about half of American households owned television sets. Advertisers flocked to this new medium and television was to show Americans that their country was the most advanced technically in the world.

American industry supported by research and development during the war was set to provide a peace dividend to society. Technology affected all aspects of life. Homes ran almost completely on electricity with new inventions like electric garbage disposals in the sink, automatic garage doors and curtains, and a large range of new electrical appliances. Nuclear energy was going to be the power of the future where Lewis Strauss, Chairman of the United States Atomic Energy Commission stated that electricity in the future *"would be too cheap to meter"*[57]. The USSR launched the first satellite Sputnik 1 in 1957 beginning the *space race* and new medicines and medical procedures were being developed that gave people confidence about the future. Within agriculture too, there were leaps and bounds in technology. Until the *green revolution* took place in the late 1940s agriculture relied primarily on traditional methods of production, based on preventative measures and local inputs. Through technology advances during the Second World War, farm productivity improved dramatically. This was achieved through chemical based fertilizers, pesticides, and herbicides, based on petroleum by-products, ironically *spin-offs* from the chemical warfare programs. This lead to the growth the American chemical companies like Monsanto and Dow Chemical. In addition a number of labour saving and automation inventions and innovations such as the tractor and plough arrays and automated harvesters enabled the development of extensive farming on a much larger scale than ever before, making people believe that the World had food security.

International trade was growing but shipping was inefficient as every package had to be unloaded from a truck or railroad car and lifted by a crane into the hold of a ship and unloaded at the destination in the same way. Malcolm McLean had built up a trucking company from a single truck to a fleet of over 1,770 trucks making his company the second largest in the United States. He saw that the way goods were shipped was totally inefficient and saw great advantages if the whole load could just be lifted on and off a ship, truck and trailer. As trucks on a ship would waste space, McLean refined his idea to just lifting on and off standardized boxes or containers. At the time in the United States the owner of a trucking company could not purchase a shipping line due to antitrust laws. Mclean sold his trucking

---

[57] http://www.thisdayinquotes.com/2009/09/too-cheap-to-meter-nuclear-quote-debate.html (Accessed 30th January 2011).

interests and purchased two shipping lines with the idea of converting the vessels to containerization. Mclean at first converted two old Second World War ships and commenced a container service between New York, Florida, and Texas in 1957. McLean's company was renamed Sea-Land Service Inc. in 1960. Although the idea was initially resisted by the unions at the beginning, containerization gradually became accepted around the world by the end of the 1970s. Although the idea was not completely new[58], Mclean had refined the concept and put it into practice, which eventually revolutionized the shipping logistics of world trade.

The 1950s came to a conclusion with a decade of continual growth. The American corporation brought a *blissful* existence to the middle class by employing and providing them with affordable television, entertainment, cars, fast food, and new urban lifestyle in carefully planned suburban situations around a nuclear family that brought conformity (Whyte 1956). The McCarthyism movement of the decade was allowed to grow out of this conformity and organizations became centres of belongingness and subservience to the greater corporate good, rather than individualism and non-conformism where creativity was a group pursuit. Thus during the 1950s the majority pursued a career rather than self employment and entrepreneurship. American business by 1960 dominated the world in so many fields automobiles, aviation, steel, entertainment, broadcasting, shipping, pharmaceuticals, and petroleum, where corporate American was unchecked by government, foreign competition, consumer movements, or class actions.

The 1960s

Whereas the 1950s had been an age of conformity, the sixties took on much more complex social and political trends. The sixties was a time when counter cultures developed which created a diverse mixture of views. This period saw modern feminism emerge, the American civil rights movement, and the aboriginal people of Australia finally granted the right to citizenship. However the sixties also saw retrograde events such as the building of the Berlin wall, the Arab-Israeli War, and a continuation of a long dragged out war in Indo-China. Many governments, particularly in Europe and Canada adopted the welfare state model, some becoming mildly socialist in their outlooks. Science moved ahead in leaps and bounds symbolized by the flight into earth orbit by Yuri Gagarin of the Soviet Union at the beginning of the decade and the landing on the moon by Neil Armstrong and Edwin Buzz Aldrin in July 1969. The world heard about the first working laser, watched television transmitted through the first Atlantic satellite, played the first computer video game, and used the first automated teller machine (ATM). Back on the ground US car makers continued to manufacture high horse-powered motor vehicles up until the end of the decade, dominated by the three major manufacturers Ford, general Motors, and Chrysler. The 1960s also saw the end of colonialism in over 30 countries and was a period of under developed and developing economies in Africa and South-East Asia. The 1960s was also the beginning of the era of mass marketing.

Post war America was an age when products were marketed with some promotional support to assist them to sell. This was more as an afterthought rather than being any central tenant to the firm's marketing strategy. But the 1960s saw a great increase in competition

---

[58] In 1929 Seatrain lines had carried railroad boxcars on its ships to transport goods between New York and Cuba.

which gave consumers much more choice. In 1958 Ford created a new division to launch a new model called the Edsel. After much fanfare the motorcar failed to live up to sales expectations and sold miserably and was taken out of production by 1960 providing a loss of more than USD 359 Million (Collier & Horowitz 1987). There have been many reasons given for the failure of the Edsel in marketing postmortems over the years (Dicke 2010), but essentially the car missed the opportunity it was designed and developed for. The market that the car had been developed for changed dramatically before it could be launched. By the time the Edsel came onto the market, the middle price segment was a shrinking market with companies serving this segment battling against becoming insolvent, Studebaker abandoned producing the Packard, American Motors discontinued producing the Nash and Hudson, and Chrysler discontinued the brand DeSoto. Sales in this segment were down as consumers were slowly shifting to smaller cars like the more efficient Volkswagen Beetle. In contrast the Edsel had a powerful engine requiring premium fuel, with very poor fuel economy. The Edsel was just the *wrong car at the wrong time* (Deutsch 1976). It was just too expensive to buy and own.

Although branding was nothing new to America[59], brand management was still in its infancy. Proctor & Gamble in Cincinnati found in the 1930's that it had a number of successful brands in the same category like *Camay* and *Ivory* soaps that needed a new way to manage so that due focus could be given to each brand. The company gave responsibility for total brand management to a single person (product manager) under a brand management system, which took over all decision making in regards to the brand in the company (Russell *et. al.* 1988). By the 1960s, brand management spread throughout most consumer goods companies and is still a widely practiced functional structuring of a marketing organization today.

Thomas Watson Senior, the founder of IBM realized that for an organization to be profitable, focus must be orientated towards the customer rather than the product. The objective of a company is to serve the customer, rather than become immersed in the product and technology it has developed. Watson developed this concept and embedded it within the core values of IBM which was based on the belief competing vigorously and providing first class customer service was the key to success. This philosophy is successfully used as a strategy in a number of companies around the world today as a source of their competitive advantage, including FedEx, Thomas Cook.

In 1960, E Jerome McCarthy conceptualized the four P's of the marketing mix; product, price, place and promotion (McCarthy 1981), as the most important ingredients in setting marketing strategy. It was not a great breakthrough in marketing thought, rather a convenient way to view strategy. It was developed at a time when mass industrial marketing was growing rapidly and in recent times the marketing orientation of strategy has dramatically changed as the 4 P's have become much more integrated and other factors from a customer point of view like customer needs and wants, cost, convenience, communication, distribution and relationships are seen as being more important. However, the concept until today is taught in marketing courses around the world and used by management in their marketing strategy development.

---

[59] Brands probably developed during the 19th century in the tobacco industry, where different tobaccos produced in regional America had to be transported to different locations and identified by brand. Coca Cola was one of the first soft drinks that carried the name to distinguish it from the number of other colas on the market.

Right into the 1960's most companies in America were production orientated, seeing the market as the means to dispose of their production. This went well until *'slow downs'* in consumer purchases create stock build ups in warehouses and interfered with production. Theodore Levitt argued that companies should become much more customer orientated in their approach to the market (Levitt 1962). Levitt's ideas were inspired by Ford providing customers with what he thought they wanted and the rise of General Motors in gaining market share by providing customers with variations of the basic product by providing new colours, more choice and new models. Although Levitt's ideas were accepted by corporate America in the 1960's, it was not until the 1980's that the marketing revolution came to fruition. Marketing departments began growing and the marketing manager became a powerful driver of the company.

Although multinational corporations were not the invention of America, as the early pioneer companies were mostly European, *i.e., Bayer (German 1863), Nestlé (Switzerland 1867), Michelin (France 1893), and Lever Bros. (UK 1890),* it was now the American companies that were at the forefront of technology that had developed through intensive local competition. The American domestic market aided US firms to become innovative, develop technologies and business methods, plan and execute strategies effectively (Porter 1990, P. 557). The major pull to US firms to develop foreign operations was primarily because of high transport costs and the high tariff regimes that many national governments built around their industries to attract local manufacturing. During this decade many leading American firms expanded to Europe, Australia, Latin America, and Asia. One of the side effects of the growth of US corporations abroad was the influence they had on local cultures and societies. There social impact was mainly through the advertising and products they made available and through the *new* working conditions they offered to local employees (Ghertman & Allen 1982). Multinational companies also developed linkages that helped to develop local suppliers, sub-contracting, and generally encouraged new entrepreneurial ventures (Watanabe 1975).

Sam Walton had been in the retail trade most of his life starting his career at a J.C. Penny store in Iowa. He eventually ran a store called *Ben Franklin* in Newport, Arkansas, going on to open his own store under the *Ben Franklin* group in Bentonville called *Walton's Five and Dime* (Walton & Huey 1993), where he found great success through discounting. Walton first opened a Wal-Mart Discount City Store in Rogers, Arkansas in 1962, and within five years expanded to 24 stores across Arkansas. By 1968 Walton expanded beyond Arkansas and the following year opened a head office and centralized distribution centre in Bentonville, operating with 38 stores, 1,500 employees and sales of USD 45 Million. Wal-Mart had by 1988 upon Sam Walton's retirement opened up more than 1,600 stores and created jobs for more than 212,000 people (Walton & Huey 1993). By 2010 Wal-Mart has over 8,500 stores in 15 countries under various banners and is considered the world's largest retailer and public company by revenue.

Sam Walton saw opportunity by cutting costs and lowering prices to consumers as a formula for success. He focused on continuous improvement of efficiency and cost control in a similar manner to John D. Rockefeller did almost a century before him. The high inflation era of the 1970s worked to his advantage as consumers became much more price conscious and willing to go without service, travel long distances, and buy in bulk to save.

Wal-Mart stores had adverse affects on the small retail sector in the area when a new store was opened, demonstrating Schumpeter's concept of *creative destruction* (Sobel &

Dean 2008). Wal-Mart saved American families money on everyday expenditures and created jobs (Mallaby 2005). Walton created a new business model now emulated by almost all retail chains in the world that redistributes costs from products they buy and transport to new logistic profit centres. Sam Walton was the richest man in the United States according to Forbes from 1982 to 1988, when his income was partially distributed to members of his family. Today Wal-Mart operates under various banners in Argentina, Brazil, Chile, China, Costa Rica, El Salvador, Guatemala, Honduras, Mexico, Nicaragua, Puerto Rico, South Korea, and the United States.

Mary Kay Ash was a divorced woman with three children and went to work for Stanley Home Products, a direct marketing company based in Houston. She obtained a respectable salary within the firm but resigned when someone she had trained got a promotion above her, which she believed she was entitled to (Leavitt 1985). Having left Stanley, she began to write a book which turned into a business plan of what she believed to be the perfect company and decided to start up the company. In 1963 with her son Richard Rogers, Mark Kay Cosmetics was formed with USD $5,000 investment.

Ash focused on skin care which was a market segment ignored by other companies at the time. She believed that simple door to door selling had its day and that the party-plan concept with a beauty demonstration in the homes of housewives that agreed to be hostesses would be the best sales strategy. Ash recruited representatives from suburban housewives who gave clinics on beauty and skin care and performed personalized make-up lessons to participants. As Ash believed that the caliber of the representatives was the key to sales, she put in lots of training, monetary rewards, and special prizes of pink Buicks and Cadillacs, which became a trademark of the company. By 2008, Mary Kay Cosmetics had 1.7 Million representatives worldwide and more than USD $2.0 Billion revenue. Mary Kay Cosmetics now operate in the United States, Australia, Canada, Argentina, Pakistan, Germany, Malaysia, Mexico, Thailand, New Zealand, Guatemala, Taiwan, Spain, Sweden, Bermuda, Brunei, Norway, Singapore, Russia, UK, Brazil, Japan, China, Portugal, Finland, Czech Republic, Ukraine, El Salvador, Hong Kong, Slovakia, Korea, India, Poland, and a number of other countries, with plants in the United States and China.

The 1960s saw a steady company growth within an environment of economic prosperity. There were large investments in research and development during the decade. Research and development since the Second World War started laying the foundation of a new industry that was to have immense influence upon the world. Computer development was currently restricted because of their massive size and limited computing capacity. William Shockley had been heavily involved in research for the war effort and went to work at the Solid State Physics Laboratories at Bell Laboratories with John Bardeen, Walter Brattain, Gerald Pearson, Robert Gibney, Hilbert Moore, and many other scientists working on solid state electronics at the time. They were attempting to improve upon vacuum tube amplifiers and in 1947 Bardeen and Brattain succeeded in creating a point-contact transistor that achieved amplification without Shockley. Bell's attorneys started the process of patenting the discovery, along with a number of others, all without Shockley's name as a co-inventor. This angered Shockley who believed his name should also be included as the work was based on his field effect data. He continued his own research secretly to build a different form of transistor based on junctions instead of point contacts, believing this to be more commercially viable. Shockley developed proof of his principals in 1949, resulting in the junction transistor and found a method to manufacture it a couple of years later. The junction transistor became dominant in the marketplace.

Shockley eventually left Bell laboratories and spent some time as a visiting professor at the California Institute of Technology (Caltech). He formed the Shockley Semiconductor laboratories with the backing of Beckman Instruments and recruited some of the best graduates in America. In 1957, a number of researchers left Shockley Semiconductors to join Sherman Fairchild and form Fairchild Semiconductors. Some of them later left to form Intel Corporation, with some leaving again to form National Semiconductor and Advanced Micro Devices[60]. Over the course of two decades, a number of Shockley's employees had founded 65 companies forming the foundation of what is to become known as Silicon Valley.

William Shockley failed to get his three-state device to work, became a controversial philosopher, acclaimed rock climber, in later life became reserved and isolated from his friends and finally died in 1989. Both Fairchild and Texas Instruments working independently succeeded in putting micro-processors onto a single chip and the computer industry could begin to develop in earnest.

At the end of the 1960s the United States was still led by the manufacturing sector, with the steel industry at the pinnacle. However the nature of the market was slowly shifting unnoticed by most US firms. The first signs of trouble were emerging within the steel industry. Wages were spiraling, demand shifting away from steel products, new economies of scale being introduced through mini-mills, profits plunging downwards, and poor management vision was hindering appropriate responses. The US industry took a *knee-jerk* reaction blaming cheaper imports as the source of their problems. These complaints resulted in the *stop-gap* measure of having a Voluntary Restraint Agreement to limit imports in the industry, in effect putting blinkers on the stewards of the industry, blinding them to the structural industry changes that were occurring (Mueller 1982). In fact Japanese steel was being produced at 70% of the cost of US steel due to better efficiencies, leading American producers to *cry* that dumping was occurring, which had little resemblance to fact (Schweikart & Doti 2010, P. 358).

Finally, American business saw the emergence of the consumer advocacy movement which was going to win some large cases against corporate America in the coming decades. In 1962 Rachel Carson wrote a book called *Silent Spring* warning of the dangers of pesticides, especially DDT within the food chain, resulting in the banning of DDT. In 1964 a young graduate of Harvard law school Ralph Nader wrote a book *Unsafe at any Speed* which raised concerns about the safety of General Motors Corvair. American corporations saw a rise in claims for any mishap however remotely associated with their products, supported by industry *'experts'* in the lawsuits, most often creating bad media publicity. Corporations at first responded by attacking the personal backgrounds of these claimants, which in the GM case led to Ralph Nader filing for damages and winning on appeal USD $425,000 from General Motors. The next decade was to be very challenging for American corporations as

---

[60] According to Blasi, Kruse, and Berstein (2003) Julius Blank, Victor Grinich, Jean Hoemi, Eugene Kleiner, Jay Last, Gordon Moore, Robert Noyce, and Sheldon Roberts left Shockley because they had difficulties with William Shockley's authoritarian management style and trait of impatiently waiting for results. These eight went to Fairchild but weren't satisfied there and went on to form a number of spin-off companies, Noyce and Moore founding Intel, Kleiner co-founding Kleiner Perkins, a venture capital firm, Roberts, Hoemi, and last founded Teledyne, Blank founding Xicor, and Grinich becoming a professor at Stanford University.

the rest of the world began to catch up with them, where all sorts of new constraints and problems were to emerge.

The 1970s

The social progression that began in the 1960s continued during the 1970s with people becoming much more politically aware. The author Tom Wolfe coined the 1970s as the *"Me Decade"*, suggesting that post war wealth has led to self-absorption and people believing in their own immortality (McNamara 2005). This resulted in a new attitude of individualism in stark contrast to the communitarianism of the 1960s. Women became much more economically independent. The hippy movement centered on the United States continued until the end of the Vietnam War and waned, being replaced by groups that advocated world peace, opposed to nuclear weapons, and became hostile to governments and big business. The environmental movement was just beginning with organizations like *Greenpeace* and *Friends of the Earth* becoming popular with fringe, alternative and counterculture groups across Europe and the United States.

During the 1970s the Organization of Petroleum Exporting Countries (OPEC) restricted oil production, resulting in radical increases of the oil price in 1973 and again in 1979, which brought petrol rationing in some Western countries. The 1970s saw the phenomena of *stagflation,* where both inflation and unemployment occurred at the same time, presenting many policy dilemmas to governments around the world. This eventually lead to neo-liberal economic policies in the 1980s which promoted monetary policy, trade liberalization, floating exchange rates, deregulation, and privatization, strongly advocated by the incoming prime minister of Britain, Margaret Thatcher in 1979.

The 1970s was also a time where China began coming out into the world, taking its seat in the United Nations and opening up dialogue and diplomatic relations with many Western countries. Japan early in the 1970s sunk into deep recession due to the oil embargo, but the economy later boomed when corporate Japan took their place in the international arena in the textile, automobile, motorcycle, camera, watch, consumer electronics, fine chemical, and steel industries[61]. The 1970s saw a rise in Middle East tensions which were to continue into the new Millennium culminating with the Munich Olympic massacre, a Middle East war, and finally in 1979 a peace agreement between Egypt and Israel brokered by the then United States President Jimmy Carter. America seemed to be held for ransom during the US Embassy hostage crisis, shortly after the Iranian revolution disposing the Shah, who was an American ally. Along with the earlier fall of the Saigon Government in 1975; this portrayed the United States as being weak. The Soviet Union invaded Afghanistan, which was going to greatly weaken the USSR and finally lead to the fall of communist regimes across Europe within the decade.

America was about to pioneer the personal computer. Microprocessor manufacturers became locked in fierce competition developing more powerful and faster processors that

---

[61] A host of books came out discussing the Japanese phenomena providing warnings and advice to American business on management, strategy, marketing, and manufacturing. These included William Ouchi's (1983), Theory Z, Richard Pascale and Anthony Athos's (1982) The Art of Japanese Management, Akio's Morita's (1987), Made in Japan, Kenichi Ohmae's (1991), The Mind of the Strategist, Philip Kotler et. al. (1985), The New Competition, and Richard Schonberger's (1982), Japanese Manufacturing Techniques.

created the platform for ever better personal computers. Personal computers would within the space of a couple of decades erode the dominance of companies like IBM that had almost completely dominated the computer industry during the 1960s. What was ironic is that a group of entrepreneurs who in the main did not finish college or university were able to spot the emerging opportunities and exploit them in the 1970s, so much better than IBM.

Two college dropouts, Steve Jobs and Steve Wozniak had assembled a small computer which they called the Apple in Job's family garage. The original Apple contained an assembly board with about 60 chips, a read-only memory (ROM), a power transformer and a keyboard packed in a case that could be connected to a small television for a monitor. Other machines at the time used either LED lights or teletype machines for readout, which made the Apple 1 the first interactive personal computer around. Jobs and Wozniak sold about 200 units and went on with the help of Ronald Wayne and funding from A.C. "Mike" Markkula to form Apple Computer, Inc. Soon after, they launched the Apple II, hired Mike Scott from national Semiconductor as CEO. By 1980 Apple achieved sales of over USD $120 Million, elevating both Jobs and Wozniak to celebrity status. Apple had joined the ranks of the Fortune 500 faster than any other company in history by making computers easy to use (Pusateri 1988). Apple went on to launch a computer that had a mouse and utilized desktop icons as the menu to make computers even easier for people to use. Apple Computer was quickly joined by other companies, including Commodore which launched the Commodore PET in 1977, Atari with the Atari 400 and 800 in 1979, and Tandy with the TRS-80 soon after. By the end of the Millennium there were 2.6 people for every computer on the Earth.

William Henry "Bill" Gates was born to a well to do family, his father an attorney and his mother a company director. During his early years at school, Bill Gates was very interested in the application of computers and continually played around with the Schools General Electric computer, where he learned to program in BASIC. Taking any opportunities to work with a computer, Gates learned FORTRAN, LISP, and COBOL becoming a very competent programmer. At age 17 Gates and his school friend Paul Allen made traffic counters based on an Intel 8008 processor, forming a company called Traf-O-Data (Gates 1995, P. 14). In 1973 Gates enrolled at Harvard University and continued pursuing his interest in computing. This is where his work habit of working up to 36 hours straight, then taking a short nap before recommencing work started showing, indicating his dedication.

After reading an issue of *Popular Electronics* in 1975 that reviewed the Altair 8800 stating that the programming language had a series of bugs in it, Gates and Allen contacted Micro Instrumentation and Telemetry Systems (MITS) to see if the company was interested in their help developing the language and interpreter. Gates and Allen's demonstration of their BASIC language and interpreter was a success and they formed a company Micro-Soft with MITS and moved to Albuquerque in November 1975. After Gates found out that his BASIC program had gone out to hobbyists before its release, he wrote in the MITS newsletter that MITS could not continue to release free software without payment from the users. This was at a time where the *'hacker's ethic'* encouraged the free flow of information to fellow hackers (Youngs 1993). This letter made Gates very unpopular with hobbyists. In 1976 Micro-Soft became independent of MITS, dropping the hyphen in its name, moving back to Washington State, and continued to produce programming language software. During these early years Gates oversaw all business details and personally wrote much of the software, reviewing every line before it went out into the market place.

IBM was preparing to launch its own personal computer using *off the shelf* components as there was no time to develop their own due to the rapid growth of the personal computer market and their need to get into the market quickly. IBM approached Microsoft to write the BASIC interpreter for the PC. However IBM needed an operating system and negotiations with Digital Research for the CP/M system failed to conclude any licensing agreement. Gates was asked again about the operating system and he recommended to IBM to use 86-DOS, similar to CP/M, which was written for some machinery. After adapting the system to the IBM-PC, Microsoft sold the operating system for a one up fee of USD $50,000 without transferring the copyright. Gates felt that a number of companies would be interested in cloning the IBM-PC and he was right. The sales of MS-DOS made Microsoft a major company within the computer industry.

Gates and Microsoft went on to develop windows that pushed the company's sales over the USD $1 Billion mark and ruthlessly guarded his market share. Gates had a reputation for being a fiery boss, often going into outbursts and berating his managers. The company also faced a number of antitrust actions, which they often lost. In some ways Gates had a similar ruthless disposition as John D. Rockefeller and by 1987 he was declared the youngest Billionaire by Forbes in history.

Meanwhile within the aviation industry new business models and deregulation were going to change the nature of civil aviation and the airline industry. Frederick Alfred Laker had been involved in aviation since leaving school, working for British European Airways (BEA) and London Aero Motor Services (LASM). Laker later left to develop his business selling surplus WWII aircraft. The advent of the Berlin blockade by the Soviet Union during 1948-49 advantaged Laker as every available aircraft was needed to carry freight to West Berlin. In 1954 Laker commenced transporting cars and their owners in Bristol Freighters from Rochford in Britain to Calais in France. Laker was made an offer by the Airwork group and sold off all his businesses, joining the group. After a merger with another company in 1960, the group became known as British United Airways and Laker became the managing director. Laker built British United Airways into Britain's largest privately owned independent airline with an all jet fleet.

After a disagreement with the British United Chairman Myles Wyatt in 1965 (Eglin & Ritchie 1980), Laker left to form Laker Airways and began operating charter flights with two Bristol Britannia 102 series turboprops. In 1967 he acquired five BAC One-Eleven 300 short haul jet aircraft partly self financed with the balance financed by a consortium of banks. Laker offered a 30% discount to travel agents to encourage them to utilize charter flights which helped create traffic to popular Mediterranean resorts. He carried out a number of cost cutting measures like using reduced thrust for takeoff, faster climbs to optimal altitudes, and limiting baggage to 15Kg rather than the usual 20Kg and passenger numbers to reduce weight and fuel consumption. Laker also set up a hub in what was then West Berlin that focused on taking holiday makers to resorts in the Canary Islands and Mediterranean. In 1992, Laker bought two wide-bodied McDonnell Douglas DC-10s into commercial service.

In 1971 Laker submitted a proposal to the UK's then Air Transport Licensing Boars (ATLB) to operate a low cost Trans-Atlantic route between London and New York. It was to operate like a *walk-on, walk-off* service without prior booking. The application was rejected and Laker appealed the ruling and he was eventually granted a license in 1972. However under pressure from the other airlines suffering from the OPEC oil embargo, the British Government revoked the license in 1975. Laker finally got the license reinstated in 1977 and commenced the Skytrain service to New York. Skytrain was an immediate financial success in the first year of operation[62], leading to expansion of new routes. Laker became very popular with the public through undertaking a series of publicity stunts (Eglin & Ritchie 1980). Skytrain continued to expand its fleet with another five DC-10s delivered from December 1979 onwards to cater for the growing number of destinations. A further ten Airbus A300s were ordered for a planned intra-European Skytrain.

However Laker's expansion had been too rapid and become very difficult to fund, as the firm did not have any significant assets and was facing growing interest repayments, and declining traffic due to the 1980-81 recession. Laker also suffered from the grounding of his DC-10s due to an American Airways crash at Chicago's O'Hare airport in 1979[63]. Laker was also the victim of price cutting by the major airlines resulting in an out of court settlement for a suit for antitrust breach. After going bankrupt, Laker tried to reestablish the airline with a public float[64], but after a short restart the airline closed for good in 2005.

Sir Freddie Laker saw the opportunity for low cost travel but had to battle policy, bureaucracy and even bullying by existing competition to create the first low cost, no frills airline in the world. His competitive strategy was based on developing high aircraft and staff productivity, low costs by reducing aircraft turnaround times (Bamber *et. al.* 2009), and seeking niche customer markets. Sir Freddie Laker was a pioneer showing up the complacency of the established industry protected by regulation and benefitting the customer greatly. Laker was followed promptly by Southwest Airlines with a modified business model, which has been emulated by so many other low cost airlines since including Easy Jet, Ryanair, Westjet, Air Asia, Virgin Atlantic, Virgin Blue, Jetstar, Cebu Pacific, Nok Air, Freedom Air, Volaris, and Pegasus Airlines.

From a very young age Frederick Wallace Smith had a love of flying and also saw the lack of accountability the post office and freight companies had with letters and parcels they carried (Sigafoos 1984). At the time mail was monopolized by the post office and parcel freight by Emery Air Freight and Flying Tigers, where an effective oligopoly existed. In 1970 Smith purchased a controlling interest in Ark Aviation Sales and traded in used jets making a good profit in the first year. He still saw the deficiencies in the air freight market and used his USD $4 million inheritance to start up Federal Express with a consortium of investors and a bank providing finance. The company raised USD $91 million, the biggest single start-up in American history in 1971. Federal Express started a service to 25 American cities using 33 French Dassault Falcon 20 executive jets, as their small sized excepted Smith in the need to comply with Civil Aeronautics Board (CAB) requirements for air forwarders. Smith modeled a hub system based on the concept of a bank clearing house where all parcels would come to a central hub located in Memphis, Tennessee and then be dispatched to their destination. Federal Express took the initiative and guaranteed a 24 hour delivery service which competitors had not been able to achieve at the time.

Federal Express had a rocky beginning with Smith forced to sell his private jet and staff often being forced to leave valuables as a deposit for fuel at airports. However in 1974, a

---

[62] See 'Skytrain profit to top £1 million?', Flight International, P. 553, 4th March 1978, http://www.flightglobal.com/pdfarchive/view/1978/1978%20-%200315.html, (accessed 7th February 2011).

[63] See 'Laker claims £13 million for DC-10 grounding, Flight International, 27th October 1979, P. 1338, http://www.flightglobal.com/pdfarchive/view/1979/1979%20-%203888.html, (accessed 7th February 2011).

[64] See 'Sir Freddie plans a comeback', Flight International, 5th January 1985, P. 5, http://www.flightglobal.com/pdfarchive/view/1985/1985%20-%200006.html, (accessed 7th February 2011).

strike at UPS gave Federal Express a virtual monopoly on some routes for a short time, giving the company the opportunity to show customers its reliability and win over customers. After deregulation the company purchased much larger aircraft and expanded its routes and services, revolutionizing the parcel service and challenging the monopoly of the post office.

Later on in the decade, the airline industry began to become deregulated. At this stage many 'flag carriers' were actually owned by their respective national governments which had a vested interest in restrictive regulation. Some airlines also began leaving the International Air Transport Association (IATA) which had very strict regulations about what could and couldn't be done by airlines. Leaving IATA benefitted many airlines like Singapore Airlines which through enhanced services were able to grow substantially during the next decade.

Until the 1970s American business had been competing among themselves with a great deal of predictability. The rise of Japan from the ashes of World War Two was seen as one of the miracles of business in the second half of the Twentieth Century. Japan had to overcome the complete devastation the allied bombing had done to the factories, its lack of resources, language, and finally image. Japanese companies employed very precise marketing practices at a time when American manufacturers thought they knew everything about marketing (Kotler *et. al.* 1985, P. ix). Japanese companies were to employ their style of market selection, market entry, market penetration, and market maintenance that made American executives ponder about this new Japanese success. Japanese companies were not frightened to buy market share through very heavy media campaigns that could not be equated to the percentage of sales like American firms practiced, and straight out buying up of their competition[65].

Many reasons have been attributed to the success of Japanese business over the years. Most probably one of the important reasons behind Japanese successes in the market place was the complacency of their competitors and failure to seek and exploit new opportunities which made them vulnerable. What American business didn't see, Japanese Business did, and they acted upon what they saw. The secret to Japanese success was seeing new opportunities that were customer based, applying new technologies to these opportunities, redefining the relationship between cost and quality at the production level, and carefully developing complex business strategies and implementing them very tightly.

The Japanese success was limited to a number of industries where they had a competitive advantage, listed in the introduction to this decade. The automobile is perhaps the best example of the Japanese rise to dominance in an industry, where Japan overtook Germany as a producer of motor vehicles in the 1960s and finally overtook the United States in 1980. In the 1960s Japanese cars were thought of as cheap and of low quality, a decade later they were considered to be fuel efficient, high quality, reliable, and trouble free. Brand names like Toyota, Datsun (Nissan), Mazda, Honda, Subaru, and Mitsubishi rose to the fore gathering high consumer loyalty. Japanese manufacturers selected the small-car segment that the American industry had ignored with fuel efficient vehicles with more standard items than the American models.

This also occurred in the motorcycle industry dominated in the 1950s in the UK by BSA, Norton, and Triumph, Moto-Guzzi in Italy, and Harley Davidson in the United States. Honda had entered the US market in the 1950s and by 1970 was the undisputed market leader in

---

[65] Two examples of this would be Kao Corporation's purchase of The Andrew Jergens Company and Sony's purchase of Columbia Pictures.

motorcycles. Honda developed an aggressive sales distribution network with a wide service support network. Later Yamaha and Suzuki also entered the market focusing on the young generation.

After the Second World War the Japanese electrical industry was technically backward and produced inferior products to their international competitors in the 1950s. They began buying up technical licenses from international companies which enabled them to learn and improve upon the new technologies. By the 1960s Japanese products began to surpass their competitors. Companies like Matsushita, Toshiba, Hitachi, Mitsubishi Electric, Sony, and Sanyo fiercely competed domestically and then internationally. This was repeated in the appliance industry with Hitachi, Toshiba, Mitsubishi, Sharp, and Sanyo and in the watch industry by Seiko, Citizen, and Orient, which had learnt to produce high precision and high quality timepieces at a low price. Japanese companies also had great success in the camera industry in the single lens, reflex cameras that took over from German camera manufacturers. Japanese companies also dominated the steel, shipbuilding, semiconductor, robotics, and copier industries.

By the end of the 1970s US industry was beginning to realize their own vulnerability and was looking for answers. The regulatory environment was going to be continually eased fostering a more competitive environment, bringing uncertainty into the next decade. Economic uncertainty also rose with growing unemployment. Society failed to learn the lessons of the two oil embargos and look for alternatives to an oil based lifestyle. The cost of homes and mortgages was at an all time home making it difficult for small entrepreneurs to start up. The era of greed was just about upon us with corporations losing great creditability as consumers grew weary and lost faith in them.

The 1980s

The beginning of the 1980s was characterized by low/negative growth, rising unemployment, high inflation and interest rates, where a number of countries were going through debt crises. However many corporations grew exponentially through acquisition and merger making them stronger and wealthier than they have ever been before. At the national level many underdeveloped countries attracted manufacturing industry that greatly aided in their development and economic growth, particularly in Mexico, East and South-East Asia. In Eastern Europe the new Soviet policies of *perestroika* and *glasnost* gave countries within the Soviet Block new economic freedoms where Poland, Hungary, Czechoslovak experienced uprisings, while Nicolae Ceausescu was overthrown by popular revolt in Romania. The Berlin Wall came down in 1989 symbolizing the end of communism in Eastern Europe. The United Kingdom and United States under the leadership of Margaret Thatcher and Ronald Reagan respectively moved towards a *laissez-faire* economy through privatization, deregulation and use of monetary policy over fiscal policy, allowing the exchange rate to float freely. The European Union continued to enlarge with the admittance of Greece in 1981 and followed by Spain and Portugal in 1986.

The age of the computer was arriving where many tasks in organizations like word processing replaced the typewriter and home ownership of personal computers was on the rise. However due to the increase in home PC ownership, video console games died out by 1983, but rose again in the late 80s with a new generation of graphics enhanced game boxes produced by companies like Nintendo and Sega. This showed the market volatility of technology based industries that could very quickly rise and just as quickly dissipate into some other form of technology – *something that would be seen many times in the computer and mobile phone industries later on.*

The American automobile industry continued to suffer with many of the large corporations nearly going into bankruptcy. This was exacerbated by their still unclear future directions, poor quality control, an economic downturn, and competition from Japan. During this decade the Korean car Hyundai made its appearance onto the US market in 1986.

The world underwent massive population growth during the 1980s, particularly in Sub-Saharan Africa, the Middle East, and South Asia. The 1980s saw the beginning of the AIDS pandemic, leading to some backlash against certain minority groups. However it was in this decade that the world had been able to cooperate together to solve the problem of depleted ozone around the South Polar cap. Western societies began to adopt the concept of political correctness as opposed to showing prejudice to minority groups in society, which influenced media content [66]. Society became less tolerant of smoking, opposed to nuclear power after the Chernobyl disaster in 1996, more accepting of gay rights, and interested in recycling and *'green'* policies. Consumers also became brand conscious with a bias towards luxury brands over previous decades but at the same time frequented discount and factory outlets for bargains. However the 1980s saw a streak of selfishness to it which is probably best epitomized by the phase *"greed is good"*, spoken by Gordon Gekko in the Oliver Stone movie of that decade *"Wall Street"*.

Enter Tom Peters. Peters was co-author of a book written at a time when Japan had severely challenged America's business dominance with many believing that many other industries were vulnerable to this Japanese *"attack"*. Tom Peters and Robert Waterman were employees at Mckinsey, one of the premier management consulting firms in the United States. They carried out research to identify common characteristics of successful companies, based on selection criteria of six financial measurements. Peters and Waterman called in two academics Richard Pascale and Anthony Athos to assist them make sense of the data and select the important characteristics of success. *Strategy, structure* and *systems* had been agreed upon and Pascale suggested *style* and *shared values* to complete five components of the *Seven S Framework.* After some weeks of discussion *skills* was added to the framework to make up six components. The seventh was decided upon as *sequencing*, but later replaced with *staff.* Peters was also proposing adding power, but this didn't eventuate (Crainer 1998).

Their basic conclusion was that excellent companies exercised commonsense and kept very close to the business basics (Crainer 1998). The book opposed analytical management that relied on numbers to make decisions. Peters and Waterman emphasized *'mindset'*, *'autonomy'*, and *"culture'*.

The *Seven S Framework* was featured in Peters and Waterman's book *In Search of Excellence*, published in 1982. The book was far from being an academic piece of literature and written in a *popularist* format, easy to read with lots of stories to get the messages across. Even though the *Seven S Framework* was sharply criticized for making organizational behavior simplistic, akin to an advertising agency developing slogans and that many of the

---

[66] Political correctness is a term to describe the foregoing of using language, ideas, policies, or behavior that might cause offence to occupational, gender, racial, cultural, sexually orientated, religious believing, disability, and/or age related minority groups.

excellent companies described in the book are not performing well now[67], the book had many relevant messages based on eight main themes, in a chapter by chapter format, which came to corporate America at the right time;

1. A bias for action, active decision making - *'getting on with it'.*
2. Close to the customer - learning from the people served by the business.
3. Autonomy and entrepreneurship - fostering innovation and nurturing 'champions'.
4. Productivity through people - treating rank and file employees as a source of quality.
5. Hands-on, value-driven - management philosophy that guides everyday practice - management showing its commitment.
6. Stick to the knitting - stay with the business that you know.
7. Simple form, lean staff - some of the best companies have minimal HQ staff, and
8. Simultaneous loose-tight properties - autonomy in shop-floor activities plus centralized values (Peters & Waterman 1982).

It was reported nearly two decades later that Peters admitted that he and his co-author falsified the underlying data used in this groundbreaking book, but this was later denied by Peters (Byrne 2001). Nevertheless, given all the criticisms *In Search of Excellence* was the top selling management book of all time and ushered in the new era of *management gurus, management fads,* and *'the quick fix'* mentality. Tom Peters is the most highly demanded speaker in the management circuit, *itself a new industry.* Peters in his way of putting things has managed to inspire many and bring up the *'management culture phenomenon'.* However, although most managers at the time had a copy on the bookcase behind their desk, actually how many read it and were able to implement any of the ideas was another thing.

Tom Peters as an influence on management thought continued with his books, more recently focusing on personal responsibility in relation to the new economy; *A Passion for Excellence (1985), Thriving on Chaos (1987), Liberation Management (1992), The Tom Peters Seminar: Crazy times for crazy organizations (1993), The Pursuit of Wow! (1994), The circle of Innovation: You can't shrink your way to Greatness (1997), The Brand You50 (1999), Re-imagine! Business excellence in a disruptive age (2003), Talent (2005), Leadership (2005), Design (2005), Trends (2005),* and *The Little Things: 163 ways to pursue EXCELLENCE (2010).*

On the night of 2-3rd December 1984 at the Union Carbide plant at Bhopal, India, a gas leak occurred and exposed thousands of people to the deadly chemical methyl isocyanate leaving thousands dead. The company was blamed for taking short cuts in the production of pesticides, having inadequate safety and emergency procedures, storing excessive amounts of toxic chemicals above safety levels on site, having malfunctioning warning systems, and being located too close to densely populated areas (Eckerman 2005). The disaster led to long and protracted litigation, criminal charges against the management, and much public condemnation.

Later near the end of the decade an oil tanker the Exxon Valdez while travelling through Prince William Sound in Alaska struck Bligh Reef and spilled an enormous amount of crude

---

[67] Companies like Wang Computer actually closed down.

oil into the sound, the largest oil spill in history. Exxon was heavily criticized for its inadequate response to the disaster[68].

A number of court cases occurred during the 1980s bringing a new term *"insider trading"* to public attention. These cases led to the public attention that the *'corporate highflyers'* who have access to information that the *'average person in the street'* does not have are able to increase their own personal wealth significantly and unfairly. That coupled with the media coverage of outrageous corporate salaries greatly disenchanted the public about corporate leadership.

This was reinforced through the news footage of the lavish lifestyles of corporate leaders. For example in Australia, Alan Bond an entrepreneur in Western Australia, famous for his 1983 high profile win of the Americas Cup with the yacht *Australia II,* an elite sport, ended up being sentenced to seven years jail after pleading guilty for using his controlling interest in Bell Resources to deceptively siphon off AUD $1.2 Billion into the accounts of Bond Corporation. Another entrepreneur Christopher Skase after his firm Qintex purchased the Seven Television Network, Hollywood's MGM Studios, the Brisbane Bears Australian Rules Football Club, and developed the Mirage Resorts in Port Douglas, putting the small town on the world map, suffered badly from rising interest rates in 1989, contributing to Qintex's collapse. Skase and his wife, well known for their lavish lifestyles fled to Majorca Spain after parceling up their personal collection of antiques, becoming Australia's most wanted fugitive. Christopher Skase died in Majorca before the authorities could gain his extradition for trial back in Australia.

Prior to the above disasters and scandals, corporations were portrayed as law abiding and patriotic entities that personified freedom and ethics (Wagnleither 1994). People found that in some cases nothing could be further than the truth. Previously corporations had only very superficially been scrutinized about their basic ethics, but these disasters and scandals led to the beginning of corporations highlighting their ethical standards in what was later going to be known as Corporate Social Responsibility (CSR).

Anita Roddick was one of the early entrepreneurs to create and build a company based on ethical consumerism and Fair-trade[69]. In the 1970s Roddick was on holiday in America and visited a shop called *The Body Shop* in Berkeley California run by sisters through marriage Peggy Short and Janet Saunders. Their ideas inspired Roddick to open her own shop in Brighton England in 1976. In 1987 after some negotiation, Roddick bought the rights to the name from Short and Saunders for a reported £3.5 Million (Bronstein 2004). Anita's husband Gordon Roddick worked out a franchising system which would enable the couple to open many shops around the United Kingdom and overseas[70]. By 1991, The Body Shop had over 700 stores and by 2004 over 2,000 stores serving close to 80 million customers around the world. Roddick sold the business to L'Oreal in 2006 for £652 million[71], a decision that many criticized her for appearing to go against her principals.

---

[68] See Baker, M. (2008). Companies in Crisis – What not to do when it all goes wrong, mallenbaker.net, http://www.mallenbaker.net/csr/crisis03.html, (accessed 9th February 2011).

[69] See Dame Anita Roddick, The Sunday Times, 11th September 2007, http://www.timesonline.co.uk/tol/comment/obituaries/article2426176.ece, (accessed 9th February 2011).

[70] See: Dame Anita Roddick dies aged 64, BBC News, 10th September 2007, http://news.bbc.co.uk/2/hi/uk_news/6988343.stm, (accessed 9th February 2011).

[71] L'Oréal buys Body Shop for £652m, The Independent, 17th March 2006, http://www.independent.co.uk/news/business/news/loreal-buys-body-shop-for-pound652m-470244.html, (accessed 9th February 2011).

The Body Shop was one of the early businesses that built their branding upon ethics. During Roddick's stewardship of The Body Shop, she ran many social campaigns about ethical issues including banning animal testing, recycling, the raising of women's self-esteem and stereotyping of women, saving the whales campaign with Greenpeace, and promoted fair-trade. In an interview before her death, Roddick claimed the The Body Shop developed from a series of brilliant accidents, had a great smell, funky name, and started in a hot year where people needed lots of sun-block lotion[72]. Roddick showed that firms could charge premium prices for *'integrity premiums'* and *'packaged idealism'* marketing strategies that would be successfully used by a number of other companies in the coming two decades.

However companies relying upon ethics in their branding are not beyond scrutiny and The Body Shop was no exception. Jon Entine (2007) reported that Anita Roddick had just copied the name and concept from the shop in Berkeley California, including store design, labeling, promotional materials, and overall marketing concept, including individual product lines. Her stories of travelling around the world looking for new products from indigenous communities were mostly fabricated as she preferred to buy at the cheapest price and only a very small proportion of products sold in The Body Shop originated from her projects or were Fair-trade products. Entine continued to report that most of the ingredients in products with not natural and Roddick herself did not seem to personally care much about these issues and in the first 11 years of The Body Shop operation the company gave nothing to charity. Entire used the term *'greenwashing'* to depict companies using ethics and sustainability issues to cynically gain sales and that companies extolling *'social responsibility'* may not in actual fact be operating any more socially responsible than other companies.

The economic growth of the 1980s saw a wave of mergers and acquisitions that was going to continue to become a permanent feature of the corporate landscape. Mergers and acquisitions started increasing in the 1980s because of the slowly relaxing regulatory environment, the development of the European Union as a single jurisdiction and market, and the easier access to funds through emerging pension funds, junk bonds, and underwriters. 1980s mergers and acquisitions consequently tended to be much more leveraged than they were in later decades. Some deals were fiercely resisted while some were friendly to achieve quick growth and synergies.

One of the largest leveraged buyouts in history was the merger between R. J. Reynolds Tobacco Company and Nabisco in 1985 and then the hostile and bitterly fought takeover of RJR Nabisco by Kohlberg Kravis Roberts & Co. three years later. In 1989 Philip Morris Corporation purchased Kraft for USD $12.9 billion and merged Kraft with their General Foods Division. General Motors purchased Hughes Aircraft Company from the Howard Hughes Medical Institute for USD $4.7 billion. Gulf Oil, one of the seven sisters, merged with SOCAL and rebranded the company as Chevron in 1985, RCA was taken over by General Electric in 1986, US Steel acquired Marathon oil in 1982, and Burroughs and Sperry merged in 1986 to form Unisys in 1986, changing the Fortune 500 listings dramatically.

Generally firms merge or acquire another firm to achieve quick growth, achieve some forms of synergy between the two operations such as cost savings through combining administration, production, and sales forces, etc, achieve some diversification like the tobacco companies tried to do due to long term uncertainty about their major product cigarettes, add to

---

[72] See Anita Roddick, capitalist with a conscience, dies at 64, The Independent, 11th September 2007, http://www.independent.co.uk/news/uk/this-britain/anita-roddick-capitalist-with-a-conscience-dies-at-64-

their product portfolios, horizontally diversify, acquire intellectual property, buy market share, or vertically integrate their business. However many mergers and acquisitions don't work out as planned and failed to bring the financial results expected. Very often in mergers that take a firm away from the core business there is often a failure to understand the new industry. In acquired companies, the acquiring company's executives may act as conquers and lose many talented people and value from the acquired company. There can also be a clash of different cultures and values between the acquiring and acquired companies. When companies merge with similar companies carrying similar product ranges, customers may rationalize the products they purchase from the new company, resulting in a loss and decrease of overall sales. Finally as was the case in General Foods after the Kraft takeover, the effort and time needed to consolidate the merging of the two companies takes focus away from new product development, which was the strength of General Foods and the market in general.

Outsourcing of goods and services from other firms and/or individual contractors rapidly grew in the 1980s as firms looked at new ways of cutting costs, increasing efficiencies and improving quality. In the 1960s many major corporations acquired goods suppliers or other service providers as a means to save costs through vertical integration. However after going through this exercise most companies found that dedicated suppliers actually raised overheads, lowered innovative creativity, became complacent toward their captive customer, and had difficulty expanding the divisions due to hesitancy of competitors to purchase from a company owned by another competitor.

Companies utilized bureaus to undertake their computing needs as mainframes, mini-computers, and software was very expensive at the time and the ability of micro computers to undertake corporate accounting, retail, and production management had not yet been achieved. Companies that had their own computer systems would hire contractors as programmers, as it was more expensive to have them as fulltime staff. Likewise companies that had in-house delivery logistics also found it cheaper and less worrisome to hire outside logistic firms. Even warehousing was contracted out to third parties. On the sales side, sales brokers and merchandising was also contracted out to third parties, sometimes ex-employees who had specifically left to undertake contractual services for their former companies. The advantage for companies that outsourced was that it could get rid of *'hidden costs'* that go with employing fulltime staff and provide certainty about monthly costs. Companies and organizations with large revenues would be able to be managed by relatively few people with a minimum number of employees. The outsourcing phenomena added greatly to the growth of opportunities for people with specific skills and networks within the service sector.

On Monday 19th October 1987 equity stock prices in Hong Kong started falling dramatically, spreading through all the markets in the world during that day. By the end of *'black Monday'* the Dow Jones Industrial Average had dropped 22.61% (Browning 2007). Within the next 10 days almost 50% of the value of the world's equities had been eroded. There is a great deal of debate about what caused the crash, although once it started electronic trading and psychological factors contributed to the downward momentum. The effect of the crash was to severely financially strain business in repaying extremely large loans due to relatively liberal lending regime of the 1980s by banks and other financial institutions. This led many firms into bankruptcy and liquidation putting strain on banks, finally leading to a

402014.html, (accessed 9th February 2011).

major recession in 1990. One of the legacies of the 1980s was that leveraging would be more conservative in the next decade.

The 1990s

The 1990s was the decade where new mass technologies began to embrace peoples' lives. There was a rapid transformation from things mechanical, to analogue, and to digital. Cell phones transformed from something a high placed executive would use at the beginning of the decade to a means of communication for the masses by the end of the decade. The *World Wide Web* emerged for public use in the early 1990s and by the year 2000, almost 50% of western households had access to it. This was supported by a rapid improvement in the speed and capacity of modems and communication transmission lines during the decade. Satellite television also emerged bringing programming around the world in a way that had never happened before.

The phenomena called *globalism* was felt much more in the 1990s with better air transport, media communications, multinational brand presence, and the quicker transfer of cultural and counter-cultural artifacts between countries and regions. Individualism became much more prevalent in western cultures, where through rapid portrayal in the media also followed in major urban centers around the world. Urban youth domed tattoos, body piercing, and retro fashion of the *'sixties'* and *'seventies'* creating urban counter-cultures all over the world. New interests emerged in extreme sports and outdoor activities like marathon running, triathlons, and bicycle riding. The baby-boom generation was reaching their forties and companies targeted products at this demographic group because of their relatively large incomes. Some radio stations also focused on the generation by presenting *rock and roll* and *easy listening* formats. Market opportunities moved with this demographic. The 1990s also saw strict ethics regarding sexual harassment and there was a general rise in the power of women in both business and politics. Prize money in major sporting events like tennis became equal for the men's and women's competitions.

The fall of the Soviet Union led to a global political realignment with the American intelligence and military complex without an enemy to focus their activity upon, until Saddam Hussein, strapped for cash after the Iran-Iraq war invaded Kuwait. The military would see action a number of times during the decade in regional and localized conflicts. Parts of Europe, the United States, and Australia drifted into the post industrial economy stage of development with East Asian economies steadily reaching a high standard of living during the decade.

Sustainable development and environmental protection became much more important in the 1990s with the 1992 Earth Summit in Rio de Janeiro and the adoption of the Kyoto Protocol in 1997.

Due to the downsizing in the 1980s and 1990s the concept of job security began to evaporate and self employment became a viable option chosen by many. The 1990s saw a dramatic rise in small business. The expansion of small business numbers started in the 1980s in the United States and skyrocketed during the 1990s where the United States was increasingly becoming an entrepreneurial economy (Case 1992, P.14). For the first time, the national level of economic growth could be correlated with the national level of entrepreneurial activity (Reynolds *et. al.* 2002). This is where Silicon Valley emerged and successful entrepreneurs were seen as the heroes of the nation with entrepreneurship taking on positive connotations in society once again.

Due to the success of many new entrepreneurs, large corporations became interested in ways they could install creativity and innovation back into their own organizations to emulate small business success. This led to the development of the concepts of *knowledge organization, innovation management,* and the *learning organization* during the decade. Demand for entrepreneurial studies at colleges and universities increased dramatically where specialized courses were developed rather than just incorporating entrepreneurship as a single elective in general courses (Finkle & Deeds 2001). This momentum brought structural change which seemed to bring on a new form of capitalism where one in ten people in the United States were now self employed (Reynolds *et. al.* 2000). Some of America's richest people were entrepreneurs and government policy in many countries started looking towards entrepreneurship as a means of creating economic growth and employment (Timmons & Spinelli 2004, P.5). This structural change made the economy an organic entity that was now always in the process of *'beginning'* rather than *'being'* (Kuratko & Welsch 2004). Entrepreneurship was now seen as a means of upward mobility (Dennis & Fernald 2000) and access the *American dream*[73], a perception followed by other societies around the world.

Satellite television broadcasting began with experimental broadcasts in the 1970s and expanded with some free to air television available on C band in the 1980s, but it wasn't until the 1990s that the concept was universally popular[74]. One early pioneer was Ted Turner who purchased a defunct UHF television station WTCG and commenced running old movies. UHF stations were not as popular as their VHF counterparts and most often had trouble surviving in these early times. He renamed the station WTBS (Turner Broadcasting System) in the early 1970s. In December 1976 WTRS was beamed by satellite and became a national subscriber station. WTBS broadcast movies, cartoons, sports, music videos, and current affairs, all on a single channel. WTBS became a regular broadcaster of sports events, becoming the home of the program World Championship Wrestling (WCW) broadcast each Saturday night.

In 1980 Ted Turner and a group of investors formed the Cable News Network (CNN), the first 24 hours news station broadcasting from its headquarters in Atlanta, Georgia at a former country club. Turner later purchased a defunct shopping centre with a tower and relocated the operation there calling it the CNN Centre, which helped to rejuvenate downtown Atlanta. It was the CNN coverage of the Gulf War in 1991 that established CNN and the concept of 24 hour news broadcasting into international prominence. CNN was the only network that was allowed to broadcast directly from inside Iraq and gave a live broadcast from the *al-Rashid Hotel* in Bagdad with reporters Bernard Shaw, John Holliman, and Peter Arnett all became household names. The Gulf War showed that live news coverage of events were to greatly influence how events played out which has been shown in numerous international events up until the fall of Hosni Mubarak in Egypt recently, coined by some in the Pentagon as the

---

[73] See: The New American Revolution: The Role and Impact of Small Business, Washington DC, US Small Business Administration, Office of Economic Research, (1998).

[74] Before the 1990s equipment was expensive and could not compete against the other modes of transmission, i.e., cable and UHF.

"CNN effect"[75]. Previously news had been broadcast in cycles allowing authorities to control the timing of events for their benefit. Live news coverage had a great impact on peoples' perceptions and views and tend to force authorities to hasten their actions in many circumstances. CNN had grown from a channel seen by 1.7 million American households in 1980, to been seen by viewers in over 212 countries today, with 10 US News bureaus and 27 international bureaus today[76]. CNN has inspired the creation of a number of similar channels including the Weather Channel in 1982, CNN international in 1985, Sky News in 1989, CNBC in 1989, Court TV in 1991, CNN Airport Network in 1992, BBC Worldwide in 1995, MSNBC in 1996, Fox news in 1996, and al Jazeera in 1996. CNN was taken over by Time Warner in 1996 and operates as a semi-autonomous division.

The concept of transmitting data between two computers was very limited before the 1980s. Packet switching protocols were developed during the 1960s that enabled messages to be broken down into arbitrary packets with routing decisions made according to the packet as opposed to rigid physical routing systems. In the late 1960s universities began building networks between their individual computer systems that allowed inter-computer communications. In the United States this network grew with new hosts situated primarily at universities being added on a regular basis to build the forerunner to what we call the internet today (Hafner & Lyon 1996).

Meanwhile the X.25 protocol was developed to allow companies to send data down telecommunications lines which eventually became and international packet network by the late 1970s and early 1980s. This would enable the connection to a computer through any telephone line. A group of researchers at Stanford University developed a universal protocol that would allow the linking of all these systems together. The control of this working network was handed over to the Defense Communications Agency in 1975 to operate the system as a gateway for defense and university communications. The government restricted commercial use at first, but government agencies became heavy users of the system right into the 1980s. Email was one of the first important applications of this network which began to be called the internet or internetworking.

In the late 1980s the first internet service providers (ISP) were formed to provide internet access to private customers. Companies like PSINET, Netcom, and Portal Software provided dial up services to the internet. In 1992 the US Congress passed the Scientific and Advanced Technology Act to allow commercial use of the internet. Finally in 1994 the centralized routing protocols or NSFNet Internet Backbone was replaced by a Border Gateway Protocol (BGP) which allowed direct communications between computers without having to go through the central system.

The internet was about to become a platform that was going to change world commerce and itself bloom into a massive industry that would have some of the largest capitalized companies in the world utilizing it. One of the early battles of the internet was over the web browser. Netscape Communications Corporation's proprietary web browser dominated the market in terms of its usage over the mid 1990s. The Netscape Browser had good features, an attractive licensing scheme, and was free for non-commercial users and became the de facto

---

[75] The CNN effect has become a theory in political science where 24 hour news broadcasting has significant effect on the conduct of a states foreign policy. 24 hour news broadcasters like CNN have brought events directly into world attention which has a great effect on how authorities play out their actions due to live public observation.

[76] See: In 20 years, CNN has changed the way we view the news, Enquirer Local New Coverage, 28th may 2000, http://www.enquirer.com/editions/2000/05/28/loc_kiesewetter.html, (accessed 11th February 2011).

standard on the windows platform. Netscape saw that the computer operating system would not be as important as the web browser which could connect to all the applications a user required.

The rise of the Netscape browser worried Bill Gates at Microsoft and so the company developed their own web browser Microsoft Explorer (IE) to enter the market. Microsoft succeeded in getting most computer vendors to distribute Microsoft Explorer on their computers and leaving out the Netscape Explorer using leverage from their windows OEM licenses. By the end of the decade Netscape lost its dominance over the Microsoft Windows Platform. Netscape launched an antitrust action against Microsoft and the court ruled that Microsoft bundling of Internet Explorer with the Windows Operating System was a monopolistic and illegal business practice, but this decision was too late as Microsoft Explorer had become the de facto web browser. In 1998 Netscape went open source, releasing the product as Mozilla. America Online bought Netscape but couldn't win back users to the Netscape navigator.

Fibre optic cables were being laid all around the world to distribute primarily cable television to households with the internet *piggybacking* upon the new infrastructure. The internet spread faster than any other technology ever developed and commercialized[77]. America Online (AOL) utilized the fibre optic network for the internet and became one of the first internet providers with novel services like on-line gaming. AOL went public in 1992 pioneering the way people spent their leisure time, but was quickly overtaken by a number of smaller internet service providers and taken over by Time Warner in 2001.

Tools that guided users on the internet were the next enhancement to the internet environment. In January 1994, Jerry Yang and David Filo, electrical engineers at Stanford University created a web site called *"David's and Jerry's guide to the World Wide Web"*. The site contained a collated list of web sites with a searchable index. The site was renamed Yahoo in April 1994 and grew in popularity over the decade. Lycos started as a research project at Carnegie Mellor University by Michael Loren Mauldin in 1994, after unsuccessfully trying to launch it as a software company. With Bob Davis as CEO the company concentrated on building an advertising supported web portal. The company listed in 1996 and became one of the first profitable internet businesses. This business model became well accepted and the company grew to become one of the most visited online sites in the 1990s. At nearly the same time a group of students at Stanford University, Graham Spencer, Joe Kraus, Mark Van Haren, Ryan McIntyre, Ben Lutch, and Martin Reinfried, developed an internet portal with a search engine, web email, instant messaging, stock quotes, and a customized web-page that could collate information from a number of web sources. The site was formally launched around the end of 1995 and although developed to become one of the most well known brands on the internet, failed to make a profit and was sold to @Home Network in 1999.

Two Stanford University students Larry Page and Sergey Brin had developed a search engine that ranked results by their search popularity. They ran the project on the Stanford University computer and in 1998 and shortly after incorporated the company Google, operating from a friend's garage in Menlo Park, California. Concerned that the enterprise was taking up too much time from study, Page and Brin tried to sell the company to Excite but the

---

[77] The personal computer took around 16 years, the telephone took 35 years, the airplane around 18 years, and the automobile around 55 years.

offer was rejected. In 1999 venture capital firms Kleine Caulfield & Byers and Sequoia Capital provided Google with USD $25 million funding. Since 2000, Google has purchased a number of companies adding to the services it provides on the internet and had a public listing in 2004 making Larry Page, Sergey Brin and a number of Google employees instant millionaires.

During the 1990s there were a number of successful web business start-ups that would dominate international e-commerce. Amazon was formed in 1995 by Jeff Bezos. The company began an online bookstore that had a massive amount of titles a physical bookstore could not compete with. Bezos made a number of acquisitions to expand the business over the years including an internet movie database, online music, print on demand e-books, e-book software company, audio books until Amazon now offers almost a full range of products. Amazon also created a lot of extra features like allowing people to write make book reviews. The firm became profitable by 2001 and is listed in the NASDAQ.

Another start-up during the mid 1990s was eBay. eBay grew out of a personal web site of French born computer programmer Pierre Omidyar in San Jose California. After being shocked by selling a broken laser pen on his website Omidyar realized the potential of that an auction web site would have. (Cohen 2003). This inspired Omidyar to develop this site and he started selling plane tickets and other travel products. The company expanded its product lines and bought out the European internet auction company IBazar in 1995. By 1997 the site hosted more than 2,000,000 auctions and the firm obtained USD $6.7 million from Benchmark Capital to list on the stock exchange the following year. The company bought out PayPal in 2002 and linked it to the eBay site. The company now has over 15,000 employees and revenues in excess of USD 7.7 billion.

Web-based business start-ups were not restricted to the United States. A Chinese entrepreneur (Jack) Ma Yun had seen the need of Chinese businesses to find international customers and the need of international customers to find Chinese suppliers. With 18 financial supporters, Ma developed the trade web-site Alibaba.com in 1999. In August 2005 Yahoo purchased a 40% interest in the company for USD $1 billion.

The internet was changing the nature of how companies were doing business and most significant companies developed their own web sites. The internet began to be used as an important aspect of a firm business model where airline, rail, and concert bookings could be made and online banking transactions undertaken.

Internet business start ups were very common in the late 1990s. A new start up based on a new idea would commence with the backing of funds by friends and family. Founders would develop a business plan with exit strategies that would attract venture capital firms to support the venture. The venture would run on initial venture capital finance and even a public offering of shares before any income would come in. Companies would then attempt to grow as quickly as possible to develop a presence and user loyalty before a competitor could come in and exploit the idea better (Spector 2000). Firms could then prepare a public offering (IPO) where founders could profit enormously and venture capital firms could exit with a massive profit, just like Yahoo had done in 1996 where the share price tripled on the first day of trading.

However these meteoric rises of new companies were not always based on fundamentals and tended to be valued on novelty and potential[78]. Few companies actually really had a business plan that made any sense. In reality there was a very long period from start-up to profits due to the need to grow before revenues would be higher than expenses to make a profit, if indeed they made any profit at all. At the end of the 1990s the Federal Reserve Bank raised interest rates a number of times and Microsoft had some bad publicity with anti-trust cases. These factors led to some sell offs of internet company stocks where values starting falling causing a panic. Several companies ran out of capital and were forced to file for bankruptcy or be acquired by traditional firms. Some firms were also found to be employing fraudulent practices to overstate profits leading to very poor confidence in internet companies generally. With a shakeout affecting almost half of the internet companies, some like eBay, Amazon, and Google were able to survive and dominate their industries within the coming decade.

The 1990s saw a dramatic increase in the amount of regulation governing business. This included food, cosmetic, chemical, equal opportunity, anti-discrimination, occupational health and safety, environment protection, transport, and public liability regulations. Many countries also introduced a value added tax system which added to paperwork compliance. The result of all these new regulations was a decrease in productivity and greatly increased cost of doing business with some estimates as being as high as 10% of national GDP (Bovard 1994), which ended up increasing the cost of living (Hopkins 1995). Any average person wishing to start-up a new business in a post capitalist society needed a large amount of extra capital just to comply with regulations.

Just as Japan and East Asia had risen dramatically in the 1970s and 1980s, South East Asia rose steadily during the late 1980s and 1990s with local family owned conglomerates becoming very powerful. A boom in foreign investment created a large manufacturing base where Malaysia became the world centre of semiconductor production. The manufacturing sector also encouraged rapid urban growth, generating new skylines and greatly increased the standard of living. Government linked companies particularly in Malaysia had also participated in the boom in growth and became wealthy. Vibrant stock exchanges emerged that attracted foreign capital and commodity prices for rubber and palm oil were high adding to a favorable balance of trade.

However suddenly in 1997 Asian currencies started devaluing rapidly causing great panic. This also occurred in East Asia and Hong Kong, where Joseph Yam the CEO of the Hong Kong Monetary Authority announced that Hong Kong and the region was facing a severe conspiracy by speculators that launched coordinated and well planned attacks across regional markets[79]. Although this was fanciful (Studwell 2007, P. 141), in Malaysia, Dr. Mahathir unlike other ASEAN countries that took IMF packages, steered alone and insulted Malaysia from the crisis by fixing the pegging the Ringgit to the US Dollar at 3.80/1.0, and bailed out a number of companies to maintain employment to prevent undue suffering by the local population. The Asian financial crisis however gave an unparalleled opportunity for

---

[78] These types of booms also developed during earlier history where new technologies were introduced. For example, the steam engine and railroads attracted high interest in the 1840s, automobiles in the 1920s, and transistors in the 1950s.

[79] See: Joseph Yam, 'Causes of and the solutions to the recent financial turmoil in the Asian region' a speech given to Asian Central Bankers in Manila, http://www.info.gov.hk/hkma/eng/ speeches/speechs/joseph/speech_050199b.htm

foreign multinationals to buy up Asian assets relatively cheaply; so many manufacturing, cement operations, hotels and resorts were bought or completely taken over from their local partners as they were strapped for liquidity (Backman & Butler 2007, P. 95).

The world before the end of the decade became concerned about the Y2K problem, where some computer programs had utilized only two-digit dates for the year instead of four. There was great concern at the time that at the stroke of midnight on 31st December 1999 computers all over the world would malfunction. A vast amount of money in the hundreds of billions, most probably unnecessarily was spent to remedy this potential problem.

Into The New Millennium

The first decade of the 21st Century was plagued by financial and economic crises, energy and food crises, two flu pandemics, and a spate of natural disasters. The decade began with fallout from the *Dot.com* collapse which disrupted financial markets and brought a general downturn in economic activity. This forced the Federal Reserve to reduce interest rates a number of times to avoid recession. In 2007 the US housing market collapsed causing loan defaults and a number of financial institutions to collapse, leading to a bailout and partial nationalization of banks, financial institutions and automobile manufacturers. Governments utilized Keynesian fiscal spending to induce economic activity again to avoid a deep recession. This was followed with a debt crisis in a number of European countries that faced trouble financing their budgets.

During the decade the price of oil slowly drifted up until it reached the mid USD $160s per barrel in 2008, caused by concern over oil reserves, crisis in the Middle East and oil speculation. This put great strain on many national economies and led to a high food prices and shortages, putting stress upon many under developed and developing countries. This triggered a renewed interest in alternative fuels and *'green'* energy development.

The September 11th attacks on the Pentagon in Washington DC and the World Trade Center in New York City led to the United States, United Kingdom and a coalition of other countries invading and occupying Afghanistan and Iraq. This occupied American Defense and foreign policy for the rest of the decade and the formation of the Homeland Security which introduced numerous security measures within the United States and abroad in what became known as *"the war on terror"*. A spate of other terror attacks occurred during the decade including Anthrax attacks in the United States during 2001, Bali during 2002, Casablanca in 2003, Istanbul in 2003, Moscow, in 2004, Barcelona in 2004, London in 2005, and Mumbai in 2008.

The world was hit by two pandemics in the decade with the SARS (Severe Acute Respiratory Syndrome) in 2003 and H1N1 (Swine Flu) epidemic in 2009. A large tsunami produced by a massive earthquake in Sumatra claimed almost 250,000 lives around the Indian Ocean rim in 2004. There were a number of severe tropical Hurricanes and cyclones of which Hurricane Katrina wiped out most of New Orleans, bringing back some focus onto the issue of climate change. Many stories emerged in the media about farming regions struggling with traditional crops like viniculture in Australia, South Africa, and California, while at the same time new regions like Nova Scotia quickly developed wine industries, due to the decline in frosts (Fraser 2007). An Australian CSIRO report put the above concerns to the Australian Government stating that *"...Australia is one of many global regions experiencing significant climate changes as a result of global emissions of greenhouse gases (GHGs) from human activities"* (Preston & Jones 2005, P.5). The report confirms that average temperatures have globally risen over the last 100 years and there are marked declines in precipitation in some regional areas, while increases in others. The report concludes that even though initially there are some benefits of longer day period and shorter winters, with increasing crop yields; rising temperatures, droughts and adverse weather conditions will negate these benefits and become a factor threatening the vitality of agriculture in the future. A more recent report released by the IPCC based on actual measurements rather than projections, establishes that greenhouse gases in the atmosphere are increasing much faster than previously estimated and are already over the threshold that could be potentially dangerous to climate change[80].

The world economy doubled in size during the decade. The United States managed to maintain its place as the world's largest economy and Japan the second largest, but its contribution to the world economy shrank dramatically as the Japanese economy sank into the doldrums. China rose dramatically becoming the third largest economy, having double digit GDP growth during most of the decade[81]. The dramatic improvement of education, a large pool of skilled labour, artificially low exchange rate, and removal of trade barriers has turned China into an export powerhouse. Many companies have outsourced their entire production to China, closing down their production facilities in their home country. As a consequence manufacturing in Japan, Europe, and The United States has declined with the creation of the of *urban prairie* phenomena in traditional industrial strongholds like the city of Detroit in the United States, while at the same time the rapid development of new industrial cities like Shenzhen along the coastal areas of China. Due to the increased demand for energy and mineral resources the Australian, Brazilian, Russian, and United Arab Emirates economies benefited greatly.

The European Union came closer again to becoming one market with the introduction of a common currency, the Euro in 15 countries with the United Kingdom, Denmark, and Sweden opting out. During the debt crisis many European states found it very difficult to manage their respective economies with no control over exchange rates, affecting both budgeting and competitiveness[82]. In 2004 the EU admitted 10 more countries, mainly from Eastern Europe and in 2007, Bulgaria and Romania joined.

Corporate America once again shook peoples' confidence. The well respected Enron energy company was involved in dubious contracts in Central and Latin America and had bribed officials in India to gain a contract. Enron executives with the complicity of Arthur Anderson & Co. formed subsidiary companies to park the losses that Enron had been making, and in 2001 both companies filed for bankruptcy. Two officers of Adelphia were found guilty of siphoning off USD $100 million from the company and the former chairman and chief financial officer of Tyco International were convicted of stealing USD $600 million from the

---

[80] Television Interview, Professor Tim Flannery discusses greenhouse gas levels, Australian Broadcasting Corporation, 8th October 2007, Text of interview at http://www.abc.net.au/lateline/content/2007/s2054168.htm, (accessed 9th October 2007), copy of draft report at http://news.bbc.co.uk/2/shared/bsp/hi/pdfs/17_11_07_ipcc4.pdf, (Accessed 17th November 2007)

81 Figures released at the end of 2010 indicate that China has surpassed Japan as the second largest economy in the world. Japan's GDP was USD $5.474 Trillion and China USD $5.8 Trillion. See: China overtakes Japan as world's second-biggest economy, BBC News Business, 14th February 2011, http://www.bbc.co.uk/news/business-12427321, (accessed 14th February 2011).

[82] See: The future of the euro: Don't do it, the euro is proving horrible costly for some. A break up would even be worse, The Economist, 2nd December 2010, http://www.economist.com/node/17629661, (accessed 25th December 2010).

company. A biopharmaceutical company ImClone was rocked by insider trading charges that put the company's CEO Samuel Waksal and media personality Martha Stewart in jail. In March 2009 the high profile Bernard Madoff was convicted of turning his wealth management scheme into a massive *Ponzi scheme* that defrauded billions of dollars from many high profile clients.

Trust in governments also went down to low levels as the invasion of Iraq had not unveiled any weapons of mass destruction (WMDs), which was the reason given as justification for the invasion in the first place. Many people, including those from outside the United States put almost *messiah like* expectations on Barak Obama's run for the US presidency, as did the Nobel Prize committee, awarding the peace prize to him in 2009. British and Australian parliamentary elections resulted in hung parliaments, perhaps suggesting peoples' skepticism of major political parties in those countries. According to the Edelman Trust Barometer released at Davos at the 2011 World Economic Forum, the level of trust in both business and government institutions in the United States was below 50% and at the bottom of 23 countries measured (Edelman & Flieger 2011).

However while political and business trust waned, the internet was becoming the means for people to get their messages across to others. Even online news had room for readers to make comments at the bottom of articles, so news was becoming two-way. People had turned from downloading music, which was becoming more difficult with the demise of Napstar in 2001 due to legal challenges and participating in the new phenomena social media, beginning with the bulletin boards, chat rooms and blogs that were used to communicate within special interest groups during the later part of the 1990s. Social networking sites had existed but until this decade had very little success, as for some reason people were not yet attracted to them[83]. However, in 2002, Jonathon Abrams and Peter Chin from California wanted to create a safer environment for meeting new people by browsing user profiles, connect to friends, and build up their own networks of acquaintances. When Friendster went live in 2002 it quickly attracted millions of users within the first few months. This rapid success generated the phenomenon of social networking (Rivlin 2006). Frienster today has over 115 million members that are rapidly rising in Asia, but declining in the United States.

Very soon after the launch of Friendster, some eUniverse employees (now called Intermix media Inc.) saw the potential of social networking and emulated Friendster, starting up MySpace which went live in August 2003. Through aggressive recruitment MySpace quickly gained millions of members and became one of the leading social networks by 2006. Other sites that opened up included WAYN an acronym for *where are you now*, that had a goal to unite travelers in 2002, LinkedIn, a business orientated social networking website in 2002, CouchSurfing in 2003, aiming to be a hospitality website, and Tagged founded in 2004, allowing people to play games, share tags and give virtual gifts.

Meanwhile, a childhood prodigy and extraordinarily talented computer programmer Mark Zuckerberg enrolled at Harvard College in 2002. Zuckerberg very quickly gained a reputation for computer programming designing a site CourseMatch which enabled students to select courses based on popularity with the other students. As an amusement, Zuckerberg also created Facemash that let students select the '*hottest*' face among paired female students and

---

[83] Probably exceptions were theGlobe.com founded in 1994 (although declined quickly after 2000) and FriendFinder founded in 1996.

rank them. Within hours of the program going live it jammed the Harvard computer system and Zuckerberg was forced to apologize for using people's pictures without their permission.

Zuckerberg then decided to develop a Facebook for students to list themselves and connect with their friends, as he saw at the time when he developed Facemash that some colleges in Harvard didn't have a student directory. He teamed up with Eduardo Saverin who provided the initial capital to go live from Zuckerberg's dormitory room in February 2004. The response was very good and Zuckerberg started expanding the project to other schools. He moved to Palo Alto California for the summer holidays with Dustin Muskovitz and some other friends and expanded. He met up with Peter Thiel co-founder of PayPal, and Sean Parker, co-founder of Napstar who arranged start-up finance for the venture. Eduardo Saverin went to New York to do an internship and in what appeared as a *coup de grace* was forced to dilute his shareholding, a matter which he sued Zuckerberg over in April 2005. Zuckerberg settled the matter outside of court for an undisclosed amount.

Another controversy around Zuckerberg was his obligation to develop a similar website for two brothers Cameron and Tyler Winklevoss and Divya Norendra called HarvardConnect.com. It was claimed that Zuckerberg stalled on this development to incorporate their ideas into his own site Facebook. The Winklevoss brothers and Norendra issued a lawsuit which Zuckerberg settled out of court.

Today Facebook is the most used social networking site worldwide with over 500 million members and Mark Zuckerberg became the youngest billionaire ever. Although some social networking websites have been capitalized into the billions of dollars, it has taken some sites a number of years to generate a good financial return. Most sites rely upon advertising revenue from third parties like Google. It actually took some of the site founders a period of time before they realized where they could attract revenues.

Two other important sites that were started include You Tube founded in 2005 and Twitter in 2006. There is no doubt that social networking sites have made a social and political contribution. Social networking sites have been utilized very heavily by American politicians during the last few campaigns, and have played a role in peoples' uprisings in Iran, Tunisia, and Egypt. Many companies now utilize social networking websites to keep in contact with consumers and run viral campaigns. Social networking is also a forum where people will use to complain and expose poor products and services.

In addition to the rise of China as a source of manufactured goods, India had been establishing itself as a service outsourcing centre. Originally multinational companies came to India for the domestic market but found that the market was not quite ready for their products (Engardio 2007, P. 81). India had a good education system, a large number of trained professionals, predominately spoke English, and by the mid 1990s the internet was versatile enough to enable new ways of doing business that would provide cost savings for firms in high cost structured countries[84]. This trend began in the early 1980s when a number of European airlines began using New Delhi as a location to undertake administrative tasks cheaply. General Electric followed in the 1990s and was the first to use voice out communications very successfully. Eventually an employee of GE ventured out with a few colleagues and the help of a venture capital firm to create the company Spectramind as a third party business processing operation (BPO).

---

[84] One important advance in the internet that allowed the outsourcing industry to rapidly grow was voice over internet protocol (VOIP) which allowed very cheap telephony communication around the world.

The industry soon expanded to undertaking general IT functions like programming and data storage with firms like Wipro, Tata, Infosys, Infolinx, HCL, and Patni entering the business. American executives could have their assistant in India undertake jobs like drawing up architectural drawings or PowerPoint presentations overnight, ready for the next morning at a fraction of the cost it could be done in their home country.

Today this booming industry is centered in Bangalore, Chennai, Hyderabad, Kolkata, NCR, Mumbai, and Ahmadabad, but as costs are increasing in the major cities, new ventures were dispersing to rural areas. More than 500,000 workers are involved, bringing in more than USD $8 billion to the Indian economy (Ram 2010). Approximately 80% of the world's top 500 companies now have offshore work undertaken in India. Although the 2008 financial crisis slowed the industry down (Bhushan 2008), its growth has put stress on infrastructure, skills availability, and is leading to rapid wage increases in India[85].

This trend has not been without its criticisms. There was a great outrage in Indiana when the local government gave a USD $15 million service contract to Tata, which had to be withdrawn (Engardio 2007, P. 47). There have been fears about the security of data and the loss of jobs to these offshore operations. This represents job migration in the service industry, which is not yet fully understood as multinationals move administrative work offshore. One of the consequences is that there are now little chances that western employees have the same opportunities to gain administrative experience and climb up the company hierarchy as they had been able to do before.

The development of new technologies that allowed the outsourcing of administrative has created a new breed of service companies which is now a competitive industry where it is the quickest and cheapest telecom lines that provide competitive advantage for future competition in this emerging industry. The need for a service company to be located near to the client is no longer applicable. Countries like China[86], Russia[87], Philippines[88], Mexico[89], Uruguay[90] and Vietnam[91] are also entering this industry competitively.

This decade also saw the demise of a century old product and the associated industry that supported it. In 2009 Kodak announced it was discontinuing Kodachrome film production, which represented the death of a technology that had been in use since the 1880s. The technology behind the digital camera was derived basically from the same technology that television images were recorded. Television images were converted to electrical impulses and stored as impulses on magnetic tape (VTR). Image capturing technology was enhanced by Eugene F. Lally of the NASA Jet Propulsion Laboratory who produced a *mosaic photosensor* to assist in guidance and navigation systems (Lally 1961). Texas Instruments patented a filmless camera in 1972 and Sony released the Professional ProMavica MVC-5000 electronic still camera where images were stored on a mini disc and then put into a video reader attached to a television monitor or printer in 1981. Kodak developed in 1985 the world's first pixel

---

[85] See: India's Outsourcing revenue to hit $50 bn, The Financial Express, 29th January 2008, http://www.financialexpress.com/news/indias-outsourcing-revenue-to-hit-50-bn/266661/2, (accessed 14th February 2011).

[86] Focusing on taking work from Japan based in Dalian.

[87] Engineering, particularly aviation engineering.

[88] BPO and voice out.

[89] IT services.

[90] India's Tata Consulting opened branch to support US businesses in same time-zone as India is in the middle of the night.

[91] Software development

sensor capable of recording 1.4 mega-pixels that produced 5 X 7"prints. In the following year a Kodak researcher Dr. Ching W. Tang developed the first multi-layer OLEDs that comprised of self illuminating pixels that did not need background light as LCD displays required. Kodak also released a number of products for recording, storing, manipulating, transmitting, and printing electronically stored images and in 1990 developed a photo CD system. In 1991 Kodak launched its first professional digital camera system (DCS) aimed at photojournalists based on the Nikon F-3 SLR.

In 1990 the Dycam Model 1 could produce black and white shots at a resolution of 320X240 pixels which was able to store 32 images on a 1 MB internal RAM with battery power. In the mid 1990s a series of cameras that could be connected to computers through a cable were released including the Apple QuickTake 100, Kodak DC40, Casio QV-11, Olympus Deltis VC-1100, and the Sony Cyber-Shot digital still cameras. The technology was still poor where film photography was still of superior quality. Kodak collaborated with Microsoft to create digital image software workstations where customers could produce photo CDs and photographs at camera kiosks.

In 1995 Ricoh introduced the first digital camera RDC-1 that could capture moving images and store audio recording. Then in 1997 Hitachi launched the MP-EGI that could transfer pictures to a computer in MPEG format. This technology was closely followed by Sony and Fuji which introduced memory cards. The further improvement of memory storage technology, especially the invention of flash cards enabled more convenient and greater image storage capacity.

The enhancement of digital photography also required printers that could provide quality pictures. In 1997 HP introduced the PhotoSmart Printer that could print on glossy paper limited to a maximum size of 8 X 11" paper. This was followed by Epson but ink and paper costs were still very high putting digital photography at a disadvantage to conventional film based photography. Cannon and Sony produced menu driven software that made digital photography much more user friendly which greatly increased consumer viability of the product.

During 2000-2009 mega-pixel capacities, battery life, memory size, lens quality, software, and printing technologies have greatly improved dramatically until the ease of use, convenience, cost, and quality of digital photography was superior to conventional film photography. "New" companies to the photography industry like Sony, Cannon, Panasonic, Samsung, and LG, were taking advantage of the new technology and provided fierce competition with traditional firms in the industry like Kodak, Nikon, Fuji, and Leica. This in some cases has been at great cost to companies like Kodak in the market place. Although Kodak was given many awards for excellence in innovation, since 2004 the company has been losing billions of dollars and half its workforce, as well as being dropped from the S&P 500 list.

New technologies like the development of active pixel sensors will further improve digital photography and produce lower product costs. With the advance of digital technology traditional camera and film processing stores have almost become redundant and those still in business are trying to adapt to servicing customers within the new digital technology paradigm. There is now a greater emphasis on camera sales through department stores, changing the way cameras are marketed to consumers. Mobile phone manufacturers have aggressively incorporated digital cameras into their phones, and now lenses and mega-pixel capacity is not far away from standard digital cameras, leading to a merging of the mobile phone industry into the digital camera industry.

The decade saw the rise of the fourth generation of modern automobile manufacturers, the first being the US automakers, then the Japanese emergence in the 1960s and 70s, and then the Korean emergence during the 1990s. The fourth Generation consists of Indian manufacturers like Tata Motors and a number of newly created Chinese manufacturers which include BYD, Lifan, Chang'an (Chana), Geely, Cheri, Hafei, Great Wall, Jianghuai (JAC), Roewe, Martin and a number of others.

Tata Motors is part of the Tata Group, the largest privately owned conglomerate in India. Tata began operations in 1945 building locomotives and then in 1954 commenced manufacturing commercial vehicles as a joint venture with Daimler-Benz. Tata entered the passenger car market in 1991 launching the Tata Sierra and a number of other models. In 1998 Tata launched the Indica, the first fully indigenous car built in India which was a great success and now exported to South Africa, the United Kingdom, and Italy. The company acquired Daewoo truck manufacturing operation in 2004, a controlling interest in Aragonese (within Spain) Hispano Carrocera in 2005, formed a joint venture with Marcopolo in Brazil in 2007, acquired British Jaguar land Rover in 2008 and took an 80% stake in Trilix of Italy in 2010. In 2008 Tata launched the Nano, a car priced around USD $2,000 so that more people could afford to purchase an automobile in India. Tata is experimenting with electric cars and compressed air engines. Today Tata has an extremely strong customer based on the Sub-continent and exports to 26 countries with manufacturing plants in the UK, Korea, Spain, Thailand, South Africa, and Argentina. Under franchise Tata cars are also assembled in Russia, Ukraine, Kenya, Bangladesh, and Senegal.

China's auto industry began in the 1950s under the guidance of the Chinese Communist Party Central Committee, with technical assistance from the Soviet Union. From the 1980s to 2000 all of the China's leading automakers were joint ventures with foreign automobile companies. Output was tightly controlled with most production focused on commercial vehicles. As China prospered, vehicle ownership has increased dramatically, where production increased from one million automobiles in 2000 to almost 14 million vehicles in 2009[92] , making China the largest automobile manufacturer in the world (Marr 2009).

Many of the local companies that commenced operations after the 1990s were owned by the Defense Ministry, *Chang'an Motors, Changhe, Hufei Motors,* or provincial authorities, *Brilliance China Auto, Cherry Auto,* and *Chang Feng Automotive.* A few private companies *BYD Auto, Greely Automotive* and *Great Wall Motors* also started up. On the whole Chinese automakers lack the efficiency and quality, but still produce cars much cheaper than manufacturers in other countries. R&D is still low at present with some companies taking inspiration from international models. The state owned Cherry Automobile Co. Ltd. is the largest independent domestic vehicle manufacturer and will be privatized soon. Some of the other major domestic manufacturers *First Automobile Works Group Corporation (FAW), Greely, SAIC,* and *Dong Feng* have built their cars upon platforms provided from international automakers while the rest have been the result been built from knowledge gained through reengineering or just outright copying (Tang 2009, P. 13). Some firms like SAIC and Nanjing Automobile Group acquired MC Rover to access technology and there is a

---

[92] See: Motoring Ahead: More Cars are Sold in China than in America, The Economist, 23rd October 2009, http://www.economist.com/node/14732026?story_id=14732026&fsrc=nwl, (accessed 16th February 2011).

tendency for domestic companies to acquire international brands rather than build them (Jian 2009). The Chinese Government is encouraging domestic automakers to merge so that three or four main domestic players exist in the industry (Tang 2009, P. 14). Due to the economic downturn of 2008 Chinese Automakers had been able to acquire struggling part manufacturers such as the Greely purchase of the Australian Drivetrain Systems International (DSI).

Chinese companies are working on developing electric cars. However costs are still too high for the average Chinese consumer, and there are still many practical problems as most Chinese live in apartments and access to power supplies may be difficult. Nevertheless China is the largest producer of electric cars in the world. One company committed to the development of electric cars is BYD, a Shenzhen based company founded by entrepreneur Wang Chuanfu in 1995 when he was 29 years old[93]. By 2005 BYD was the largest manufacturer of batteries in the world for mobile phones, iPods, digital cameras, and other electronic goods. While he still eats in the company canteen and lives in the company housing block, Wang Chuanfu is now considered one of the richest people in China[94]. Warren Buffet is an investor in BYD.

The idiosyncratic and evangelistic entrepreneur Steve Jobs who co-founded Apple but was deposed as CEO in 1984, made a massive impact upon the computer industry again this decade. After Apple bought out Job's NeXT corporation, Job returned to the tenure of CEO at Apple in 1997. Much of NeXT's technology was used in Apple products including Mac OS X operating system. The company widened its focus away from computers and launched the iPod portable music player, iTunes digital music software, the iTunes stores, Apple TV, consumer electronics stores, and introduced the iPhone, a multi-touch display cell phone which included the features of iPod and was equipped with a mobile browser. The iPhone revolutionized the mobile phone industry, merging it with the computer and internet industry beginning the era of the *cyber cloud*, where Apple became the third largest mobile phone supplier (Chen 2008). In January 2010 Apple launched the iPad, a touch screen tablet using a similar operating system to the iPhone and uses the same apps which are already a billion dollar business for Apple (McLaughlin 2008). Apple was now a company that exceeded Microsoft's capitalization with a capital value of USD $ 222[95]

Steve Jobs is either primary or co-inventor of over 230 patents of computers and other portable devices and the largest shareholder in Disney after Disney's takeover of Job's former company Pixar in 2005. Jobs is seen as a larger than life character whose career has influenced the computer, entertainment, music, and mobile electronic device industries over a 40 year period, iconic of the Silicon Valley culture (Appleyard 2009)- the epitome of how an individual can influence events and the way our society develops.

With the almost replacement of the personal computer by the notebook and the emergence of IPads, consumer book reading is undergoing tremendous change, even though many believed that people would not pay for a e-book when they could buy the physical copy for the same price. But by 2010 e-books designed for Amazon's Kindle had for the first time

---

[93] Wang Chuanfu: Building electric dreams in China, CNN.com/asia, 20th April 2009, http://edition.cnn.com/2009/WORLD/asiapcf/04/20/byd.wangchuanfu/index.html, (accessed 14th February 2011).

[94] See: http://www.forbes.com/lists/2010/10/billionaires-2010_Wang-Chuanfu_39SU.html

[95] See: Apple passes Microsoft to be biggest tech company, BBC News, 27th May, http://www.bbc.co.uk/news/10168684, (accessed 17th February 2011).

surpassed Amazon's sales of hardcovers and was soon about to surpass paperbacks as well[96]. This will again lead to changes in how the book industry will be structured in the near future.

The decade ended with the financial crisis and civil unrest around many parts of the world and some sense of disappointment in political leadership. Commodity prices were beginning to rise, once again bringing concerns about future energy and food crises and terrorist attacks were continuing. China emerged as a superpower and the first signs that China would flex its muscles in the foreign policy and international arena were showing. Currency exchange rates were also beginning to become a major political issue as it had a great impact on terms of trade and competitiveness between countries. The decline of the US currency also undermined it as the major trading currency, but the Euro as well was weak and had its own problems.

Smart-phones and wireless internet enabled many in urban societies to remain connected to the internet on a continual basis. Generation Y was beginning to enter the workforce while many of the baby-boomer generation were beginning to enter retirement age. Although there were leaps and bounds in the advances of medicine, the widening gap between North-South may mean that only the privileged few would benefit for it. This had already been an issue with medicines for the treatment of HIV and related diseases earlier in the decade, threatening respect for patent law. These issues along with climate change would most probably become more important issues as the next decade continued.

The Future

We know many things about what will happen in the future from past events, trends, and the present. We know that it will be extremely likely that the US economy will be surpassed by China as the largest economy in the not too distant future. This will bring in a completely new set of geo-political, military, social, economic, cultural, and business dynamics. We may have some doubt, but *where is the world's fastest train? Where is the world's tallest building? Where is GDP growth fastest? Where are the most cars sold? Which country uses the most cement? Which country uses the most steel?* and *which country has the most engineering graduates?* Compare this to the country which produces mostly arts, sociology, and communications graduates.

We know that industry is relocating to Asia, which is eroding Western tax bases and will also erode standards of living. China and India are catching up and closing the technology gap through education and research and development. It may take a number of years but it will happen. We are not certain that the next person who walks on the moon will be an American.

Post industrial economies are less controllable that people think and cannot be relied upon for continual growth. This is bolstered by the loss of employment due to *offshoring* of work and the West's future maybe similar to Japan's deflationary economy (King 2010). Other authors add that firms in post industrial societies invest in primarily unproductive enterprises and that capitalism in general has lost its creativity (Harvey 2010).

Some of the above is inevitable due to demographics. The population in most post-capitalist societies is generally aging as babyboomers retire. Aggregate incomes will

---

[96] See: Amazon Kindle e-book downloads outsell paperbacks, BBC News, 28th January 2011, http://www.bbc.co.uk/news/business-12305015, (accessed 29th January 2011).

decrease, thus decreasing the standard of living in those countries. As a consequence savings will decrease, as will domestic investment. GDP in the future will be more dependent on exports to the growing economies of China, Asia, and Brazil.

It is generally agreed that by 2050 world population will be around 9 billion, which brings up many issues about consumption, technology, and resource usage. This population increase will mainly occur within Sub-Saharan Africa, India, and Latin America, which will bring questions about the gap between North and South. Population will be expected to fall in China, Eastern Europe, and the former Soviet Bloc countries. Population in 2050 will most probably be more urban and witness the emergence of mega-cities. The UN predicts that by 2025 Tokyo will have 30 million, New Delhi, Sao Paulo, and Mumbai 20 million, with Dhaka, Ciudad de Mexico, New York-Newark, Kolkata, and Shanghai, very close behind[97].

Although we can see many trends concerning the future, predictions about what will happen are extremely difficult as we don't know what crises the world and individual countries will face, and how these crises will be overcome. Any shock that is large enough may put a country or the world on a completely different trajectory, look at Haiti and Japan. This could be a financial accident, a pandemic, an international security crisis (think of Iran and North Korea), or an extreme earth or climate event that may potentially put the world off course. On the other side there may also be technological breakthroughs that may change some aspects of life that we cannot foresee at this point. It is very difficult to always immediately know what the implications of new technologies are on business. For example the internet's influence on British GDP occurred in spurts, rather than linearly and has disrupted some industries but empowered others (Kalapesi 2010).

Predicting the future is difficult and as Bremmer & Keat (2009) point out that back in the 1950s nobody was predicting that the Soviet Union would be transformed into a number of capitalist successor states in the 1990s, or that China would become a capitalist powerhouse. What we certainly don't know is where a new Oprah, Bill Gates, Thomas Edison, John D. Rockefeller, Sam Walton, or Steve Jobs will appear and what they will do. This is the most unpredictable element of the future but also the most important driver of the future.

Some of the issues that will influence opportunity in the future will be;

- Continued volatility of commodity prices, levels of economic activity, employment, aggregate demand, and exchange rates,
- Global warming and the necessary changes to our lifestyles to compensate for the effects. Also the need to find solutions to these emerging problems.
- Declining oil reserves and higher petrochemical prices.
- Water shortages in some regions.
- Food shortages in some regions.
- The emergence of new technologies.
- Higher unemployment in post industrial societies.
- Increasing world population size and changing demographics.
- A likelihood that this generation will not be as financially well off as the last.
- An increase of immigration around the world, and
- Changing political scenarios.

---

[97] United Nations Department of Economic and Social Affairs Population Division, *World Urbanization Prospects: The 2009 Revision,* New York, United nations.

If we draw lessons from the 1974-84 period, we will most likely experience mooted economic growth in post industrial societies which will place pressure on SMEs and make it more difficult for new start-ups[98]. How self employment will be able to compensate for growing loss of jobs due *offshoring* remains to be seen. 2007 also showed us that the capitalist system works well during times of growth and comes under strain during times of retraction. The new green economy may become a big bubble itself with unsatisfactory technologies, rip offs, and a big burst, just like what has happened before with other new technologies. However what we will see are new electric cars with perfected battery technology, the massive leapfrogging of technology by China and India with the west, the development of safer and more compact nuclear technologies like the pebble bed reactor, new ways of diagnosing diseases with *nano*-sensors that roam inside our body, new cures to diseases based on new genome knowledge and biotechnology processes, a move away from the petroleum based economy, and new business models to supply our wants and needs.

The Significance of Time and Space to Opportunity

The world is undergoing convergence which is seen in the way products and industries are developing and merging which each other. These are primarily the products of insight. For example we see computers and mobile phones as one, mobile phones and cameras as one, the merging of line based telephones, the internet and television, insurance coupled with the medical profession, shopping and banking merged through the debit card, airlines, hotels and rental cars, books and computers with the e-book, GPS and telephones, tourism and medicine, tourism and education, tourism and aid, business and foreign aid and the merging of natural therapies and massage, etc.

This also requires convergence in the R&D processes that create new inventions, products and business models. This requires a trans-disciplinary approach where for example being an engineer is not good enough in isolation. In order to create, an engineer must have knowledge across a number of disciplines so that knowledge can be synergized into some meaningful expressions in the form of new applications and inventions. This would normally be triggered by some deep insight that relates trans-disciplinary knowledge with some issues facing society that need to be solved, as is shown in figure 2.11. This creates new knowledge and new knowledge itself is a source of exponential growth of opportunity.

Industries undergo a lifecycle and therefore have a finite existence before dying away or transforming into another industry. Within each stage of a lifecycle there are different forces at work. In the infancy stage, pioneers will see some form of opportunity and exploit it with a start-up. If the pioneer is successful in the marketplace or onlookers spot errors in the pioneering firm's strategy, they may enter the industry and attempt to reap the potential benefits of the newly identified opportunity. During the growth stage there is potential for new firms to enter the market due to the continued growth of the industry. However at some point of time, one or more firms will develop a new source of competitive advantage. This could result from introducing a new technology, gaining control of the distribution channels, creating a new one, or developing some other form of power that pushes away the weaker

---

[98] This is from an aggregate point of view as there will always be individuals starting up new enterprises.

firms from the industry. Through this process the industry will become concentrated leaving little opportunities for new firms. This often happens in the consumer goods industry when major retailers stock only a couple of brands of each product type on their shelves[99].

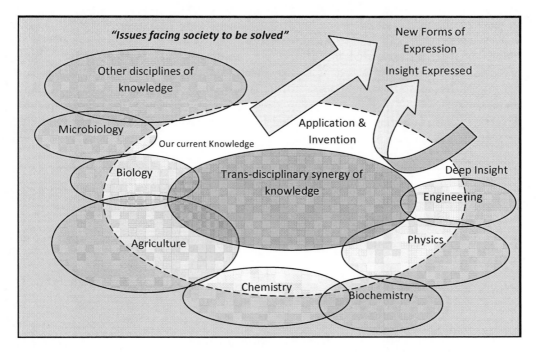

Figure 2.11. Trans-disciplinary knowledge and the expression of new knowledge as application or invention.

However eventually the market will begin to segment and fragment through consumers developing different preferences, desires, and ways they would prefer to acquire the product, *i.e., Amway and Mary Kay Cosmetics exploited this and created completely new channels of distribution served by a different business model.* The astute companies that can see these new potential niches can exploit them as new segments which may initially be too small for other competitors to notice.

New market niches don't just occur, a firm has to recognize the potential for one and create it from the latent demand it sees. An industry may quickly decline with the introduction of a new technology, *i.e., replacement of the typewriter with personal computer,* or very slowly, *i.e., the replacement of safety matches with disposable lighters.* Although the lifecycles of the products may be relatively short, *i.e., digital camera megapixel capacity,* the lifecycle of the general industry will be much longer. However an industry may evolve and sometimes radically change its structure during its lifespan. This can be seen with the auto industry where a number of years ago large models were replaced by small, more fuel

---

[99] Today the modus operandi that chain stores operate under is category management where the products kept on the shelves are only reviewed periodically and kept very limited. In a concentrated market where only a small number of retailers dominate the market, a company not on the retail chains list of products will virtually have no sales and go out of business unless alternative points of distribution can be found. The result of this is that in each supermarket category only 3-6 companies may be active in any product segment.

efficient models and smaller segments like sports cars, 4XD, and MPVs have appeared and disappeared over the years.

When a firm incorporates the features of a product from another industry into their own products, this may merge one industry into another, effectively creating a new industry. For example many mobile phones have digital cameras incorporated into them, contain a MP3 and are connectable to the internet. Flickr statistics show that introduction of cameras in mobile phones has depressed the competitive medium priced camera segment, people preferring to use their mobile phone to take snap pictures or purchase DSLRs which have become much more affordable (Hearn 2010). The offering of new product features across traditional industries is a means of creating a new source of opportunity and gain competitive advantage is also occurring in the internet and computer industries. The industry lifecycle and some of the forces discussed are shown in figure 2.11.

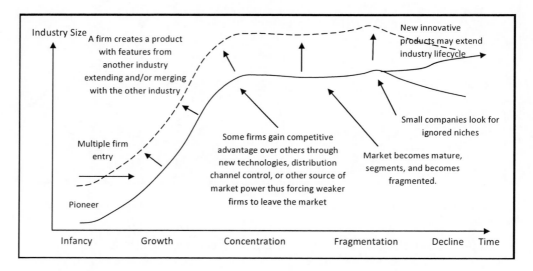

Figure 2.11. A depiction of some forces acting upon each stage of an industry lifecycle.

Opportunities can only be exploited when the relevant technology is available. Any missing piece of technology renders an opportunity just an idea. For example chocolates produced in the desert from goat's milk was just an idea until the packaging technology existed to protect the product from heat and a feasible supply chain existed to transport the items without allowing damage to the product. Al Nassma Chocolates was only able to exploit the opportunity to produce goat's milk chocolates in Dubai when a German firm developed a tight aluminum packaging system with layered ice packs and UPS provided a dedicated route to a runway to enable direct aircraft loading. Paperless customs clearance allowed speedy passing through customs procedures at the destination (Chibber 2010). This example shows the growing importance of logistical chains in developing opportunity concepts.

Opportunity and innovation is a function of a region's underlying factors that support its propensity. Geography plays a central role in terms of the availability and type of expertise existing within a region, peoples' skills and experience, types of industries and support services, existing knowledge and networks of talent. The local industries may also influence what types of education and research is undertaken in the region. The region's own culture will have its own values about what types of things are important, beliefs about risk taking, and self employment, etc. The long legacy of this development will create a level of interest, interrelationships and technical capability for innovation that tends to be clustered in particular areas (Sweeney 1987, Tassey 1991). For example certain areas will tend to specialize in certain activities. Silicon Valley has attracted those involved in electronics, communications, and internet related innovation (Saxenian 1985), and New Jersey has attracted expertise related to drug and medicine development (Feldman & Schreuder 1993).

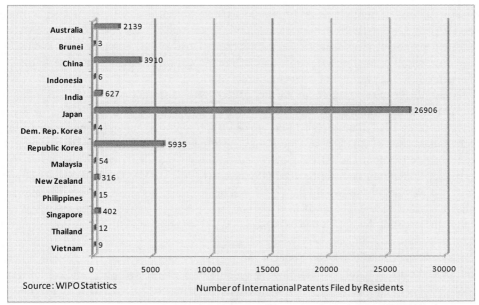

Document originally produced by the World Intellectual Property Organization (WIPO), the owner of the copyright.

Figure 2.12. International Patents Filed by Residents in Asia-Pacific Region 2010.

This phenomenon can be seen at a national level if one looks at the number of resident patents filed per million population in each country. Focusing on the Asia-Pacific region, Figure 2.12. shows the number of resident international patents applied for in the region during 2010. International patent filings are more relevant than domestic patent filings as the international filings figures are a better indicator of the country's international influence in the global business arena. Countries like Japan, Republic of Korea, China and Australia are far in front of the rest of the Asia-Pacific Region. In the Asian Grouping, India had 627 international patent filings during 2010 and Singapore 402. Both countries have invested in R&D very heavily, with India expected to become an industrial giant in the near future and Singapore publically emulating the Korean research model in cluster development, in large investments like the biotechnology Biopolis. Although aggregate filings are low in the rest of the Asian Region, Malaysia stands out with some relative success with its national policies on projects like the Multimedia Super Corridor (MSC) in generating new patent filings. The

Asian region still has a long way to go, however issues like innovation, research and development, and commercialization are on top of the policy agendas at this time.

Schumpeter (1954) argued that economic growth requires innovation – the generation of higher quality products at lower unit costs. The future of regions and nations depend on new ideas and new products that energize those places and facilitate economic growth (Feldman & Florida 1994). Therefore opportunities contribute towards economic growth and economic growth towards opportunities – a circular relationship. Geography plays an important role in this. Innovation is not as much about individual firms, but rather the assembled resources, knowledge, and other inputs and capabilities that agglomerate in specific places, and the innovators either as individuals or firms that exist or are attracted there (Storper & Walker 1989). History (Arthur 1988, 1990), the available resources, networks (DeBresson & Amesse 1992) and the social processes are very important (Dosi 1988). Serendipitous events don't create opportunities in the same way that economic growth, infrastructure, resources, and capacity produce innovation in a particular area.

As has been seen throughout history, there is a distinction between invention and innovation. An invention is the first occurrence of an idea as a physical object or process. Innovation is the first commercialization of the idea. Sometimes invention and innovation are closely linked, but in many cases there may be a period of time separating the two. This period is reflective upon the difference between making a practical demonstration of a theory and creating something that can be used in practice (Rogers 1995). The first powered manned aircraft, the Wright Flyer I would hardly be practical for any commercial purpose and it took another decade to develop aircraft to the point that it could be used commercially. We also saw that an invention without a business model, a way to commercialize it, is not very useful, a fact that Thomas Edison was very well aware of.

Business opportunity usually reflects the period an entrepreneur is surrounded within. Business in the 17th Century would have operated along established trade routes that went to the colonies. Today a new business may consider utilizing the internet or going through the channels of distribution that Wal-Mart and other retailers provide. Inventions and innovations are usually based upon situations and resources that exist in a region the entrepreneur/inventor exists within. Eli Whitney's was living in a cotton producing areas when he invented the cotton gin in Southern states of America in the late 1700s. The invention of packaged goods machinery led to more packaged goods being produced, the automobile brought more automobiles, and the jet engine changed the way we saw the world. It is the ability to break out of current surroundings and invent things that extend what already exists, is where real innovation occurs.

Innovation is not a static, homogenous, or an ordered entity, it occurs at its own pace and has various effects and levels of influence on the surrounding environment (Kline & Rosenberg 1986).Different innovations will have different economic significance. The innovation of micro-credit by Grameen Bank had a different significance than the innovation of incorporating a GPS on top of an electronic map reader, although both innovations are very significant. What is important here is that innovation will have a *flow-on effect*, creating more opportunities for others to exploit. Take for example the development of a resort Hotel along a beautiful piece of a country's coastline, the *flow-on effect* will be evident with the other businesses that are created around it in a cluster (see figure 2.13).

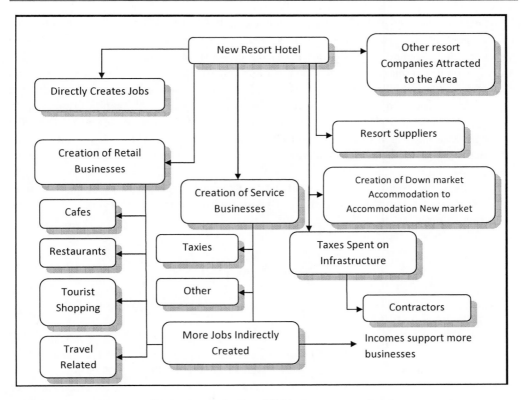

Figure 2.13. The *Flow-on Effect* as the result of establishing a new resort hotel.

CONCLUSION

The recent closing down of 200 Angus & Robertson and 26 Borders Bookstores in Australia (Lloyd & bell 2011) and the boom of online retailing highlights the importance of time and space. It looks that the business model is becoming a much more important factor of success than strategy, as a physical retail outlet is restricted in what business models it can employ, if the firm is committed to physical retailing. Thus one will expect more start-ups and re-creations of firms in the future to redefine and re-align themselves with the new opportunities they perceive based on changing values and costs of resources. Even commodities like sugar in Mauritius are being recreated as a sustainable zero waste crop and rebranded as *'organic sugar'* to meet changing EU consumer values[100].

The highly desirable strategies of today may be losing strategies of tomorrow just as Fletcher Jones, Blockbuster Video, and Bethlehem Steel encountered, leading to their demise. What more we live in uncertainty, as a massive investment of laying down fibre optic cable today for cable TV and internet broadband may be a completely redundant technology tomorrow with a firm that has only invested a fraction of the infrastructure cost is able to dominate the market with a new technology. Due to demographics, regional conditions,

---

[100] Gurib-Fakim, A. (2010) *Sugar Processing in Mauritius – A case Study on Zero Waste,* a powerpoint presentation provided to the author.

incongruities, resource endowments, available technologies and capital, the right competitive environment, a large enough market with sufficient buying power, there is a time and place for everything. Change, as it was defined in the last chapter is a factor of seeing and being able to exploit what has been seen. One must be persuasive to suppliers, investors, staff, and customers to make things happen. Access to capital is critical, as well as being passionate, but not blind, energetic and relentless, prepared to face adversity, with a little bit of ruthlessness. History has also shown that an adequate IP regime was extremely important in fostering the invention and innovation of the 19th and 20th centuries. Knowing what is happening around you, networking, and being competitive with ones rivals were also factors that were present during these times.

To make the analogy, our environment is like an organism going through constant recombination of new and existing ideas, of which the sum of this generates opportunity and our society's progress.

REFERENCES

Ackroyd, J.A.D. (2002). Sir George Cayley, the father of aeronautics, *Notes Rec. R. Soc.*, Vol. 56, No, 2, pp. 161-181.

Appleyard, B. (2009). Steve Jobs: The man who polished Apple, *The Sunday Times, 16th August,* *http://technology.timesonline.co.uk/tol/news/tech_and_web/article6797859. ece?token=null&offset=0&page=1*, (accessed 17th February 2011).

Arthur, W.B. (1988). Urban Systems and Historical Path Dependence, In: Ausubel, J. & Herman, R. (Eds.), *Cities and Their Vital Systems,* Washington, D.C., National Academy Press.

Arthur, W.B. (1990). Silicon Valley Locational Clusters: When Do Increasing returns Imply Monopoly? *Mathematical Social Sciences*, Vol. 19, pp. 235-251.

Backman, M. & Butler, C. (2007). *Big in Asia: 30 Strategies from Business Success,* New York, Palgrave Macmillan.

Baldwin, N. (1995). *Edison: Inventing the Century,* New York, Hyperion.

Bamber, G.J., Gittell, J.H., Kochan, T.A., von Nordenflytch, A. (2009). *Up in the Air: How airlines can improve performance by engaging their employees,* New York, Cornell University Press.

Bhushan, S. (2008). Indian BPOs hit by financial meltdown, *NDTV.com,* 17th October, *http://www.ndtv.com/convergence/ndtv/story.aspx?id=NEWEN20080069056*, (accessed 15th February 2011).

Bienhocker, E.D. (2007). *The Origin of Wealth: Evolution, Complexity, and the Radical Remaking of Economies,* London, Random House.

Blasi, J., Kruse, D., and Bernstein, A. (2003). *In the Company of Owners: The Truth About Stock Options (and why every employee should own them),* New York, Basic Books.

Bloom, D.A. & Canning, D. (2001). Cumulative causality, economic growth, and the demographic transition, In: Birdsall, N., Kelley, A., & Sinding, S. (Eds.)., *Population matters: Demography, Growth, and Poverty in the Developing World,* Oxford, Oxford University press, pp. 165-197.

Bloom, D.A. & Canning, D. (2004). Global demographic change: Dimensions and economic significance, Paper presented to the Federal reserve bank of Kansas City Symposium on *Global Demographic Change: Impacts and Policy Challenges,* Jackson Hole, Wyoming, August 26-28.

Bovard, J. (1994). *The Destruction of American Liberty,* New York, St. Martins.

Bremmer, I. & Keat, P. (2009). *The Fat Tail: the power of political knowledge for strategic investing,* Oxford, Oxford University Press.

Bronstein, Z. (2004). Made in Berkeley: Berkeley's Body Time the Original Body Shop, *The Berkeley Daily Planet,* February 4th, *http://www.berkeleydailyplanet.com/issue/2004-02-03/article/18201?headline=Made-In-Berkeley-Berkeley-s-Body-Time-the-Original-Body-Shop,* (accessed 9th February 2011).

Browning, E.S. (2007). Exorcising the Ghosts of Octobers Past, *The Wall Street Journal,* 15th October, 26667758592.html?mod=mkts_main_news_hs_h, (accessed 10th February 2011).

Bryant, K.L. & Dethloff, H.C. (1990). *A History of American Business, 2nd Edition,* Englewood Cliffs, Prentice-Hall.

Byrne, J. A. (2001). The Real Confessions of Tom Peters: Did *In Search of Excellence* Fake Data? A Magazine suggests it did, *Bloomberg Businessweek,* 3rd December, *http://www.businessweek.com/magazine/content/01_49/b3760040.htm,* (accessed 9th February 2011).

Case, T. (1992). *From the Ground Up,* New York, Belknop Press.

Chandler, A. D. (1962). *Strategy and Structure: Chapters in the History of American Industrial Enterprise,* Cambridge, MA, MIT Press.

Chen, B.X. (2008). Jobs: Apple is Third Largest Handset Supplier, *Wired,* 21st October, *http://www.wired.com/epicenter/2008/10/with-iphone-app/#,* (accessed 17th February 2011).

Chernow, R. (1998). *Titan: The Life of John D. Rockefeller,* New York, Random House.

Chibber, K. (2010). Logistical leaps help small companies go global, *BBC News,* 10th December, *http://www.bbc.co.uk/news/business-11929742,* (accessed 21st January 2010).

Cohen, A. (2003). *The Perfect Store,* Boston, Back Bay Books.

Collier, P. & Horowitz, D. (1987). *The Fords: An American Epic,* New York, Simon & Schuster.

Conn, C.P. (1977). *The Possible Dream: A candid look at Amway,* Grand Rapids, MI, Revell.

Cooke, P. & Morgan, K. (1998). *The Associational Economy: Firms, Regions and Innovation,* Oxford, Oxford University Press.

Crainer, S., (1998), *Key Management Ideas, 3rd Edition,* London, Financial Times.

Creighton, M.S. (1995). *Rites and Passages: The Experience of American Whaling 1830-1870,* Cambridge, Cambridge University Press.

Crouch, T.D. (2003). *The Bishop's Boys: A life of Wilbur and Orville Wright,* New York, W.W. Norton & Company.

Davies, H. (2004). *George Stephenson: The remarkable life of the founder of the railway,* Stroud, Gloucestershire, Sutton Publishing Ltd.

DeBresson, C. & Amesse, F. (1992). Networks of Innovators: A Review and Introduction to the Issues, *Research Policy,* Vol. 20, pp. 363-380.

Dee, R. (2007). *The Man Who Discovered Flight: George Cayley and the First Airplane,* Toronto, McClelland and Stewart.

Dennis, W.J., Fernald, L.W. (2000). The chances of financial success (and loss) from small business ownership, *Entrepreneurship Theory and Practice,* Vol. 26, No. 1, pp. 75-83.

Deutsch, J.G. (1976). *Selling the People's Cadillac: The Edsel and Corporate responsibility,* New Haven, Yale University Press.

Diamond, J. (1997). *Guns, Germs, and Steel: A short history of everybody for the last 13,000 years,* London, Vintage.

Dicke, T. (2010). The Edsel: Forty years as a symbol of Failure, *Journal of Popular Culture,* Vol. 43, No. 3, pp. 486-502.

Diesel, E., Goldbeck, G., & Schildberger, F. (1960). *From Engines to Autos: Five pioneers in engine development and their contributions to the auto industry,* Chicago, Henry Regnery Company.

Dosi, G. (1988). Sources, Procedures, and Microeconomic Effects of Innovation, *Journal of Economic Literature,* Vol. 36, pp. 1120-1171.

Drucker, P.F. (1993). *Post-Capitalist Society*, New York, Harper Business.

Eaton, L. (1998). William Kelly, 92, Founder of Temporary Jobs Company, *Business Day, The New York Times,* 8th January, *http://query.nytimes.com/gst/fullpage.html?res =9802EED61030F93BA35752C0A96E958260*, (accessed 29th January 2011).

Eckerman, I. (2005). *The Bhopal Saga-Causes and Consequences of the World's Largest Industrial Disaster,* New Delhi, India, Universities Press.

Edelman, R. & Flieger, N. (2011). The United States and the Trust Barometer, *Davos Dairies, The Washington Post,* 25th January, *http://voices.washingtonpost.com/davos-diary/2011/01/the_united_states_and_the_trus.html,* (accessed 27th January 2011)

Eglin, R. & Ritchie, B. (1980). *Fly Me, I'M Freddie!,* Worthing, West Sussex, Littlehampton Book Services.

Engardio, P. (2007). *Chindia: How China and India are Revolutionizing Global Business,* New York, McGraw Hill.

Entine, J. (2007). Queen of Green Roddick's 'unfair trade' started when she copied Body Shop Formula.

Essletzbichler, J. & Rigby, D. (2005). Technological Evolution as Creative Destruction of Process Heterogeneity – Evidence from US Plant level Data, *Economic Systems Research,* Vol. 17, pp. 25-45.

Feldma, M.P. & Schreuder, Y. (1993). Pharmaceutical Compound: An Historical Investigation of the Geographic Concentration of the Pharmaceutical Industry in the Mid-Atlantic Region, Working Paper, Hagley Museum and Library, Washington, Delaware.

Feldman, M.P. & Florida, R. (1994). The Geographic Sources of Innovation: Technological Infrastructure and Product Innovation in the United States, *Annals of the Association of American Geographers,* Vol. 84, No. 2, pp. 210-229.

Filion, L. J. (1997). From entrepreneurship to entroprenology, *Journal of Enterprising Culture,* Vol. 16, No. 1, pp. 1-23.

Finkle, T.A. & Deeds, D. (2001). Trends in the market for entrepreneurship faculty during the period 1989-1998, *Journal of Business Venturing,* Vol. 16, No. 6, pp. 613-630.

Ford, H. (in collaboration with S. Crowther) (2008). *My Life and Work,* Akasha Classics

Fraser, S. (2007). Hot properties in vineland: Rising temperatures, cheaper land are starting to lure Ontario grape-growers to the Maritimes, *The Star.com,* 4th October, *http://www.thestar.com/travel/article/263748,* (accessed 6th October 2007).

Friedel, R., Israel, P., & Finn, B. S. (1988). *Edison's Electric Light,* Camden, NJ., Rutgers University Press.

Galbraith, J.K. (1980). *The Nature of Mass Poverty,* Cambridge, Mass, Harvard University Press.

Gates, B. (1995). *The Road Ahead,* New York, Viking Books.

Ghertman, M. & Allen, M. (1982). *An Introduction to the Multinationals,* London, Macmillan Press.

Gibb, A. A. & Ritchie, J. (1982). Understanding the process of starting small businesses, *European Small Business Journal,* Vol. 1, No. 1, pp. 26-46.

Golding, B. (2001). Great divides in learning: youth learning pathways in rural and remote Australian towns, Proceedings of the *ACER Research Conference 2001, Understanding Youth Pathways,* Hilton on the Park, Melbourne, 15-16th October, pp. 13-18, *http://acer.edu.au/documents/RC2001_Proceedings.pdf* (accessed 29th November 2008).

Grabher, G. (1993). The weakness of strong ties – The Lock-In of Regional Development in the Ruhr Area, In: Grabher, G. (Editor), *The Embedded Firm,* London, Routledge, pp. 255-277.

Gras, N.S.B. & Larsen, H. (1939), *Casebook in American Business History,* New York, F.S. Crofts.

Hafner, K. & Lyon, M. (1996). *Where Wizards Stay Up late: The origins of the internet,* New York, Simon & Schuster.

Harford, T. (2006). *The Undercover Economist,* London, Abacus.

Harvey, D. (2010). *The Enigma of Capital: and crises of capitalism,* London, Profile Books.

Hearn, L. (2010). Shuttered: are the camera's days numbered?, *The Age,* 13th December, *http://www.theagecom.au/digital-life/cameras/shuttered-are-the-cameras-days-numbered-20101209-18r5d.html,* (accessed 13th December 2010)

Hopkins, T.D. (1995). A guide to the regulatory landscape, *Jobs & Capital,* Vol. 4, pp. 28-31.

Hudson, S.W. & Ruhen, O. (1977). *Lawrence Hargrave: Explorer, Inventor and Aviation Experimenter,* Cassel, Sydney.

Hunter, M. (1993). The Challenge of South East Asia for the Australian Cosmetic Manufacturer, *Cosmetics, Aerosols & Toiletries in Australia,* Vol. 8, No. 1.

Israel, P. (1998). *Edison: A life of Invention,* New York, John Wiley.

Jakab, P. L. (1997). *Visions of a Flying Machine: The Wright Brothers and the process of invention,* Washington, DC, Smithsonian.

Jian, Y. (2009). Chinese Car Companies Resort to Buying Brands Rather Than Creating Them, *Advertising Age,* 15th July, *http://adage.com/china/article?article_id=137900,* (accessed 16th February 2011).

Kalapesi, C., Willersdorf, S., & Zwillenberg, P. (2010). *The Connected Kingdom: How the Internet is Transforming the U.K. Economy,* Boston, The Boston Consulting Group, Inc.

Khan, Z. (2005). *The Democratization of Invention: Patents and Copyright in American Economic Development,* New York, Cambridge University Press.

King, S. D. (2010). *Losing Control: The Emerging Threats to Western Prosperity,* New Haven, CT., Yale University Press.

Kline, S.J. & Rosenberg, N. (1986). An Overview of Innovation, In: Landau, R. & Rosenberg, N. (Eds.). *The Positive Sum Strategy: Harvesting Technology for Economic Growth,* Washington, D.C. National Academy Press, pp. 275-304.

Kotler, P., Fahey, L. & Jatusripitak, S. (1985). *The New Competition: Meeting the Marketing Challenge from the Far East,* Englewood Cliffs, NJ., Prentice-Hall.

Kujpvich, M. Y. (1970). The refrigerator car and the growth of the American beef industry, *Business History Review,* Vol. 44, pp. 460-482.

Kuratko, D.F. & Welsch, H.P. (2004). *Strategic Entrepreneurial Growth, 2nd Edition,* Mason, Ohio, Thomson South-Western.

Lally, E.F.(1961). Mosaic Guidance for Interplanetary Travel. In: proceedings of *Space Flight Report to the Nation,* New York, American Rocket Society, 9-15th October, pp. 2249-61.

Landier, A. (2006). Entrepreneurship and the stigma of failure, *mimeo,* New York University.

Langewiesche, W. (1944). *Stick and Rudder: An explanation of the art of flying,* New York, McGraw-Hill.

Lawson, C. (1999). Towards a Competence Theory of the Region, *Cambridge Journal of Economics,* Vol. 23, pp. 151-166.

Leavitt, J.A. (1985). *American Women Managers and Administrators,* Westport Conn, Greenwood Publishing.

Levitt, T., (1962), *Innovation in Marketing,* New York, McGraw-Hill.

Loris, R. S. (2003). *A Heritage of Light, Lamps and lighting in the Early Canadian Home,* Toronto, University of Toronto Press.

Lottman, H.R. (2003). *The Michelin Men Driving and Empire,* London, I.B. Tauris.

Lloyd, P. & Bell, L. (2011). Internet spells the death of bookstores, *702 ABC Sydney,* 18th February, *http://www.abc.net.au/local/stories/2011/02/18/3142172.htm,* (accessed 18th February 2011).

McCraw, T.K. (2006). Schumpeter's Business cycles as Business History, *Business History review,* Vol. 80, pp. 231-261.

McLaughlin, K. (2008). Apple's Jobs Gushes Over App Store Success, *CRN,* 11th August, *http://www.crn.com/blogs-op-ed/the-channel-wire/210002313/apples-jobs-gushes-over-app-store-success.htm,* (accessed 17th February 2011).

Maddison, A. (2007). *Contours of the world economy, 1-2030 AD: Essays in Macro-Economic History,* Oxford, Oxford University Press.

Mallaby, S. (2005). Progressive Wal-Mart. Really, *The Washington Post,* 28th November, *http://www.washingtonpost.com/wp-dyn/content/article/2005/11/27/AR2005112700687.html,* (accessed 4th February 2011).

Marr, K. (2009). As Detroit Crumbles, China Emerges as Auto Epicenter, *The Washington Post,* 18th May, *http://www.washingtonpost.com/wp-dyn/content/article/2009/05/17/AR2009051702269.html,* (accessed 15th February 2011).

Martin, R. & Sunley, P. (2006). Path dependence and regional economic evolution, *Journal of Economic Geography,* Vol. 6, pp. 395-437.

Maskell, P. & Malmberg, A. (1999). Localized learning and industrial competitiveness, *Cambridge Journal of Economics,* Vol. 23, pp. 167-185.

Matschoss, C. (1939). *Great Engineers,* Essay Index Reprint Series (reprinted 1979 and translated by Hatfield, H.S.), Freeport, New York.

Maurer, N. (2002). *The Power and the Money. The Mexican Financial System 1876-1932,* Stanford, Stanford University Press.

McCarthy, E. J., (1981) *Basic Marketing: A Managerial Approach, (9th Edition),* Homewood, Illinois, Irwin.

McGuire, J. (1964). *Theories of Business behavior,* Englewood Cliffs, NJ, Prentice Hall.

McGuire, J. (1976). The Small business in Economics and Organization Theory, *Journal of Contemporary Business,* Vol. 5, No. 2, pp. 115-138.

McNamara, C. (2005). The pursuit of happiness, American style: Tom Wolfe's study of status and freedom, *Perspectives on Political Science,* Vol. 34, No. 1, pp. 16-26.

Meier, G.M. (1984). *Leading Issues in Economic Development, Fourth Edition,* New York, Oxford University Press.

Morita, A, Reingold, E.M. & Shimomura, M. (1987), *Made in Japan,* London, Collins.

Mueller, H.G. (1982). The Steel Industry, IN: Finger, M & Willett, T.G. (Eds.). *The Internationalization of the American Economy, The Annals of the American Academy of Political and Social Science,* Vol. 460, pp. 73-82.

Nevins, A. (1953). *Study in Power: John D. Rockefeller, Industrialist and Philanthropist, Vol. 1,* New York, Charles Scribner's Sons.

Newman, P.C. (1981). *The Acquisitors,* Toronto, McClelland and Stewart.

O'Brien, P. Griffiths, T., & Hunt, P. (1991). Political Components of the Industrial Revolution: Parliament and the English Cotton Textile Industry, 1660-1774, *Economic History Review,* Vol. 44, pp. 395-423.

Ohmae, K. (1991). *The Mind of the Strategist: The art of Japanese Business,* New York, McGraw-Hill.

Ouchi, W. G. (1983). *Theory Z: How American Business can meet the Japanese challenge,* New York, Avon Books.

Pascale, R.T. & Athos, A. G. (1982). *The Art of Japanese Management: Applications for American Executives,* New York, Warner Books.

Perez, C. (1983). Structural change and the assimilation of new technologies in the economic and social system, *Futures,* Vol. 15, pp. 357-375.

Perez, C. (1985). Micro-electronics, long waves and world structural change, *World Development,* Vol. 13, pp. 441-463.

Peters, T. and Waterman, R., (1982), *In Search of Excellence,* New York, Harper & Row.

Porter, M.E. (1990). *The Competitive Advantage of Nations,* New York, Free Press.

Prasad, B.K. (2003). *Urban Development: A new perspective,* New Delhi, Sarup & Sons.

Preston, B. L., and Jones, R. N., (2005), Climate Change Impacts on Australia and the Benefits of Early Action to Reduce Global Greenhouse Gas Emissions: A consultancy report for the Australian Business Roundtable on Climate Change, Melbourne, CSIRO.

Pusateri, C.J. (1988). *A History of American Business, 2nd Edition,* Wheeling, Ill., Harlan Davidson Inc.

Ram, C. (2010). India's Next Outsourcing Wave, *Bloomberg Businessweek,* 9th March, *http://www.businessweek.com/globalbiz/content/mar2010/gb2010039_433787.htm,* (accessed 14th February 2011).

Reynolds, P.D., Hay, M., Bygrave, W.D., Camp, A.M., & Autio, E. (2000). *Global Entrepreneurship Monitor, 2002 Executive Report,* Babson College, London Business School, and Ewing Marion Kauffman Foundation, *http://www.gemconsortium.org/ download/1297391076714/GEM%20Global%202000%20report.pdf,* (accessed 11th February 2011).

Reynolds, P.D., Bygrave, W.D., Autio, W.D., Cox, L.W., and Hay, M. (2002). *Global Entrepreneurship Monitor, 2002 Executive Report,* Babson College, London Business School, and Ewing Marion Kauffman Foundation, *http://sites.kauffman.org/pdf/GEM 2002.pdf,* (accessed 11th February 2011).

Rivlin, J. (2006). Wallflower at the Web Party, *The New York Times,* 15th October, *http://www.nytimes.com/2006/10/15/business/yourmoney/15friend.html?_r=2,* (accessed 14th February 2011).

Robinson, J.W. (1997). *Empire of Freedom: The Amway story and what it means to you,* New York, Prima Publishing.

Rogers, E. (1995). *Diffusion of Innovations, 4th Edition,* New York, Free Press.

Rolt, L.T.C. & Allen, J.S., (2007). *The steam engine of Thomas Newcomen,* Ashbourne, Landmark Publishing.

Rostow, W. W. (1960). *The stages of economic growth: A non-communist manifesto,* Cambridge, Cambridge University Press.

Russell, J.T., Verrill, G., & Lane, W.R. (1988). *Kleppner's Advertising Procedure (10th Edition),* New Jersey, Prentice Hall.

Saxenian, A. (1985). Silicon Valley and Route 128: Regional prototypes or Historical Exceptions?, In: Castells, M. (Ed.) *High Technology, Space and Society,* Beverly Hills, Sage, pp. 81-115.

Saxenian, A. (1994). *Regional Advantage: culture and competition in Silicon Valley and Route 128,* Boston, Harvard University Press.

Schonberger, R.J. (1982). *Japanese Management techniques: Nine Hidden lessons in Simplicity,* New York, Free Press.

Schumpeter, J. (1954). *Capitalism, Socialism, and Democracy, 3rd Edition,* New York, Harper & Row.

Schweikart, L. & Doti, L.P. (2010). *American Entrepreneur,* New York, AMACON.

Segall, G. (2001). *John D. Rockefeller: Anointed with Oil,* Oxford, Oxford University Press.

Shane, S. & Venkataraman, S. (2000). The promise of entrepreneurship as a field of research, *Academy of Management Review,* Vol. 25, pp. 217-226.

Sigafoos, R.A. (1984). *Absolutely Positively Overnight!,* New York, New American Library.

Sobel, R. & Sicilia, D.B. (1986). *Entrepreneurs: An American Adventure,* Boston, Houghton-Mifflin.

Sobel, R.S. & Dean, A.M. (2008). Wal-Mart on Self-employment and Small Establishments in the United States, *Economic Inquiry,* Vol. 64, No. 4, pp. 676-695.

Spector, R. (2000). *Amazon.com: Get Big Fast,* new York, HarperBusiness.

Stapleton, D. (1987). *The Transfer of Early industrial technologies to America,* Philadelphia, American Philosophical Society.

Starbuck, A. (1989). *History of the American Whale Industry,* Secaucus, NJ., Castle Books.

Storper, M. & Walker, R. (1989). *The Capitalist Imperative: Territory, Technology, and Industrial Growth,* Oxford, Blackwell.

Studwell, J. (2007). *Asian Godfathers: Money and Power in Hong Kong and Southeast Asia,* New York, Grove Press.

Sweeney, G.P. (1987). *Innovation. Entrepreneurs and Regional Development,* New York, St. Martin's Press.

Swift, L. F. & Van Vlissington, A. (1928). *The Yankee of the Yards: The Biography of Gustavus Franklin Swift,* Chicago, Ill, A.W. Shaw & Company.

Tang, R. (2009). The Rise of China's Auto Industry and its Impact on the U.S. Motor Vehicle Industry, Washington D.C., Congressional Research Service, *http://www.fas.org/sgp/crs/row/R40924.pdf,* (accessed 15th February 2011).

Tassey, G. (1991). The Functions of Technology Infrastructure in a Competitive Economy, *Research Policy,* Vol. 20, pp. 329-343.

Thirlwall, A.P. (1983). *Growth & Development: with special reference to developing economies, Third Edition,* London, MacMillan Press.

Timmons, J.A. & Spinelli, S. (2004). *New Venture Creation: Entrepreneurship for the 21st Century,* Boston, McGraw Hill Irwin.

Tobin, J. (2004). *To Conquer the Air: The Wright Brothers and the Great Race to Flight,* New York, Simon & Schuster.

Van Andel, J. (1998). *An Enterprising Life,* New York, HarperCollins.

Veblen, T. (1899). *The Theory of the Leisure Class: An economic study in the evolution of institutions,* New York, Macmillan.

Wagnleither, R. (1994). *Coca-Colonialization and the Cold War: The Cultural Mission of the United States in Austria after the Second World War,* North Carolina, University of North Carolina Press.

Walton, S. & Huey, J. (1993). *Sam Walton: made in America: My Story,* New York, Bantam Books.

Watanabe, K. (1975). Sub-contracting, industrialization and employment creation, *International labour Review,* Vol. 104, No. 1, pp. 61-79.

Weightman, G. (2007). *The Industrial Revolutionaries: The making of the modern world, 1776-1914,* New York, Grove Press.

White, J.H. Jr., (1995). *The American Freight Car: From Wood-Car Era to the Coming of Steel,* Baltimore, The John Hopkins University Press.

Whyte, W.H. (1956). *The Organization Man,* New York, Simon & Schuster.

Williamson, O.E. (1991). Comparative economic organization: the analysis of discrete structural alternatives, *Administrative Science Quarterly,* Vol. 36, pp. 269-296.

Wilson, K. & Kerr, R. (1996). *Half Luck and half brains: The Kemmons Wilson, Holiday Inn Story,* Nashville, TN, Hambleton Hill Publishing.

Xardel, D. (1993). *The Direct Sellign revolution: Understanding the Growth of the Amway Corporation,* Hoboken, NJ, Blackwell Publishing.

Youngs, W.T. (1993). Bill Gates and Microsoft, In: Youngs, W.T. (Ed.). *American realities: Historical Episodes, Vol. 2, From Reconstruction to the Present, 3rd Ed.,* New York, HarperCollins. Pp. 282-301.

Chapter 3

THE VISION PLATFORM OF OPPORTUNITY

INTRODUCTION

We see people and the world around us but what are we really seeing? Why do we get trapped into our favorite ways of thinking? For opportunity to be seized, someone must recognize it as a viable opportunity. Can I make it? Do I want to make it? Does it fit into my self-view? Does it fit into my intentions? The way we see things and make decisions upon what we see is influenced by our belief structures and cognitive maps (Walsh & Fahey 1986).

This chapter gives a description and explanation of the social, cognitive and psychological processes related perception and decision making so that the influence of cognitive traps and other psycho-distortion processes can be understood and their role in the opportunity process appreciated. This chapter is an attempt to list and give some commentary about the major factors that have some influence over perception, thought and conceptualization. This list covers factors from the fields of anthropology, behavioral and cognitive areas of psychology, philosophy, psychoanalysis, religion, economic geography, political economy, and sociology. Many links and relationships between the various areas discussed and opportunity are only conjectural in most cases as specific research is generally lacking in many of these areas. One factor may heavily influence perception in some cases and have no influence in others. Sometimes factors act individually and at other times in conjunction with one or a number of other factors to influence perception. The chapter is only meant to be a guide to what may be important factors within what the author calls the *vision platform* of opportunity.

PART ONE: THE SOCIOLOGY OF THE VISION PLATFORM

FAMILY AND PEERS

Within the United States nearly 90% of private businesses and 60% of all public companies are family dominated businesses in one form or another (Shanker & Astrachan 2003). Australia, Brazil, Italy, New Zealand and Spain also reflect this. Many well known and Fortune/S&P 500 companies including Marriot, Ford, Walgreens Drugstores, Nordstrom's

Department Stores, Tyson Foods, Mars Candies, Wrigley, SC Johnsons, Coors, Anheuser Busch and Sun Oil were once or still are family dominated companies (Habbershon 2007). Based on this information one would expect the domain of the family to exhort great influence over children. However this is far from the case as parents exhibit only minimal influence over their children in their choices about career and self employment (Kim *et. al.* 2006).

Parental influence tends to follow three distinct stages over their child's development; childhood, adolescence and adult life. The parents influence over the occupational choice of their children generally lessens as their children grow up and are influenced by other factors outside the family environment.

Parents have the most influence over their children during early child hood through both parenting and genetic inheritance. Parents are the only role model to children in early life and during this period where they learn the social role of family and gender[1]. This is where children pick up many of their early values and behavior which are reinforced with some genetic similarities of their parents. The family environment tends to reinforce the genetic traits of children during this time (Shanahan & Hofer 2005).

Values are instilled in children through child rearing practices, interaction with their siblings, the types of activities the family undertakes, the schools that they go to and the peers they have access to. Children become socially conditioned where they start to pick up the values of their socio-economic class. Sons begin to emulate their father's socio-economic values through their early childhood socialization, which may lead to the child aspiring to having the same social position in the future (Lichtenstein *et. al.* 1995). Parents who have high self directive occupations like lawyers, doctors, or university lecturers may install values of high self direction into their children, whereas parents with low self directive occupations like transport drivers and process workers may install the values of conformity into their children (Kohn *et. al.* 1986). Middle class children may develop a greater sense of entitlement giving them self-confidence to mobilize resources where working class children may like the autonomy they have in childhood and seek occupational autonomy in adult life (Lareau 2002).

During childhood parents play a moderately significant role in influencing specific vocational and occupational choices in their children (Barak, Feldman & Noy 1991). This influence is very strong where the family is immersed within the vocational domain of a farm or a solo country doctor's practice. However these types of professions are declining rapidly (Aldrich & Kim 2007). During childhood children are heavily influenced by fantasy and may develop aspirations for *'fantasy occupations'* like an astronaut, fireman, oceanographer, pilot, train driver or policeman, rather than wanting to directly mirror their father's occupation.

During adolescence children move into their teenage years with very general vocational interests and expectations, having shed their childhood *'fantasy occupations'*. They are in awe of the range of possibilities as teenagers become exposed to teachers, friends, parents of friends, relatives and other people they meet along the road of their upbringing. The blending of their personality traits with the stimulation from the environment and discovery of their own self identity opens up new vocational possibilities and closes others. Only a small number of high school students actively seek information about potential career paths by

---

[1] In early life individuals may select their parents, brothers, sisters or other relatives as role models. They may with exposure also look to other outside people such as sportspeople as inspirational figures.

seeking information or joining in appropriate activities, even though almost all teenagers will have vocational aspirations when asked (Schneider & Stevenson 2002). Teenagers who perceive their families as supportive and having high expectations of them, have higher occupational aspirations (Whiston & Keller 2004). If the father has a prestige occupation, sons may aspire to the same, or if not something with similar prestige (Mortimer 1974, 1976).

Only a minority of children of self-employed parents begin working in the family business at a young age. The children's time in the family business is usually very short, where they tend to leave for other jobs before they are 21 years old (Aldrich & Kim 2007). Exposure to entrepreneurship within the family may not be enough for a child to learn the tacit knowledge necessary to be successfully self employed (Aldrich *et. al.* 1998).

Parental influence on career choices by the adolescence years depends upon how their children perceive their parents occupations, which can be either a positive or negative influence (Mortimer 1976).

Research shows that parents and family have little influence on adult children in their career choices, once they reach adulthood (Aldrich & Kim 2007). After adolescence an adult has too many influences upon them. Work experience builds upon what they learnt from their parents, and the number of years of managerial experience is probably more important an influence on a person to enter self-employment to exploit perceived opportunities (Kim *et. al.* 2006).

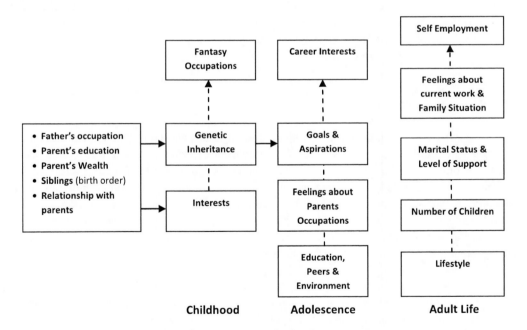

Figure 3.1. The probable influences of parents and family upon their children's career choices.

Adults tend to get advice from professional experts in particular areas like lawyers and accountants, etc. (Renzulli *et. al.* 2000)[2]. Parental assistance to children tends to be restricted

---

[2] The parents may still play a strong moral support role during a person's life and career. Individuals will select the person they feel closest to, empathize with and feel comfortable discussing things with, whether a parent, sibling, partner or friend.

to providing loans and gifts to children for start-up capital and providing moral support and advice. If children are in the same industry as their parents, then parental advice may save the expense and time of undergoing trial and error during the start-up phase of the business (Sorensen 2006). However the majority of children enter different industries than their parents, so previous work experience in similar businesses before they start their own is likely to be more valuable (Fairlie & Robb 2005). Decisions about career and the potential of self-employment opportunities will in adulthood depend more upon the person's chosen lifestyle, the number of children and potential risks and opportunity costs of career or self-employment, marital status and support, particularly to female entrepreneurs (Hisrich & Brush 1983). Figure 3.1. shows the probable influences of parents and family upon their children's career choices.

The family, particularly the father and mother play a powerful role in establishing the desirability and credibility of entrepreneurial action for the child (Shapero & Sokol 1982). However, this does not explain why individuals tend not to follow their parents career as one child may consider entrepreneurship as an exciting career option while another may feel that this direction is only for people who cannot get a regular job (Katz 1992). Therefore family background, although having great influence on a person's attitudes and behaviour can only provide us with a very limited insight into what shapes a person's aspirations and desires.

There is a tendency for people to seek out the advice of others particularly in the research stage before making a decision or commitment. This can be seen as a mechanism utilized to gain confidence about making a certain move or decision. However too many people delude themselves and listen only to what they want to believe and may avoid seeking advice from people they feel will not agree with them.

Domicile Outlook

Domicile outlook can be defined as the beliefs, attitudes and views one develops from the position where they live and social status. The concept of brings together factors like social status, income, location, state of employment and immigrant status. Together these factors contribute to a person's basic beliefs and attitudes and outlook towards opportunity and their potential to exploit it. Domicile outlook is closely related to social status. Social status is itself a multidimensional concept made up of numerous factors including education, occupation, sex, marital status, area of residence and family (Hollingshead 1975). Social status has a strong influence in creating domicile outlooks and domicile outlooks play a role in creating social status.

Social status can enhance or hinder a person's ability to exploit opportunities. It is generally postulated that social status will increase a person's likelihood of exploiting entrepreneurial opportunity by the position they are in to convince others of the value of an opportunity, gather resources and organize (Shane 2003, P. 92). According to research, social status increases a person's power of persuasion (Stuart *et. al.* 1999). For example inventors with high university rank in Britain are statistically more likely to be involved in start-ups than lower ranked university scientists (Shane and Khurana 2001). Once again in Britain, people of higher social classes were more likely to become self employed (Dolton & Makepeace 1990).

Social status is an important source and determinant of the level of empowerment a person feels they have. Social status also determines how others perceive you and how you connect and interrelate with others. Research shows that 50% of jobs are filled through informal social channels by connections of family, neighbors, and other friends, etc, showing the influence of social status on our lives (Granovetter 1985).

People who become unemployed change their social status, *i.e., how they perceive themselves and how others perceive them.* For example, unemployment brings a change in a person's circumstances which often forces consideration of alternatives that would not normally be considered. As the opportunity cost of self employment decreases (i.e., there are few if any employment options), looking for an opportunity and turning to self-employment becomes more likely (Mesch & Czamanski 1997). The probability of taking the self-employment option during times of unemployment increases with time (Evans & Leighton 1989), unless unemployment benefits keep the opportunity cost of self employment high (Eisenhauer 1995, Alba-Ramirez 1994).

Migrants with language and cultural unfamiliarity seem to be able to undertake the transition through poverty that local indigenous minorities may be locked within (Portes & Min Zhou 1992). Immigrant groups fleeing from wars, political and religious persecutions have been able to transform the economies of the countries they have settled in, such as the Cubans in Florida, displaced colonialists in Morocco, Tunisia and Algiers, East Germans in West Germany, and Koreans and Vietnamese in the US (Krueger 2002, P. 100). Local minority groups may not have the skills that and capital that immigrants have or accumulate and therefore face barriers to self employment. Minority groups with little social capital are consequently restricted to self employment pursuits that require little start-up capital in marginal enterprises (Boyd 2007). Some migrant groups may be aided by the existence of their own communities with their own concepts of social status. These communities may be large enough to start community specific businesses like newspapers, restaurants, and car dealers, etc (Wilson & Martin 1982).

The advantages of social status can be seen where the children of self-employed also have a tendency to become self-employed themselves, either through their family business or their own start-up (Dunn & Holtz-Eakin 2000). Children of self-employed may observe their parents use tacit skills required for any enterprise start-up and carry goodwill through their family name. Likewise people with high education and a relatively high net worth are most likely to engage in self employment to exploit an opportunity (Bates 1995).

A person's locality has great impact upon the continuum of opportunities available to them. This continuum is widened or narrowed by their social status, skills, access to capital and market access within the area they reside.

Urban areas are usually a large source of opportunity due to the high concentration of people, the high consumption nature of the population, the need for income to survive in the consumption oriented society and the diversity of needs and wants within the metropolitan area. An urban market contributes to potential economies of scale due to close proximity of the business to consumers. The larger the urban area, the greater the scale of opportunities exist. An urban environment attracts increasing human habitation requiring infrastructure, housing, food, waste disposal systems, transport, communications, employment, and governing mechanisms. Although viewing an urban area as an ecosystem maybe radical (McDonnell & Pickett 1990), it operates as a human driven system where opportunity is created out of the need to solve urban generated problems, *i.e., needs for housing, transport, consumption, employment and commerce.* Social status will effect to some degree the level and scale of opportunities a person is able to realistically contemplate and exploit.

Massive structural changes are occurring in urban areas around the world, changing domicile outlooks. In the industrial countries most craft based and manufacturing industry has exited inner suburban areas where they once thrived. Some areas have made way for trendy inner city living lifestyles where service businesses like launderettes, coffee shops, delicatessens and other specialty service businesses have taken over to capitalize on lifestyle demand. In urban areas that have lost the very industries that once drove urban growth, unemployment, poverty and even destitution are left behind (Guarino 2010). Spurred on by the housing crisis in 2009, now 47.6 Million Americans or 1 in 6 people in the United States are now in poverty according to the US Census Bureau (Muir & Bass 2009). Many of the unemployed are in their 50s with obsolete skills competing with those very much younger for the few jobs now available.

In contrast, cities in Asia are rapidly growing in a similar fashion as the industrial cities of the west did in the 1960-70s. This is particularly the case along coastal China, Bangkok, Kuala Lumpur, Jakarta and a number of cities in India. Manufacturing industries bring with them new middle classes and opportunities for business ventures that are needed to satisfy the needs and wants of these emerging classes.

Opportunity in rural areas is influenced by a number of factors, which are summarized below;

1. Geography is one of the most important determinants of opportunity. Topographical features and the transport and communications infrastructure will determine the cost structure of operating a business in any particular area. Isolated areas are basically inaccessible by road and other transport and may not have mobile phone coverage. The population within an isolated area may not have access to much education above primary school and tend to be isolated from knowledge and technology. Any products and inputs for a potential business will be relatively expensive (Maleck 1994). Markets will be extremely small with not enough population to promote any economies of scale. Remote areas are disadvantaged to a lesser degree than isolated areas. Remote areas have access to populated areas through roads and communications. Still the costs of doing business may be significantly higher than in urban areas, but opportunities may exist for higher value contributing businesses in these areas. General access to capital in both isolated and remote areas will usually be very limited or non-existent. Areas adjacent to urban populations provide access to large markets where operational costs may be competitive to urban based businesses. Adjacent rural areas over time may be eaten up by the growing urban sprawl.
2. The scenic aspects of geography provide potential for tourism. Areas where tourism exists may have a wide spread of opportunities for local entrepreneurs to exploit.
3. Transport is critical for opportunities, potential markets and the cost of exploiting them. Transport infrastructure is vital for the wellbeing of a community. The establishment of transport infrastructure like a high grade road, rail or air link may dramatically increase opportunities. Likewise the diversion of vital road arteries away from major towns has a dramatic effect on the wellbeing of local communities that traditionally supported travelers. Road diversion can usually have a devastating

effect on local economies. On a national scale, international transport links will partially determine a country's international competitiveness.

4. Basic infrastructure like utilities, health and education services influence a region's desirability for settlement. Without basic facilities an area will not be attractive for general settlement, leaving it unpopulated and lacking in potential income earning opportunities. Such areas will be both socially and economically isolated from the rest of the region.

5. Over the last two decades land governance issues has affected the economic viability of land. Government authorities in countries like Australia charge resource rents through water charges to farmers. Farms are also given water allocations which they must pay for. This together with drought has changed the viability of producing crops on the land. In many developing countries land issues are governed by customary law and inheritance. As families of the last generation tended to be large, family parcels of land have been divided up to the point of being uneconomic to work. This has created much idle land in some countries where reform of these customary laws is required to enable farmers to access economic plots of land. Land around the world has generally degraded through salinity, erosion of top soils and the effects of climate change, changing the set of crop options to open to farmers.

Many rural areas around the world are in crisis. Australia has been hit by a long drought which is slowly grinding rural communities to a halt. With tightening credit, many rural families are being forced off the land. Chronic shortages of labour are affecting harvests and production. The inequality of educational pathways between rural and urban youth will potentially inhibit the ability of today's rural youth to scan the environment for opportunities and exploit them in the next generation (Golding 2001).

In countries like Papua New Guinea, economic and social inequality is increasing between the rural and urban population. Rural population has fewer opportunities from limited economic activity in their regions. Their disadvantages are caused by remoteness from urban markets, the high cost and deterioration of transport services, poor access to services, lack of private and government investment and environmental pressure on the eco-system due to illegal activities such as logging. In Papua New Guinea nearly half the people living in rural areas live under the poverty line (Baxtor 2001).

Through South-East Asia, rural areas are facing similar problems. Many rural areas lag behind in national development, unable to benefit from the high levels of growth in the region. Some countries are focusing on building infrastructure in urban areas due to the very rapid urban population growth at the expense of rural areas. Lack of rural investment is leading to higher rural unemployment rates where a large percentage of rural youth population is leaving for the cities in search of job opportunities (Hunter 2006). This leaves an aging farmer population in rural areas with low education levels, resources and capital. In some parts of the region there is a feeling of powerlessness, with a lack of ideas, opportunities and matching skills, so very few are willing and able to embark upon new business ventures, due to a general feeling of hopelessness and despair (Hunter 2008).

Communities in isolated and remote locations may have adequate food and housing to survive and live a relatively comfortable life of which they have known for generations. Some of the younger people from these isolated communities may go outside and work so they can remit funds back to their families for buying of staple goods, so there is no financial poverty.

However these conditions create a *poverty of opportunity* where isolation and lack of market access deprives them from making a sustainable livelihood. The *poverty of opportunity* is a situation which prevents a community from leading productive and satisfying lives. Due to the sparse population any business without outside markets will not be economical or even able to survive (Tafuna'I 2002). More often than not these communities are also subject to external threats such as logging and rising sea levels along coastal areas and islands.

Poverty is a major barrier to opportunity in a number of ways. Poverty is characterized by lack of capital, financial, physical and human, capital depreciation, through over fishing, over harvesting and over logging, etc. Land in rural areas is derogated through loss of top soil and nutrients, lacking any infrastructure for irrigation during dry seasons. Communities may be isolated through almost inaccessible mountain ranges, poor roads and high transport costs. Often communities may have social customs which create barriers and blocks to advancement, like views on women's role in society, etc. This may be aggravated with high fertility rates. However the single most important hindrance to getting out of what Jeffrey Sachs (2005, P. 62) calls the *poverty trap* is the ability to be creative and innovative, so opportunities can be constructed or discovered.

The concept of domicile outlook is shown in figure 3.2.

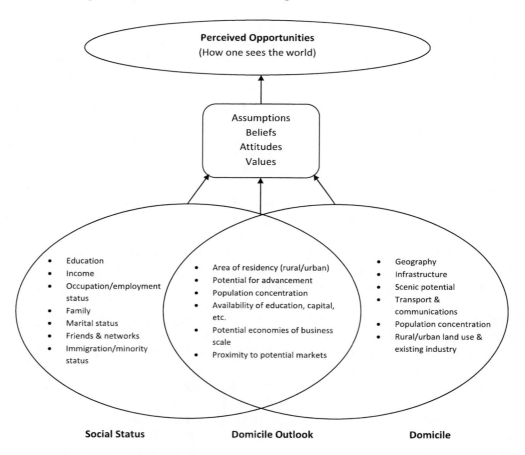

Figure 3.2. The Concept of Domicile Outlook.

However opportunities exist within the lowest income earning communities around the world as a market and a source of production. Some of the world's largest companies have developed new and innovative ways to develop markets within the bottom income strata of society. For example Kao Philippines many decades ago developed shampoo in the form of a powder sold in satchels for daily use through *'moms and pops'* stores throughout the archipelago. Likewise Indonesian detergent manufacturers developed low cost crème detergent for laundry and dish washing that was affordable by the poorest communities in Indonesia. Hindustan lever has followed the lead of their local competitor Nirma in India with low cost detergent that could be used on a daily basis (Prahalad and Hart 2002).

Further, the advent of micro-credit has enabled increased consumption by the poor of things they would not normally be able to purchase. CEMEX a transnational cement company based in Mexico, found a novel method of accessing low-income customers by sending their sales representatives into villages to sell material packages with small monthly repayments to build home extensions, that would otherwise take years to complete without micro-credit. In Mexico, once children are married they stay at home according to tradition. CEMEX through encouraging the formation of savings clubs and offering materials packages *(Patrimonio Hoy)* with micro-credit has enabled families that normally couldn't afford home extensions undertake them. Grameen Bank was formed to service the poor using a *"peer lending model"* that other banks could not consider because of the small loan size, need for collateral and contractual enforcement. This success led to the formation of Grameen Telecom which offers a village phone service in Bangladesh.

In Thailand, a number of companies manufacture and distribute ingredients for simple street stall dishes like noodles. To make it easier for a street stall vendor to start-up, the companies supply everything including the physical stall itself. This innovation in Asian street stall food has gone so well that most street stall foods in Thailand now carry franchised brand names, which give consumers the confidence in the quality and taste they will get. New innovations like selling products in kit form to create new cost structures, decentralizing and miniaturizing production, using micro-credit, developing new channels through new alliances will enable the creation of new markets that were not there before among the poor.

Creating small decentralized production within communities of the poor of the world was a vision of E. F. Schumacher (1973) in his seminal book *Small is Beautiful*. Production is being broken down into nodal production units, saving on tremendous capital costs (Prahalad 2004, P. 16). For example, Nestle collects dairy milk from individual smallholders to produce their milk products in India, thus saving on investment in their own large dairy farm estates and Jaipur Rugs has 40,000 contract workers weaving at home producing their carpets.

Building new supply and value chains is the key to empowering the poor in remote locations to potential markets. For example, the 'One Tambon One Product'[3] program in Thailand was initiated nationwide by the government in 2001. Products are selected for promotion on the basis of their quality and export potential and include food items, textiles, woven handicrafts, and non-edible herbal products, etc. The project is supervised by a national OTOP committee with regional and provincial level committees. The local committees help not only to identify potential products but also provide advice on production (e.g. quality control, packaging and designs that make them attractive to domestic and/or export markets).

---

[3] Village sub-district.

The original objective of "One Tambon One product *(OTOP)*" project was to enhance social protection through;

1. A social protection and risk management system with participation from the private sector and the people,
2. The sustainability of local handicraft products, social protection and skill development, changes of livelihood and coping strategy in relations to the OTOP project,
3. Collaboration modules among public agencies (Ministry of Labour, Ministry of Social Development and Human Security, Ministry of Commerce, Ministry of Industry) and local government organizations for expanding social protection to informal workers,
4. Culture: role of producers, consumers and modes exchange Best practices in area-based sufficiency economy, e.g. provincial development or provincial cluster development, and sufficiency economy index/indicators,
5. Survey of the application of sufficiency economy in various sectors, e.g. agriculture, industry, and
6. tourism, etc., and possibility for expansion in different areas, sectors
7. Fiscal and financial measures to promote green and clean products and technology, and
8. Marketing strategies/plans to promote green and clean products and technology.

The Thailand OTOP program is based on the Japanese *"One Village One Product Movement (OVOP)"*. The OVOP movement started 1979 in Oita Japan as a means to promote regional revitalization and autonomy. Each community identified one or more products or industry that was locally specific and distinct. Resources were then concentrated on the production of these products, establishing them as local brands, and marketing them to the entire country or beyond. The program is based on the following principles: 1) Local yet global –the development of globally accepted products that reflect pride in the local culture; 2) Self-reliance and creativity; and 3) Human resource development – Rewarding creativity and industry. Villagers found that their local products turned into national brands, which encouraged interest in their local traditions and products – leading at times to an increase in tourism. Publicized through mass media, research and guidance facilities were established to provide technical support to varying industries; a sales and distribution mechanism for OVOP products was organized, and education and training was offered to industrial and regional leaders. A reward system was also set up for those who successfully implemented the program.

OTOP Thailand is an umbrella concept where multiple programs are combined to enhance product development, skill, technology and marketing through exhibitions, local, regional and international development. OTOP uses a multiple channel strategy framework, utilizing;

1. Regional Retail Outlets,
2. Retail outlets in Tourist precincts,
3. Exhibitions (regional, domestic and international),
4. Roadshows (domestic and international),

5. Internet Marketing,
6. Catalogue marketing,
7. Permanent central exhibition centre in Bangkok,
8. Through hypermarkets like MAKRO, Carrefour[4], Tops and Tesco,
9. Direct marketing organization, and
10. International OTOP trade offices.

OTOP now covers all product areas including handicrafts, cosmetics, herbs, essential oils, foods, beverages, wine, produce, textiles and clothing, and many other categories. The OTOP program is now in its third strategy phase of developing international markets and is making agreements with international companies and department stores to carry OTOP products in Europe and Japan (MCOT 2006).

The Fair-trade movement is a trading partnership based on community dialogue, transparency and mutual respect that seeks to develop trade along an equal and equitable partnership. Fair-trade also strives to contribute to sustainable community development through the improvement of trade conditions. Fair-trade was originally developed through religious groups and NGOs work in developing countries to open up trade links with more equity. The formal Fair-trade movement grew out the 1960s student and activist movements against neo-colonial and multinational companies, where the concept of *"trade not aid"* gained acceptance. Handicrafts during the 1960s were sold through OXFAM stores in the United Kingdom, and eventually volunteer shops opened throughout the rest of Western Europe, and later the United States selling products from the Third World.

During the 1980s the Alternative Trading Organisations (ATO) was formed and widened their scope from handicrafts to focus on the wider issues of commodity trade from South to North. This led to the sale of tea, coffee, fruits, cocoa, sugar, spices, and nuts. Fair-trade also widened its retail scope around Europe and the United States to achieve more than USD 3.6 Billion sales in 2007, increasing at the rate of almost 50% each year[5]. This is still only a very small proportion of total World trade, but according to the Fair Trade 2007 annual report, sales in specific traded product categories represented between 1.0 to 20.0% of total trade in that item in Europe and the United States[6].

The basic principles of the Fair-trade movement are;

- The sharing of a common vision where justice and sustainable development are the basis of trade structures and practices, so that everybody can enjoy a dignified life and develop their full potential,
- That Fair-trade will be a fundamental driver of poverty reduction and contribute to sustainable development, by connecting those in the South who most need change with citizens of the North who seek greater sustainability and justice,

This will be achieved through;

---

[4] Now known as Big C Extra.
[5]   See: http://www.fairtrade.net/single_view.html?&cHash=ec8730e426&txttnews[backPid]=168&tx_ttnews[tt_news]=41, (accessed 23rd September 2008)
[6] See: An Inspiration for Change: Annual Report 2007, Bonn, Fairtrade Labelling Organizations International, 2008, P. 11., http://www.fairtrade.net/uploads/media/FLO_AR2007_low_res_01.pdf, (accessed 24th September 2008)

- Gaining market access for those excluded from the mainstream and value-added markets or those with only access to them through lengthy and inefficient trading chains.
- Encourages the use of traditional forms of production so that social benefits can come back to the community.
- Helps to shorten the trade chain so that more funds will come back to the producers of primary goods, where the basis of the transactions takes account of the costs of production, both direct and indirect, including the safeguarding of natural resources and meeting future investment needs, and
- To assist producers connect with the consumer, so producers can learn concepts of social justice and opportunities for change[7].

The Fair-trade system provides two prices to the producer. The first is the Fair-trade Minimum Price which is a guaranteed price that covers the direct and indirect costs of sustainable production, which moves up and down according to the market. The second price is the Fair-trade Premium which is a separate payment for social and economic development in the producer's community.

In 1988 a Fair-trade certification initiative was developed so Fair-trade products could be sold through wider distribution channels. This led to the formation of the Faired Labelling Organizations International (FLO), an umbrella organisation responsible for the setting of Fair-trade standards, support and certification of producers[8]. The first trademark system identified to people products that met agreed environmental, labour and development standards was launched in 2002 under the authority of FLO-CERT. FLO-CERT is a certification body responsible for inspecting the producers and traders, licensing them with authority to use the trademark.

Fair-trade standards specify the requirements producers must meet to be certified. These standards specify the improvements that producers must make each year. Two basic standards exist, one for small farmers' organisations and another for hired labour situations. Small farmer organisation standards specify democratic decision making systems and how Fair-trade premiums are invested in the community, as well as requirements for capacity building on both an individual and organisational basis. Standards for hired labour specify that workers receive decent wages and enjoy the freedom to join unions and bargain collectively. Plantations must ensure that there is no forced child labour and occupational health and safety requirements are met. Standards also require that a joint worker-management committee is set up and that premiums be spent to the benefit of plantation workers.

Fair-trade marks are now issued for coffee, tea, rice, bananas, mangoes, cocoa, cotton, sugar, honey, fruit juices, nuts, fresh fruits, dried fruits, canned fruits, quinoa, chutney, muesli, biscuits, jams, sauces, herbs and spices, cakes, wine, beer, cosmetics, baby-food, cotton products, yoghurt, and footballs, etc., sold through department stores, supermarkets and convenience stores in around 50 countries.

Although some communities have benefitted by the innovations described above, there are so many other communities that suffer from relative and absolute poverty and the *poverty*

---

[7] http://activistnotes.wordpress.com/2008/06/06/a-draft-charter-of-fair-trade-principles-   flo-and-ifat/, (accessed 25th September 2008)
[8] See: http://www.fairtrade.net/

of opportunity. Table 3.1. shows the number of people and percentage of total population living in rural areas and officially in poverty according to various country measurements of poverty in a number of selected countries.

Table 3.1. Summary of Rural Population and Poverty Levels in Selected Countries[9]

Country	Rural Population	%	Population in Poverty	%
Argentina	3,273,086	8.0%	12,274,075	30.0%
Australia	2,338,890	11.0%	-	-
Austria	2,627,289	33.0%	484,405	5.9%
Azerbaijan	3,954,562	48.0%	1,977,281	24.0%
Bangladesh	120,159,179	77.0%	56,646,470	36.3%
Belarus	2,219,162	22.0%	2,614,752	27.1%
Belgium	312,430	3.0%	1,582,979	15.2%
Bolivia	3,323,583	34.0%	5,965,147	60.0%
Bosnia and Herzegovina	2,445,109	53.0%	1,153,353	25.0%
Botswana	796,350	40.0%	601,244	30.2%
Brazil	27,823,497	14%	51,672,209	26.0%
Bulgaria	5,115,327	71.0%	1,015,860	14.1%
Burma	32,252,286	67.0%	15,741,041	32.7%
Burundi	8,560,197	90.0%	6,467,704	68.0%
Cambodia	12,754,977	88.0%	5,073,002	35.0%
Cameroon	8,684,478	46,0%	9,062,064	48.0%
Canada	6,697,441	20.0%	3,616,618	10.8%
Chad	8,572,412	83.0%	8,262,566	80.0%
Chile	1,992,204	12.0%	3,021,510	18.2%
China	763,009,391	57.0%	37,481,163	2.80%
Columbia	11,356,116	26.0%	21,489,267	49.2%
Congo, DR	45,337,077	66.0%	-	-
Cuba	2,748,396	24.0%	-	-
Czech Republic	2,757,214	27.0%	-	-
Dominican Republic	2,991,516	31.0%	4,0723,322	42.2%
Ecuador	4,954,854	34.0%	5,566,924	38.3%
Egypt	44,953,981	57.0%	15,773,327	20.0%
Ethiopia	70,746,990	83.0%	32,986,849	38.7%
France	21,779,649	34.0%	3,971,583	6.2%
Germany	27,992,117	34.0%	9,056,273	11.0%
Ghana	11,943,906	50.0%	6,808,026	28.5%
Greece	4,187,596	39.0%	-	-
Guinea	6,638,263	66.0%	4,727,248	47.0%
Hungary	3,169,790	32.0%	851,881	8.6%
India	821,397,413	71.0%	289,224,441	25.0%
Indonesia	115,330,330	48.0%	42,768,330	17.8%
Iran	21,257,270	32.0%	11,957,271	18.0%
Iraq	9,552,037	33.0%	7,236,392	25.0%

---

[9] Source: CIA Fact Book https://www.cia.gov/library/publications/the-world-factbook/ (accessed 24th February 2010)

Table 3.1. Continued

Country	Rural Population	%	Population in Poverty	%
Italy	18,699,387	32.0%	-	-
Japan	43,206,750	34.0%	-	-
Kazakhstan	6,467,763	42.0%	2,125,122	13.8%
Kenya	34,322,439	88.0%	15,601,108	40.0%
Korea, North	8,386,177	37.0%	-	-
Korea, South	9,216,704	19.0%	7,276,345	15.0%
Laos	4,715,698	69.0%	1,776,929	26.0%
Madagascar	14,664,024	71.0%	10,326,778	50.0%
Malawi	12,173,293	81.0%	7,965,241	53.0%
Malaysia	7,714,745	30.0%	1,311,506	5.1%
Mali	9,141,393	68.0%	4,853,004	36.1%
Mexico	36,699,890	33.0%	52,269,540	47.0%
Morocco	14,391,180	46.0%	4,692,776	15.0%
Mozambique	13,651,645	63.0%	15,168,494	70.0%
Nepal	23,707,602	83.0%	7,055,154	24.7%
Netherlands	3,008,879	18.0%	1,755,179	10.5%
Niger	12,857,251	84.0%	9,642,938	63.0%
Nigeria	77,599,126	52.0%	104,460,363	70.0%
Pakistan	111,730,277	64.0%	41,898,853	24.0%
Peru	8,568,619	29.0%	13,148,398	44.5%
Philippines	34,291,181	35.0%	29,392,980	30.0%
Poland	15,008,338	39.0%	6,542,096	17.0%
Portugal	4,390,249	41.0%	1,927,426	18.0%
Romania	10,219,093	46.0%	5,553,855	25.0%
Russia	51,815,261	37.0%	22,126,517	15.8%
Rwanda	8,811,975	82.0%	6,447,786	60.%
Senegal	7,952,726	58.0%	7,404,262	54.0%
South Africa	19,130,470	39.0%	24,526,244	50.0%
Spain	13,373,250	33.0%	8,023,950	19.8%
Sri Lanka	18,126,072	85.0%	4,904,701	23.0%
Sudan	23,420,060	57.0%	16,435,130	40.0%
Syria	10,010,969	46.0%	2,589,794	11.9%
Tanzania	30,786,399	75.0%	14,777,471	36.0%
Thailand	44,218,952	67.0%	6.599.843	10.0%
Tunisia	3,460,491	33.0%	775,993	7.4%
Turkey	23,809,712	31.0%	15,361,104	20.0%
Uganda	28,161,515	87.0%	11,329,345	35.0%
Ukraine	14,624,126	32.0%	17,229,048	37.7%
United Kingdom	6,111,320	10.0%	8,555,848	14.0%
United States	55,298,182	18.0%	36,865,454	12.0%
Uzbekistan	17,391,784	63.0%	9,109,982	33.0%
Venezuela	1,877,039	7.0%	13,952,825	37.9%
Vietnam	63,775,265	72.0%	13,109,360	14.8%
Zambia	7,710,781	65.0%	10,201,956	86.0%
Zimbabwe	7,177,356	63.0%	7,746,987	68.0%

The Need to Survive

Many people for various reasons are unable to gain stable employment. This may be for reasons of age, location, education, disability, necessity to care for young dependents, or economic downturn, etc. As a consequence large numbers of people throughout both developing and developed countries are only able to consider economic activities within the informal sector as a casual employee or in some form of self employment. People from developing countries are driven by poverty, the need to survive and lack of employment choices into starting small business ventures (Reynolds *et. al.* 2002). Engaging in self employment for survival tends to be higher in countries with lower GDP per capita (Reynolds *et. al. 2002*). States with social welfare systems with safety nets tend to have less people opening small micro-enterprises in need of survival (Henrekson 2005).

People who engage in self employment within the informal sector are only able to exploit a very limited set of local opportunities based on the existence of local clientele with very limited and meager resources (Bruderl *et. al.* 1992). The poorer the circumstances and greater the necessity, the less will be the inclination to start a business. This is because of the minimum amount of cash investment needed to start (Rosa *et. al.* 2008). Some saving must be undertaken first, so self-employment usually comes after some casual work for someone else or borrowing from a relative. Some people will have assets like a piece of land and home, but little cash. These micro-enterprises will be opened in industries with little market barriers like newspaper vending, shoe polishing or repair, car washing, grass cutting, baby minding, laundry, ironing, housework, home assembly (piece work), a market shop, food vending or catering, etc. Approximately 70% of these types of businesses will be single person start-ups (Niefert & Tachouvakhina 2006).

The intention of these micro-enterprises is to achieve certain family goals like send the children to school, build a home back in their village, buy a piece of land to work or raise their own social status (Rosa *et. al.* 2008). These would be seen as basic needs in developed countries but they are aspirations in developing countries, which require forgoing consumption in the short term for achieving these longer term aspirations.

These micro enterprises tend to grow at much slower rates than opportunity based enterprises with higher capital injections because the person in the micro-enterprise has little time and spare labour capacity left over to develop and expand the business. There may not be any aspiration for business expansion as there may be little opportunity other than satisfying a small niche of local clientele. Also the area of business is likely to be very competitive where gaining extra business will unsettle the micro-social situation in the area leading to anger and even violence from poaching other vender's customers. Government regulations like HACCP in the food retailing industry, taxation[10], and the cost of employing someone act as further disincentives to expand and get out of the informal sector. People are trapped where they are and become habituated in what they are doing to think of anything different. High competition leads to only a marginal income, leaving little room for saving once weekly living expenses are paid.

The income circumstances of people in developing countries with land and family can also be very complex with multiple sources of income and some self-sufficiency in the

---

[10] In countries like Malaysia sales tax if required to be paid on sales above a certain threshold. Provisional tax in countries like Australia, require the payment of tax on expected earnings.

production of food[11]. Family members working away from home may supplement incomes, as would a harvest of some crop like paddy in the tropical countries. Alternatively, they may receive some rental income from their rural land and the enterprise they work in is more of a supplemental income. This provides freedom from the necessity to be employed full time and an opportunity to raise their social status, progress with their lives, and/or be independent as a single parent, etc. In this circumstance self-employment is a way of staying out of poverty (Minniti & Arenius 2003) and to some degree being able to determine their own destiny. Thus the most important factor in the ability to start-up a micro-enterprise is the ability to save the initial capital, rather than education skills or employment situation (Rosa *et. al.* 2008).

Work Experience

Numerous studies have supported the proposition that work experience has positive effects on a person's skills, abilities and knowledge. Work experience enhances a person's ability to see opportunities and develop strategy scenarios in industries they are involved. Intimate understanding of an industry leads to less uncertainty. A person within an industry can interpret its meanings in ways outsiders cannot easily understand, leading to advantages in the ability to discover opportunities and develop subsequent strategies to exploit them.

There are a number of different types of work experience that aid the ability to discover opportunities, develop strategy and organize a start-up in an industry where a person has experience in. General and functional business experience includes knowledge and skills in the basic principles and functions of business including finance, sales, technology, logistics, marketing, and organizational skills (Romanelli & Schoonhoven *et. al* 2001, Klepper & Sleeper 2001). These general and functional business skills assist a person make decisions about business location, product development, quality control, setting of prices, customer service and innovation issues (Lerner *et. al.* 1995).

Some business skills like sales are more useful than others, where other skills like financial management can be picked up during later periods (Roberts 1991). The closer work experience is related to the specific tasks required to exploit an opportunity, the more proficient the person will be at a start-up and organization of a new firm. People with experience in marketing, new product development and management are more likely to exploit opportunities than people in the financial and accounting areas (Boyd 1990, Klepper & Sleeper 2001).

Specific industry knowledge is of prime importance in reducing uncertainty around any attempt to exploit opportunities (Shane 2003, P. 79). Familiarity of the market, channels of distribution, products, competitors, suppliers, consumers and the *'general ways of doing business'* allow better understanding of the market than outsiders to the industry (Johnson 1986). Founders of new ventures tend to keep in industries that they are familiar with. This helps to reduce the likelihood of failure (Bruderl & Preisendorfer 1998, Bruderl *et. al.* 1992, Wicker & King 1989). In contrast, public sector employees in general are less likely to become self employed than those from the private sector (Praag & Pohen 1995), unless specific opportunities to provide services to government evolve.

---

[11] Having village or traditional land is common in countries like Malaysia, Thailand, and Fiji, etc., but there are many countries like Bangladesh, India and Indonesia where many of the poor are landless.

Prior experience in venture start-ups is invaluable in knowing what to do when an opportunity has been discovered. Many things must be attended to during a start-up that is based on tacit knowledge and situational events; therefore it is difficult to teach these skills through formal education (Jovanovic 1982, Herbert & Link 1988). Prior start-up experience assists in deciding what information to collect to aid in decision making (Duchesneau & Gartner 1990), how to deal with suppliers and customers (Campbell 1992), and what actions to take in what sequence, etc.

Skills relevant to exploiting opportunities can be learned through the observation of others (Shane 1996). Children of entrepreneurs are more likely to exploit opportunities than others because of close observation of their parents during their adolescent years which provides tacit knowledge (Minniti 1999). People who grow up in entrepreneurial environments are more likely to become entrepreneurs themselves (Matthews & Moser 1995). General exposure to friends, neighbors and other entrepreneurs generally increases the likelihood that a person will seek to exploit opportunities (Landry et. al. 1992).

Generally people with little organizing ability are less likely to exploit opportunities (Shane 1996). People with previous business experience are more likely to approach a new venture by analyzing customer's needs than those who have not started a business before (Shuman et. al. 1985). People with business experience will be more concerned about cash flow and profitability of a business. Previous work experience helps a person develop managerial, financial, attitudinal and general business competence (Goss 1991). Skills that can be learned through work experience and their potential benefits to opportunity exploitation and start-ups are listed in Table 3.2. below. Business experience is in many ways better than formal education because it provides tacit knowledge which is difficult to disseminate through formal structured education. Therefore experience is greatly beneficial when it comes to the opportunity identification and exploitation. According to Kolb et. al. (1985) the most powerful way to learn is by experience.

Finally it must be mentioned that many companies particularly in the high technology industries like microchips, hard-drives and lasers were formed as the result of employees leaving a firm to set up their own. Examples of spin-offs companies set-up by ex-employees of companies include Intel, Advanced Micro Devices, National Semiconductors (spin-offs from Fairchild Semiconductors) and 3Com and Adobe (spin-offs from 3M). Bhide (1994, P. 151) in a study of found that 71% of innovations in new companies were replicated or modified from their concepts in previous employment. When new industries develop, those with experience in a related industry have an advantage over those with no experience in related industries (Klepper & Simons 2000)[12]. People are more likely to take up opportunities if they feel their resources and capabilities are compatible with the potential opportunity (Helfat & Lieberman 2002).

---

[12] One interesting study by Shane (2000) showed that individuals with different backgrounds saw different potential applications opportunities for a three-dimensional printing technology developed at MIT. This indicates that people perceive opportunities based on their own prior knowledge.

Table 3.2. Skills that can be learned through work experience and potential benefits to opportunity exploitation and start-ups

Skills –General	Sales and marketing, finance and accounting, budgeting, product costing and cost control, manufacturing, sourcing and procurement, general management (personnel, operations, logistics, etc.). Provides practical rather than theoretical knowledge.
Skills – Specific	Product development, standards, technology, how to organize, how to gather market information, competitor information, consumer information and industry trends. Provides practical rather than theoretical knowledge.
Skills - Tacit	How to *'feel'* the market instinctively, how to behave according to market and industry norms, how to acquire resources necessary in the industry, how to identify opportunities, how to extrapolate corresponding product/market/industry specific strategies, how to behave in the market, the steps and sequence needed to exploit an opportunity. Very difficult to learn these skills through formal education.
Industry Specific Knowledge	The industry's values and norms, the culture of doing things, close up knowledge about stakeholder (suppliers, customers, competitors, regulatory mechanisms, and other agents within the supply chain), selecting the best locations, products and strategies to exploit opportunities. Specific industry knowledge in many cases too narrow for formal education.
Potential Inside Industry Advantages	Experience reduces uncertainty about a potential opportunity Industry experience increases confidence Experience develops skills needed to exploit opportunities (in practical rather than theoretical teams). Reduces the likelihood of failure. Assists in making efficient start-ups with low resource bases. Know what type of information to collect and how to use it *i.e., what is relevant and irrelevant.* Should lead to better focused strategies and management. Enables intimate knowledge of specialized technologies.

Life Experience

A person's life experience can assist a person see and discover opportunity and contribute to their sense of self-efficacy, which may provide them with the necessary self confidence to exploit an opportunity once discovered. Life experience is a framework of time and space that serves as a reference for viewing the environment.

Certain life experiences provide familiarity to areas that a person has little previous experience. A person with a general background in marketing and sales may be able to see areas where customers are not satisfied, preferences (Johnson 1986) and gaps within the marketplace (Von Hippel 1986). General knowledge of marketing provides information necessary where opportunities can be discovered (Klepper and Sleeper 2001). Likewise people involved in product development and applications tend to be more alert for new product opportunities (Roberts 1991).

Metaphorically opportunity discovery can be seen like having a puzzle with a missing piece required to complete the puzzle. A new piece of information may be the missing link that creates an opportunity (Romanelli & Schoonhoven 2001). People who have a wide life experience through having a number of jobs and/or travelled may have information that others don't (Casson 1995) to complete the metaphoric opportunity puzzle. For example, a Malaysian student studying in the U.K., U.S. or Australia may become exposed to concepts that are yet to exist in their homeland and constitute an opportunity. A sports person or hobbyist with marketing experience may see a potential opportunity within the sport they play or the hobby they partake that is worth exploitation. People with specialized skills like carpentry may see opportunities related to their skills that are difficult for people without those skills to see. People who travel to other countries and return home (McCormick & Wahba 2001) and people who have knowledge others don't are able to discover opportunities others don't see (Shane 2003, P. 48). The more geographically mobile a person is the more chance of seeing opportunities (Delmer & Davidsson 2000, Lerner & Hendeles 1993).

Diverse life experience particularly with some relevant skills and competencies will provide a knowledge angle to approach the development of a new business. Relevant knowledge can be built upon with the addition of new knowledge creates a *'snowball effect'* in building competence to develop and run the business. Businesses can be developed from different knowledge angles, a marketing approach, technical approach or a channel approach to developing the business. For example a person with marketing experience may be able to build up their technical product knowledge as they go along or a person with technical product knowledge may be able to build up their marketing skills as they go along with the venture. This experience is invaluable in providing tacit knowledge which can be applied to specific problems, enabling a person to think of practical solutions based on past events.

A person's level of self-efficacy is determined by their general success and achievement throughout their life. If one's life experience has contributed to a feeling of self-efficacy a person is more likely to feel confident about exploiting an opportunity they feel can be exploited successfully (Markman & Baron 2003). Self-efficacy creates optimism that a person can achieve a desired outcome (Bandura 1993). This optimism lowers the amount of perceived risk that a person associates with the opportunity. Life experience sets the limitations of the will. This may sometimes be divided against itself with both the urge to do and the urge to hold back.

Finally, life experience can set the domain limits on the set of ideas that an individual may consider. This self definition upon what is within personal focus creates attention to specific events, objects, and people. Therefore any may see scope for growth. For example, the American railroads stopped growing because managers saw themselves as the in the railroad business. This narrow self definition prevented further growth (Levitt 1960). When a company manufactures electric light globes for example, is the company in the electric business? Or is the company in the consumer products business? Each answer may be right at a given time for a given company, but each answer would lead to the viewing of a very different environment where the company would put its efforts (Drucker 1992, P. 190). Ideas and opportunities are restricted by the narratives we live by.

Education

It is generally believed that that the higher the level of education in the community, the higher will be the propensity to exploit entrepreneurial opportunities (Shane 2003, P. 69). This is supported by a number of research studies that found people with a higher level of education than the general population are more likely to exploit opportunities and engage in self employment (Robinson & Sexton 1994, Storey 1994, Reynolds 1997, Bowen & Hisrich 1986). Further studies have reinforced this hypothesis with statistical studies showing that those with professional qualifications (Dolton & Makepeace 1990) and with over 16 years of schooling were more likely to exploit entrepreneurial opportunities and engage in self employment than others (Borjas & Bronars 1989, Bull & Winter 1991).

However there are important questions that need to be asked about any education system and the facilitation it brings to opportunity discovery, strategy crafting and implementation. *How much does an education system stimulate a person's spirit of discovery?* and *Does the right structure, content and delivery style exist within the education system to build personal creativity, opportunity discovery, and evaluation tools?* The answers will vary according to each system. Various systems are based on different objectives, philosophies, outcomes, content and pedagogy. Teachers are trained at different levels and approach teaching from different perspectives. People have different social expectations from the education system that provides for their learning.

Consequently the influence of education is situational and conditional upon the relevance of structure, curricula and pedagogy that students are exposed to. The influence an education system has on a person also depends upon other outlooks one obtains through family, peers and society's culture (Gupta 1992). *Are these factors supportive or contradictory to what a person learns through the formal education system?* A poorly framed and structured education system may actually hinder creativity and entrepreneurship (Charmard 1989, Plaschka & Welsh 1990) and promote a *'get a job'* mentality (Kourilsky 1994).

Many of the entrepreneurial education courses in existence are not put together carefully, nor evaluated or correlated with objective measures of subsequent venture performance by those who have undertaken courses (McMullan *et. al.* 2001). Many programs are confused about their objectives. Should the course teach about entrepreneurship, entrepreneurship skills, small business or creativity and innovation as life concepts? These all have very different orientations and cultures (Gibb 1987). To enhance a person's creativity, opportunity discovery and evaluation skills, resource acquisition skills and strategy crafting and organizing skills requires specific concept teaching (Knight 1987). Secondly this material must be taught in ways that maximize learning, such as experiential learning concepts? (Ulrich & Cole 1987, Stumpf *et. al.* 1991). Education programs must have skill building components like negotiation, leadership, creative thinking, as well as exposure to technical innovation and product development to enhance a person's ability to exploit opportunities (McMullan & Long 1987).

For an education system to be relevant to opportunity discovery, evaluation, and exploitation, it must improve entrepreneurial judgment by providing people with the analytical ability and an understanding of the entrepreneurial process (Clouse 1990, Casson 1995). Education should reduce the perceptions of difficulty in starting a business (Jackson & Rodney 1994). Most importantly education should increase a person's perception of their own self-efficacy. Self efficacy is an important trait that enables a person to have the confidence in discovering opportunities and contemplate the feasibility of starting a business (Shapero 1975, Shapero & Sokol 1982). However it must be remembered that self-efficacy is not solely created through education, family, peers and the surrounding society also have great influence (Ajzen 1987, Boyd & Vozikis 1994). For these reasons the effect of education will not be the same on all people.

However some of the most famous entrepreneurs of our time did not complete college. Thomas Edison finished school at 12, Steve Woznick and Steve Jobs did not graduate, and Bill Gates dropped out of Harvard to start Microsoft, while Michael Dell quit the University of Texas to start Dell Computers (Bhide 2000).

Yet another challenge is how to structure an education system so it can be coupled with technical knowledge to enhance a person's ability to be innovative. Entrepreneurship education without the specific technical knowledge needed to drive particular ventures is not a full education. In general entrepreneurship training courses the student will generally lack any specific technical background and is forced to pick this knowledge up somewhere else. Thus technically educated people who take up some entrepreneurial courses during or after their technical studies will have advantages over those who study a dedicated entrepreneurship course. Those with industry experience will also accumulate tacit knowledge that education has difficulty in providing. This is one of the dilemmas of entrepreneurship education at undergraduate levels at least. Graduate programs may apply incubator programs from engineering and science schools.

Positive education should provide a person the basic skills of how to seek knowledge and use it for whatever purpose it has been sort, *i.e., how to learn how to learn.* In industries where technology is constantly evolving technical knowledge very quickly becomes outdated. Skill building programs are much more valuable than knowledge building programs, especially in view of the dynamics of technologies and markets. Education must build self learning abilities to assist people develop new knowledge schema for their specific opportunity applications.

Skills and Abilities

There are various skills and abilities a person needs to exploit any opportunity through an enterprise framework (Casson & Della Giusta 2007). Some of the major skills and abilities a person needs are;

1.   General Business Skills

Some of the general business functions required to successfully exploit an opportunity within a business environment include; marketing, production operations, human resources, financial, business laws and regulations and general administrative skills. Particular day to day skills required to operate any business include sales, purchasing, supply chain management, general book keeping and accounting, cash flow and general business management. These basic skills enable a person to understand and operate a business within the basic principles of management. There may be a need for more specialized knowledge depending on the type of business operation, *e.g. retail, wholesale, importer, exporter, wholesaler, marketing company, assembler or manufacturer, etc.* There is usually a tendency that a person has better competencies in some areas than others and any business orientation and operational style will be biased towards those competencies. For example a person with a strong sales background may give the company a sales emphasis, whereas a person with a production background may position the operation as a production orientated company.

2.   Technical Skills

Technical skills are important for the processing, manufacturing or some other specific aspect of a business. Strength in particular technical skills provides a person with product, processing and manufacturing knowledge. Without a strong core of technical skills a business has no technology base which may or may not be needed within the gamut of the chosen industry the entrepreneur has chosen to operate within. Technical knowledge also functions as an anchor between the enterprise and the industry. Technology empowers the enterprise and at the same time can lock a business into a specific industry based on a specific technology. Nevertheless knowledge in specific technologies may be a necessary prerequisite for industry entry, existence and product competition. Any specifically developed proprietary knowledge or intellectual property may assist in creating some sort of competitive advantage or barriers to entry for other potential competitors.

3.   Start-up Skills

Start-up skills are very important for converting an idea into an enterprise to exploit the perceived opportunity. This phase usually commences after the opportunity has been identified. Start-up skills range from the tacit knowledge necessary to undertake the preliminary steps needed to commence trading operations and the more specialized aspects of the business that need to be specifically created for the enterprise, like specialized production layouts or retail configurations. The general start-up tasks include registering a business entity, setting up a bank account, finding a premises, creating accounts with suppliers, employing early employees if need be and purchasing immediate necessities like office equipment etc. The specific specialized aspects of the enterprise that require setting up and development include the identified technologies that will be exploited, the new product development process and the initial identification and building up of early customer relationships. It is during this stage that the planned innovations that will provide an anchor for the enterprise within its chosen industry are developed, whether it is a technical, process, organizational or supply chain innovation.

4.   Planning Skills

Planning skills are required to map out the direction of the enterprise so it can successfully exploit the perceived opportunity it was formed for. This involves simultaneous planning concerning marketing, sales, product development, organizational development, financial and resource acquisition. Only after all these aspects are coordinated and developed together will the enterprise platform physically exist with the ability to exploit the selected opportunity.

5. Analytical and Conceptual skills

Analytical and conceptual skills are needed to both visualize any opportunities, enable the visualization of an enterprise to exploit perceived opportunities and continue guiding the strategic direction of the enterprise once it is in operation. Analytical skills gather and organize information in such a way that conclusions can be drawn upon its meaning, significance or importance to the enterprise, that may lead to future action. Conceptual skills are about broad thinking and the general outlook of particular situations based on the environment, enterprise and self.

6. Interpersonal Skills

Interpersonal skills involve the interaction with others for the purposes of resource acquisitions, sales, communications with potential funding organizations and communications with potential employees. Interpersonal skills are also very important in the process of persuading people to support certain aspects of the enterprise, whether as a customer, employee, supplier or other form of stakeholder.

7. Networking and negotiation Skills

Networking skills are needed to develop relationships with people and companies that are potential stakeholders and have some influence over the enterprise's future. The enterprise founder/manager should be an extravert to some degree and be comfortable about meeting people. Negotiation skills are very important in the negotiation of leases, rents, purchase prices of inputs, salaries, and last but not least with customers. Without sound negotiation skills there is a great chance that the enterprise will suffer cost disadvantages from paying high prices for leases and other inputs and lower revenues because of selling goods or services below the price someone may be able to get if they were a better negotiator. Negotiation sells are a key determinant of cost efficiencies for the enterprise, where poor skills in this area would be a great disadvantage.

8. Leadership Skills

Leadership skills are very important to develop loyalty, commitment, dedication, motivation and sharing of the enterprise vision with others, especially employees. Good leadership creates extra energy within an enterprise. Leadership involves the playing of various roles which include nurturing, guiding, advising, showing example, directing, showing the way and focusing the organization. In start-ups and young enterprises the leader sets the vision and is one of the most important influences on the development of the culture within the enterprise. Good leadership also requires a good rounding of all the other skills mentioned above and any weaknesses would denigrate the quality of enterprise leadership, most possibly leading to a less effective operating organization.

In order for a person to exploit any opportunity they must perceive that they possess the required skills, personal competencies, and knowledge needed to start and operate a business (Tutkimusraportteja 2009). This comes from self-efficacy, the belief that one can execute a certain set of tasks and behaviour (Boyd & Vozikis 1994). Self perception reflects a person's innermost thoughts and feelings on whether they have what it takes to successfully perform the tasks needed. One's actual abilities only matter if a person has self-confidence in those abilities, and also the self confidence that they can convert their skills into the means to achieve their desired outcomes (Bandura 1986, 1997). General self efficacy is central to a person's human functioning and is based on what people believe rather than what is actually the case (Markman *et. al.* 2002). High levels of self-efficacy can act as a motivator for someone to take action upon a perceived opportunity, while low self-efficacy may explain why some groups in society do not act upon perceived opportunities. For example, when people in poverty have no drive, no energy and no self-esteem, they become defeatist. If they are placed in an environment which encourages and supports them, *i.e., a windfall in a lottery or a good job,* the same people would become go getters and self confident (Kao *et. al.* 2006). Self-efficacy is a reasonable predictor of the propensity for someone to perceive opportunities (Krueger & Carsrud 1993).

Persistence is a very important attribute in the start-up and consequent development of an enterprise and this is influenced by how a person perceives themselves and their situation. According to Shapero (1975) self-efficacy is central to a person seeing the feasibility of starting a business. Self-efficacy is believed to be influenced by experience and other social factors like observational learning, vicarious experience, social persuasion, parental and peer support, and personal judgments, physiological state and age (Ajzen 1987a, Boyd & Vozikis 1994, Shapero 1975, Shapero & Sokol 1982). Therefore any new venture decision will be influenced by a person's perception of the skills necessary to initiate tasks, regardless of any other triggers (discussed later in this chapter) that motivate any desirability. Someone who feels that they don't have the necessary skills, even in the situation of necessity, will tend to look for other ways of surviving before looking at the option of starting a business, as they don't feel personally capable of taking a risk of that magnitude (Morales-Gualdrón & Roig 2005).

Finally, our perceived opportunities are to some degree based on our self perception of our skills and abilities. Our self-efficacy influences our courses of action, level of effort, how we perseverance, our amount of resilience in the face of barriers and obstacles, how we cope with adversity and whether our own thoughts are self-hindering or self-aiding to our actions (Woods & Bandura 1989, Markman *et. al.* 2002).

Age

Age is one of the clearest factors that influence the propensity to exploit opportunities (Parker 2004, P. 106). According to Scott Shane (2003, P. 89) there is a curvilinear (inverted U-shape) relationship between age and opportunity exploitation (start-up). Start ups increase with age for a number of reasons, Younger people have just reached maturity and are ready to focus upon something. They have been educated and have little restriction because of mortgages and loan payments to consider when making decisions. They are used to living through odd hours and are at their physical peaks. Available employment opportunities are less than previous generations had access to so settling into a new business is just as much of an adjustment to make as settling into a new job.

Age continues to increase the likelihood that people will exploit opportunities until the mid 40s (Holtz-Eakin *et. al.* 1994). This is because people have gathered skills and experiences that are necessary to exploit opportunities, are competent in communicating with others and able to use networks of contacts to gather resources (Freeman 1982) and connect to potential customers, if they remain in the same industry. However once people get higher salaries and age, opportunity costs of starting new businesses increase and their willingness to live with uncertainty begins to decline (Shane 2003, P. 89). People who have not gone out into their own businesses by their mid forties are likely to be satisfied and complacent, unless some major shock like redundancy occurs.

A recent study of age and exploitation of opportunities has uncovered a trend in baby boomers over 50 engaging in start-ups (strangler 2009). Start-ups by the 20-24 age group at this point of time very low, according to statistics in the United States (Ballou *et. al.* 2008). According to Ballou *et. al.* (2008) in every year since 1996, Americans aged between 55 and 64 had a higher rate of entrepreneurial activity (roughly 33% higher) than those aged 20-34. There could be several reasons why this could be so. For example, the availability of less *'lifetime'* work available to baby boomers has decreased the opportunity cost has increased the attractiveness of going into one's own business (Farber 2006). Further, as life expectancy is increasing *(78 for females and 76 for males),* baby boomers are changing their attitudes and are looking for activities like further education, work and leisure to pursue (Hansen 1993). Figure 3.3. shows the propensity for start-ups by age.

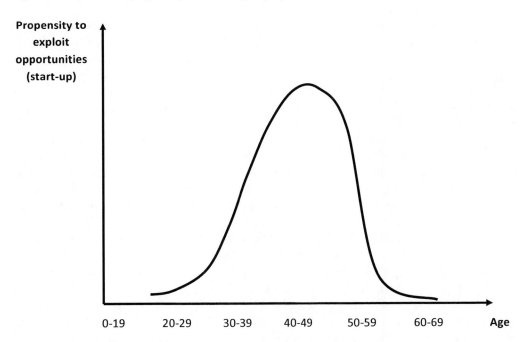

Figure 3.3. Age Distribution of Propensity to Exploit Opportunities (Start-Ups) in the United States.

The above are U.S. trends and few studies exist to determine whether other countries are following suit with start-ups during later age. Differences in start-up trends between countries will affect national innovation and productivity levels, which will affect aggregate economic growth in the future (Bloom *et. al.* 2007). It is not knowledge creation itself that creates innovation, but the use of knowledge in start-ups that creates economic activity (Aces *et al.*

2006). Therefore start up and age distributions trends will be expected to affect the exploitation of opportunities in individual countries.

Gender[13]

There has been a dramatic rise in the number of women who have taken up self employment over the last thirty years. Generally speaking, female self employment around the world is approximately 60-70% of male self employment levels. Primarily due to cultural reasons, countries like Tonga and Guatemala actually have greater rates of female self employment than males and countries in the Middle East countries like Saudi Arabia have extremely low levels of female self employment. The gender gap is very low in efficiency driven economies[14], especially the Latin American countries, with women exceeding men in Brazil. The Eastern European countries exhibit much lower rates of women self employment than men. Male self employment in the innovation driven economies is approximately twice that of women, excepting Germany, where almost the same number of females are self employed and in Japan, Italy and France where female self employment rates are extremely low (Bosma & Levie 2010).

Statistically[15] women are attracted to the extremely competitive services sector where it is difficult to develop any competitive advantage and therefore only marginally profitable. Women are locked into the services sector in aggregate because they know and have experience in this area, frequently lack technical skills for manufacturing and high-tech sectors, have difficulty obtaining the resources needed (Bruni et. al. 2004) and have minimal access to the necessary networks (Aldrich et. al. 1996, Brush 1992). Due to these disadvantages women's businesses tend to exhibit slower growth than male owned and operated businesses (Brush 1997). However, female participation in both management and self employment in both the traditional and non-traditional sectors is expected to increase in the coming decades as more females are staying single pursuing careers (Hamer 2010) and universities are experiencing large surges in enrollments in business and technical degrees by more women than ever before (Guess 2007, Jaschik 2006), especially in Asia (Shirahase 2000).

Gender is a culturally specific pattern of behavior that is associated with each sex and influences social relations, values and roles in family and society (Oakley 1972). Until recently women were locked into their socially constructed view of the world as primary care givers to their families (Burrell 1992, P. 72) and had relatively little public power, authority and influence (Black 1989). Women lacked a science and technical education, thereby forcing them to participate in the retail, food and service industries rather than manufacturing and construction, etc. This fitted in with their previous experience in the vocations of teaching, middle management, nursing and secretarial work (Hisrich & Brush 1983). Cordelia Fine

---

[13] Management theory usually takes a gender neutral approach (Baker et. al. 1997), so this section is focused on highlighting some of the special issues related to women.

[14] The Global Entrepreneurship Monitor classifies countries according to their stage of development based on their GDP per capita and the extent to which countries are factor driven in terms of shares of primary products as exports. Factor driven economies are primarily extractive in nature, where efficiency driven economies exhibit scale intensity as the major driver of the economy. An innovation driven economy is characterized by the production of innovative products and services created by pioneering and sophisticated means of production.

[15] Many statistical and quantitative studies have shown this. See Rosa et. al. 1994.

(2010) believes that gender casting is a product of culture and upbringing rather than genetic inheritance. There are no major neurological differences guiding men and women's behavior and it is nurture rather than genetic inheritance that influences skills, attributes, and personalities, beginning in their infancy and continuing through their schooling and cultural exposure within society.

Women's motives for starting a business are very different to men. One major difference is that women are responsible for the caring of family and children, requiring flexibility and balance between their family and work responsibilities. This according to research at the time weighed very heavily on their decisions to enter into self employment (Chaganti 1986, Goffee & Scase 1983, Scott 1986). Women's careers on the whole are characterized by interruptions due to child bearing, etc, where career is perceived as taking second place to family duties (Bruni et. al. 2004). This brings upon women feelings of guilt and stress in their careers that men do not feel (Winn 2004). This concern for balance and flexibility probably explains why businesses operated by females tended to grow slower than those operated by males (Cromie 1987).

Another important factor that the literature cited during the 1980s and 90s was the 'glass ceiling'[16], an invisible barrier reinforced by male dominated networks, quasi male nepotism and discrimination against women's promotions to the top managerial jobs (Bowen & Hisrich 1986). A woman's career commitment is often treated with suspicion (Cordano et. al. 2002), thus self employment is an option for those that believe they are being discriminated against within the workplace (Cowling & Mitchell 1997). Other reasons why women become entrepreneurs through choice is independence, self fulfillment, entrepreneurial drive, and desire for wealth, power and social position (Orhan & Scott 2001). Women tend to start businesses with the ambition of *making a difference*, where they are more client focused, ethical in operations and orientated towards making a social contribution rather than pursuing economic rewards (Still & Timms 2000).

Women in developing countries have traditionally had to find ways of converting home based duties into revenue seeking activities. They tend to have very small networks and are lass able to more to different geographical location than men in search of work or opportunities (Minniti & Arenius 2003). Therefore the majority of businesses developed are low skilled, labour intensive and providing little profit. Women's self employment activities tended to reflect their home responsibilities, i.e., child minding, home sewing and assembling, street venders, washing and ironing services, home based restaurants, and secretarial services, where face to face contact was the basis of customer relationships (Ng & Ng 2003). These micro enterprises tended to be invisible within the informal economy where the profits were used to pay for family living expenses and children's schooling, etc (Singh et. al. 2001). Some of the traditional differences between women's entrepreneurship in developing and developed countries is summarized in Table 3.3.

Due to geographic, educational and work experience diversity today there are many categories of female entrepreneurs who engage in a diverse range of activities with a diverse range of situations. Based on the trends mentioned above a number of typologies can be outlined that may provide some better understanding of the female entrepreneurship continuum.

---

[16] The glass ceiling can be termed a situation where a qualified person is prevented from rising through the hierarchy of an organization because of some form of sexual or racist discrimination.

Table 3.3. Some of the Traditional Differences between Women Entrepreneurs in Developing and developed Countries

Variables	Developing Countries	Developed Countries
Education	Little education maybe up to secondary level (this is rapidly changing).	Secondary to tertiary education.
Previous Experience	No or little experience other than doing home duties.	Maybe business started after some experience in another business.
Skills	Very little, only what is picked up doing the job.	Some specialized skills learnt through education and/or experience.
Areas of Business Interest	Mostly in the informal sector with very low skill base, usually as an extension of household work (food, catering, cleaning, piecework, etc.)	Mostly in the services sector with some specialized skills (i.e., secretarial, artistic, computer, nursing, etc,)
Business Environment	Serving informal customers who are neighbors or regular passers-by.	Serving a specialized industry or retail sector.
Business characteristics	Business in areas which require manual labour, large time commitment, low profitability, face to face customer relationships, reliant on local customer bases, maybe utilizing family labour to assist.	Tasks that require some personalized and specialized attention, either home or office based servicing target clients within a local area or industry, maybe employing up 4-5 people.
Customer Loyalty/Competition	Customer loyalty gained through personal contact/very competitive area, no opportunity for branding as a means to create loyalty or value.	Customer loyalty gained through service and quality of job. Very competitive market but some opportunity to create some goodwill by the quality of service.

- The male subservient entrepreneur is a woman who is undertaking a business with their husband or partner. In this traditional dual self-employment family business, the male is usually the dominant partner making all the major decisions, controlling finance and external sales, etc. The female is usually allocated the tasks of running the shop or shop-floor in any manufacturing situation under directions of the husband partner. This is culturally the case among Southern Asian communities both in South Asia and abroad (Dhaliwal 2000). However these power dynamics vary greatly between ethnic groups, where for example women traditionally hold and control the finances in Chinese family businesses.
- The need entrepreneur is usually a single mother, widowed or divorced women who has to take up self employment to earn income to survive. Self employment is seen as a flexible alternative to salaried employment because of the flexibility it gives in caring for the children. The woman usually has a modest education and opens a home based business as an extension of her home duties, like catering, child care, housework, laundry and ironing or piecework at home, etc. These types of businesses are labour intensive, time consuming and marginally profitable, usually being the primary income for the single parent family.
- Professional women are usually highly educated (professional and/or technical) and have made a conscious decision to pursue a career as their major priority in life. They

will be single, married or partnered to another highly motivated career person who has a career of their own. These women compete directly with men in the corporate world. They will stay in the corporate hierarchy until they find disappointment with inability to go any higher up the *'corporate ladder'* due to perceived nepotism and favouritism, or other dissatisfaction with their career.

- The professional mother like the professional woman is highly motivated and ambitious but is forced to balance her working life with family life. This may have the result of preventing her to rise to a level in management in line with her true ability or potential. She may wait until her child care and other responsibilities are completed and seek to go into self employment in pursuit of some long held ambition.

- The returning professional may be the professional mother seeking a return to work after a period of absence from the workforce due to family responsibilities. Her previous dissatisfaction with the workforce or inability to get a job may influence the option of self employment. She may plan to undertake a long held ambition to develop something that she thinks is important and will *'make a difference'*, building an organization that she hopes will not only give her fulfillment but also provide satisfaction to those that she may employ. It is also likely that the firm will be ethically based trying to live up to some philosophy that she thinks is important. Her business will be client centered most probably within the service sector.

- The mature entrepreneur is a woman in later life after her child care responsibilities are completed looking to fulfill a lifelong ambition or entrepreneurial fantasy. This maybe a boutique, a line of products like cosmetics, or a retail operation like a restaurant. The woman may or may not be educated and will have varying degrees or commitment to the venture, from being a hobby to a major commitment. A variation of this typology is a woman who is forced to take the reins of a family business following the death of a spouse. She may or may not have had previous experience within the business, but must take on the role as the major decision maker.

These career journeys a woman may take will be greatly influenced by her family environment (Orhan & Scott 2001). The parents have great influence upon what education the daughter undertook and have provided a home environment full of the values which would influence her life decisions to some degree. Financial needs will also influence the decisions to obtain a higher education and the age that a woman enters the workforce. Once in the workforce a person's level of satisfaction, family responsibilities, perceptions of self-efficacy, potential networks and access to potential resources will also influence what directions will be taken in the future, *i.e., whether self employment is a viable option.*

The Combined Influence of Demographic Factors

The combined influence of parents, family and peers, a person's domicile outlook, the need to survive, life and work experience, education, age and gender coupled with a person's perceptions of their own skills and abilities become a set of predisposition factors. A person's general attitude to opportunity and self employment are influenced to some degree by this set of factors, summarized individually in Table 3.4. below.

Table 3.4. A Person's General Attitude towards Opportunity Based on Selected Demographic Traits

Parents, Family & Peers	Some behavior is reinforced through children's genetic similarities with their parents. The parents influence over the occupational choice of their children generally lessens as their children grow up and are influenced by other factors outside the family environment. Research shows that parents and family have little influence on adult children in their career choices, once they reach adulthood. Decisions about career and the potential of self-employment opportunities will in adulthood depend more upon the person's chosen lifestyle, the number of children and potential risks and opportunity costs of career or self-employment, marital status and support, particularly to female entrepreneurs.
Domicile Outlook	The concept of brings together factors like social status, income, location, state of employment and immigrant status. Together these factors contribute to a person's basic beliefs and attitudes and outlook towards opportunity and its potential exploitation. A person's locality also has great impact upon the continuum of opportunities available to them.
Need to Survive	Engaging in self employment for survival tends to be higher in countries with lower GDP per capita. People who engage in self employment within the informal sector are only able to exploit a very limited set of local opportunities based on the existence of local clientele with very limited and meager resources. The poorer the circumstances and greater the necessity, the less will be the inclination to start a business.
Work Experience	Numerous studies have supported the proposition that work experience has positive effects on a person's skills, abilities and knowledge. Specific industry knowledge is of prime importance in reducing uncertainty around any attempt to exploit opportunities. Familiarity of the market, channels of distribution, products, competitors, suppliers, consumers and the *general ways of doing business* allows better understanding of the market than outsiders to the industry.
Life Experience	A person's life experience can assist a person see and discover opportunity and contribute to their sense of self-efficacy, which may provide them with the necessary self confidence to exploit an opportunity once discovered. Certain life experiences provide familiarity to areas that a person has little previous experience.
Education	There are important questions that need to be asked about any education system and the facilitation it brings to opportunity discovery, strategy crafting and implementation. *How much does an education system stimulate a person's spirit of discovery?* and *Does the right structure, content and delivery style exist within the education system to build personal creativity, opportunity discovery, and evaluation tools?* The answers will vary according to each system. Consequently the influence of education is situational and conditional upon the relevance of structure, curricula and pedagogy that students are exposed to. Some of the most famous entrepreneurs of our time did not complete college.
Skills & Abilities	In order for a person to exploit any opportunity they must perceive that they possess the required skills, capabilities knowledge needed to start and operate a business. One's actual abilities only matter if a person has self-confidence in those abilities, and

	also the self confidence that they can convert their skills into the means to achieve their desired outcomes. High levels of self-efficacy can act as a motivator for someone to take action upon a perceived opportunity, while low self-efficacy may explain why some groups in society do not act upon perceived opportunities.
Age	Age is one of the clearest factors that influence the propensity to exploit opportunities. There is a curvilinear (inverted U-shape) relationship between age and opportunity exploitation (start-up). Start ups increase with age for a number of reasons. Age continues to increase the likelihood that people will exploit opportunities until the mid 40s. This is because people have gathered skills and experiences that are necessary to exploit opportunities, are competent in communicating with others and able to use networks of contacts to gather resources and connect to potential customers, if they remain in the same industry. However once people get higher salaries and age, opportunity costs of starting new businesses increase and their willingness to live with uncertainty begins to decline. People who have not gone out into their own businesses by their mid forties are likely to be satisfied and complacent, unless some major shock like redundancy occurs.
Gender	There has been a dramatic rise in the number of women who have taken up self employment over the last thirty years. Generally speaking, female self employment around the world is approximately 60-70% of male self employment levels. Primarily due to cultural reasons, countries like Tonga and Guatemala actually have greater rates of female self employment than males and countries in the Middle East countries like Saudi Arabia have extremely low levels of female self employment. The gender gap is very low in efficiency driven economies, especially the Latin American countries, with women exceeding men in Brazil. The Eastern European countries exhibit much lower rates of women self employment than men. Male self employment in the innovation driven economies is approximately twice that of women, except Germany, where almost the same number of females are self employed and in Japan, Italy and France where female self employment rates are extremely low.

The predisposing factors can be considered pull factors which create either a positive or negative disposition towards undertaking self employment.

These factors assist in creating a person's self-perception as an entrepreneur or small business operater. This self perception of their general competence will influence future actions towards self employment should some form of trigger in the form of personal crisis occur. Their vision may be linked to the triggering factors. The trigger is some form of realization that may consist of sudden unemployment, being passed over for promotion, not being taken seriously at work, or being discriminated against, etc (Connolly *et. al.* 2003). These push factors are usually the result of some external event as mentioned previously.

There should be some form of idea for a business venture along with the trigger to support consideration of entering self employment. If a person then sees the potential availability of resources, can visualize some form of strategy and has aspirations to exploit the opportunity, then there is a chance the person will move into action to exploit the perceived opportunity. Thus all the factors (predisposition, trigger, idea, potential resources, strategy and aspirations) all combine together improve the ability to recognize opportunities and have new ideas and take the risk of start-up (Scott & Twomey 1988). This process model is shown in figure 3.4. below.

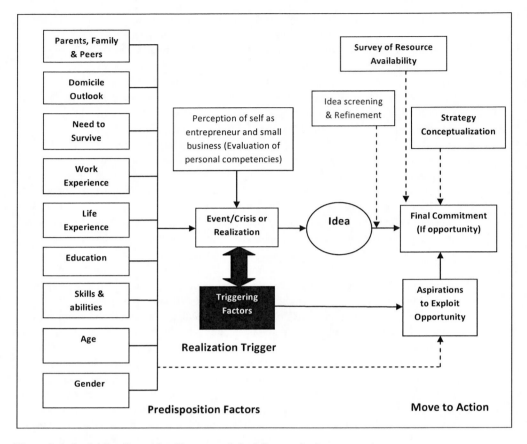

Figure 3.4. Social Predisposition Factors and the Move to Action.

Generational Attitudes

It can be clearly seen that generational attitudes have influence upon thinking and behavior. A generation can be considered a segment of the population who have shared experiences and have a sense of history that influences their thinking and behavior today. In Western countries like the United States and Canada in North America, most countries in Western Europe, Australia and New Zealand can be considered to have three distinct generations that influence society today, the baby boomers, generation X and generation Y. The baby boomer generation came in a mass population bubble after World War Two until around 1964. Generation X are the children of the baby boomers born between 1965 and 1979. Generation Y are the children of generation X couples and include those born between 1980 and 1999.

The baby boomer generation were the children of parents of the silent generation. Fathers of the baby boomers were generally too young to have served in World War II and both parents would have gone through the great depression. This would have had a profound effect upon the values baby boomers were brought up upon. Their parents would have had a grave, conventional, conservative, fatalistic outlook on life and were also perhaps confused morally, indifferent, unadventurous and disappointed with what life had brought them.

The baby boomer generation was extremely large because of the relative political stability after the Second World War. They were much more optimistic than their parents due to the economic boom from post war reconstruction and the following years of steady industrial development. Baby boomers tended to reject the traditional values of their parents, religion and became much more individualistic and liberal.

Baby boomers idealistically looked for social change. They experimented with different ideas, lifestyles, sexual freedoms, ways of thinking, as the hippy movement exhibited during the late 60's. Baby boomers were free spirited, open, tried to be fair and took up social causes. This was the time when the civil rights, anti-war and women's movement emerged and politics became a mass event where two clearly defined sides (liberal and conservative) developed. The heroes to many at the time would have been John F. Kennedy, Martin Luther King, and Malcolm X, etc.

Baby boomers were witnesses to rapid development of technology and came to appreciate and accept it. They saw the space race, the arms race, the invention of the transistor, television, the green revolution in agriculture, and great improvements in medicine, *i.e., the first heart transplant*. Baby boomers probably got the idea that mankind could control and harness nature during this time. They became the healthiest generation so far and life expectancies increased dramatically.

Baby boomers in their mature working years accepted the system, not only becoming part of it, but being the ones responsible for building it to what it is today. The 70's and 80's were the time of rapid corporate growth where the baby boomers were workaholics. They competed with their peers and became a relatively financially well off group. They respected success and achievement as an important institutional foundation. Having the latest gadgets (colour TV, Mobile phone, luxury car, etc) became the baby boomer status symbols defining class to some extent.

When baby boomers got to the top of the corporate and political ladders, their conservatism came out. The words *'politically correct'* became a euphemism for taboo subjects, Gordon Gekko's cry of *'greed is good'*[17] reflected a desire of many and much of the western world adopted the philosophies of *'Reaganomics'* and *'Thatcherism'*[18]. Subconsciously the baby boomers hoped for immortality, which could be seen in what was built during the baby boomer era was something meant to last as a legacy. Baby boomers believed what worked yesterday will still work tomorrow and try to deny the transition of time and change. This is reflected in some baby boomers still eager to maintain the helms of the empires and institutions they helped to build and their failure to provide for retirement provisions and death[19] [20].

---

[17] Gordon Gekko was the arch villain or anti-hero of the film Wall Street in 1990 played by Michael Douglas. He would raid company stocks, take them over and break them up for quick profits without regard for the workers of the companies involved.

[18] One can remember the Reagan-Thatcher era during the 1980s. Reagan's election promise was for lower taxes and smaller government, i.e., reduce govt. spending reduce taxes, reduce govt. influence over the economy and the use of monetary policy to control inflation. Thatcherism can be explained as the above with conservative values. These policies were emulated in New Zealand through 'Rogernomics' and in Australia through 'economic rationalism'.

[19] One of the reasons many companies collapsed in the 2009 economic downturn was the shortfall in retirement funds. One of the major responsibilities of the baby boomer children is to provide for their parents old age.

Generation X is a dramatically smaller population group than the preceding baby boomer generation. Generation X grew up during the final years of the Vietnam War, Watergate, and through the Reagan and Bush Senior era in the United States. They also witnessed the end of the Cold War, the expansion of globalism, the introduction of the early home computers, radical changes to the media industry and the early days of MTV. Generation X grew up with continual change and continual introduction of new technologies. As a consequence, Generation X is accustomed to a changing environment.

Generation X is generally better educated than their parents. They became adults during the late 1980's and have been described as pragmatic, perceptive, savvy but amoral, and more focused on money than on art (Strauss & Howe 1992, P. 365). They believe in sex before marriage but not the free sex that was practiced during the baby boom era, probably because of the event of HIV/AIDS. Generation X is also known as the divorce generation. Couples tend to break up rather than stick out and work through relationship problems like previous generations. There is not the same social stigma about divorce and it has become the easiest option. Generation X as a group has tended to respect their parents less than previous generations (Asthana & Thorpe 2005).

Generation X'ers generally earn less than their fathers, but the combined incomes of couples, where the female has her own career, is more than the family incomes of the baby boomer generation. Generation X is also generally hocked in debt through heavy credit card utilization and paying off mortgages and student loans. Generation X has had to struggle financially harder than their parents due to a number of economic downturns over the last two decades. Although some became millionaires, there are many that have had to struggle to make ends meet in this generation.

Generation X is now beginning to turn 40 and starting to replace the baby boomers as they retire from corporate life. Generation X tends to work in highly skilled and specialized jobs, like working in a *'collegial'* manner and like to be valued for their talents. They are attached more to their profession than the company. They also accept changing technologies and new ways of doing things much more readily than the baby boomers. Generation X sees entrepreneurship as a viable and challenging career option.

As parents, Generation X has looked after their children well and struggled to give them all they want. Although they have many things in common with their children, the excitement of new technologies and multitasking, etc, the children of Generation X have generally seen things very differently than their parents.

Generation Y is another large populous group like the baby boomer generation. They have grown up with computers, multi-channel satellite and cable TV, mobile phones, instant messaging and other high-tech gadgets like iPods, etc. They have been the most cared for generation in history, and even though news is accessible in an instant exposing the problems of the world, they are most sheltered and protected (Strauss & Howe 2000, P. 119). Generation Y, also known as the *Millennial Generation* has been shaped by the events and trends of the late 1990's and Millennium decade, where 9/11, the Gulf War, Afghanistan, global warming, the *dot.com* boom and bust have had profound effects on their sense of morality and civic natures. The advent of the internet, mobile phones, instant communications

---

[20] This can also be seen from the view that baby boomers believe that there is no one to take their place and younger people are not visionary, competent, committed or as well trained as they are. From the Generation X point of view, the boomers are sitting too long at the top of the organization and ignoring new blood and views. (See Kunreuther 2003).

and social networking sites have connected this generation to their peers around the clock, where this generation is truly socially orientated.

The *Millennial personality* according to Strauss and Howe (2000) is based on a rejection of the perceived laxness of their parents during the 60's and 70's and their exposure to globalization, multiracial and multi-ethnic diversity. Their traits therefore contrast with their parents. They ignore tradition and religion, where they were bored going to church and didn't see the point of it. Generation Y have become agnostic, secular, unengaged, or picked up their own mix of beliefs as they have gone along. They have a religious apathy as they have been taught to be materialist (Mason *et. al.* 2008). Generation Y is idealistic, reactive, and adaptive, even though they are perceived by those outside their generation as problematic and irresponsible. The majority are not interested or even apathetic towards politics and politicians (Bates & Papadopoulos 2008). However paradoxically young people were at the front of the rebellion in Burma during 2007, the 2009-10 Iranian election protests and the overthrowing of the Mubarak regime in Egypt in February 2011. Friends and relationships are very important to them. Personal networks form part of their own support system and are also the source of entertainment and news, which filters the way the deal with the world. Many generation Y'ers have both a real and virtual world, with the average person spending around 5 hours a week playing on-line games and the heavy players spending 5 to 6 hours per night playing (Lahiff & Hamilton 2008).

Generation Y has become over-reliant on their parents, often returning to live with them after graduation in their adult life. Although this is seen as an easy way out to life by some, their attachment to their parents may have more to do with genuine family orientation (Noveck & Thompson 2007). This has probably come about as a reaction to the divorce culture of the previous generation, where Generation Y appears to be strongly attached to their mothers (Strauss & Howe 2000, pp. 185-186).

Generation Y appears to be a self confident generation. Based on influence from their workaholic parents, Generation Yers believe they must build strong resumes and become skilled to get on in life (Novech & Tompson 2007). They believe that success comes through hard work and this external drive is what motivates them, rather than inner ambitions (Strauss & Howe 2000, P. 184). They are not like the previous generations where college was a place of enlightenment. Although they enjoy school and university they don't forget the reason why they are there is to get good grades. Generation Y has a *'work hard, play hard'* outlook to life (Clydesdale 2007, P. 3).

Although Generation Y tends to be externally motivated, they are still very calculative and rationalistic about long range plans, thinking carefully about finance, the value of certain degrees and potential salaries, etc (Strauss & Howe 2000, pp. 182-183). However with this powerful external motivation and lifestyle, many young people are coming down with anxiety and stress (Kadison & DiGeronimo 2004, Robbins 2006 and Twenge 2006).

Generation Y have a sense of entitlement, feeling the workplace should be built around them (Alsop 2008) and have a high expectation of their employers. They tend to question and what to know why things are done the way they are. They seek responsibility and flexible deadlines have a desire to be praised by their employers. They seek praise almost instantly in a similar manner to receiving rewards in video games that they play during leisure (Johnson

2005).They seek a fun workplace with meaning attached to the work they do and approach their tasks in a participative manner[21]. Balance in work and leisure is important to them.

Generation Y is generally good at multitasking and have entrepreneurial initiative. They generally want to make a difference and feel strong about social responsibility. However, although most like to follow rules, increasing competitiveness is increasing and for some, cheating in exams is seen as a way to get ahead (Twenge 2006, pp. 27-28). Cutting and pasting any information from any source to do an assignment is something they do without thinking of where the information comes from and issues of copyright (Holliday & Li 2004). They are used to getting immediate answers to any question through the internet (Lucan 2008).

Recent economic conditions have made things very difficult for this generation where many are facing difficulties in getting work after graduating. Youth unemployment is very high and causing social unrest as youths face many hardships (Lowry 2009). This generation is less likely to be able to afford buying a home than the ones before them.

Generation Yers have high expectations of themselves, constantly trying to solve their own problems and take the challenges that come their way. They can work quickly but need definite objectives to motivate (Cochran 2007). Traditional motivational measures such as promotions and bonuses don't excite them much (Alch 2008). Due to their upbringing, generation Y is adaptable to change and value mentoring and training (Cennamo & Gardner 2008). Generation Y has an entrepreneurial spirit, tremendous energy that can give them an advantage, but they are still naïve about the business world (Cochran 2007). However they are prepared to go into business and fail if necessary and move forward after that. They prefer to start with partners as they know the value of collaboration and cooperate learning (Audet et. al. 2009). However entrepreneurship tends to be a means to an end rather than an end in itself unlike previous generations.

Generation Y has many implications for the market environments now in the present and in the future as more join the workforce and collective income dramatically increases in the next few years. Millennials expect a greater range and variety of things whether it is in the classroom or workplace (Sweeney 2006). They expect a continual flow of new and exciting products entering the marketplace. This generation is more cautious about new products than any generation before it. Although they are loyal to brands, they expect brands to earn their loyalty. It is estimated that 50% of 18-24 year olds have personal debts totally more than $14,000 in Australia (Arthur 2008).

Conventional marketing campaigns are felt to be intrusive and Millenials prefer to get their information from their peers with recommendations from *'thought leaders'* and follow *'urban trend setters'*. Traditional TV, radio and leaflet advertising is not effective with Generation Y. Thus marketing campaigns must put propositions directly to consumers through the means that they use to communicate, *i.e., internet, You Tube, Facebook, blogs, etc.* Products must reach across to individual personalities and reflect the way they see themselves. Methods like *underground marketing* that utilize direct approaches through the consumers own world are more effective. *Underground marketing* uses multi-media approaches with viral advertising (often through social media) to create a sense of shared meaning and experience through participative activities with target consumers (Johnson

---

[21] Some companies hire groups of friends to keep social networks together (see Tohmatsu 2006). Wilson and Gerber (2008) found that students performed better when they had input into the design of the assessment, assignment

2006). The product offered although mass produced can be highly differentiated bringing a sense of uniqueness to the consumer who will identify with his or her *'one off'* product. Such an example would be the Toyota Scion which is marketed separately from other Toyota cars and can be highly differenced through selecting from a wide range of accessories available at the retail outlet (Jones 2007). Other examples of successful products or services that have utilized *underground marketing* strategies include Harley-Davidson, Red Bull Energy Drink and the US Army recruitment computer game.

Table 3.5. Some comparisons between the generations

	Baby Boomers	Generation X	Generation Y
Time Period	1946-1964	1965-1978	1979-1999
Events	Their parents experiences during the depression and WWII, the Korean and Vietnam wars, Television, Nuclear era, Space race, Cold war, Civil rights, Rock and roll, JFK, RFK and Martin Luther King assassinated.	Watergate, US hostages in Iran, Computers, Reagan era, HIV/AIDS, the women's movement, the environmental movement and the end of the Cold war.	9/11, The Gulf war, Dot.Com boom and bust, internet, mobile phones and SMS and social networking.
Attitudes and values	A general optimism and satisfaction, feeling of social responsibility, work, health and wellbeing, personal growth, personal gratification.	Work is a challenge. Work is a contract and obligation, self reliance, life/work balance, pragmatism, fun.	Work is a means to an end, optimism, social responsibility, ambition, morality, integrity, ethics, self confidence, sociability.
Communication Technologies	Newspapers, written correspondence, post, time delays between communications, broadcast news, TV, radio, etc.	Printed media, TV, radio, telephone, computer, telex, fax, multimedia and internet.	Broadcasting, cable and satellite TV, email, SMS, chat and other real time internet based teleconferencing.
Motivations	Money, promotion, public recognition, peer recognition and desire to be in control.	Time off, meeting one's own goals, recognition from boss, skills training, mentoring and work/leisure balance.	Time off, skills training, meeting own goals, mentoring, work and play intermixed and being valued.
Working style	Workaholics, working efficiently according to the ways they know how to work, Work for causes and personal fulfillment, consensual and collegial, team players, like meetings, good at forming relationships and reluctant to go against peers.	Self reliant, want structure and direction, skeptical of authority, equality within the workplace, don't respect authority, very direct in speech, strongly independent, cynical and want proof of concept.	Like short time spans, multitasking goal orientated, entrepreneurial, consensus and participative and collective action, like to be challenged, thrive on change, in constant electronic communication and always want feedback.
Problem solving	What has worked in the past can be replicated on the current problem and will work in the future.	Develop a list of potential scenario/solutions and then discuss each option.	Brainstorming, web search, peer discussion.
Concerns	Stability and retirement	Work and leisure/family balances, whether they are appreciated.	The problem of the day, career.

---

types and grading systems within the class.

Not all countries followed the same evolutionary generational path described above. Different histories, events and outlooks affected different countries in various ways. China went through turmoil and upheaval during the 1940's and 50's with the civil war between the KMT and the communists, the Japanese invasion, world war II and the eventual formation of the Peoples Republic of China in 1949. Even after 1949 there was poverty all over the country as it had to rebuild after all the turmoil. The time 1950 to 1970 was the period of the lost generation, first participating in the *great leap forward* and then the *Cultural Revolution*. This left a generation relatively uneducated and indoctrinated with the socialist way of life. It was not until prosperity came to China after its opening up to World trade in the 1970s that the coastal and city areas started to develop and prosper.

Children born between the years of 1970-90 are known as the *lifestyle generation* in China[22]. They are a product of the *'one-child'* policy and number between 230-260 million. Parents tended to spoil, pamper and spend the majority of their incomes on their children's education and material wellbeing. They have become to be known as the little *'emperors'* and *'empresses'* in the family (Lasserre & Schutte 2006, P. 75). These children became differentiated and individualist as opposed to the traditional and socialist orientation of their parents. There is a noticeable generation gap between this generation and those before them. They are optimistic but tend to be amoral due to the absence of religion in China for many years. The *lifestyle* generation is intensely urban yuppyish. They are fashion conscious but with less brand loyalty and more individuality, wanting to be noticed. They are ostentatious consumers and entrepreneurial. Due to the imbalance between males and females in the males favor, females are very selective of their future husbands. In terms of management, they are creative, want to be heard and look towards quick promotions, whilst lacking team spirit (Demoor & Zhang 2007).

With succeeding generations in Japan, traditional values are being replaced with modern Japanese values, which have a number of similarities with western values. Japanese today are much more leisure orientated than the past generation. They look more for quality of life and are larger consumers than the past generation. They follow fads and fashions and seek outside leisure amusement with computer games, etc. They seek instant gratification and are much more individualistic than the last generation that valued collectivity, conformity and loyalty. However, young Japanese don't have the same job security as their predecessors and have different views on loyalty and trust.

In India the boomer generation came after independence and became suspicious of traditional Indian institutions and government. Both Generation X and Y in India see economic growth and more prosperity as an opportunity to advance and consequently work hard to find their place within it. The rest of Asia is developing at different rates, the post war generation generally had to struggle. As this *development* generation saw independence from colonial rule and became more economically comfortable they gave birth to children who are more exposed to modern technology and global influences. The young generations of Asia now have many resemblances to Generation Y of the west.

---

[22] Stanat (2006) classifies those born between 1980-89 as the after-eighty generation, especially those born along the coastal areas of China. According to Stanat this generation is not dissimilar to generation Y in the west.

Culture

Peter Berger and Thomas Luckmann (1967) hypothesized that we live within a socially constructed reality based on the sociology of knowledge[23] about which we take for granted. The sociology of knowledge is information about how we see, live and do in our everyday lives, providing our truths and meanings. The sociology of knowledge is unique to each society. What is real to an Australian may not be real to a Korean and the knowledge of a brick layer will differ from the knowledge of a carpenter. Our very thinking cannot be independent of our own social context.

Perception, thinking and problem solving differs among cultures as different aspects of intelligence are required. Wertsch and Kanner (1992) define culture as shared notions about what counts as efficient problem solving. For example, Western societies heavily utilize verbal, mathematical and spatial skills, while former hunting and gathering cultures a sense of direction and animal knowledge to survive was required.

Geert Hofstede (1991) drew analogies between culture and mental programming, where every person carries with them certain patterns of thinking, feeling and acting based upon what they have learned throughout their life by experiences. Hofstede (1991, P. 4) goes on to explain how this programming begins to be instilled at infancy within the family, then influences from the neighbourhood, school, youth groups, the work place and so on continue as one travels through life. People in different countries develop different mental programs which are as right for them, just as another program is right for someone else in another country. These programs are a product of social environments and are called culture.

Edgar Schein (2005) of MIT adds to our understanding of culture by describing culture as *patterns of shared basic assumptions* that enable groups to learn how to solve both external adaptation internal integration problems. As these basic assumptions have worked in the past, they are retained and passed onto new group members as the correct way to perceive, think, feel, and solve their problems. These basic assumptions filter into the group's belief and value systems through what Clifford Geertz (1973) called the *'symbols of meaning'*, i.e., *language, stories, rituals, artifacts, signs, heroes and villains, etc*[24]. Clyde Kluckholm (1944) enhanced our understanding even further by providing a number of descriptions of culture as *"the total way of life of a people"*, *"the social legacy an individual acquires from his or her group"*, *"a way of thinking, feeling, and believing"*, *"an abstraction from behaviour"*, *"a storehouse of pooled learning"*, *"a set of standardized orientations to recurrent problems"*, *"learned behavior"*, *"a mechanism for the normative regulation of behaviour"*, *"a set of techniques for adjusting both to the external environment and to other people"*, *"a precipitate of history"*, and *"a behavioural map, sieve or matrix"*. This suggests that humans have two

---

[23] The sociology of knowledge is the study of the relationship between thought and social context, and the effect on society. These ideas came from the German sociologist Max Scheler in the 1920s and were used by Berger and Luckmann as a means of gaining a qualitative understanding of socially constructed reality. In cognitive science these concepts may not be too far away from schemata and scripts that give a person structure and meaning to their perceptions, i.e., the means to turn their perceptions into their realties.

[24] Our culture manifests itself in all of society's institutions. Culture itself cannot be seen, but the instruments and effects of culture can be seen in the way the organization is structured, the rites and rituals, the rules and protocol of the organization, the role of status, formal documents like vision, mission and strategy, etc, logos and designs, slogans, rules and ways of control, informal rules and the way people work and behave, stories, office decor and furnishings and the rhetoric, dogma, actions and behaviour of the leader. See Deal and Kennedy (1982), Schein (2005) and Parker (2000).

basic issues to resolve, that of how to achieve integration with society and how to deal with the external environment.

Culture may appear homogenous at a national level, but usually there are subtle differences at a regional level. Culture exists at a number of levels and influences us at all of these levels (Fan 2000, George & Zahra 2002). Culture also exists at an international level, *i.e., East verses West.* We are also a citizen of a nation and may also identify ourselves with a number of groups within it, *i.e., socio-economic, religious, ethnic, gender, generational or geographical group, etc.* We may be a member of a school or university, have a certain occupation, be a member of some specific issue group and/or be a member of a sub-group in society that has counter views to the rest of the nation.

A heterogeneous society does not mean that there is not a national culture, even though some members maybe of different ethnic, social and/or religious backgrounds. Members of these sub-groups usually conform to many of the norms of a national culture while also holding onto norms of their sub-culture, where they deviate from the national culture (Decrop 1999, P. 110). The amount of influence each sub-culture exerts on the national culture and *vice versa* depends upon the individual strength and numbers within each sub-culture. For example, in Malaysia, the tolerant Malay culture has some reminisce of a Hindu past, old colonial institutional trimmings which are overlaid with a dominant Islamic culture (Asrul Zamani 2002). The influence of the layers of culture upon society and its individuals is shown in figure 3.5.

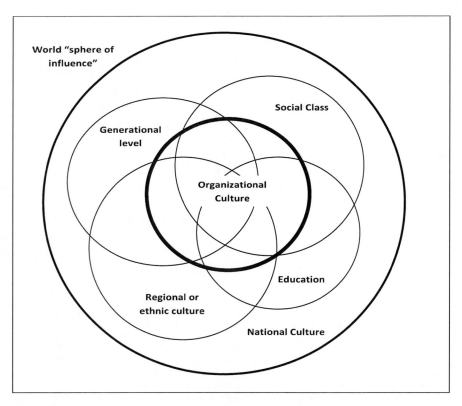

Figure 3.5. Some of the Spherical Influences of Culture upon an individual.

Although it may be easy to understand what culture is by seeing its manifestation, it is extremely difficult to develop hypotheses that lead to any predictability (Grief 1994), or understanding of the deep meanings behind it without our own biases (Geertz 1973). Culture influences a person at two levels. The first level is at a macro-national level from elements of the social history, religion, political philosophies, economic institutions and organizations, language and customs and media influence. External global influence also affects national culture along with other issues like technology that bring social change. The second level of factors are environmental that are much more localized in their influence upon the individual. These factors include the local geography, location and history, local economic environment, the basis of existence for the local society, family influences, education, community expectations and finally mentors, peers and other examples that an individual is exposed to. These are summarized in the next few paragraphs. The cultural process is shown in figure 3.6. and summarized in the following paragraphs.

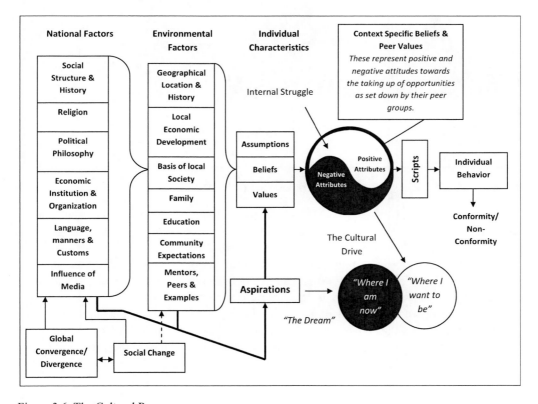

Figure 3.6. The Cultural Process.

Social Structure and History

The social structure defines the way members of society organize themselves and interrelate to each other. Society can organize itself along very formal, structured and hierarchical lines, something towards the direction of a feudal society. This resembles many old agricultural based societies, some still existing in parts of Africa and Asia today.

Alternatively a formal society may resemble a patriarch type of society like Japan. At the other end of the spectrum, society may be very egalitarian like Australian society where respect is earned through achievement. There are also socialist type societies like Cuba, Vietnam and North Korea and Religious based societies like Saudi Arabia and Iran. How society is organized will have some bearing on how relationships interact. Feudal and patriarch type societies tend to have high respect for elders and as a consequence a wide power-distance relationship between leaders and subordinates. Other societies may be segregated by socio-economic boundaries where two different sub-sets of social structure operate like Brazil, Fiji, Thailand, and Indonesia, etc. Figure 3.7. shows how social sub-sets based on income will look like in some countries of the Asia-Pacific Region.

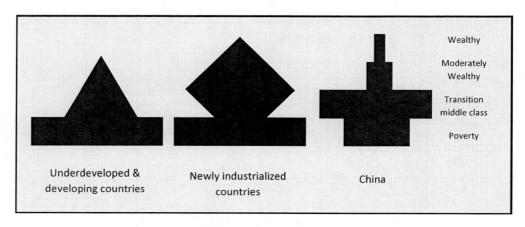

Figure 3.7. Social Group Sub-Sets based on Income in LDC, NIEs and China.

Some societies may have a collective orientation in the way they handle relationships, where the group is seen as more important than any individual wants, while other societies like the United States value the freedom of the individual. In some societies males are expected to act out their masculine traits and the showing of feminine traits is considered a weakness. In other societies like Western and Southern Europe, some feminine traits in males are desired, *i.e., mode of greetings in Southern Europe and Spain, etc[25]*. When looking and comparing social structures, one will usually find odd contradictions. For example, Malaysia could be considered a collective society but decision making is usually the discretion of the leader[26], where in Japan's patriarch system one would expect senior leaders to have a large

---

[25] The discussion in this paragraph basically outlines Hofstede's (1980) cultural values. 1. Power distance: the degree that members of a society accept the right of authority of another over them. In a high power distance culture, a subordinate will expect direction from a superior. In a low power distance culture a participative style of management is preferred. 2. Uncertainty avoidance: the extent to which individuals become stressed due to lack of structure or uncertainty. 3. Individualistic verses collectivist: An individualistic culture is where people tend to look after their own interests and consider their own goals and achievements to be important, where a collectivist culture tends to put group interests over individuals. 4. Masculine and feminine cultures: Masculine societies stress material acquisition and success, while feminine cultures are characterized by interpersonal and interdependency in relationships.

[26] This has certainly been the decision making style of political leadership and is also the style of the public sector and larger organizations.

discretion in decisions, but according to Ouchi (1981) decisions are made collectively through the process of *ringi*[27].

Many social values are the result of unique historical events, evolution and development. For example, the Thai people have a proud sense of history that they were never colonized by a European power and this is important to their sense of freedom and individualism. Thai people are very nationalistic and support community product programs with strong enthusiasm[28]. Likewise Indonesians and Vietnamese have a strong sense of national pride about their struggles against western powers for independence. Chinese tend to be supportive of their Government over general issues that outsiders are critical of China, especially over issues like Tibet[29]. The love-hate relationship that Mexicans feel about the United States has something to do with the legacy of the Mexican-American wars of the 19th Century[30]. The slow evolution of Japan from Shogun feudal rule, Confucian education and agrarian society has influenced the development of strong family values, company and national loyalty. Urbanization in South-East Asia has influenced women to disregard their traditional roles in favour of workforce careers. Urbanization has also broken down the traditional closeness of families. Values develop as the result of unique historical events that shape different national views of the world. Culture is dynamic, where development and urbanization causes values to continually evolve and eventually form new value sets.

Religion

Religion defines a person's relationship with life and eternity. This in varying degrees is reflected in social values, the taboos within interpersonal relationships, ethics and a person's view of their place in the world. Weber (1930) argued that protestant ethics promoted a rational pursuit of economic gain, which gave worldly activities a spiritual and moral meaning. Weber believed that these values made some contribution to the success of industry during the 16th Century in England. However this has been refuted by a number of other scholars (Tawney 1926). Islam is a religion where it's very doctrine, the *Al Qur'an* is written in the metaphor of business and that the Prophet Muhammad (SAW) himself was born into a trading family. Within many parts of the *Al-Qur'an* life is paralleled to a business venture, where one earns profits to gain entry into heaven – profits meaning faith and good deeds to others and those that accept *Allah's* (SWT) guidance as a bargain to save them from punishment on judgment day[31]. Islam urges individuals to strive their utmost to earn large monetary rewards and spiritual profits, while at the same time being inspired to be successful and honest people (Hunter 2008). However, even with Islam's strong pro-business stance, entrepreneurship in many Islamic countries is below that of other comparable countries.

---

[27] Ringi is a bottom-up, consensus based decision making process. It is used as a way of gauging support for various ideas in informal sessions before decisions are made.

[28] One example is Thai consumer support for the "One Tambun One Product" program (OTOP).

[29] This sentiment could be seen in the Chinese backlash to Tibetan supporters attempted disruptions to the Olympic touch relay prior to the 2008 Olympics in Beijing.

[30] Many Mexicans see United States intentions in Latin America as an offensive expression of US influence. This is not only because of the more recent Monroe Doctrine, but also because of US territorial expansion at the cost of Mexico's sovereignty during the 1700-1800s (see Skirius 2003).

[31] See: Al-Qur'an (92:4), (29:69).

Religion does influence many patterns of life. Religion helps to define authority relationships, develop a sense of individualistic duty and responsibility to society, and define the boundaries and taboos of behaviour within relationships. How religion influences opportunity and entrepreneurship is really unknown due to lack of research and conclusive results in this area.

While Islam is on the rise in many countries, the influence of religion in many Western countries is in decline. Many people are taking up alternative spiritual practices as a substitute for the institutionalized religions.

Political Philosophy

Political institutions provide the formal and informal *"rules of engagement"* in the consumer and business sectors of a country. They define how business is viewed by society. Political institutions are made up of a formal level which includes laws and regulations about property rights, etc., and informal influences made up of norms, customs, traditions and moral codes, etc. (Williamson 2000). The philosophical direction of these institutions and informal influence are deeply embedded unconscious values that will influence policy and regulation (Licht, Goldschmidt & Schwartz 2004). These values and beliefs will shape the business culture over a period of time. Political action will influence whether business pursues innovative and productive activities or tends to pursue rent seeking activities, organized crime, bribery and corruption. For example, studies made by Johnson, McMillan and Woodruff (2000, 2002) found that innovative entrepreneurship was inhibited in the post-Soviet economies of Eastern Europe because of insecure property rights, corruption, with inefficient courts to back-up the law. Values and beliefs emerging from political philosophies will also influence how consumers deal with manufacturers and suppliers, and how management deals with labour, etc.

Political philosophy is important in creating the *"business culture"* of a country by setting up the ability of businesses and innovators to enforce their rights in society. Government makes laws, regulations and defines business procedures that impact on firm values and behaviour. The legal system adopted or inherited helps define legal relations. Enforcement helps to shape responses and respect for the *"basic playing rules"* in the economy. For example strong property and intellectual rights stimulate, reinforced by the court system (Khan 2005) will support an innovative and entrepreneurial business culture (North 1990, North and Davis 1971, North and Weingast 1989).

Economic Institution and Organization

The economic philosophy of the country is very important in shaping general business and economic conditions. A country's economic institutions involve basic infrastructures and transport and communication networks, level of professional infrastructure and the country's research and development base. Important areas of economic philosophy include attitudes towards manufacturing, trade and business restrictions, philosophy towards managing the economy, exchange rates and balance of trade, company governance, regulation, and overall trade policies, etc. These factors will play a role, along with political institutions in the general orientation of business, *i.e., export or import substitution orientated, manufacturing or trade orientated, etc.*

Generally the stage of economic development will have great influence upon the structure of the economy and level of employment (Acs & Armington 2006). Basic agricultural production dominates the early stages of economic development. This stage would be characterized by basic farming enterprises, some small manufacturing and supply type enterprises. This stage is also characterized by large rates of self-employment and some of the early traditions and ways of doing business begin to develop[32]. During the development phase, manufacturing will increase either as an export orientated sector based on low cost labour or as an import substitution sector protected by tariffs. This will accelerate the growth of cities and wage based employment where people move from rural to urban areas. This changes society from an agrarian trading community to an urban purchasing community, which in turn will shape new ways of life, relationships, where new sets of values emerge. The first signs of a general rise in wealth will be seen in the urban areas. Eventually the economy develops into a more focused manufacturing sector, accompanied by a developing service industry. Consumer choice increases along with rising incomes and consumer expectations, influenced by advertising for branded and luxury products.

The emerging services sector provides opportunities for entrepreneurs to establish specific specialized enterprises in urban areas. However another effect of the post industrial phase is the decline of urban areas where large scale manufacturing was based, creating a massive reshaping of society. Employment becomes more difficult to obtain, where people require massive vocational retraining. Within society more intense competition makes it more difficult to select economically viable opportunities for individuals to exploit through small to medium enterprises[33]. This leaves large pools of urban unemployment in the cities of the western world (see issues facing generation Y). These large pools of youth unemployment become the breeding ground for sub-cultures in society where they begin to set themselves apart from the mainstream culture, forming alternative assumptions, beliefs and values as a way to cope with anxiety.

Language and Customs

Language can be seen as the pride of a culture. Many countries still use their respective national languages as the official language and language of education. Language includes not only written and spoken words, but expressions which have specific cultural contexts and meaning, signs, symbols, gestures, mannerisms and pauses. Words although translated similarly, may in actual fact have wider or narrower meanings, which can change its emphasis and connotation. Language is embedded into custom and manners where it becomes the narrative of meaning for people. Table 3.6. below explains the meaning of the word

---

[32] This is where the early signs of "how people approach doing business". These signs can be seen in how farmers approach business, i.e., whether they are satisfied to produce for middlemen to come and purchase their produce or whether they themselves participate in the marketing process. Other signs can be seen in how rural suppliers do business, i.e., they suppliers restrict their operations to retail, or wholesale as well?, do they offer credit, etc? Future business will tend to operate within these early set 'modus operandi', until some entrepreneurs or enterprises in the future change the business models.

[33] An alternative view is that a post industrial economy will provide more opportunities for small sized SMEs because of lower barriers to entry and low initial capital requirements for industry entry (EIM/ENSR 1997).

"entrepreneurship" in a number of languages and shows some differences in cultural contexts[34].

Table 3.6. The meaning of the Word *"Entrepreneurship"* in various Language Contexts

Language	Pronunciation	Meaning
Finnish	Yrittäjyys	The person who tries; a Trier, trialship, to try.
French	Entrepreneur	Entrepreneur; taking yourself into something that takes hold of you; to undertake
Greek	επιχειρηματικότητας	The ability to do business, to try something, to take a chance.
Hebrew	יזמות {Yazam}	To do something from the beginning or scratch.
Hungarian	Válavosás	To volunteer, to undertake
Icelandic	Frumkvöplastrfsemi	Going first, taking the initiative, the first to take on an activity.
Indonesian	Wirausaha	A courageous effort.
Irish	Fiontraí	A person involved in an adventure, taking risks.
Japanese	Kiyokasashi	To create new business, people with spirit.
Malay	Usahawan Perniaga	To do something, usually a commercial activity. Someone who does business
Mandarin	創業	I have a dream to change the way.
Spanish (Spain)	Emprendedorismo	To move on, the achiever, to do something.
Swedish	Företagane	He or she that undertakes something
Tagalog	Negosyo	A business person, the one who starts a business.
Thai	เป็นผู้ประกอบการ {Puphratg okgan}	To assemble people and do things together.

Embedded customs can create obstacles for business. Customs may affect the meaning and the way credit can be utilized as a way of doing business. For example, the Fijian style of observing credit responsibilities within clan *(i.e., friends and relatives)* is through the concept of *kerkere,* where there is little compulsion or obligation to pay back the money borrowed. This creates burdens on native Fijian entrepreneurs while Indian and Chinese Fijians do not have this same burden (Benedict 1979). Business practices are also affected by a culture's sense of time (Coulter 1967, Qalo 1997), property rights, and family relationships, etc[35].

The Influence of Media

The media plays an important role in forming and reflecting opinion and culture in a country. The media influences what people think is important, funny, serious, taboo, acceptable, sacred, scary, what people want, what people aspire, how people live and how people like to be seen and not be seen. The relationship between the individual and the media is a complex one, although the media appears to be able to have some influence on elections in democracies and consumer behaviour through editorial and advertising.

[34] See Frederick, H. (2006). Definitions of Entrepreneurship in World Languages (DVD), Auckland, New Zealand, Ten3 Asia-Pacific ltd.
[35] In many parts of the world a business cannot be run and operated according to western concepts of efficiency for various cultural reasons.

According to McQuail (1983) the mass media plays a number of roles in society. Firstly, media reinforces a person's behaviour by connecting him or her to defined role values and gender identification. Secondly, media provides a means where a person can connect and identify with others. Thirdly, the media provides a person a sense of security. Fourthly, the media provides a window to the world and opportunity to learn and gain information. Finally, the media offers a sense of escape and emotional release.

The media can influence social agenda over issues and be a change agent of peoples' values and beliefs. The media has been used numerous times as an instrument of control in many countries over the last fifty years. It is also a powerful carrier of the influence of *"globalism"* to many societies. This has had great influence of the *"westernization"* of Asian societies, over the last twenty years[36].

The media is heading into a transformation with the advent of the internet and almost immediate transmission of information around the world by citizens of countries through social media and hand held media devices. The effects of individual interaction with the internet are seen in mass political movements and direct consumer involvement in corporate advertising strategies. This is changing the way politics is played out in both democratic and undemocratic regimes, product and corporate promotion. Social media increases the exchange of information between people on a direct basis. How the traditional television, radio and print media redefine their roles within the new technologies is yet to be fully seen. There is no doubt that relationships between culture and the media will be one of the most important factors in shaping peoples values and beliefs.

Globalization: Convergence/Divergence

The concept of globalization is very abstract and has many different dimensions including, communication, corporate, cultural, economic, environmental, information, market, political, social, travel and security. Globalization is also confused with the issues of modernization, technology development, especially communication and information technology and issues of transfer. Globalization is not a new phenomenon it dates back to the pre-history period when *Homo sapiens* left the African continent to inhabit Eurasia, empires and religions developed and spread, and seagoing vessels enabled old Europe to colonize most of the *new worlds* from the 1400-1800s. Many of the characteristics of globalization today are the consequence of improving transport, communications and government policy changes over the last century. Many claim that the world is becoming more globalized than ever before, but some historians of political economy claim that the world is only returning to the integration it once had before WWI[37].

The major issue from our point of view is the impact of globalization on a culture. There is both some convergence and divergence within the concept of globalism. Cultural convergence leads to homogeneous cultural values between cultures and divergence leads to

---

[36] This "westernization" reflects more changes in consumer habits rather than changes in core assumptions, beliefs and values. The rapid influence of "western consumerism" and fashion was seen when television was first introduced to Bhutan in the early 1990s.

[37] International migration was much greater before World War I with almost 60 million people from Europe travelling to the United States, Canada, New Zealand and other countries. This does not include Chinese and Indian migration around the world (see Gilpin 2000, pp. 18-19, 295, and 311-14).

cultural diversity and localism in cultural outlooks. The dynamics of global convergence and divergence are extremely complex. These issues are subject to fierce and emotional debate and as an issue to stir up political support in many Asian countries. These debates play on fears about western corporate control over national economies, the loss of culture and values to the influences of western media agendas.

However, within a country there are forces that counter or block the impacts of global influences, just as there are also forces that promote the acceptance of global influences. Thomas Friedman (2005) believes that there are two aspects of culture that determine convergence or divergence in a country: *how outward is the culture (or how inward)?* And *how open is it to new ideas?* Friedman (2005 pp. 421-423) continues on to say that some cultures are more outward and open than others to foreign influence, contrasting the differences between the more moderate Islamic countries like Turkey, Lebanon, Bahrain, Indonesia, Dubai and Malaysia to the more fundamental Islamic nations. Some of the forces for convergence and divergence are listed in Table 3.7. below.

Table 3.7. Some Forces for Convergence and Divergence

Forces Promoting Convergence	Forces Promoting Divergence
Migration	Backlash to migration
Trade	Trade barriers and restrictions
Capital inflow and direct foreign investment.	Capital and exchange rate restrictions
Growth in communications, especially satellite TV and internet.	Use of internet to promote local culture and language.
Knowledge	Lack of knowledge
Communications technology	Censorship
Liberalization of economic policies and deregulation	Trade barriers, economic nationalism
Technology and innovation	Poor intellectual property protection
Transport and logistics	Underdeveloped infrastructure
Transnational companies	Restrictive investment regulation
Need of greater economies of scale in production and corresponding markets.	Import replacement policies
International sport	Local sport preferences
Popular culture (movies, music, etc.)	Local popular culture (local movies, music)
Concentration of Retail sector	Fragmentation of retail market
Education	Poverty, lack of education and knowledge dissemination
Urbanization	Rural Stagnation, Feudalism
Religious tolerance	Religious fundamentalism

Social Change

Social change evolves in most cultures over time, except in the most rigid and dogmatic societies. There are a number of factors that can be considered precursors for altering social, political and economic structures and changing social patterns.

One of the most influential factors affecting social change is economic development. Economic development disturbs the *'ways of how things have been done'* through transformation. As economic development is usually urban centred cities will often quickly develop at the expense of rural areas. This brings with it great shifts in lifestyle and behaviour patterns where people become wage and salary earners and live and work within *industrial timetables*. Often the values of new professionals within society as managers are in conflict with their traditional values as seen in Malay society (Rashid 1988). More changes affect the structure and interrelationships within the family as more women enter the workforce, families rely on dual incomes and those left in rural areas tend to stagnate. Good technical skills become the currency where people advance themselves so education becomes a valuable currency.

Increasing per-capita incomes brings on new patterns in consumer behaviour. Choice becomes an important aspect of consumerism and opportunities open up for new concepts to satisfy sophisticated consumers. As economic development reaches a mature stage, manufacturing industries tend to decline. Companies seek out lower cost countries to manufacture in especially when tariff regimes are taken down and there are cost advantages in sourcing externally or relocating. Such trends can be seen in the US, Canada, EU, Australia, New Zealand, sourcing from China and South-East Asia. Consequently, this post industrial phase sees a rise in service industry which creates another radical change in the *'ways of how things have been done'*, leading to new types of supply chains and new sets of skills and influences. These processes are continual and as they evolve peoples' attitudes and culture changes without society being aware until the changes have occurred. The edge of social change is where opportunity can be both discovered and created.

Another set of more local environmental factors also influences the cultural environment for individuals. These factors are more specifically local and group specific and can also explain differences in culture across a single country.

Geographical Location and History

A community's way of life is dictated by the local geography, topography, resources and history of an area. Being close to the sea, bay, inlet, harbour, mountain, plain, jungle, isolated, urban or rural, between two major cities or resource endowed will influence the range of occupations and general outlook on life. Economic and social life in most areas can be explained by the surrounding geography and history of an area.

Geographical characteristics such as the availability of farmland and ease of access to potential markets, physical resource endowments like mineral resources, and the physical ability to access markets through any topographical obstacles will partially determine economic development.

Why some communities grow and prosper and others stagnate and decline is partly a function of natural and man-made topography and features. Airport, road, rail and sea links tend to bolster economic activity, while lack of them may inhibit growth or even cause decline. One can see the economic decline in many towns where highway extensions by-passed by the town, as has occurred in many places around the world.

The English Channel tunnel between the UK and France and the Loetschberg tunnel between Germany and Northern Italy under the Alps were built to enhance economic activity between nations. These massive transport infrastructure projects improve links between countries that where traditional foes through European history. Not all man-made infrastructure projects have helped all people. The building of irrigation schemes by the Soviets that diverted water from rivers flowing into the Aral Sea since the 1960s has destroyed a prosperous fishing industry, bringing poverty and death to 3 million people in the region (Lean 2006). Another type of problem occurred with the construction of the Three Gorges Dam across the Yangtze River in China. Although the dam is producing massive hydro-electricity aiding in economic development, cutting down on greenhouse gases, aiding transport through better shipping and assisting in flood control, more than 1.2 million people have been displaced and silts are no longer being carried downstream to help replenish soil fertility (Kuhn 2008).

Table 3.8. The Different Influences Geographical Features Could Have on Lifestyle/Occupation/Opportunities

Geographical Eco-System Type	Lifestyle/Occupation/Opportunity
Arid Semi-Desert	Usually agro-horticultural-pastoral activities under small subsistence, semi-subsistence, partly commercial farm living. Other communities may have large commercial farms and commercial mono-cropping. Intermittent towns would serve the surrounding hinterland with suppliers and consolidate produce for transport to major markets. Would expect unified assumptions, beliefs, and values.
Coastal Agro-Ecosystem	Usually livestock, fishing, agriculture and horticultural industries. Can range from small subsistence, to semi-subsistence and partly commercial farms. In some areas small to large commercial farms managed along estate lines. Town may support hinterland and because coastal may also have a port, which may attract larger populations due to trade activities. Area may also support tourism. Would expect unified assumptions, beliefs, and values, except where occupational diversity may occur.
Hill and Mountain	Agricultural, horticultural and livestock. May also support tourism. Small subsistence, semi-subsistence and small specialized commercial family farms. Towns support local inhabitants would be expected to be small. Group diversity may occur due to influence of tourism.
Irrigated Agro-Ecosystem	Rice, wheat, sugar cane, cotton, soy, dairy and fishing. Small subsistence, semi-subsistence and small specialized commercial family farms. Towns would support hinterland. The extent of growth will determine how diverse groups will become within society.
Rainfed Agro-Ecosystem	Arable farming, agro-forestry and livestock. Small subsistence, semi-subsistence, and both small and large mono-crop estates. Towns would support hinterland. The extent of growth will determine how diverse groups will become within society.
Urban Environment	Usually a major town or city ranging from several thousand people to over one million carrying out urban activities of various types. Would expect cosmopolitan population with transport links to other cities via air, road and rail. Large metropolitan areas would also house majority of manufacturing industry with support service sector. Some act as seat of government.

How communities react to economic development through tourism, industrialization, increases in trade through their region is very complex, with research providing different conclusions. One can see that communities with a long history of exposure to outsiders appear to be tolerant and appreciative of the opportunities this brings. Conversely, communities with little exposure to outsiders appear to be less open to new ideas and change[38]. Table 3.8. shows the different influences geographical features could have on lifestyle, occupations and opportunities.

Local Economic Development

Local economic development will have some influence over a person's hopes, aspirations, mobility, employment and opportunity potential. Economic development may diversify activities and occupations beyond traditional ways of earning income. Alternatively economic development within a country can eventually lead to rural decline in certain regions. The level of economic development may influence peoples' optimism or pessimism about the future. If the general population is involved through employment opportunities, there will most likely be some optimism, whereas if new industries don't create employment opportunities, pessimism may develop.

The Basis of Local Society

The basis of existence of a local society is primarily historical and will influence the types of traditions and views of life people have. As the basis of the local society may change through development, some traditions and outlooks may stay with the senior populations. Examples of towns built on specific reason include the old coal mining towns of the UK, the fishing towns along the coasts of countries around oceans like UK and Australia and the mining towns in Northern and Western Australia, etc. Towns may have developed because of a specific reason like a *gold-rush,* peak and then decline. Unless new activities can help define new roles like farming, the town's prosperity may decline and eventual survival threatened.

Family

People born into and brought up in a family will tend to reflect some, if not most of the assumptions, beliefs and social values from their parents. From an early childhood children within the family environment learn what is safe and dangerous, what is acceptable and taboo, what the truth is and what are not, what ideas are good and what are not and their relationship with the rest of the world, etc. Family fundamentally defines social class for the children, as the school, outside groups they become involved in, and perhaps even sports they play will be influenced by the parents. Social peers and friends are likely to be members of the same or

---

[38] The literature on community acceptance of tourism even though there would be economic benefits showed that there would more than likely be negative attitudes towards tourism (see for example Hjalager 1996, Murphy 1981). One can only observe that communities that have a long history of trade and tourism are more open in outlook to communities with much less exposure. In making these comments the author has cities like London, Paris, Bangkok, Jakarta and Vientiane in mind as cities with positive outlook on outsiders, where negative outlooks would come from country towns in many countries where "outside" traffic is infrequent. However the author is also sure that there will be many exceptions to these cases.

similar social background which verifies their assumptions, beliefs and social values. Children will tend to model themselves upon their parents and may even follow in similar career patterns (Hofstede 1980, P. 32)[39]. Family, social class, education, peers and occupation are closely linked and generally reinforce each other as influencing factors upon a person.

Basic assumptions about life differ from society to society (Douglas 1966). Ethnic values are instilled in children early, helping them learn how to relate to others. For example, children in cultures like Japan and Korea learn to respect their parents and elder people in society. In contrast, parents in western societies like the United States want to teach their children independent behaviour, with the hope that they will learn how to take control of their own lives. The upbringing in Japan leads to a patriarchal society where senior managers have a lot of power and influence over decision making with formal rules of relationship. Children in the United States will tend to grow up doing part time jobs for pocket money and upon adulthood will have a relationship with their parents as friends rather than parent-child.

Children develop their personal sense of risk taking propensity in their early teens. However as risk taking is situational, a person's propensity to take risks, particularly in the business area may not come out until later life because as young people, the personal risk of starting a business may be enough to dissuade them due to the responsibilities of buying a house and starting a family (Bolton & Thompson 2003, P. 40).

Finally family background is not a good predictor of who can discover or construct opportunities and act upon them. Entrepreneurs come from both rich and poor backgrounds, with both solid and broken homes. Children of wealthy comfortable families may not have the passion or desire for business and instead of entering a family business, go and do something else. However the key attribute that comes from a family is a sense of self and self assurance.

Education

Education, along with national media and language factors create a strong integration force on a national culture level (Hofstede 1980, P. 12). Both formal and informal education affects culture and the capacity of the human capital quality, which is measured on a macro scale through literacy rate, general education level, range of skill competencies and potential career paths and technical competence, etc. Education instills a degree of mental programming within the citizenry that affects the types of technology people will look to, the type of business models people will use, the types of resources and networks that will be favoured and the types of strategies and supply chains that will be utilized (Le 1999). A person with information and skills will be more likely to exploit opportunities in areas where those competencies and skills are required (Shane 2003, P. 69).

The type and level of education a person undertakes is influenced by social class and what career opportunities a person desires. Diplomas and degrees have a special symbolic purpose of increasing both economic and self worth. In a sense a diploma or degree is an achievement that is recognized by society. The diploma/degree enables someone to associate

---

[39] From a Freudian perspective a male may be driven by an unresolved rivalry with his father. The grown up child may be striving unconsciously to rid himself of control from the father. The mother strongly urges the son to achieve more than the father due to her disappointments of the husband. Anger is the main driver for success and for this they will work hard.

with higher status groups in business and obtain higher status marriage partners, etc. A degree is traditionally thought of as a *'meal ticket'*. To some extent, undertaking an education can be seen as the beginning of one's pursuit of their aspirations and dreams, both at the individual and collective level. To a great extent the equality/inequality of a country is influenced by access to education[40].

Education produces professional groups within a culture that have their own cognitive patterns of thinking. For example a mechanic will be able to diagnose symptoms of an engine problem through their hearing from where they can diagnose the problem. In a similar manner doctors identify a patient's medical problem through examining symptoms and match these symptoms to a probable disease or pathology that fits the symptomatic description. Learning patterns also differ between generations. As people tend to learn only what they need to know. For example, most of the younger generation is poor at mental arithmetic because they rely on pocket calculators which the last generation did not have access to. There are also differences between languages where Chinese students must learn between 5,000 to 15,000 characters by heart to read and write the Chinese language.

Cultural differences also affect learning styles. The extent to which students learn, or don't learn, may be a product of teaching style used. Therefore the situation arises within national education systems where the majority of students may be congruent with the teaching style, but a minority will be deficient in learning because the teaching style is inappropriate for their learning style. Ramírez and Castarñedu (1974) described Mexican-American students as field dependent learners where white students tended to be field independent *(discussed later in this chapter)*. Although culture has some influence in this situation, it cannot be argued that it is the sole influence on learning ability (Irvine & York 1995). Every society places a different value on learning and achievement at school (Oybu 1991). Minority groups may develop sub-cultures with specific norms or values that deter a person achieving in fear that they may be labeled someone trying to emulate the dominating culture (Kunjufu 1986).

Many highly technical fields like biotechnology and electronic engineering often require very highly educated people (Zucker *et. al.* 1998), who have undertaken specific research in the field to commercialize new ideas based on new knowledge (Aldrich & Wiedenmeyer 1993). Similarly, a lot of the internet entrepreneurs attended business schools where they had a long time to develop their ideas, access banks, venture capitalists and network with their fellow students. However, education can be restrictive on impatient people who cannot take the discipline of learning things which they do not see relevant to their ideas. This is why many entrepreneurs leave school or university before getting a diploma or degree, as they don't see the value in it. For this reason education does not necessary correlate with entrepreneurial achievement.

Education is experience and this can be obtained in alternative and informal ways like selling lemonade outside the family home during youth, or undertaking some sort of business activities while at school, etc. Doing small things in youth that are entrepreneurial and fun is a learning experience which can lead to bigger things as Michael Dell, as founder of Dell computers testified to in his semi-autobiographical book (Dell & Fredman 1999). Although it

---

[40] For example, in the political turmoil in Thailand, the disposed Prime Minister Dr. Taksin Shinawatra is supported by the peasants in the North and North-East of Thailand (red shirts), where the current Government of Mr. Abhisit Vejjajiva draws his support from the more educated middle class in Central and Southern Thailand.

is not certain what effect education has on a person's ability to discover and construct opportunity. Table 3.9. below lists the advantages education provides people in this regard.

Table 3.9. Skills and Abilities derived from education and the Advantages they Bring

Skills and Abilities	Advantages
Planning, bargaining, decision making, problem solving	These are general cognitive business skills which help with evaluation, planning and running of a business. These skills help to teach a person to learn. They are fairly generic with very minor cultural differences.
Judgment	Venture and strategy evaluation. Helps to reduce uncertainty.
Labour law knowledge, consumer law knowledge, accountancy and book-keeping knowledge, finance knowledge, business law, intellectual property knowledge, etc.	These represent content business information which is usually country and cultural specific to many aspects.
Marketing, selling, customer, supply chain and value chain knowledge	These are specific skills which enable a person to enter an industry. If an entrepreneur understands the customers, markets and *modus operandi* of markets he or she has little or no experience in, he or she should be able to operate within it. This is generally country and culturally specific knowledge.
Technical engineering, scientific and manufacturing knowledge.	This represents the technical knowledge required to manufacture and support products of any venture. This technology is not restricted to *'hard'* things as *'software'* *(i.e., manufacturing and process procedures)* is also required to utilize technology. These are usually generic and not culturally specific considerations except where manufacturing procedures may be influenced through cultural and economic factors *(i.e., labour verses capital intensive production methods).*

Community Expectations

As people become better educated, wealthier and join an amassing middle class, community expectations will over a wide range of issues become more sophisticated. These include expectations about standards of governance, government services, customer service by companies, wider range of choice, lifestyle, opportunities for advancement and quality of work life. Community expectations influence the *'buoyancy'* of a culture, *i.e., whether a community is generally content or dissatisfied about the present, optimistic or pessimistic about the future, and whether the general outlook is one of hope or despair.* This general *'buoyancy'* influences assumptions and beliefs and will set the background from where individuals will develop their collective and individual aspirations for the future.

Mentors, Peers and Role Models

A mentor is a senior and experienced person who could be a parent, close friend or teacher who assists, advises, helps and guides a usually younger, less experienced person, sometimes called a protégé. Mentorship can be both formal and informal and involves the dissemination of knowledge in a practical way so that the protégé can develop both the explicit and implicit aspects of a trade, art, job or entrepreneurial venture, etc. This way of passing knowledge onto another also passes across attitudes, beliefs and values about the skills and abilities in focus. Mentorship through both formal and informal apprenticeships is a powerful way of transferring beliefs, values and skills to younger people. For this reason organizational mentor programmes are very popular as a means to develop people (Murray 1991, Schlee 2000).

Peer groups usually contain people of similar social status and education, have similar interests and have a common source of bonding. Peer groups form a basis of shared cognitive, social and emotional development in a way that fosters intimacy and security. Peer groups assist a person develop their own personality through their interactions with others which creates their own perceptions and views of themselves. Erik Erikson (1975) argues that this development goes on into adulthood and that there are eight stages of development. These are;

- *Trust verses Mistrust:* in infancy when children are dependent upon others, *'wonder who is going to take care of them?'* and *'how are they going to be taken care of?'* etc. If children are well taken care of and their needs met, they will develop a sense of trust in their caregivers. Erikson believes that this trust will form the basic assumptions of future relationships and consequently in adulthood the person will approach potential relationships in a trusting manner. If infants are not taken care of, the opposite will occur where the person will develop a sense that no one is to be trusted.

- *Autonomy verses Shame and Doubt:* Once children are on their feet, they will test both their physical abilities and boundaries. This results in children running around the room and screaming until they are told to be quiet. Often they will test this authority to find out how much control they really have over the situation. When a child feels a sense of control and mastery over things, they will develop self confidence. If parents inhibit their children's actions, then their maybe a loss of self confidence and retardation of the want of the child to explore and encounter a wide variety of life events.

- *Initiative verses Guilt:* Children in their toddler years will often imitate adults. They will receive their first experience doing adult tasks during play. They learn how to work with people, follow others, lead and settle disputes. When this goes well, children will develop a sense of initiative, which can translate into ambition. If things don't go well, children may become resigned to failure and not take any initiative in life.

- *Industry verses Inferiority:* around the age of four children start to compare themselves to others, especially those their own age. Many develop a sense of competence and achievement and belief that if they work hard enough they can do most things they desire to do. However if they experience enough failure, they may develop a sense of inferiority, feeling they don't have the talent and ability to get by in life.

- *Identity verses Role Confusion:* During adolescence people go through all sorts of physical and emotional changes. Where people transition from childhood into adulthood they develop their identity achievement asking questions of themselves *"Who am I?"*, and *"do others recognize me for who I am?"* etc. This is also a period of experimentation where different identities are tried (Erikson 1968). Teenagers search for this identity in many places. Eventually most people make the decisions about who they are, what is important to them and what they want, etc. People who don't resolve these issues wonder in confusion and enter adulthood without a sense of identity and meaning in their lives. People differ to the extent that they commit themselves to the values, careers, relationships in their lives and personal ideologies (Marcia 2002).

Most people go through this stage of identity confusion until they find meaning. Some people develop a negative identity which is founded on undesirable social norms, roles and rules. They often take cues from undesirable role models. Most people have to go through some crisis or realization to find their identity. If they don't, they may pick up a shallow identity with values and beliefs that they cannot backup with any real rationale or meaning. People with this identity display moralistic and conventional characteristics, but also have a dark and hidden side suppressed inside them.

- *Intimacy verses Isolation:* In adulthood connecting to others is a prime concern. People need to develop relationships that are mutually satisfying and intimate. This is the time when people grow emotionally and develop into caring nurturing and providing adults. This often means making a commitment to a single person in life through marriage. On the other hand, isolation is the failure to find and maintain intimacy.
- *Generativity verses Stagnation:* During the rest of a person's years the main issue is whether the person has generated something that he or she really cares about in life. This may take the form of a career, commitment to children, a hobby, volunteering, or something that is generative. When people stop and think back over their years and feel that they have not achieved anything, they feel disappointed. Other people don't care and just go along in life, not really caring about what they are doing. They go through life and can be seen as phonies.
- *Integrity verses Despair:* At this last stage of development, occurring near the end of life, a final crisis occurs. When we let go of our generative role when we retire from the job we loved or maybe the children take on their own lives, or we stop doing the volunteer work we loved and prepare to face death, we look back on our lives and make judgment. *"Was it all worth it?"*, *"did I accomplish anything?"* If positive a person will take satisfaction in their lives and go through our passing with integrity. If dissatisfied with our lives, wishing we had more time to make changes, to repair relationships, and right the wrongs, etc, we experience despair. People who have a lot of regrets in old age will become bitter people.

Consequently, through our life development, the peer group is an important reference and influence upon our lives, especially from infancy into adult life. Peoples motivations and wants are situational and partly come through comparison and observation with others. Through this peer conformity, people develop similar desires, wants and/or aspirations. This is how research clusters and business incubators develop an environment where peer values assist in driving innovation where *Silicon Valley* is perhaps the most famous example (Larson & Rogers 1986).

The influence of leadership within organizations is particularly important, especially when the leader is also the founder. The founder imposes his or her assumptions, beliefs and values onto new groups during the formation of the organization. The leader's assumptions, beliefs and values are espoused to the other members of the organization through what issues the leader focuses upon, how he or she reacts to events, where resources are allocated, what things he or she controls, through talking, speeches and by his or her very own day to day actions (Schein 2004, P. 246).

Basically culture will influence every aspect of life and how things are done. Some examples of areas of everyday life that is affected by culture are listed in table 3.10. below.

Table 3.10. Some Areas of Life that Culture Affects

Acceptability of society	Government system	Puberty customs
Art	Greetings	Range and types of foods
Artifacts	Hairstyles	Religion and religious rituals
Basis of respect	Heroes	Residence rules
Body adornments	Historical interpretation	Rest times
Calendar	Home decor	Rights (legal and moral)
Community organizations	Hospitality	Sexual restrictions
Consumer tastes	Housing	Soul concepts
Courtship and marriage customs	Inheritance	Standard of Cleanliness
Dancing and performing arts	Jokes and humour	Status and social structure
Dreams and dream interpretation	Kinships	Superstitions
Driving rules and etiquette	Labour organization	Symbols
Education	Language	Television shows
Education philosophy	Magic and esoteric	Tipping
Entertainment	Mealtimes	Transport
Ethnics and morals	Medicine	Type of news reported
Ethno botany	Mental health	View of aged people in society
Etiquette	Modesty	View of nature and the environment (relationship and control)
Expectations	Mourning	View of place in society
Family	Music	View of the world
Folklore	Mythology	Visiting
Food taboos	Numerals	Ways of doing jobs and work
Funeral rites	Obstetrics	Weaning
Games	Parties and celebrations	What sports are played
Gestures	Penal sanctions	Work patterns
Gift giving	Personal names	Writing
Government spending	Property rights	

Aspirations

An aspiration can be a national ethos, which is a set of ideals that the majority of people can identify with through cultural conditioning. The national aspiration is a wide and general like principal, extolling something like *'having a richer and happier life'* or *'owning our house'*, etc. Aspirations create desires and ideals the country's citizens hope to achieve. These aspirations have developed through a nation's history and been shaped by some of the cultural factors discussed previously.

Aspirations are an important part of culture and translate through the assumptions, beliefs and values of the culture and often become reflected in individual desires and drive. Aspirations of individuals are orientated to the basic questions of *'Where am I now?'* and *'where do I want to be?'* People will have different views on their ability to achieve cultural aspirations based on their own views of self efficacy and control over their own destiny. These aspirations become a person's motivating drive. Different levels of self motivation may partly explain why people vary in their rates of learning at school (Riessman 1962), vary in their alertness for opportunities, and vary in their business growth aspirations (Tominc & Rebernik 2007).

The entrepreneur through literature and the media has become symbolized as a person who is a brave frontiersman like the mythical cowboy of the past. Entrepreneurship is portrayed as a road to freedom and reward. Therefore to some, entrepreneurship may be a spirit of expression and perceived as a way of turning one's own ideals into a reality. This mythology has its basis both in history through the pilgrim settlements in America and entertainment, where characters *"Rocky"* are personified as the *'underdog'* who wins against all odds (Hammond & Morrison 1996).

Assumptions, Beliefs and Values

Assumptions are the deep inner core of culture. We all have developed shared sets of assumptions about our place within the environment, the nature of man, the nature of human relationships, the nature of reality and truth, the nature of time and space, and how to adapt to the external environment as a means to achieve our goals.

Kluckhohn and Strodtbeck (1961) described mankind's three basic environmental orientations as;

1. *The Doing orientation:* assumes man can control and manipulate the environment. Consequently a person with a doing orientation will take a pragmatic and proactive orientation towards nature. In such an orientation, people take charge and formulate strategies that try to control the environment. This doing orientation is seen traditionally as a *'western orientation'*, focusing on objectives, task, goals with efficiency. Individuals with this orientation would tend to formulate strategies in an attempt take control and dominate the market.

2. *The Being orientation:* is opposite to the doing orientation and assumes that nature is so powerful that all humans are subservient to it. This fatalistic approach has a sense of weakness that one cannot influence events facing him or her and must take what comes along. One focuses on *'here and now'*, *'enjoyment'* and *'accepting whatever*

comes'. Individuals in this frame would look for niche markets with little competition and operate with the goal to survive.

3. *The Being-in-Becoming orientation*: is somewhere in the middle of *'doing'* and *'being'* orientations where the basic assumption here is that the individual must achieve harmony with the environment by fully developing his or her own capabilities and sense of achieving full unity with nature. In this orientation the focus is on developing full integration so the person rather than what the person has achieved is important.

Every culture has shared assumptions about the nature of human nature, *i.e., 'what it means to be human', 'what are our basic instincts',* and *'what kind of behaviour is considered appropriate for a human',* etc. Humanity itself is a cultural construction and differs slightly from culture to culture. Through both religion and work, our assumptions about the nature of human nature can be seen clearly.

In most religions man is seen as a figure that can be redeemed and that once shown the *'right'* path, man is intrinsically good. Salvation is promised in the next life as a reward. However the problem with religion today is that many in the west now live spiritually rather than religiously and the level of commitment to religion varies greatly from person to person. Religion in some parts of the world has taken on a *'pathological zealotism'* and been used to justify political positions and terrorism (Todd 2010), just as it was once used to justify the persecution of the Christians in Palestine and the Roman Empire and slavery in North America during the 18th Century.

Through looking at the nature of work, one can very quickly pick up the assumptions about the nature of human nature through the observations of policy and action and the relationships between managers and employees.

All management theory is built upon assumptions of the nature of human nature. Very early on in the emergence of modern management Frederick Taylor developed a philosophy called *scientific management* that assumed that man could not be trusted and had to be controlled. Decades went by until this was disproven through *The Hawthorne Experiments* carried on by Elton Mayo which lead to a new set of assumptions that man was a being that wanted social interaction and could be motivated through intrinsic means. A clear expression of the two polarized assumptions of the nature of human nature can be seen in McGregor's (1960) *Theory X and theory Y. Theory X and Y* are two sets of broad assumptions where *Theory X* sees man as basically untrustworthy, needing to be closely supervised and extrinsically motivated and *Theory Y*, which sees man as trustworthy, not needing to be closely supervised and intrinsically motivated. Some of the major characteristics of *Theory X and Y* are shown in Table 3.11.

Managers often have the view that workers are untrustworthy and behave in a manner that itself could be the cause *(i.e., the work group will react to the manager with type X behaviour)*[41]. One can still see today *Theory X* type management in so many organizations. *Theory X and Y* are two extremes and other management theories have bridged the gap between them with much more sophisticated and less polarized theories.

---

[41] A Type X manager would be expected to be result driven, intolerant, always give deadlines and ultimatums, be distant and detached, aloof and arrogant, elitist, short tempered, directs without listening, demanding, etc.

Table 3.11. Basic Premises of Theory X and Y

Theory X	Theory Y
Major Assumption: Employees are inherently lazy and will avoid any work if they can.	Major Assumption: Employees are ambitious and self motivated people.
Dislike work and will avoid it if possible.	Enjoy work as it is like play.
Have little ambition and must be motivated by extrinsic incentives.	Seek and accept responsibility and seek self control.
Out for themselves.	Group orientated.
Disloyal.	Loyal to group.
Not creative.	Under right conditions creative at problem solving.

Our basic assumptions also define the nature of our relationships with others. Rules emerging from our cultural assumptions provide orientations into how to make our relationships safe, comfortable and productive. To achieve this we must resolve the issues of our own identity and role within the group, our power and influence, our needs and objectives, whether we are accepted and have intimacy within our relationships (Schein 2005, P. 179). How we relate to each other is culturally defined through group and relationship characteristics which are based on the degree of individualism and collectivism, power distance and acceptable ways of communication between people within the culture.

Our assumptions shape what reality and truth is. Reality and truth are also social constructs that we learn to share with others. Our outermost reality is the physical external reality which we can see, perceive, measure in some objective manner. However meaning is shaped by our two deeper realities, our social and personal realities. Social reality is a consensus reality that is shared with the rest of society, particularly the groups we identify with. We are taught how to identify and interpret people, objects and events through our social reality. Our innermost realty is our own identity which is developed through learned knowledge, experience and ways we have developed to interpret perceptions.

Time and space are social constructs to make them exist. Without social construction there is no time. Time is a defined concept which society accepts and operates by. Our behaviour is determined by how we define and understand the concept of time. For example, *'does society think in the short or long term?'*, *'what is meant by short and long term?'*, *'Is the past important to society?'*, *'Does society value the future?'*, i.e., plan and have visions about the future, *'How is the present valued?'*, i.e., as time to prepare for the future by working hard or time for enjoyment, etc.

Space has a symbolic meaning within culture. How space is allocated, distributed, and shared defines many relational aspects of self and others within society. For example, *'How does one define their own space?'*, *'Is it important to have space exclusively?'*, *'What constitutes sharing and invasion of space?'*, and *'How does space define ownership and authority?'* etc. Intimacy, privacy, and authority are often symbolized through space.

Finally society must have assumptions about how to adapt to the outside environment and how to achieve its goals. From the individual point of view, assumptions that enable one to function coherently within a group must be discovered. This is a process of using assumptions and testing their validity within a group. When feedback is positive, assumptions are validated. When feedback is negative, inappropriate assumptions will be discarded and new assumptions adopted and tested, until a working set of assumptions exists. This is a learning process shown in Figure 3.8.

Strategy is the basis by which we maintain our existence and survival. Developing strategy for personal, group interaction or business strategy is a cultural matter. We consider our goals and formulate strategies to achieve them. Our strategies are therefore a reflection upon our own inner assumptions. If they are valid, then the very way we develop organization, plan and develop products, sell, and treat employees and customers will have some cultural reflection. Any chosen strategy must be within cultural assumptions and values otherwise it will fail and affect our own views of our self efficacy, self esteem and self confidence.

Assumptions manifest into beliefs and values based on upbringing, social structure, religion, political and economic philosophies, education, media influence, and that of peers and others around them. Beliefs and values influence perception and behaviour in complex ways. There is a significant correlation between national or regional cultural beliefs and values and those of an individual (Mueller & Thomas 2001). Beliefs and values are deeply engrained standards that justify past action and determine future actions (Braithwaite & Scott 1991). Values can be considered transitional goals or objectives that vary in importance but act as guiding principles of life (Schwartz 1996).

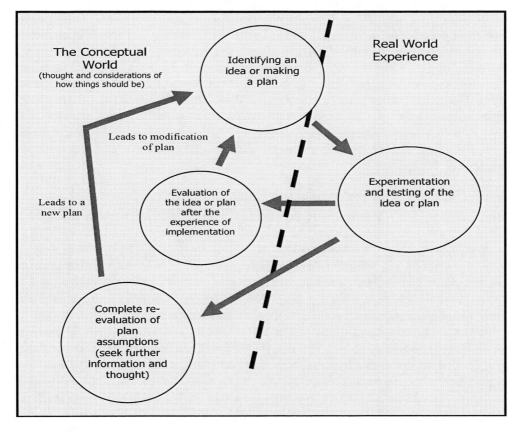

Figure 3.8. The Learning Process (Hunter 2009).

Scripts

Beliefs and values form schemata or scripts with specific information that are used during the cognitive process for perception and the creation of meaning. According to Mitchell *et. al.* (2000) these scripts are composed of culturally specific information. Therefore the perception of opportunities and crafting of strategy is attuned to the specific culture in question. Each script contains heuristics that are rules of thumb that guide a person's perceptions and judgments *(These are discussed later in this chapter under cognition and cognitive biases).* Studies by Kitayama *et. al.* (2003) also postulate that perceptions between cultures also vary. North Americans tend to be field independent in their perceptions while Japanese appear to be field dependent *(This will be discussed in its own section).*

The sophistication and development of scripts within the individual are believed to provide the knowledge, confidence and drive to undertake certain actions. Mitchell *et. al.* (2000) postulate there are three important scripts related to opportunity and action. These are arrangement scripts, willingness scripts and ability scripts. Arrangement scripts contain knowledge that will support someone doing a certain activity, *i.e., about resource combinations, supply chain knowledge, potential customer needs, etc.* They show the arrangements people know are needed to do something *(see figure 3.6.).* Arrangement scripts have the knowledge, but the willingness scripts drive a person into consideration of taking action. They drive someone to seek out new opportunity and give thought about pursuing them (McCelland 1968, Sexton & Bowman-Upton 1985). Willingness scripts help to reduce uncertainty (Heath & Tversky 1991) and without this willingness script people will not be motivated to act (Krueger 1993). Ability scripts provide the knowledge of capabilities, competencies, knowledge and skills required to start any action (Bull & Willard 1993, Herron 1990). Situational scripts enable someone to draw on prior knowledge from previous experiences and apply it to a specific situation (Cooper & Dunkelberg 1987, Stuart & Abetti 1990). Finally ability – opportunity scripts enables a person to see ways of how to create the necessary combinations of people, resources, networks and products to make the idea work (Glade 1967, Kirzner 1982).

Internal Struggle – Positive and Negative Cultural Attributes

Within every culture (national, regional or organizational) there are attributes which are irrational, contradictory and negative towards certain types of behaviour. Different cultures will reward or punish behaviour that may be considered innovative, entrepreneurial and positive towards achieving certain goals. What can be worse in some cultures is that the espoused values are positive, but the actual values practiced in action are negative. This is a common trait in many organizations where the mission and vision seems to encourage innovation, but by coming up with new innovative ways to assist the organization, one comes up against covert forces that try to sabotage these initiatives. Cultures that value and reward positive behaviour, promote a propensity to be innovative, while cultures that reinforce conformity, group interests and try to control the future are not likely to develop much risk-taking and entrepreneurial behaviour (Herbig & Miller 1992, Hofstede 1980).

An examination of the difference between what is espoused and what is practiced and what kind of behaviour is rewarded and punished both formally and informally will assist in identifying the positive and negative attributes. Table 3.12. provides guideline questions to assist in evaluating positive and negative attributes of a culture according to some main assumptions areas.

Table 3.12. Guideline Questions to determine Positive and Negative Attributes of Culture

Attitude	Continuum	Comments
Interaction between people and the environment	Individualistic/collective Group welfare/self interest Authoritarian/egalitarian Authoritarian/consultative Trust/mistrust Personal/impersonal Direct/indirect Formal/informal Conservative/liberal Ostentatious/modest To exploit/to nurture	*How do people interact during social occasions, play, sport?, What type of leadership is usually practiced?, What qualities are respected in people?, How do people of different social classes, genders and ages interact?, how do people communicate?, how do people like to communicate?, do people like to offer opinions?, Is non-normal behavior accepted, shunned or condemned?, are dress codes uniform, individualistic and rigidly adhered to?, are there big differentiators between social classes?, how are people addressed?, is status respected?, how is the environment viewed?*
Family/Community Support	Employment/self employment Public/private Supportive/non-supportive family	*How do people make their living? are there a large number of self employed/employed people?, are there many professional people?, are there many public servants, i.e., teachers, etc?, how do members of the family make a living?, how do neighbors and friends make a living?*
Innovation/Change	Traditional/evolving Ritualistic/progressive	*Is tradition important? , is society ritualistic? is open discussion encouraged?, are people frank and open with opinions?, do members of society easily get jealous of those who progress?, do organizations tend to practice meritocracy or nepotism?, are new ideas valued?*
Institutional Support	Regulated/de-regulated Fair/unfair practices Negative/disinterested/ supportive	*Are political institutions pro-business?, are political institutions pro-market and believe in a level playing field approach to business?, what are attitudes and remedies like for issues of corruption and other business dishonesty?, are there institutional entrepreneurship programs available?, Is credit easy of difficult to get?, Is it relatively easy to go through the formal steps of opening a business?, are there incentives available?, is it easy or difficult to look after your legal rights?*
Time	Valuable/not valuable Think short term/long term	*How do people use their time? do people keep busy or relax?, how do people view those who don't work or are unemployed?, do people plan for the future or take each day as it comes?*
Success/failure	Acceptable/not acceptable	*How is success viewed by others? how is failure viewed by others?, are people giving a second chance?*
Reliance	Independent/dependent Reliant/self-reliant	*How do people view education?, do people rely on govt. and/or family hand outs to survive, if not employed, self-employed?, Is it easy to survive as someone unemployed?, If unemployed, are people prepared to move to other locations for work?*
Self-confidence/efficacy	Confident/non-confident Not seeking new knowledge/life-long learner	*What are peoples' general aspirations?, do they believe that somehow they can achieve them?, people are willing to have a go at new things?, people have ambition?, are willing to take more education?, have a learning disposition?, people believe they have some control over their own destiny?*
Location	Rural/urban	*This is a rural/urban situation?*

The key is to look at what values in a culture support entrepreneurship and innovation and what don't. Values that support a strong work ethic, individual accountability, and a sense of independence are required. Fatalism can destroy any sense of self-efficacy on the part of an individual. Cultural values that are most supportive will be those that support optimism and improvement of one's own situation. A culture should support cooperation and the concept that cooperative effort pays off. This will be an important determinant of growth. Societies that believe in a *'fixed pie'* approach to competition will find it very difficult to cooperate with others, as all are competing for a piece of it without considering the possibilities of change and growth. Cultures that support experimentation will provide a better platform for innovation than those which discourage it. Fundamental, collective, and heavily censored societies tend to stifle innovation. It is not necessarily a need for a democracy but an allowance for its citizens to undertake novelty. Finally it is a matter of how a society looks at time, *do they live for today? Are they mired in past traditions?* Or *look optimistically to the future?*

Individual behaviour will likely conform to cultural value and attributes unless there is strong influence from a group counter culture. Culture cannot predict behaviour but only provide some contextual background environmental knowledge that individuals and groups operate within[42].

PART TWO: SENSORY PERCEPTION AND COGNITION

How we sense, perceive, acquire knowledge and think is governed by cognition, so it is important to have some basic understanding of the process. The advent of functional magnetic resonance imaging (fMRI) and position-emission tomography (PCT) which can measure cerebral blood flow in the brain through sensing magnetic signals or low level radiation respectively to determine brain activity levels have greatly deepened our understanding of the processes of cognition (Posner, DiGirolamo & Fernandez-Duque 1997). Quite remarkably, the cognitive process has many similarities with computer information processing steps of acquisition, storage, retrieval, processing, data organization and artificial intelligence structures (Reed 2007).

Perceptual Cognition

Perception is such a complex brain activity that a very large part of the brain function is totally dedicated to this process. All external stimuli are detected by the five senses and environmental energy is transformed into neural electricity via complex biochemical conversions called *transduction*[43]. Neural electricity carrying information maintained in its

---

[42] This can definitely be seen in the business models and strategies selected in various countries. In some countries SMS advertising would be considered invasive of peoples' privacy, but in other countries accepted as a fair means of advertising, just as vans with speakers blaring advertising are accepted in some developing countries. Noodle and Asian stall food franchising is culturally acceptable in South-East Asia, while multi level marketing is accepted in some countries and not others.

[43] Transduction occurs in different ways depending upon the receptor. The eye contains photoreceptors which contain photopigments. When exposed to light these photopigments breakdown and produce electricity that is

original format from the senses travels, cell to cell to the sensory store by the process of neural transmission[44]. The sensory store is not actually a single area within the brain. Different areas of the brain process sensory information as indicated in figure 3.9. showing an overview of the cognitive system. The sensory store can only keep unanalyzed sensory information for very brief periods for identification through pattern recognition. Information that cannot be identified through the pattern recognition process will be lost.

Many stimuli can enter the sensory store at one time but only one pattern at a time can enter the pattern recognition stage. This is controlled through perceptual limitation which prevents people from being overloaded with too much information at any one time (Broadbent 1958). The attention function determines the sequence and amount of information that will be identified at one time. This restricts the amount of information that can enter the memory. The filtering stage sorts and limits information entering the memory like a bottleneck (Broadbent 1957). This bottleneck occurs at the entrance to the pattern recognition stage, where only one piece of information can be processed at a time (Deutsch & Deutsch 1963, Norman 1968), thus preventing information overload. This is metaphorically shown as marbles being poured down a funnel as shown in Figure 3.10.

Pattern recognition is the stage where information is matched with known patterns. There are a number of different theories as to how the brain identifies patterns. Template theories explain pattern identification through matching information with stored shapes or templates. Feature theories explain the use of discovered features that distinguish one pattern from another and structural theories use the relationship between features to recognize patterns. A complete theory and understanding of the pattern recognition process does not exist as yet because identification of an object involves so many visual cues and spatial issues, and the knowledge needed to see any of these cues is so extensive. For example, we can read with ease but the process of understanding words may rely on a number of different and flexible word recognition strategies. There are multiple levels of identification at the feature, word and letter levels which interact to assist comprehension (McCelland & Rumelhart 1981). Our ease in reading presents many problems to theories of how we identify and comprehend words (Grainger & Whitney 2004).

---

transported through neurons to the retina. In the ear small hair-like outgrowths called cilia make up mechanoreceptors where vibrations caused by sound waves disrupt the cilia causing an electrical charge in the receptor. Olfactory receptors at the base of the nasal cavity called the olfactory epithelium. These receptors are located on cilia and when they come in contact with an odour molecule they transmit neural electricity. There are approximately 1000 different types of receptor in the nose to differentiate various odour molecules (Ressler, Sullivan & Buck 1994). There are also a number of free nerve endings that can detect sensations like coolness, tingling and warmth, etc. The tongue contains about 10,000 chemoreceptors on our taste buds or papillae. Each bud contains around 150 receptor cells. Molecules of the food or other substance carrying a taste connect with the receptors via saliva and bind. Changes in membrane permeability will cause changes in electricity potentials. Taste is detected through different chemical molecules causing different charge micro-voltages. Finally haptic receptors are varied and range from free nerve endings to specialized receptors that are at various locations on and in the body that work on a number of different principals.

[44] Neural transmission from cell to cell occurs through impulses that travel from the dendrite of a cell (a branched tree like structure projecting from the neuron cell) to terminal buttons at the end of axons (the thin branches of neural cells) of other cells. The terminal buttons connect to the dendrites of other cells at the synapse (junction between the terminal button of one neuron and the dendrite of another neuron). When an electrical impulse reaches the synapse, this triggers the release of neurotransmitters (electrically charged enzymes and proteins) that pass along an electrical charge to the next neuron.

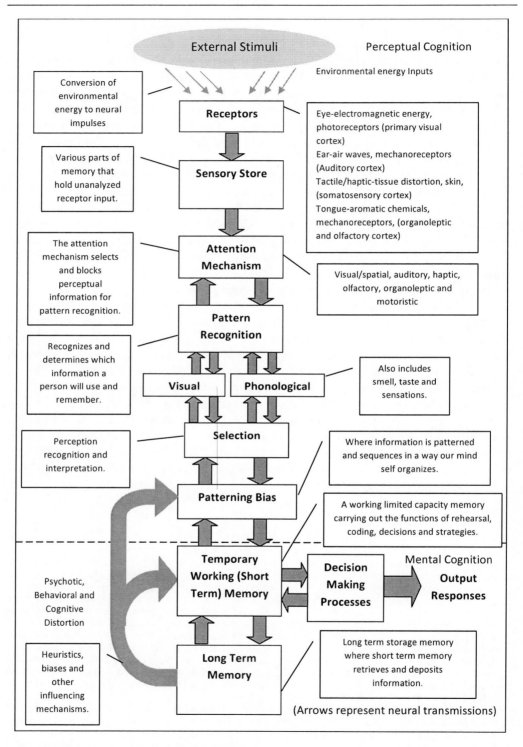

Figure 3.9. An Overview of the Cognitive System.

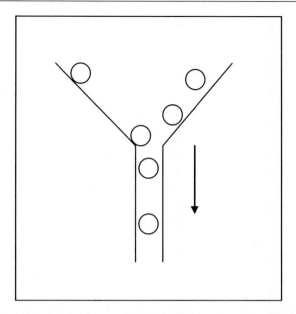

Figure 3.10. Limited Capacity Entrance Channel into the Pattern Recognition Stage.

Yellow Blue Orange

Black Red Green

Purple Yellow Red

Orange Green Black

Blue Red Purple

Green Blue Orange

Figure 3.11. Demonstration of Colour-Word Conflict.

Perception tasks occur both at the conscious and unconscious level. Different perception tasks require different effort and compete for limited capacity. Some tasks are so well practiced that they become routine and processed automatically. However when one comes up against unusual objects, then a great conscious effort is required to process and recognize them. For example if you look at figure 3.11. and say the colour and not the word, you will most likely find that this is not so easy as two recognition processes (word and colour) come into conflict which requires conscious resolution.

Probably one of the closest explanations to how our brain processes information in the recognition process is the neural network model (Rumelhart, Hinton & McClelland 1986). This metaphoric concept hypothesizes a network of linked concepts (called nodes) are linked to other nodes, where they interact through excitatory or inhibitory electrical charges. Node activation above a threshold makes us aware of a letter in a word, etc. Neural networks accommodate learning through changing the weights of node activation through excitatory or inhibitory actions. This improves the efficiency of the network in making identifications through being able to process information in parallel, both top-down and bottom-up processing. A pictorial example of a neural network is shown in figure 3.12.

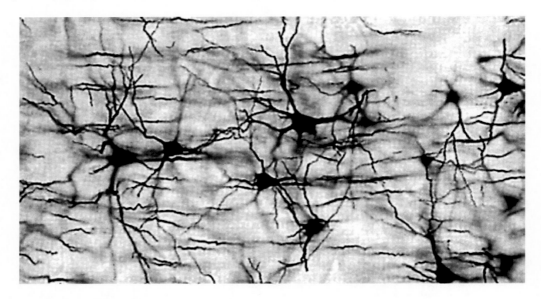

Figure 3.12. An Example of a Neural Network.

One of the advantages of a neural network is the ability to process information either top-down, where information in our memory helps us recognize information or bottom-up, where information from the sensory store is sent to the short term or working memory to enable quick identification of information. Information held within a neural network enables a person to look, in the case of writing, at either the word level, letter level and feature level, which implies where we can interpret incomplete words and sentences (McCelland & Rumelhart 1981, Grainer & Whitney 2004). Figure 3.13. shows this process pictorially.

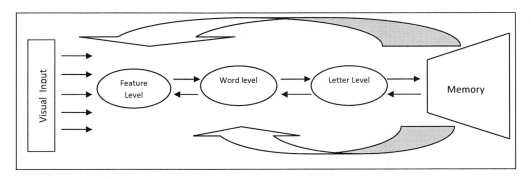

Figure 3.13. The Word Recognition Process.

Another bottleneck occurs between pattern recognition information entering the short term working memory. This is not a perceptual problem but one of the selection of which sequence of information goes into memory. This is more a capacity limitation on how much mental work can be undertaken at any one time. Factors that influence the sequence of information entering the short term working memory include memory capacity, arousal, enduring dispositions, momentary interventions and conscious and unconscious evaluations (Kahneman 1973).

The patterning mechanism is a channel or bias that screens, distorts or otherwise patterns information in particular ways. This can also be thought of as knowledge structures which put information into patterns we already understand. Thus the content of the knowledge structure will influence perception. Hillerbrand (1989) postulates that this mechanism is another way the brain cuts down on information overload, so that information can be easily encoded into memory. This assists a person make sense of things out of confusion and uncertainty where thinking is focused on finding things that one is already familiar with. For example, when we learn to drive a car, we must concentrate on every decision and action we take. Once we are familiar with the skills of driving a car, we do this without taking any conscious actions. This is the advantage of patterning. This mechanism may also partly explain why people have different perspectives from the same stimuli and may also partly explain why some people see opportunity while others don't (Baron & Ward 2004), although this process is far from understood.

The patterning mechanism could be the beginning of the brain's *self organizing system* where incoming information is organized into patterns and sequences that can be processing according to already established meanings. According to de Bono (1993, P. 49) patterning is a fixed way of seeing things and inhibits creativity, as it is part of the fixed mental model we have.

Therefore perception is influenced by prior knowledge and other preconceptions, heuristics and biases we have (these will be discussed later during the chapter). Thus ideas are the result of *logical hindsight,* rather than foresight to gain insights into things and issues (Pang 1972). This is extremely useful for people carrying out their work like doctors making a diagnosis, mechanics inspecting an engine for faults, airline pilots, and farmers, etc, doing the routine parts of their jobs. It helps give them their specialist intuition. Thus returning to our previous funnel metaphor, there are really a number of funnels, each representing certain pre-existing mental models through which we perceive. This affects our perception, reasoning and decision making processes. Figure 3.14. shows a metaphorical diagram of the patterning process.

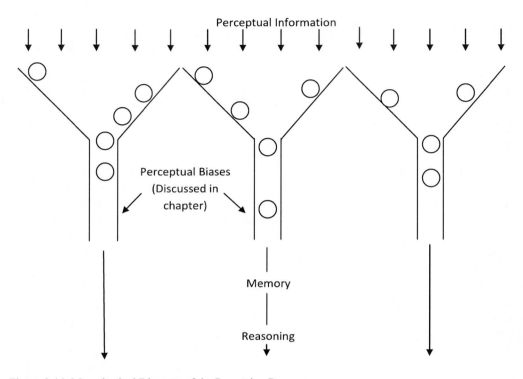

Figure 3.14. Metaphorical Diagram of the Patterning Process.

According to Uchasaran, Westhead & Wright (2004) the ability to manipulate or change patterns (which are like lenses or glasses we look through), gives the person the ability to look at perceived information in different ways[45]. Patterns thus guide our approaches to reasoning, decision making and problem solving and are affected by bias, delusion, distortion, heuristics and socio-cultural influences that influence the structure of our schemata.

Mental Cognition

There are two memory functions, the working or short term memory and the long term memory. The working or short term memory is where text comprehension, reasoning and

---

[45] The metaphor of seeing things through tinted or coloured glasses has been used for hundreds of years to describe various delusions or biases people may have. L. Frank Baum's character Dorothy in the Wonderful Wizard of Oz asked the guardian of the gates why everyone has to wear green glasses in the Emerald City. The guardian replied so everything in the Emerald City would look green, so that people would think it really is an Emerald City (Baum 1999, pp. 130-131). Today for example, green is associated with envy, i.e., "green with envy", blue is associated with depression, i.e., "the blues", and rose or red is associated with optimistic delusion, i.e., "a rosier world". Popular media has adapted this metaphor and used many ad hoc terms like 'green glasses', Dole-coloured glasses' and 'private sector glasses', etc (Doyle 2001). Edward de Bono (1985) uses the colour metaphor to change patterns of thinking through his "Six Thinking hats".

problem solving takes place. The working or short term memory has a very limited storage capacity and can only hold information for a very short length of time. The working or short term memory is the interface between stimuli and information from the environment and information from our long term memory.

Research has shown (Baddeley 1992, 2001, Baddeley & Hitch 1974) the working or short term memory is made up of a phonological part, a visual-spatial part, a memory and a central processing function. A different part of the brain handles the phonological information (Awh *et. al.* 1996), where information is identified and new words can be learned and stored in the long term memory (Saarilouma 1992). The working memory function plays a major role in how logical reasoning and decisions are reached (Gilhooly, *et. al.* 1993). A pictorial model of the working or short term memory is shown in figure 3.15.

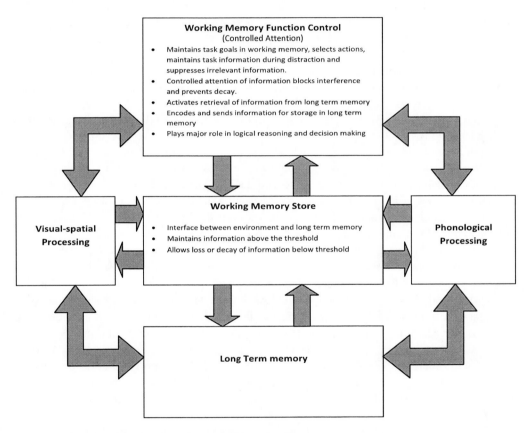

Figure 3.15. A pictorial model of the working or short term memory.

Varying levels of controlled attention in individuals partly explains differences in peoples' perception and reasoning. Controlled attention is important for maintaining task goals in working memory, scheduling actions, maintaining task information during distraction, and suppressing irrelevant information (Engle & Oransky 1999). Another major difference between people is how people group and structure information in collective chunks. A study by de Groot (1965) found that the difference between master and ordinary chess players was the difference in perception and memory, rather than differences in deciding planned moves. Master chess players would tend to group the pieces on the board into familiar patterns of past games to remember. However where pieces were placed randomly on the board, there was no difference between the master's and ordinary player's ability to recall the placement of the pieces on the board. Further studies showed the memory depends on being able to retrieve certain chunks of information from the long term memory when required (Chase & Simon 1973). This indicates that prior knowledge influences our perception and the way we code and retrieve information.

There is no known limit in long term memory capacity. The long term memory is where information is stored for the working or short term memory to retrieve or deposit information as required. Three basic processes occur within the long term memory. The first is acquisition of information. This is our ability to learn. Secondly, information must also be retained until it is needed by the short term or working memory, as required. Finally information must be able to be retrieved for use by the short term memory, through a particular retrieval strategy.

The long term memory contains three main types of memory, the *episodic* memory, the *semantic* memory and the *procedural* memory. The semantic memory stores temporary information about recollections of events and personal experiences. The semantic memory contains general knowledge that is not associated with any time or context. Procedural memory stores actions, skills and operations, rather than factual information like the first two. Factual information seems much easier to lose than procedural information (Warrington & Weiskrantz 1986).

Both our experience and theoretical knowledge influences our judgments. Our judgments and ideas develop through learning and are stored as various cognitive devices called heuristics, which are logic rules that assist with decision making. There are also a number of mechanisms that can influence the logic and reasoning process that enter into the working or short term memory and patterning bias processes from the long term memory. These will be discussed later during the chapter.

The ability to recall information depends upon the kinds of operations and the way information is organized and encoded in the long term memory (Tulving & Thomson 1973). Memory codes can differ in how they elaborate and store information in memory. Additional associations and elaborations are stored along with the basic information (Anderson & Reder 1979), so that information is easier to retrieve. Very often mood and emotions are stored with autobiographical events to assist recall (Eich, Macaulay & Ryan 1994). Information is often stored as visual images for better retention. Visual storage enables easy elaboration on perceived information. Visual memory is much better than the memory of words, thus staying in memory much longer, although susceptible to distortion through elaboration over time. Therefore memories will contain both information from the external environment and elaborated information from our memory, shifting our recollection of actual reality to the point where it becomes impossible to distinguish between real and imagined events.

The future perceptions of people are influenced by the way they categorize information in memory. The patterns of categorization are the means by how we identify objects in the external world. How relationships between chunks of information are developed will relate to how a person sees the environment. This helps reduce complexity, but the way things are related can also affect meaning. For example we tend to try to classify objects together for simplicity of understanding, rather than look at their unique characteristics. This reduces our need for constant learning.

The categorization of objects aids our perception and prompts quick responses in relation to them, *i.e., fire, hot, keep away.* How we organize memories greatly influences our views on things. For example, through the stereotyping of objects, people and events we create manageable views of the world. Categorization creates simplicity but when they are based on erroneous assumptions they add to the creation of distorted views of things (Canter & Genero 1986). Through stereotyping we tend to view people of the same social category as being similar. Once we categorize a person, his or her traits become exaggerated, which distorts actual reality. People tend to discard information that differentiates one person from another and focus upon our stereotyped knowledge to form our views (Reed 2007, P. 194). Other psychotic pathologies also tend to create distorted perception of actual reality and meaning. This will be extensively discussed later in the chapter.

People who develop an efficient organization system to encode and retrieve information will have good memories. Memories are usually organized through hierarchical and relational structures (Ericsson 1985) in what is called a semantic network, consisting of concepts and links that specify relationships between them. Within a semantic network, information is clustered in schemata. A schema is a cluster of knowledge that represents a general procedure, an object precept, an event or event sequence or a social situation (Thorndyke 1984). A schema is an organization of past experiences which have been encoded into abstract concepts to fit into a cognitive structure. There are a number of models which propose how a schema is constructed, as we are not completely sure how knowledge is actually organized. Structures continually develop and change as new information is blended with existing information.

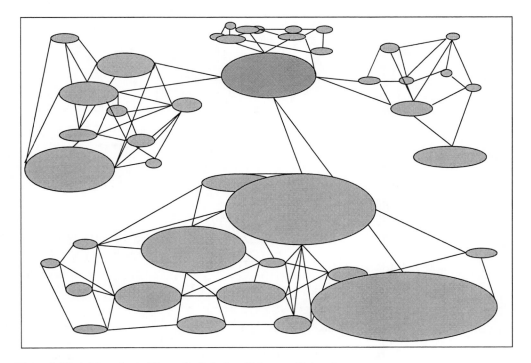

Figure 3.15. A Metaphoric View of a Relational Memory Network.

This form of information organization can be represented as a relational network which emphasizes concepts linked to various bits of relevant information that create a holistic picture in memory. This relational structure shown in figure 3.15. bares some physical resemblance to the neural networks shown in Figure 3.12. previously. The relational concept allows for ease of information retrieval via multiple paths. This kind of relational network, although not yet proven to physically exist, is consistent with the way we think in many situations (Collins & Loftus 1975, Meyer & Schvaneveldt 1976, Ratcliff & McKoon 1988).

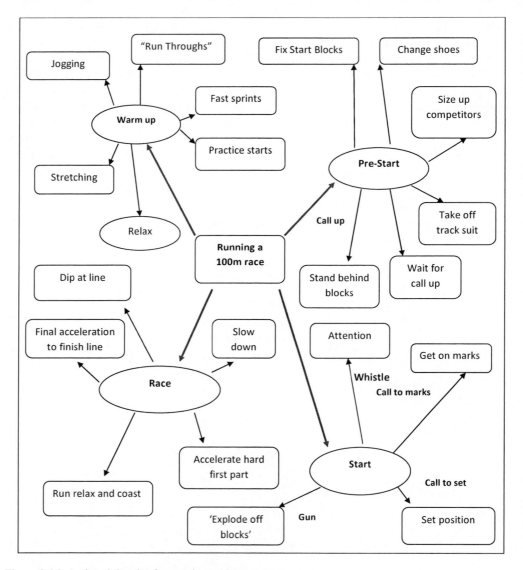

Figure 3.16. A pictorial script for running a 100 metres race.

Routine activities which make up a large amount of our knowledge are encoded into specific schema called scripts (Schank & Abelson 1977). A script is simply a sequence of knowledge about what happens during routine activities in a structure like a flowchart.

Schemas and scripts help a person to make sense and meaning of the world around them. Incoming information is understood much easier when it is integrated with information a person already has stored in memory. Present information is immediately compared with prior information, ideas and judgments to look for similarities from where meaning can be inferred. Through this process we are able to construct a mental model based on both the new information and abstracts from our memory (Glenberg, Meyer & Linden 1987). Figure 3.16. shows a script for running a 100 metres race.

Mental models have both advantages and disadvantages. Through mental models, a person can make inferences, *i.e., to make conclusions based on unconscious rules of logic or heuristics.* This helps create very quick meaning out of a situation. This was very necessary in previous times when mankind was a hunter and came across dangerous situations where they had to make very quick *fight or flight* decisions. Inferences activate meaning and cut down on uncertainty.

Actual reality can have many different interpretations. For example, what appears to be a snake at the bank of a river could in reality be a stick or branch of a tree. Inferences cut down the risk of the situation through erring on potentially dangerous versions of reality. Therefore abstracted inferences in complex situations can distort actual realities. We see this process in how people reinterpret history making inferences about past people and events (Erickson & Mattson 1981) and how witnesses in court can give unreliable descriptions based on abstract inferences of their memory (Loftus 1975, Harris 1978).

Prior Knowledge

Prior knowledge is knowledge that accumulates in our memory from previous experiences. Prior knowledge assists us in both perceptual and conceptual cognition. Prior knowledge is extremely useful in understanding complex topics, in learning and as an important tool for making sense of objects, people and situations.

Through the use of metaphor, prior knowledge assists in problem solving by providing simpler analogies where complex cause and effect can be easily understood and evaluated. For example business strategy is often referred to as sport and war analogies which make them easier to understand and visualize. In a similar manner, blood circulation is often explained in pumping and pressure analogies. Prior knowledge is also a powerful tool for the interpretation of situations where things are missing, *e.g., puzzles, missing words, missing number patterns etc.*

Prior knowledge influences our general perception of the world. We tend to build our knowledge based on a pool of metaphors which are available to us as a way to create understanding of our existing knowledge [46](diSessa 1993). The advantage of metaphor is that it can be loosely applied to current situations in a flexible manner to help clarify any uncertainty. Metaphors make things more familiar to us. If metaphors successfully explain our created interpretations of new experiences to our satisfaction, then they go onto reinforce the current schemata of prior knowledge and emotions we already have. However if current metaphors cannot explain our interpretations of current experiences and solve particular

---

[46] In this case, metaphors are analogies that help to explain something complex using a simpler example.

problems, then these new experiences will blend with prior knowledge to create a modified schemata and new emotions.

New knowledge comes from our ability to merge new information through the interpretations of our experiences with our prior knowledge. Our schemata become more sophisticated as we develop. More sophisticated schemata assist us in interpreting our experiences much more comprehensively (Dewey 1938). This is how learning occurs through the transformation of schemata over time (Roschelle & Clancey 1992). The key to our ability to continue learning is to be able to integrate the knowledge we acquire with the knowledge we already have in our schemata. Figure 3.17. diagrammatically shows this process.

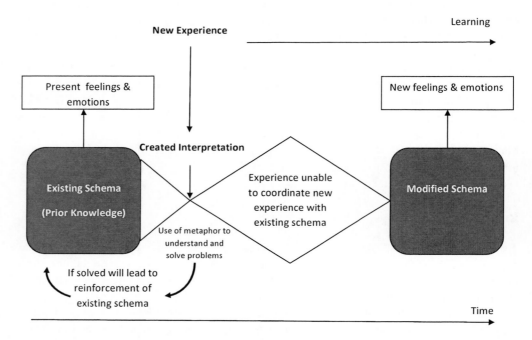

Figure 3.17. How Schemata Transform as Learning Takes Place.

Prior knowledge may also instigate distorted interpretations of experiences through the use of heuristics and other cognitive biases that lead to implications on the decisions we make.

Problem Solving and Decision Making

The primary objective of reasoning, problem solving and decision making is to find ways out of difficulties, achieve aims or objectives, make a selection or overcome some form of obstacle. Decision making requires special sets of skills, which not only set us apart from the animal kingdom but also set human apart from human. In his book *Sources of Power: How People make Decisions*, Gary Klein (1998) goes further and states that decision making skills are a source of power for an individual.

There are numerous theories about problem solving, decision making and creativity in cognitive psychology. This reflects upon the numerous types of problems that need to be solved and require different reasoning strategies and thought patterns that can be applied to specific types of problems. Many different situations exist where selected cognitive styles employed will maximize accuracy and minimize the effort required to make a decision or solve a problem (Payne, Bettman & Johnson 1993). This section will outline a number of them.

Each type of problem a person encounters will require a different set of skills to solve them. A better understanding of problems can be gained by classifying them according to the skills required to solve them. Greeno (1978) postulated that there are three main types of problems requiring different skills to solve them[47]. These three basic types include problems of *arrangement,* problems of *inducing structure* and problems of *transformation.* Although this is not exhaustive it provides a useful indication of the differences in approaches needed to solve problems.

Problems of arrangement require the problem solver to arrange things or objects in a way that meets a specific criterion. There are usually a number of ways to arrange these things or objects, but only one way to meet the criteria specified in the problem. A good example of this type of problem is an anagram where a set of letters can be rearranged to make up a new word or phrase, e.g. MARY-ARMY or ELVIS-LIVES. Solving this type of problem requires the ability to generate numerous potential solutions which can be evaluated and discarded if it doesn't meet the specified criteria, in a *'trial and error'* sequence. This requires a focused vocabulary and understanding the various constraints, *i.e., letters/word combinations that fall within the specified criteria.* An example where this skill would be required is in the board game called *Scrabble.*

To discover the correct arrangement of objects may require a flash of insight to discover the right combination of sequence. This may sometimes occur after a number of attempts to arrange and rearrange the objects through *'trial and error'.* The necessary arrangement or sequence of items to solve the puzzle or problem may only be discovered after a number of attempts to find the correct sequence[48]. The key characteristic of insight that separates it from other forms of discovery is the suddenness of the insight occurring over other more planned and systematic means to discover things.

One reason why people often don't find solutions is because they put unnecessary restrictions on the possible set of potential solutions. For example if you were asked to construct 4 equilateral triangles with 6 matches, how would you go about solving this problem? Many people would be constrained by thinking only in two dimensions, where the correct answer would require thinking in three dimensions and constructing a pyramid as shown in Figure 3.18.

---

[47] This does not imply that all problems fall within these categories. Some problems may be very complex and have attributes from all the basic problem types.

[48] This was demonstrated well in a sequence of the film Apollo 13, directed by Ron Howard. The level of oxygen was rapidly declining in the lunar module of the ill-fated Apollo 13 mission, so a solution was needed to maintain adequate filtering of the air to rid it of CO2 build up. The technical team in Houston was given the problem of finding …"a way to make this (a square air scrubber filter from the command module) fit into a hole like this (the shape of a round air scrubber filter in the lunar module) using nothing but that (items that are available to the astronauts in either the command or lunar module). This problem could only be solved through trial and error until a solution was found.

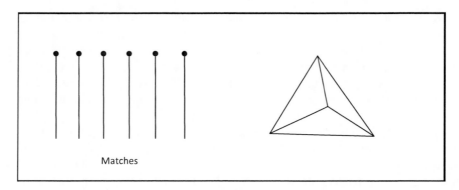

Figure 3.18. An illustrational representation of 4 equilateral triangles constructed with 6 matches.

Problems of inducing structure involve determination of the relationships between sets of numbers, words, symbols, ideas, or other objects. This occurs in series extrapolation or completion and analogy type problems. The cognitive process in solving these types of problems involves finding the relationships within the patterns. Examples of this would include verbal analogies like *"clouds are to the sky as waves are to the sea"* and number analogies would include sequences like *"2, 4, 9, 11, 16"*. Robert Jeffrey Sternberg (1977) postulated that there are four steps in solving analogical problems; encoding which identifies characteristics that maybe important in establishing relationships between each object; inference which establishes a valid relationship between two objects; mapping which extends the potential relationship to the next set of objects; and application which runs out the process to create new objects or fill in missing objects, as the problem requires. Analogical reasoning is makes up a large part of the Miller Analogies Test which was widely used for student admission to graduate school and the US Graduate Record Exam (GRE) and Scholastic Aptitude Test (SAT).

Problems of transformation require making a sequence of transformations to reach a specific goal. Transformation problems differ from the previous two forms because the goal is known, but not the way to get there. Puzzles are often transformation problems. According to Greeno (1978), Transformation problems require skills in planning in what are called a *means-ends analysis*[49] to solve them.

Newell and Simon set up an experiment to determine how humans thought during problem solving experiments. As a person's thinking is not observable (Newel & Simon 1972), they instructed the subjects to say aloud everything that came to their head when working on the puzzles (Simon & Newell 1971). From this information a computer program was developed that could be run to see if the instructions were sufficient to solve the problem and there was not any other *'mysterious'* processes used to solve the problems. This work enabled Newell and Simon to develop a general framework on how information is processed to solve problems.

Newell and Simon found that it is the basic characteristics of the cognitive system itself, *i.e., working memory capacity, storage time, retrieval time of working and long term memory*

---

[49] Means-end analysis is a way to solve goal based problems. This requires undertaking a series of actions that lead to this goal. The ability to solve this type of problem rests with making associations between changes that particular actions will cause. Each action should reduce the difference between the two positions until the goal is achieved.

that influenced problem solving performance. Problems often require calculations that exceed the capacity of the working memory so long term memory is needed to assist in storing information. When long term memory is utilized for problem solving, access and retrieval delays can confuse the steps in a problem, leading to confusion, decreasing the efficiency of the problem solver (Atwood & Polson 1976).

Within a problem there are a specific number of ways that can be followed to find a solution and the problem solver will make a decision as to which paths he or she will take. To quickly solve a problem, it is important that the correct paths are taken without wasting time going down *'dead-ends'*(Reed 2007, P. 309). The sources of information a person draws upon to evaluate the set of choices open to him or her include; the task instructions and description of the problem, previous experience with similar and other analogous tasks, stored schemata in the long term memory and any other information discovered during the problem solving process.

Problems are generally solved through the use of heuristics, which are general rules of thumb that assist in solving a problem, but are no guarantee of solving the problem. Means-end analysis mentioned previously is an example of a heuristic and there are others that also can be employed in problem solving.

Sub-goals divide a problem into parts, where each sub-goal is much easier to solve. This can make the total problem generally easier to solve than seeking to make a total solution. This method is useful when dividing a problem into sub-goals is possible. However it is not always helpful if sub-goals are not obvious.

Analogy is another heuristic where a solution strategy for a similar problem can be used on the current problem. This success of this strategy depends upon recognition of the similarities between the problem and a schema a person has in their long term memory. This is not often easy to identify. The ability of a person to develop general abstract schema that can be applied to a range of problems is how people develop expertise in particular fields (Ross & Kennedy 1990).

Finally another method of solving problems is by drawing diagrams which transfers the problem from a temporal perspective to a spatial perspective.

There are a number of barriers to effective problem solving that impede efforts to come up with solutions;

- Many problems contain irrelevant information which is not easy to separate from what is relevant, particularly in the early stages of the problem. Focusing on irrelevant information has adverse effects on developing problem solving strategies. For example, people often wrongly assume that all available numerical information is relevant to the problem and attempt to find numerical solutions with first trying to gauge the relevance of the information (Sternberg 1986).

- People tend to look at objects in relation to their most common use and discount other possibilities. This is called *functional fixedness* which blocks a person from developing a solution to a problem because they fail to recognize other potential uses for objects other than their common use.

- A person's mental set has a tendency to keep people using problem solving strategies that have worked well in the past. People with expertise in a particular area will tend to use the diagnostic tools they are used to rather than utilize other means of problem diagnosis (Leighton & Sternberg 2003).

- Often problem solvers sub-consciously set themselves constraints in solving problems. As we have seen with the problem of creating 4 equilateral triangles with 6 matches, it requires moving from a two-dimensional paradigm to a three-dimensional paradigm.

Turning away from problem solving, decision making is an important aspect in our daily life which involves making choices between alternatives. Some choices are relatively unimportant like what we will wear and have for lunch, while others are much more important like selecting a new car, buying a house or choosing a job, etc. Decision making is far from a rational process. As we have seen, our cognitive processes are limited in the volume of information it can handle which makes it difficult to consider and evaluate all relevant information before making any decision. Herbert Simon (1957) asserted that people tend to use simple strategies in decision making that focus on only a few aspects of available information and options that result in irrational decisions that are less than optimal. Thus, beside our limited capacity to process information, the availability of too many choices (Schwartz 2004)[50] and just getting tired of looking at alternatives, *i.e., looking for an apartment* (Reed 2007, P. 357) contribute to a person just taking a good choice option rather than an optimum choice option. Also, all sorts of mechanisms and biases interfere in the decision making process.

As people are faced everyday with numerous choices to make, they must utilize a variety of strategies to assist them in these processes, so a preferred choice can be arrived at (Goldstein & Hogarth 1997). Various decision making strategies are summarized below;

Additive strategies provide systematic ways to evaluate alternatives. The *additive strategy* works by giving a score to the desirability of each attribute of a choice and then totaling up the scores and selecting the choice with the highest score as the example of making a choice between two cars is shown in Table 3.13 below.

In the case above car one would be selected because the total score for the car was 2 points higher than car B. An *additive-difference strategy* would focus on the difference between the score of each attribute of both cars. The differences are shown in Table 3.14.

Table 3.13. The Attribute Rating Totals of the two cars

	Car 1	Car 2
Cost	+2	+1
Power	+1	+2
Economy	+1	-1
Comfort	+2	+2
Total	+6	+4

---

[50] Schwartz also postulated that through having an abundant number of choices available there is greater room for remorse and regret about poor decisions, which can lead to unhappiness and less well-being.

Table 3.14. Difference in the Scores of Each Attribute of the Two Cars

	Car 1	Car 2	Difference
Cost	+2	+1	+1
Power	+1	+2	-1
Economy	+1	-1	+2
Comfort	+2	+2	0
Total	+6	+4	+2

The difference +2 which means that car 1 is 2 points more attractive than car B. Even though the conclusions of the *additive* and *additive-difference strategies* are the same, the information evaluated is different. The *additive strategy* looked at total utility or appeal, while the *additive-difference strategy* looked at the value of each attribute.

Another way of making choices is by eliminating choices whose attributes fail to meet certain criteria, until there is only one option left. This is called *elimination by aspects strategy*. For example if a person is looking to buy a new house and only has $100,000 to spend, a house costing $110,000 will be outside the attribute limit, so eliminated as an option. This strategy assumes that attributes differ in their importance; however the order of which attributes are selected to evaluate can influence the result. A *conjuncture strategy* is a variation of elimination by aspects strategy, where all attributes of an alternative must satisfy a minimum criteria before that alternative can be selected. This alternative means that one alternative must be fully evaluated before moving to the next alternative.

These four strategies show different ways a person can make decisions. According to studies made by Payne (1976), people tend to change strategies as the demands of the task change. When there are a high number of alternatives people tried to reduce complexity by using the *elimination by aspects* or *conjunctive strategies*. When alternatives are smaller in number people tend to use the more cognitively demanding *additive* and *additive-difference strategies*.

Decision making is also affected by our emotions and moods. Emotions have a substantial impact on what type of information we retrieve from our long term memory. Happy moods make it more likely that we will retrieve more positive events, while sadness will make it more likely that we will recall more negative events (Blaney 1986). The greater the number of positive events that are in our mind, the greater the chance we will take a positive outlook on events in the future, while the greater availability of negative events in memory, the greater the chance will view future events in a negative light (Wright & Bower 1992). Mood also affects our perception. When we are in happy moods our visual cortex takes in more information, while in unhappy moods the visual cortex creates *'tunnel vision'* (Schmitz, De Rosa & Anderson 2009).

Business decision making is much more complex than the simple strategies outlined above. Jury decision making is much more complex and has more similarities. Studies have shown that there are a number of factors that influence a juror's decisions. Like business decisions, jury decisions are made over a period of time. Jurors like business people are exposed to continuous inflows of information, some relevant and some irrelevant to the sets of decisions they have to make. Hastie and Pennington (2000) postulate that we accumulate information in complex situations like a developing story. Evidence becomes an evolving narrative where new facts are interpreted according to the overall direction the story is going, in the situation of a court case either a guilty or not guilty verdict (Carlson & Russo 2001).

Story construction eliminates detail and makes the incoming information more cognitively manageable. Prior knowledge also comes to play in complex decision making situations like a trial in assisting a person in how to comprehend the story and judge the plausibility of the constructed story, bringing in their own judgments and biases (Hastie & Pennington 2000). This is where stereotyping can bring bias to story construction. So in complex decision making facts and information are likely to be distorted during the cognitive construction processes.

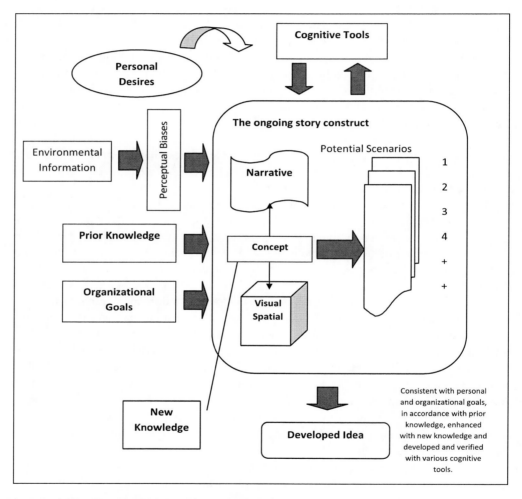

Figure 3.19. The Cognitive Thinking Process and Idea Evolution

Complex decisions in relation to potential opportunities and suitable strategies cannot be explained by simple models. These types of decisions are multiple, sequential and must be decided in a flexible manner to suit different situations within an overall changing environment. The characteristic environment where these decisions are made will be;

- Related to ill-defined and ill-structured problems where a lot of effort has to be made to understand what is happening.
- In a dynamic environment under situations of uncertainty where information will be incomplete and ambiguous.
- Where there are multiple players within the environment, whose actions and reactions are not always known.
- Where objectives may shift during evaluation periods and during strategy execution.
- Where strategy and work within the environment is complex and requires a high amount of coordination.
- Where relationships between variables are not fully clear and these relationships can even change over time.
- Where there is considerable time pressure where stress exists.
- There are costs involved with failure, and
- Where both organizational and personal goals are a guide to the direction decision making will go.

Table 3.15. A List of Some Cognitive Tools that Assist the Decision Making and Idea Evolution Process

Cognitive Tool	Comments
Detecting Anomalies	The ability to detect anomalies, weaknesses and defects in arguments, concepts, logic and strategies, etc.
Experience	Knowledge and skills gained through doing and observing over a period of time.
Identifying Gaps and barriers	The ability to identify and appraise gaps in strategy, competence, resources, abilities, skills, etc and identify potential barriers to entry, execution and/or operation.
Imagining	To form a mental picture, image or concept of something.
Improvising	The principal of responding to some stimulus through intuitive thinking often ending up in creating something.
Intuition	Perceiving, feeling or seeing something without cognitive effort.
Mental Simulation	To learn about the mental states of others by mentally simulating their behavior.
Metacognition	Knowledge or wisdom about knowing what strategies are required for decision making and problem solving.
Pattern Matching	To test whether things like arguments, concepts and ideas have a believed or desired structure.
Problem Detection	Where people become concerned about the potential consequences of events taking unacceptable directions.
Rational Analysis	To identify goals, build a hypothesis and test it.
Situation Awareness	The perception of environmental elements within a particular volume of time and space.
Spotting Leverage Points	Looking for places where a small effort can make an out of proportion achievement.
Strong Feeling	A feeling some certainty or conviction about something.
Tricks of the Trade	Knowledge and tools specifically from your profession and experience.
Vision	Foresight.

Decision making under the above circumstances will most likely involve people with expertise in this area and they will tend to rely on both prior knowledge and their set of cognitive analytical skills to make decisions. As we have seen, they will also be affected by perception biases, moods, heuristics and other biases in the decision making process.

Decision making in relation to opportunity and strategy under these kinds of complex situations involve a saga where the nature of the of the opportunity will evolve through image and narrative into an open ended running story that continues to be created and evolve as information keeps coming in and different styles and tools of reasoning refines or expels the emerging concept in focus. Figure 3.19. shows this process of idea evolution and some of the cognitive aspects that influence it and table 3.15. Lists some of the Cognitive tools that can be used to aid and develop the decision making process.

Field Dependence-Independence

Herman Witkin spent over 30 years researching differences in visual perception. Witkin and his associates constructed a test where the respondent would sit on an adjustable chair to change orientation in a dark room and look at rod and tilted frame, where they would be asked to turn a knob to move the rod to an upright position inside the frame. In this rod and frame test (RFT), Witkin and his associates found that one group of respondents used the tilted frame as a reference to move the rod to an upright position and the other group would go by the sensation of their body to move the rod to an upright position. The first group was considered field dependent as they were dependent on the frame as the reference while the second group was considered field independent as they used their body as a frame of reference, which is outside the field. Later Witkin developed the embedded figures test (EFT) which consisted of a complex picture with hidden figures within it as an easier alternative to the rod and frame test (see figure 3.20).

Field dependence is a situation where a person tends to perceive the whole environment and has difficulty separating individual items within it. Such a person will look at the whole field in an undifferentiated manner. Field independence is a situation where a person perceives the individual items within the field, rather than the field as a whole. Field dependence-independence is also called global-analytical thinking as global thinking (field dependence) is holistic and analytical thinking (field interdependence) breaks down the whole into simpler parts and re-organizes them. Field dependence-independence is considered by some as a dimension of cognitive style[51], but Jonassen and Grabowski (1993) define it as a cognitive control because it regulates visual perception.

Witkin et. al. (1954, Witkin 1977, Witkin & Goodenough 1977) believed that a person's personality can be seen through the way they perceive the environment. People who are field dependent would tend to rely on more social interaction for getting information, ask opinions of others and be attentive to social stimuli. They would be good at seeing connections between categories of information, look at the environment holistically, and process information in chunks. These people tend to favor social science and education as a profession. People who are field independent on the other hand, tend to be impersonal and

---

[51] Cognitive styles include traits and characteristics like impulsive-refectivity, complexity-simplicity, visual-haptic, and visualizer-verbalizer.

detached towards others, not very interested in others opinions, and have a low preference for social events. They are however more autonomous and display a focused and analytical approach to issues in complex settings, discarding what to them is not important. These people tend to favor science, mathematics and engineering as a profession.

Figure 3.20. An example of an embedded figures test diagram.

Field independence can be related to left side brain activities as those who are field independent tend to be better at learning languages, better at mathematics (Vaidya & Chasky 1980) and better at reading, where field dependent people were better at right side brain activities like social literature. Field independence was probably a very important characteristic for hunting in nomadic societies and field dependence characteristics important in agriculture (Yiu & Saner 2007). Field independency aids analysis and cognitive restructuring, while field dependence assists interpersonal skills as it is more sensitive to emotional stimuli. Field dependency is more common in women and field independency is more common in men (Yiu & Saner 2007). A study by Silverman et. al. (1966) found that more left handed people were field dependent than those that were right handed. Another study (Pizzamiglio 1974) found that more ambidextrous people tend to be field dependent than right handed people. These studies hint that field dependence-independence may be influenced by the dominant lateral hemisphere of the brain. Table 3.16. below shows some of the important field dependence-independence characteristics.

Most people at an early age are field dependent where field independency develops at early adulthood. As people age they tend to go back to field dependency (Witkin et. al. 1977). Witkin believed that field dependence-independence tendencies were the result of how children were brought up by their parents. Those that were kept under strict control tended to become field dependent and those brought up in a less strict environment tended to be more field independent (Korchin 1986). Field dependency is more common in developing countries and agrarian societies and field independence is more common in Western and industrialized societies (Yiu & Saner 2007).

Table 3.16. Field Dependent-Independent Characteristics

Field Dependent	Field Independent
Perception: Holistic (global) perception, adheres to existing structures, looks at broad concepts, able to see connections and links between different stimuli, social orientation and relates to own experiences.	**Perception:** Perceives things in isolation to rest of field, categorizes stimuli, can impose own structures, detached and impersonal.
Cognitive Characteristics and Learning: Requires externally defined goals, reinforcements and structure, likes visual information, looks at field as a spectator deductive conclusion, looks for concepts before going down to details, needs social interaction, sensitive to criticism.	**Cognitive Characteristics and Learning:** Can set own goals and objectives, likes figures and statistics with visual reinforcement, interested in new concepts for the sake of new concepts, uses a hypothesis-testing approach to attain concepts, takes a step by step (sequential) approach to develop concepts, attempts to conclude tasks, less sensitive to criticism.

Witkin (1977) stated that the dominance of one side of field dependence-independence is not any better than the other side as it only indicates how a person perceives the environment. Those people who are field dependent process information holistically. They do not look at specific detail or concerned with more of the socially orientated issues (Frank & Davis 1982). Field dependent people are better able to find connections between things than field independent people. However field independent people can quickly break down an environment into individual parts and analyze them in a more detached manner. Field independent people are able to go beyond structure and reorganize information. Field independent people are less distracted by peripheral things and able to focus on particular people, things or events[52]. Field independent people are able to remember small details much better than field dependent people, i.e., small details in photos etc. (Bastone & Woods 1997).

Both field dependent and independent perception have their advantages and disadvantages. However both modes of perception are able to view the same environment in different ways, which can provide vastly different perspectives.

Cognitive Style

Cognitive style refers to the thinking strategy used to perceive, remember and use information for solving problems. Cognitive style defines a person's preferred and habitual approach to organizing, representing and processing information and a built in way of responding to situations (Riding & Rayner 1998). Cognitive style could be considered a set of higher ordered heuristics which give a person a consistent approach to problem solving (Brigham & Castro 2003). As we have seen that patterning is a normal aspect of our

---

[52] A study of police officers in the United States found that officers that were field independent are much better at ignoring distractions and focusing on important information during an event like a shoot-out (Vrij, van der Steen & Koppelaar 1995).

perception in the last section, people may differ in their abilities to discover opportunities because of their search and scanning techniques and thinking style (Ko & Butler 2002). Ideas also exist in interrelated patterns where one idea will lead on to another (Koestler 1976). The ability to be creative requires one to move between matrixes and string things together such as resources, networks, skills and capabilities, etc (Ko & Butler 2002).

For a long time we have known that different parts of the brain fulfill different thinking functions where the left hand side of the brain thinks analytically, systematically, logically, and controls speech and the right hand side of the brain thinks artistically, musically, spatially, intuitively and emotionally (Lumsdaine & Binks 2003). Ned Herrmann (1996) a physicist who worked within the human resource department of General Electric after years of research in creativity of the human brain developed a metaphorical model of how the four quadrants of the brain have specialized functions (Lumsdaine & Lumsdaine 1995).

Herrmann believes the brain works as a coalition of four quadrants that carry out specialized functions. Quadrants A and B are superimposed over the left side of the brain which is sequential and time-bound and quadrants C and D are superimposed over the right hand side of the brain which is holistic and timeless. Quadrant A thinkers think in terms of words and numbers, logically and analytically. They are achievement orientated and most people are trained and educated in this way (Arora & Faraone 2003). Quadrant B thinkers are task-orientated and result driven in the way they organize facts and plan. Quadrant C thinkers are intuitive and rely on interpersonal stimulations and quadrant D thinkers are conceptualizing, imaginative and holistic (Herrmann 1996). Each quadrant works in tandem in varying degrees within individuals. Figure 3.21. depicts the brain metaphor model.

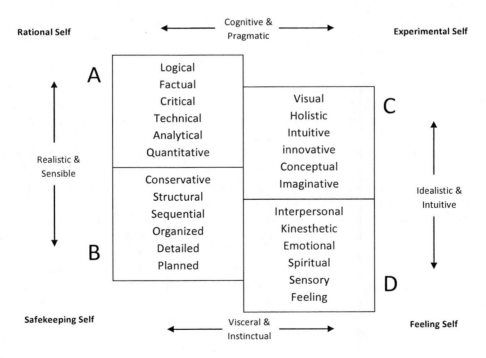

Figure 3.21. The Brain Metaphor Model.

Each quadrant has dominant ways of thinking which suits different tasks. Quadrant A is rational and will suit tasks like applying formulae to problems, analyzing data, and diagnosing problems, etc. Decisions will only be made on hard facts and data and there is complete focus on the tasks at hand. This style tends to be more directive often putting people's feelings in the background. Quadrant A thinking suits scientists, engineers, technical, financial, medical and legal people. Quadrant B is organized and will suit the tasks of building things, paperwork procedures, establishing order, planning, getting things done according to a schedule, detailed and administrative jobs. This style is very detailed, structured and without ambiguity, while strictly following protocols. There will be focus on efficiency and procedure but hesitancy towards new ideas. This style suits administrative, accounting, supervisory and assembly work. Quadrant C is emotional, spiritual and feeling which suits tasks like team based activities, building relationships, teaching, listening, persuading people, being a member of a team, helping people and counseling. This style is inclusive, participative and team orientated and suits counseling, teaching, social work, care giving and service orientated occupations. Quadrant D is imaginative, creative, and experimental and will suit tasks like inventing solutions to problems, bringing about change, selling new ideas, developing new things and designing. This style will enable people to see things through to the end, be adverse to risk, creative, excited about new ideas and adventurous and suit entrepreneurs, artists, developmental people, sales and entertainers.

The four quadrants are the basis of our thinking preferences which determine how we prefer to learn, understand and express things in what are called cognitive preferences or preferred modes of knowing (Herrmann 1995). When faced with a situation or problem we use our preferred way of thinking to make sense and solve the problem. When people are anchored toward one mode, other modes of thinking are avoided. This greatly affects our intake of information, comprehension of a situation and overall learning capabilities (Sadowski *et. al.* 2006).

People tend to think from different positions within the whole brain metaphor. Only a small percentage of the population thinks within a single quadrant. However single quadrant thinking develops little conflict with thinking patterns within the other quadrants which provides cognitively consistent perceptions and decision making. However single quadrant thinkers have difficulty in changing to other quadrants for understanding. This creates an issue when communicating to others who think from other quadrants. As each quadrant has its own patterns and meaning[53] which creates its own *'mental language'* (Herrmann 1995, P. 173), which can be mistaken as to the actual meaning intended by others who operate from other quadrants and other *'mental languages'* (Herrmann 1996, P. 161).

Around 30-40% of people think with dominant double quadrant thinking preferences. This can be either in the same hemisphere or between hemispheres. When people are dominant double quadrant thinking between A and B in the left cerebral hemisphere or C and D in the right cerebral hemisphere, the strength and quality of their thinking will increase. This is because A and B are both verbal and structured quadrants, where a person will tend to be realistic and sensible and C and D are both intuitive and holistic quadrants, where a person will tend to be idealistic and intuitive. However whenever people think with dominant double quadrants within the same hemisphere, those with right dominance will appear to be vague about things at times while those with left dominance will appear to be more directive and authoritative.

When double dominance occurs between two hemispheres *i.e. A and D or B and C,* various conflicts will occur like ideas verses action, feelings verses rationality, the future verses the past, and risk verses security being impetuous verses cautious, etc. Under pressure these people find they tend to switch between modes of thinking and can become confused and unable to make decisions. However when a person is in harmony this dominance configuration can bring powerful combinations of abilities where for example, a person may be able to be a careful planner with equally strong abilities for action and implementation. People who think dominantly across two opposite quadrants in different cerebral lobes will tend to be pulled by opposite and conflicting perspectives. Under pressure these people will become indecisive and feel paralyzed to make any decision and act.

About one third of people use three quadrants in perception and thinking. Triple quadrant thinkers are able to perceive lots more information than either single or double quadrant thinkers and communicate their ideas to a wider group of people. Only a small number of people utilize all four quadrants equally. Quadruple quadrant thinkers have immense advantages over other thinking types and tend to have balanced views of things in any given situation.

How does this relate to opportunity? People dominated by quadrant A would tend to seek familiar information and use existing patterns in the perception of opportunity. They tend not to be creative and innovative and are thus not original in their ideas. Quadrant B thinkers are conservative, risk conscious, careful and hesitant to evaluate potential opportunities without security. They seek only familiar information based on established patterns rather than being original or creative. Quadrant C thinkers have the ability to pick up emotional under-currents when looking at situations and assessing opportunities. This greatly affects their judgment. Like quadrant A and B thinkers, quadrant C thinkers look at existing patterns but are influenced by feelings and emotion. Quadrant D thinkers thrive on excitement of new ideas and possibilities, but tend to not function well according to time. They are risk takers and impetuous, but able to see *'the big picture'* of things and consequently can develop spectacular visions. They are very creative, intuitive, experimental and innovative when evaluating potential opportunities by looking outside existing patterns. People whose thinking is dominated by a single quadrant may miss much environmental information that other quadrant patterning will pick up, thus being disadvantaged at picking up opportunities. Double and triple dominant quadrant thinkers will tend to include more information than single dominant people but miss out the types of information the absent quadrant is attuned to. Quadruple dominant thinkers have the ability to take all sorts of information into account in seeing opportunities and are able to evaluate them much more comprehensively.

Dr. Saras D. Sarasvathy (2001) described two distinctly different types of thinking processes and mental construction that are important for ideation and strategy conceptualization; - causation and effectuation. These two ways of thinking can be best illustrated by imagining how a person cooks a meal after coming home from work. If a person has a predetermined dish in his or her mind, the person will list each food ingredient needed and then look for each of them in the food pantry and refrigerator, and then go on and cook

---

[53] According to Herrmann (1995, P. 175) what we say reflects our values, beliefs, assumptions, expectations, biases, prejudices, experiences and brain quadrant dominance. The 'mental language' we use reflects all this in our

the meal. Alternatively the person could look at what food ingredients are in the food pantry and refrigerator and then use these ingredients to cook something that comes to mind.

In the first case this is the process of causation. The process of causation occurs when a person looks at an existing market for a new product opportunity and systematically works back to create a product that would fit into the market. This is quite similar to how the general strategic marketing process works to create a competitive strategy and would be very suitable for allocative and discovery opportunities. Causation focuses on achieving an expected goal that is predetermined within an existing market field. Crafted strategy depends upon undertaking a competitive analysis using pre-existing knowledge about the market and competition.

The second case is the process of strategy effectuation. The process of effectuation is about thinking of possibilities that may have potential and then evaluating and confirming the potential. Effectuation does not rely on preconception, which is something akin to a painter sitting in front of a blank painting canvass thinking about what to paint. Effectuation is about creating something that will extend the market field or create a new market field. This would be very suitable for construction opportunities. The thinking concepts of causation and effectuation are illustrated in Figure 3.23.

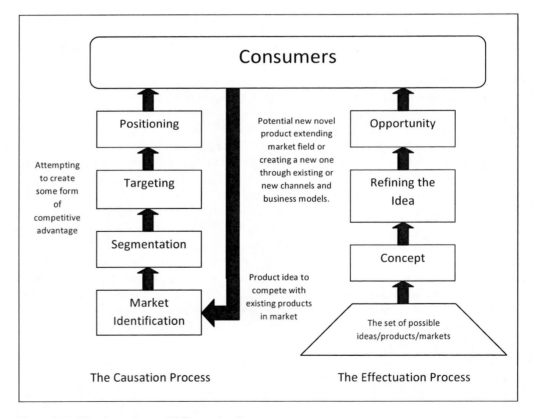

Figure 3.22. The Causation and Effectuation Processes.

narrative.

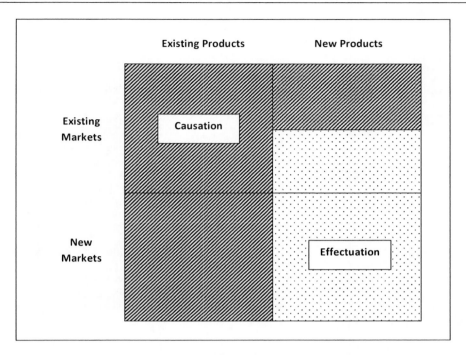

Figure 3.23. The relevance of causation and effectuation on the strategy matrix.

Causation and effectuation are two cognitive styles important in opportunity construction. Effectuation predominates entrepreneurial thinking through creating divergent concepts in new market space (Sarasvathy 2003). Causation is based on *the logic of prediction*, where the future is predicted and an attempt to control it is made through strategy. Causation is thus about analyzing the future through historical reflection to make predictions about trends which form the basis for strategy decisions. Effectuation relies on creativity and has *the logic of control* where the means are controlled to arrive at an unknown future and uncertain goals, as it is not constrained by pre-existing goals (Sarasvathy 2001). Effectuation allows the moving from a single product and single customer to multiple products and multiple customers without this end first in mind. It's about incremental growth and steering a direction according to where opportunities arise in the future. The focus is on matching means with opportunities[54]. The characteristics of the processes of causation and effectuation are listed in Table 3.17. below.

The thinking style of a person is characteristic upon how a person will perceive information from the environment, make decisions and solve problems. Some people carefully collect all types of data and information, carefully evaluating it before using it, while others will only see selective data and information before using it. Some people will rationally and sequentially make decisions while others will base their decisions on intuition, feeling and hunches. Cognitive style will be influenced by how adverse a person is to risk, how excited they will be to new ideas and how they will approach a particular situation, *i.e., cautiously, impetuously, conservatively or sequentially, etc.* Finally cognitive style will

---

[54] Saras Sarasvathy (2003) uses the metaphor of a patchwork quilt that is added to over time to grow and also cut down and torn where need be, if the growth is disliked or to suit the situation in a continuous manner.

influence how a person deals with ambiguity and uncertainty. Can a person take action without knowing what the end will be or does a person need to have the end in mind before taking action?

Table 3.17. The Characteristics of the Processes of Causation and Effectuation

Characteristic	Causation	Effectuation
How Objectives are Developed	A given objective is reactive to the existing market set.	To creatively develop a new market field or extend an existing market field.
General Strategy Outlook	To the extent the future can be predicted, it can be controlled.	If the processes can be controlled, the future can be controlled, but it is not important to predict the future.
Decision Making Criteria	To select the means to achieve goals where the criteria is based on costs/returns. Choice of means according to what traditionally available, according to present knowledge.	To evaluate potential combinations of means and assess probable effects. Driven by the personal characteristics of the person.
Competencies	Based on experience, existing knowledge, competitors and markets.	Existing base plus what is learnt as go along.
Environment	Stable, if not static where linear strategy can be utilized.	Dynamic, uncertain, changing constantly, results unknown.
Focus	Focus on predictable aspects of strategy.	Focus on controllable aspects and adjust for what is not controllable.
Outcomes	Market share in existing markets through developing new products and entering new markets with existing products. Strategies based on competitive strategies.	New products, new markets.

Multiple Intelligences

Howard Gardner began developing his multiple intelligences theory through taking an interest in the research of Norman Geschwind[55] who was concerned with what happened to normal or gifted individuals after the misfortune of a stroke or some other form of brain damage. Gardner was amazed at how a patient, counter to logic would lose the ability to read words, but could still read numbers, name objects and write normally (Gardner 2003). Gardner synthesized his knowledge of the study of brain damage with his study of cognitive development.

There is no conclusive agreement about what the concept of intelligence really means. Concepts of intelligence before Gardner's work were narrow with most definitions focused on achievement, *i.e., how much a person knew relative to others in an age group*, or aptitude orientated, *i.e., the person's ability to learn*[56]. Intelligence was generally thought of as a general trait, *"g"* for general intelligence where people would differ in the amount of intelligence they processed. However as separate abilities *(e.g. verbal, memory, perceptual, and arithmetic)* were recognized as intelligence, the concept of intelligence widened[57].

---

[55] Norman Geschwind is considered the pioneer of behavioral neurology.

[56] The traditional measure of intelligence was the IQ test to predict school performance and vocational potential.

[57] This can be seen in tests which measured more than a single variable like the Scholastic Aptitude Test (SAT), which gives a verbal and mathematic score. Another test, the Wechsler Intelligence Scale for Children gives 11 subtest scores of which 6 are concerned with verbal abilities and 5 with non-verbal abilities.

Gardner (2004, P. 4) believes intelligence can be shown in numerous ways. Obtaining a high level of competence in a field should be seen as exhibiting intelligent behavior, and as such intelligence must also have a cultural base[58]. Western society heavily values verbal, mathematical and spatial competencies while in other competencies may have more importance in other cultures, *i.e., hunter-gatherers will value body-kinesthetic competences*. Intellectual competence must therefore entail the possession of a set of skills that can enable someone to solve problems, resolve difficulties they may find in day to day living, have the potential to find or create problems, and have the ability to acquire new knowledge from these experiences (Gardner 2004, pp 60-61). Multiple intelligence theory is recognition that broad mental abilities are needed in society and that every person has a unique blend of different intelligences (Gardner 1999, P. 45).

Gardner (2004) initially listed seven intelligences (later adding one more) which are briefly summarized below[59]:

The Body-Kinesthetic intelligence is the ability of controlling bodily movement. This involves learning bodily movement and coordination. People with strong body-kinesthetic intelligence would be good at sports, dance, acting performing, and making things. This would have been a very important intelligence in the early history of mankind when hunting and protecting themselves was important. People tend to learn by doing things physically with repetitive practice within this intelligence.

The Verbal-Linguistic intelligence involves the use of the spoken and written language. People with strong verbal-linguistic intelligence have good language capabilities and will be skilled at explaining things, teaching, orating, writing rhetorical and poetic narrative, etc. They have good verbal memory and recall and can learn languages quickly. People with verbal-linguistic intelligence learn by reading, listening, taking notes, and discussion, etc.

Logical-Mathematical intelligence involves the ability to use logic, scientific thinking, reasoning, abstract patterns of recognition, and traditional mathematical operations to solve problems. People with logical-mathematical intelligence would be expected to be excellent at chess, computer programming, and other logic driven pursuits. However Gardner (2004, P. 145) points to a difference between the mathematician and Scientist. The mathematician tends to be interested in abstract systems and making order from chaos through logic, the scientist on the other hand uses mathematics as a tool for building models and hypothesizing new ideas. This intelligence equates closely with more traditional concepts of intelligence.

Visual-Spatial intelligence involves spatial ability, *i.e., the ability to see visual patterns and make spatial judgments*. This intelligence allows a person to perceive a visual object and mentally reshape, recreate and manipulate the object-patterns. People with strong visual-spatial intelligence are good at solving visual puzzles, conjuring up visual imagery and manipulate it, etc. They also possess the feelings of balance and composition, needed in artwork like painting or sculpture. A person with strong visual-

---

[58] Gardner cites the example of a boy at 12 years of age being selected by the village elders to become a sailor, an Iranian youth learning the Koran by heart and a boy in Paris that has learned computer programming and is composing music with the aid of a synthesizer.

[59] Gardner used a criterion to select each intelligence type. In the absence of any algorithm, selection according to Gardner was more reminiscent of an artistic judgment (Gardner 2004, P. 63), therefore each selection should be seen as provisional. The criterion used (Gardner 2004, pp 63-69) included; the intelligence could be potentially isolated by observing a patient with brain damage, the existence of idiots savants (where someone is mentally impaired but also have some extraordinary mental abilities), prodigies and other exceptional individuals, support from psychometric findings, susceptibility to encoding in a symbol system, a set of operations that can be identified and a distinctive history.

spatial intelligence will also have very good visual thinking skills, memory, sense of direction and eye-hand coordination.

Musical intelligence involves abilities in rhythm, music and hearing. Those who have strong musical intelligence have a greater sensitivity to sound and can very easily pick up rhythms, pitch and tones. People with musical intelligence would themselves have good pitch, be able to sing, play musical instruments and compose. Musical intelligence is the first intelligence an infant picks up and this intelligence is very heavily influenced by culture.

One's own self the intrapersonal intelligence is the range of feelings, emotions, and the ability to recognize them and draw upon them to understand their influence on behavior. The intrapersonal intelligence is nothing more than the capacity to distinguish the feelings or pleasure and pain at its basic level. At higher levels intrapersonal intelligence enables one to sense and symbolize complex and differentiated feelings and emotions (Gardner 2004, P. 239). The intrapersonal intelligence is the capacity to understand one's self. People with strong intrapersonal intelligence will be intuitive and introverted. They will understand their own strengths and weaknesses and what makes them a unique person.

The interpersonal intelligence focuses outward to others. Interpersonal intelligence is the ability to notice and access other people's moods, temperaments, motivations and intentions. In the crudest form the interpersonal intelligence is the infant's ability to access and discriminate the moods of others around him or her. In its highest form, the interpersonal intelligence enables a person to read others desires and intentions. Interpersonal intelligence is also the ability to communicate effectively and influence other people. People with strong interpersonal intelligence are able to lead others. They learn through social interaction, discussion and debate with others.

While on sabbatical leave during 1994-95 Howard Gardner reviewed evidence for the existence of new types of intelligences (Gardner 2003, P. 7). He concluded that there was enough evidence for the existence of a naturalist intelligence and possibly an existential intelligence (the intelligence of big questions).

The naturalist intelligence is about empathy with nature and understanding our own place within it. Naturalist intelligence is about the ability to grow things, the ability to care for and understand animals, and a general sensitivity towards the operation of natural eco-systems (Gardner 1999, P 52).

Existential intelligence is the capacity to think about and reflect on philosophical questions about life, death and the universe met most but not all criteria. Gardner also looked at spiritual and moral intelligence but they could be better described as personality traits and beliefs rather than separate intelligences (Gardner 1999, P. 77).

Multiple intelligence has been heavily criticized over the years, viewed as rhetoric rather than science supported by empirical data (Demetriou & Kazi 2006)[60]. Others argue that the different intelligences are really just separate abilities that correlate with general intelligence (Eysenck 1994, Scarr 1985, Sternberg 1983, 1991). Ironically, Gardner himself states that he could have easily used the title the *"Seven Talents"* rather than Seven Intelligences (Gardner 2003, P. 3), which would have defused much criticism. However what is important to our

---

[60] Although Multiple Intelligence has not been widely accepted by the psychology community, it has been widely accepted in education circles and forms the basis of many curriculum structures. Mindy Kornhaber (2001, P. 276) claimed that the theory of multiple intelligence actually validates what teachers have known for years i.e., that students learn in many different ways.

argument is that multiple intelligences recognize different skills coming from different areas of the mind and offers a different insight into how we think. Singularly and combined multiple intelligences offers an understanding that there are multiple paths of perception, perspective and reasoning patterns. Multiple intelligences as a metaphor is a powerful way of understanding how we can see and understand things in different ways. These special skills influence how we see, think and learn from the environment. Each type of intelligence has its own source of enquiry (Gardner 2004, P. 290) which can provide a means of reflection based on selected patterns and principals (Gardner 2004, P. 169). Learning the logics of these intelligences can act as powerful tools to see the environment and find new sources of creativity. However, one must remember that entrepreneurial success does not necessarily correlate with intelligence (Dollinger 2003, P. 13).

PART THREE: OUR PSYCHOLOGICAL AND PSYCHOTIC WORLD

Our Emotions as a Gateway between Ourselves and the Environment

Understanding the causes and the impact of emotions is important to the study of opportunity and strategy development. It is important to recognize our emotions and the role they play in influencing decision making. Emotional states can influence a person's thinking and make behaviour irrational (Nesse 1998). The increase of the cognitive influence in psychology has brought emotional processes into focus (Greenberg & Safran 1989), especially within the context of entrepreneurship. These next two sections look at emotions and the ways they influence us.

Our basic emotions are primal urges that we share with many other members of the animal kingdom, except that the majority of animals do not have any cognitive capacity to turn them into higher order feelings, thoughts and concepts[61]. Emotions are part of our basic schemata and semantics at the imaginative and conceptual levels (Buck 1985) and their intensity assists us with memory retrieval. Higher order emotions tend to be socially constructed and occur within social interaction and relationships. Emotions can evolve, transform, change and take new directions in different situational contexts. Emotions can be positive or negative, expressed or not expressed and vary in intensity. Emotions play a role in our perception, thinking, decision making and communication with others.

Emotions, although not directly part of our cognitive systems, are very closely intertwined and have great influence over perception and decision making. Emotions add subjectivity to our experiences and trigger accompanying physiological responses which in many cases have motivational influences and behavioural consequences. Emotions are biological, social, cultural and personal.

If we subscribe to the notion that the process of opportunity identification and subsequent exploitation is not an entirely rational process, then exploring these activities through emotions may create some valuable texture and understanding to the subject that we miss through examining the process through the '*more rational'* management process theories. Using metaphors such as nurturing and bringing up a child conjure up analogies that portray events as emotional, that traditional management process theories do not take into

---

[61] Some theories of emotion see all emotions as socially constructive and not evolutionary.

consideration and thus lack full meaning. The nurturing metaphor would bring understanding to the persistence someone would put into a business when results are poor *(i.e., where a parent would not give up)*, exercise long term commitment with self sacrifice *(i.e., the nature of life with dependent children)*, being an over-controlling founder of an enterprise *(i.e., parents attachment to children)*, reduce the perception of risks *(i.e., love may be blind)*, and treat the business like it is an offspring through commitment *(i.e., a passion for work)*, etc (Cardon *et. al.* 2005). This enables us to *'feel'* rather than think about opportunity exploitation in an emotional context with an intensity that exists within these processes that we cannot understand through using management process theories.

To understand who a person is, it is necessary to understand emotion. Emotions help us to learn and are an integral part of how we make sense of our lives. We find ourselves feeling strongly about something without really knowing how these feelings come. Our basic emotions come from inner extra-rational dynamics within our psych (Chodorow 1999) that are expressed as feelings, dreams, fantasies and other imagined aspects of our lives. Emotions are part of our fundamental irrational and unpredictable side to our self. Emotions show our basic urges, desires, repulsions and dislikes about what we see, feel and perceive in the environment. This subverts our sense of rationality, sometimes giving us multiple and contradictory feelings at the same time. One example would be getting angry at someone and then felling guilty about it. Yet behind these conflicting emotions maybe deeper emotions exist, as the feeling of been left out or not being part of the group – even a low feeling of self esteem. In a Jungian way, emotions are a window into our deep inner selves that are exposed through our daily experiences in the world.

Emotions provide personal meanings for everyday occurrences (Chodorow 1999). Emotions animate our thoughts into actions and behaviour which connects us to an event and social interaction. Thus emotions connect our inner selves with the outside environment and also with our interrelationships with others. We reflect using our emotions and touch our spiritual and moral inner world through what we feel through our emotions (Dirkx 1997). Emotions can amplify or circumvent the power of our ego and desires, thus encouraging or restraining any actions we take through specific feelings *(often manifested with multiple feelings)* that are generated within us. These urges are usually able to be controlled through the discipline of our reasoning, but in extreme situations become uncontrollable (Jaggar 1989), showing the inner conflict between our rational and irrational selves.

Emotions usually exist in multiplicity and as such often conflict with each other. In an ongoing enterprise where decisions have to be made, a person may be *"pulled in two conflicting directions"* by the emotions he or she has. Take for example in a family company where a long time employee must be disciplined or terminated for some grave misconduct. There may be mixed feelings that create tension and reluctance to take action when at the same time there are feelings that action must be taken in the interests of the enterprise (Fuller-Love & Thomas 2004).

Each event, object or person we perceive will bring about some form of response. This will occur in the form of emotion which is a form of psychic energy and generally provides driving or restraining forces behind a person's intent. Emotions may be short lived or persist for long periods of time. They may be dependent on internal processes or a reaction to the outside environment. Emotions can vary in intensity and be shaped by our cultural and social situations. While undertaking any tasks, emotions will tend to fluctuate widely and affect our level of creativity, energy, passion and persistence.

Table 3.18. The Positive/Negative Consequences of Positive/Negative Emotions

Positive Emotions – Positive Effects	<ul><li>Emotions indicate to others what we feel and think about something. This can be a motivator to others to share the specified emotions in some form of social situation.</li><li>Leads to more efficient decision making.</li><li>Leads to higher task involvement.</li><li>Able to tolerate higher levels of stress (Baron 2008).</li><li>With positive attitudes better able to persuade potential customers, financiers, suppliers and other stakeholders.</li><li>Leads to increased creativity.</li></ul>
Positive Emotions – Negative Effects	<ul><li>By showing positive emotions during certain negotiations may give signals to other parties of what one is thinking at that particular point of time.</li><li>May lead to hasty decisions without full deliberation.</li><li>Stop the search for information needed to make fully informed decisions (incomplete information search).</li><li>Increase the willingness to take risks.</li><li>Create feelings of overconfidence as expect positive outcomes.</li><li>Strong emotions increase the propensity to use heuristics rather than systematic thinking.</li><li>Reduces cognitive activity that can lead to judgment areas.</li></ul>
Negative Emotions – Positive Effects	<ul><li>Like positive emotions and positive effects, the showing of negative emotions can be a queue to others that something is not encouraged or wanted.</li><li>Negative emotions may be a warning that something is not right and requires further investigation.</li><li>May become more careful in decision making.</li><li>Tend to evaluate all alternatives of action before acting.</li></ul>
Negative Emotions – Negative Effects	<ul><li>The showing of negative emotions can show the weaknesses of a person and be socially undesirable. The showing of negative emotions may also show that someone is unable to exercise self control and emotionally immature.</li><li>Leads to avoidance behaviour.</li><li>Leads to risk aversion.</li><li>Discourage action due to over analysis of the situation.</li><li>Negative emotions can prevent a person undertaking necessary change that may be in the best business interests, *i.e., fear of the consequences of shutting down an enterprise may prevent a person from closing down, even though there may be drastic financial consequences.*</li></ul>

Emotions relate to our general temperament and functioning in life. They provide feeling states which influence what we want, what we do and don't do, and who we meet and interrelate with. Emotions influence our general beliefs and attitudes, providing feelings upon which courses of action we intend to take, places we want to go and people we want to associate with (Ashkanasy & Daus 2002). They create states of caution, persistence, patience, excitement, restraint, boredom, encouragement, confusion, hesitancy, challenge, mastery and enthusiasm within us. Therefore it stands that with changing emotions we also change our physiological state and behaviour.

Our higher emotions are a message to others and are interpreted according to our culture and social situations. Emotions are part of communication and colour our perceptions of organizations and relationships with others. People observe our emotions and read meaning based on the types of emotions we display or fail to display within any situational context (Brundin *et. al.* 2008). Examples of everyday use of emotion in our society include the supermarket cashier's smile and an undertaker's expression of sadness when in the presence of the widow (Rafaeli 1989). People expect to experience certain types of emotions in certain social and cultural situations to create an atmosphere of safety and stability. Perceiving a different set of emotions would create tenseness, frustration, anxiety, discomfort and even fear in a social situation.

Positive emotions in a social context lead to higher involvement in tasks (Lyubomirsky *et. al.* 2005), tolerate higher levels of stress (Baron 2008), and lead to more efficient decision making (Isen 2000). A negative emotional environment may result in avoidance behaviour (Krause 2004) and the hesitancy to take risks (Higgins 2005). Positive emotions can also have negatives consequences as well as negative emotions having positive consequences as Table 3.18. indicates.

Organizations have been designed to eliminate emotion that would interfere in rational decision making (Weber 1978, 1981, Simon 1997). So much effort has been made in business schools and throughout the rest of our education systems to promote rationality as the basis on action. Although rationality is given this supreme position, the reality is that many issues are decided upon by emotional rather than rational thinking. Emotion is sublimed through the education process, although taking a central part in our cognitive and learning processes.

In the entrepreneurial context many decisions are made under ambiguity and uncertainty. There is a high probability that the entrepreneur will have very intense emotions when making decisions (Baron 2008). Decisions are made in the absence of precedent and information, thus relying upon one's reasoning, intuition, feeling and reckoning.

Opportunity is a prediction of a potential future outcome, but any accurate prediction of the future is impossible. Emotions influence the process of decision making, as it is impossible to make any rational type of decision regarding the future (Elster 1999). It can only be an objective, goal, aspiration or hope. People will make decisions based on intuition and wisdom, which rely on stored knowledge in the long term memory and its retrieval, rather than the present situation in the environment. Before making any decision, a person will tend to weigh up the issues on the matter and take some form of *'calculated risk'* in the decision they reach. This is the work of using tacit knowledge or heuristics and emotion. Emotion prioritizes what heuristics to use by recalling the pleasantness, unpleasantness and intensity of the associated emotions. Stimulated by events, our emotions attract our attention to heuristics that are associated with the more intense emotions[62]. Our cognitive processes will retrieve

---

[62] Albert Ellis postulates that when we experience undesirable events about which we may have rational or irrational beliefs, we will become emotional over the event, leading to cognitive and behavioral consequences (Ellis & Dryden 1997). Irrational beliefs will be based on our deep subconscious self assumptions like the feeling of hopelessness, self-esteem and self-efficacy, etc (Ellis 1991). David *et. al.* (2002) classified these irrational beliefs

mental models associated with intense happiness, sadness, anger, frustration, grief, worry, complexity, etc (Simon 1997a).

The range of emotions we have are wide and it is not generally agreed how many emotions actually exist and what they actually are (Frijda 1986). The basic emotions may have been biologically derived from our earlier primal existence which aided our survival within a dangerous environment (Greenberg & Safran 1989). Some of our most basic emotions include anger, fear, sorrow, joy, envy and greed. These appear to be wired into the human organism (Arnold 1960, Leventhal 1984) and specific codes of behaviours correspond to specific primary emotions (Ekman 1972, Ekman & Friesen 1975).

The basic emotions (particularly the unpleasant ones) also generate physiological responses such as needed in the fight/flight mode when we came in proximity of a threatening animal. The brain would release adrenaline and noradrenaline into the bloodstream to enable faster thinking and actions. The brain would drastically increase its activity. The body would freeze with all senses focused on the perceived threat. The heart would beat faster, ready for a quick getaway. Blood is diverted from the skin to the limbs to enable quick and powerful movement. Blood pressure rises and respiration increases. The muscles are tensed and sweating increases to cool the body. Appetite is suppressed and the bowels relaxed so that a person will be lighter for a getaway. These emotions are involuntary and often experienced without recourse to our consciousness or intervening thought processes[63].

The key to our emotion generation is the appraisal process within our cognitive system. As the situation gets reinterpreted and reinterpreted, secondary emotions begin to be generated at a more conscious level. Emotions occur when a person is aroused after detection of some form of stimuli. This immediately changes the base level of arousal where perhaps a genetically encoded response is triggered, such as a response to the danger of a snake or spider, etc. This response immediately prepares our senses and body according to the significance of the threat. There will be a physiological response and behavioural intention after identification and a clear understanding of the situation is gained.

From the evolutionary viewpoint, the properties of stimuli that create pleasant emotions aim towards sustaining life and the properties of stimuli that take aversion to things that are incompatible with life (Panksepp 1988). Though essentially our basic emotions were biological responses to danger, threat or loss, as well as an aid to seek out ways to nurture human needs, in the modern world, threats and dangers don't exist as they did in the primal world. These physiological states are only intended to last a few moments while one deals with a perceived threat. With the stress of today's society and the prolonged emotional state many people experience, some of the above described physiological actions like high blood pressure become pathologies in individuals trying to cope with long terms stress.

---

in four categories; evaluation of self-worth, low frustration tolerance, awfulizing, and demandingness. Therefore rational beliefs will result in functional behavior and irrational beliefs will result in dysfunctional behavior.

[63] What is interesting is that Charles Darwin (1872) postulated that emotional expressions are not cultural and part of our global genetic makeup.

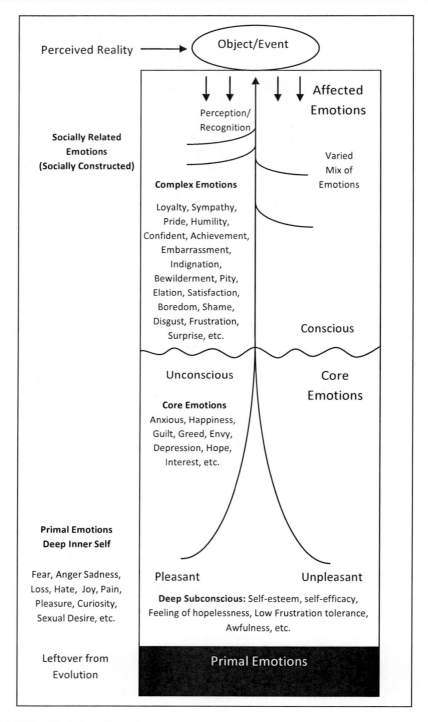

Figure 3.24. The Hierarchy of Emotions.

There is a range of emotions that are much more complex than the basic emotions. The higher ordered emotions are more socially related and usually show to others our feelings and the meaning we make of the situation. They are our response to meaning (Lazarus 1999). Socially constructed meaning is a large part of what emotional experiences are about. We answer a situation from mental models built upon our experiences stored in our long term memory. Upon subsequent appraisal, our cognitive processes determine the intensity we respond to the situation with our emotions (Lazarus & Folkman 1984). Learned *'core related themes'* are believed to influence this automatic appraisal process (Smith & Lazarus 1993). Therefore higher order emotions are social constructs. To be angry, disgusted, humiliated and proud are moral positions (Harre 1991). These social emotional positions are coded into memory schemata and they become automatic responses (Leventhal 1982). These socially related emotions will also have some relationship to the basic core emotions (Greenberg & Safran 1989). The hierarchy of our emotions is shown in Figure 3.24.

Socially related emotions have evolved through the influence of family, social and cultural influences. We learn the basic forms of these higher level emotions and tend to use them when culturally and socially appropriate (Stanley & Burrows 2001). All the higher level emotions can be represented as complex interactions of the basic emotions.

Emotions may not have direct opposites like happiness and unhappiness. Both these emotions can be experienced at the same time, as they are independent dimensions (Bradburn 1969). For example, lack of happiness does not necessarily mean unhappiness and vice versa. Some of the more common socially derived emotions are listed in Table 3.19. Below.

Our core emotions help maintain a unitary feeling within us along a particular mood theme. However the more socially related emotions provide us with mixed and complex feelings, which are often conflicting and flowing backwards and forwards in their individual intensities, leaving us in indecisive decision making capacity or in the more extreme situation, confused disposition. We experience a whole range of different emotions at the same time which partly overlap and partly conflict with each other. This would be something like the wait at an amusement park for some sort of exhilarating ride where expectation, excitement would be accompanied by some fear and hesitancy. Whether one decides to get on the ride or not will depend upon the balance of emotions at that very time, *i.e., the excitement and exhilaration would be stronger than the fear and hesitancy.* Decisions about opportunity and strategy may be just like the amusement ride but with less immediate intensity for many entrepreneurs.

Our whole emotional state is affected by a balance of affected and socially related emotions, core emotions and primal and deep sub-conscious emotions. What drives the higher emotions comes from both the environment and what is deep within our sub-conscious. Therefore in understanding our own emotional state it is important not just to look at the expressed higher emotions, but at the deeper emotions that may be driving them. Thus our experience of reality is a meta-experience made up of the set of all our emotions, the environment, and our self.

To some degree our decisions are influenced by the moods we are in. Therefore according to research, happy entrepreneurs with positive emotions tend to be more successful than sad entrepreneurs because happy people focus on learning new knowledge, new skills, and maximize their social contact with others. This increased involvement with their environment leads to more success (Baron 2008, Fredrickson 2001).

Table 3.19. Some Common Socially Derived Emotions

Emotion	Comments
Aggression	Aggression is a defence against threats to one's self-identity, or in the physical sense one's own survival. It can also be used as a tactic of dominance over others. Aggression is derived from anger (Lazarus & Cohen-Charash 2001).
Bewilderment	Failure to understand and seen as a type of ambiguity experience (Meyerson 1990). A sign of weakness.
Compassion	Compassion is being moved by another person's suffering and wanting to help. Compassion is closely related to empathy.
Depression	A longer lasting emotion than sadness. It occurs as a more global state of mind and usually follows major life events like a loss of reputation, humiliation, business or personal failure, etc. (Brown *et. al.* 1995). A person in a business *'going nowhere'* may also develop depression. Depression can be seen as a motivator to disengage from something (business or relationship) that is going nowhere (Carver & Scheier 1990). Derived from loss of self-esteem. Depression is also considered in the extreme form as a psychotic pathology.
Frustration	Worry, bewilderment, strain and other negative emotions. Derived from the basic emotion of anger (Fineman 2003).
Guilt	A self righteous feeling of having a moral lapse where remedy is attempted by performing acts of contrition (Lazarus & Cohen-Charash 2001). It can be considered a loss to our identity and is closely related to shame.
Pride	Pride stems from something favourable or positive that perceptually elevates the persona or feelings of superiority of a person in front of others. It is associated with achievement and happiness. Pride is also the opposite of shame.
Regression	As in crying, acting below one's age, etc. A social means of gaining attention or affection from others by causing emotional disturbance in others (Barr 1990). A baby crying for food is an emotional tactic for gaining more food or affection from the parents.
Sadness	An emotion based on the deeper emotion of loss. Sadness usually comes after an event, maybe as a way to prevent further losses (Nesse 1991).
Shame	The feeling after doing something defective or feeling inadequate in front of a public. It is a grave failure of living up to the expectations of the ego. Shame is closely related to guilt.
Spite	An urge to revenge a person out of disappointment and a feeling of betrayal in reciprocation or obligation by another person. This may be mixed with anger, mistrust, rejection and hatred. Spite is an intent to revenge and obtain reparations from the other through some form of malicious or harmful action (Nesse 1998).
Strain	A form of tiredness, exhaustion and depression arising from high job demands (Fineman 2003). Continuous strain can lead to physical symptoms such as increased blood pressure and cardiovascular diseases (Schnall *et. al.* 1994).
Submission	A tactic to maintain membership of a group by allowing one to be dominated by others.
Worry	A negatively affect emotion where there is an uncomfortable chain of thoughts and images (Borkovec *et. al.* 1983). Leads to insecurity, intolerance of uncertainty.

Most psychotic states are emotional states and driven by the person's social conflict (Nesse 1998). When emotions become very intense and prolonged, they create a dysfunctional state, leading to deep fears and anxieties. This develops in the extreme into pathologies like paranoia, compulsion, schizophrenia, depression, dramatic behaviour tendencies and narcissism. Within any of these situations a person will always look for danger and threats and maintain an aroused nature of anxiety, fear or depression. This will greatly affect a person's cognitive processes and rationality when holding underlying believes of fear, pessimism and danger, etc. Our emotions affect the relationships we have. Some people fly into rages at the slightest irritation, while their partners stay with them for years out of infatuation, security or the fear of leaving. Couples can spend a great amount of time and energy fighting but stay together. Some parents will feel the excitements of having children, while others will feel neglect from their partner and seek intimacy and affection from third parties. Some people will spend a whole career of helping others, but neglect their own family and children. Parents mourning a loss of a child may neglect their other children and subconsciously blame the other partner for the loss. Our behaviour is rarely rational because of our emotions.

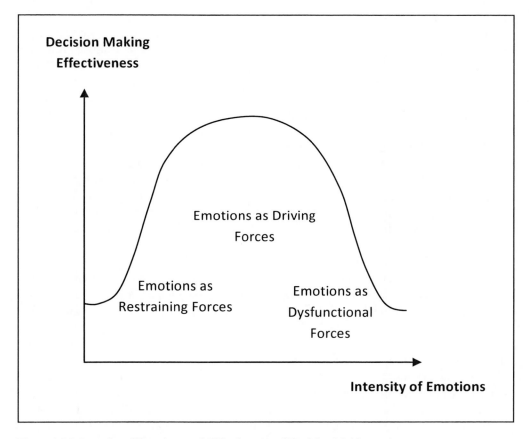

Figure 3.25. Intensity of Emotions and Effectiveness of Decision Making.

Emotions can enhance or impede our learning. Emotion is a very important part of our individual learning experiences and enables newly learnt knowledge to become psychically connected with our selves through the intensity of our emotions (Dirkx 2001). Emotionally charged images and other information are more vividly remembered and thought about than material that does not invoke any emotions. This is partly why shock enables a person to quickly make changes to their personal lives[64]. The emotions we experience with learning gives meaning to new information within our self and social setting.

Emotions affect enterprise effectiveness through acting as restraints on action or driving forces towards action. Emotions can signal potential danger, thus cautioning a person to examine a situation more carefully before making a decision and acting. The sublimation of emotions also has the effect of restraining action. Honest acceptance of our own emotions act as one of the prime driving forces of a person behind our passion, persistence and determination. Finally we will see in some of the psychotic states examined ahead, that emotions can become delusions biasing perceptions, judgments and decisions a person makes thus reducing the effectiveness of perception and decision making. Figure 3.25. below shows graphically the influence of the intensity of emotions on effective decision making.

Emotions affect a person's propensity to pursue growth, recognize potential opportunities, achieve balance between work and leisure, and manage effectively. Their personal performance is affected by the nature of their experiences and corresponding emotions that are generated. This issue is not the event itself, but whether it was a pleasant or unpleasant experience. The list of potential emotions with each experience is wide. Everyday activities like dealing with customers, competitors and the market will generate ambiguity, anger, bewilderment, concern, confidence, fear, frustration, impatience, loneliness, resignation, satisfaction, strain and stress which will either endear or discourage a person from making like decisions and actions in the future. There will be periods of a sense of control and stability and other periods of stress and a feeling of being out of control. Metaphorically this may be like sailing a yacht within calm seas and a light wind and sailing in rough seas with strong winds where one struggles to keep the yacht from capsizing. As people have different dispositions, some will enjoy the calm and dread the wild, while others will be impatient during the calm periods awaiting the challenges of the rough seas. This takes a person away from rational thinking and actions. How emotions influence our perceptions, thinking and decision making is shown in Figure 3.26.

As Figure 3.26. shows our judgments and decisions are influenced by our emotions and thus our affected states at the time of making decisions are very important. Our emotions and their intensity affects us at the point of perception through attention and patterning, within our cognitive processing through the heuristics and cognitive biases we utilize and through to influencing our motivations to seek, see, construct and discover opportunity and make any decisions. Emotion also continues its influence on perception, cognitive thinking and motivation through the reappraisal process.

The people, objects and events we experience partly influence our emotional experiences based on any prior experiences with similar people, objects and events. Each experience has a positive or negative impact with a specific degree of intensity. This positive/negative valence with its level of intensity will have some effect on our cognition and behaviour. These factors will help in deciding the persistence, dedication, commitment, focus and energy we will allocate to our chosen behaviours. However each effect from emotions will be very specific to individuals depending upon the type and intensity of core emotions and the balance and mix of socially related emotions. The types of emotions each individual feels will also be driven by some deep subconscious and primal emotions that one has suppressed below their

---

[64] For example when a doctor provides a patient with a diagnosis that is threatening, the patient will easily change their lifestyle to rid themselves of the sickness.

consciousness. A person must be aware of the influence and attachment one has to these deeper sub-conscious emotions as they are sublimely guiding thinking. We may not realize the influence of these deep sub-conscious emotions as they are manifested in our core and complex socially related emotions. The next section will consider emotional attachment.

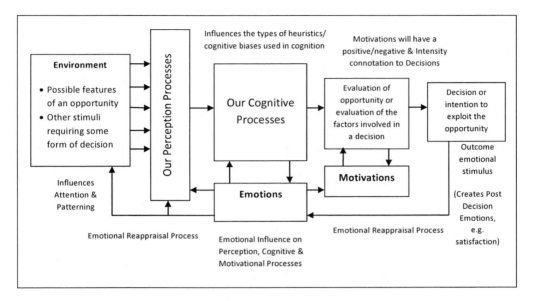

Figure 3.26. How emotions influence our perceptions, thinking and decision making.

Emotional Attachment

A person's perception continually ebbs and flows on a daily basis with changes in intelligence, knowledge and understanding, based on the type of emotions one feels and their individual strength, pull and intensity. This process makes a person happy, sad, excited, hesitant or anxious about people, things and events around them. One may feel angry, greedy, jealous, trusting, lustful, and confused all in one day. More often than not, we are not aware of the influence of our feelings upon how we perceive things and behave, as this process is partly sub-conscious (Tashi Tsering 2006). Feeling is what drives a person, whether it is to seek shelter and food, clothing and medical care, love and sex, career and comfort, etc. According to Buddhist Dharma *(theology)*, desire is a major part of our motivation and psych.

Within the *Abhidhamma Pitaka*, the last of three parts to the *Pali Cannon (the scriptures of Theravãda Buddhism)* are a number of texts concerning psychology, philosophy and metaphysics. The *Abhidhamma Pitaka* describes the structure of the human mind and perception with amazing accuracy to the accepted views of modern neuro-science. The mind is described as a continual conscious process or experience in the metaphor of a *'mindstream'* (something similar to phenomenological psychology)[65]. Buddhism sees mankind living in a

---

[65] The early concept of phenomenology was developed by G.W.L. Hegel, who was interested in exploring the phenomena of conscious experience. These concepts were further developed by Edmund Husserl and Martin Heidegger, later enlarged upon by numerous philosophers including Franz Brentano, Maurice Merleau-Ponty,

deluded reality caused by infatuation, *attachment*[66] and clinging to desire for objects and permanence in the world as the source of all suffering. The pathway to wisdom[67] is found through understanding *'The Four Noble Truths'*[68] and practice of the *'Eightfold Path'*[69]. Many of these practices are being used in modified forms for therapy today (Epstein 2001).

Within Buddhist philosophy, consciousness and metaphysics are combined in the concept of *Pratîtyasamutpada* or dependent origination. This is where reality is seen as an interdependent timeless universe of interrelated cause and effect. A human's existence is interwoven with the existence of everything else and the existence of everything else is interwoven with the human's existence in a mutually interdependent way. Because this concept is past, present and future, everything in the universe is only transient and has no real individual existence.

This is a very important concept because it is only our ability to free ourselves from attachment and delusion about our sense of self and values unconsciously placed on others, will we be able to see the world as it really is, rather than what we wish it to be. In fact our view of self and existence is created through our clinging and craving which blinds us to the reality of dependent origination. Buddhism is about transcending these delusions so human perception is clear and unbiased. This makes Buddhism an ethical philosophy of life, rather than a religion in strict terms (Watts 1996).

Since the beginning of the Twentieth Century, especially after World War II, there has been a growing interest in Eastern philosophy in the West. The teachings of the *Abhidhamma Pitaka* have inspired and influenced many psychoanalysts and psychologists (Trungpa 1975, de Silva 1991, Claxton 1990, Epstein 1995), including Carl Jung, Erich Fromm, Albert Ellis, Jon Kabat-Zinn and Marsha M. Linehan. There has been a great leap forward in humanitarian and transpersonal philosophical influence both in therapy and management theories (Goleman 2004). Dialogue between philosophy theorists and practitioners of East and West has led to mutually influential relationships between them (Safran 2003). This has led to new insights into therapies and new schools of thought on both sides (Grossman 2004, Safran 2003, Sherwood 2005). Aspects of Buddhist Dharma are also incorporated in the works of Western philosophers including Caroline A. F. Rhys David and Alan Watts.

Buddhist Dharma describes the mind as five *Skandhas (*layers) consisting of;

Max Scheler, Edith Stein, Dietrich von Hildebrand and Emmanuel Levinas. Phenomenology looks at the consciousness as a process of experience rather as a static state. Consciousness is seen as a continual process where something is always in view, whether it be a perception of an object, event or fantasy. Therefore to consciousness it is not important whether the object is real or imaginary – the conscious intention exists of the object. In phenomenology the truth is what is intelligible based on one's subjective opinion rather than physical reality. The perceived reality comes from the individual's emotions, which are within the consciousness. The consciousness exists in the lifeworld, which in addition to the physical world includes all life experiences and memories. Some view the world as being completely transparent before the consciousness.

[66] Attachment in Buddhism is a much wider concept than attachment in psychotherapy where it is primarily concerned about infant/caregiver relationships in early life. Although there are many similarities, the two concepts should not be confused.

[67] Wisdom in Buddhism can be interpreted as acceptance of Karma and conscious awareness of those actions that will bring us happiness and those that will bring us suffering and the understanding of the concept of non-duality, recognizing that there is no permanence.

[68] The Four Noble Truths are: 1. Our delusions of self cause our suffering, 2. Suffering is a fact of life resulting from our attachment to what we desire, 3. If we extinguish our attachment, we reduce our suffering, and 4. By following the Eightfold Path and developing wisdom, we can alleviate our suffering.

[69] The Eightfold path consists of right understanding, right intention, right speech, right action, right livelihood, right effort, mindfulness and right concentration. Practice of the Eightfold Path may assist in raising consciousness to a completely non-dualistic view of subject and object.

The body including sight, hearing, taste, smell and tactile feeling *(rupa)*,
Sensations and feelings *(vedana)*, (contact between the body senses and objects),
Perceptions and ideas *(samjña)*, (our ability to recognize objects and ideas),
Mental acts *(samskara)*, (willpower and attention), and
Basic consciousness *(vijnaña)*[70].

The last four layers make up the psych *(naman)*. Under *Mahayama*, but not *Theravāda* Buddhism there exists a *'storehouse'* consciousness of inborn templates[71] designating how to perceive the world resulting from one's karmic history *(bijas)*. *Bijas* combines with *naman* to form an ego or collective consciousness[72] creating the conscious illusions of everyday life.

The senses (eye, ear, nose, tongue and body) when see, hear, smell, taste or feel an object do so without identifying and giving any label to it. The senses collect raw data which must be identified through the process of discernment where the object's characteristics are matched against templates in the mind (memory). Once the object is identified, pleasure or pain feelings develop from the sense consciousness. This feeling then develops into like or dislike for the object which triggers feelings of desire or repulsion. Desire or repulsion varies in its intensity from a mild to a strong attraction or repulsion for the object. It is this feeling which gives any object value to a person.

Feelings can be generated from our natural condition, mental disposition, personality and training. Our natural condition is the intuitive tendency we feel whenever an object comes in contact to the senses. There will be a natural tendency to go towards or away from the object. In contrast our mental disposition is affected by our moods and can also be influenced by altered mind states like intoxication. Our life experience, environment and cultural influences all contribute the development of our personality, which also influences how we react to something. Finally through mental conditioning developed by training, we can change our programmed responses to objects. This can be seen when learning to drive a car. When just learning we need to concentrate on every action taken but once driving is conditioned within our mind, we do not require the same concentration, and actions taken appear to happen intuitively naturally.

Once we have a feeling about any object, our intention coordinates and directs the rest of the elements of our mind in respect of the object. Intention activates any action that will be taken based on the strength of our feelings. Our feelings and intention are very strongly related to our motivation. Our decision to act on anything is intention.

Our thoughts, speech and actions create karma. Karma is the law of cause and effect in relation to our mind, speech and actions, *i.e.,* moral causation. New karma is continually generated through our *'mindstream'* and is kept within us like a storage bank. Karma can be good or bad depending on the nature of the actions. Our stored karma determines how we perceive and respond to stimuli in the world. These are considered our natural or intuitive responses.

Due to the large number of stimuli within the world we live within, attention focuses our mind on specific objects in a similar way a filter takes away things that are unwanted. There

---

[70] See Tejguru Sirshree Tejparkhiji, (2006). Detachment from Attachment – Let Bliss Succeed, Let Sorrow Fail, Bombay, Tej Gyan Foundation.
[71] This would be something like psychic inheritance.
[72] This would be something like Carl Jung's concept of collective unconscious.

are many stimuli and corresponding mental factors operating at once, however the mind is unable to process them simultaneously. In this situation only data from one sense can be processed at a time. This means for example if driving a car and speaking on a phone at the same time, stimuli from outside the car and from the phone can only be processed sequentially meaning we are experiencing an illusion that both are operating together (Tashi Tsering 2006, P. 26).

There are a number of higher mental processes which are sometimes present. Aspiration, similar to intention, moves a person closer to an object of attachment or away from an object of aversion. This can occur both consciously and unconsciously. Aspiration is much stronger and not always present. Aspiration is the basis for enthusiasm. Appreciation develops aspiration by signaling positive or negative qualities of the object in attention. This has the effect of directing the mind closer to or further away from the object. Appreciation also develops the feeling of desire and secures its recollection in the mind. Recollection is the ability of the mind to return to any object, and forms part of the memory. Concentration is the ability of the mind to remain focused on any object. Intelligence is the ability to examine an object and determine its value. It does this by examining an object's characteristics to determine whether it is attractive or repulsive. These decisions are made on what information the mind can retrieve about the object from memory. Therefore for the mind to carry out these functions there must be an object whether physical or imaginary.

The process of attachment begins at birth where we are quickly dependent on our mother and create likes and dislikes for things. As these emotions are so strong, the majority of people are incapable of withdrawing from these attachments in later life[73]. The thought processes that lead to attachment are important to how we identify our own sense of self and being. This is agreed upon by many psychoanalysts, including Freud, who see traits like anger, aggressiveness, craving, hatred and lust make a large contribution to how we see ourselves (Metzner 1997, Engler 1993, 2003, Epstein 1995, 2007). Attachment also gives things value or meaning, rather than the perception of the actual reality (Tart 1997). It becomes the *"lens"* through which the environment is experienced and interpreted (Welwood 2001, Zimberoff & Hartman 2002).

There are different forms of attachment[74]. Sensual attachment occurs when we like processing objects that we are enchanted with. These objects include colours, shapes, sounds, odours, flavours, other objects of desire, images *(whether real or imaginary)* of the past, present and future that are in the mind. Sensual attachment can lead to feelings of envy, anger, arrogance, hate and can even lead to acts of murder and suicide. Everything a human does has some origin in sensual attachment and it is the power that drives people to study, work and earn money in the search of pleasure. Because of the desire to feel good, one can become a slave to another for the trappings of status, power, wealth and comforts that it brings, even though it forces one to agree all the time. Such a relationship brings out arrogance, ostentation and blind-less attachment. The desire to go to heaven preached in most religion also has its roots in sensuality. Sensuality is the primary form of attachment.

---

[73] This has many similarities to some of the concepts in Freudian Psychoanalysis, see Wallin, D. J., (2007). Attachment in Psychotherapy, New York, The Guilford Press, P. 31.

[74] For a discussion on the various types of delusions and attachment see: Buddhadasa Bhikkhu (2007). Handbook for mankind: Realizing your full potential as a human being, Bangkok, Amarin Publishing (Translated from the Thai edition by Aniyanada Bhikkhu Roderick S. Bucknell).

To have one's own opinions is very natural. However when ideas and opinions become cemented into a person's mind and they cling to them, this becomes attachment. Many of these opinions are bound up in customs, professions, religions, traditions and rituals and our perceptions become dogma based upon the beliefs a person subscribes to (Vajiranama 1962). They become stubborn convictions which cannot be changed due to the cement of long held traditions, professional practices and/or beliefs. The clinging to views and opinions is based on original ignorance, where existence becomes very mechanical with programmed type responses. If we see wrong we rarely admit it, often leading to anger and even violence or war, where naïve doctrines are held. When we become attached to our sheltered culture, imagination and perceptions, the potential for progress and development is hindered. When things are considered sacred and cannot be changed under any circumstances, i.e., beliefs about *'artifacts'* like qualifications, *'magical processes'* like strategic planning and *'secret procedures'* like employee selection, rationality is distorted and becomes a barrier to change.

Finally, one can be attached to the belief of the idea of *'self'* or *'I'*. This is also a common occurring form of attachment and like attachment to opinion, is very hard to detect. The paradigm of *'me and mine'* is based on our primal instincts to hunt and gather, procreate and protect, etc. We also tend to see our existence as eternal and fear the concept of death. This form of attachment eliminates any beliefs in transience where the person unconsciously develops delusions of permanence and solidity. This creates the fear of loss and desire to defend and protect both time and space as something needing to be held onto. Freud (1926) also saw the importance of the sense of loss to a person – love, object or experience, and saw that loss *(and potential loss)* can lead to manifestations of depression and anxiety. This most often leads to the search for pleasure seeking experiences to avoid further pain and suffering.

Another consequence of the *'me and mine'* paradigm is the development of aversion. When something threatens our self image, aversion steps in to maintain our self notion of permanence. Aversion may range from simple avoidance of the issue, to dissatisfaction, frustration or intense anger. The source of all these symptoms is our ignorance of our self at the unconscious level where the mind exaggerates the negative parts of our self image (Tashi Tsering 2006, P.54). Attachment can also feel good as it may be covered in love, *i.e.,* slave of a person, or anger with oneself may be covered with hate for something or someone external to oneself. These symptoms develop a number of defense mechanisms discussed in the next section.

According to Buddhadasa Bhikkhu (2007, P. 65) suffering arises because of unsatisfied desire and infatuation, leading to a vicious cycle. This is known as the *Wheel of Samsara* which pictorially depicts the endless cycle of suffering continually flowing through our life in the past, present and future, leading to endless births, deaths and rebirths through various realms (mind-states) for all forms of life.

Central to the *Wheel of Samsara* is the concept of *Paticcasamuppada* or *dependent origination* which is a perception state based on ignorance. Through sensual *(eye, nose, ear, tongue, body or mind)* contact with something, feelings are derived. This is because of our notion of self *("I and mine")* and desire, always bringing suffering through feelings, attachment and clinging. Buddhadasa Bhikkhu (1992, pp. 32-41) gives numerous examples of *dependent origination* like when a baby is upset when her doll is broken, a boy fails an exam and ends up fainting or crying, a girl sees her boyfriend walking with another girl and becomes inflamed and furious and people become attached to foods they like. In each case Buddhadasa explains that the sensual consciousness is aroused giving rise to feelings, bringing a conditioned response based on ignorance, triggered by one or more of the types of desire, discussed above.

Dependent origination occurs within the context of flowing through a number of states of ignorance and types of attachment, being continually re-birthed within one of the realms *(mind-states)*. Thus living things are just transient beings through each realm *(mind-state)*, which infers that the perception of an independent self life existence is an illusion. The Twelve *dependent origination* links, which resemble a person's thought processes on the outer part of the *Wheel of Samsara* are explained below:

Ignorance is the first of twelve situations in dependent origination. A blind woman who is about to fall over a cliff is metaphorically depicted. This shows that a person with a mind deluded in ignorance will stumble through rebirth, after rebirth ignorant of what really constitutes her individual existence and reason for her suffering. Therefore unable to break the *cycle of samsara*.

Karma or action is the second link where we shape our lives by the actions we take. This is symbolically depicted by the potter creating pots. Good karma leads to our transition to the higher realms *(mind-state)* and bad karma leads us to the lower realms. Ignorance leads to being imprisoned within the *cycle of samsara*.

Consciousness of mind is the third link, usually depicted by a swinging monkey representing how our mind moves from object to object through boredom without examining oneself. This is confused and ignorant consciousness where understanding of the concept of non-permanence is impossible. If the consciousness cannot be transformed from ignorance to enlightenment, then the person will continue going around the *cycle of samsara*.

Name and form make up the forth link referring to the five forms that constitute a person, physical being (the senses), contact with objects, perception, mental labeling and consciousness. If our consciousness still retains some ignorance before death then the forth form will go to the intermediate period between death and rebirth. This is depicted by a man rowing a boat halfway across a river, yet to reach the other side.

The five senses are the fifth link following on from the last link where a person is about to undergo rebirth. The five senses, sight, hearing, smell, taste and touch are physically formed in the mother's womb but yet to have the power of sight, hearing, smell, taste and touch because as depicted in the picture, the house is still empty.

Contact is the sixth link which is the point where the senses make contact with an object but are yet to form any reaction to the contact. This is usually depicted by two embracing lovers.

Perception is the seventh link where contact with an object gives a basic intuitive feeling of pain or pleasure. This stimulus is not felt as something liked or disliked at the perception stage. The power of perception is usually depicted in the *cycle of samsara* as a man with an arrow through his head.

Attachment is the eighth link. A person begins to mentally label perceptions as good or bad according to our self-centered desires and aversions. This attachment builds our desires, contributing to our suffering. The person addicted to alcohol in the *cycle of samsara* is symbolic of the attachments we create.

Craving is the ninth link, which is more intense form of attachment. People are not content with what they have and desire to seek pleasure and avoid pain, even at the cost of harm to others. This is intensely selfish and leads to bad karma which traps one to going around the *cycle of samsara*. This is depicted by a monkey reaching out on a tree for more fruit.

Another birth within *samsara* is the tenth link. A person with a life of craving through ignorance will be doomed to be re-birthed within the *cycle of samsara*. This is depicted by the pregnant woman.

Existence is the eleventh link where the woman has already given birth. The karma from selfish attachment and craving of the last life has caused an existence within the *cycle of samsara* in the next life.

Death is the final link in the *cycle of samsara*. If death occurs with any semblance of ignorance in the mind, then birth will occur again and again in the *cycle of samsara* until it can be broken through an understanding of dependent origination. This is depicted in a picture of a person taking a corpse out for burial.

The links in the cycle of *Paticcasamuppada* (dependent origination) are states conditioned by the previous link and go onto condition the following link. Through ignorance there is karma that creates a conditioned consciousness of despair. The physical senses condition the mind consciousness through perception, creating feelings that trigger attachment and craving. This escalates into clinging which conditions karma, the force which determines which realm *(mind-state)* the person will enter into at rebirth, continuing the *cycle of samsara*. This links the past, the present and the future.

The six realms *(5 in Theravada Buddhism)* inside the links of *Paticcasamuppada* can be seen as metaphors for various *'mind-states'* one experiences during life [75]. The depicted realms can be correlated to psychotic pathologies (Buddhaghosa 1991). Existence in each realm creates a different sense of self (Mitchell 1993) reflecting distorted views of their own ego (Moacanin 1986), leading to certain types of behavior. Unless one can break free of their karma, one is trapped into moving between these different realms or *'mind-states'*. Ones actions of body, speech and mind extend beyond the present life will determine what realm one will be re-birthed into in the next life. Each realm has particular advantages and disadvantages for obtaining enlightenment.

The Realm of the *Deva* (gods) is a world where the *Deva* have great power, are very wealthy, have a long life and are relieved of all forms of suffering. They have got to this realm because of amassing lots of good karma. The *Deva* are complacent and therefore blind to the suffering of others and cannot learn compassion and wisdom. During their long life in this realm they use up all their good karma and are re-birthed in lower realm in the next life as they are still tempted by sensual pleasures and distracted from meditation. In *Theravada Buddhism* the *Deva* share a realm with the *Asura*. The *Asura* are depicted in the *wheel of samsara* as gods with access to the wishing tree and are waging war with the *Devas* for control of the tree. The white Buddha is playing the vena to remind the gods that their time in this realm is only temporary.

The Realm of the *Asura* is a world of envy, jealousy and hate. The *Asura* have the same comforts as the *Deva*. They have gotten into this realm because they had good intentions but committed bad acts, most likely harming others. They have enough good karma to get into the *Asura* realm above the lower worlds but their hate and jealousy prevents them from entering the realm of the *Devas*. The *Asura* see themselves are superior to all others with no patience for inferiors and usually look down and belittle others. Outwardly they show themselves pious, wise, just and fair, devoted to worship. The *Asura* are mortal enemies of the *Deva* and are fighting a continual feudal war over the wishing tree. The

---

[75] Individuals can have several views of themselves which can change over time depending on life circumstances and on personal and interpersonal processes. External experiences are absorbed into the consciousness and given form through both sense of self and projection onto others.

roots of the wishing tree are in the realm of the *Asura* but the wishing fruit only grows in the realm of the *Deva*. The Buddha depicted in the realm is holding an arrow and preaching moral restraint.

The *Manusya* or the Human realm is based on passion, doubt, desire and pride, all qualities of human existence. This realm is the most advantageous and most precious, as there are fewer humans than other creatures, except for *Devas*. Only humans have the wisdom to practice Buddhism. Therefore the human realm is the only realm where one can obtain enlightenment because humans have much more potential when life is pursued correctly. However most people waste their lives in the pursuit of material objects which end up reinforcing attachment, craving and clinging. Therefore most descend to a lower realm in rebirth. The scene depicts Buddha teaching the benefits of mental discipline and *The Four Noble Truths* to his disciples.

The *Naraka* or Hell Realm is the most terrible of all the realms containing a number of cold and hot hells. People are rebirthed into the Hell realm because of burning hatred, coldhearted cruelty and aggression. People remain in the hell realm until all their bad karma is extinguished and they are propelled into another realm. The lord of death is depicted in the top right hand corner of the realm where he holds a mirror so people can see their own bad karma. One the top right hand side is a Buddha holding water to signify patience and a flame as the light of hope.

The *Tiryagyoni* or Animal Realm is a world based on stupidity, prejudice, complacency with little intelligence. People who are ignorant, act upon primal motivations without any moral reflection and contented are destined for rebirth in the Animal Realm. Within the realm one lives a sheltered life of slavery trying to avoid discomforts. As animals cannot reason they are incapable of learning Buddhism and will stay there for many rebirths. The Buddha is depicted in this realm as holding a Dharma scroll to show the benefit of perfect wisdom and ethical conduct.

The black and white circle inside the realms shows that karma drives people around the realms. The white side shows ascension into the higher realms of the *Asura, Manusya* and *Deva*, while the black side shows the dissension into the lower *Tiryagyoni, Preta* and *Naraka* realms. The very centre of the *wheel of samsara* shows the tree poisons we develop from birth. The snake shows anger which is very powerful as it can destroy previously collected good karma. The Rooster represents high sexual drive and the pig represents ignorance. These three animals are shown chasing each other because each poison reinforces the other two. This is the reason why people keep having rebirths within the *wheel of samsara.*

The *wheel of samsara* is held by the demon *Yama* who depicts death and suffering as an inevitable fate within *samsara*. One is encouraged to forsake attachment for the pleasures of wealth, material things, beauty, youth and reputation that hinder an enlightened mind free of anger, greed and ignorance. The Buddha on the top right hand side points to the moon which represents *The Third Noble Truth,* the cessation of desire, *i.e.,* there is a way to end suffering and escape *samsara*.

Although the *wheel of samsara* specifically refers to individual delusion, analogies can be drawn out to organizations. The physicist David Bohm (1965) conceptualized consciousness as a collective stream of thought where meaning is developed through language and individuals make sense of it. As a 'collective consciousness' where individuals share the assumptions, beliefs and values of the group, an organization can also be seen as being trapped within the *wheel of samsara*, unable to see though its collective delusions. The 'collective consciousness' of the organization would hold views about how much the organization can influence the environment it operates within, the nature and strength of their

own competencies, how competitors will react to their actions, how consumers think, how
employees are motivated and what constitutes an opportunity to the organization. The story of
the CEO and the three letters has probably been told in many countries with local variations:

(With permission Wat Suan Mokkh, Chaiya, Thailand)

Figure 3.27. The Wheel of Samsara.
The Realm of the *Preta* or Hungry Ghosts is where people have an insatiable hunger and craving which
cannot be satisfied. A hungry ghost is always looking outside himself for new things that will satisfy his
hungry and craving. People are rebirthed into this realm because they are addicted to something,
obsessed, compulsive or possessive in their previous lives. The hungry ghosts are depicted as beings
with big empty stomachs, long necks that cannot shallow and a pinhole mouth, so their desires will
always torment them. They have fire coming out of their mouths because their cravings cannot be
satisfied. A Buddha is seen carrying a container of nourishment to sooth their pain.

After a poor year of corporate performance the company was about to have its annual board meeting. The CEO felt responsible and decided it was necessary for him to resign. The board accepted his resignation and appointed a new CEO. The new CEO met with the outgoing CEO in his office as he was packing his things and asked what advice he could give. The outgoing CEO replied *"I have put three letters in the top right hand drawer, if you get stuck, open them for my advice."*

A year went by and company performance had not improved. The new CEO had to face the board the next day and was stressed for what answer he could provide at the meeting. He remembered the letters the outgoing CEO had placed in the top right hand drawer. Hoping for an answer he opened the drawer, took out the first letter and opened it. The letter told him *"to advise the board to carry out a complete restructuring and reorganization"*.

The CEO was excited and went to the meeting suggesting the restructuring and reorganization. The board was very happy with the plan and gave him another year to implement it.

Another year went by and company performance was still poor. It was the night before the annual board meeting and the CEO knew he had to face the board again. He remembered the letters in the drawer the last CEO had left and rushed for the letter. Opening the letter and reading the advice he was excited. *"Advise the board that the company's strategy has to be realigned with its structure"*. The CEO went into the meeting confident and got another year to implement the plan.

Another year went by and there had been no improvement in company performance. The CEO was really perplexed and didn't know what to say. He remembered the letters the former CEO had placed in the drawer and took the last letter out and opened it. The letter read *"put in your resignation tomorrow and leave three more letters in the top drawer"*.

Contemporary Buddhism is taking a more liberal view of attachment/detachment (Ghose 2004). Some detachment could actually be apathy towards anything and everything by a person. Detachment itself can be a sign of the inability of a person to handle life situations, for example use detachment as a defense mechanism to cope with distress; *such as a child coping with the distress of the absence of a parent* (Kobak 1999). This can possibly leave unresolved issues between the child and parent, which can be considered unhealthy and detrimental to emotional growth and learning. There is a difficulty of distinguishing apathy from the type of detachment that liberates the consciousness. Therefore a possible reason for and effect of detachment, is people become apathetic losing any care about the world and being unhappy.

There can be distinctions made between desires that are unwholesome like greed and desires that are consistent with Buddhist practice like the desires for auspicious virtues. This also implies some distinction could be made between *'positive'* and *'negative'* desires (Govinda 1991). The test here is whether any desires emotions or thoughts are ego-centric or not? (Ghose 2004). Even the desire to do virtuous things can be ego-centric in nature.

Thich Nhat Hanh (1976, P. 38) stated that every feeling whether good or bad, powerful or light should be paid attention to with mindfulness[76] that can be used as a force to protect the psych. This has two important implications. The first is to be aware of our own biases and distortive tendencies in our perception of objects. The second implication is that we protect ourselves from harmful influences and *'emotionally'* learn. Psychotherapy advocates a healthy ego which requires some *'healthy attachment'* like identification in the creation of a sense of self (Winnicott 1965, 1971). Das (2003) expands on identity as being something we experience spiritually, sexually, sensually, intellectually, economically, philosophically, and so on. Identity is situationally dependent upon the role one plays as a mother, father, worker, student, etc. However from the Buddhist perspective, this can lead to an ego produced out of mistaken identity, based on anxiety and confusion about *'who I am'* (Engler 2003, P. 36).

John Bowlby's (1980) seminal work on attachment theory defines attachment as one of the prime motivational systems with its own workings and interfaces with other motivational systems. What may be important is understanding desire as a driver of motivation (Smith 1987). Thus some attachment is considered to be a healthy part of a person's psychological make-up, a driver for action. However it should be noted that the motivation behind our actions is usually desire, which unchecked can develop into many abnormal pathologies like depression, anxiety, aggression, etc (Epstein 2005). It is not the desire that causes the suffering, but what we do with our desire. People need to feel secure and have loving relationships to provide a base for life exploration, which requires some attachment. Michael Porter (1980, P. 267) also recognized that emotional attachment can influence rationality of strategic decision making where one may be committed to a business, have a sense of pride, be concerned about the stigma attached to a decision, identify with the program or venture, etc.

A true understanding of the concept of attachment and detachment from the Buddhist perspective may have been lost in the semantics of translation, especially with the institutionalization of most of Buddhism's doctrinal interpretations. Modern Buddhist and psychology scholars with the benefit of hindsight have added new perspectives by taking more liberal semantic interpretations of translations providing new insights (King 1994).

Dharma seeks to make us aware of the emotions one is attached and clinging to so that we can be freed from the suffering it produces. We make sense of the world we see through the filters of our own attachments which distort reality. Griffiths (1986) used a very useful metaphor of a mirror that cannot reflect light because of dust that has settled upon the surface clouding any clear view. So Buddhism and psychoanalytic-theory may assist in helping one see the manifestations of attachment and their underlying causes. The task is to let go of the distortions of perception created through sub-conscious attachments. This means understanding illusion from biased judgments, aversion, prejudice and greed in us and seeing the environment for what it really is. Buddhist Psychology provides a non-linear model for seeing a non-linear world. According to Freud (1912, P. 112), one is ....*"in danger of never finding anything but what he already knows: and if he follows his inclinations he will certainly falsify what he may perceive"*.

We in adulthood have become a product of our own eyes, prisoners of our own mind, observing things with a construed reality (Welwood 1996, P. 122). Our attachment to thoughts, feelings and experiences continually reinforce and strengthen our narratives and rationalizations. In modern Western psychology the tool to remedy distortion is termed cognitive reconstruction. One can learn to recognize weaknesses in beliefs, dysfunctional emotions that produce irrational thinking and resulting behaviors like stress, depression and

---

[76] Mindfulness is a state of open acceptance of one's own perceptions and sensibilities that helps our experience of being calm, relaxed and alert state of mind and be aware of our thoughts without identifying with them (Ladner

anxiety, etc. Once these emotions are seen, and the motivations behind them are recognized, one can take responsibility for them. Then one's cognitive streaming can be changed, which will allow one to freely explore their internal and external worlds without the distortions of attachment and clinging. This may require changing cognitive streaming that has developed from early childhood.

Our Self and the World

Our own self view and that of reality occurs primarily in our unconscious. It is in our unconscious that our innermost desires and wants exist and these impulses shape our personality and drive us. Some of these impulses must be controlled so that we can co-exist in society with others. There are many theories about how our psych works and influence the way we have emotions, feelings, thinking and reasoning. Each theory can make some contribution to how we understand these processes. Like the previous section on emotional attachment, each theory is a metaphor and gives some unique explanation of our psych and how we see ourselves and the world.

Concepts of our Self: The Ego, Id and Superego, Archetypes, Habitus and Soul

Fundamental to our self, is our own identity, existence, basis of reason, and our sense of morality, etc. There are many different ideas about the existence of our very consciousness and what it does. The best way to understand consciousness and the influence it has on our perceptions and reasoning, is to briefly look at a number of conceptualizations.

The Ego, Id and Superego

Sigmund Freud studied human personality and behavior from the perspective of early childhood sexuality. Freud believed that children go through different phases of sexuality and that different experiences can lead to different forms of repression that reappear in later life. Foremost in Freud's theory is that the mind is a *'store'* of powerful primitive motives of which one is unaware. Therefore behavior can be motivated by both conscious and unconscious drivers[77], some of which a person can control and others that cannot be easily controlled because of being in the unconscious. Some unconscious motives are driven on sexual-aggressive impulses which usually find a release outlet through dreams, behavior and other pathological symptoms[78].

Freud (1933) described three levels of personality as the *id, ego* and *superego.* The *id* according to Freud is the most primitive part of a person's mind where primordial instincts and impulses such as selfishness, anger and pleasure originate. The *id* controls all primary

---

2005, P. 19).

[77] Drivers are also known as psych energy, tension, instinct or what Freud called libido.

[78] These pathological symptoms are referred to as defence mechanisms which act to help discipline and redirect these unconscious drivers. They are discussed in the next section.

process thoughts which are concerned solely about seeking pleasure and avoiding pain without regard to anything else. The *id* therefore doesn't exist in any social reality as it is only concerned with self gratification, regardless of concerns for other people, morals, cultural norms or rules. The *id's* outlet is often dreams and fantasy which can satisfy its desires temporarily.

The *id* exists at birth and is the source of a person's psychic energy. The *id* does not use logic and generates only selfish childlike behavior with little or no patience. For example the *id* would urge a person to jump queues and not let people out of a lift or elevator before entering inside, etc. The *id* is best seen when a child is refused something they like, where they will usually get angry and turn on a tantrum. There is no time for the *id*; nothing happens in the past or the future as only instant gratification in the present is of concern.

The *ego* starts developing in an infant around 6 months and becomes fully operational around the age of two where it learns the constraints of social reality. The *ego* continually constrains the primal urges of the *id* into less socially problematic behavior where consequences can be minimized. Where compromises between the *ego* and the *id* are not achieved, anxiety, tension and stress develop. Anxiety and stress require different socially acceptable strategies to cope. For example, when a child is angry with a sibling, instead of hitting a brother or sister the person may decide to tease him or her, which may satisfy both the *ego* and the aggressive part of the *id*.

The *superego* begins to develop around the age of five in a child, although not maturing until some years later. The *superego* internalizes values, morals and the ideals of society within a person. They are instilled into a child through identification with the parents who have great influence in the early years of the child's development, especially in the realms of self-control and conscience. Through children identifying with their parents, aspirations and ideals, motivated by the emotions of love, fear and admiration, social values are able to be transmitted from generation to generation. Other figures like teachers and religious people also contribute to the child's *superego* development.

The *superego* as a moral conscience has a punishment and reward function to control the behavior of the other parts of the person's personality. The person will feel pride when they do something good and feel guilty, ashamed or embarrassed when they do something wrong. The *superego* is the source of our moral judgments which uses guilt as the primary enforcement mechanism. However as each person's sense of morality is different, those with low moral standards may not feel guilty when they do harm to others, while those with high moral standards will feel worthless when they cannot meet their own standards. Like the *id*, the *superego* is not bounded by reality so may set virtues and standards far out of proportion to reality.

The *id, ego* and *superego* are in continuous interaction. Each of them has different goals which provoke internal conflicts within a person. The ego works to satisfy *id* impulses by producing thoughts and corresponding behavior without generating strong guilt in the *superego*. The strong *ego* will find ways of achieving gratification in socially accepted ways, so that the individual is satisfied, without any feelings of guilt or worthlessness from the *superego*. If the *ego* is weak, then it will be ineffective against the *id, superego* and the demands of reality, where guilt or worthlessness will develop, thus causing anxiety. Anxiety is an unpleasant state and is a signal that something must be done to prevent the *ego* being threatened by reality. For example, an adolescent has strong pressure upon him or her to conform to a peer group, which behaves contrary to the moral standards of the *superego*.

Anxiety may develop into pathological symptoms as a way of coping with the person's internal conflict.

As the *ego* gets stronger, it pushes the *id* and the *superego* into the unconsciousness. The *id* under control of the *ego* manifests itself through dreams and fantasy. The *superego* also descends into the unconscious but leaves the *ego ideal* within the consciousness. Then most of the interaction between the *id, ego* and *superego* occurs in the unconscious. The ego partly remains in the consciousness as it has to deal with the realities of life, especially in protecting oneself and finding new objects that will satisfy its basic drives or *libido.*

The *id, ego* and *superego* are not part of the brain, but a metaphor of how our reasoning works.

Freud believed that everybody passes through five stages of personality development. Each stage carries with it certain types of conflict. Each stage requires more mature ways of dealing with conflict. How each person deals with these conflicts provides insights into their eventual personalities. Once a person has passed through all the stages of development, a full personality has developed. If a child gets into difficulty resolving conflicts at any stage, he or she may get stuck at that stage in a state of what Freud calls *fixation.*

The first stage within the first eighteen months of life is called the *oral stage.* During this period pleasure and frustration comes from the mouth, lips and tongue. The main conflict at this stage is weaning, where the child is slowly withdrawn from the mother's breast or bottle. Here the *id* wants immediate gratification from taking nourishment. However there is also a conflict of pleasure verses dependency, with the fear that one may be left to fend for themselves. For some people the process of weaning can be traumatic, leaving them with an *oral fixation.*

People fixed on the *oral stage* may seek gratification through eating, smoking, biting nails and pencils, and sucking thumbs, etc. They may be overly dependent on others, wanting to be nurtured with others making decisions for them. These people are passive and take in experiences. During this period they learn to delay gratification and become aware of self and others.

During this period children will also begin to grow teeth and may seek to bite things as a source of pleasure. This may be discouraged by the parents particularly if the child is biting the breast, other people or chewing on things like toys and plastics, etc. This brings conflict between the pleasure from biting and parental restriction. The child becomes aware that all wishes cannot be satisfied. When fixated on this stage, people may become hostile and quarrelsome.

The second stage of development occurs between the eighteen months and three years of age is called the *anal stage.* At this stage the child gains pleasure through expelling feces and through toilet training learns to retain feces through self control. The *id* requires immediate release of any feces as soon as there is any pressure on the rectum. This results in feces being expelled anywhere and at anytime. Parents through toilet training teach the child self restraint. The conflict during this stage is subordination of the child's will against the will of others, i.e., parents teach the child to use the toilet.

According to Freud, those achieving little control may grow up to be sloppy and dirty, while those who practice self control may take pleasure in acts of self control. Adults who become fixated on the *anal stage* may become rigid, fixed in ideas, time conscious, highly organized and compulsive. Too much self control can also develop into stinginess, selfishness, overly willful and stubbornness.

The third stage occurs between the age of three and six and is called the *phallic stage*. During this stage the child discovers their own genitals and they feel pleasure when touching them. According to Freud, this is where sexual desire is first awakened.

In the *phallic stage* the little boy falls in love with his mother and sees the father as a competitor for her affections. As there is some lust involved, the father is seen as preventing the boy from possessing the mother entirely for himself, in what Freud called the *Oedipus complex*. The boy becomes fearful of the father and believes that as he is all and powerful, he may make a preventive strike on him and take away his genitals in what is called *castration anxiety*. This stops the boy from having sexual desire for the mother. The boy decides the best option is to become like the father. Through this identification the boy discovers his gender and the *Oedipus* conflict is resolved.

Development through the *phallic stage* is not as well thought out for girls and Freud believed that some issues in girls remain unresolved. According to Freud, the conflict is centered on the absence of a penis where the girl blames her mother for the lack of one. The girl desires the father and at the same time envies his penis in what is called *penis envy*. As the girl doesn't fear the mother in the same way the boy feared the father as a competitor, the girl maintains a strong desire for the father[79].

The dynamics during the *phallic stage* are very complex where conflicting desires and wishes occur within the mother-child-father relationship. There are a number of paradoxes the child faces and must learn to resolve (Newman & Newman 2007, P. 55). These paradoxes include that there is conflict in wanting to satisfy ones sexual desires and that self-stimulation is not socially acceptable. The child faces conflict in wanting to remain a child and be loved and cared for by both parents and the desire to assume a more mature role in the eyes of the opposite sex parent. There is the anger and rivalry towards the same sex parent and at the same time the need for the parent's love and admiration. There is also pressure to embrace one's own gender identity and the envy one has for the opposite sex. During this period most of these paradoxes remain repressed and the ego emerges with self esteem and some confidence about his/her place in the family structure (Tyson & Tyson 1995).

During the *phallic stage* the *superego* emerges as a strong entity that assists the ego control the unacceptable impulses of the *id*. The process of identification with the father's moral and ethical values enables the child to obtain some autonomy and at the same time still receive love and admiration from the parents.

The next stage from about seven years to puberty is called the *latent stage*. Freud believed that this time during the child's life very little psychological happens in personality development[80] until the on setting of puberty, which brings on the final stage called the *genital stage*.

The *genital stage* begins at puberty and lasts through a person's whole adult life. People only reach this stage if they have resolved their conflicts in prior stages. Their adult personality to a great degree will depend upon how conflicts were resolved during earlier stages. In the *genital stage*, the *libido* focuses upon the genitals. One must satisfy their sexual impulses in mature adult relationships without the conflicts of earlier stages. Freud believed

---

[79] Freud believed that women were morally inferior to men and this has drawn great criticism over the years. See Helson & Picano (1990).

[80] Many psychoanalysts since Freud have argued that during this period a person learns how to make decisions for themselves, how to interact socially with others, develop their interests and self-identity and learn the meaning of society and its institutions like work and religion, etc.

that psychological conflicts that arise during adolescence do so because of unresolved childhood wishes. Therefore suppressed childhood wishes and impulses surface so gratification can be obtained in later life. This result in a number of pleasure-seeking, anxiety reducing behaviors that are appropriate to earlier stages of development. The stronger these impulses the more psychic energy they take up that deprive normal behavior patterns. This sublimation of the past forms into a person's life orientation where the *id* still exerts some control over the *ego* and *superego.*

Klein's Concept of Ego and Object-Relations

Melanie Klein looked at the issue of adult anxiety, tracing the causes back to early childhood defences. She made some enhancements upon Freud's ideas which were overly concerned with the child's relationship with the father in early childhood experience. Klein originally followed Freud's concept of *id, ego* and *superego*, but upon studying children's anxieties and fantasies, she developed a different conceptual world of the child than Freud[81].

Klein saw the infant's world as an extremely basic one with only a single object, the mother's breast. The relationship was with the breast and not the mother. The infant identified 'good' with the breast when he or she fed upon it and was secure and nourished. When there was trouble feeding or the breast was not available, it became the 'bad' breast. The child unconsciously splits the breast into two, the 'good' and 'bad', where this experience creates specific feelings, object relations and thought processes. According to Klein, this process in the child's mind continues to operate into adulthood and is the basic explanation of both normal and abnormal behavior.

Klein hypothesized that the child goes through a paranoid-schizoid state where the dual mechanisms of projective and introjective identification come into play with the *'good'* breast and the *'bad'* breast. This is the child's first object-relation with the mother's breast. These feelings form a persecutory anxiety where the infant is in fear of annihilation. This gives rise to anger and even a destructive *'death wish'* for anything that threatens their survival (Klein 1975, P. 287).The infant uses splitting to separate the good feelings from the bad feelings as a means of dealing with the existence of threatening forces by projecting them onto something external. Life or *libido* comes from the *'good'* breast. These processes are all undertaken by the *ego* in a rudimentary basic state that forms at birth.

After a period of time the infant realizes that the 'good' and the 'bad' breast are in fact the one and the same. This leads to a state of depression where the infant realizes that he/she has in fact attacked and hated what he/she loves. This gives rise to mourning and feelings of guilt and a transition away from the paranoid-schizoid phase to the depressive phase where all the feelings of fear, hate, envy, greed, frustration, guilt, paranoia, sadism, obsession, depression and fantasy are carried into the unconscious. Klein suggests that these early defences are used against anxiety in adult life through splitting, introjection, idealization, denial and sublimation, etc (these are discussed later on in this chapter).

---

[81] Klein's hypothesis had been based on observations of children, whereas Freud's theories were based on analysis of adults, particularly neurotic middle aged women of the Victorian era.

Klein believes that the above processes are just as much a part of normality as they are in abnormality and it is in childhood the person learns these defence mechanisms that will continue to be used throughout life to protect against anxieties and fear.

Jung's Ego, Archetypes and the Collective Unconscious

Carl Jung's theories have appeared as being something esoteric to many, yet at the same time form some of the basis of modern personality psychology today. Jung took a radical departure from Freud's emphasis on bodily sexuality and aggressiveness, seeing the mind as part of something more consistent with modern cognitive science, psychic inheritance and quantum physics.

According to Jung, our self unity comes from balancing opposing forces in our conscious and unconscious, where the ego plays the role of unifier. The unconscious is made up of the 'collective unconscious' and the 'personal unconscious'.

Our 'collective unconscious' is a prehistoric collection of information, instincts, myths, stories, images, universal symbols that are universally understood across all cultures. The 'collective unconscious' embeds all our ancestral experience and concepts of religion and morality. This inherited content is passed from generation to generation and is part of a transcendental reality, linking mind to mind and mind to nature. All people are born with this reservoir of our experience as a species. Although we are not conscious of it, this collective past influences our present behavior. Some experiences that may come from the 'collective unconscious' include, love at first sight, déjà vu experiences, immediate recognition of some symbols, reactions to music *(like the drum beat)*, and near death experiences.

The contents of the 'collective unconscious' are called archetypes. Archetypes are templates or schema through which we organize images and ideas in a way that we understand. Each archetype is a structure of information and experience through which we see ourselves and see the world. Archetypes pattern our thinking according to specific logics, temperaments, and feelings, i.e., an unlearned tendency to experience something a certain way. Archetypes are living ideas that shape our view of reality, revolving around a number of themes interpreted into new sets of experiences forming new realities. We may move through a number of archetypes as we go the sequence of life events, i.e., birth, nurturing, separation from parents, initiation, marriage, old age and wisdom and death. There is no fixed number of archetypes. Archetypes blend and combine to form new sets of logic and meaning. Some of the major archetypal images are described below;

> The *mother archetype* is actualized in the mind of a child when being nurtured by the mother or other surrogate figure. This is built into the child as a mother complex which like other complexes becomes a functional mechanism within the unconscious.
> The *shadow archetype* represents our weaknesses and basic pre-modal instincts. The shadow is one of the most powerful archetypes as it contains 'our dark side' of life. Through the shadow we are capable of being both loving and caring, but also vicious and brutal to people. It is a possible link to our *prehistoric* life where basic animal instincts drove us. The shadow is instinctive and irrational, often with conflicting desires and tries to turn our moral and personal inferiority into strength through projecting to the outside world. Many unresolved elements within the shadow are projected onto others and external situations. This archetype if not checked can take control and cause dangerous

delusions between the real world and self, effecting judgment and decision making (Jung 1964, P. 72). The shadow and ego are usually entangled in continual conflict for dominance. Failure to deal with the repressed shadow can lead to neurosis and psychic mal-adaption. How a person develops their personality will rest with their ability to recognize the rival elements the shadow exposes to the rest of the psych. However the *shadow archetype* also has some good qualities. The shadow is a source of creative impulses (Jung 1964, P. 110).

The *persona* represents our image of how we would like others to see us in the external world. The persona serves two purposes. The first is to present to the world the impression we would like to give and the second is to conceal our inner self from others (and maybe our own self). A strong persona can trick us into believing who we are pretending to be. The persona is strongest in our adolescent youth and its influence tends to weaken with age. The persona is the most distant archetype from the *'collective unconscious'*.

Anima and *animus* are the two archetypes representing masculine and feminine roles and behavior. Both these archetypes are bisexual in nature but are influenced by sex organs, hormones, physical features and social constructs and constraints. Although *anima*, the female archetype exists in the *collective unconscious* of men and *animus*, the male archetype exists in the *collective unconscious* of women; they are socially locked into only one gender role thus restricting our full potential. *Anima* and *animus* can take on many forms and variations with different meanings. For example *anima* can be a young girl, very spontaneous and intuitive person, a witch or mother earth herself. *Animus* can be a wise old man, a saint or prophet, a wild and aggressive animal, or a sorcerer, etc. These roles take on different logics and rationalities and by discovering the masculine or feminine side of us, new ways of thinking can be unleashed. For example, the personification of the *anima* in men can release feminine psychological tendencies like vague feelings and moods, hunches, receptiveness to the irrational capacity for personal love, feeling for nature and his relation with the unconscious (Jung 1964, P. 186). The anima in conjunction with the shadow can also be very destructive as a siren in creating dreams that are delusional and cannot be fulfilled, i.e., fall in love with a woman seen with fairy tale qualities that are simple projections of the *anima* within the males. The *animus* in women can lead to strong conviction and create masculine tendencies in women like cold rationality and logic. However they can also be destructive, stubborn and inaccessible.

The *trickster* archetype elates to our early life where only physical appetites dominate life. He is cruel, cynical and unfeeling. The *trickster* lacks any purpose and seeks only gratification jumping from exploit to exploit in the form of usually an animal. This archetype through initiation and maturity can transform into some type of hero.

Some other archetypes are *mana*, representing spirituality, the *animal*, representing our association with nature, the *father*, representing authority, security and blood relationship, the *child, original man, God*, the *hero,* the *villain*, and the *hermaphrodite*[82].

Through archetypes we experience and see things within the configuration of meaning they promote. Archetypes are very useful in seeing themes behind myths and stories and at a deeper level understanding some of the assumptions and beliefs behind peoples' ideas within their own world of meaning, particularly as a cognitive template or schema patterning perception of things, people and events. It is impossible to directly see these archetypes in people, except through observing the manifestation of peoples' behavior.

---

[82] Numerous archetypes exist and their traits may depend upon life experiences. Many follow Greek mythology for example, where there can be many forms of gods.

Mitroff (1984) used archetypes as a tool to understand meaning and behavior within organizations. He looked at organizational life as interrelationships between fools, magicians, warriors, high priests and lovers, etc, in dramatic, tragic, comic and ironic circumstances.

The 'personal unconscious' includes everything that is not presently conscious, but can be. This includes all experiences in the form of memories that can be retrieved back into conscious thought. The actualization of archetypes within the self and personal experiences determines the degree of personal individualism.

In Jungian psychology the ego plays the role of moderation between the conscious and unconscious. Within these conscious and unconscious forces are morally good and bad opposites, expressed in sentiments and acts of external reality. As the ego itself is amoral, it is the opposing forces that create an urge, emotion, and psychic energy to act. The stronger the opposites and the more energy they create. This is evident in young people, who tend to think a lot about sexual differences, i.e., their masculinity or femininity, etc., their sexual drive, drive to achieve in sports or energy to follow a cause. As opposites start coming together in entropy, the energy differential decreases, where there is less psychic energy. This is evident in older people who don't feel the same need to extenuate their differences, see both sides of argument and don't carry the same polarized convictions as in their youth (disillusioned, skeptical, cynical, etc). They feel comfortable with opposing points of view and different ideas, etc., so are said to rise above the world of opposites in transcendence[83]. The *self* is an archetype that represents transcendence of all opposites, where all one's personality is expressed equally without the influence of the *anima, animus, ego, persona* or *shadow*.

The denial of *'evil thoughts'* will move energy towards an archetype where a complex of suppressed thoughts and feelings will develop. This will give one particular archetype extraordinary power over the psych which can cause some particular form of reasoning and behavior as a personal bias (Jung 1964, P. 68). If this strengthened archetype combines with the shadow, it will begin to develop a strong character of its own, which could be diagnosed as a psychiatric pathology[84].

Another concept Jung develops is synchronicity. Unlike Freudian psychology where present behavior is based on the past, Jung describes a world that has connection without necessarily having causality. For example Jung (1964, P. 226) gives the example of someone ordering a blue frock and having a black one delivered by accident the next day from the shop, when at the same time there is a death in the family. There is meaning but no causality. Jung (1964, P. 41) goes on to give a number of examples like a mirror cracking or a clock stopping when someone dies, where there is a common denominator of a symbolically expressed message.

To Jung this proved some connection with all nature through the *'collective unconscious'*. Jung likens the external world to one of illusion, something similar to the world of *Maya* in *Hindu* theology (Burke 2004, P. 16). Our egos *(jivatman)* are individual souls which are actually extensions of the one and only *Atman,* universal energy or God who allows an independent identity to manifest itself in part of himself. Through this we are all

---

[83] Jung (1964, P. 146) describes transcendence as man's release from confining patterns of existence towards a more mature stage of in development. In transcendence man can reach his highest goal of achieving a realization of the potential of his individual self. This completeness comes from the union of conscious and the unconscious contents of the mind. This is where maturity, spiritualism and where the unconscious can reach the conscious mind.

connected, independent, but interdependent. When we die we realize the illusion that we actually existed as we are part of God.

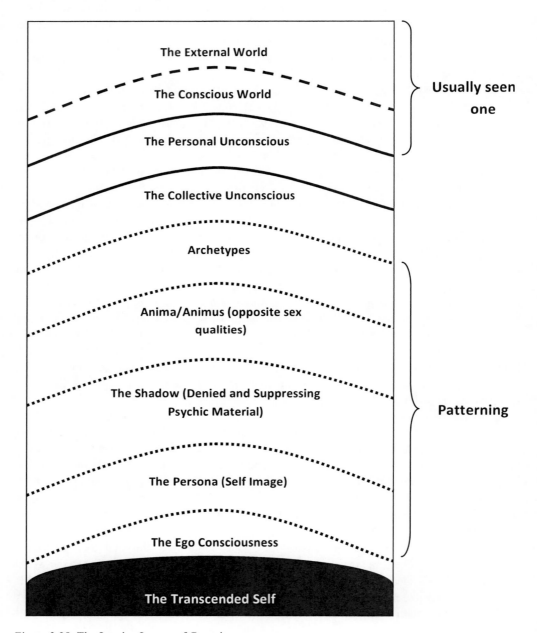

Figure 3.28. The Jungian Layers of Consciousness.

---

[84] Jung used the metaphors of the archetype casting a spell and the shadow with the archetype possessing the person, i.e., in medical terms – schizophrenia.

Jung drew distinction to one pair of personality trait opposites – introversion and extraversion. These two traits show a person's orientation towards the world and are easier to recognize than other traits. An introvert is orientated inward towards the world of thoughts, feelings, fantasies, and dreams, whereas the extrovert is orientated out towards the external world of things, people and activities. An extrovert will tend to choose and follow majority views while and introvert will keep his or her own views, even if just for the reason because it is not fashionable. Given that an introvert is orientated inward towards the physic does not mean that the introvert will not gain valuable insights into things, people and events, as introspection and self knowledge can be very powerful.

Jung states that the self has four distinct ways of perceiving and interpreting reality called the four ego functions, thought-feeling and intuition-sensation. These are composed as two opposite pairs and function as follows;

The *thought* function is an analytical, rational and logical way of evaluating things, where it involves decision making, rather than just taking in information. This is a very highly developed way of reasoning and involves putting ideas together to form some understanding. Thinking can be detached and unemotional.

The *feeling* function is diametrically opposed to the thinking function and involves empathetic, value-based, heart-felt way of dealing with information. Decisions are made through weighing up one's emotions as to what is best in terms of being pleasant or unpleasant. Feeling is an undeveloped way of thinking as facts are often suppressed and discarded.

Thinking and feelings are both rational as they require making choices and judgments.

The *intuition* function is orientated inward to the psych where perception is influenced by some unknown guide, set of rules, template or schema. It is a hunch or a *'gut-feel'*. The process senses things out from large and complex amounts of information rather than seeing or hearing argument. Intuition jumps out from images and can be the source of inspiration, creativity and novel ideas. One of the interesting observations Jung (1964, P. 29) made about our conscious mind was that our psychic associations may vary in intensity according to the relative importance we place on ideas and concepts at the time. Therefore when things slip into our unconscious they are able to change their character of concept and return to us as something different through intuition at a later point of time. Thus this is one of the potential processes of how we develop ideas.

The *sensation* function is orientated out towards the external environment where things are sensed through the sense organs, i.e., seeing and listening. The process involves coming to conclusions based on perception rather than actual decision making. An *introverted-sensation* type will experience the physical world through the perspective of the psych and for this reason maybe artistic. The *extroverted-sensation* type would be someone who is only interested in material and pragmatic things.

Sensation and intuition are both irrational ways of making decisions because no reason is used and judgments arise directly from stimuli.

All these four functions exist in everybody however they exert difference levels of influence. Thinking is more common in men, while intuition is more common in women. More men tend to be extroverted-sensation types than women. More people are extroverted in the world than introverted. More use sensing than intuition and thinking-feeling is fairly evenly distributed in the population, although more men are thinkers rather than feelers, while more women are feelers than thinkers. Most people only develop one of two of these functions[85]. Some of the characteristics and traits of each function are listed in Table 3.20.

Jung helps to explain how our mind works, how we pattern and influenced from the inside and how we perceive things, think and develop ideas through the ego functions. Some of Jung's explanations are very close to how cognitive processes are mapped out and may help to deepen our understanding of them. Jung's theories are powerful metaphors when used with other theories greatly strengthen our understanding of people and thought.

Bourdieu's Habitus and Field

Pierre Bourdieu was an eminent French sociologist who was interested in the concepts of power relations within social life. Bourdieu borrowed concepts from philosophy, sociology and anthropology to develop a structured framework to understand the dynamics and interrelationships of power relations through a theory of *habitus, agents, capital* and *fields*. The theory created mechanisms which defined and enabled the potential scope of perception, thought and action in the field for an individual agent. Through Bourdieu's theory we can understand that we are ourselves a conditioned product of the social environment as well as the social environment is a product of our collective actions.

The influence of the social environment imposes its presence upon us through the *habitus*. The *habitus* houses the conditioning of embodied dispositions associated with a particular class involving principals that generate and organize practices associated with their *field* (Bourdieu 1990, P. 53). This means a person is a free agent but is also predisposed to function according to embodied conditionings within the *habitus.*

To understand clearly the role of the *habitus* we must understand the *field* that it operates within. The *field* is a sphere or plain of social life where each person or *agent* is operating within it according to a practical logic with the objective of achieving some end. The field can be a society, a village, a market, an industry, an organization or any other social structure. A person's power to influence or dominate the *field* depends upon the amount and type of *capital* they possess in relation to other *agents*. To Bourdieu the concept of capital was much wider than financial resources. Four types of capital exist;

> *Economic capital* – access to money, buildings, plant and equipment, etc,
> *Cultural capital* – knowledge which equips the social agent with empathy toward for, or appreciation for, or competence working within the cultural rules and norms within the field,
> *Social capital* – consisting of resources obtainable through connections and group networks, and
> *Symbolic capital* – which include socially derived symbols like university degrees, or acceptance by social institutions within the field (Drummond 1998, P. 104).

---

[85] Jung's ego functions are the basis of the test developed by Katherine Briggs and her daughter Isabel Briggs Myers, known as the Myers-Briggs Type Indicator. This is one of the most popular psychological trait tests used today. The test will assign a respondent one of the 16 personality typologies according to the answers to 125 questions. Each typology is based on four scales, extroversion-introversion, sensing-intuiting, thinking-feeling and judging-perceiving which was added in to help determine which of a person's functions is superior.

Table 3.20. Some Traits and Characteristics of the Ego-Functions

Extroversion	Introversion
Expressive, outgoing, energized by things, people and events, act or speak before they think, share information easily, prefer the company of others, easily distracted, have a lot of friends, uninhibited, like working in groups, easily approachable, like meeting new people, develop ideas through discussion.	Quiet, shy, energized by ideas, feelings and impressions, think before they speak, reluctant to share information, prefer to be left alone, can concentrate well, have a small close group of friends, inhibited socially, like to work alone, prefer to keep to themselves, ideas come from thinking alone.
Thinking	**Feeling**
Value facts and figures, look for the truth, use logic and reasoning to make decisions, driven by rationality, notice wrong reasoning and illogical thinking in arguments, speak their mind, firm with people, use justice in speaking with others, can be seen as cold and heartless, impersonal, objective, critical, prefers a logical impersonal atmosphere, thick-skinned.	Value harmony, use personal feelings in making decisions, passionate about issues, empathetic with people, merciful, takes things personally, subjective, prefers a warm friendly atmosphere, thin-skinned.
Sensation	**Intuition**
Focused on the physical world, live by their senses, concrete, interested in 'what is', realistic, practical, understands details and particulars, sees only the obvious, down to earth, uses words literally, lives in the present, needs evidence and facts, traditional and simple, sees the trees instead of the forest.	Focused on the mental or spiritual world, uses hunches and gut feeling, abstract, interested in what can be, idealistic, imaginative, understands meaning and generalities, looks beyond the surface, head in the clouds, deep thinker, uses metaphors, analogies and hidden meanings, lives in the future, speculative and theoretical, original and complex, and sees the big picture.

Capital is a major determinant of the capacity to exercise influence over the field and thus control our own future (Bourdieu & Wacquant 1992, P. 162). Capital is the essence of exploiting opportunity.

The field is the place where social life is played out[86]. The field as a social sphere has its own set of practical logic, producing a habitus embodied with the logic making it uniquely suited to operate within it. Due to social background and social grounding through families and education, a habitus will be more predisposed to operate in certain fields rather than others or the field will draw the person with the appropriate habitus to play the game in that field. This is an explanation of why it is difficult for people to move into businesses outside fields their habitus is not conditioned to. The modus operandi of the field is foreign and the agent does not have the necessary practical logic within their habitus, or the necessary capital to gain any influence within the field. There are embedded social barriers unseen to potential agents. This exists in the great divide of society within the countries of South-East Asia, Latin America, Africa, and to even some degree in the US. People lacking education, social disposition, social and symbolic capital are unable to play on the same fields as those who have the necessary capital to do so. This is the major barrier between the uneducated rural peasant class and the educated urban middle classes around the world today. Thus the habitus

---

[86] Pierre Bourdieu used the game metaphor in agent-field interactions.

and field are closely related and encompass a structure where agents can play out their long historical struggles within social space consistent with their position (Bourdieu 1990a, P. 14).

Given the relationship between the habitus and the field, it can be seen that the social structure (field) produces the mental structure (habitus), that produce social structure (field), that produce mental structure (habitus), that produce social structure (field). Everybody is unaware of this process as they are within it. Therefore the individual's rationality is a social bounded phenomenon where our practical logic, disposition towards to perceptions, appreciation, view of the world, and action content is created through experience within a social structure.

The person is always trapped within the limits of the brain, which is limited by the system it owes its upbringing and training to (Bourdieu & Wacquant 1992, P.126). The habitus both shapes our identity and provides schemas of perception, thought and action. These schemas operate below the level of consciousness and language beyond our introspective scrutiny or control of our will (Bourdieu 1989, P 466.). The habitus interprets and categorizes information from experience in ways that protect itself (Bourdieu 1990, P. 61) by systematically selecting information that reinforces it, rejecting and discarding anything that may threaten its position. Thus the habitus acts as a filter which can lead to bias.

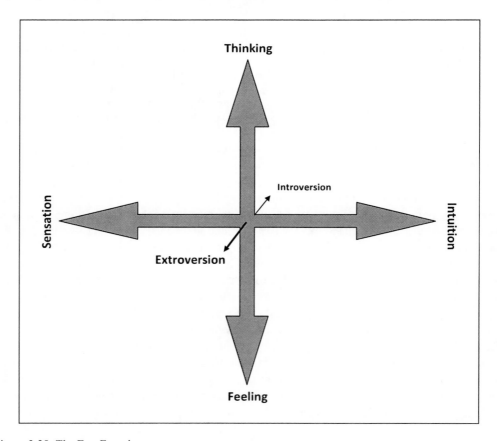

Figure 3.29. The Ego Functions.

The habitus can generate new principals of strategy and practice that flow from experiences that produce it, taking into account of specific social content within the field the individual is playing in (Boudieu 1991, P.14). When the habitus is in line with the field and vice versa, a coherent logic of practice develops. This logic is called doxa. Doxa is the basic belief and value system of the habitus where it accepts its social position and place in the world. Doxa operates at the pre-conscious level.

The habitus is not a individual but is a group mechanism, i.e., people don't have a habitus they share one. Thus the habitus contains the practical knowledge and regulatory mechanism of interaction between themselves and the world. A person is part of a larger group where the single person represents diversity within the group homogeneity. Identity is thus socially authored. Society shapes the meaning for us, so a social agent not only understands him or herself but others in terms of their social roles and how to act within their social structures (Sewell 1992). Society also makes fields emerge which are governed by their own laws which agents understand (Bourdieu 1998, P. 83). The habitus reflects social position with a certain social trajectory (Bourdieu 1990, P. 66).

Bourdieu's habitus and field theory is able to provide an explanation as why opportunities are sometimes missed in changing fields. If conditions within the field are going through change where the conditions operate somewhat differently to conditioning within the habitus, there will be a hysteresis effect. Hysteresis is the phenomena where a magnetic effect will lag behind the source causing the magnetism (Brubaker 1985, P. 759). Habitus hysteresis will occur when the social conditioning in the habitus lags behind social conditions within the field. Therefore the agent or individual will not be able to perceive new opportunities because of this structural gap (Bourdieu 1977, P. 83). Where the field changes without corresponding changes in habitus conditioning, there will be an inability to cope with the changed field. As all agents have similar conditions within the habitus, the response from all will be similar. Such an example was the US Car industry unable to change strategy with the arrival of the energy crisis in 1974, new competition from Japan in the late 1970s and changing customer environment.

The Soul and Conscience

The soul in theology and religion is believed to have great influence over a person through the conscience. The soul can be considered a deep dimension of a person's identity and character, where the most fundamental stance is taken about life (Burke 2004, pp. 1-2). The soul also influences a person's belief about their mortality, i.e., the existence of life after death. The soul implies basic meaning of life[87] which is translated into behavioral actions through the intervention of the conscience[88]. Moral meaning is influenced by various religious doctrines upon the person. The soul is not a physical thing or phenomena that can be seen within the working of the mind. From a psychological standpoint the soul develops a set of schema *(the conscience)* that influences our cognition, particularly in perception and

---

[87] According to many religious theologies, the soul has a separate existence from the body and upon death transcends the body. The soul is considered the spiritual and eternal part of a person.

[88] For the purposes of this discussion the conscience is a set of moral schema that are considered during decision making.

decision making. The conscience is primarily developed through learning in the growing up process, from parents, school, religious teachers and general social exposure.

Qutb (1953, P. 95) explains the role of conscience as the guardian of the legal processes to see that they are obeyed and one is accountable. Freud (1950, P. 98) saw the conscience as an internal perception of the rejection of a wish within us. The conscience is our spiritual and moral schema that enforces responsibility and self control upon us. The conscience embodies our sense of good and evil, a sense of responsibility to self, family, community and country, a sense of what matters morally and how far we should feel responsible. The conscience maps out what is taboo. It helps to ensure a person doesn't cross any forbidden line that society and theology has set[89].

When a person thinks or acts about something they will usually experience a feeling of right or wrong, which may install hesitancy if what they intend to do is contrary to the schema of the conscience. When a person actually does something that the conscience schema considers a wrong act or taboo, feelings of guilt will usually develop. Religious theologies and state legal codes specify punishments for things that are taboo in society, which in most cases lend external weight to the influence of the conscience. As the conscience is the law of the spirit and the spirit is eternal, a person may be deterred because of the knowledge they must face the *'day of judgment'* in the afterlife[90]. The influence of the conscience mechanism on individuals will vary according to a person's sense of moral importance, knowledge of religious theology and legal codes and sanctions, their socialization within the community and their own sense of judgment.

Psychotic States and Disorders

Peoples' perceptions and views of the world are influenced by both conscious and unconscious phenomena. The world is a totally socially constructed reality where the people make sense of it from their culture, experience and learning. Within the bounds of culture and experience, each person has some unique interpretation of the environment and understanding of its dynamics. Thus everything can be viewed with multiple perspectives or realities.

A person's psychological state will directly influence perception of people, objects and events. This can potentially lead to perceptive distortion, especially if the person has any psychotic tendencies[91]. Therefore any construed reality, decisions made, strategies crafted, resulting actions and consequential behavior would be based upon biased perceptions. Thus everything that develops within a firm including culture, management style, interpersonal relationships, rules and procedures, strategy, symbols and behavior will have some unconscious basis to it (Kets de Vries & Miller 1984).

As different psychotic states channel perception and thinking into specific frames, this becomes relevant to how people see opportunity and take action to exploit it. Thus perception and thinking processes that identify opportunities and shape subsequent actions have their origins both in the psych and the external world. Identifying an opportunity and exploiting it

---

[89] The religions of Semitic origin Judaism, Christianity and Islam have very detailed codes of what is taboo. Legal systems also legislate and codify to society what the state considers taboo.

[90] Judaism, Christianity and Islam all have their day of judgment or reckoning in the afterlife.

[91] The continuum from normal to any type of psychotic behavior should be seen in steps and degrees, rather than in any absolute terms.

may have as more to do with inner needs i.e., *recognition, love and affection, power and control, self esteem, or grandeur, etc.,* as with any rational thought processes.

Cognitive distortion and delusion are more likely to occur at the extremities of the psychotic continuum. However, most people whose personalities can be considered within the bounds of normality will exhibit some psychotic traits. This can include compulsion, anxiety, depression, attention seeking, fantasies, irrational fears, paranoia, shyness or narcissistic behavior, etc. For example, psychographic research shows there are large variations in the levels of depression across regions (Cohen, Slomkowski & Robins 1999).

It is usually very difficult to see abnormality as many psychotic traits are also important drivers of manager and entrepreneur behavior. Many well known business leaders could be considered narcissistic in nature (Maccoby 2000). Some forms of psychosis *(attention-seeking, paranoia, obsessive-compulsiveness & narcissism)* are actually qualities that help bring people to the top of their fields. However these same qualities in excess can lead to an arrogant and overconfident delusion, once at the top. Many managers have fallen from corporate grace for this reason (Kramer 2003).

Psychosis can prevent firms seeing the environment in new ways and hinder the process of creativity and innovation. US industry faced this situation in the 1970s and 80s when rising energy costs changed the competitive environment and new competition came from Japan and East Asia. The leaders of US industry failed to see the need to adapt to the changing market environment. Many companies hung onto their old perceptions and failed to see the realities of their new environment and the need to change. This cost many companies very dearly for this delusion (Schoenberger 1994).

Firms and organizations can also show *'collective'* patterned behaviors just like individuals and groups. Individual and group psychosis has been well researched and written about. However *'collective'* firm and organization psychosis has been the subject of only a small handful of articles and books, and generally ignored in management theory. The psychotic paradigm is useful in looking at the issues of how a person sees and constructs meaning, how a person's needs influence the decisions they make, and how psychological pathologies affect behavior.

There are a number of basic psychotic pathologies which can affect both perception and behavior. These pathologies include the paranoid, obsessive-compulsive, attention-seeking, depressive, schizoid and narcissistic typologies. These are not absolute disorders and may vary in intensity from organization to organization. Some psychotic conditions may act in together with other forms of psychosis creating part of a complex personality[92]. Looking for evidence of these typologies can assist in seeing the way others see the world and form their underlying assumptions.

---

[92] Personalities are very complex and most psychological profiling methods measure them simply missing much of the depth of a personality. Thus personalities really cannot be accurately understood through a 5 or 7 point scale, etc, as a personality is made up of thousands of traits or attributes which vary in influence according to time of day, mood and situational occurrences. What even makes personality more difficult to understand is that a person's 'self-view' may be very different to what they portray to the world, i.e., an attention seeker shows

The Paranoid Typology

Paranoia is based on an intense fear, suspicion of others (both internal and external to the organization) that is exaggerated or irrational. Paranoia usually brings with it deluded perceptions that the person *'is being singled out by enemies',* who are harming or intend to harm him/her. Paranoia is ego-centric because it is about *'I'* and *'me'* and usually sees another as *'out to get him/her'* (persecutory complex). People with paranoid tendencies tend to see the world as a threatening place and are usually very guarded until they know their fears are groundless. This leads to little loyalty towards others.

Relationships and interpersonal behavior is generally governed with the belief that *'people somehow have it in for him/*her'. Paranoid people tend to avoid relationships. However relationships they do form tend to be cold, lack intimacy and involve jealousy and suspicion, *i.e., the other person is doing something harmful behind his/her back.* They are usually very sensitive to criticism and will brood for long periods of time if criticized. Criticism can also invoke anger, argumentation, and uncompromising stands which often lead to great antagonism, if challenged. Even though they are very sensitive to criticism themselves, they are very critical of others. Anything that goes wrong is someone else's fault and not theirs.

Paranoia is usually focused on the present where someone is trying to undermine him/her and the future, where someone is plotting a plan to harm him/her. Suspicions based on past experience cannot be classed as paranoia when experience as a basis of concern. However, if this concern is blown out of proportion to any potential harm that can be done, paranoia is present.

Paranoid people have the urge to collect as much information about the market as possible. They will scan for information of threats and spend a large amount of time thinking how to formulate reactions to them. They are in fact looking for evidence that reinforces their suspicions but at the same time pride themselves on their rationality and objectiveness. They centralize organization decision making because of lack of trust in other peoples judgments and their beliefs that people are looking for ways to sabotage him/her. Consequently budgeting and controls will be very strict. The organization culture will be one of suspicion where looking for problems and wrong doers (scapegoats) is the norm.

The resulting crafted strategies are primarily designed to protect the company's position and defend it from any potential competitor attacks rather than be proactive moves in the marketplace and take risk. Therefore the firm will miss many opportunities to be creative and innovative in the market. Paranoid companies tend to lag behind the competition and muddle through with disconcerted and inconsistent strategies. They will follow the market leader rather than risk being innovative with their own ideas. However they will very easily revert to legal litigation if they believe harm has been done to them. Paranoid people will tend to avoid certain products and markets if they believe there is a more powerful competitor in the market.

Paranoia usually occurs when there is some form of traumatic and stressful issues or some challenge arising. In many cases paranoia will be a temporary condition until the immediate sources of stress pass. Paranoia can also be a selective phenomena where an

---

grandiosity but may have a very low self-esteem. Our general surface observation of a person can only see what that person wants us to see and what they want to be, rather than whom they are.

object, event or situation. For example, the belief that *'multinational companies always target local companies for takeover'* will influence perception and behavior.

Paranoia can also merge with the schizoid typology where a strong persecutory complex develops. Paranoia sufferers can also develop grandiose delusions where he/she believes they have particular skills or abilities to carry out a special mission, but someone has a master plan to prevent him/her from successfully fulfilling their calling. Such a fantasy was shown in the movie The Blues Brothers where Jake and Elwood believed they were on *'a mission from God'* and being prevented from carrying out their calling by a number of groups (the police, the sheriff, the other group and eventually the whole United States armed forces).

A mild form of the paranoia typology could be positive where the organization will have good knowledge of its external threats and opportunities and internal strengths and weaknesses. This would be well suited to extremely dynamic environments where there is rapid change going on.

The Obsessive-Compulsive Typology

The obsessive-compulsive typology has many similarities to the previous paranoid typology where there is great emphasis on control of the organization and surveillance of the environment. A leader with this type of behavior will tend to be stubborn and frustrated with his/her subordinates because of his/her inner need to pursue perfection. This behavior is often a characteristic of many high achievers in society.

Compulsive people are usually perfectionists and take great care and diligence in their own work to the point of being very slow to complete tasks. As a manager of others he/she will have great difficulty in delegating work. To maintain control, they will develop many rules, procedures and policies to keep a check on their subordinates work. The firm's preoccupation with planning, budgets, procedures, rules and action plans will greatly influence how the company is internally organized and how the environment is seen and interpreted. Strategy will also be crafted taking into account the firm's existing rules and procedure structure, limiting its own strategy options.

Productivity will be sacrificed for perfection of work. Obsessive-compulsive people also expect perfection from others and become very frustrated when people don't live up to their standards and expectations. In extreme situations this leads to get mistrust of coworkers and subordinates, leading to the loss of respect and falling out of relationships. This is generally part of a wider inability to develop and carry on relationships with people because of their feeling that socializing is wasting time.

Strategy is usually developed and implemented with a very clear concrete objective and underlying and uncompromising philosophy which serves as the organization's reason for being. This philosophy based on the founder's sense of ethics will remain steadfast within the company's mission and strategy, even at the cost of exploiting some potential opportunities arising during the life of the company. Strategy will tend to be based more on this philosophy than what is happening in the competitive environment.

Success is often jeopardized with to the reluctance to commit the necessary resources in the implementation phase. The obsessive-compulsive organization will tend to hoard and hang on to resources, being reluctant to use them.

The entrepreneur who started the firm will in most cases also manage the firm during the growth and maturity stages. A person may find it very difficult to release control and delegate power and authority. Where compulsiveness and centralized decision making worked well in the early stages, this style of management in later stages of development becomes an obstacle to firm creativity and innovation. This form of positional status can increase the power-distance relationships in the organization[93]. Formal controls and organizational hierarchy creates a very static and stable internal environment. Formal authority is through position in the hierarchy rather than experience. This status and dominance over subordinates is clearly shown in these types of organizations.

Obsessive-compulsive behavior in organizations may tend to be a defense mechanism against some form of anxiety or fear, in a similar way to the paranoia typology. Obsessive-compulsive people hold the belief that some form of calamity will happen if action is not taken to prevent it. To them this means that work must be completed to the upmost highest standards possible. This scenario is often reinforced by organizational stories about a previous major problem that occurred because the firm was not adequately prepared. In times of great uncertainty this typology can lead to organizational breakdown.

The obsessive-compulsive typology is useful during entrepreneurial start ups, in very stable environments and repetitive manufacturing operations, etc. However the resulting organizational form created out of this typology will become very rigid because of the core philosophy and the high number of controls in place. If controls become too excessive, organizational motivation, creativity and innovation will decline. This will hinder the organization from identifying and exploiting new opportunities. However in a moderate form the organization will have a well integrated check and balance system and focused product strategy. When new products/opportunities are discovered, the underlying need of producing perfection will make the development process very slow.

The Attention-Seeking (Dramatic) Typology

The attention-seeking (dramatic) typology is manifested when a person is hyperactive, impulsive and dramatically venturesome in their lives. They work tirelessly to impress others, often appearing flamboyant, craving novelty and excitement. Attention seeking people base their actions on hunches and intuition, without any formal analysis before making decisions. An organization within the attention-seeking (dramatic) typology will have very centralized decision and command structures. The attention-seeking leader sees the primary role the organization is to carry out his/her bold and dramatic ideas thought out by the leader.

Attention-seeking (dramatic) leaders are usually great charmers of people they want to impress. They continually seek positive feedback and admiration of their actions. They are very opinionated on topical issues, but lack substance to support their ideas and will change their position to suit their audience. They have very low self-esteem and rely on others to

---

[93] The power-distance relationship was a concept developed by Gerard Hendrik Hofstede to describe how people in the lower part of the organization accept power from higher up the organisation hierarchy. In the case of an obsessive-compulsive organization it would be expected that the power-distance relationship to be high where relationships would be very autocratic. See: Hofstede, G. H., (2001). Culture's Consequences: Comparing values, behaviors, institutions, and organizations across nations, 2nd Ed., Thousand Oaks, CA., Sage Publications.

suppress this. Being at the centre of attention relieves this tension and the insecurity they feel. Consequently it is hard to get along with these people unless one helps to fulfill this craving for attention. These leaders tend to surround themselves with people who will always agree with them.

Decision making is unreflective and borders on the impulsive. The larger and more complex the organization grows, the more opportunity for dramatic events and less time there is for the leader to focus on detail in the decisions he/she makes on behalf of the organization. Decisions tend to be made on the potential to gain attention rather than any factual analysis. Narcissistic behavior also can occur, where bullying, manipulation and deception become tools of control and domination. Subordinates usually see through the insincerity and become de-motivated, uninspired, skeptical, and stop giving creative suggestions to the leader. This uncreative environment is reinforced by the way managerial posts are filled through politics and nepotism. Those who have real influence are those who are favoured by the leader. The leader sees employees only as tools to implement his/her grand plans. The views of subordinates are rarely taken into account for major decisions.

Strategy is based on the general craving for visibility and exposure. Consequently strategy often diverges from previously set goals and objectives because other circumstances have created opportunities where attention can be quickly gained. As a consequence, strategy becomes very disjointed and *ad hoc*. Organizational structure is hap-hazard and does not take account for the needs of the environment. The structure is developed with the need of the leader to control decision making. It is not uncommon for the leader to meddle in even the most mundane decisions and give out assignments that are very difficult to satisfy. Short term advantages are sort at the cost of long term gains for the organization. Resources are used very inefficiently. Attention-seeking (dramatic) organizations may borrow heavily and become highly geared companies.

Attention-seeking (dramatic) people my start projects with great enthusiasm, as it seemed a good idea at the time, but very quickly loses interest. The general motivation behind what they do is to gain notoriety and attention rather than create something of long term substance. This trait may be very valuable in start ups in high profile industries like entertainment where there are no shortages of examples. However this form of strategy can be disastrous in a mature organization, where new strategy will be inconsistent, with an unnecessary high risk with rash expansion.

The Depressive Typology

The depressive typology is characterized by a feeling of hopelessness, inaction, passiveness, low confidence and conservatism. There is a feeling that there is little control of the outside environment and even if they intervened there is little chance of success, so the best option is to carry on as usual and not be proactive.

In a depressive state cognitive information coming in will become distorted resulting in a stream of negative thoughts. Beck (1967) suggests that people who themselves are depressed will develop a cognitive schema that organizes incoming information in a negative way. Things about self, the world and the future will be subject to *overgeneralization distortions* which will create negative outlooks into matters of competency, ability, luck, fate and potential outcomes, etc. Other cognitive distortions (Beck 1976) like *arbitrary inferences* (jumping to negative conclusions about everything), *personalizing* (assuming everything is one's own fault), and *castastrophizing* (thinking the worst case scenario about everything) will also distort incoming information, leading to the feeling of being a total failure, where a self fulfilling prophecy develops.

Within the organizational context, there will not be much interest in anything, leading to a number of stifling consequences such as failure to replace assets, little, if any new product development, little market intelligence gathering, poor customer service and leader indecisiveness. There is a basic pessimistic outlook towards the outside environment. The organization will tend to be very bureaucratic and hierarchical, the same it has been for decades before (if it is an established company). Managers will not take any initiative and leave major decisions for the board and committees to make. The company operates through procedures with little impact from happenings in the marketplace. This brings complacency which brings strong barriers to any form of change.

Strategy tends to develop from within, rather than from the market as managers feel they already understand the market well enough and there is little point doing any further field analysis. The competition is seen as being the same and customers are homogenous as far as managers are concerned. Too much field analysis could bring uncertainty, shock and anxiety about the need to change which is what the organization is trying to avoid.

This typology is common in very established firms in stable market environments where technology in production processes have been already automated. Examples of these types of industries would include the steel, automotive (prior to the 1980s), agriculture and some industrial chemical industries. Industries that have been protected through tariffs and formed oligopolies would be very susceptible to depression. Because these industries have been stable for many years, environmental change is very difficult to see from inside the industry, something like *the goldfish not being able to see the water it is swimming in.* In an organization with a moderate form of pessimism, one would expect a high degree of management involvement in strategy formation, resulting in firm focus. However where complacency has developed, anarchistic strategies and stagnation in a declining market would be very characteristic.

When firms become pessimistic bringing on complacency, this leaves them open to takeover by stronger and more ambitious competitors. For example, CEMEX the Mexican cement giant took the opportunity to takeover cement companies in South-East Asia during the 1997-1999 Asian financial crisis, where many firms became very pessimistic. Novel strategies in very stable markets can shake complacent competition. Singapore Airlines left IATA and shook up competition by providing better in-flight service in the 1970s. Existing TV networks were caught off-guard when CNN launched its 24 hour news network in 1980.

The Schizoid Typology

The schizoid typology is relatively rare in new enterprises as someone in this state would be unlikely to develop an enterprise unless it is of solitary nature, like graphic design or computer programming. The world to the schizoid is unhappy, unpleasant and empty of meaning. Nothing really excites the schizoid who tries to remain detached from everything. Sometimes schizoid tendencies carry an eccentric nature or beliefs with them such as belief in the supernatural, UFOs or conspiracy theories, etc. In private life the schizoid person is greatly devoid of personal relationships except for parents and closest relatives. He/she would have very few friends as they are seen as intrusive and a waste of time. For these reasons the person lives a very sheltered life, where any social support network will not likely exist.

Under the schizoid typology, any leadership in an organization would appear directionless, always changing and confused, indifferent to praise and criticism, and seemingly detached from the reality of what is going on. The leader would appear to be in a world of fantasy or daydreams. Deep down this state would be caused by anxiety or fear of being attached to intimacy from either the feeling self conscious, worthless and at the same time superior to others (Stone 1993).

Firms in the schizoid state would carry out very little environmental scanning. There is no firm philosophy to follow, resulting in undisciplined and uncoordinated product/market strategy. Little direction would come from the leader who will tend to be withdrawn, indecisive or uncommitted. It is likely that the leader will not even have any close advisors to fill in his/her apathetic void. Such a company would tend to pay little, if any attention to criticism and complaints by customers, stakeholders and authorities. Due to this underlying apathy there is great risk that strategies developed will operate with little regard to rules and regulations. If these breaches are serious and the company is caught out, it could lead to heavy consequences.

Company strategy and operations will just continually muddle along unless one or more groups within the organization takeover and dominate the decision making process, e.g., marketing, finance or operations departments. There may be a struggle between two or more groups within the company, where demarcation lines with will be created with an *"us and them"* mentality. If this occurs then the organization will become a political battleground, resulting in little collaboration. These barriers between departments would lead to very little flow of information around the organization.

If conflict is managed within the organization this could promote many different points of view. However this may be difficult if political competitiveness destroys any potential cooperation. Most strategy and operational decisions will be very inconsistent because they are based on political processes. The organization will lack the strength in the top leadership to steer it all subordinates in the same direction and overcome the climate of suspicion and non-cooperation.

The Narcissistic Typology

Narcissistic behavior can occur from extreme behaviors within the paranoid, obsessive-compulsive and the attention-seeking (Dramatic) typologies or it can occur as a psychological response to the need to manage self-esteem. Narcissistic individuals have a strong need to be admired, a sense of self importance and a lack of insight and empathy into the needs and feelings of others. They see themselves as great achievers, even if they haven't achieved anything, which can lead to an overconfidence bias (discussed later in this chapter). They seek to associate themselves with those who have been successful to seek more acclaim through the association. Narcissists find it very difficult to cope with their own emotions, particularly when their self view comes under scrutiny. For this reason they find it very difficult to learn from others, are poor listeners and don't teach, but indoctrinate their subordinates.

Narcissists are highly ambitious people. They are attracted to business and driven by their need for power and glory. This is a trait of many successful entrepreneurs, where self confidence and ambition assisted them. The dream of success and the accolades it brings is something they think about a lot. Some narcissists are truly experts in their field and they will extend their knowledge and skills into other areas. Where narcissists have little intellectual knowledge in their field, they will think very shallow, but at the same time they will be very *'street-smart'*.

Narcissists expect a lot from their subordinates. When they don't receive the total devotion and dedication they expect of their subordinates, they will punish them in Machiavellian ways. The narcissist is highly distrustful and overly exploitive of his/her subordinates. However he/she is extremely sensitive to criticism and will very quickly grow into childlike deep anger and rages if they are not given the respect they think they deserve.

Strategy will be underlined with a great desire to compete and win at any costs. This drive to win can be positive but at the extreme, devious methods will be employed which can border on the unethical and illegal. In extreme narcissism, objectives can be unrealistic as they are based on fantasy. This results in grandiose strategies objectives which are impossible to achieve (Brown, 1997, P. 648). The arrogant nature of the narcissist will lead to intuitive decisions where little analysis and interpretation of the market is undertaken (Brown & Starkey 2000). The narcissist likes to think in terms of the big picture and leave details to his/her few trusted loyalists who tend to tell their leader what he/she wants to hear. The narcissist wants to leave a legacy and be ready for a fight. However he/she will always look for potential enemies along the horizon. There is a reluctance to change strategy even when it is not working as the narcissist views this as a sign of weakness and failure. This weakness can lead to large scale disasters.

The firm will become self-absorbed and seek to capitalize on opportunities that show greatness. These are very inward looking (Christensen & Cheney 2000), where stakeholder interests are rarely considered, often leaving them to drop off support. Self rhetoric can become so intense an echo of unrealistic dreams and grand schemes, that in telling himself who he is and what he stands for, that he will forget who he is and what he stands for (Hatch & Schultz 2002).

The typologies above have some influence in how the world is perceived. Structure, management style and strategy reflect or mirror how the leader and members of the organization see the world. This is heavily influenced by the leader at the top (Mitroff 1984), especially if the leader was also the founder of the organization.

Defence Mechanisms

Defence mechanisms evolved thousands of years ago to protect humankind from the dangers of the environment. They originate from man's need to hunt, protect, nurture and generally survive on the Earth (Tiger & Fox 1972). When man faced danger, he had two basic choices open to him; fight or flight. This primal defence mechanism is ready to be activated only after a number of very quick physiological changes in the body creating stress and anxiety occur, so the person can make the decision to defend himself or flee from the scene[94].

Living today in a modern society creates stress and anxiety that is sustained in the person much longer than the *'hunter'* who only dealt with short skirmishes. Anxiety is a primal response to danger and in modern society it builds up in us, something akin to us making regular deposits of money into our savings account. Stress manifests itself with a number of symptoms like high blood pressure, digestional problems and insomnia, which can lead to the danger of blood clots, stroke and heart attack. These are now the highest causes of death in both middle and high income countries (WHO 2004). The effect of stress and anxiety is to hinder concentration, restricting thinking to only immediate problems, without consideration of the long term consequences (De Board 1978, P. 113). Stress and anxiety also leads to a number of behavioral responses which are based on a defence mechanism.

Anxiety today is not externally produced as it was for the hunters. Anxiety comes from within, manifesting subjective dangers with corresponding feelings and emotions over longer periods of time than the hunters. This anxiety is neurotic rather than objectively caused anxiety originating externally. The approaches the psych takes to managing anxiety have also evolved in sophistication over thousands of years and form an important part of our personalities.

Human Personality has a strong influence on every aspect of life. A person continually experiences objects, people and events that create pain, suffering or pleasure, happiness or sadness, with other emotions, that largely go unnoticed during the day (De Board 1978, P. 25). Emotions create various human feelings may originate from either external events, *i.e., threats to physical safety*, a feeling of pain or pleasure, *i.e., rapid sexual arousal,* or to a moral issue, *i.e., some feeling of guilt* (Larsen & Buss, 2005, P. 284). These emotions and feelings can distort perception, where external and internal stimuli become confused and often exaggerated, sometime leading to psychotic behaviors[95], discussed previously. Our psych acts to control and stabilize these emotions so a person can cope with everyday life through a number of defence mechanisms.

Defence mechanisms are psychological strategies that the psych develops to cope with the emotions generated through everyday life (Larsen 2000). They try to preserve a person's self-image and view of the world. Normality often contains neurotic traits which can be triggered by anxiety and dominate one's perception over a period of high emotion. In such situations, defence mechanisms can over compensate and develop distortions and misperceptions, preventing productive behavior, making things worse (Cramer 2000).

---

[94] When a person is exposed to some sort of external danger arteries near the skin begin to clamp down, muscles begin to tense and blood pressure rapidly rises. The heart begins beating at a rapid rate and blood is redistributed to the limbs, ready for any quick moves. Bowels release to reduce weight and adrenalin is pumped into the blood stream to help the blood clot quickly if any injury occurs.

[95] This is the basis of psychoanalytical theory. Psychoanalysis looks at the whole personality, rather than individual traits, and behavior. Psychoanalytical theories consider object-relations which begin with a person's relationship with a mother's breast and develop throughout childhood, and ones basic instinctual needs as the major factors influencing the development of personality. A child develops a world of pleasure and pain, hate and love, where he/she forms their own self view and view of the world. This development continues through life and these mental representations become the way that a person perceives, interprets and constructs their own meaning of the world. A person's instinctual base develops into a continuum of needs and wants, which becomes fantasized into unconscious schema, creating a subjective world in a person where potential urges and behavior originates. We are interested in this from the point of view as how a person perceives the environment, develops ambitions, sets objectives, develops strategy and reacts to potential opportunities.

Defence mechanisms used in their extreme take away both psych and physical energy from other tasks which weaken a person, pushing him/her into some degree of psychosis. They can cloud perception and thinking and affect the way problems are seen and approached (Larsen & Buss, 2005, P. 292).

Table 3.21. Six psychotic typologies, characteristics, associated thoughts and beliefs

Typology	Characteristics	Associated Thoughts & Beliefs
Paranoid	People influenced by this typology will; Be distrustful of others, Misinterpret social events as threatening, Harbor resentment towards others, Is prone to envy and jealousy, and Is argumentative, hostile and stubborn.	"People are all out to get me" "We must get others before they get us" "All people have ulterior motives and cannot be trusted" "People say one thing but do another" "Don't let people get away with anything" "I have to be on my guard all the time" "People are only friendly because they want something"
Obsessive-Compulsive	People influenced by this typology will; Be preoccupied with order, Seek perfection in what they do, Be workaholics Have little time for friends and holidays, Usually be miserly and stingy, and Be rigid and stubborn.	"Rules and high standards keep order" "Other people are reckless and irresponsible in their work" "If don't look into the details there may be possible flaws" "My way is the right way to do things" "It is not worth doing something unless it is done perfectly" "I must not waste any time on frivolous things that interfere with my work" "I can only depend on myself"
Attention-Seeking (Dramatic)	People influenced by this typology will; Engage in excessive attention seeking activities, Exhibit excessive emotions, Have shallow opinions, Have a strong need for attention, and Be very political, Machiavellian in their decision making.	"I am in charge of everything" "People are here to work for me" "High profile actions promote my image" "Politics, manipulation and deception are ways of achieving ends" "I get by on my hunches without really having to think about things" "It feels good to be at the centre of things" "The world is a stage – dramatic acts lead to greatness" "Look at me, aren't I great" "I can impress and entertain anybody because I'm an exciting person" "Boredom is the worst feeling" "If I can do it – just do it"
Depressive	People influenced by this typology will; Tend to give up or not even try, Believe they are not capable of achievement, See their position as hopeless, and Tend to give up if problems arise.	"I am likely to fail" "The world is against me" "If anything will go wrong, it will" "Why bother trying" "Everything is my fault" "We cannot beat the competition"
Schizoid	People influenced by this typology will; Be detached from personal relationships, Be indifferent to opinion, Have very little pleasure in life, Be socially inept, Be very passive and uncommitted when events are occurring, and	"I hate being around and tied up with other people" "I like my privacy and not being close to others" "Its best not to confide in others" "Relationships are always difficult and end up badly" "I am best working on my own" "I don't need an intimate relationship"

	Prefer to work alone.	
Narcissistic Typology	People influenced by this typology will; Need to be admired, Have a strong sense of self importance, Have a lack of insight into other people's needs and feelings, Have a sense of entitlement, Have a sense of superiority, Have a strong but very fragile self-esteem, and Be envious of others.	"I very special and deserve VIP treatment" "Rules don't apply to me" "I look after No. 1" "If others don't give me the praise and recognition I deserve, they should be punished" "Who are you to criticize me?"

Defence mechanisms can be considered as a group of personality traits that originate in the psych[96] and function to protect a person's self image and assumptions, values and beliefs that make up his/her view of the world. They act to reduce anxiety, fear, stress and guilt. They defend a person from the painful realizations that will challenge one's identity. They reduce the inconsistencies between one's view of self and world and any external evidence that would refute that view. They simplify the complexities of situations that contradict a person's simple view of reality. Defence mechanisms reduce fear and build security so that a person can live with the dangers and threats in the world.

Therefore defence mechanisms have some influence upon the construction of opportunity, which itself is a desire of a certain reality. Defence mechanisms can obstruct one seeing opportunity and inhibit action out of the fear of uncertainty new opportunities can potentially bring. Defence mechanisms have something to do with how we reconcile the paradox of an opportunity bringing potential success and also the potential fear and uncertainty of failure that goes along with it.

Defence mechanisms can be classified into four levels (Valliant 1977). The first level defences can be considered psychotic where external experiences are distorted in some way to cope with reality. These include denial, distortion and delusional projection, all common in psychotic disorders. The second level defences are immature defenses. They are common in childhood and carry their way through to adulthood in many people. These defenses inhibit a person ability to cope socially and effectively reduce any anxiety. They are common in depressive disorders. These include fantasy, projection, passive aggression, acting out and idealization. Level three defences are neurotic, fairly common in the adult population. These types of defences can destabilize relationships general life. They include displacement, isolation, intellectualization, reaction formation, repression, regression and rationalization. Level four defences are the most common and include altruism, anticipation, humor, identification, introjections, sublimation and suppression. These defence mechanisms are developed by individuals throughout their life and become very unique to a person's personality. A person using these defences would usually remain productive, being able to control and use his/her emotions to their benefit.

There are numerous more defences that the psych develops against anxiety (A. Freud 1936). Some of the major ones mentioned above are listed in Table 3.22. below.

---

[96] According to Freudian psychology defence mechanisms originate from the ego. The need for defence mechanisms occurs when the id (a primal, instinctual pleasure orientated part of the personality that is impulsive) comes in conflict with the super-ego (the social morality aspect of the personality). Un-satisfaction, desire, anxiousness and/or fear will eventually rise to the consciousness and needs to be suppressed by the ego through defence mechanisms to block the id.

Table 3.22. Common Defence Mechanisms

Defence Mechanism	Description and Comments
Acting out	Acting out is a defence mechanism which involves undertaking actions based on unconscious desires that are socially unacceptable. Acting out can be related to regression. Acting out is a loss of self control which will bring guilt and shame later on, thus requiring the use of other defence mechanisms like denial. Acting out may be an unconscious attempt to gain attention through drug addition, temper tantrums, self mutilation, and other anti-social or damaging behaviors. Acting out is the opposite of sublimation.
Altruism	Altruism is the wish or intention to do good for others without reward. However sometimes altruism occurs out of a motivation to feel good about oneself.
Anticipation	Anticipation is a defence mechanism to reduce anxiety by looking forward to a coming event. Anticipation can be shown either by enthusiasm or feeling ill or sick. People react differently before performing on stage or in a sporting event through the phenomena of stage fright.
Denial	Denial is one of the most common defence mechanisms. This involves the refusal to accept the facts or reality, creating arguments against any anxiety forming event, refusing to admit something exists or refusing to perceive something that will cause pain, etc. *When a person after being demoted continues to act as if he/she is still in the same position*, is an example of denial. Denial aims to keep things out of memory to minimize any potential pain the object, person or event may cause. Denial is also used to put the blame for something on other causes other than oneself to escape responsibility. This is called fundamental attribution error. This is common when external causes are sort to explain a failure that is really caused by the person or group themselves, *i.e., externalize the problem*.
Devaluation	Devaluation occurs where a person or object creates ambivalent feelings is seen as flawed, not living up to expectations. This creates feelings that the person or object is worthless, fake or phony. Devaluation is the opposite to idealization.
Displacement	Displacement occurs when something threatening, often a personal aggressive or sexual impulse, is redirected away from its original target onto a non-threatening target, *i.e., being told off by a supervisor at work, only to go home and get angry at a spouse.* This is usually an unconscious process where anger and/or aggression is built up, so a person can avoid the consequences of being angry or aggressive at the *supervisor* and let all their anger out at their spouse without the same consequences[97]. This defence attempts to release unacceptable anger, aggression and/or sexual tension, etc.
Distortion	Distortion is a less functional response to anxiety produced by facts that threaten a person's self image. This defence mechanism involves reshaping facts to suit a person's self image. For example, *a person failing a driving test may claim to friends that the examiner is unfair.*
Fantasy	When some people are put under stress and pain they sometimes withdraw themselves into fantasy (McWilliams 1994, P. 100). Fantasy encumbers desires based on primal instinctual needs (from the id) in mental representations. These become the basis of some behavior (Klein 1948). Fantasies develop in a person's subjective world when something in the external world that causes

[97] However this may create other long term relationship problems with the spouse.

	pain, stress, fear and unease. Fantasies can also develop in group and organizational situations and can give rise to shared fantasies that will influence organizational functioning, culture (Kets de Vries & Miller 1984, P. 20), policy and decision making (Mitroff & Kilmann 1976). Fantasy can also border on the paranoid where groups develop *persecutory group fantasy* (deMause 2002, P. 111), for example where executives fear a new boss after their company has been taken over.
Fixation	Fixation originates from Freud's psychosexual development theory where a child gets stuck in a particular stage of development. He/she trapped in an earlier stage of development will seek pleasure in immature ways. In adult life a person may not be able to emotionally pass through a crisis and will continue to focus on the issues of that past event. People display fixation when they cannot budge from the attitude, point of view and ideas they hold, resulting in a fixed type of behavior pattern.
Humor	Humor is a mature defence mechanism which shows control of emotions, unless it is used in a compulsive or attention seeking manner. Humor is used to lessen the anxiety caused by situations which bring fear or attack self-esteem.
Idealization	Idealization occurs when groups split and project all exaggerated "ideal" qualities onto a leader (or a leader can do the same to his/her subordinates). This creates a leader that is considered faultless and "superhuman". Subordinates in such a situation will always agree with their leader and when they have to make decisions themselves will try and emulate their leader's thinking. When strategies are poorly thought out, there will usually be no disagreement from any subordinates. This often occurs in entrepreneurial start-ups or when a new CEO is appointed in troubled times. This defence mechanism will inhibit innovation greatly (Kets de Vries & Miller 1984, P. 82).
Identification	Identification is a defense mechanism which rarely occurs in isolation. This defence mechanism can help people adjust to social situations and culture. It starts in early life where boys may want to be like their fathers, as they wish to have the same patterns, attitudes and beliefs. Some people take on the attributes of people they fear, like a boss as a way to cope with the anxiety generated (Kets de Vries & Miller 1984, P. 140).
Introjection	Introjection is where external meanings are taken into a person's psych where it becomes their own meaning. Ferenczi (1916, P. 41), the psychoanalyst and colleague of Freud believed that introjections is an important process in creating personal meaning of the external world, which has great influence on behavior and personality (Freud 1950, P. 89). In a group situation where members wish to identify with the leader will incorporate his/her ideas into their own. This creates very closely knit groups through what is called *introjective identification.* The traits people introject into themselves will idealize what they want to be. This can be seen in religious identification.
Isolation & Intellectualization	Isolation is a defence mechanism which separates any feeling from a given event, so the person has no emotional response. Intellectualization is a form of isolation where an event is described in a clinical way, without emotional description. These defences are used to distance and detach oneself from any painful emotions and anxiety.

Table 3.22. Continued

Defence Mechanism	Description and Comments
Passive Aggression	Passive aggression is a partly conscious defence mechanism. It has a characteristic negative and passively antagonistic disposition where a person is obstructive, stubbornly resistant in a group or occupational situation. Passive aggression is also characterized by resentment and sulkiness against something or someone. Passive aggression usually occurs as a reaction to competition, resistance against dependency and intimacy.
Projection	Projection is a common defence mechanism with some paranoid tendencies. Through projection a person puts all their unwanted and hated traits onto another person, which they come to hate and despise instead of hating themselves. They also don't admit they have these traits within themselves. Projection is a method to deal with guilt and anxiety by blaming others for what they are responsible for. Projection leaves a person with a self perception of only virtuous and moralistic traits. Projection is the source of prejudice, jealousy and paranoia. Jaques (1955, P. 478) considers projection as a defence against anxiety at the group level to be one of the most powerful forces binding people together.
Rationalization	Rationalization is another common defence mechanism where a person develops a very elaborate explanation to disguise their own intentions or feelings. For example, if a person's spouse leaves, that person may say the relationship was really long over and they would have separated anyway. Failure at some given task may be explained away by saying that things were not explained clearly, they didn't have the right tools or there was not enough time, etc. The objective of rationalization is to maintain self-esteem and reduce anxiety from any personal trauma.
Reaction Formation	Reaction formation is an attempt to change an urge a person would have into its opposite impulse. For example where a person has been told off by a superior, instead of using displacement as a defence mechanism, the person will be overly kind to the superior. Reaction formation can lead people to do the opposite of what one might predict they do. However the original emotion will still persist in the sub-conscious. Reaction formation can cause behavior in extreme which hinders the ability to adapt to change (Kets de Vries & Miller 1984, P. 141).
Regression	Regression reverts a person back to some child like behavior when self-esteem is threatened. An example of someone reverting to regression as a defence mechanism is shown in J. D. Salinger's (1951) novel *The Catcher on the Rye,* where Holden Caulfield, the main character reverts to regressive behavior as a way to cope with the stress and fear of growing up.
Repression	It is reported that Freud considered repression as the forerunner of most other defence mechanisms (Larsen & Buss 2005, P. 285). Repression is a defence mechanism that represses anxiety producing thoughts into the sub-conscious. This probably occurs in situations where there are two contradictory beliefs that cause anxiety. For example, *'I like smoking'* and *'smoking can cause cancer'* are two contradictory beliefs. The person can repress the fact that smoking can cause cancer to repress any anxiety about smoking. Tavris and Aronson (2007) argue that we use this method *(dissonance reduction)* to 'fool' ourselves about facts so we can live our lives with self-justification, thereby reducing guilt and anxiety generated by our actions.
Somatization	Somatization is not a common defence mechanism. It occurs when there are

	some unconscious psychological conflicts that are channeled onto oneself in the form of pain, illness or anxiety.
Splitting	Splitting is the process where people, objects and events are seen as either all good or all bad, i.e., thinking in extremes. Splitting helps to preserve one's own "good" self-image by splitting all the bad parts and projecting them onto another (usually weaker) person or group. According to Jaques (1955, P. 479) this is how scapegoating and persecution occurs. For example the Nazis projected all their hatred onto the Jews who could be attacked, abused and exterminated. This is similar to how an organization *(and even a country)* develops its own myths about heroes and villains. Splitting works alongside projection, idealization and devaluation. Menzies (1960) looked at the use of these defence mechanisms to cope with the anxieties of their work in the nursing profession. Nurses transformed their intra-personal struggle into an interpersonal struggle through splitting irresponsible impulses onto subordinates, treating them hard as a consequence of the blame unconsciously attributed to them.
Sublimation	Sublimation is a very useful defence mechanism as it channels potentially destructive psychic energies and transforms them into more socially accepted psychic energies. People have urges and impulses which are socially destructive and can that focus away from other aspects of life. These can be anger or sexual urges that distract a person. Sublimation is the mechanism that transforms destructive urges into socially accepted urges. For example, the psychic energy from a person's need to dominate others can be channeled into leadership or entrepreneurship roles.
Suppression	Suppression is the conscious process of putting off the consideration of doing something, or doing something to suppress any anxiety. An example of this is putting off going to the dentist due to the unpleasantness one anticipates, or in a corporate situation putting off discussions about painful issues of closing a factory, discontinuing a product or making retrenchments, etc.
Maintaining Routines	Organizations develop work routines that have the affect of assisting people avoid risks. For example, when an issue that is uncomfortable and requires taking some risk comes up, the safe way is to pass it up the organizational hierarchy for a decision (Bardwick 1995, P. 27). People use routines to cope with anxiety, fear and uncertainty. This can lead to unproductive or *pseudowork* where there is emphasis on getting things done through following procedures, rather than accomplishment.
Addiction	An addiction is a conditioned, reflexive, and compulsive behavior that momentarily reduces stress, *i.e., eating, smoking, or drinking* (Hollis 2007, P. 67).

Group Reality

Cartwright and Zander (1960) believe groups mobilize powerful forces which produce effects of the utmost importance and influence to individuals. Schein (1980, pp. 150-151) specifies some of these psychological functions as including giving its members a sense of affiliation, providing a sense of shared identity contributing to security and self-esteem and most importantly, giving the group a shared social reality. Social reality is a common understanding of what exists, what is happening and why? Group perception of social reality gives a sense of meaning, where anxiety arises from phenomena that are not understood, do not fit into the group's schema of understanding and consequently feared.

Like individuals, groups also utilize defence mechanisms to cope with group anxieties, as the Hawthorne studies in the 1920s and 1930s showed[98]. Jaques (1955, P. 478) postulated that defence against anxiety is one of the most powerful elements that bind a group together and that maladaptive behavior will be exhibited. These types of behaviors will depend upon the group's shared view of reality and the various types of defence they utilize against anxiety to minimize group distress.

Groups develop fantasies which become a symbolic reality to the individual members. According to Robert Bales (1970, P. 150) unified fantasies develop in groups through the items and elements that the group is interested in, events that are given symbolic meaning, and elaboration of selected elements, carried out through a process that reinforces itself through interest, excitement and involvement of the group. A group mentality will develop that is uniform throughout the membership[99], where according to Wilfred Bion (1959, P. 42) contrasts itself with the diversity of individual mentality.

Wilfred Bion developed much of his group theories while he was a member of the Tavistock Institute of Human Relations and from his work in the British Army, trying to select potential leaders during World War Two. Bion postulated that every group has two aspects to it. The first aspect is the group has its formal role to perform according to the reason it was set up. Formally the group will have its objectives, tasks to perform, rules and procedures, membership and formal leader. The second aspect of the group is the basic assumptions that underlie the members manners of coping with anxiety developed through different group situations. Thus the assumption aspect operates at the unconscious fantasy level, and tacit to the group's membership. Bion further postulates that there are three types of basic assumptions group will operate by.

---

[98] Elton Mayo, an Australian researcher in the United States was investigating the reasons for high employee turnover at the Philadelphia Textile Mill in 1923 and 1924. After interviewing and consulting with employees, Mayo's group set up a number of rest periods during work which resulted in reduced turnover and more positive work attitudes. At the same time a scientific management study was being undertaken at the Western Electric Plant in Hawthorne, Illinois. Between 1924 and 1927 these studies examined the effect of lighting illumination, which would be expanded upon and continue into the 1930's. The experiments were intended to examine the effect light intensity on productivity and expected to see a direct correlation between light intensity and productivity. However to their surprise, the researchers found that no matter the light intensity, productivity would increase. Something else was influencing increased productivity. This led to a completely accidental discovery. The research group concluded that it was the novelty of the situation that was the factor in increases of productivity (Mayo 1945). The studies continued with Elton Mayo joining the group, which experimented with changes in job design and pay incentives as new variables. The results indicated that pay schemes and incentives were not as importance as group influence on productivity in the workplace through the norms they develop. Group norms developed to protect the group in the organisation from external influences such as management. For example, the group would restrict production out of fear they would work themselves out of a job or that management would raise quotas. The group developed it's own sanctions against errant members through ridicule, ostracism and name calling. The results showed the importance of the informal group on productivity and satisfaction in the workplace and issues like job security can be considered more important than financial rewards. Mayo himself argued that self esteem was vital to performance and management must take account of human nature as social motives. Failure to do this will lead to lower productivity, through covert activities like restricting production or in extreme cases sabotage, a defence mechanism (Mayo 1947). Consequently, non-directive styles of supervision would be best to promote harmony and avoid conflict, allowing strong interpersonal bonds between the group members to develop as a means of satisfying social needs and inducing high productivity (O'Brien 1986).

[99] Bion is not arguing that a form of group mind exists or there is any natural 'herd' mentality in humans. A group mentality can only be the sum of the members of a group and without the members there cannot be any group mentality or consciousness. How strong the group mentality is will also be dependent upon the group homogeneity in values and beliefs. A group could be in a 'storming' stage for a long period of time where there may be a polarity of values and beliefs within the group.

The first basic assumption type is where members must be sustained by a leader who is seen as stable, dependable, so is idealized. The group believes that this person, if willing can solve all their problems. If there is evidence to the contrary they will deny it. Under such a leader no real work or learning can be done. There is no real cooperation among the group. The group is inward looking and will tend to not look at the environment, as its own fantasies replace the need to do so. The outside world is a cold, complex and an unfriendly place where the members fear being outside by themselves and relish the security the group provides. The leader defends the group from reality, so the group doesn't need to know it.

On the surface, the primary emotions of the group are elation, unity and security. However these cover the deeper feeling of depression, where they are dependent yet at the same time like to be nurtured, which also leads to feeling of inadequacy. At the same time they are envious of the leader, but feel guilt for feeling envious. There is also the presence of greed where the group has regressed to childlike behavior in demanding *'parental care'* from the leader. This often creates a paradox to the member having both *'childlike'* and *'adult'* needs at the same time. Although anger and frustration exist, there is little fear as the leader is present to protect them.

It is very easy for the leader to slip into the role as the messiah to the group. The stronger the leader, the more power he/she can exert over the group. At the extremity, the group dynamics may resemble something like a *pseudo religious cult.* The words, writings and doings of the leader become sacred and in the leader's absence these artifacts can take his/her place.

However over time, the leader will disappoint the group and anger will begin to emerge. Sometimes an attitude reversal may occur, transforming idealization into devaluation. There is often an oscillation of emotion from *'good'* to *'bad'* and to *'good'* again which makes the group very emotionally explosive. In some cases the leader maybe overthrown and replaced with a new leader, if the group is strong enough. If the leader is strong enough, the rebel group members will be expelled.

When the group no longer has a leader, there will be a big vacuum. Many will draw their strength from the history, stories and myths and fantasy of the leader, until a successor can be found. The group may split into two sub-groups where one sub-group manipulates the artifacts of a leader or traditions to control the rest of the group. This allows the group to delay the need to look outside into the environment and do anything until the next leader arrives.

The second basic assumption type is the fight/flight group which sees the environment as a highly dangerous one. This group relies on one of the most primitive emotions against fear and anxiety; either to be the aggressor towards the enemy or flee from the enemy. This all resides in a very stressful environment where people are mistrusted. There is no tolerance for weak in this environment and any member will be easily sacrificed by the others for the sake of preserving the rest of the group.

The fight/flight group sees the world as either good or bad. The group is excessively paranoid about potential enemies. If there isn't one, one must be created. The bad attributes of group members are projected onto outside *'enemies'* so the group remains *'good'* and *'pure'*. A common enemy is one of the facets that bind the group together. Consequently the leader must be willing to attack the enemy, show bravery and valor on a regular basis to keep the group together and stay in power. Thus leadership is paranoid, non-reflective in decision making, insular and impulsive[100].

There is very little self-reflection in the group and anybody intellectual is shunned by the membership. Attitudes may be frozen by a past experience or trauma. The group tends to be intuitively impulsive in its reactions to things and will either immediately engage or flee. Timescales for action are very short. There tends to be a continual state of panic and willingness to either be aggressive, or quickly retreat from things. The leader must continue to maintain the group in this state of readiness to fight or he/she will be ignored. This takes a lot of emotional energy out of the members making it difficult for the group to do any real work as its energies are put into its fantasies. The leader really has little power over the group other than direct it to fight or flight, so is actually *'unknowingly'* only a captive of the group. The prominent emotions of the group are hate, fear, mistrust and suspicion. The group lacks any introspection and looks only at the surface of things. The world is static and there is no vision. Reality is suppressed, otherwise the group will discover that the real enemy is not outside but is within the group itself.

The third basic assumption type is pairing where the group has formed in the hope of bringing the messiah to lead the group. The group waits in anticipation while two members *'pair off'* on behalf of the group to create a new, as yet unborn leader. This act of creation is essentially sexual, although the sex of the pair is unimportant. What is important that the group is always in anticipation about any news about the coming of the new leader. The new leader may not necessarily be a person. It could be a new idea, thought or philosophy. It is the hope of the new life and deliverance from hatred, destructiveness and despair, the *'coming'* will bring.

A general feeling of hopelessness is within the group but relationships and interactions are soft and agreeable. The group is deluded with the illusion of this new potential that will come and solve all their problems and bring them into a utopian existence. Fantasy and daydreams settles conflicts and gives the group gratification. Hope or anticipation is the defence mechanism that protects them from fear and anxiety.

The group may go on without a leader, as it is the hope itself which drives the group. This type of group would tend to be visionary, enthusiastic, optimistic and creative in the way they approached the environment. However, if anybody became leader they would very quickly fail to meet the group's expectations. This would shatter hopes and aspirations and be devastating, which would bring despair and disillusionment. This would create a defeatist attitude to the environment.

The basic assumption types outlined above can increase and decrease in the intensity of influence over time. Any basic assumption type will not be necessarily exclusive to any group as there may be elements of more than one type within the group. Groups can also change their basic assumptions over time. For example a dependency type of group without a leader could transform into a utopian type group. In moderation basic assumptions can play a positive role. However in their extreme, basic assumptions can distort perception and influence the formation of rash and ill-conceived strategy based on fantasies. Thus group

---

[100] However paranoia can also bring out a ruthless competitive spirit in an organization. Avoidance based on flight can be the basis of an organization building up a set of internal operating procedures that builds up a barrier to the outside environment, thereby encouraging members to focus on internal procedures that take attention away from its enemies.

dynamics and shared fantasies have some influence on the opportunity discovery process. Table 3.23. shows some of the expected group characteristics of each basic assumption type.

Everybody has some tendency to become part of group life and be influenced by the dynamics described above. Individuals will have a tendency and preference for one style. There are expectations about the types of leaders and function groups perform for individuals. For example, a person who may be seeking stability and trust will therefore prefer to be in a dependency group. A fight/flight group will suit those who require inspiring and courageous leadership or membership in a fellowship, something like a religion. A creative person may prefer the optimism of a pairing group, etc.

Generally basic assumptions are not orientated out towards the environment, but orientated inwards towards fantasy, which is the driver of group acting-out (Rioch 1971, pp. 61-62). In this way, the group is another filter through which the individual views the environment. Reality is one step further away to an individual who will see the environment through the eyes of the group. This allows generally little reality testing and consideration about any consequences. These distortions are hard to detect as these processes *(except for the emotions generated)* tend to stay in the unconscious. Members' values and beliefs manifest themselves from their assumptions in stories, interpreted history, symbols and artifacts. Time and space are distorted, blurred and confused into symbolisms which contain meaning for them. This inhibits group learning through experience, as experience itself is continually distorted to fit into the existing schema.

Group defence mechanisms usually go unnoticed and according to Argyris (1985) cover the ways we are thinking, suppressing any flaws in logic, insufficient information or failure to consider other alternatives. Defence mechanisms hide the way we think and inhibit any learning potential from experience. Defence mechanisms also hide our anxieties and fears so that we cannot examine the reason for them. Therefore the most effective groups will be those who can see through their own defence mechanisms and obtain clear insights into 'what is really going on' in the environment.

The operation of basic assumption patterns in dependency groups can be seen in everyday organizational life fulfilling non-task functions. For example dependency can be seen in organizations that have a very flat hierarchy, where decision making tends to be centralized. Hospitals and junior schools show where patients/students are dependent on nurses/teachers. Dependency is usually in place where an organization has a charismatic leader who surrounds him/herself with agreeable subordinates who do little analytical work as decisions are left up to the boss. This also occurs in the early stages of a firm's life, like an entrepreneurial start-up, where the leader/founder dominates. As the leader holds most power, decisions will be made more on an *ad hoc* basis than according to some long term plan. Decisions would tend to be made on the spot and action is centered on the present, so the company would be very inconsistent, but flexible in strategy.

Fight/flight types can be seen in many direct door to door marketing organizations, event managers, and property developers, etc, who work on short term, highly focused projects. They will not spend time on anything that doesn't lead to almost instant results. Fight/flight assumptions can also be seen in marketing departments, where market-share percentages and distribution points are the metaphors of their function. There is almost paranoia about statistics and results. Incentive-control systems are very important in the operation and peoples working lives. The sales and marketing staff almost become antagonist towards their competitors. There will be little constant surveillance of competitor activity in the marketplace. This antagonism also can become interdepartmental where each department sees the other as a competitor and always ready to criticize the other for things that go wrong. People affiliated with a department will also see themselves as superior to others in another department, where comments like *"the salesmen are the batters and the accountants are only the scorers"*, will be commonplace to explain departmental interrelationships.

The powerful influence of pairing assumptions can be seen where the citizens of countries with royalty are excited about the Royal marriages and the birth of a new Aire to the throne. Immense hope and anticipation of a utopian future was the reason many voted for Barack Obama in the US Presidential Election in November 2008. In the business world biotech and electronic companies that undertake research for future products can be seen as giving birth to new *"influential objects"* that can take on *"messiah like'* attributes or qualities. Steve Jobs and the legend developed by Apple can be seen in this *"messiah like"* light, where even the props where speeches are given have symbolic *"alter like"* qualities. Utopian type groups carry with them large amounts of optimism and even grandiosity, where they seek to inspire. Sir Richard Branson is an inspirational hero to many, taking on the major record companies with Virgin Records, British Airways with Virgin Airlines, with his risky ballooning exploits and support for visionary ideas like *Virgin Galactic*. These ventures required strong vision and fantasy to achieve, where rational thought would have dismissed many of these ideas as unfeasible.

Utopian aspirations can also lead to eventual company failure as well. Fletcher Jones in Warrnambool, Australia tried to maintain the principal that high quality clothing could continue to be manufactured in Australia, even though the company faced much cheaper offshore competition. The company refused to go offshore keeping to the utopian concept of staff equity and share in management until its idealism forced it the closure of its Australian plant and into bankruptcy in the 1980s.

Senge (2006, P. 209) believes that fear and aspiration are the two fundamental sources of emotional energy that motivates an organization. Fear is the basis of a negative vision, which is very common in society. These would include anti-smoking, anti-war, anti-drug, anti-rape and anti-animal cruelty organizations, etc. However the problem with negative emotions is that when the threat or problem either ceases to exist or becomes less important to the membership, commitment to the vision and cause decline. Senge continues to point out that aspiration is the basis of positive visions, and is a much more long-term motivator, where he believes learning and growth can occur.

Transference

Transference is a situation where relationships in the present are influenced unconsciously by important relationships from the past. The past relationship was an intimate one, with perhaps a parent, where some unresolved issues bring out more emotional intensity than would normally be the case in the present relationship. From the Freudian perspective, transference represents a person's self refusal to let go of the pleasures or traumas of the *id*-dominated past, where the self is suffering from a compulsion to repeat and relive the past (Kalin 1974, P. 146).

Table 3.23. Some of the expected group characteristics of each basic assumption type.

Basic Assumption Type	Basic Assumptions/*Defence mechanisms*	Organizational Characteristics	Vision & Perception Orientation	Advantages	Disadvantages
Dependency	Members desire to be nourished and protected by a leader. Group idealization (sometimes devaluation) of a leader or leadership myth.	Centralization of all power and decision making Bureaucratic: rule and procedure orientated.	Present and future orientated. Only leader deliberates, other opinions carry little weight. Flexible strategies. Both means and goals orientated. Charismatic or autocratic management style.	Very goal orientated Cohesive Focused strategy Clearly defined organizational roles.	Very passive to the environment. No environmental scanning. Lack critical judgments of subordinates. Little if no innovation. Lack of moderation in decision making by leader. Excessive reliance on rules and regulation. Resistance to change.
Fight/Flight	There is an enemy inside and/or outside. Members must attack or flee if necessary Projection of group hostile emotions onto others, splitting world into good and bad	Paranoia: Continually searching for an enemy Avoidance of the environment through setting up sophisticated internal procedures.	Orientation in the past. Short term attention span. Impulsive and very rigid. Means orientated as ends (goals) can change. Insular management style.	Very rapid ability to mobilize resources and capabilities towards any problem. Sense of commitment by group members. Excellent organization design. Efficiency.	Poorly conceived strategy. Organizational infighting. Poor cooperation within organization. Stereotyping and scapegoating. Insularity. Very poor environmental analysis and ignorance of competitive threats. Large risk taking.
Pairing/Utopian	There is a philosophy, idea or person, still yet to arrive, that will deliver the group from all its hatred, destruction and despair. Anticipation and fantasy about a leader and utopian ideas.	Technically and organizationally creative & innovative.	Long term future orientated. Highly deliberate decisions by leader and group. Flexible strategies. Goal orientated with no means. Democratic and participative style management.	Creativity. Innovation and adventurism with new ideas and technologies. Harmony and collaboration, democratization and very good adaptation ability.	Waste resources, large risk taking. Lack of realistic external analysis replaced with Idealism. Denial of realities. Floundering from one idea to another.

Transference is a common phenomenon and can vary from the normal to the neurotic in intensity where past conflict, fantasy, wishes, hopes and desires resurface into part of a present relationship (Storr 1979). All human relationships have some degree of transference mixed into the relationship (Fenichel 1941). When interpersonal responses are over-reactive or out of proportion to the situation, most probably a high amount of transference exists within the interpersonal exchanges. A transference phenomenon utilizes a number of defence mechanisms and types of behaviors discussed previously in this chapter.

There are a number of different types of transference, some being positive with emotions of affections, while others negative with emotions of hostility. Kets de Vries and Miller

(1984, pp. 79-92) outlined three basic types of transference: *Idealization, Mirror* and *persecutory,* which are described below.

> Idealizing transference is motivated by the feeling of being lost and untrustworthy; unless there is someone they can admire and idealize (Kohut & Wolf 1978). Idealizing transference returns a person to a part of early life where he/she wishes to recreate an original state of bliss through developing a relationship with someone they see as perfect. They may idealize this person for their power, intelligence, moral position or beauty. Their weaknesses are usually passed over, while their strengths are greatly exaggerated. The people develop a dependency on the person to some degree. People who idealize superiors in a company tend to be contented, enthusiastic and supportive. However they tend not to have any ideas themselves, lose their own judgment, independent thinking and ability to solve problems on their own[101]. They will tend to make decisions the way they believe the superior will make them without using any of their creativity and innovation. This is very dangerous within an organization as idealization transference it will allow only one point of view without any opportunity for criticism or evaluation.

People who idealize others will put so many expectations put upon the other person, who will find it difficult to live up to. This may cause great disillusionment and could result in hostility and rebellion. Idealizing transference is good for an organization undergoing change where subordinates will not question any changes and tend to enthusiastically implement them. This form of leadership is common where there are strong entrepreneurial visionaries and charismatic leaders. Companies with this type of leadership will verge on the dramatic/attention seeking type with a dependency culture, described previously. The types of people attracted to this type of organization are those who want to be loyal and subordinate to others. Any different types of people will bring conflict, politics and resistance. Any new leader is best selected from outside the group, as no one in the group will have the strength and vision to provide adequate leadership to the others.

Idealizing transference can occur in reverse where the superior idealizes his/her subordinates. In this situation the leader will give the group tasks that have ambitious objectives that cannot be achieved. The failure to achieve and meet the leader's expectations will most likely lead to feelings of low self-efficacy within the group.

> Mirroring transference occurs when a person wants to return to a state of early life bliss by seeing him/herself as a grandiose, perfect and all powerful figure (Kohut & Wolf 1978). They have accumulated feelings of worthlessness and low self esteem from early childhood, where it was likely they were neglected by their parents. Mirroring transference is complementary to idealizing transference, where the subordinate idealizes and the superior mirrors.

> People exhibiting mirroring transference tend to be narcissistic in character and are attention seeking, insensitive and exploitive of their subordinates. They crave admiration and plaudits from others and surround themselves with *'yes-men'* who are blindly agreeable due to their idealization of him/her. These leaders also attract followers who are politically ambitious who want to climb by flattering and agreeing with him/her. This way they can carry favour with the leader who supports their position and doesn't

---

[101] Idealizing transference can range from 'normal idealization' where the subordinates respect the superior, looking at his/her characteristics as examples, where they show some sort of initiative, to a more extreme 'clinging idealization' where subordinates blindly imitate the superior without question and thinking.

scrutinize the lack of work and achievements by them. Any other subordinates who are strong and reflective will have great difficulty existing under a mirroring leader. They will likely leave on their own accord or be forced to leave by the Machiavellian leader, as they are seen as a threat to him/her.

A mirroring leader will not listen to the advice of subordinates and look only to their grandiose fantasies. They overvalue their own talents and abilities which leads them to reckless and ill thought out strategies. The will ignore the external world and come up with high risk, high resource draining plans and strategies where failure will have grave consequences, but success will lead to great recognition of others. The leader will seek to take credit for everything and see subordinates only as part of the stage he/she is performing on. People can only be for or against the leader. There is no room for people to sit on the fence. The failure of subordinates to give the leader accolades or disagree is a sign that they are against him/her, where the leader will react with rage and act vindictively against them. This type of behavior destroys any morale within the organization and suppresses any new ideas, creativity and innovation from subordinates.

As a result of this type of environment, plans and strategies will go un-scrutinized which can lead to massive disasters in the future. For example, Proton the Malaysian national car was started as a grand project with high ambitions but almost 30 years on is struggling to survive. The company has a large plant capital investment and only small domestic and limited export markets to serve. The increase of competition not just from traditional rivals, but a handful of new more efficient automotive companies has taken large market share away from Proton of late. Without the subsidies and trade barriers, Proton would probably not have survived so long.

Mirroring subordinates try to look better than their peers and superiors. They are motivated by their own gain rather than making contributions to the company or organization the work for. They want to impress the others and particularly the leader. They have the hope of becoming indispensible to the leader and the organization. Mirroring subordinates tend to seek out the formal extrinsic awards like promotions, pay rises, company car, office and status, etc, rather than the intrinsic satisfaction that the work itself brings. They are *'political animals'*, not hesitant to take others ideas, work on schemes to make others look poor in front of the boss, and may even attempt to develop their own projects.

Persecutory transference involves splitting bad attributes away from the self and projecting them onto others as a defence against aggressiveness. Interpersonal relationships tend to be laced with hostility, moral masochism and envy. These deep emotions most probably developed during infancy and enter the dynamics of existing relationships.

Leaders may display hostility in relationships as they see others out to destroy them through slow work, incompetence or malingering, etc. Due to this perception the leader may tighten formal controls and closely supervise his/her subordinates to the point where they lose their self-esteem and even conduct acts of overt and covert sabotage. The leader may also hold back salary increases, training and promotions, which adds to unhappiness and employees holding back on contributions to the firm. The bright employees with no prospects leave the firm, thus decrease the pool of talent available. When subordinates display transference hostility, they are uncooperative towards the leader and disruptive within the working environment. They are mistrustful, suspicious and will incite others to also be uncooperative and sabotage the firm.

Situations of transference hostility lead to decision making that protects one side and hurts the other, in a *'win-lose'* manner. A transference hostile employee may have the informal power to challenge the authority of the superior to implement anything substantial. Decisions with sanctions on employees will just lead to another round of hostile responses by the other side. Strategy developed will be simplistic, lacking any vision other than representing the aims of the leader, rather than the organization. Strategy implementation will be marked with conflict and perhaps even sabotage, resembling the paranoid and schizoid type firms discussed previously.

Moral masochism occurs when someone feels they are being persecuted and at the same time guilty about wishing to persecute others. Instead of taking anger out on others, the anger is taken out on oneself through self masochism. This is the person's way of fleeing their own anxiety and feelings of helplessness and worthlessness. The major characteristic of masochistic transference is seeking punishment as redemption for their feelings and guilt. In an organization setting this may manifest itself in someone failing in the tasks they are given. A masochistic leader will tend to develop grand and risky strategies that can end in disaster.

Envy transference occurs when a person is unhappy about things other people have, that they don't have. This brings unhappiness and feelings of inferiority. In the organization the superior will look for ways to take the things they want from other people through selfish, spiteful management decisions based on a hidden agenda of trying to sabotage others. Envious subordinates feel the superior is not being fair to them and they are missing out. This would create a very selfish, spiteful and political environment where information would be withheld and distorted, leading to very poor decision making and strategy implementation.

Symbolic and Ritualistic Processes as a Delusion

We have seen that defence mechanisms are a means of protecting a person or group from anxieties of some sort. Sometimes we do things for indirect reasons in the assumption that these acts will protect us from something or have some influence over our destiny. The energy we put into things is for something symbolic rather than for the overt functional reasons of the task. This is seen in some religious rituals where symbolic cleansings are undertaken to rid one of *'metaphoric dirt'* or clean ourselves of sin[102].

Many studies have been undertaken to examine work practices as a means to defend on against anxiety in the nursing profession (Menzies 1960). Nurses in hospitals have developed many rituals around birth, death, status and power to assist them cope with the daily anxieties (Chapman 1983) and to help prevent them from beginning emotionally evolved through job specialization. According to Varma and Chakraborty (cited in Jaipal 2004, P. 304) ritual plays an important role in maintaining psychological health. Ritual is a cultural defence mechanism against loss, anxiety and conflict in the therapeutic, social and political senses. Rituals help people deny, sublime, project or gratify things. They serve as preventative measures to ensure the smooth functioning of the organization in question.

---

[102] Such rituals could be the ritual splashing of holy water and the release of smoke at benedictions in the Catholic Faith and the cleansing of self before prayers with water in the Islamic faith.

Just like hierarchy, ritual and symbolism is used as protection against anxiety and to produce meaning in the nursing profession, the same processes occur commonly throughout other types of work and organizations. Formal and informal work rituals are often used to hide feelings of vulnerability and danger in the workplace. Boland and Hoffman's (1983) study of the use of humor showed that practical joking between co-workers at a machine shop was a very important mechanism to reduce boredom and monotony, bringing equal status to all workgroup and reducing general anxiety about the dangers involved with heavy metalwork. Gareth Morgan (2006, pp. 220-221) surmises that the very hierarchies, setting of goals and objectives, strategic planning processes, rituals and symbols of an organization may also fulfill the function of reducing anxiety, making things feel right, making people feel good, projecting things onto others, etc. Thus the real meaning of these things to members is that it creates security and a feeling of shared confidence among its members.

Creating an organization can also be seen as a means of denying our mortality. Ernst Becker (1973) believed that a person's character is primarily built around the process of denying their own mortality[103]. Man is basically afraid of the reality that death and seeks means to suppress this thought though building or becoming part of something that is bigger than himself to feel less vulnerable. This can lead to a person building an organization or fighting for a cause as a means to forget about mortality. They dedicate their life to the mission with the knowledge that this mission, cause or organization will last longer than themselves. This way their own symbolic immortality is achieved. This can be a very powerful evangelistic type of motivation to act and build something. The denial of death as a motivation is seen when people strive to leave a legacy after their death for society in some way or the other. However the quest for this legacy can also act as a block to change.

Groupthink

The groupthink hypothesis provides us with another mode of understanding how groups perceive opportunity, how exploitation decisions are made, how strategy paths are chosen, and what biases and distortions of reality exist. The term groupthink was first used by Irving Janis in 1972 to refer to the phenomena of a group coming to a consensus without critically analyzing all the various issues involved. The striving of the group for unanimity overrides the motivation to objectively appraise alternative courses of action (Janis 1972, P. 9). Janis (1982, P. 175) postulates that when the symptoms of groupthink are evident, decisions are likely to be poor.

Groupthink is a very popular term used in literature carrying with it very negative connotations. The word is usually used to describe decisions and their resulting disasters[104].

---

[103] Ernst Becker was a cultural antrapoligist and saw that people need to find a way to separate themselves from nature to deny mortality. This would be achieved through transference where there would be identification with the external object that would take on a godlike character of its own. This allows the person to co-exist with the knowledge of death – where everything would have a sense of urgency. This transference involves creating an illusion of something that maximizes the person's freedom, dignity and hope (Becker 1973, P. 202), which can partly explain why people tend to turn to spiritual and religious endeavors in the latter part of their life.

[104] The 'groupthink' phenomenon only exists if the symptomatic conditions are present. 'Groupthink' decisions may not necessary result in a poor decision and failure. There are many other reasons besides groupthink that can lead to a poor decision and failure, for example; the lack of necessary information, poor judgment, lack of experience

Groupthink is a widely studied phenomenon and has been used to explain many historical political decisions and their resulting consequences[105]. This metaphor can lead to a better understanding how groups make their decisions, what information they used and didn't use, what were their underlying group assumptions and what other influential factors were involved.

The groupthink phenomenon arises where individual inclinations to be critical and independently analyze issues are sacrificed in the interests of maintaining harmony within the group so a state of cohesion can occur. This results in people providing only opinions that they believe fall into the gambit of acceptable thinking. Members sub-consciously want to be part of the group and fear embarrassment, appearing outspoken and stubborn or disruptive to the flow of the group. This is likely to be based on a feeling of low self-efficacy (Baron 2005), and results in a consensus at the cost of rationality, with potentially faulty premises and failure to look at important pieces of information and potential consequences. As any doubts are suppressed, each member of the group believes that the decision made had full support of all the members.

According to the hypothesis, groupthink is most likely to occur when a group is very cohesive, insulated with lack of impartial leadership, lack procedure methodology, and have a homogeneous social background and ideology (Janis 1972). The groupthink process is actually triggered by some form of an external crisis, event or failure which induces stress and feelings of low self efficacy on the group, challenging their existing decision making processes and sometimes creating moral dilemmas.

Janis (1972) postulated that the symptoms of groupthink are;

> The illusion of invulnerability which creates over optimism of potential success and willingness to take high risks,
> An inherent belief of their own morality where the consequences of their decisions are ignored,
> Collective rationalization where warnings, signs and messages are rationalized according to existing group assumptions,
> Negatively generalized and stereotyped views of external people and entities, where they view others as weak and foolish,
> Self censorship and pressure on dissenters to carry the group line and not express any disagreements, including the suppression of outside views disagreeing with the group,
> The illusion of unanimity in the belief that individual views conform to the majority view and silence means consent,
> Social pressure on those who have doubts about group consensus, and
> There are self appointed 'mind-guards' to protect the leader and group from information that may threaten any potential group cohesiveness.

Kowert (2002) also added that an overload of information may also contribute to causing the groupthink phenomena.

---

of the issues, luck, unexpected actions by competitors, government, and suppliers, etc., group competence, the heuristics used (discussed later in this chapter), and inadequate time for proper decision making.

[105] Janis (1972) first used the concept to appraise the Korean War stalemate and Vietnam War escalation. In 1982, Janis examined the Watergate cover-up. Kramer (1998) examined the Bay of Pigs and Vietnam decisions, with additional evidence casting some doubt on Janis's analytical conclusions. Hart (1994) and Whyte (1998) enhanced the groupthink hypothesis. Smith (1984) analyzed the US rescue mission to Iran in 1979. Vaughan (1996) and Schwartz and Wald (2003) looked at the way NASA operated in relation to the Challenger and Columbia disasters.

The result of this is a defective decision making process characterized by;

The decision had an incomplete consideration of possible alternative courses of action, 2. The problem will have clearly specified objectives, 3. There was a failure to properly analyze risks of the preferred choice, 4. There was a failure to reassess earlier discarded options, 5. There was a poor information search, 6. There was bias in the selection and processing of information, and 7. No contingencies were conceived.

The result of this process is a decision that has a very low probability of a successful outcome. A diagram of the groupthink process is shown in Figure 3.30.

The effect of groupthink is to strengthen group cohesion at the cost of increasing the influence of group bias and lowering of the quality of decisions. The groupthink hypothesis doesn't say that all decisions will be poor ones, only that there is a high probability that they will be poor. The hypothesis just shows one way that groups can get trapped within their own insular thinking and decision making process. It shows where groups are vulnerable, especially cohesive and harmonious groups which can very easily create their own information filters and allow biases to influence them.

When a group of people such as managers share a similar background, then there is danger of the groupthink phenomena occurring. This may be the case in many businesses and particularly of the Chinese SMEs in South-East Asia. This situation can impair the ability of the company to grow and change into new trajectories. Diversity of thinking in strategy is needed in environments that change quickly because of changing consumer demand, technologies, and intense competition (Hambrick 1995).

The important lesson from the groupthink hypothesis is to understand the steps that can be taken to avoid this phenomenon. There are many methods that can assist groups avoid biases and selected patterning[106]. After the Bay of Pigs fiasco, the then US President John F. Kennedy took steps to avoid the groupthink phenomenon happening again. He used outside expertise and promoted the thorough questioning of different viewpoints, both within the closed group and outside the group in departmental sub-groups. John F. Kennedy was also deliberately absent at some meetings to allow a freer flow of opinions and prevent group bias towards his own thinking (Janis 1972 pp. 148-149).

Group problem solving can be very useful, particularly when a group is socially diverse and '*cognitive diversity*'[107] can exist and operate. A diverse and functioning group can greatly enhance the problem solving because greater knowledge is available, more ideas can be generated with better evaluation, an improved ability to find errors and a wider diversity of experience. Under the right circumstances, group thinking has much superior capabilities than individual thinking (Klein 1999, P. 245).

---

[106] Janis (1982) suggested that a number of processes be included in group processes to eliminate the pitfalls of groupthink and develop more impartiality. These steps include; assigning each member of the group the role of a critical evaluator, higher people should abstain from expressing opinions when assigning tasks to the group, several independent groups should be set up to bring in more ideas and points of view, all alternatives should be examined, each member should discuss the issues with trusted people outside the group, invite outside experts to give their opinions, and a group member be assigned the role of 'Devil's advocate'.

[107] See section on multiple intelligence in this chapter.

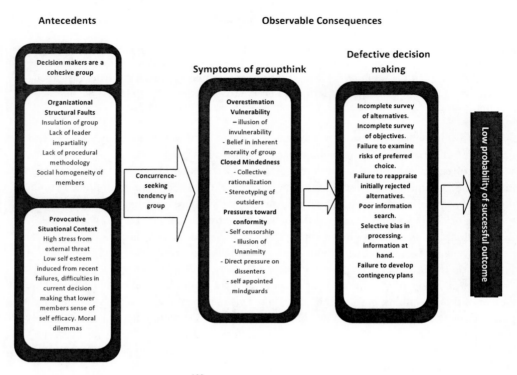

Figure 3.30. The Groupthink Process[108].

Motivational Bias

Motivational biases are another group of mechanisms that influence perception and decision making. Unlike defence mechanisms which tend to be emotionally driven and cognitive biases (discussed later in this chapter) which are based on what someone expects to see, motivational biases are based upon what someone wants to see. Motivational biases occur when a person has an interest in reaching certain conclusions or see things go a certain way. Motivational biases can be both unconscious and conscious phenomena, where in some cases a person is aware of the bias in their thinking, i.e., *'plain wishful thinking' may motivate perception and decisions*.

Motivation influences perceptions and decisions made in most areas of life. For example, people in a high income bracket may have a negative attitude towards the poor and blame them for their own plight, while people in a low income bracket may see poverty as a situational factor such as government failure (Sinha, Jain & Pandey 1980). People who are declared bankrupt tend to blame the petitioner and not themselves (Lerner & Miller 2001).

Motivational biases are built into occupations, where for example an architect will tend to under or over estimate the materials required as the situation requires and the building contractor may tend to overestimate the materials required because there is an interest in building a strong structure (Vick 2002, P. 218). Technical experts may under-estimate

---

[108] Modified from Janis (1982, P. 244)

potential risks with technologies they are familiar with in their own disciplines (Burgman 2005, P. 89). Salespeople may have a tendency to underestimate their sales budgets if incentives are based on those figures. Loyal employees of a company may make decisions which they feel may please their superiors. Upper management may lower risk probabilities in annual reports for the benefit of stakeholders. People may stick to a particular line of argument, rather than agree to change because they believe that maintain the same cause of action is the most beneficial for the firm. Likewise, public figures will be reluctant to give credence to alternative views in the risk of been seen as weak (Morgan & Henrion 1990, P. 142). Ego-centric people may just want to impress others that they are knowledgeable about a subject area.

Motivational biases are present in our self-view of the world. Taylor and Brown (1988) see motivational bias as part of healthy cognition, as it assists with making quick decisions in life. Motivational biases often disappear when a person is depressed (Alloy & Abramson 1979) and when they are asked to estimate the probability of the same events happening to others (Mirels 1980).We tend to overestimate our skills and abilities and influence on *'making things happen'*, even if we have no influence at all over the event (Weinstein 1980). This boosts our self-esteem, which may be a very important aspect of opportunity. An underestimate of one's success could bring apathy about potential opportunities, resulting in missing out (Evans, Heuvelink & Nette 2003). Without seeing ourselves as capable people we would not have any confidence to take up any new opportunities.

Motivational biases are often difficult to detect as they are well concealed. Looking at ourselves is very difficult, just like a fish trying to see water. Each of us believes that we take an objective view of the world and impartial, while others are partial and biased (Pronin, Lin & Ross 2002). One should be vigilant in looking for motivational biases in external information like conference papers, newspaper and consultant's reports where the authors' may have a vested interest in them. It is a very common situation where a person has a *vested interest* or *conflict of interest* that is not obvious to his/her audience.

Motivational Biases affect cognition in both perception and thought. Motivational emotion combines with cogitative processes to help form judgments (Kruglonski 2001). Sometimes motivational biases can challenge cognitive biases in an antagonistic manner. Put in Freudian terms, the rational *super-ego* and the logical *ego* conflict with the impetuous and passionate *id.* This conflict can lead to several types of neurosis that undermine and disrupt adaptive functioning. Therefore in modern psychology the cure of neurosis echoes the victory of reason over desire, *i.e., ego and super-ego forces winning over the id* (Freud 1923). Therefore all cognition must have some motivational underpinning in certain circumstances[109].

Motivational factors act to direct cognitive activity according to interest: giving great weight to desirable information and low weight to undesirable information (Kruglanski & Webster 1991). Therefore motivational biases can be seen as a kind of cognition itself. A motivational bias is an intrinsic knowledge structure, a schema which can be activated through semantic priming from cognition, resulting in human judgment (Kriglanski 2001, P. 42).

---

[109] Both Petty and Cacioppo's (1986) Elaboration Likelihood Model (ELM) and Chaiken and Eagly's (1989) Heuristic-Systematic Model (HSM) assume where an individual's motivation toward a topic is high they will engage in different cognitive processes in making judgments, than individuals whose motivation towards a topic is low.

Tiredness and Complacency

A leader after a period of time often becomes tired and complacent. This is very common in founder/entrepreneurs who have led a company from initial start-up and corporate leaders who have been in their position for a long period of time[110]. The phenomena of complacency can be seen as a major reason contributing to the changeover of governments at elections within some democratic systems[111]. After some time, governments become perceived as being out of new ideas, tired, complacent and arrogant, where they are voted out of office.

Complacency is a characteristic that gradually sets into a person who becomes very comfortable, gets bored, and is tired of the same issues and problems each day. Past success tends to bring high self confidence in people, where they are satisfied with their success and wish to *'rest on their laurels'*. Sometimes this over confidence brings arrogance. Leaders believe that they know all there is to know about the market and cease to scan the environment for new threats and opportunities. Within this scenario, motivation will slowly decline and new ideas, self discipline, general focus and concentration will wane. The leader's complacency will eventually spread to the rest of the organization where subordinates also lose interest, their sense of creativity, motivation and passing of information around the organization. This affects general productivity, customer service, supplier and other stakeholder relationships.

Complacent people never see themselves as complacent as they are proud of their past success, believe that they are invincible and that life will go on as it is. In an organizational context, the meaning of its very existence and the qualities which gave it the original success start eroding. The company will begin falling behind its competitors without company members really realizing it. The ambition to do new things lessens, opportunities and threats start being ignored, and a bias for action becomes a bias for complacency – the opposite quality to what made it once successful. Complacency is a state of mind and becomes a screen hiding the environment. The founder/manager becomes personally scared of the consequences of any change that involves taking risks again.

Judith M. Bardwick (1995) argued that complacency has seeped into Western corporations through the loss of traditional work ethics. The work culture that has evolved since the 1950s has developed a number of informal ways in which people avoid taking risks. Organizations have developed bureaucracies, hierarchies, rules and procedures which make people comfortable, where good, bad, and no performance are all treated the same. People are encouraged to do *'pseudowork'* to look good (Bardwick 1995, P. 25), following rules rather than achieving goals[112]. People look at their leaders for direction rather than building strategy upon the environmental situation.

---

[110] It is not uncommon for shareholders to dismiss a founder CEO from his/her position, even where the company was formed from this person's ideas and they were responsible for the company's early successes. One example is in Australia where Jim Penman, the founder of the highly successful Jim's Mowing Group, which owned 28 different franchises, faced being forced out of the company through a franchisee referendum, resulting from a class action.

[111] This can be clearly seen in countries like Australia, New Zealand, Britain, Italy, US Congress majorities and the Presidency. In East Asia the KMT Government was defeated a few years ago by the opposition, only to return again in another election. In Japan the LDP Government which ruled for the last 50 years was defeated by the opposition.

[112] Bardwick (P. 27) explains pseudowork as forming committees to examine issues, holding meetings, where the appearance of being busy is all that is important. Long reports which nobody reads are prepared and follow up

Complacency is based on fear and anxiety about being helpless and having no control over what is happening. People seek power over others to protect their own existence through controlling their immediate internal environment. This leads to ignoring the outside environment where strategy becomes very passive due to denial of change and the wish to cling to the present (Bardwich 1995, P. 41). People use up all their psychic energies to cope with the anxiety and fear of feeling helpless. This brings on narcissism, paranoia, rigidity, cynicism and politics where people become too *burned-out* to deal with the external environment.

John Kotter (2008) elaborated of the concept of *pseudowork* and described a phenomenon opposite to complacency called *'false urgency''*. *False urgency* is a situation where the organization is busy undertaking tasks for things that are not important to its progress or survival. *False urgency* takes up a lot of energy for what many see as causeless activities. Employees become angry, anxious, frustrated and tired. Similarly, leaders who continually drive their staff to higher and higher levels of activity, drain their energy until fatigue sets in. Both these situations takeaway focus from the environment where potential threats and opportunities that may emerge are not seen, and if seen, ignored.

Complacency can be widely seen in many government departments, where there are no alternative services available to the client. Complacency was tackled through benchmarking and customer quality programs in the 1980s. Complacency can also be seen in industries that are highly regulated and/or a near monopolistic or oligopolistic situation exists. Examples include telephone services, which held monopolies before deregulation and the advent of mobile services, the post office, before the advent of couriers, facsimile and email and airlines and public transport before deregulation and privatization was implemented.

Cognitive Traps: Heuristics, Bias, Misconceptions, Fallacies and Abstract Inferences

To handle the enormous amounts of incoming information and perform the decisions that have to be made requires some form of mechanisms that can *'short-cut'* the interpretive and decision processes (Finucane *et.al* 2000). Heuristics and biases are a means to achieving this and as a consequence have an influence on our perception and reasoning. Heuristics assist decision making under uncertainty because of insufficient information from the environment. Heuristics and other biases compensate and thus assist people in seeing potential opportunities that others don't (Gaglio & Katz 2001). They also influence how strategies are developed (Busenitz & Barney 1997, Mitchell *et al.* 2002, Alvarez & Busenitz 2001).

Heuristics are *'short-cuts', 'rules of thumb'*, decision rules or templates that aid quick judgments and decisions. Heuristics become embedded within our belief system. They can also be influenced by our deep motivations and reflect our social conditioning. Heuristics and other biases become intertwined within our knowledge structures and become a factor of influence in the assessments, judgments and decisions we make involving opportunity evaluation (Mitchell *et al.* 2004). They are part of the decision making process (Wright *et. al.* 2000). In effect heuristics are our programmed system of *'common sense'*.

---

rarely occurs. People lose sight of what is important and success in the marketplace is of secondary importance. Pseudowork is preoccupied with meeting schedules, rules and procedures.

Heuristics have the potential to assist the decision making process by cutting down on the person's information load (Gowda 1999). They allow a person to make quick decisions about opportunities without undertaking formal analysis which would tend to highlight problems, thus preventing its exploitation[113]. Heuristics are important when windows of opportunity are very short (Tversky & Kahneman 1974). They also help in making quick strategy choices, saving time and adding to flexibility. Heuristics make up for lack of experience (Alveraz & Busenitz 2001) and drive intuition, which is independent of inputs from the cognitive perception process (Gowda 1999). This will trigger off the creativity process by imposing an alternative reality to what is perceived through the senses.

On the negative side, heuristics can become cognitive biases. Cognitive biases are errors of judgment based on misconceptions of the facts, memory errors, probability errors, motivational factors, and/or social influences. These are the basis of irrational reasoning which can lead to all sorts of mistakes in judgment (Baron 1998). The general conditions that people work under, particularly if it an entrepreneurial environment will normally be characterized with information overload, uncertainty, strong emotions, time pressure, fatigue and the need to do unfamiliar things with little prior experience. This type of situation is a stressful one and a potential trigger for distortion in perception and reasoning. This usually occurs without a person's conscious knowledge of the fact (Wilson *et. al.* 1996). Human reliance on heuristics and biases tends to increase in busy environments described above (Gilbert, *et. al.* 1988), especially when immediate answers are required (Gilbert & Osborne 1989). This is where lots of irrelevant information works its way into the reasoning process (Chapman & Johnson 2003) and leads to cognitive biases that contribute to irrational and less than optimal decisions.

Heuristics and cognitive biases are believed to be caused by the process of *attribute substitution*. *Attribute substitution* occurs when a person has to make a judgment (of an attribute target) that is very complex. As a consequence of the complexity, the mind substitutes a more easily calculated heuristic attribute to simplify complexity (Kahneman & Frederick 2002). This occurs when the target attribute is relatively unavailable through reasoning *(answer cannot be easily retrieved through memory)*, so an associate attribute (heuristic) is substituted. This process occurs because the heuristic is easily available in memory *(i.e., a neural perception or primed in memory[114])* and this process is not detectable through the person's reflective system. The attribute substitution process combines available knowledge and experience into heuristics that drive a new idea forward.

It is very difficult to detect heuristics and biases. However they can sometimes be picked up in narrative, as phrases like *'I think', 'I feel', 'I believe', 'I reckon'* or *'it is unlikely that'*, etc. It is also very difficult to split heuristics from cognitive biases. In pragmatic terms, heuristics and cognitive biases are built upon a person's belief system. However the cognitive

---

[113] This is one area where entrepreneurial thinking may be very different from management thinking. An entrepreneur without perfect information will act on intuition and hunch. Any analysis will be mental rather than through the formal processes which managers in a company situation will tend to follow. Management analysis of new ideas will tend to frame the question; what is wrong with this idea?, why should it not be exploited?, what will be the potential problems?, etc. Thus analysis can become a very negative paradigm in management preventing new ideas emerging into new strategies.

[114] Priming occurs when an earlier stimulus influences a response to a later stimulus. For example, a person watches a television program the night before on conservation of forests. The next day someone asks the person for their views on conservation. It is likely that the person will give views and ideas that originated from the program on conservation the night before. This is assuming the person does not already have any strong views on the subject.

bias is tended to be founded on misconceptions. Table 3.24. is a list of some heuristics and Table 3.25. is a list of common cognitive biases.

Table 3.24. A List of Some Heuristics

Type of Heuristic	Description
Availability Heuristic	The tendency to recall or imagine frequently occurring and critical events more easily than less occurring events.
Hindsight Heuristic	Using the decisions made in similar events of the past as a guide to the decision.
Imitation	Use of a similar decision made previously.
Input Biases	The reliance of selective data due to availability which leads to false perception of situations.
Misinterpretation of Principal of Sampling	Thinking there is a correlation between two variables when there really isn't.
Operational Biases	A limited amount of information from the past forms the basis of a decision.
Output biases	Decision makers unconsciously influence the result.
Representativeness Heuristic	Generalization about a person or event that leads to the consideration of only a few variables.
Satisfying representativeness	The search for a solution that is acceptable to all rather than the optimal one.
Simplification	Facts about a situation are ignored to reduce the complexity of the problem.

Heuristics and biases have developed through evolution and learning. Our everyday experience continually reinforces them. In healthy situations heuristics will slowly change over time as experience confirms or disproves their validity and application to life situations. This slowly evolves our mental map so it remains relevant with the demands of the environment, so that we perceive things differently over time[115]. Peter Drucker (1994) calls vision the ultimate heuristic, our theory of how we do business. Therefore to survive in times of rapid change, our vision must also continually change.

Misconceptions

Misconceptions are false, flawed or mistaken views, opinions or attitudes. Errors and misconceptions are more likely to occur when knowledge about a specific area is inadequate and supports only partial understanding. Generalizations are needed to develop any understanding of a situation or event. This develops misconceptions which are taken as fact and used to grapple with new situations (Nesher 1987, Resnick *et. al.* 1989).

Misconceptions are wide through the community and form the basis of many heuristics and biases. They are particularly evident in the media. Tversky and Kahneman (1982) found that even professionals widely used the *representativeness heuristic* and *law of small numbers* in their work. Misconceptions can be strongly held and resistant to change (Clement 1987).

---

[115] A mental map is a mental model made up of our schema, perceptions of things, people and events, our feelings and personal points of view.

Therefore misconceptions can retard and prejudice learning as new information coming in will tend to be rearranged to support existing misconceptions.

Table 3.25. A List of Common Cognitive Biases

Type of Bias	Description
Affect Infusion	Affected states produced by one source influence judgments and decisions about other unrelated sources.
Ambiguity Effect	Avoiding options where missing information make the probability appear 'unknown'.
Anchoring	A tendency to over rely on past or irrelevant information or references in making a decision.
Attention Bias	A tendency to neglect relevant information when making decisions.
Authority Bias	A tendency to give extremely important weight to the opinions of people in authority.
Availability Cascade	A process where collective belief is strengthened through regular public discourse.
Bandwagon Effect	A tendency to do and/or believe things because many others do or believe it.
Belief Bias	Where someone's evaluation of the logical strength of an argument is biased by the believability of the conclusion.
Black Swan Effect	A tendency to be blind to random events[116].
Clustering Illusion	The tendency to see patterns when patterns do not exist.
Confirmation Bias	A tendency to search of look for information that confirms one's own preconceptions.
Congruence Bias	The tendency to test one hypothesis without considering possible alternative hypothesis.
Consistency Bias	Remembering previous attitudes and behaviour as present attitudes.
Contrasting Effect	Enhancing or diminishing the importance of a measurement when compared with another object.
Counterfactual Thinking	A tendency to imagine what might have been the case, given a particular situation.
Distinction Bias	A tendency to evaluate two options as more dissimilar when they are evaluated together than when they are evaluated separately.
Egocentric Bias	The desire of a positive image.
Endowment Effect	Where people demand much more for giving up an item than they would be willing to pay to acquire it.
Escalation of Commitment	A tendency to keep on investing time, effort and money in losing courses of action because of the initial commitment.
Expectation Bias	The tendency to believe data that agrees with a person's expectations and discard data that is outside their expectations.
Exposure Effect	A tendency for people to express a liking for something only because they are familiar with it.
Framing Effect	Where presenting a problem in a different way (frames) will lead to a different conclusion.
Fundamental Attribution Bias	A tendency for people to over emphasize personality based explanations for behaviour observed in other people while under estimating situational influences.
Halo Effect	The tendency for people to make attributions about something based on past performance[117].
Hawthorne Effect	A tendency for people to perform or perceive differently when they know they are being observed.
Hindsight Bias	Seeing past events as being predictable .i.e., 'I knew it all along'.
Hyperbolic Discounting	A tendency for people to have a preference for an immediate pay out rather than a delayed pay out.
Illusionary Correlation	A belief that there is a relationship between two factors (a correlation) when there isn't.
Illusion of Control	A tendency for people to believe they control or have influence over certain outcomes where they do not.

[116] See Nassim Nicholas Talab (2007), The Black Swan, New York, Random House Inc.
[117] See: Phil Rosenzweig (2007), The Halo Effect, London, Pocket Books, pp. 51-64.

Impact Bias	A tendency for people to overestimate the length or intensity of influence of some type of event, effect or happening.
Information Bias	The tendency to seek information although the extra information does not affect any decision.
Irrational Escalation	A tendency to make irrational decisions based upon past rational decisions or justify decisions already made.
Law of Small Numbers	Where a person uses a limited number of population data and generalizes it over a much larger population.
Loss Aversion	The disutility of giving up something that is greater than the utility associated with acquiring it.
Need for Closure	A need to reach a conclusion in a matter to reduce the feeling of doubt and uncertainty.
Neglect of Probability	A tendency to ignore probability when making a decision under uncertainty.
Observer Expectancy Effect	Where a researcher expects a given result and unconsciously manipulates or misinterprets the data to achieve that result.
Omission Bias	The tendency to judge effects as being more harmful than they actually are.
Optimism Bias	A tendency to be over optimistic about the outcomes of planned actions.
Ostrich Effect	Ignoring something obvious in a negative situation.
Overconfidence Bias	A tendency to overestimate one's knowledge and ability to do a task.
Planning Fallacy Bias	A tendency to underestimate the time it will take to complete a project, to overestimate how much can be completed in a given time or underestimate the amount of funds required for the task.
Positive Outcome Bias	A tendency to believe that good things usually happen to them.
Post Purchase Rationality	A tendency to persuade oneself through rational argument that a previous purchase was the right decision.
Prediction Bias	When people place too much importance on one aspect causing error in making accurate predictions.
Primacy Effect	A tendency to weight initial events more than subsequent events.
Professional Bias	A tendency to look at things according to the ideas of one's own profession without considering broader points of view.
Projection Bias	A tendency to unconsciously assume that others share the same or similar thoughts, beliefs, values or positions.
Recency Effect	A tendency to weight recent events more than earlier events.
Recollection Bias	A tendency to recall past decisions and events as more rational than they really were.
Restraint Bias	A tendency to overestimate one's ability to show restraint in a matter or happening.
Rosy Retrospection	The tendency to rate past events more positively than they had actually rated them when the event occurred.
Self Serving bias	A tendency to claim responsibility for successes but not failures.
Selective Perception	A tendency for an expectation to influence perception.
Status quo Bias	A tendency for people to like things to stay relatively the same.
Stereotyping	A tendency to see someone and assign them traits and characteristic based on either generalization or prejudice.
Von Restorff Effect	A tendency for something that 'stands out' to be remembered.
Wishful Thinking	Making decisions according to what the person wants to happen or imagines rather than according to evidence of alternative outcomes.
Zero-Risk Bias	A tendency to reduce a small risk to zero.

Table 3.26. Some Common Types of Fallacies

Fallacy	Description
Ad hominen	An argument that attacks the person who holds a view rather than the view itself.
Appeal to Authority	Where something is deemed to be true just because of the position of the person asserting it.
Appeal to emotion	An argument made to appeal to the emotions of prejudice, what might be pleasing and desirable (i.e., utopian), bitterness and spitefulness or flattery to gain support.
Appeal to probability	An argument that assumes because it can happen, it will happen. Murphy's law is an appeal to probability.
Appeal to Ridicule	An appeal through emotion where an opponent's argument is made to look ridiculous.
Appeal to tradition	Where something is deemed correct because of the tradition behind it.
Argument by Repetition	When an argument has been discussed extensively and nobody wants to discuss it anymore.
Argumentum ad populum	Where something is claimed to be true just because many people believe it to be true.
Base Rate fallacy	An argument using weak evidence to make a probability judgment, often excluding empirical statistics about the probability.
Cherry Picking	Using selective cases to confirm a particular position while ignoring the bulk portion of the data.
Correlation does not imply causation	Where a correlation between two items does not imply causation.
Existential Fallacy	An argument has two universal premises and a specific conclusion, but the premises do not establish the truth of the conclusion.
False Compromise	An argument that a compromise between two different positions is the best course of action.
False Dichotomy	Where two options are given as the only two options, where there are clearly more.
Gambler's fallacy	A belief that the outcome of a random event can be predicted from other independent events.
Historian's fallacy	An assumption the decision makers of a past event viewed the situation from the same perspective and having the same information as those analyzing the decision.
Moving the Goalpost	When evidence is presented to rebuke a specific claim and is dismissed with demands for more evidence.
Naturalistic Fallacy	An argument that natural is good and right, when this may not be the case.
Negative Proof Fallacy	When an argument cannot be proven false, it is presented as being true or because a premise cannot be proven true, then it must be false.
Package-Deal Fallacy	This assumes that because things are grouped together by culture or tradition, then they must be grouped together in that way.
Poisoning the Well	Where adverse information is released about someone in order to discredit anything they say.
Proof by Example	When an argument is given credence through an example.
Psychologist's Fallacy	When someone observing an event presupposes their own objectively.

Fallacies

A normal argument consists of one or more premises and a conclusion. An argument can be either deductive where the premises provide complete support for the conclusion or inductive where the premises provide some degree of support for the conclusion. The stronger the premises, the stronger will be the case of the argument. A good deductive argument is therefore forms a valid argument. A good inductive argument is known as a strong inductive argument. A fallacy is an error in the premise or reasoning of the argument. It is not a factual error as the premises may be correct with the conclusion in error. A deductive fallacy is a deductive argument that is invalid. Fallacies therefore have poor premises, poor support for their conclusions, use irrelevant data, or analogies or make claims that are too wide and sweeping for their related premises.

Fallacies are very common in the way we think, reason, and argue cases to both ourselves and others. Fallacies are particularly common when one is very passionate about something. Fallacies can be very persuasive and difficult to detect unless one is continually alert. They are very common in newspapers and the media. Some common types of fallacies are listed in Table 3.26. below.

Abstract Inferences

Due to our minds being saturated with information, it is impossible to remember detail. To cope with this volume of information our mind develops abstractions or generalizations, simplifying the massive information we have to deal with. Therefore throughout everyday situations inferences are made from specific things we see to help us make quick assessments and decisions. We are usually unaware of the generalizations and inferences we make.

Abstract inferences help us to unconsciously develop emotions for people, things and events. These emotions trigger thoughts that influence the quick decisions we make about these situations. For example, if we were a salesperson we probably wouldn't wait extra time for a store owner to return if we believe that *'he never orders anything anyway'*. Likewise we won't undertake extra study for an exam where we believe that *'I'm not good at this subject anyway'*. We regularly make generalizations that we rarely question. These abstractions become a type of *schema* that influences our decisions and behavior. This is the process that leads to stereotyping.

Figure 3.31. summarizes our discussion on cognitive traps. The diagram shows the various informational and cognitive mechanisms that influence decision making. When humans face repetitive or similar decision making circumstances there is a tendency for heuristics to develop through attribute substitution. However heuristics are also influenced by misconception, fallacy and abstract inferences. Where these forces are overbearing on perception, cognitive biases will develop which that distort the reasoning process. Reasoning affects both the decision making process and the construction of fallacies and misconceptions as well. When reasoning is affected by biases, the decision making phase may produce less than optimal decisions. On the positive side, heuristics can block perception, replacing it with intuition which can trigger the creative process. The vertical axis shows the volumes of types of information available and the horizontal axis shows the increasing usefulness of information for decision making purposes.

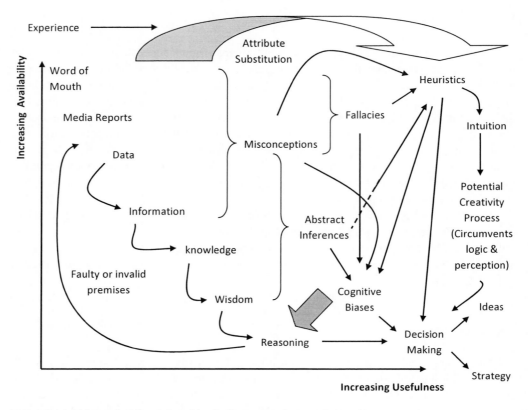

Figure 3.31. Informational and Cognitive Influences upon Decision Making.

Personality Traits, Attributes and Behavior

The exploitation of any opportunity unifies all energy, creativity, innovation, effort, skills, competencies, resources and networks into a single behavior. Researchers have tried to link this behavior with psychological traits and characteristics. Back in the 1960s researchers began looking into the concept that behavior was somehow related to a number of personality traits with the hope of answering questions like '*why do some people see opportunity, when others do not?*', ' *is there any difference between people who are entrepreneurs and non-entrepreneurs?*', and '*can a psychological profile be developed for entrepreneurs?*', etc.

Over the years a large number of personality traits have been explored and reported upon. Early work by McClelland in the 1960s postulated that the key to entrepreneurial behavior was the need for achievement as a source of motivation (McClelland 1961). According to McClelland (1967) people with a high need for achievement wanted to take responsibility for their decisions, set goals and accomplish them through their own effort. They also desire some form of regular feedback (Begley & Boyd 1987, Johnson 1990). High achievers wanted challenging tasks with concrete goals and succeed by their own efforts rather than by chance (Chell, Haworth & Brearley 1991). Based on the logic of the need for high achievement, people with this need would become entrepreneurs (Smith-Hunter, Kapp & Yonkers 2003).

However the need for achievement is not an exclusive trait for entrepreneurs and it fails to predict entrepreneurial tendencies (Sexton & Bowman 1985).

Research turned their attention to the study of the locus of control. The locus of control generally refers to a person's perceptions of the outside world and the reasons they believe are the causes of events impacting on their lives. People who believe they can control the environment through their actions have what is called and internal locus of control. Whereas people who believe they have little control of the environment have what is called an external locus of control. Generally it was believed that people with an internal locus of control would gravitate towards being entrepreneurs and people with an external locus of control would be reluctant to become entrepreneurs (Chen, Greene & Crick 1998, Sexton & Smilor 1986)[118]. Rotter (1966) hypothesized that people an internal locus of control would be more likely to strive for achievement than people with an external locus of control. Although there was much research that supported these ideas, this was not a trait exclusive to entrepreneurs and was found in people of other professions (Hull, Bosley & Udell 1980, Chen, Green and Crick 1998, Sexton & Bowman 1985).

The propensity to take financial, family or career risks are often attributed to entrepreneurs. Thus it was assumed by researchers that entrepreneurs would take moderate risks in trying to satisfy their need for achievement (Bowen & Hisrich 1988), and propensity to take risks would be higher than managers. Some research studies concluded that the propensity to take risks, among other personality characteristics was important in identifying entrepreneurial types (Hull, Bosley & Udell 1980). However many other results have shown to the contrary (Sexton & Smilor 1986). Peter Drucker (1986) took the point of view that the entrepreneurs don't take risk, they actually try and minimize risks before acting and the entrepreneur as a risk taker is a myth. Taking this view, entrepreneurs are capable risk managers who defuse risk through their knowledge and confidence of situations that others may view as high risk (Amit, Glostent & Muller 1993). Other studies have shown that the amount of risk a person is willing to take is situational upon specific conditions (Kent, Sexton & Vesper 1982) and entrepreneurs don't take any more risks than managers (Sexton & Bowman 1985).

Research on specific psychological traits did not identify any typology type profiles of entrepreneurs or any exclusive traits that would lead to the prediction of entrepreneurs. Nor did trait studies give any insights into the belief systems or behavior patterns of entrepreneurs. Behavior is too complex a phenomenon with too many factors influencing how one perceives the world, feels emotionally and perceives their own self esteem for the trait approach to explain[119]. Any psychological profile would be too theoretical and too general to have any real meaning. For example, under the Myers-Briggs description of ENTP – *(extrovert intuitive thinker and perceiver)*, a person would look for one exciting challenge after another. They would be highly inventive and their enthusiasm would lead to lots of different activities. Their inventiveness is attributable to their rich intuition which would give them a world of endless possibilities, when combined with their objective decision making facilities and

---

[118] However people with an internal locus of control may believe that fate and luck have a great influence in their lives and take action based on these beliefs. Likewise a person with a strong internal locus of control may undertake strategies that have little or no realistic chances of success due to overwhelming competition and other odds against success. Therefore locus of control cannot necessarily predict behavior and reactions of people.

[119] There are in fact about 5000 traits that make up a person's personality. Not more than half a dozen of these traits have been examined about causality with entrepreneurship.

directed outwardly converts everything to ideas and schemes. Such a *horoscope like* description really doesn't bring much deeper understanding of who is an entrepreneur and why they see opportunity, when others don't.

If one undertook several case studies of successful entrepreneurs and identified important traits that assisted in their respected successes, these traits would not necessarily be common to all cases. Therefore the study of psychological traits as a means to answer the question of *'why some people see opportunities and others don't'*, etc, should be widened to include other internal and external factors as well as situational circumstances (Gartner 1988, Ardichvili, Cardozo, Ray 2003, Smith-Hunter, Kapp & Yonkers, 2003). For example, extroversion would be a much more important trait in a situation where an employee had direct contact with customers than in a position that dealt in paperwork (Vinchur *et. al* 1998).

Each entrepreneur will have a number of positive and negative personality characteristics that will not direct behavior but be ancillary to behavior. Therefore as broad dispositions, these traits cannot be expected to be a very good predictor of individual behavior (Epstein & O'Brien 1985, P. 532). A person's general orientation, situation and personal motives also come to play in influencing behavior (Shaver & Scott 1991). A list of some commonly mentioned traits are shown in Table 3.27.

Table 3.27. Some Commonly Mentioned Characteristics of Entrepreneurs.

Ability to learn from mistakes	Foresight	Product knowledge
Able to take calculated risks	Goal orientated	Profit orientated
Aggressive	Honest	Quick decision maker
Balanced	Imaginative	Resourcefulness
Charismatic	Independent	Responsible
Committed	Influential over people	Responsive to criticism
Confidence	Initiative	Responsive to suggestions
Cooperative	Integrity	Self-reliant
Courageous	Intelligent	Sense of power
Creativity	Leadership	Sensitive
Customer orientated	Market knowledge	Sociable
Determination	Maturity	Street smart
Diligence	Need for achievement	Technical knowhow
Dynamism	Non-conformist	Thorough
Efficacy	Optimism	Tolerant of ambiguity
Efficient	Passion for work	Trustful of others
Egotistical	Perceptive	Trustworthy
Energy	Perseverance	Versatility
Flexible	Positive to challenges	Visionary

As can be seen from the list above, the traits themselves are very narrow and cannot on their own or combined predict who the entrepreneur really is and why they can see opportunities. Some traits maybe helpful in opportunity identification and venture creation but may tend to be destructive during growth and maturity stages of a business. For example, the need to control others will be very useful when the early stages of a new business must focus on production and sales. As the company grows and needs new opportunities and strategies to grow centralized control and decision making may stifle creativity and innovation within the firm. Another issue is that behavioral relationships between different traits can be totally unpredictable. For example, a self-centeredness will have influences on the locus of control, need for achievement and propensity to take risks in ways where behavior cannot be predicted, especially where situational aspects are varied between people.

Most traits also have opposites like *independent-dependent, thorough-lax, sociable-unsociable,* and *responsible-irresponsible, etc.* Many personality traits like the need for power (Peay & Dyer 1989), recklessness, over confidence and unrealistic optimism (Kidd & Morgan 1969, Laurie & Whittaker 1977), and sociopathic tendencies (Solomon & Winslow 1988), can have very counter-productive results on behavior. As mentioned, the need for control can stifle creativity and innovation. A sense of distrust of others can bare many negative consequences on the firm and other individuals (Kets de Vries 1985). Osbourne (1991) postulated that the ownership of an enterprise itself can actually corrupt and change people for the worse. People might not be driven by their traits but by their flaws, as flaws may be motivated as defence systems, discussed earlier in this chapter. For example, behind the need to achieve may be the fear of being found out (Kets de Vries 1985). People may work hard for success to compensate for failed (or failing) relationships and easily become obsessive.

The search for opportunity, subsequent strategy development and execution has multidimensional factors influencing it. Without these other multidimensional factors, psychological characteristics will not drive these processes. Opportunity is a socio-psycho phenomenon and from this point of view, the potential factors that influence entrepreneurial behavior[120] are shown in Figure 3.32.

What factors, situations and emotions determine how people behave is so complex that no diagram or explanation can cover all behavioral contingencies. However for a person to start looking with intention at ideas that can turn into opportunities and be acted upon through a set of strategies requires a *trigger situation*. A trigger situation can be activated from an external event and/or internal consideration. External events could be shocks that may occur through sudden unemployment, being overlooked for promotion or some other personal tragedy that sets the process off. This may not be a sudden response to the tragedy, as alternative courses of action like looking for another job may precede the setting off of the situational trigger. Other internal triggers may occur when a person may be dissatisfied at work, feel they can do it better or have immense difficulties working under others. This internal *'cooking'* of desire or frustration may take time and itself require some event in the workplace like being passed up for promotion or having a new ideas ignored to *'tip the balance'*.

When an idea exists and there is a *"gap"* between the present situation and the potential reality that the new idea could create, there is enough tension to activate the motivational trigger discussed in the last section of this chapter. An idea is needed to set off the situational trigger because without any idea there can be no opportunity alternatives available to the person to think about and act upon.

---

[120] There is no agreed definition of entrepreneurship. For the purpose of these arguments we are interested in behavior towards exploiting opportunities through selected strategies.

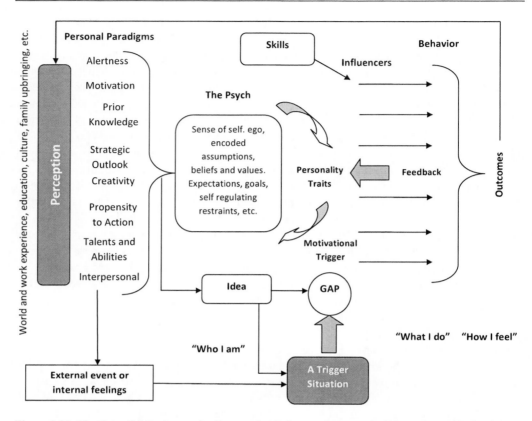

Figure 3.32. The Potential Socio-psycho Factors that Influence Opportunity Discovery and Behavior.

Acting as a filter through our perception mechanisms is a group of attributes called *personal paradigms. Personal paradigms* act to pattern or filter information going into the psych where cognitive decision making processes take place. The author believes that it is these *personal paradigms,* which are particular attributes related to how opportunity is seen, appraised and acted upon, have great influence over our decision making and behavior. They are a buffer between our internal and external world where *'what we see'*, *'how we feel'*, and *'what we think'*, relates back to our *personal paradigms.* A brief description of some *personal paradigms* follows below;

- *Alertness* or entrepreneurial alertness (Kirzner 1973) is the ability to be sensitive to information about objects, incidents and patterns in the environment where ideas and potential opportunities can be constructed. To perceive potential opportunities there must be a heightened perceptual and cognitive alertness (Ray & Cardozo 1996). Without alertness, any information will not gain any cognitive attention and be forgotten almost immediately. Alertness is a product of our psych and the environment (Shapero 1975, Sathe 1989, Hisrich 1990, Gaglio & Taub 1992).
- *Motives* push people to perceive, think and act in specific ways that attempt to satisfy needs (Larsen & Buss 2005, P. 339). Motives often stay unconscious in a person, as the person doesn't know exactly what they want, yet these motives remain powerful

influence behind thoughts, feelings and behaviors (Barembaum & Winter 2003). People differ in their types and strength of motives, taking them on different lifetime journeys with different outcomes. For example, Anita Roddick, the founder of The Body Shop may have been personally committed to the environment, education and social change, while Jack Welch and Bill Gates were more motivated by competition and winning, leading to completely different types of organizations and operational philosophies, while all being considered more than successful. Motivation is also situational where for example one can see the higher rates of entrepreneurship among migrant populations in developed countries (Kloosterman & Rath 2003). Studying motives can assist in answering the question of *'why people do what they do?'*

Motivation is not static. There are two sets of motivational factors. The first set that motivates a person initially usually involves need, responsibilities and obligations that may have arisen from some form of trauma like job retrenchment. A second set of motivators come into influence once a person has established something and involves motivational factors related to the tasks themselves. These higher order motivations have a lot to do with achievement, satisfaction, recognition and fulfillment. Motivational goals often keep moving as one progresses thus maintaining tension and drive in the person. For example, an original motivation may have been to serve a particular geographic area, but as time goes along, ambitions and motivations grow to new and larger areas. When one does meet a goal or objective, then that goal or objective ceases to be a motivator and complacency can set into the person. A list of common motivational factors is listed in Table 3.28.

Motivation appears to come from the ego portion of the psych (Bolton & Thompson 2003, P. 78.). The ego gives a person a sense of purpose and this is where *'the urge to make a difference'*, *'to be respected'*, *'to be admired'*, *'to be wealthy'*, *'to be successful'*, *'to control others'* and *'to be the best originates'*. The ego holds emotions of self esteem, the sense of achievement, envy, greed, hate, anger, anxiety, fear, guilt and empathy which are the building blocks of motivators.

- *Prior knowledge* is information and knowledge a person accumulates over a period of time (Von Hippel 1994). Prior knowledge assists a person discover opportunities as it patterns incoming information with familiar knowledge already known. This recognizes the specific value of incoming information in the light of prior information. Shane (1999) postulates that a person will tend to discover only opportunities related to their own prior knowledge. Thus people without specific prior information related to incoming information will not see the same opportunities as those that have (Kirzner 1997). As everybody's prior information has its own idiosyncrasies, each person will have their own unique *'knowledge corridor'* that allows them to see certain types of opportunities but not others (Hayek 1945, Ronstadt 1988).

  In relation to opportunity, there are three dimensions of prior knowledge; 1. Prior knowledge of markets, 2. Prior knowledge of ways to serve markets, and 3. Prior knowledge of customer problems (Ardichvilli, Cardozo & Ray 2003). This can be further broken down two areas. The first is knowledge of special interests to a person, which can provide them with profound insights into their special interest areas. The second area is knowledge accumulated from their work experience over a number of years (Sigrist 1999). When information from the first area is mixed with information from the second area, new insights may be gained which lead to the discovery of unique opportunities. For example, a salesperson that goes yachting every weekend may discover unique business opportunities related to the leisure sailing industry through the mixing of both phases of his or her prior knowledge.

- *The strategic outlook* paradigm is concerned about vision, the ability to recognize and evaluate opportunities by turning them into mental scenarios, seeing the benefits, identifying the types and quantities of resources required and weight up all the issues in a strategic manner. A vision helps a person focus upon the types of opportunities suited to their disposition. This sense of vision is guided by their assumptions, beliefs and values within the psych. Vision has varying strengths in different people depending upon their ego characteristics and motivations. The ability to spot and evaluate opportunities is closely linked with a person's creativity paradigm, their propensity to action and their perceptions of their own talents and available skills. According to Bolton and Thompson (2003, pp. 92-93) entrepreneurs spot particular opportunities and extrapolate potential achievable scenarios within the limits of their skills and ability to gather resources to exploit the opportunity. These extrapolations from opportunity to strategy require both visual/spatial and calculative thinking skills at a strategic rather than detailed level.

  Adequate concentration is required in order to have a strategic outlook upon things. This requires focus in strategic thinking, creativity, ego values and interpersonal paradigms. Too little focus will result in random jumping from potential opportunity to opportunity without undertaking any diligent mental evaluations. Too much focus may result in narrow mindedness and even obsessive thinking which would result in either blindness to many potential opportunities or action without truly "objective" evaluation. Table 3.29. below shows the potential effects of focus on behavior.

- *The element of creativity* expresses itself through other facets and talents. It is a competence that gives a person the ability to make connections between unrelated things, thus creating new ideas, concepts through what can be called an innovation. Creativity is the element that creates opportunity constructs from the fusion of external stimuli and internal information or prior knowledge of the person. Creativity develops innovation which becomes an element behind most opportunities, problem solving, combining resources, generally using talents and skills, and in overcoming barriers and obstacles. Motivation is required to drive creativity and focus maximizes the sensitivity of creativity. Creativity will be discussed in much more detail in the next chapter.

- In Tom Peters and Robert Waterman's seminal book *'In Search of Excellence'*, they listed *'a bias for action'* as the first of their eight basic principles. *'A bias for action'* is a preference for doing something rather than getting into the inertia of doing nothing (Peters and Waterman 1982). Many people spot opportunities but for various reasons fail to do anything about them. The propensity for action is about energy, both cognitive and physical to act upon a perceived opportunity. Cognitive energy is required during the mental evaluation stage and physical energy is required to actually put strategies into effect. Without any propensity for action, no other personal paradigm will have any constructive effect.

- *Personal talents* are natural aptitudes, abilities, skills and intelligence to assist a person pursue their life goals according to their interests, motivations and contexts (Moon 2003). Talents according to Cattell (1966) are almost fully inherited. *Abilities* are also aptitudes, skills and intelligence to enable someone to do physical or mental things, but are developed through lifetime learning. Talents and some abilities through learning can be developed into excellence. To utilize and enhance talents and abilities a person must have temperament, attitude, motivation, and interest (Allen 2003, P. 388). Temperament encompasses the ability to manage talent and maintain perseverance. Many talented careers, particularly in sport and the performing arts fail because of the wrong attitudes and temperament. Personal talents and abilities link closely with the personal creativity paradigm and may act as both an anchor and a primer for creative action. Personal talents and abilities may also heighten patterning attention towards stimuli and information close to a person's span of talent and ability areas.

- *The interpersonal paradigm* will almost directly influence how large an opportunity a person may consider, dependent on their ability to communicate, collaborate, and work with others. Those with extrovert personalities and leadership qualities are able to bring others onboard and acquire talents and abilities they themselves lack. This means that a person can generally imagine larger potential opportunities because in their assumptions exists the possibility of building large organizations, than would be the case if they were considering or only comfortable working by themselves. How people view others is partly influenced by how they tend to view trust. Those people who tend to be trusting of others will tend to build organizations that may be more open for creativity and innovation than those that are built on assumptions of mistrust of people.

For the purpose of entrepreneurial behavior, the ego drives a person. This is especially so in the creativity, strategic outlook, motivation, alertness and propensity for action paradigms. A very weak ego would lead to a sense of apathy, where a strong ego would lead to a much stronger sense of self. Without a healthy ego, talents and abilities would be wasted. The ego provides our temperament and influences our basic assumptions, beliefs and values. On our external side, the ego along with the rest of the psych forms our personality traits. The world sees us through our personality traits and to a certain degree our traits along with our psych are precursors to our behavior[121].

Bolton and Thompson (2003) describe the ego as having two parts. The inner part of the ego is concerned about our internal manifestations of self assurance, dedication and motivation. The inner ego produces our interest and passion about things and is the psychic driver of a person. The facets of the outer ego are more behavioral and concern more about a person's outward qualities. These qualities include a person's sense of responsibility, accountability and courage. Courage is perhaps the element that makes one feel confident, face reality and stand up to their beliefs and values. The ego tends to be shaped by our self perceptions, experience and unconscious primitive drives and basic morality.

---

[121] However as we have seen the relationship between our traits, psych and behavior is extremely complex.

Table 3.28. Some Common Motivational factors[122]

Motivator	Description
Achievement	A need to master, manipulate, organize and arrange objects, people and events in an accomplished way by overcoming obstacles and excelling.
Exhibition	A need to be seen and heard by others and be the centre of attention and make an impression on others.
Order	A need to put things in an orderly arrangement, balance and in precision.
Dominance	To seek and direct the behavior of others by persuasion, command, coercion or seduction. To seek to control the environment.
Abasement	To accept injury, criticism and blame. To submit to the force of others and resign yourself to fate. To admit wrong doing, inferiority and error.
Aggression	To overcome any opposition forcibly. To avenge injury and hurt with attack and oppression.
Autonomy	To maintain free of others restraints, to break out of confines, to be one's own master.
Blame-avoidance	To avoid blame and humiliation at all costs, to avoid situations that may lead to embarrassment, to refrain from action because of fear of failure.
Affiliation/Intimacy	To seek cooperation with others, to draw near and close to others, to win affection of others, to be liked to develop loyalty and receive loyalty from others.
Nurturance	To take care of others in need, to give sympathy and gratify the needs of helpless others.
Succor	To receive help from other, to have one's needs gratified by another, to be indulged, nursed, supported and protected by others.

Our perceptions, experience, prior knowledge and psych help shape *"who I am"* though a continual molding and shaping process. When set off by a trigger, our perceptions, psych, traits and skills combine to form ideas and some behavioral response, *"what I do"*, which produces certain outcomes. As we produce outcomes, we measure them against our personal goals and go back through our perception system as feedback or *'how we feel"*.

A person reacts to the environment they are within. However it is impossible to predict the behavior that will come from the combination of the personality and environment. Predicting behavior is difficult because all behavior is situational upon the environment. In other words, behavior is both personality and environmentally dependent.

Not only is behavior environmentally influenced, a person with a particular personality leaning will attempt to seek out or create an environment that is suitable to them (Scarr & McCartney 1983). For example, an introvert will seek a quiet, unobtrusive environment which is secluded and personal, where an extrovert will prefer a social environment with interpersonal interaction. Personal paradigms are not static, their will shift in their influence and dominance over times and according to life circumstances (Mitchell 1993).

Finally, personality can act as a type of memory filter. People tend to remember things that are compatible with their personality traits. Therefore a person with a calm and non-

---

[122] Adapted from Murray, H. A. (1938). Explorations in Personality, New York, Oxford University Press.

confronting disposition will remember events that promote these attributes, rather than conflicting and divisive situations (Larsen & Buss 2005, P. 186).

Table 3.29. The Potential Effects of Focus on behavior

Variable	Absent Focus	Mean Focus	Extreme Focus
Strategic Outlook	Switch off, insensitive to environment, blind to opportunity.	Able to spot opportunities, work towards exploiting them, able to see required resources and identify potential sources.	Look in too much detail so fail to get overview or big picture.
Creativity	Unimaginative	Able to think both laterally and serially and construct opportunities.	Over-imaginative, lose sight of big picture.
Ego Values	Purposelessness not interested.	Able to contemplate some form of action with some form of motivators driving ego.	Self-delusion, delusions of grandeur.
Interpersonal	Individualistic and independent.	Able to communicate and work within social sphere.	Hesitant to take responsibility, dependent.
Overall	Random scanning of environment, jump from opportunity to opportunity, apathetic.	Focused on opportunity possibilities and drawbacks. Orientated towards action.	Tunnel vision, fanatical and/or blindness.

Entrepreneurial Typologies

With the disappointment with the traits approach not being able to predict who would become an entrepreneur, some researchers looked at typologizing entrepreneurs as a way to understand anchor traits, value systems, and thinking for given typologies of entrepreneurs (Filion 2004, P. 325). Typologies can be considered theories that can be modeled according to traits and variables into a synthesized conception of an entrepreneur type (Miner 1997).

Landau (1992) proposed that entrepreneurs could be classified according to their innovative and risk bearing characteristics and proposed four basic typologies. The consolidator is a person who develops a business on a low innovation, risk bearing platform and aims to consolidate and slowly improve, usually bringing low returns. The gambler is characterized by a low degree of innovation and high level of risk where he or she takes big chances in what they do, but is able to deliver through breakthroughs if successful. The dreamer attempts to combine a high level of innovation with a low level of risk. However without risk the dream can never be realized. The entrepreneur takes a high level of risk and innovation and succeeds on the basis of how they are able to manage the risk. Research has also focused on the typologies of the entrepreneur as a craftsman with a blue collar and limited educational background, who prefer technical work and are motivated by the want of personal autonomy, and opportunists who are well educated and motivated by building a successful organization and financial gains (Woo & Cooper 1991). Another typology is an inventor-entrepreneur who has a strong commitment for new product development and rapid market entry with an orientation towards the future (Miner, Smith & Bracker 1992).

Siu (1996) developed five typologies of entrepreneurs in China; the senior citizen, who seeks to work by him or herself, the workaholic, the swinger who jumps from deal to deal, the idealist who tends to think in longer timeframes, and the high flyers. Jones-Evans (1995) suggested four technical categorizations of entrepreneurs. The research based technical entrepreneur is in a research environment where his or her ideas have been incubated for a long period of time. He or she is purely a research based entrepreneur without much business experience. The producer technical entrepreneur is an individual who has some exposure to business decision making, probably within manufacturing. The user technical entrepreneur is an individual whose main experience is commercially based with some technical background, and the opportunist entrepreneur is one who has no previous exposure to technology but has seen a commercial opportunity.

Although typologies are not absolutes, as individuals may have characteristics from more than one typology, a good typology fit can be predictive of behavior. The typology approach can be widened to include any number of potential typologies to describe an entrepreneur and the way they seek and exploit opportunities. Some examples of potential typologies may include;

- The entrepreneur as a gamesman,
- The entrepreneur as an actor,
- The entrepreneur as a creator,
- The entrepreneur as a scene artist,
- The entrepreneur as a visionary,
- The entrepreneur as a dreamer,
- The entrepreneur as a salesman,
- The entrepreneur as a hustler,
- The entrepreneur as an administrator,
- The entrepreneur as a soloist,
- The entrepreneur as a team player,
- The entrepreneur as an innovator,
- The entrepreneur as an empowerer,
- The entrepreneur as an industrialist,
- The entrepreneur as an acquirer,
- The entrepreneur as a trader,
- The entrepreneur as a transformer,
- The entrepreneur as an adventurer,
- The entrepreneur as an intrapreneur,
- The entrepreneur as a crusader,
- The entrepreneur as an evangelist,
- The entrepreneur as a conglomerator, and
- The entrepreneur as a speculator.

The traits, styles, types of strategy, types of appropriate preferred businesses and strategies, timeframes, etc. would be specific to the stated typology and suited to different types of opportunities and entrepreneurship.

The typologies approach provides some understanding of an individual's skills, abilities, and personal competencies, and their strengths and weaknesses. Typologies also enable a judgment about an entrepreneur's style and approach to opportunity and venture development.

Power and Conflict

So far it has not been possible to establish a psychological profile that can explain the behavior of an entrepreneur. When research focused on personality characteristics in an attempt to find the entrepreneurial typology back in the 1980s, the need for power was a neglected trait.

One of the early pioneering researchers on motivation factors during the 1950s and 60s was Harvard psychology professor David McClelland. While best known for his work on the need for achievement (nAch), it was one of his students David Winter carried on McClelland's early work on the need for power (nPow). Winter (1973) defines the need for power as readiness or urge for having an impact on other people. This urge is assumed to influence behavior when opportune occasions develop. People with a need for power would be expected to hold firmly to their ideas if opposed by others, take higher risks in gambling situations and tending to behave assertively in groups. They would be more inclined according to Winter (1973) to seek "prestige" objects and privileges like luxury cars, club memberships and gain positions of respect through election to public or society office, etc. The need for power creates a desire to influence and lead others. A person's thinking and perhaps fantasy would be concerned with how to influence others, set trends, win arguments, control agendas and be an opinion leader (Kirkpatrick & Locke 1991). If the need for power influences peoples' behavior then opportunity discovery and any corresponding strategy development may not be completely rational processes.

There are two basic motives behind the need for power (Hornaday & Aboud 1971). The first is the personalized power motive where a person sees power as an end in itself. These people have little self control over their impulses. They focus almost solely on gaining the trappings of prestige such as position, status, high profile, authority and control over others, etc. Their main objective is to gain power over others just for the sake of having power over others. Behind this motivation is a deeply profound sense of self-doubt and lack of self-efficacy, where through the domination of others they seek personal gratification to deny their own self doubts.

In contrast, a person may have a socialized power nature of desire which is linked to their personal desires to make a positive difference. They seek to lead others in a mission to achieve a vision or set goals by encouraging cooperation, resolving conflicts and generally encouraging others to work together in striving for these goals. Rather than dominate and suppress others, a person with socialized power will attempt to empower others. Individuals with socialized power nature tend to be more emotionally mature than those with a personalized power nature. They exercise power for the benefit of the group and are less likely to engage in manipulative behavior. These leaders are less defensive and more prone to seek the advice of others.

On the positive side, power is a means to get things done through other people, either by persuasion or by force. In these terms it can be thought of as a resource which assists in the execution of strategies crafted to exploit opportunities. This may involve the use of power through prestige and status to utilize networks and resources that others may not have access to. When used in a positive manner power is closely related to trust, which leads to an effective running organization where people are influenced through various rewards and coercions.

However the need for power and control is a major aspect of our psych (De Vries 1989). A person's preoccupation with control affects the way power relationships are handled. Each of the two typologies outlined above may at the extreme have personality and behavioral inconsistencies. For example where power is used to create a rigid and controlled environment, this structural situation will stifle people, thus hindering creativity and innovation. Such an example would have been Xerox in the 1980s that was too rigid to be innovative in the new emerging home copier market, allowing more innovative companies to come into the market. At the other extreme where power empowers others, this environment may create numerous ideas without resulting product innovation because of indecision. The Netscape web browser once had a 90% market-share in the mid 1990s, which has fallen to less than 1% now, as the company failed to retaliate to Microsoft Explorer's advancements.

Power as a motivator can be very dangerous, especially during the early stages of firm growth. Too much power without restriction could put an organization at risk and too little power may retard a person's drive and business judgment (Wagner 1991). People with a high need for power usually have difficulty working within structures, unless they have created them. People with a high need for power do not handle frustration and conflict well. The need for power at the extreme is related to paranoia. Suspicion will motivate rigorous external and international environment scanning for evidence to confirm their suspicions. This may make an organization very externally alert for opportunities, which may be looked at in an ad hoc way, but will be damaging to the organization. Strong internal control will hinder independent action and creativity within an organization. Strong checks on behavior would exist like time clock systems which would force people to stay on site where they are better monitored. These checks would bring an environment of distrust to protect against acts of misbehavior and assist in protecting the power and authority of the boss. Meetings to make decisions would be dominated by the intuition and whims of the leader. Gamesmanship and politics would be rife in competition for favoritism of the leader, leading to sub-empires led by those in favor within the organization. With all decisions made by the leader, the organization will have trouble functioning when he is away. A cynical counter-culture would develop leading to a very dysfunctional organization.

Many organizations are run through authoritarian methods throughout the world. Most owner/managers of family firms have almost unlimited power as a result of being the owner/founder, member of the family and/or have other skills that aid in developing power and authority. There are numerous sources of power which have different implications on power can be used and how beneficial a source may be for opportunity construction and exploitation. Formal authority is based on the legal or social legitimacy one has for a position of authority. This may also be underpinned by charisma, tradition (as in royalty), the rule of law or another source of power. The control of resources is another source of power. This source may create certain opportunities for those that yield these resources and enable the implementation of strategies that others may not be able to utilize. Control of knowledge or technology is another source of power that may lead to the construction of opportunities that have a monopolistic situation for a time period until others are able to access this knowledge.

This could be tacit knowledge about something in the market environment where opportunities can be developed or technical knowledge which can be protected through intellectual property mechanisms like patents and trademarks, etc.

Where boundaries are managed or restricted by others for some reason, the person that is managed will only get a view of the world that others wish them to see. This is common for prime ministers and presidents who are insulated away from the real world and rely on others for information. Networks, peer groups and alliances are another source of power which assists in opportunity discovery, resource acquisition and strategy implementation. Networks and alliances are now a very important opportunity and strategy tool. In high technology firms with turbulent environments a technical background is important as a base of power. However as technology become more generic and the environment stable, technical backgrounds are less important. Organizations within the industry may also exercise counter power which restricts opportunity or the ability to do something. This would include government and trade unions as regulators and monopolies of resources.

Our perception of power influences how one sees goals, objectives and strategy. The need to dominate, for prestige, to influence and to be seen can run through the opportunity and strategy processes. A business may be seen by an owner as an extension of themselves and because of this will have trouble delegating authority. Organizations, especially entrepreneurial ones tend to be a primary source for a person's power needs. This may lead to the desire to build large empires that reflect their fantasies for power, as a monument to themselves and symbol of their power (Peay & Dyer Jr. 1989). However a socialized leader will understand the general intrinsic needs of his insiders such as growth for managers, moderate perpetual change for analysts, and excellence for skilled operators, etc (Mintzberg 1983, P. 182).

One's own perception of power will influence whether a company acts unilaterally with its own resources and competences or enters into a joint venture, strategic alliance or agency relationship, particularly with supply chain strategies. The sense of power may also influence the extent of risks that will be taken. This will influence decisions about technology development, expansions, diversifications, and niche verses mass market decisions. Finally the sense of self power may influence whether business is undertaken to win-win, or win-lose as a zero sum game. Multi-national approaches to strategy will thereby greatly differ from those of an SME based on a sense of power.

Politics and the balance of power within an organization is a means of resolving conflicts and arriving at decisions upon matters of importance to the organization. Most organizations are structured where conflict is inevitable because limited resources have to be shared between a number of different divisions and departments within the structure. This can be seen in an organizational chart of almost any organization where multiple divisions are pitted against each other and report to one office that yields authority over them (Burns 1961).

Processes, both formal and informal are utilized to make resource decisions within the structure. This may involve strategic planning, annual budget and management meetings as mechanisms where competing divisional managers advocate, appeal, compete, negotiate, and compromise on specific resource allocation formulas and strategies. This also infers that much of this process is informal as it is formal and the actual deals and compromises may be done outside of the formal mechanisms. This is a method for making diverging interests agree on common directions, but due to the political rather than rational approach to decision making, there is a fair chance that less than optimal decisions are made for the point of view of the organization. Logic is lost to power and conflict and compromises may override good ideas and potential opportunities.

Conflict can lead to good and bad performance, but politics leads to less than rational decision making. Whether compromise and support for a particular company direction is more effective than determination of the most effective direction is the matter of debate. A rational manager would desire to obtain a strategy that is both supported and optimal for maximum strategy effect in competitive markets. Conflict can be positive in achieving good and careful decision making, but it can also be destructive with fighting and bickering leading to stalemates or compromise strategies which provide less than optimal company positions in the market.

However, the existence of a number of points of view within an organization can aid good decision making processes. An organization without conflict can develop complacency and conformity which leads to a lackluster sense of creativity, innovation, reactivity and opportunity blindness within the organization. Healthy conflict within an organization may be reflective of the turbulent environment outside which can trigger (or gestalt) a rapid change internally. Power and conflict may be a necessary part of an organization to function (Morgan 2006, P. 150).

Genetic Inheritance

The study of behavioral genes is controversial, where researchers have been trying to determine the degree to which individual differences in personality are caused by genetic and environmental differences. For example, a person's height is determined by both genetic and environmental causes, however to what extent genetic inheritance is responsible is still unknown. In fact, both genetic makeup and environment influence a personality. Our hereditary genetic endowment influences our brain development and consequently our cognitive system (Goos & Silverman 2006). Thus genetic inheritance influences our intelligence, motor capabilities, perceptual abilities, personality and temperament, etc. This is why one will often see children and grandchildren displaying similar traits of mannerisms to their parents and grandparents.

However our cognitive traits and personality also depends upon the environment. Intelligence can be seen to run in families. However family members don't just share the same genes but the same environment, so it is really not possible to be sure of whether similarities come from the shared environment or hereditary genes. Behavior is the result of the two ingredients together, like making a jelly. What is it that makes the jelly, water and gelatin? It is a mixture of the two, where different proportions will give the final jelly different textures and hardness. Therefore jelly will differ in texture from batch to batch, and likewise family members will also differ in their cognitive traits and personality, even though they have a similar genetic and environmental background.

Twin and adoption studies provide some greater insights into the debate about hereditary and environmental influences. One can see many similarities between genetically identical twins that were separated at birth (Segal 1999). This is some indication of substantial hereditary influence on personality traits (Bouchard & McGue 1990, Tellegen *et. al.* 1988). However quantifying hereditary influence has not been conclusive. Studies examining different traits show different levels of hereditary/environmental influence. Correlations between psychopathic personality traits and inheritance were higher than traits like fearlessness (Blonigen *et. al.* 2003). Factor model studies of personality have generally shown around 40% correlation with hereditary genes (Borkenau, *et. al* 2001). Hereditary also seems to influence certain attitudes (Abrahamson *et.al.* 2002) and occupational preferences (Ellis & Bonin 2003). One of the highest correlations with hereditary studies showed up was intelligence (Bouchard 1998, Plomin & Spinath 2004), even when identical twins were separated from their parents at birth (Plomin *et. al.* 2008).

Some specific studies about hereditary genes and entrepreneurship have shown some interesting results. Recent studies have shown that that the propensity for people to become entrepreneurs is genetic rather than shared and non-shared environments, *i.e., little effect from family upbringing* (Nicolaou *et. al.* 2008). However complementary cognitive mechanisms are required such as extroversion which is also hereditable (Bouchard & Loehlin 2001). Other studies has shown that genes also affect the way that people look at the environment (Scarr 1992) and opportunity (Nicolaou *et. al* 2009), where the existence of the gene DRD4 increases salience in an individual (Volkow 2004) which assists in opportunity identification (Shane 2000).

However, although inherited genes have been identified as having some influence in personality traits, attitudes and assists in opportunity identification, studies still show that environmental influence is very important. This leads to issue of why is there a difference in people's attitudes that are shaped by the same environmental influences, *i.e., reading, books, TV, music, friends, treatment by parents, etc,* as a similar environment will not cause a similar personality in a person. It must be a combination of inherited genes and the environment (Plomin & Daniels 1987). Some researchers suggest that the critical thing that influences personality and other traits are unique experiences that an individual has – a gestalt that brings very personal insights to an individual. This puts people on specific paths in life where they pick up their own skills, attitudes and competencies. These gestalts bring very personal realizations, where no two lives are exactly the same and it is these combinations of small experience differences which shape unique personalities (Willerman 1979).

Mid Life Crisis and Transition

Through the passage of life, people go through periods of regret, remorse, and depression about their achievements and existence. Economic conditions over the last 40 years have challenged the concept of traditional employment. Today secure jobs and long term employment is less common than in the immediate post war and industrial development years (Bridges 1980). Downsizing, retrenchments, layoffs and bankruptcies are more common than ever before, creating trauma crisis and a vacuum in peoples' lives.

People develop their own self concept through their careers (Super *et. al.* 1996). Working is a form of self-expression which brings satisfaction, happiness, frustration and stress in a person's life. A person's career is an important anchor in their life, providing the basis of their own self identity. People express who they are through their skills, competencies, position, status and values. This career anchor is an important sphere of influence on a person's choices and decisions (Schein 1978, P. 125).

Abrupt career termination, job dissatisfaction, remorse about *"what one has failed to achieve"* in a person's life leads to a *"personal crisis"* and as a consequence, a transition is required[123]. According to Erikson (1968), a person also goes through a number of stages during their life where their identity, achievements and self worth are questioned. These periods whether caused by external trauma or internal self doubt and questioning lead to very strong emotional states challenging a person's reason and meaning of existence.

Personal crisis has its beginnings in adolescence where a career choice was made, that was not to a person's liking. They wanted to please their parents and fulfill their father's unmet dreams by proxy. They had taken on their father's values in their early years without really questioning whether these values are consistent with their own self identity. In later adult life a person realizes the mismatch between their own ideals and what they are actually doing (Levison 1978). This comes as a shock, as they realize time is running out and instead of doing something that has meaning to them, they are trapped in a job that brings dissatisfaction and resentment. Change is very difficult because of financial and family commitments; they are a prisoner of their own making, locked in the treadmill of life that is taking them nowhere. This can create great anxiety, depression and panic.

Up to middle age people usually focus on the external aspects of life which attracts the trimmings of career success in way of career, position, prestige, status and a reasonable standard of living for all those around them. However this is usually at the cost of the inside which is empty and neglected. Life has little meaning or emotional identity. His sacrifice of the inner self for the external world has been a costly one and a sense of grief sets in[124]. This realization can spring a set of behavioral changes as defence mechanisms against grief. This may be hostility towards his wife and children and in extreme cases result in separation and divorce. One response is to try and return to their youth and buy a sports car and take up new interests as a way to deny their emptiness.

Another reaction to the feeling of emptiness is the creation of fantasies and daydreams to help a person escape any inner feelings of depression. Melbourne psychologist Dr. Peter O'Conner (1981) found a number of recurring themes in these fantasies. Each of these fantasies represent inner struggles, represented as *"if only I"* aspirations. Each fantasy may provide some hints of how an individual can solve them, if the underlying needs can be seen.

The Farmer Fantasy is where a person visions himself controlling a farming domain where he exists with the rhythm of nature and produces crops with his own hands. There is a yearning for some feeling of integration with the land with the life as a farmer, owning, living and working the land. This fantasy represents a desire to go back to natural simplicity where satisfaction comes from producing things with his own two hands. Contrary to the hard work a farm demands this fantasy is also seen as an escape or freedom from the perceived shackled present life. The farm fantasy can also be seen as a seeking of purity and morality that has been missing. The farmer fantasy according to O'Conner (1981, P. 60) is the most common of all the fantasies.

The Nurseryman Fantasy is similar to the farmer fantasy with a greater emphasis on creation, growth and nurturing. This fantasy relates to man's need to promote the growth of living things and escape the harsh realities of everyday life, where there are many demands upon him. He has worked hard to provide things for himself and his family in his earlier life at the cost of fulfilling his inner needs. This fantasy is a wish for inner growth, which has

---

[123] Other trauma like a death of a close loved one in the family, or an event or tragedy will also bring about a crisis where transition or "moving on" is eventually required after grief and mourning.

[124] Although grief is an emotion for the loss of someone or something, the feeling of emotional emptiness and that life is coming to an end can trigger grief.

been lacking. There is also a need for self-care, intimacy and nurturing. Once these needs are realized, a person can change their lifestyle to seek what is needed. This fantasy is common in professional people.

The Helper Fantasy is about wanting to help others in some form of social work. This desire often comes after years of sacrificing the wellbeing of their family while in the pursuit of material wealth. Although the desire to help others is genuine, unconsciously this is a way of paying reparations for the neglect of their family in the past. A little deeper there may be a yearning for a relationship where they can care for and be cared for by someone. Just like the nurseryman, adjustments to lifestyle can be made to allow more time for relationships. Those who don't find intimacy go on to undertake some social work. This fantasy is common in self made, high energy, and successful people.

The Writer (or creative) Fantasy is about having the opportunity to be creative in some way. This could be the desire to write a novel, become a sculptor, a musician, a painter, potter or other creative activity. There may be a yearning to create some great piece of creative work, if only they could devote all their time to this activity. They see this as the key to ridding themselves of their despair and unhappiness. This fantasy tends to appear in intellectuals who have ignored the spontaneous and irrational side of themselves. So this fantasy is about rebalancing oneself so that there is time to just *'be oneself making sandcastles by the sea".* People are sometimes prevented from being themselves out of fear their behavior will not fit into the view that they believe people have of them. They may also fear failure which prevents them from picking up a brush, guitar or spade. This fear is denying their personal growth and psychic balance as a human being, keeping them out of touch with their creative and emotional side.

The Dropping-out Fantasy is a way of perceived escapism from grieving. This is quite a common reaction where simply dropping out is a form of regression to adolescence where one just runs away from the problem to make it go away. This fantasy may be symbolized by wanting to live on an island, a mountain, backpack through Asia or go into the outback of Australia, etc. Dropping out is about trying to find one's misspent youth again, but any relief will only be temporary as the crisis will only catch up with the person again sometime in the near future.

If the dropping out fantasy is reframed from dropping out from something to dropping into something, the process can be a constructive one. A complete reassessment of goals and priorities, seeing what their real identity could be, may lead to doing something like opening a motorbike tour operation through the Himalayas, a scuba diving tour in the Great Barrier Reef or Andaman Sea, etc. Such a change may carry considerable risk but at the same time be something that the person always wanted to do, and thus be considered a move forward.

These fantasies can all be seen as typologies not too dissimilar to Jung's archetype personalities. They are about what we aspire to be. There may be small cultural variations, but the fantasies represent some yearning or desire for change. Failure to change will lead to inertia of failure and emotional death. The feeling of *'time running out'* becomes an excuse for doing nothing, most likely leading to inner anger and disappear and eventual bitterness for the rest of their lives. However, many see the rest of their life as an opportunity and resurrect themselves as the *'hero'* that they once aspired to be. They battle with their own logic and rationality, where often rationality prevents the fulfillment of aspirations dismissing them as silly. There may be a fear of letting their emotions take over, thus transforming them into a realm that they have never experienced and thus fear. They deny their inner self.

If this is overcome, there will be change in existing relationships, the taking up of new activities or the commencement of self employment with a sense of spiritual guidance influencing their future path. Therefore it is not uncommon to see people changing jobs in their late thirties and early forties. Thus the chosen activities, whether it is a new job, a desired business activity or some form of social entrepreneurship should more closely reflect their skills, competencies and aspirations than what they were doing before their crisis. However taking up new activities and keeping oneself busy with a new hobby or venture will not solve this crisis if their fundamental fear is not faced and challenged. The inner world will remain empty and void with a feeling of continual regret and emptiness.

In these cases opportunity does not come completely from perception of the external environment but is also part of one's inner psych and suppressed self. To them any opportunity and subsequent exploitation becomes a persona of how they want to see themselves.

Women encounter their personnel crisis differently to men in many respects. A woman's early work life is basically concerned with looking after the needs of others at their own expense. After a number of years of having to balance work, childcare and family life, women look for new challenges in life and will move on from their existing careers if it is not meeting their needs (Marshall 1994). Women want to spend more time on relationships that are important to them and seek activities that reflect their own true values (Borysenko 1996).

Women during midlife appear to adopt new cognitive perspectives about their views on family, career progress and responsibilities (Borysenko 1996). This cognitive shift usually provides a new positive frame on things where success is defined in new ways[125]. Women tend to develop a more focused holistic perspective about their life's goals as they see there is no time to waste after their children have grown up and become independent and their own parents have aged (Gordon and Whelan 1998). Women see midlife as an opportunity to become involved in the world and want to make their contribution. As child care is no longer an issue, they seek to pursue both intellectual and financially rewarding challenges. Women look for challenge, the chance to live up to their true talents and abilities, which can lead to radical career change midlife. Within this frame opportunity and its exploitation becomes an expression of talents, abilities and aspirations as they would like to see themselves.

The phenomenon of personal crisis is not restricted to midlife. Situational changes will influence people to react and respond to newly perceived circumstances (Collin 1990). Crisis can occur at anytime during life, particularly when some form of trauma occurs. Trauma can occur through retrenchment or injury. Trauma may also be the result of a slow build up of job stress, career burnout, increasing or decreasing family responsibilities, a desire for control over one's destiny, or lack of challenge in a person's job. This may trigger changes in work and life values, which lead people to question and re-evaluate their life decisions, behaviors (Kanchier & Unruh 1989) and careers (Doering *et. al.* 1983), according to these new values.

Change can also occur due to a number of other factors. During a career a person may feel that they have reached a plateau where they have mastered their current job (Hall 2002, P. 122). This can lead to the questioning of a present work situation (Leong & Boyle 1997) where greater challenges are sought. Many people realize that they are looking for job achievement rather than job advancement (Zabusky & Barley 1996). There may be some realization that salary, position, status and prestige may be at the expense of their values and psychological needs, leading to a re-evaluation about their own self concept and beliefs about themselves (Fiske & Taylor 1991). This may lead to a shock which proves either positive or negative. They may see themselves as how others see them which violate their own sense of basic values, leading to shock and confusion. Consequently change becomes necessary to pursue their career goals according to their newly found values, rather than external measures of success. This may result in a want to fulfill a dream, gain control of their working life, autonomy, quality of work-life, flexibility, or work within a specific ethical framework of prime importance in their life. People may simply want to revive passion in their work. These feelings and wants are conscious rather than the unconscious fears that occur through a midlife personal crisis. People see change as a *'spiritual response'* to what they perceive outside and feel within (Gibbs 2005). Factors triggering transition are shown in Figure 3.33.

There has been a rise in job mobility in recent years due to financial need to continue working (Mirvis & Hall 1996) and a decrease of loyalty to organizations (Bridges 1994). People are staying longer in the workforce. The growing importance of professional social networks is also adding to increased job mobility and options of self employment (Saxenian 1996). High self confidence from a feeling of self mastery and strong social networks tends to make perceived market opportunities seem more viable to a person, leading to high rates of self employment in post industrial societies. Consequently contemporary outlooks about career differ greatly from more traditionally accepted outlooks over the last decades as shown in Table 3.30.

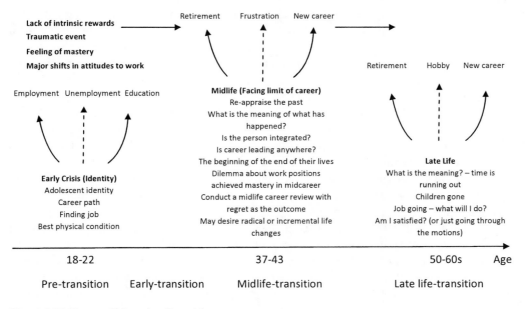

Figure 3.33. Factors Triggering Transition.

---

[125] For example, women realize the political realities and the 'glass ceiling' that exists, preventing any further promotion in their existing career. They see politics as de-motivating, energy wasting and eventually destructive, so opt for new challenges in different walks of life.

Table 3.30. Traditional and Current Outlooks towards Career and transition

Traditional Outlook	Current Outlook
Loyalty for job security	Performance for continuous learning and marketability
One or two firms during lifetime	Multiple firms during lifetime
Firm specific skills	Transferable skills
Success measured by salary, promotion and skills	Success is about psychologically meaningful work
Organization responsible for career development	Individual responsible for self career development
Milestones aged related	Milestones learning related
Authority based on position	Authority based on knowledge
Specific tasks, functions	Functions based on knowledge, expertise
External motivations, salary, position and status	Intrinsic motivations, job and task satisfaction

Imagination

The concept of imagination is deeply embedded in culture (Kearney 1988), folk psychology (Brann 1991, Sutherland 1971) and spirituality. Imagination is closely linked to vision and opportunity and may have something to do with our personal motivation. Imagination enables us to see the world as it hasn't been seen before, to see things in new ways. Imagination has helped see new scientific realities where Kepler saw the notion of the Earth revolving around the Sun, Faraday saw a magnet surrounded by a field of electromagnetic force and Darwin saw the animal kingdom as a competitive field of fierce struggle (Thomas 1999). Some people find it hard to use their own imagination fully, difficulty using the illogicality of imagination to develop the mental imagery and fantasy needed to develop new ideas (Hicks 2004, P. 56).

Imagination helps us to see patterns and similarities between unrelated things, to analogize things through metaphor, to work across our specialized intelligences, bringing them into synergy as one (Homer-Dixon 2001, P. 395). Imagination allows us to form mental images and/or semantic constructions that are not perceived through our senses within our minds. The mind can build or construct visual scenes, objects, people or events that do not exist, not present or in the past (Garry *et. al.* 1996). Imagination makes it possible to experience the world within our mind.

The images that imagination creates enable us to develop meaning through the generation of contextual feelings and emotions (Chodorow 1999). Through the feelings and emotions generated, imagination is linked directly to our conscious thoughts, as a go-between our internal and external world. In this way our imagination helps us make sense of our experiences, our relationships, and ourselves (Denzin 1984, Lupton 1998). Our imagination reinterprets events, people, objects and events with emotionally charged meaning that creates a world view that we would prefer and is compatible with our inner selves. Imagination often reinterprets our daily lives in our own sense of spirituality (Hillman 1975, Moore 1992, Sardello 1992, Ulanov 1999, Woodman and Dickson 1996).

Imagination plays a number of other roles within our cognitive processes. New patterns can be created and seen when cognitive cues or stimulation from the outside environment is interpreted by our own inner knowledge (Bandura 1986), leading to new assumptions. Imagination can complete schemata that lack complete information, thereby *"filling in the gaps"* of our knowledge (Matthews 1969) that enables us to make meaning out of uncertainty in situations where information is lacking (Gunderman 2000). This partly explains why people react differently to the same external stimulation due to the unique interpretations people make with differing knowledge in their memories at their disposal.

Imagination can prevent our minds from becoming rigid and set in fixed ways. The ability to change our basic assumptions about things, events, problems and people allows new concepts and ideas to emerge from within us. For example mankind versioned the concept of flight long before the Wright Brothers made the first flight in the early 1900s. Imagination preceded technology in many science fiction films like *Star Wars, Star Trek, James Bond,* and *2001*, etc.

Imagination is also behind some of our basic fears about technology where science fiction films like *"The Hulk"* and *"Frankenstein"* shows us extreme examples of what happens when technology gets out of hand (Renn 2004). This fearful view (imagination) of technology has contributed to people's poor perceptions of GMO foods and contributed to Monsanto's failure as a life science company specializing in genetically modified seeds because of public resistance (Hart & Sharma 2004).

Every time we see television, read a book, hear a story, etc., we allow our imagination to permeate and become empathetic towards a character, a situation or event. Imagination allows us to feel what others feel and understand the emotions of others. Empathy created through imagination is a linking mechanism between the individual and the larger community.

How we remember the past has great bearing upon how we think and feel about people, objects and events. We often create fantasies about the past which emotionally influence how we feel about the present and future. What we remember may be far from the factual reality and more in line with how we want to see the world (Tversky & Kahnemarn 1973). We remember the past in more socially desirable ways where we feel more confident (Abelson *et. al.* 1992). We often remember information but cannot specifically recall the source and time of past events (Johnson 1988, Johnson *et. al.* 1993). Our day dreams and fantasies can be confused with our past experience (Garry *et. al.* 1996). Although they may be false memories, they are real to those experiencing these attached emotions[126]. Our imagination acts within a timeless domain. The past and future is blurred in our imagination where everything is constructed from our present standpoint, where our views on the past are always changing (Johnson & Sherman 1990). Our own personal experiences are subject to distortion (Loftus 1993).

The reinterpretation of our memories can lead us to be more confident about achieving our goals and objectives. Imagining a future event increases the likelihood that the event will actually occur (Carroll 1978, Gregory *et. al.* 1982, Sherman *et. al.* 1985). This idea on the surface appears to support the esoteric concept of the *"Law of Attraction",* recently made

---

[126] This is the reason why witness testimony in a court of law is sometimes questioned in regards to the changing interpretation of memories and influence of suggestions made in the presence of police prosecutors to witnesses. The effect of outsiders trying to bring back past memories in interview situations often leads to the creation of false memories. Imaginative activities may unknowingly promote a belief that particular episodes actually occurred when they actually didn't.

famous by Rhonda Byrnes (2006) bestselling book *The Secret*[127]. The *Law of Attraction* appears to have some degree of compatibility with Jung's concept of *"collective unconscious"*. However current opinion in regard to the validity of *'the Law of Attraction"* fails to live up to scientific scrutiny (Kaptchuk & Eisenberg 1998). It is more likely as Tvershy and Kahnemarn (1973) postulate, that when we imagine things people think of more *'cognitively available'* outcomes that are more likely to occur, *i.e.*, reframing and re-interpreting the past in a way that inflates our confidence. Imagination is configured around the facts and scenarios that we know, where alternative realities fit into plausible events making people more confident in potential outcomes (Koehler 1991).

Imagination links us to a vision of where we may want to go and how we want to get there (Gunderman 2000). Imagination helps us set goals and objectives. The emotive thoughts generated by imagination give us the momentum to move forward, a determination to reach the goals we desire to achieve. Imagination helps us overcome complacency and fear. Our imagination provides us with the ability to undertake mental rehearsals of the things we have to do in order to be successful. Mental rehearsal creates familiarity of tasks making us better at what we do. This is very common in sport where a sportsperson will imagine the race they are to participate in over and over again with potential winning scenarios. You have to imagine winning to feel the emotions associated with the event to build up the determination to achieve the desire.

In entrepreneurship, imagination is about how the world may be and how we see and act within it (Gartner 2007). The high rate of technology in products today requires imagination to trigger creativity and innovation within a firm to remain competitive (Marshall 2001). Future competitive advantage will require the ability of firms to create new technologies that will disrupt and change markets (Hart & Sharma 2004), rather than the traditional strategic modes of lowering costs and differentiating products (Porter 1980). The top companies in the S&P or Fortune 500 in the year 2020 are most likely to be companies that we don't know today (Foster & Kaplan 2001). Corporate imagination is what will change markets and industries in the future (Christensen 1997, Hart & Milstein 1999).

This implies thinking will be predominately in the effectuation mode (see cognitive styles) in future where people and firms create new concepts rather than react to existing technology, product and market situations. The companies in the future that look at new and disruptive products and strategies rather than react through causal reasoning are the ones that will have the greatest impacts in the market[128]. This will be particularly relevant for firms in technologically turbulent industries (Chandler 1962), where predictive rationality, pre-existent firm goals and quick technology redundancies are taking place. Creative and imaginary strategies will prevail over fixed outcome approaches that would be derived from standard strategic planning methods that lock one into a single product/market paradigm[129]. Vision will be based on imagination. The way our imagination develops ideas, motivation and determination is shown in Figure 3.34.

---

[127] The Law of Attraction is a concept that believes our thoughts actually influence what will happen to us in the future. This occurs through a person's thoughts becoming a transmitted force that will attract similar forces back to the person in the universe. So if a person wishes for positive things, then positive things will occur and likewise if a person has negative thoughts, negative things will occur.

[128] However one must not forget that for every successful new company there will be many others that fail for various reasons.

[129] This requires changing thinking processes from making judgments between alternatives to constructing or mentally creating new alternatives.

Imagination can also be dysfunctional to people. Personality disorders develop emotions and feelings which takeover the imagination with fear, anxiety, paranoia and/or narcissism, etc. This prevents a person from imagining new alternatives to their goals and behavior, thus allowing their past fears and anxieties to control them (Hollis 2007, P. 77). Imagination can consciously or unconsciously dissociate a person from the reality of their everyday life where they fall into lives of fantasy. Abstract imagination can quickly take a person away from reality where current problems are ignored in favour of fantasy (Rowe 2004). The imaginations created by psychotic pathologies are major blocks to creativity.

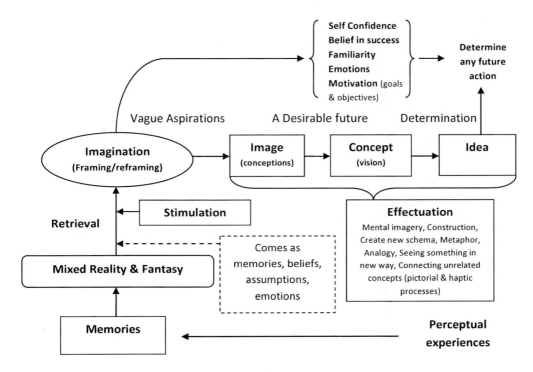

Figure 3.34. The way our imagination develops ideas, motivation and determination.

Imagination is a manifestation of our memory and helps us to construct opportunities through making it possible to experience the world inside our mind. It gives us the ability to see things from other points of view and empathize with people. Imagination enables us to examine our past and construct hypothetical future scenarios that do not yet, but could exist. Imagination is one of the tools that can separate complacent firms from the ones that have relied on imagination as its guiding principal. Imagination separates companies like Apple and IBM, where the lesser resource rich Apple was able to create a very different destiny for itself in the home computer market than did the much more resource rich IBM. Likewise Microsoft and Sun Microsystems had very different destinies with the different approaches to strategy they initially imagined. Finally there is some concern that our current education system, the way that people over schedule their time, the reliance on multi-media and video games for entertainment is stunting the potential imagination of the coming generation (Ouellette 2007).

Passion

Entrepreneurs carry an immense amount of emotions and feelings with them (Baron 2008). Emotions are usually triggered by events that carry some amount of stress, while feelings on the other hand can be triggered by thought and experiences. Emotions can make us feel and act in certain ways (Watson & Clark 1984), while feelings are more reflective upon a thought, person, object or event (Drnovsek, *et. al.* 2009). Passion is an enduring rather than a momentary emotion. Passion is a quality that brings tenacity and stability over a long period of time, but it can also be a negative influence on a person.

Although passion has long been associated with activities like sport, business and entrepreneurship, its effects on these processes have only recently been studied. By passion, we mean continuously intense positive feelings a person experiences because of being engaged in something that is meaningful to their self identity. Passion creates a deep identity connection between a person and an object, activity, idea or thing. Passion gives an opportunity some personal identity.

Passion affects our ambitions, cognitions, behavior and decision making processes. Passion is instrumental in the creation of our own visions and motivates the implementation of the corresponding mission. Passion develops emotions that can be positive or negative on a person.

Passion is a very important aspect of seeing and prioritizing our goals, view of self efficacy and commitment to carrying out things (Baum & Locke 2004). Positive emotion can aid in the opportunity and idea generation process through cognitive flexibility (Baron 2007, 2008), lead to positive decision making (Estrada *et. al.* 1997) and enhance our action in relation to these ideas, opportunities and decisions. Passion enables a person to be more adaptive to external stimuli and more likely to pursue problem solving strategies (Isen 2000, Isen & Labroo 2003). Positive feelings facilitate perceptual processing of stimuli and direct attentive systems (Pham 2004). Passion enables a person to make quick and hasty decisions about exploiting opportunities (Klaukien & Petzelt 2008) and leads people to setting challenging goals (Seo *et.al.* 2004). Passion activates and guides our actions in pursuit of our desires and chosen goals (Brush *et. al.* 2001) and overcoming obstacles that come in the way (Sy *et. al.* 2005).

By its very nature, passion sustains us, makes us persistent and absorbed in what we are doing (Cardon *et. al.* 2008). Passion affects our very creativity and persistence (Cardon *et. al.* 2005), and a sense of mission. Passion is something that motivates and inspires us to work harder and longer and go through emotional ups and downs that come from doing something (Chang 2001, Shepherd 2003). Some researchers now believe passion is a key element of the entrepreneurial process (Cardon *et. al.* 2008).

However Passion can cause us to be blind to risks in the decision making process (Cardon *et. al.* 2005) through discarding negative information (Branzei & Zietsma 2003). In addition to causing blindness to risks, passion can be the cause of irrational attachment to people, objects or ventures that may not be rationally worthwhile to pursue (Brazei & Zietsma 2003). Passion can lead people to believe that they are responsible for successes and failures (Shephard 2003) leading to overconfidence (Cardon 2008) or to anxiety or depression (Rosseau & Vallerard 2003). Finally passion can lead to obsessive dysfunctional behavior (Vallerand *et. al.* 2003). An obsessive person will find it very difficult to disengage him or herself from focusing on something (Vallerand 2008), which can lead to social problems like strained relationships with loved ones due to neglect, etc.

Passion is now seen as an important ingredient in being able to *"win"* in extremely competitive environments that are dominated by much larger and stronger competitors (Drnovosek, *et. al* 2009) Passion is a powerful motivational force that directs attention, creates focus and drives activity, motivating people to work hard (Baum *et. al.* 2001), be dedicated and desire to make a difference (Bierly *et. al.* 2000) and make personal sacrifices (Cooper *et. al.* 1988, Odiorne 1991).

Enjoyment

People engaged in entrepreneurial activities have different personality characteristics and personal traits but all have one thing in common; enjoyment for what they do. Like passion, enjoyment is a tremendous intrinsic motivational force that makes a person focused, lose their sense of time and follow their interest to the limits of their ability. Interest in something gives drive to get out of our natural entropy, the urge to relax and do nothing[130]. A person becomes motivated by the challenges their interest brings and the thrill of learning and achieving new things. Doing what interests a person is a reward in itself. Doing an activity, whether considered risky, painful, difficult or challenging is something that brings immense pleasure to a person.

Csikszentmihalyi (1996, pp. 111-112) explains that when something is enjoyable, a person develops an inherent flow for an activity, like climbing a rock or riding a bike, etc. This contributes to a person's mastery over their interests. Each action provides a person with immediate feedback about their performance assisting in keeping individual standards high. In this way a person both acts and is aware of what is going on around him. A person understands what they can and can't do with their current skill levels and will usually work with a level where skills and challenges match each other. When skills are higher than the challenge a person will get bored and when the challenge is higher than the existing skill level a person will become immensely anxious and frustrated.

Energy and Personal Discipline

Recently, the concept of energy has been related to a person's ability to be creative and achievement. However there is very little agreement on the definition of energy, what it really is, what it does and no way has been found to actually measure it directly (Lykken 2005, O'Connor 2006). This is an area that will probably be given much more attention in the near future, particularly in the discipline of entrepreneurship. A number of different types and terms for human energies have been cited, but probably out of these, three are of importance and cover different overlapping descriptions. The first of three energies is our physical energy that we use to do physical things like moving from place to place, running, sports, and any

---

[130] Michaly Csikszentmihalyi (1996, P. 109) describes the urge when we feel secure to do nothing but curl up and relax as our natural entropy. Entropy is a survival device that prevents us using up all our energy and wandering around aimlessly. According to Csikszentmihalyi we have a strong urge for entropy which makes us inoperative unless there is a stronger motivational force to drive action.

other activity that requires kinetic movement. Our physical energy is managed by food for fuel, rest and exercise to build strength and discipline. The next energy is our emotional energy which carries our general emotions like happiness, surprise, hate, envy, and jealousy, etc. Emotional energy helps to give us focus, interest and attention to different things we sense, encounter, or exposed to and is one of our primal mechanisms to keep us alert to danger in the environment[131]. Finally there is our mental energy which fuels our ability to make calculations and undertake judgments. Mental intelligence is where our problem solving skills and creativity are generated. Sometimes emotional and mental intelligences are called psychic energy, but breaking them into two separate energies allows us to understand the very different roles they play in our life. These three energies are all interrelated, where for example a physically tired person will not perform mental calculations well, or an emotionally tired person will not be able to undertake either physical or mental things very well.

Our energy is chemo-electric in nature, where proteins, enzymes and other electrically sensitive chemicals produce and transfer electricity through our neuro-system to make us move, feel and reason[132]. Our energy links our cognitive and kinetic systems together as one interdependent system something like the Chinese concept of Qi[133] that governs our bodily, mental and emotional disposition. Energy is a dynamic force that fuels all our processes and like all energy behaves according to the first law of thermodynamics where it can be stored, released, focused and drained according to stimulation, demands, needs and distractions coming from the environment and our inner self.

Our physical energy is responsible for our kinetic movements, however, like nutrients, rest and training; our emotional energy also affects our levels of physical energy. Take for example an athlete overly nervous before a race, feeling *'butterflies in the stomach'*. With extreme anxiousness and fear (presumably of losing or performing poorly), the athlete's physical energy will begin to drain making the person feel lethargic, tired and weak. This contrasts with the athlete who is ready to do their best, focused and determined to perform well and ready for the challenge without allowing doubts and anxiousness to drain his or her energy. Another example is the inability to reason logically when one is in a state of anger and the tiredness one feels after being angry. These different states show the interconnection between our various types of energies.

Emotional energy helps a person to deal with everyday frustrations, conflict and pressure. Our emotional energy is influenced by the surrounding environment, people, objects and events. Emotions in the form of moods[134] ebb and flow during the day, week and month. We

---

[131] Emotional energy could be a primal defence against danger. For example something strange has been seen or heard in the distance and the mind has an opportunity to consider the response to the potential sign of danger. There is a normal reflexive response to freeze and then consider what to do next. The response will be emotional rather than reasoned, as emotions are much quicker to generate than thoughts and reasoning.

[132] For a superb account of how our cognitive, emotional and physical systems function see chapter 5 of Michael A. Jawer and Marc S. Micozzi, The Spiritual Anatomy of Emotion.

[133] There are many definitions and descriptions of the concept of Qi. Qi is a concept describing our life-process, our bodily flow of energy that sustains our life. According to the principals of Traditional Chinese Medicine (TCM), Qi circulates around our body where metaphorically it could be viewed as a biological plasma that maintains our general functioning and health. However like emotional and mental energy Qi cannot be detected through any form of scientific instrumentation.

[134] A mood is a long lasting emotional state that is less intense that the emotions they are based on. Unlike emotions, moods are not necessarily triggered by crisis events. A mood will usually have a positive or negative feeling orientation, such as a good or bad mood.

are most often unaware of our moods which tend to influence the way we think about things[135]. Our emotions are triggered by a potential crisis, a crisis, our health, our concern for something or general stress. A person with a high level of emotional energy will be able to cope with the normal stresses of the day while a person with a low level of emotional energy will quickly succumb to any crisis, becoming stressed, anxious and/or frustrated very quickly. Under such situations a person losses focus, where their attention becomes diverted on other tasks that lower general energy levels.

Emotional energy is a source of determination providing a person with the emotional motivation to get on with a job whether it is physical or mentally orientated. Emotional energy provides our enthusiasm, drive and resilience to do things. This is fine in a person who has a clear mission to attend to, but where a person's emotions are deluded with paranoia, compulsiveness, depression, or other forms of neurosis, their emotional energies are diverted into the fantasies that these various pathologies generate[136]. For example, a paranoid person will spend all their emotional and mental energies on suspecting conspiracies against them, leaving little energy available for creative or other problem solving issues facing them. These types of emotions lead to immense fatigue and inability to function logically. Emotional balance is very important so that both our physical and mental capacities are at their optimum.

Mental energy is very important for creativity and supports two types of cognitive operations. The first is the ability to make mental calculations and draw inferences from logical and spatial relationships. The second is the ability to make judgments, recognize similarities across different categories of information using induction and logical reasoning (Csikszentmihalyi 1996, P. 122). We tend to slow down in the ability to make quick and accurate mental calculations during aging but on the contrary improve in our induction and logical reasoning with age. Intelligence is not as important to creativity as is attention and focus without distraction. Mental energy is created through our interest, desire, curiosity, passion and concern for something. Our mental energy levels can be affected by drugs, food, sleep deprivation and disease states (Lieberman 2007).

Creativity can be blocked through a number of situations. As mental cognition requires attention, the mental energy required to think can be lost through just being *'too busy to think'*. Too many demands upon a person take up full cognitive attention, leaving no cognitive capacity for anything else. Therefore people working all day without time to think will tend not to be creative. Likewise distraction will divert attention away from potential creative tasks. People looking after children, working all day, watching television will be distracted and not have the time and focus to be creative. People concerned about survival will not have time to ponder on novel things unless it is directly related towards self preservation. A person concerned about monitoring threats to their own ego will also divert their mental energies away from creative effort (Csikszentmihalyi 1996, P. 345). As we have seen earlier in this part of the book, people who are paranoid or compulsive are too distracted by their delusions to be creative, unless it is tied up with their delusions. The utilization of defence mechanisms to deny realities takes up a lot of mental energy. Lazy people without self discipline will not have any motivation to apply any mental energy to looking at novel issues. They will not be bothered to question anything as their objective is to remain detached

---

[135] Rather than look at a situation and run through a series of potential options to find the optimum action, we tend to judge everyday things based on our emotions.

[136] Psychotic disorders are actually emotional disorders that arise through situational and social conflict dealing with issues of anxiety, low self esteem, feelings of hopelessness, resentment or persecution, etc.

and apathetic towards anything requiring the use of energy. Finally there are a number of people who don't know what to do and where to look for things. They rely on the guidance of others and don't know how to question things. Table 3.31. provides a list of situations that drain a person's energy levels. Lack of stress on the other hand seems to build a person's energy and sensitivity (Goldberg *et. al.* 2002).

Table 3.31. Some situations that can drain energy

Ambiguity both in the workplace and within relationships.	Inter-personal conflict and politics.	Over or under promotion at work.
Conflict between preferences and divided loyalties.	Introduction of new technologies.	Physical injury.
Excluded from decision making processes.	Lack of group bonding.	Poor inter-relationships with boss and other work colleagues.
External locus of control	Loss of self identity.	Responsibility
Focus on seeking short-term results (i.e., tight deadlines, pressure, etc.)	Lack of skills and experience.	Restrictions on freedom and behaviour.
High and demanding workloads	Lack of support networks	The sense of being trapped in something, work, marriage, life, etc.
High responsibility for decisions made.	Making mistakes	Thwarted ambition
Impatience	No job security, fear of redundancy or retrenchment.	Too much idle time.
Information overload.	Not being recognized for achievement or contribution made.	Unsatisfied needs and wants from a relationship

Creativity is about energy, attention and focus rather than great intelligence. Creativity requires long hours with great concentration, consideration and reconsideration rather than brilliance. Creativity requires strong mental energy. Creative people are not hyperactive, but have high amounts of mental energy (Lykken 2005), which they can control. People with average intelligence can be very creative if they have the time and curiosity to look at things in novel ways. People with very high intelligence may not have any curiosity and as a consequence not consider novelty and accept things as they are.

Personal discipline is the ability to control one's energy and maintain focus on what one wants to do. Self discipline maintains focus and prevents a person from needlessly wasting energy on unnecessary issues. Personal discipline is important in keeping momentum towards desired goals and objectives. Poor self discipline leads to an inability to make completion of tasks and the failure to get things done.

Personal discipline is not a given in people and can only be slowly developed through repetition and training. This is something similar to training for cycling, swimming, tennis or running, etc. One needs to build general fitness (physical energy), a positive and confident frame of mind (emotional energy) and calculate out strategies and tactics to achieve optimum performance and achieve set goals. Training can only be built up gradually to prevent injury and exhaustion through building capacity incrementally on strength. The process of creativity must be disciplined to be relevant to what the person wants to be and where the person wants to go.

A Motivational Trigger

An opportunity is potential change and change needs energy to accomplish. Motivation is needed to trigger the process of seeing new realities that can replace the present situation. Motivation is also needed to act upon the vision of the new reality. Robert Fritz (1991) conceptualized the phenomena of *'structural tension'*, using an elastic band to demonstrate the concept and energy involved[137]. When an elastic band is between two fingers and the fingers are close together, there is little or no tension. However when the two fingers move apart, the tension on the elastic band increases. If one finger represents the current reality and the other finger represents a vision or potential reality, the tension of the elastic band can demonstrate the relational tension between the fingers at different distances. So if the elastic band is not stretched, no energy exists and nothing happens. If the present reality and vision or potential reality are far apart then there is great tension and potential energy ready for action.

According to Peter Senge (2006, P. 140-143) *structural tension*[138] also produces *'emotional tension'* represented by anxiety, sadness, discouragement, hopelessness, or worry. These emotions can act counter to the *structural tension*, as these feelings discourage a person from taking action upon any vision. It all depends upon how people cope with emotional tension to determine whether action is taken or ideas just remain as passing daydreams. People cope differently to *emotional tension* – some people are better than others in handling negative emotions. Strategies to reduce emotional tension may include abandoning the vision or moving the vision closer to the present reality.

Motivation is both situational and relational. How we react to things always depends upon the situation and our relationship to others. According to Edgar Schein (1980, P. 40) the human psych is not fixed as there are differences between people. Money incentives may not motivate someone who already has a lot, and status may not matter if one sees themselves as already having a higher status that a proposed activity provides. Yet another person may see the same opportunity as a chance to make a living or gain some attention and notoriety[139]. Therefore a great determinant of what we do is learned from our social environment. This includes our family, education, socio-economic standing, culture, our own sets of beliefs and the circumstances of the immediate time and place we are present. Thus different people will have different patterns of motivation, attitudes, perception from different relative positions of status, need and wants.

---

[137] See Robert Fritz's short clip at http://www.robert fritz.com/index.php?content=principals (accessed 1st December 2009).

[138] Peter Senge (2006, P. 140) calls structural tension, 'creative tension'.

[139] For example, a student may be very happy to get a part-time job washing cars while studying. However upon graduation washing cars for a living would be very disappointing for him or her.

CONCLUSION

What determines new opportunities is not seeing what others do, but seeing what others are not doing. Opportunities can come from various insights where; one can see improvements for existing products, new resources that can be made use of, new materials that can be made use of, new processes that can be made use of, possibilities for new products, possibilities for new ways of doing things, new ways to get a product to customers, new customers, technologies that can be used for different applications, and technologies that can produce existing products more efficiently and/or superiorly and even create new industries.

The seeing, discovery or construction of an opportunity is one thing, but imagining a combination of resources, skills, networks, technologies, innovations and strategies to exploit it is another. This involves a creative process. In addition, a person needs motivation, persistence, focus, determination and energy to move. These are all the ingredients that move a perceived idea to the realm of opportunity. An idea needs to be capable of being exploited before it can be called an opportunity.

We can explain in detail how to go to the moon, land on it, walk around the surface and return safely but we cannot satisfactorily explain how people find opportunities. There is no generally accepted theory about how people see, discover or construct opportunities. It is still very much the unopened black box of entrepreneurial activity (Fiet 2002), yet to be fully understood. To date it has only been explained by anecdotes and fragmented approaches (Shane 2003, P. 12).

Generally it is explained that opportunity gaps arise out of environmental change, driven by changes in the social, economic and technology conditions (Cagan & Vogel 2002, P. 9.). Government and regulation also create opportunity gaps through the allowance of certain things and the disallowance of others. Consequently changing laws and regulations are another source of product opportunities (Shane 2003). These are the environmental factors that together drive product, market and industry evolution (Hunter 2009).

The social and cultural environment is an important aspect of the overall environment and an important source of opportunity. As the social and cultural environment evolves, so do opportunities along with new expectations arising from changing perceptions and wellbeing. This spreads across all fields of life where for example, there may be new desires in lifelong education, health, age care, infant care, public transport, leisure and entertainment, travel, apparel and attire and so on. This implies there are continuous opportunities due to the incongruities continually being created due to social evolution.

Changing demographics due to different birth and death rates, inflows or outflows of immigration also change the demand patterns for products and services in a similar way to social and cultural change. Market and outside influences such as global trends, the availability of products, advertising and other forms of promotion create new sets of product and service acceptance. This is also internally influenced by the level of disposable income, age, employment status, and their perception of the future, etc. Through complex market and social factors various products become socially acceptable and desirable over time. This creates potential for different styles of a product, new fashions and fads that create continuous opportunity streams in the consumer market. The complex heterogeneous mix of things can perhaps best be seen in the rising popularity of *fusion foods* which are uniquely new and novel, based on foods we know from different cultures. This skillful mix of things can also be seen in innovative new business models like low cost airlines, internet businesses and eco and medical tourism, etc.

The greater the availability and choice of products, the more rapid will existing products be superseded with new models, versions and complete new designs. This together with rapidly changing technologies, are driving change in the computer, communications and mobile phone industries. On the whole consumer tastes and preferences are very different from what they were a decade ago and what they will be in the decade to come. The social environment requires a person to see change so incongruities can be recognized and opportunities constructed into a concept that can be exploited.

The economic environment influences opportunities through the macroeconomic environment, general industry conditions, the financial environment and the geographic environment. Factors influencing opportunity under the general macroeconomic environment include the stage of economic development, the size and type of economic growth, and economic stability. Opportunities are dependent upon the size of a market or potential market for products and services. Another factor under this category would include the business expertise and sophistication of domestic businesses[140]. High expertise and sophistication would be positive towards opportunities, while low expertise and sophistication would tend to be negative towards opportunities. The general fiscal environment may have some influence on opportunities and incentives to exploit them. Factors within the fiscal environment include income and capital gains taxes, resource rents and taxes, the access and rules around gaining venture finance and rules concerning the transfer of assets.

Industry conditions include issues such as the break up between primary, manufacturing, service and high tech industries, the protection of intellectual property, the intensity of research and development within the industry, the origin of innovation within the industry, *i.e., is it locally derived or purchased from offshore?*, the conditions of the markets industry serves, *i.e., size, growth, competition, and segmentation,* the stage of the industry lifecycle, elements of domination, *i.e., designs, industry consolidation and firm density*, barriers to industry entry, and the learning curve needed to become competitive within the industry. Opportunities are directly influenced by the relevance of external sources of innovation, the needed tacit knowledge, the size and concentration of the industry, the lack of dominant designs, and the existence of a large number of firms within the industry (Shane 2003, P. 118).

The financial environment influences opportunities through the cost of capital and the characteristics of the ways funds can be raised for new ventures. How banks view new and novel ventures and risks is an important factor. The availability of a market to raise venture capital is also very important. This can be considered a very important factor in new ventures contributing to economic growth from new technologies and products, giving in most cases developed economies advantages over developing economies where the venture capital markets are not as developed.

The geographic environment influences what types of opportunities may exist through the distance from markets and availability of resources, skills and capital. Fast growing urban areas offer generally greater opportunities to smaller urban areas of massive metropolises where very high levels of self employment already exploiting a wide range of opportunities exist. Industry clusters, particularly those based on higher level technologies tend to offer more opportunities than general industrial regions. This is because specific skills, specialized infrastructures, equipment, and firms already operating within the industry already exist. Resources needed for the specific industry tend to be found more easily in an industry cluster than if it is isolated. Clusters tend to have lower operational costs and in many circumstances share information (Dosi 1988).

Economic conditions have many influences upon consumers. The economic environment heavily influences a person's disposable income from the level of salary, taxation, size of family and extended family, required living expenditure, level of debt, consumption patterns and future expectations. The propensity to save, take credit and mortgages also influences consumption and consumption patterns which influences the types and sizes of potential opportunities available.

New technologies create new opportunities not just for new products, but for new industries as well. We have seen the evolution of written communication from the letter requiring a postal system, to the cable and telex requiring the telephone company, to the facsimile at first requiring bureaus and then the invention of office facsimiles, to electronic mail through the internet over the last two decades. We have evolved from a landline based telephone system, to a basic cellular telephone network carrying analogue, to a greatly enhanced cellular network that can carry all forms of data communications. We have gone from data communication speeds of bits per second (BPS) to gigabytes of information travelling through our personal handheld devices uploading and downloading all types of media. Product evolution is influenced through the development of new technologies based on completely new concepts, processes or materials that are better and more cost effective than existing ones.

However technology change is more important to some industries than others. Some industries like the chemical industry are slower changing than the electronics and communications industries. But through the interdisciplinary application of genome and biotechnologies even more stable technology industries are changing the basis of their technology platforms. With environmental issues gaining importance, carbon credit schemes will force the development of carbon neutral green technologies and practices, resulting in new products in the marketplace. Industries with closer ties to science will have more entrepreneurial opportunities in the future (Klevorick *et. al.* 1995). Technology is wide and varied in magnitude. Incremental technology changes will change products on a more regular basis and shorten products lifecycles greatly, while larger technology changes will be a source of opportunities outside of existing industry value chains, often creating new industries.

Opportunities are influenced by government and regulation. The government sets the environment for the protection of physical and intellectual property, the legal and administrative systems and supports their effectiveness. The political philosophy of the country will influence issues such as protectionism, level of market intervention, market regulation, consumer protection, the level of government owned businesses, the extent of foreign owned business allowed, industrial policy, labour regulation, and the level of monopolistic competition allowed, etc. One can see how positive political change in the way

---

[140] Factors under business expertise and sophistication would include the education level of general business managers and entrepreneurs, their general business awareness, business and ethical standards, the level and

the market is regulated has increased business activity in countries like China, Vietnam and Indonesia over the last decade. Market deregulation in the airline, transport, entertainment, communication, banking, and utilities industries has allowed the creation and success of many new novel business models that increases value to the consumer and promotes economic growth. Generally the higher the intervention into the economy by a government, the more resources will be used ineffectively and the less opportunities available for entrepreneurs to exploit. This type of environment usually ends up with the development of firms that rely on political connections and bribery (Cuevo 2005).

Government subsidies also influence the viability of certain opportunities. For example, subsidies given on daycare for working parents will open up new opportunities for day care centres (Baum & Oliver 1991). The government is also a consumer of products and services and the transparency of the contracting and tendering processes is also instrumental to the level of opportunity within an economy.

The education system is a key institution. The *'market of* ideas' and the technology and innovation to support it requires active academic institutions (Kenney 1986) that produce management talent (Higgins & Gulati 2003). Education coupled with the level of domestic research and development has influence over the types of technology and caliber of people that enter the marketplace in the future.

Opportunities are also affected by government regulation. For example new regulations making safety helmets and seats beats mandatory for motorcycles and cars respectively open up markets for new products and services. The banning of CFCs and increasing pollution controls for cars forces improvements in technology. Changing regulations concerning raw materials in the cosmetic, personal care and agro-chemical areas require complete product reformulations and even complete rethinking of products. Changing occupational safety and health issues force change in work practices. In fact changing regulation can cause global opportunity shifts. For example the increase in pollution abetment requirements in the US and EU during the 1990s had a large influence in the relocation of many chemical industries from developed to developing countries with less stringent laws.

Some opportunities appear to be random or unexpected. For example, where a shop front becomes vacant in a shopping strip and a restaurant is openmed, it may be very successful, while another will fail. Undertaking any amount of market research and strategic planning will not provide any accurate indication of potential success or failure. Some opportunities come to exist through the errors, omissions or successes of others. Drucker (1985) called unexpected successes or failures a source of innovation, but it is more likely to be a source of opportunity to learn because it highlights to someone the potential of doing something the same *(in case of success)* or different *(in the case of failure).*

In addition, each variable has a very complex web of interrelationships between each other; thereby what happens within the social, economic, technological, or regulatory domains will have an effect on the others. There is a continued ebbing of cause and effect from all elements within the environment which creates new relationships that arise in new potential opportunities. Some of these forces bring things together like mobile telephones and digital cameras, while some of these forces break things apart like analogue telephone technology broke up the telephone industry in the 1980-90s.

standards of business law and enforcement, levels of corruption and general levels of respect for the system.

However it is not the external environment that has opportunities *'labeled'* for the individual to select and exploit. Different people see the environment in different ways, putting different weights on different stimuli and coming up with their own feelings and ideas about what they see. People see differently as their perception and thinking is shaped uniquely by their psychological and non-psychological characteristics, their cognitive patterning and biases, their cultural assumptions, beliefs and values, and their emotions and so on about the environment, competition, availability of resources, networks, as well as to their perceptions about the governing principals of the environment (Cuervo 2005). These factors influence how a person sees opportunity and influences his or her desirability to exploit it.

The perception of opportunity is as much a product of our self as it is of the environment. Our consciousness was once regarded as a mirror of the environment where we passively saw images projected to us from the outside world (Rorty 1980). The environment was seen as a lamp which shone outwards into the world, which we reflected our experience like a metaphorical mirror towards a passive and receptive consciousness (Abrams 1953). Except what we know today is our consciousness actually reaches out into the world where our conscious experience is shaped by our understanding, meaning and imagination of the world (Thomas 1999). It is our creativity through our imagination that can create the mental imagery that can assemble the components of opportunity together.

Opportunity is dependent upon the limits of our knowledge which shape our cognitive frames and allow us to give attention to environmental stimuli that we are familiar with. Emotion plays a role in the intensity of focus and feelings we have about what we perceive. We view from our own competencies and knowledge (Teece *et. al.* 1994, Winter 1988). Our knowledge, experience, technological understanding and commercial sense all combine together within our imagination to convert a perceived idea into how to exploit it (Loasby 1976, 1991). The opportunity conception is both a product of ourselves and the environment. It is our subjective imagination that plays a major role in our future business behavior (Witt 1998). Conceiving the future business venture is an important and necessary part of the process of seeing and creating an opportunity and developing the strategies to exploit it (Day 1987).

Our preferences, identities and expectations are formed to make sense of the complex and confusing world (March 1996). Opportunities are created inside our minds through the creation of cognitive maps in a new way of making sense of the information we have (Weick 1979). Individual make sense of their past and present natures and perceive the future (Fiske & Taylor 1984). The key is the way a person thinks about reality, not the external reality, but external and internal.

Thus opportunity has two sets of forces, one working within the field and one working within our inner self. A new idea is a form coming from inside to correspond with what is seen on the outside. The new idea is the interrelationship between our inner self and the environment. Ideas themselves are another force that changes the field. Ideas are also a product of the interrelationships and history of the field and could not exist until the field has evolved to the point where an idea is possible[141]. Ideas are captured by our minds and expressed as a form such as in banking, a check, a loan, a telegraphic transfer, etc. Ideas reveal the numerous interrelationships between elements within the environment and

---

[141] For example, a car cannot exist until thousands of other ideas like rubber, the engine, the transmission, fuel, traffic laws and roads exist.

ourselves, that allow the society to evolve and creates the potential source of growth for a venture, *i.e., the railroads, aircraft, automobiles, fast food, medical equipment, etc.* An idea creates energy that brings change (Low 1976, P. 23).

Perhaps one of the individual differences in how we develop new opportunities is how we prioritize information through our psychic, emotional and cognitive processes. This prioritization helps us to make new connections between different bits of knowledge that previously haven't been made. Chapter four will look and examine our creativity processes and look at how we come to make new connections between things and discover, see and construct opportunities.

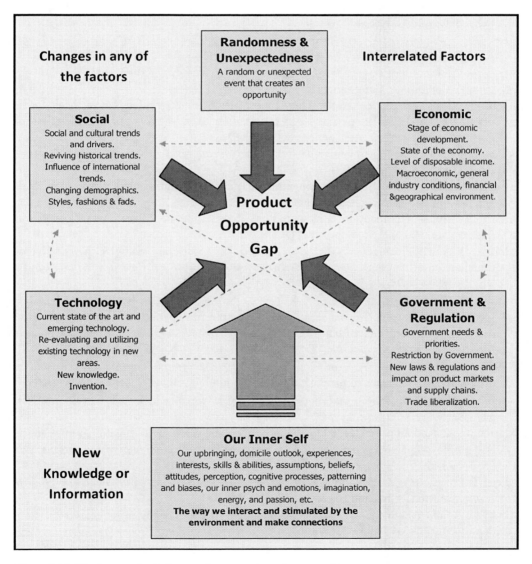

Figure 3.35. The factors that influence the perception of opportunities.

REFERENCES

Abelson, R. P., Loftus, E. F. and Greenwald, A. G. (1992). Attempts to improve the accuracy of self-reports of voting, In: Tanur, J. M. (editor), *Questions about survey questions: Meaning, memory, Expression, and Social Interactions in Surveys,* New York, Russell Sage, pp. 138-153.

Abrahamson, A. C., Baker, L. A. and Caspi, A. (2002). Rebellious Teens? Genetic and environmental influences on the social attitudes of adolescents, *Journal of Personality and Social Psychology,* Vol. 83, No. 6., pp. 1392-1408.

Abrams, M. H. (1953). *The mirror and the lamp: Romantic theory and the critical tradition,* Oxford, Oxford University Press.

Aces, Z. J., Audretsch, D. B., Braunerhjelm, P., and Carlsson, B. (2006). *Growth and Entrepreneurship; An Empirical Assessment,* CEPR Discussion paper No. 5409.

Acs, Z. J. And Armington, C. (2006). *Entrepreneurship, geography and American economic growth,* Cambridge, Cambridge University Press.

Ajzen, I. (1987). Attitudes, traits and actions: dispositional prediction of behavior in personality and social psychology, In: Berkowitz, L (Ed.). *Advances in Social Psychology,* New York, Academic Press, pp. 1-63.

Ajzen, I. (1987a). Theory of planned behaviour, *organizational Behavior & Human Decision Processes,* Vol. 50, pp. 179-211.

Alba-Ramirez, A. (1994). Self-employment in the midst of unemployment: The case of Spain and the United States, *Applied Economics,* Vol. 26, pp. 189-204.

Alch, M.L. (2008). Get ready for a new kind of worker in the workplace: the net generation, *Supervision,* Vol. 69, No. 6, pp. 18-21.

Aldrich, H. And Weidenmeyer, G. (1993). From traits to rates: an ecological perspective on organizational foundings, *Advances in Entrepreneurship, Firm Emergence and Growth,* Vol. 1, pp. 145-195.

Aldrich, H., Elam, A. B. and Reese, P. R. (1996). Strong ties, weak ties, and strangers: Do women business owners differ from men in their use of networking to obtain assistance? In: Birley, S. and MacMillan, I. C. (Eds.). *Entrepreneurship in a global context, International Business and the World Economy,* London, Routledge, pp. 1-25.

Aldrich, H., Renzulli, L. A. And Langton, N. (1998). Passing on privilege: Resources provided by self-employed parents to their self-employed children, In; Leicht, K. (editor), *Research in Stratification and mobility,* (Vol. 16.), Greenwich, CT, JAI Press, pp. 291-317.

Aldrich, H. E. And Kim, P. H. (2007). A life course perspective on occupational inheritance: Self employed parents and their children, *research in the Sociology of organizations,* Vol. 25, pp. 33-82.

Allen, B. P. (2003). *Personality Theories: Development, Growth and Diversity, Fourth Edition,* Boston, Allyn and Bacon.

Alloy, L. B. and Abramson, L. Y. (1979). Judgment of contingency in depressed and non-depressed subjects: sadder but wiser? *Journal of Experimental Psychology: general,* Vol. 108, pp. 443-479.

Alsop, R. (2008). The trophy kids grew up: How the millennial generation is shaking up the workplace, New York, Jossey-Bass.

Alvarez, S. A, and Busenitz, L. W, (2001). The Entrepreneurship of resource based theory, *Journal of Management,* Vol. 27, pp. 755-775.

Amit, R., Glostent, L. and Muller, E. (1993). Challenges to theory development in entrepreneurship research, *Journal of Management Studies,* Vol. 30, No. 5, pp. 815-834.

Anderson, J. R. and Reder, L. M. (1979). An elborative processing explanation of depth of processing, In: Cermak, L. S. and Graik (Editors), *Levels of processing in human memory,* Hillsdale, NJ, Erlaum.

Ardichvili, A., Cardozo, R., and Ray, S. (2003). A theory of entrepreneurial opportunity identification and development, *Journal of Business Venturing,* Vol. 18, pp. 105-123.

Argyris, C. (1985). Strategy, Change and Defence Routine, Boston, Pitman.

Arnold, M. B. (1960). *Emotion and Personality (Vols. 1-2),* New York, Columbia University.

Arora, V. K. and Faraone, L. (2003). 21st century Engineer-Entrepreneur, *IEEE Antennas and Propagation Magazine,* Vol. 45, No. 5, pp. 106-114.

Arthur, B. (2008). *MyGeneration Y21,* Sydney, Special Broadcasting Service, (Documentary).

Asrul Zamani, (2002). *The Malay Ideals,* Kuala Lumpur, Golden Books Centre Sdn. Bhd.

Ashkanasy, N. and Daus, C. (2002). Emotion in the Workplace: The new challenge for managers, *Academy of Management Executive,* Vol. 16, pp. 76-85.

Asthana, A. and Thorpe V. (2005). Whatever happened to the original Generation X?, *The Observer, http://observer.guardian.co.uk/uk-news/story/0.69031/396618,00.html,* (accessed 16th December 2009).

Atwood, M. E. and Polson, P. G., (1976). A process model for water jug problems, *Cognitive Psychology,* Vol. 8, No. 2, pp. 191-216.

Audet, J., Gasse, C., Gasse, Y., & Tremblay, M. (2009). Aspiring Entrepreneurs: The Case of Generation Y, *Papers and Proceedings of the Southern Academy of Entrepreneurship 2009 Annual Conference, Southern Journal of Entrepreneurship,* pp. 5-19.

Awe, E, Jonides, J., Smith, E. E., Schumacher, E. H., Koeppe, R. A. and Katz, S. (1996). Dissociation of storage and rehearsal in verbal working memory: Evidence from PET, *Psychological Science,* Vol. 7, pp. 25-31.

Baddeley, A. D. (1992). Is working memory working? The fifteenth Barlett Lecture, *Quarterly Journal of Experimental Psychology,* Vol. 44A, pp. 1-31.

Baddeley, A. D. (2001). Is working memory still working?, *American Psychologist*, Vol. 56, pp. 851-864.

Baddeley, A. D. and Hitch, G. (1974). Working Memory, In: Bower, G. H. (Editor), *The Psychology of learning and motivation,* Orlando, FL, Academic Press, (Vol.8), pp. 17-90.

Baddeley, A. D., Gathercole, S. and Papagno, C. (1998). The phonological loop as a language learning device, *Psychological Review,* Vol. 105, pp. 158-173.

Baker, T., Aldrich, H., Liou, N. (1997). Invisible entrepreneurs: the neglect of women business owners by mass media and scholarly journals in the USA, *Entrepreneurship and Regional Development,* Vol. 9, No. 3, pp. 221-238.

Bales, R. (1970). *Personality and Interpersonal Behavior,* New York, Holt, Rinehart and Winston.

Ballou, J. (2008). *The Kauffman Firm Survey: Results from the baseline and follow-up surveys*, The Kauffman Foundation, March, *http://www.kauffman.org/uploadedFiles/kfs_ 08.pdf,* (Accessed 20th January 2010).

Bandura, A. (1985). *The Social Foundations of Thought and Action,* Englewood Cliffs, Prentice-Hall.

Bandura, A. (1986). *Social Foundations of Thought and Action – A Social Cognitive Practice,* Englewood Cliffs, NJ, Prentice-Hall.

Bandura, A. (1993). Perceived self-efficacy in cognitive development and functioning, *Educational Psychologist,* Vol. 28, No. 2, pp. 117-148.

Bandura, A. (1997). *Self-Efficacy: The Exercise of Control,* New York, W.H. Freeman.

Barak, A., Feldman, S. And Noy, A. (1991). Traditionality of children's interests as related to their parents' gender stereotypes and traditionality of occupations, *Sex Roles,* Vol. 24, pp. 511-524.

Bardwick. J. M. (1995). Danger in the Comfort Zone: From the Boardroom to the Mailroom – How to Break the Entitlement Habit That's Killing American business, New York, American Management Association.

Barembaum, N. B. and Winter, D. G. (2003). Personality, In: Freedheim, D. K. (Ed.), *Handbook of Psychology: History of Psychology,* New York, John Wiley & Sons Inc., pp. 177-203.

Baron, R. A. (1998). Cognitive mechanisms in entrepreneurship: why and when entrepreneurs think differently than other people, *Journal of Business Venturing,* Vol. 13, No. 3, pp. 275-294.

Baron, R. A. (2007). Behavioral and Cognitive factors in entrepreneurship: Entrepreneurs as the active element in new venture creation, *Strategic Entrepreneurship Journal,* Vol.1., pp. 167-182.

Baron, R. A. (2008). The role of affect in the entrepreneurial process, *Academy of management Review,* Vol. 33, pp. 328-340.

Baron, R. S. (2005). So right it's wrong: Groupthink and the Ubiquitous Nature of Polarized Group Decision Making, In: Zanna, M. P. (Ed.), *Advances in Experimental Social Psychology,* San Diego, Elsevier Academic Press.

Baron, R. A. and Ward, T. B. (2004). Expanding entrepreneurial cognition's toolbox: potential contributions from the field of cognitive science, *Entrepreneurship, Theory and Practice,* Vol. 28, No. 6, pp. 553-575.

Barr, R. G. (1990). The early crying paradox: A modest proposal, *Human Nature,* Vol. 1, pp. 355-389.

Bastone, L. M. and Woods, H. A. (1997). Individual Differences in the Ability to Decode Emotional Facial Expressions, *Journal of Human Behavior,* Vol. 34, pp. 32-36.

Bate, M., & Papadopoulos, V. (2008). *MyGeneration Electioneering,* Sydney, Special Broadcasting Service, (Documentary).

Bates, T. (1995). Self-employment across industry groups, *Journal of Business Venturing,* Vol. 10, No. 2, pp. 143-156.

Baum, J. and Oliver, C. (1991). Institutional linkages and organizational mortality, *Administrative Science Quarterly,* Vol. 36, pp. 187-218.

Baum, L. F. (1999). *The Wonderful World of Oz (republished),* Lawrence, University of Kansas Press.

Baum, J. R. and Locke, E. A. (2004). The relationship of entrepreneurial traits, skill, and motivation to new venture growth, *Journal of Applied Psychology,* Vol. 89, pp. 587-599.

Baum, J. R., Locke, E. A. and Smith, K. G. (2001). A Multidimensional Model of Venture Growth, *Academy of Management Journal,* Vol. 44, pp. 292-303.

Baxtor, M. (2001). *Enclaves or Equity: The rural crisis and development in Papua New Guinea: A Summary,* Canberra, Australian Agency for International Development,

November,   *http://www.ausaid.gov.au/publications/pdf/enclaves_equity_summary.pdf,* (accessed 29th November 2008).

Beck, A. T. (1967). *Depression: Clinical, Experimental, and Theoretical Aspects,* New York, Hoeber Medical Division, Harper & Row.

Becker, E. (1973). *The Denial of Death,* New York, Free Press.

Beck, A.T. (1976). *Cognitive Therapy and Emotional Disorders,* New York, International Universities Press.

Begly, T. M. and Boyd, D. P. (1987). A comparison of entrepreneurs and managers of small business firms, *Journal of management,* Vol. 13, No. 1, pp. 99-108.

Benedict, B. (1979). Family firms and firm families: A comparison of Indian, Chinese and Creole firms in Seychelles, In: Greenfield, S. M., Strickon, A., and Aubey, R. T. (Eds.), *Entrepreneurs in Cultural Context,* Albuquerque, University of New Mexico press.

Berger, P. and Luckmann, T. (1967). *The Social Construction of knowledge: A Treatise in the Sociology of knowledge,* London, Penguin.

Bhide, A. (1994). How Entrepreneurs Craft Strategies that Work, *Harvard Business Review,* Vol. 72, pp. 150-161.

Bhide, A. (2000). *The Origins and Evolutions of new Businesses,* Oxford and New York, Oxford University Press.

Bierly, P. E., Kessler, E. H., Christensen, E. W. (2000). Organizational learning, knowledge, and wisdom, *Journal of Organizational Change and Management,* Vol. 13, pp. 595-618.

Bion, W. R. (1959). *Experiences in Groups,* London, Tavistock Publications.

Blaney, P. H. (1986). Affect and memory: a review, *Psychological Bulletin,* Vol. 99, pp. 565-578.

Blonigen, D. M., Carlson, S. R., Krueger, R. F., and Patrick, C. J. (2003). A twin study of self-reported psychopathic personality traits, *Personality and Individual Differences,* Vol. 35, pp. 179-197.

Bloom, D. E, Canning, D., Fink, G, and Finlay, J. E. (2007). *Does age structure forecast economic growth?* NBER Working paper No. 13221. 2009

Bohm, D. (1965). *The Special Theory of Relativity,* New York, W. A. Benjamin.

Boland, R. J. and Hoffman, R. (1983). Humor in the Machine Shop: An Interpretation of Symbolic Action, In Pondy. L. R., Frost, P. J., Morgan, G. and Dandridge, T. C., *Organizational Symbolism,* Greenwich, Connecticut, Jai Press Inc., pp. 187-198.

Bolton, B. and Thompson, J. (2003). *The Entrepreneur in Focus: achieve your potential,* London, Thomson.

Borjas, G. J. and Bronars, S. G. (1989). Consumer discrimination and self employment, *Journal of Political Economy,* Vol. 97, pp. 581-605.

Borkenau, P., Riemann, R., Angleitner, A, and Spinath, F. M. (2001). Genetic and environmental influences on observed personality: evidence from the German observational study of adult twins, *Journal of Personality and Social Psychology,* Vol. 80, No. 4., pp. 655-668.

Borysenko, J. (1996). *A Women's Book of Life: The Biology, Psychology, and Spirituality of the Feminine Life Cycle,* New York, Riverhead Books.

Borkovec, T. D., Robinson, E., Pruzinsky, T. and DePree, J. A. (1983). Preliminary exploration of worry: some characteristics of the processes, *Behaviour Research and Therapy,* Vol. 21, pp. 9-16.

Bosma, N. and Levie, J. (2010). *Global Entrepreneurship Monitor 2009 Annual Report,* London-Babason Park, MA, Global Entrepreneurship Research Association.

Bouchard, T.J. (1998). Genetic and environmental influences on adult intelligence and special mental abilities, *Human Biology,* Vol. 72, No. 2, pp. 257-279.

Bouchard, T. J. and Loehlin, J. C. (2001). Genes, Evolution and Personality, *Behavior Genetics,* Vol. 31, No. 3, pp. 243-273.

Bouchard, T. J. and McGue, M. (1990). Genetic and rearing environmental influences on adult personality: An analysis of adopted twins reared apart, *Journal of Personality,* Vol. 58, pp. 263-292.

Bourdieu, P. (1977). *Outline of a Theory of Practice,* New York, Cambridge University Press.

Bourdieu, P. (1989). *Distinction: A Social Critique of the Judgment of Taste,* (translate3d by Richard Nice), London, Routledge, (first published by Les Editions de Minuit, Paris, 1979).

Bourdieu, P. (1990). *The Logic of Practice,* Cambridge, Polity Press.

Bourdieu, P. (1990a). *In Other Words: Essays Towards a Reflexive Sociology,* Stanford, Stanford University Press.

Bourdieu, P. (1991). Editor's Introduction, In: Thompson, J. B. (Ed.), *Language and Symbolic Power,* Cambridge, Havard University Press, pp. 1-31.

Bourdieu, P. (1998). *Practical Reason: On the theory of action,* Cambridge, Polity Press.

Bourdieu, P. and Wacquant, L. J. D. (1992). *An Invitation to Reflexive Sociology,* Chicago/London, University of Chicago Press.

Bowen, D. D. and Hisrich, R. D. (1986). The female entrepreneur: A career development perspective, *Academy of Management Review,* Vol. 11, No. 2, pp. 393-407.

Bowlby, J. (1980). *Attachment and Loss*, New York, Basic Books.

Boyd. N. G. And Vozikis, G. S. (1994). The influence of self-efficacy on the development of entrepreneurial intentions and actions, *Entrepreneurship Theory and Practice,* Vol. 18, No. 4, pp. 63-77.

Boyd, R. L. (2007). Urbanization, Disadvantage, and Petty Entrepreneurship: Street Peddling Among African Men in Southern and Northern Cities During the Early Twentieth Century, *Sociological Inquiry,* Vol. 69, No. 2, pp. 216-235.

Boyd, R. (1991). Black Entrepreneurship in 52 metropolitan areas, *Social Science Research,* Vol. 75, No. 3, pp. 158-163.

Boyd, N. G. and Vozikis, G. S. (1994). The influence of self-efficacy on the development of entrepreneurial intentions and actions, *Entrepreneurship: Theory and Practice,* Vol. 18, No. 4, pp. 63-77.

Bradburn, N. M. (1969). *The structure of psychological well-being,* Chicago, Aldine.

Braithwaite, V. A. And Scott, W. A. (1991). Values, In: Robinson, J. P., Shaver, P. R. And Wrightsman, L. S. (Eds.), *Measures of Personality and Social Psychological Attitudes, Vol. 1,* New York, Academic press, pp. 661-753.

Brann, E. T. H. (1991). *The world of imagination: Sum and substance*, Savage, MD. Rowman and Littlefield.

Branzei, O. and Zietsma, C. (2003). Entrepreneurial Love: The enabling functions of positive illusions in venturing, *Paper presented at the babsen-Kauffman Entrepreneurial Research Conference,* Babsen Col Bridges, W. (1980).*Transitions: Making Sense of Life's Changes,* Reading, MA., Addison-Wesley Publishing Company.

Bridges, W. (1980).*Transitions: Making Sense of Life's Changes,* Reading, MA., Addison-Wesley Publishing Company.

Bridges, W. (1994). The end of the job, *Fortune,* 19th Sept., pp. 62-74.

Brigham, K. H. and De Castro, J. O. (2003). Entrepreneurial Fit: The Role of Cognitive Misfit, In: Katz, J. A. And Shepherd, D. A. (Eds.), *Cognitive Approaches to Entrepreneurial Research: Advances in Entrepreneurship, Firm emergence and growth, Vol. 6.,* Kidlington, Oxford, Elsevier Science Ltd., pp. 37-71.

Broadbent, D. E. (1957). A Mechanical Model for human Attention and Immediate Memory, *Psychological Review,* Vol. 64, pp. 205-215.

Broadbent, D. E. (1958). *Perception and Communication,* London, Pergamon Press.

Brown, A. D. (1997). Narcissism, identity and legitimacy, *Academy Management Review,* Vol. 22, pp. 643-686.

Brown, A. D. and Starkey, K. (2000). Organizational identity and learning: A psychological perspective, *Academy Management Review,* Vol. 25, pp. 102-120.

Brown, G. W., Harris, T. O. and Hepworth, C. (1995). Loss, humiliation, and entrapment among women developing depression: A patient and non-patient comparison, *Psychological medicine,* Vol. 25, pp. 7-21.

Brubaker, R. (1985). Rethinking Classical Theory: The Sociological Version of Pierre Bourdieu, *Theory and Society,* Vol. 14, No. 6, pp. 745-775.

Brüderl, J, Preisendörfer, P. and Ziegler, R. (1992). Survival chances of newly founded business organizations, *American Sociological Review,* Vol. 57, No. 2, pp. 227-241.

Bruderl, J. and Preisendorfer, P. (1998). Network support and the success of newly founded businesses, *Small Business Economics,* Vol. 10, pp. 213-225.

Bruderl, J., Preisendorfer, P. and Zieler, R. (1992). Survival chances of newly founded business organizations, *American Sociological Review,* Vol. 57, pp. 227-302.

Brundin, E., Patzelt, H. and Shepherd, D. A., (2009). Managers' emotional displays and employees' willingness to act entrepreneurially, *Journal of Business Venturing,* Vol. 23, pp. 221-243.

Bruni, A., Gherardi, S. and Poggio, B. (2004). Entrepreneur-mentality, gender and the study of women entrepreneurs, *Journal of Organizational Change Management,* Vol. 17, No. 3, pp. 256-268.

Brush, C. B., Greene, P. G., and hart, M. M. (2001). From initial idea to unique advantage: The entrepreneurial challenge of constructing a resource base, *Academy of Management Executive,* Vol. 15, No. 2, pp. 64-78.

Brush, C. (1992). Research on Women Business owners: Past trends, a unique perspective and future directions, *Entrepreneurship, Theory and Practice,* Vol. 16, No. 2, pp. 5-30.

Brush, C. (1997). Women-owned businesses: Obstacles and opportunities, *Journal of Developmental Entrepreneurship,* Vol. 2, No. 1, pp. 1-24.

Buck, R. (1985). Prime Theory: An integrated view of motivation and emotion, *Psychological Review,* Vol. 92, pp. 389-413.

Buddhadasa Bhikkhu (1992). *Paticcasamuppada: Practical, Dependent, Origination,* Bangkok, Vuddhidhamma Fund.

Buddhadasa Bhikkhu (2007). *Handbook for mankind: Realizing your full potential as a human being,* Bangkok, Amarin Publishing (Translated from the Thai edition by Aniyanada Bhikkhu Roderick S. Bucknell).

Buddhaghosa, (1991). *The Path of Purification (Visuddhimagga), 5ᵗʰ Ed.*, (translated by Bhikku Ňãnamoli), Kandy, Buddhist Publication Society.

Bull, I. and Willard, G. E. (1993). Towards a theory of entrepreneurship, *Journal of Business Venturing,* Vol. 8, pp. 183-195.

Bull, I. and Winter, F. (1991). Community differences in business births and business growths, *Journal of Business Venturing,* Vol. 6. No. 1, pp. 29-43.

Burgman, M. (2005). Risks and Decisions for Conservation and Environmental Management, Cambridge, Cambridge University Press.

Burke, T. P. (2004). *The Major Religions, 2ⁿᵈ Edition,* Malden, MA., Blackwell Publishing.

Burns, T. (1961). Micropolitics: Mechanisms of organizational change, *Administrative Science Quarterly,* Vol. 6, pp. 257-281,

Busenitz, L. W, and Barney, J. B, (1997). Differences between entrepreneurs and managers in large organizations, *Journal of Business Venturing,* Vol. 12, pp. 9-30.

Byrne, R. (2006). *The Secret,* New York, Atria Books.

Cagan, J. and Vogel, C. M. (2002). *Creating Breakthrough Products: Innovation from Product Planning to Program Approval,* Upper Saddle River, NY., Financial Times/Prentice-Hall.

Campbell, C. (1992). A decision theory model for entrepreneurial acts, *Entrepreneurship, Theory and Practice,* Vol. 17, No. 1, pp. 21-27.

Cantor, N. and Genero, N. (1986). Psychiatric diagnosis and natural categorization: A close analogy, In: Milton, T. and Klerman, G. (Eds.), *Contemporary directions in psychotherapy: Toward DSM IV,* New York, Guilford.

Cardon, M. S. (2008). Is Passion Contagious?, The transference of entrepreneurial passion in employees, *Human Resource Management Review,* Vol. 8, pp. 77-86.

Cardon, M. S., Wincent, J., Singh, J. and Drnovsek, M. (2005). Entrepreneurial Passion: The nature of emotions in entrepreneurship, In: Weaver, K. M. (Ed.), *Proceedings of the Sixty-fifth Annual meeting of the Academy of Management.*

Cardon, M. S., Zietsma, C., Saparito, P., Matherne, B. P. and Davis, C. (2005). A tale of passion: New insights into entrepreneurship from a parenthood metaphor, *Journal of Business Venturing,* Vol. 20, pp. 23-45.

Cardon, M. S., Wincent, J., Singh, J. and Drnovsek, M. (2005). The different faces of entrepreneurial affect: why entrepreneurial emotion and passion are distinct, *Paper presented to the 2008 Academy of management Conference,* Anaheim, CA.

Carlson, K. A. and Russo, J. E. (2001). Biased interpretation of evidence by mock jurors, *Journal of Experimental Psychology: Applied,* Vol. 7, pp. 91-103.

Carroll, J. S. (1978). The effect of imagining an event on expectations for the event: an interpretation in terms of the availability heuristic, *Journal of Personality and Social Psychology,* Vol. 36, pp. 1501-1511.

Cartwright, D. and Zander, A. (1960). *Group Dynamics: Research and Theory,* London, Tavistock Publications.

Carver, C. S. and Scheier, M. F. (1990). Origins and functions of positive and negative affect: A control process view, *Psychological Review,* Vol. 97, pp. 19-35.

Casson, M. (1995). *Entrepreneurship and Business Culture,* Aldershot, Uk and Brookfield, US, Edward Elgar.

Casson, M., and Della Giusta, M. (2007). Entrepreneurship and Social Capital. Analysing the impact of social networks on entrepreneurial activity from a rational action perspective, *International Small Business Journal,* Vol. 25, No. 3, pp. 220-244.

Cattell, R. B. (1966). *The Scientific Analysis of Personality,* Baltimore, Penguin.

Cennamo, L. & Gardner, D. (2008). Generational differences in work values, outcomes and person-organization values fit, *Journal of Management Psychology,* Vol. 23, No. 8, pp. 891-906.

Chaganti, R. (1986). Gender differences in full-time self employment, *Journal of Small Business Management,* Vol. 24, pp. 18-29.

Chamard, J. (1989). Public Education: Its Effect on Entrepreneurial Characteristics, *JSBE,* Vol. 6, No. 2, pp. 23-30.

Chandler, A. D. (1962). *Strategy and Structure: Chapters in the History of the Industrial Enterprise,* Cambridge, MA, MIT Press.

Chell, E., Haworth, J. M., and Brearley, S. (1991). *The Entrepreneurial personality: concepts, cases, and categories,* London, Routledge.

Chen, C. C., Greene, P., and Crick, A. (1998). Does entrepreneurial self-efficacy distinguish entrepreneurs from managers?, *Journal of Business Venturing,* Vol. 13, No. 4., pp. 295-317.

Chodorow, N. (1999). *The Power of Feeling: Personal Meaning in Psychoanalysis, Gender, and Culture,* New Haven, Yale University Press.

Christensen, C. (1997). *The Innovator's Dilemma,* Boston, Harvard Business School Press.

Christensen, L. T. and Cheney, G. (2000). Self-absorption and self-seduction in the corporate identity game, In: Shultz, M., Hatch, M. J. and Larsen, M. H. (Eds.) *The Expressive Organization: Linking Identity, reputation and the Corporate brand,* Oxford, Oxford University Press, pp. 246-271.

Chaiken, S., Liberman, A. and Eagly, A. H. (1989). Heuristic and systematic information processing within and beyond the persuasion context, In: Vlelmen, J. S. and Borgh, J. A. (Eds.), *Unintended Thought: Limits and Awareness Intention and Control,* New York, Guilford.

Chang, R., (2001). Turning Passion into Organizational Performance, *Training and Development,* Vol. 55, No. 5, pp. 104-112.

Chapman, G. E. (1983). Rituals and Rational Action in Hospitals, *Journal of Advanced Nursing,* Vol. 8, No. 1, pp. 13-20.

Chapman, G. B, and Johnson, E. J, (2003). Incorporating the Irrelevant: Anchors in Judgments of Belief and Value, In: Gilovich, T, Griffin, D, and Kahneman, D, (Eds.), *Heuristics and Biases: The Psychology of Intuitive Judgment,* Cambridge, UK, Cambridge University Press.

Chase, W. G. and Simon, H. A. (1973). Perception in chess, *Cognitive Psychology,* Vol. 4, pp. 55-81.

Claxton, G. (1990), Meditation in Buddhist Psychology, In: West, M. A. (Ed,), *The Psychology of Meditation,* Oxford, Clarendon Press.

Clement, J. (1987). The use of analogies and anchoring intuitions to remediate misconceptions in mechanics, Paper presented to the *Annual Meeting of AERA,* Washington, DC.

Clouse, V. (1990). A controlled experiment relating entrepreneurial education to student's start-up decisions, *Journal of Small Business Management,* Vol. 28, No. 2, pp. 45-53.

Clydesdale, T., (2007). *The first year out: Understanding American teens after high school,* Chicago, Il., The University of Chicago Press.

Cochran, J. (2007). Generation Y Not Now?, *Franchising World,* Vol. 39, No. 1, pp. 91-94.

Cohen, P., Slomkowski, C., and Robins, L. N., (1999). *Historical and Geographical Influences on Psychopathology,* Mahwah, NJ., Lawrence Enblaum Inc.

Collin, A. (1990). Mid-life career change research, In Young, R. A. and Borgen, W. A. (Eds.), *Methodological approaches to the study of career,* New York, Praeger Publishers, pp. 197-220.

Collins, A. M. and Loftus, E. F. (1975). A spreading activation theory of semantic processing, *Psychological Review,* Vol. 82, pp. 407-428.

Connolly, R., O'Gorman, B., and Bogue, J. (2003). Are the barriers to business start-up greater for female recent graduate entrepreneurs (FRGES) than recent male graduate entrepreneurs (MGGES)?, In: Butler, J. E. (Editor), *Women Entrepreneurs: A volume in research in entrepreneurship and management,* Greenwich, Connecticut, Information Age Publishing, pp. 151-180.

Cooper, A. C. and Dunkelberg, W. C. (1987). Entrepreneurial research: Old questions, new answers, and methodological issues, *American Journal of Small Business,* Vol. 11, No. 3, pp. 1-20.

Cooper, A. C., Dunkelberg, W. C., and Woo, C. Y. (1988). Entrepreneurs' perceived chances for success, *Journal of Business Venturing,* Vol. 3, pp. 97-109.

Cordano, M. Scherer, R. F. and Owen, C. L. (2002). Attitudes towards women as managers: sex verses culture, *Women in Management Review,* Vol. 17, No. 2, pp. 51-60.

Coulter, J. W. (1942). *Little India of the Pacific,* Chicago, University of Chicago Press.

Cowling, M. and Mitchell, P. (1997). The evolution of U.K. self-employment: A study of government policy and the role of the macro-economy, *Manchester School,* LXV, pp. 427-442.

Cramer, P. (2000). Defense Mechanisms in Psychology Today: Further Processes for Adaptation, *American Psychologist,* Vol. 55, pp. 637-646.

Cromie, S. (1987). Motivations of Aspiring Male and Female Entrepreneurs, *Journal of Occupational Behavior,* Vol. 8, pp. 251-261.

Csikszentmihalyi, M., (1996). *Creativity: Flow and the psychology of discovery and invention,* New York, Harper Perennial.

Cuervo, A. (2005). Individual and Environmental determinants of Entrepreneurship, *International Entrepreneurship and Management Journal,* Vol. 1, pp. 293-311.

Darwin, C. (1972). *The Origin of Species,* London, John Murray.

Das, L. S. (2003). *Letting Go of the Person You Used to Be,* London, Bantam Books.

David, D., Schnur, J. and Belloiu, A. (2002). Another search for the "hot" cognitions; appraisal, irrational beliefs, attributions, and their relation to emotion, *Journal of Rational-Emotive & Cognitive-Behavior Therapy,* Vol. 20, pp. 93-131.

Day, R. R. (1987). The general theory of disequilibrium economics and of economic evolution, In: Batten, J., Casti, D., and Johansson, B. (Eds.), *Economic Evolution and Structural Adjustment,* Berlin, Springer, pp. 46-63.

Denzin, N. (1984). *On Understanding Emotion,* San Francisco, Jossey-Bass.

Deal, T. E. And Kennedy, A. A. (1982). *Corporate cultures: The Rites and Rituals of Corporate Life,* Harmondsworth, Pengiun Books.

De Board, R. (1978). The Psychoanalysis of Organizations: A Psychoanalytical Approach to Behavior in Groups and Organizations, London, Tavistock Publications.

de Bono, E. (1985). *Six Thinking Hats,* London, Penguin Books.

de Bono, E. (1993). *Sur/petition,* Bodmin, Cornwall, Hartmolls Ltd.

Decrop, A. (1999). Tourists' decision-making and behaviour processes, In: Pizam, A. And Mansfeld, Y. (Eds.), *Consumer Behavior in Travel and Tourism,* London, Haworth Hospitality, pp. 103-133.

De Groot, A. D. (1965). *Thought and choice in chess,* The Hague, Mouton.

Dell, M. and Fredman, C. (1999). *Direct from Dell,* New York, HarperCollins business.

Delmer, F. And Davidsson, P. (2000). Where do they come from? Prevalence and characteristics of nascent entrepreneurs, *Entrepreneurship and Regional Development,* Vol. 12, pp. 1-23.

De Mause, L. (2002). *The Emotional Life of nations,* New York, Karnac.

Demetriou, A. and Kazi, S., (2006). Self-awareness in g (with processing efficiency and reasoning), *Intelligence,* Vol. 34, pp. 297-317.

Demoor, P., & Zhang, W. (2007). China's Y Generation, *Orion Journal of International Hotel Management,* No. 2, pp. 15-19.

de Silva, P. (1991). Buddhist Psychology: A review of theory and practice, *Current Psychology: Research and Reviews,* Vol. 9, No. 3, pp. 236-254.

Deutsch, J. A. and Deutsch, D. (1963). Attention: Some theoretical considerations, *Psychological Review,* Vol. 70, pp. 80-90.

Dewey, J. (1938). *Experience and Education,* New York, Macmillan Company.

Dhaliwal, S. (2000). Entrepreneurship – a learning process: the experiences of Asian female entrepreneurs and women in business, *Education & Training,* Vol. 42, No. 8, pp. 445-453

Dirkx, J. M. (1997). Nurturing Soul in Adult Learning, In: Cranton, P. (Editor). *Tranformative Learning in Action, New Directions for Adult and Continuing Education,* San Francisco, Jossey-Bass.

Dirkx, J. M. (2001). The power of feelings: Emotion, imagination, and the construction of meaning in adult learning, *New Directions for Adult and Continuing Education,* Vol. 89, pp. 63-72.

diSessa, A. A. (1993). Towards an epistemology of physics, *Cognition and Instruction,* Vol. 10, Nos. 1 & 2, pp. 105-225.

Doering, M., Rhodes, S. R. and Schuster, M. (1983). *The Aging Worker: Research and Recommendations,* Beverly Hills, Sage Publications.

Dollinger, M. (2003). *Entrepreneurship: Strategies and resources, 3rd Edition,* Englewood Cliffs, NJ., Prentice-Hall.

Dolton, P. and Makepeace, G. (1990). Self employment among graduates, *Bulletin of Economic Research,* Vol. 42, No. 1, pp. 35-53.

Dosi, G. (1988). The nature of the innovative process, In: Dosi, G., Freeman, C., Silverberg, G. and Soete, L. (Eds.), *Technical change and economic theory,* New York, Pinter, pp. 221-238.

Douglas, M. (1966). *Purity and Danger,* London, Routledge.

Doyle, C., C., (2001). Seeing through colored glasses, *Western Folklore,* Vol. 60, No. 1, pp. 67-91.

Drucker, P. F. (1986). *Innovation and Entrepreneurship,* New York, Harper Business.

Drucker, P.F. (1992). *The Age of Discontinuity: Guidelines for changing our society,* New York, Harper & Row.

Drucker, P. (1994). Post-Capitalist Society, New York, HarperCollins Publishers.

Drummond, G. (1998). New Theorizing About Organizations: the emergence of narrative and social theory for management, *Current Topics for Management,* Vol. 3, pp. 93-122.

Drnovsek, M., Cardon, M. S. and Murnieks, C. Y. (2009). Collective passion in Entrepreneurial Teams, In: Carsrud, A. L. and Brännback, M. (Eds.), *Understanding the Entrepreneurial Mind: Opening the Black Box,* New York, Springer, pp. 191-215.

Duchesneau, D. and Gartner, W. (1990). A profile of new venture success and failure in an emerging industry, *Journal of Business Venturing,* Vol. 5, No. 5, pp. 297-312.

Dunn, T, and Holtz-Eakin, D. (2000). Financial Capital, Human Capital, and the Transition to Self-Employment: Evidence from Intergenerational Links, *Journal of labor Economics,* Vol. 18, No. 2, pp. 282-305.

Eich, E., Macauley, D. and Ryan, L. (1994). Mood dependent memory for events of the personal past, *Journal of Experimental Psychology, General,* Vol. 123, pp. 201-215.

EIM/ENSR (1997). *The European Observatory: Fifth Annual Report,* EIM Policy and Research, Zoetermeer

Ekman, P. (ed.), (1972). *Darwin and facial expression: A century of research in review,* New York, Academic Press.

Ekman, P. and Friesen, W. V. (1975). *Unmasking the face,* Englewood Cliffs, NJ., Prentice-Hall.

Ellis, A. (1991). The revised ABC's of rational-emotive therapy (RET), *Journal of Rational-Emotive & Cognitive behaviour Therapy,* Vol. 9, pp. 139-172.

Ellis, A. And Dryden, W. (1997). The practice of rational-emotive therapy (RET), New York, Springer.

Ellis, L. and Bonin, S. L., (2003). Genetics and occupation-related preferences, Evidence from adoptive and non-adoptive families, *Personality and Individual Differences,* Vol. 35, pp. 929-937.

Elster, J. (1999). *Alchemies of the Mind,* Cambridge, Cambridge University Press.

Evans, D. and Leighton, L. (1989). Some empirical aspects of entrepreneurship, *American Economic Review,* Vol. 79, pp. 519-535.

Eisenhauer, J. (1995). The entrepreneurial decision: Economic theory and empirical evidence, *Entrepreneurship Theory and Practice,* Vol. 19, No. 4, pp. 57-79.

Engle, R. W. and Oransky, N. (1999). The evolution from short-term memory: Multistore to dynamic models of temporary storage, In: Sternberg, R. (Editor), *The nature of Cognition,* Cambridge, MA, MIT Press.

Engler, J. (1993). Becoming somebody and nobody: Psychoanalysis and Buddhism, In: Walsh, R, V, (Ed.), *Paths beyond ego: The transpersonal vision,* New York, G. P. Putman & Sons, pp. 118-121.

Engler, J. (2003). Being somebody and being nobody: a reexamination of the understanding of self in psychoanalysis and Buddhism, In Safran, J. D, (Ed.), *Psychoanalysis and Buddhism: An unfolding dialogue,* Boston, Wisdom Publications, pp. 35-86.

Epstein, M. (1995) Thoughts Without a Thinker: Psychotherapy from a Buddhist Perspective, New York, Basic Books.

Epstein, S. and O'Brien, E. J. (1985). The person-situation debate in historical and current perspective, *Psychological Bulletin,* Vol. 98, No. 3, pp. 513-537.

Epstein, M. (2001). *Going on Being,* New York, Broadway Books.

Epstein, M. (2007). Psychotherapy without the self – a Buddhist perspective, London, Yale University Press.

Ericsson, K. A. (1985). Memory Skill, *Canadian Journal of Psychology,* Vol. 39, pp. 188-231.

Erikson, E. H. (1968). *Identity: Youth and Crisis,* New York, Norton.

Erikson, E.H. (1975). *Life History and the Historical Moment,* New York, Norton.

Erickson, T. and Mattson, M. (1981). From words to meaning: A semantic illusion, *Journal of Verbal learning and Verbal Behavior,* Vol. 20, pp. 540-552.

Estrada, C. A., Isen, A. M. and Young, M. J. (1997). Positive affect facilities integration of information and decreases anchoring in reasoning among physicians, *Organizational Behavior and Human Decision Processes,* Vol. 72, pp. 117-135.

Evans, D., Heuvelink, A., and Nette, D. (2003). The evolution of optimism: a multi-agent based model of adaptive bias in human judgment, *Proceedings of the AISB '03 Symposium on Scientific Methods for the Analysis of Agent-Environment Interaction,* University of Wales, pp. 20-25.

Eysenck, M. W., (1994). Intelligence, In: Eysenck, M. W. (Ed.). *The Blackwell Dictionary of Cognitive Psychology,* Cambridge, MA. Blackwell Publishers, pp. 192-193.

Fairlie, R. W. And Robb, A. (2005). The absence of African-American owned businesses: An anlaysis of the dynamics of self-employment, *Journal of Labour Economics,* Vol. 17, No. 1, pp. 80-108.

Farber, H. S. (2006). *Is the company Man an Anachronism? Trends in long term employment in the U.S., 1973-2005,* Network on Transitions to Adulthood Research Network Working Paper, May, *http://www.transad.pop.upenn.edu/downloads/farber%20with%20cover%20sheet.pdf,* (accessed 20th January 2010).

Fan, Y. (2000). A classification of Chinese culture, *Cross Cultural Management,* Vol. 7, No. 2, pp. 3-9.

Fenichel, O., (1941). *Problems of Psychoanalytic Technique,* Albany, NY, Psychoanalytic Quarterly.

Fiet, J. O. (2002). *Systematic Search for Entrepreneurial Discoveries,* Westport, Quorum Books.

Filion, L.J. (2004). Two types of self-employed in Canada, In: Dana, L.P. (Ed.), *Handbook of Research on International Entrepreneurship,* Cheltenham, UK, Edward Elgar Publishing, pp. 308-337.

Fine, C. (2010). *Delusions of Gender: How our minds, society, and neurosexism create differences,* New York, WW Norton & Company, Inc.

Fineman, S. (2003). *Understanding Emotion at Work,* London, Sage.

Fiske, S. T. and Taylor, S. E. (1991). *Social Cognition,* New York, McGraw-Hill.

Fiske, S. T. and Taylor, S. E. (1984). *Social Cognition,* Reading, MA., Addison-Wesley.

Foster, R. and Kaplan, S. (2001). *Creative Destruction,* New York, Currency.

Frederick, H. (2006). *Definitions of Entrepreneurship in World Languages (DVD),* Auckland, New Zealand, Ten3 Asia-Pacific ltd.

Fredrickson, B. L. (2001). The role of positive emotions in positive psychology: the broaden-and-build theory of positive emotions, *American Psychologist,* Vol. 56, pp. 218-226.

Freud, S. (1912). *Recommendations to Physicians practicing psycholanalysis,* (1912 edition, Vol. 12), London, Hogarth Press.

Friedman, T. L. (2005). *The World is Flat: The Globalized World in the Twenty-First Century,* London, Penguin Books.

Frijda, N. (1986). *The Emotions,* Cambridge, Cambridge University Press.

Fritz, R. (1991). *Creating,* New York, Fawcett Columbine.

Ferenczi, S. (1916). *Contributions to Psychoanalysis,* Boston, Richard Badger.

Finucane, M. L., Alhakami, A., Slovic, P., and Johnson, S. M. (2000). The affect heuristic in judgments of risks and benefits, *Journal of Behavioral Decision Making,* Vol. 13, No. 1., pp. 1-17.

Freeman, J. (1982). Organizational life cycles and natural selection processes, *Research in Organizational Behavior,* Vol. 4, pp. 1-32.

Freud, S. (1923). The ego and the id, In Strachey, J. (Ed.), *Standard Edition of the complete psychological works of Sigmund Freud,* London, Hogarth Press.

Freud S. (1933). New introductory lectures on psychoanalysis, In: Strachey, J. (Ed.). *The Standard Edition of the Complete Psychological Works of Sigmund Freud (Vol. 22),* London, Hogarth Press, (Reprinted in 1964).

Freud, A. (1936). *The Ego and Mechanisms of Defense,* London, Hogarth Press and Institute of Psycho-Analysis.

Freud, S. (Ed.). (1926). *Inhibition, Symptoms and Anxiety.* (1964 edition, Vol. 19), London, Hogarth Press.

Freud, S. (1950). *Totem and Taboo,* London, Ark Edition (1983).

Fuller-Love, N. and Thomas, E. (2004). Networks in small manufacturing firms, *Journal of Small Business and Enterprise Development,* Vol. 11, No. 2, pp. 244-253.

Gaglio, C. M, Katz, T. A. (2001). The psychological basis of opportunity identification: entrepreneurial alertness, *Small Business Economics,* Vol. 16, No. 2, pp. 95-111.

Gaglio, C. M. and Taub, R. P. (1992), Entrepreneurs and opportunity recognition, In: Churchill, N. C., Birly, S. Bygrave, W., Muzyke, D., Wetzel, W. E, (Eds.), *Frontiers of Entrepreneurship Research,* pp. 136-147.

Gardner, H. (1999). Intelligence Reframed: Multiple Intelligences for the 21st Century, New York, Basic Books.

Gardner, H. (2003). *Multiple Intelligence After Twenty Years,* Paper presented to the American Educational Research Association, Chicago, Illinois, 21st April, 2003.

Gardner, H. (2004). Frames of Mind: The Theory of Multiple Intelligence (Twentieth Anniversary Edition), New York, Basic Books.

Garry, M., Manning, C. G., Loftus, E. F. and Sherman, S. J. (1996). Imagination Inflation: Imagining a Childhood Event Inflates Confidence that it Occurred, *Psychonomic Bulletin and Review,* Vol. 3, No. 2, pp. 208-214.

Gartner, W. B. (1988). "Who Is an Entrepreneur?" Is the wrong question, *American Journal of Small Business,* Vol. 12, No. 4, pp. 11-32.

Gartner, W. B. (2007). Entrepreneurial narrative and a science of the imagination, *Journal of Business Venturing,* Vol. 33, pp. 613-627.

Geertz, C. (1973). *The Interpretation of Cultures,* New York, Basic Books.

Ghose, L. (2004). A Study in Buddhist Psychology: Is Buddhism truly pro-detachment and anti-attachment?, Contemporary Buddhism, Vol. 5, No. 2, pp. 105-120.

Gibb, A. A. (1987). Education for Enterprise: Training for Small Business Initiation – Some Contrasts, *JSBE,* Vol. 4, No. 3, pp. 42-47.

Gibbs, N. (2005). Midlife Crisis? Bring it on!, *Time, Vol. 165, No. 20,* May 16, pp. 52-60, 63.

Gilbert, D. T. and Osborne, R. E. (1989). Thinking Backward: Some curable and incurable consequences of cognitive busyness, *Journal of Personality and Social Psychology,* Vol. 57, pp. 940-949.

Gilbert, D. T., Pelham, B. W., and Krull, D. S., (1988), On cognitive busyness: When person perceivers meet persons perceived, *Journal of Personality and Social Psychology,* Vol. 54, pp. 733-740.

Gilhooly, R. H., Logie, R. H., Wetherick, N. E. and Wynn, V. (1993). Working memory and strategies in syllogistic-reasoning tasks, *Memory & Cognition,* Vol. 21, pp. 115-124.

Gilpin, R., (2000). *The Challenge of Global Capitalism: The World Economy in the 21st Century,* Princeton, NJ., Princeton University Press.

Glade, W. P. (1967). Approaches to a theory of entrepreneurial formation, *Explorations in Entrepreneurial History,* Vol. 4, pp. 245-259.

Glenberg, A. M., Meyer, M. and Linden, K. (1987). Mental models contribute to foregrounding during text comprehension, *Journal of Memory and Language,* Vol. 26, pp. 69-83.

Goffee, R. and Scase, R. (1983). Business ownership and women's subordination: A preliminary study of female proprietors, *Sociological Review,* Vol. 31, pp. 625-647.

Goldberg, W. A., Clark-Stewart, A. K., Rice, J. A. And Dellis, E. (2002). Emotional Energy as an Explanatory Construct for father's Engagement with Their Infants, *Parenting,* Vol. 2, No. 4, pp. 379-408.

Golding, B. (2001). Great Divides in Learning: youth learning pathways in rural and remote Australian towns, Proceedings of the *ACER Research Conference 2001: Understanding Youth Pathways,* Hilton on the Park Melbourne, 15-16th October, pp. 13-18, http:acer.edu.au/documents/RC2001_Proceedings.pdf, (accessed 29th November 2008).

Goldstein, W. M. and Hogarth, R. M. (1997). Judgment and decision research: Some historical context, In: Goldstein, W. M. and Hogarth, R. M., (Editors), *Research on Judgment and Decision making: Currents, Connections and Controversies,* Cambridge, Cambridge University Press, pp. 3-65.

Goleman, D. (2004). Destructive emotions and how we can overcome them: A dialogue with the Dalai Lama, London, Bloomsbury Publishing.

Goos, L. M. and Silverman, I. (2006). The Inheritance of Cognitive Skills: Does Genomic Imprinting Play a Role?, *Journal of Neurogenetics,* Vol. 20, No. 1 & 2, pp. 19-40.

Gordon, J. R. and Whelan, K. S. (1998). Successful professional women in midlife: How organizations can more effectively understand and respond to the challenges, *Academy of Management Executive,* Vol. 12, No. 1, pp. 8-24.

Goss, D. (1991). *Small Business and Society,* London, Routledge.

Gowda, M. V. R., (1999). Heuristics, biases and the regulation of risk, *Policy Science,* Vol. 32, pp. 59-78.

Grainger, J. and Whitney, C. (2004). Does the huamn mnid raed wrods as a whole?, *TRENDS in Cognitive Sciences,* Vol. 9, No. 2, P. 59.

Granovetter, M. (1985). Economic action and social structure: The problem of embeddedness, *American Journal of Sociology,* Vol. 91, No. 3, pp. 481-510.

Greenberg, L. S. and Safran, J. D. (1989). Emotion in Psychotherapy, *American Psychologist,* Vol. 44, No. 1., pp. 19-29.

Greeno, J. G. (1978). Natures of problem solving abilities, In: Estes, W. K. (Ed.), *Handbook of Learning and Cognitive Processes (Vol. 5),* Hillsdale, NJ., Erlbaum.

Gregory, W. L., Cialdini, R. B. and carpenter, K. M. (1982). Self-relevant scenarios as mediators of likelihood estimates and compliance: does imagining make it so? *Journal of Personality and Social Psychology,* Vol. 43, pp. 88-99.

Grif, A. (1994). Cultural beliefs and the organization of a society: a historical and theoretical reflection of collectivist and individualist societies, *Journal o Political Economy,* Vol. 102, pp. 912-950.

Grossman, P, (2004). Mindfulness Practice: A unique Clinical Intervention for the Behavioral Sciences, In: Heidenreich, T., and Michalak, J., (Eds.), *Mindfulness and acceptance in Psychotherapy,* Berlin, DVTG Press, pp. 16-18.

Govinda, L. A. (1991). *Buddhist Reflections,* York Beach, S. Weiser.

Grainer, J. and Whitney, C. (2004). Does the Human Mind Raed Wrods as a Whole?, *Trends in Cognitive Science,* Vol. 8, pp. 58-59.

Griffiths, P. J. (1986). On being mindless: Buddhist Meditation and the mind-body problem, La Salle, Open Court.

Guarino, M. (2010). Poor in the Suburbs: Smaller Towns Dealing With Surge of Poverty, *abc News,* February 14th, *http://abcnews.go.com/print?id=9819964,* (accessed 15th February 2010).

Guess, A. (2007). Enrollment Surge for Women, *Inside Higher ED,* 7th August, *http://www.insidehighered.com/layout/set/print/news/2007/08/07/enrollment,* (accessed 14th February 2010).

Gunderman, R. B. (2000). Strategic Imagination, *AJR,* Vol. 175, pp. 973-976.

Gupta, S. K. (1992). The Informal Education of the Indian Entrepreneur, *JSBE,* Vol. 9, No. 4, pp. 63-70.

Habbershon, T. G. (2007). The Family as a Distinct Context for Entrepreneurship, in: Rice, M. P. and Habbershon, T. G. (Eds.). *Entrepreneurship: The engine of growth,* Westport, Connecticut, Praeger Perspectives.

Hall, D. T. (2002). *Careers in and out of Organizations,* Thousand Oaks, CA., sage Publications.

Hambrick, D.C. (1995). Fragmentation and the other problems CEOs have with their top management teams, *California Management Review,* Vol. 37, pp. 110-127.

Hamer, M. (2010). Aussie Girls Prefer Single Life, *Sunday Herald-Sun,* 14th February, http://www.herald   sun.com.au/news/aussie-girls-prefer-single-life/story-e6fri716-1, (accessed 14th February 2010).

Hammond, J. and Morrison, J. (1996). *The stuff Americans are made off: The seven cultural forces that define Americans – A new framework for quality, productivity, and profitability,* New York, MacMillan General References.

Hanh, T, N. (1976). *The Miracle of Mindfulness,* Boston, Beacon Press.

Hansen, L. S., (1993). Career Development Trends and Issues in the United States, *Journal of Career Development,* Vol. 20, No. 1., pp. 7-24.

Harré, R. (1991). *Physical Being: A Theory of Corporeal Psychology,* Blackwell, Oxford.

Harris, R. J. (1978). The effect of jury size and judge's instructions on memory for pragmatic implications from courtroom testimony, *Bulletin of the Psychonomic Society,* Vol. 11, pp. 129-132.

Hart, P. (1994). *Government: A Study of Small Groups and Policy failure.* Baltimore, The John Hopkins University Press.

Hart, S. and Milstein, M. (1999). Global sustainability and the creative destruction of industries, *Sloan Management Review,* Vol. 41, No. 1, pp. 23-33.

Hart, S. L. and Sharma, S. (2004). Encouraging fringe stakeholders for competitive imagination, *Academy of Management Executive,* Vol. 18, No. 1, pp. 7-18.

Hastie, R. and Pennington, N. (2000). Explanation based decision making, In: Connolly, K., Arkes, H. R. and Hammond, K. R. (Eds.), *Judgment and Decision Making: An interdisciplinary approach, 2nd Ed.,* Cambridge, Cambridge University Press, pp. 212-228.

Hatch, M. J. and Schultz, M. (2002). The Dynamics of Organizational Identity, *Human Relations,* Vol. 55, pp. 989-1018.

Hayek, F. (1945). The use of knowledge in society, *Am. Econ. Rev.,* Vol. 35, No. 4, pp. 519-530.

Heath, C. and Tversky, A. (1991). Performance and belief – ambiguity and competence in choice under uncertainty, *Journal of Risk and Uncertainty,* Vol. 4, pp. 5-28.

Helson, R. and Picano, J. (1990). Is the traditional role bad for women? *Journal of Personality and Social Psychology,* Vol. 59, pp. 311-320.

Herbig, P. A. And Miller, J. C. (1992). Culture and technology: Does the traffic move in both directions? *Journal of global marketing,* Vol. 6, No. 3, pp. 75-104.

Herbert, R. and Link, A. (1988). *The Entrepreneur: Mainstream Views and Radical Critiques,* New York, Praeger.

Herron, L. (1990). *The effects of characteristics of the entrepreneur on new venture performance,* Columbia, University of South Carolina Press.

Hicks, M. J. (2004). *Problem Solving and Decision making: Hard, Soft and Creative Approaches, 2nd Edition,* London, Thomson Learning.

Higgins, M. C. and Gulati, R. (2003). Getting off to a good start: The effects of upper echelon affiliation on underwriter prestige, *Organization Science,* Vol. 14, pp. 244-263.

Hillerbrand, E. (1989). Cognitive differences between experts and novices: implications for group supervision, *Journal of Counseling and Development,* Vol. 67, No. 5, pp. 293-296.

Hillman, J. (1975). *Re-visioning Psychology,* New York, Harper.

Hisrich, R. D. (1990). Entrepreneurship/intrapreneurship, *American Psychologist,* Vol. 45, No. 2, pp. 209-222.

Hisrich, R. D. And Brush, C. (1983). The Women entrepreneur: Implications of family, educational, and occupational experience, In: Hornaday, J. A., Timmons, J. A., and Vesper, K. H. (eds.), *Frontiers of entrepreneurship research,* Wellesley, MA, Babson College, Centre for Entrepreneurial Studies.

Hjalager, A-M, (1996). Agricultural diversification into tourism: Evidence of a European Community Development Programme, *Tourism management,* Volume 17, No. 2, pp. 103-111.

Hofstede, G., (1980). *Culture's Consequences: International Differences in Work Related Values,* Newberry Park, CA, Sage.

Hofstede, G. (1991). *Cultures and Organizations: Intercultural Cooperation and its Importance for Survival; Software of the Mind,* London, McGraw-Hill.

Hofstede, G. H., (2001). Culture's Consequences: Comparing values, behaviors, institutions, and organizations across nations, 2nd Ed., Thousand Oaks, CA., Sage Publications.

Holliday, W. & Li, Q. (2004). Understanding the Millennials: Updating Our Knowledge About Students, *Reference Services Review,* Vol. 32, No. 4, pp. 356-366.

Hollis, J. (2007). *Why Good People Do Bad Things: Understanding our darker selves,* New York, Gotham.

Holtz-Eakin, D., Joulfaian, D., and rosen, H. (1994). Sucking it out: Entrepreneurial survival and liquidity constraints, *Journal of Political Economy,* Vol. 102, No. 1, pp. 53-75.

Homer-Dixon, T. (2001). *The Ingenuity Gap: Can We Solve the Problems of the Future?* Toronto, Alfred A. Kropf.

Hornaday, D. A. and Aboud, J. (1971). Characteristics of successful entrepreneurs, *Personal Psychology,* Vol. 24, pp. 141-153.

Hull, D., Bosley, J. and Udell, G. (1980). Renewing The Hunt for the Heffalump: Identifying Potential Entrepreneurs by Personality Characteristics, *Journal of Small Business*, Vol. 18, No. 1., pp. 11-18.

Hunter, M. (2006). Mindset Barriers Against the Development of Malaysian Agriculture, *Proceedings of the SME-Entrepreneurship and Global Conference 2006,* Kuala Lumpur.

Hunter, M. (2008). Revolutionary Empowerment: A Relook at Spirituality, Cultural Integrity and Development, Proceedings of the *SME-Entrepreneurship Global Conference 2008,* 2-4th July, Melbourne Australia.

Irvine, J. J. And York, D. E., (1995). Learning Styles and Culturally Diverse Students: A Literature Review, In: Banks, J. A, and McGee Banks, C. A. (Eds.), *Handbook of Research on Multicultural Education,* New York, Macmillan.

Isen, A. M. (2000). Positive affect and decision making, In: Lewis, M., Haviland-Jones, J., (Eds.), *Handbook of Emotions,* New York, Guilford Press, pp. 417-435.

Isen, A. M. and Labroo, A. A., (2003). Some ways in which positive affect facilitates decision marking and judgment, In: Schneider, S. L. and Shanteau, J. R. (eds.), *Emerging perspectives on Decision Research,* New York, Cambridge Press, pp. 365-393.

Jackson, J. and Rodney, G. (1994). The attitudinal climate for entrepreneurial activity, *Public Opinion Quarterly,* Vol. 58, No. 5, pp. 467-488.

Jaggar, A. (1989). Love and Knowledge: Emotion in Feminist Epistemology, *Inquiry,* Vol. 32, pp. 151-176.

Jaipal, R. (2004). Indian conceptions of mental health, healing and the individual, In: Gielen, U., Fish, J. M. and Draguns, J. G. (Eds.), *Handbook of Culture, Therapy and Healing,* Mahwah, NJ, Lawrence Erlbaum & Associates, Inc., pp. 293-310.

Janis, I.L. (1972). Victims of Groupthink: A Psychological Study of Foreign Policy Decisions and Fiascos. Boston, Houghton Mifflin Company.

Janis, I.L. (1982). Groupthink: A Psychological Study of Policy decisions and Fiascos. Boston, Houghton Mifflin Company.

Jaques, E. (1955). Social Systems as a Defence Against Persecutory and Depressive Anxiety, In Klein, M., Heimann, P. and Money-Kyrle, R., (Eds.), *New Directions in Psychoanalysis,* London, Tavistock Publications.

Jasnchik, S. (2006). New Take on the Gender gap, *Inside Higher ED, 26th April,* *http://insidehighered.com/layout/set/print/news/2006/04/26/gebder,* (accessed 14th February 2010).

Jawer, M. A. And Micozzi, M. S. (2009). *The Spiritual Anatomy of Emotion: How feelings link the brain, the body and the sixth sense,* Rochester, Park Street Press.

Johnson, M. K. (1988). Reality Monitoring: an experimental phenomenological approach, *Journal of Experimental Psychology: General,* Vol. 117, pp. 371-376.

Johnson, S., McMillan, J., and Woodruff, C. (2000). Entrepreneurs and the ordering of Institutional Reform: Poland, Slovakia, Romania, Russia and the Ukraine Compared, *Economics of Transition,* Vol. 8, pp. 1-36.

Johnson, S., McMillan, J., and Woodruff, C. (2002). Property rights and Finance, *American Economic Review,* Vol. 92, pp. 1335-1356.

Johnson, M. K. and Sherman, S. J. (1990). Constructing and reconstructing the past and the present, In: Higgins, E. T. and Sorrentino, R. M. (Editors), *Handbook of motivational and social cognition: foundations of social behavior,* New York, Guilford Press, pp. 482-526.

Johnson, M. K., Hashtroudi, S., and Lindsay, D. S. (1993). Source Monitoring, *Psychological Bulletin,* Vol. 114, pp. 3-28.

Helfat, C., and Lieberman, M. (2002). The birth of capabilities: market entry and the importance of pre-history, *Industrial and Corporate Change,* Vol. 11, pp. 725-760.

Henrekson, M. (2005). Entrepreneurship: A weak link in the welfare state, *Industrial and Corporate Change,* Vol. 13, No. 3, pp. 447-467.

Herrmann, N. (1995). *The Creative Brain: Insights into creativity, communication, management, education and self-understanding,* Lake Lure, NC, The Ned Herrmann Group.

Herrmann, N. (1996). *The Whole Brain Business book: Unlocking the power of whole brain thinking in organizations and individuals,* New York, McGraw-Hill.

Hollingshead, A. B. (1975). *Four factor Index of Social Status,* Unpublished Working Paper, Department of Sociology, Yale University, New Haven, CT., *http://www.yale-university.com/sociology/faculty/docs/hollingshead_socStat4factor.pdf,* (accessed 15th February 2011).

Hunter, M. (2008). Towards an Islamic Business Model: A Tawhid Approach, In; Buttigieg, D. And Ndubisi, N. O. (Eds.), *Proceedings of the SME-Entrepreneurship Global Conference 2-4th July 2008,* Monash University, Melbourne, Australia.

Hunter, M. (2009). *Essential Oils: Art, Science, Industry, Agriculture and Entrepreneurship: A focus on the Asia-Pacific Region,* New York, Nova Science Publishers.

Johnson, B. R. (1990). Toward a multidimensional model of entrepreneurship: The case of achievement motivation and the entrepreneur, *Entrepreneurship: Theory & Practice,* Vol. 14, No. 3, pp. 39-48.

Johnson, L. (2006). Mind Your X's and Y's: satisfying the cravings of a new generation of consumers, New York, Free Press.

Johnson, P. (1986). *New Firms: An Economic Perspective,* London, Allen and Unwin.

Johnson, S. (2005). Everything bad is good for you: How today's popular culture is actually making us smarter, New York, Riverhead Books.

Jonassen, D. H. and Grabowski, B. L. (1993). Cognitive controls, In: Jonassen, D. H. and Grabowski, B. L. (Eds.), *Handbook of Individual Differences, Learning and Instruction,* London, Lawrence Erlbaum Associates.

Jones, R. (2007). Can Toyota's Scion Keep its Edge?: Brand aimed at famously fickle Generation Y buyers, *msnbc,* 21st March, *http://www.msnbc.msn.com/id/17688646/,* (accessed 17th December 2009).

Jones-Evans, D. (1995). A Typology of technical based entrepreneurs, *International Journal of Entrepreneurial research and Behaviour,* Vol. 1, No. 1, pp. 26-42.

Jovanovic, B. (1982). Matching turnover and unemployment, *Journal of Political Economy,* Vol. 87, pp. 1246-1260.

Jung, C. G. (1964). *Man and His Symbols,* London, Dell.

Kadison, R. D. and DiGeronimo, T. F. (2004). College of the overwhelmed: The campus mental health crisis and what to do about it, San Francisco, Jossey-Bass.

Kahneman, D. (1973). *Attention and Effort,* Englewood Cliffs, NJ, Prentice-Hall.

Kahneman, D. and Frederick, S. (2002). Represetativeness Revisited: Attribute Substitution in Intuitive Judgment, In: Gilovich, T, Griffin, D., Kahneman, D., *Heuristics and Biases: The Psychology of Intuitive Judgment,* Cambridge, UK, Cambridge University press, pp. 49-81.

Kalin, M. G. (1974). The Utopian Flight from Unhappiness: Freud against Marx on Social Progress, Chicago, Nelson-Hall.

Kao, R. W. Y., Kao, R. R., and Jing, Y. (2006). *An Entrepreneurial Approach to Corporate Management, 2nd Edition,* Singapore, Pearson-Prentice-Hall.

Kanchier, C. and Unruh, W. R. (1989). Factors influencing career change, *International Journal for the advancement of counseling,* Vol. 12, pp. 309-321.

Kaptchuk, T. and Eisenberg, D. (1998). The Persuasive Appeal of Alternative Medicine, *Annals of Internal Medicine,* Vol. 129, No. 12, pp. 1061-1068.

Katz, J. A. (1992). A psychological cognitive model of employment status choice, *Entrepreneurship, Theory and Practice,* Vol. 17, No. 1, pp. 23-33.

Kearney, R. (1988). *The wake of imagination: Ideas of creativity in western culture,* London, Hutchinson.

Kenney, M. (1986). *Biotechnology: The university-industrial complex,* New Haven, Yale University Press.

Kent, C., Sexton, D. and Vesper, K.(1982). *Encyclopedia of Entrepreneurship,* Englewood Cliffs, NJ, Prentice-Hall Inc.

Kets de Vries, M. F. R. (1985). The dark side of entrepreneurship, *Harvard Business Review,* Vol. 63, No. 6. pp. 160-167.

Kets de Vries, F. R. and Miller, D. (1984). The Neurotic Organisation, Diagnosing and Changing Counterproductive Styles of Management, San Francisco, Jossey-Bass, Inc.

Kets de Vries, M. K. (1989). Can you survive as Entrepreneur?, In: Kao, J. (Ed.), *Entrepreneurship, Creativity, and Organization,* Englewood Cliffs, Prentice-Hall.

Khan, Z. (2005). *The Democratization of Invention: Patents and Copyrights in American Economic Development,* New York, Free Press.

Kidd, J. B. and Morgan, J. R. (1969). A Predictive information system for management, *Operational Research Quarterly,* June, pp. 149-170.

Kim, P. H., Aldrich, H. E. and Lisa, A. K. (2006). Access (not) denied: The impact of financial, human, and cultural capital on entrepreneurial entry in the United States, *Small Business economics,* Vol. 27, pp. 5-27.

King, R. (1994). Early Yogacara and its Relationship with the Madhyamaka School, Philosophy East & West, Vol. 44, No. 4, pp. 659-686.

Kirkpatrick, S. and Locke, E. A. (1991). Leadership: do traits matter? *Academy of management Executive,* Vol. 5, No. 2, pp. 48-60.

Kirzner, I. M. (1982). The theory of entreprenurship in economic growth, In Kent, C. A., Sexton, D. L. And Vesper, K. H. (Eds.), *Encyclopedia of Entrepreneurship,* Englewood Cliffs, NJ, Pentice-Hall, pp. 272-276.

Kitayama, S., Duffy, S., Kawamura, T., and Larsen, J. T. (2003). Perceiving an Object and its context in Different cultures: A cultural look at new look, *Psychological Science,* Vol. 14, No. 3, pp. 201-206.

Kirzner, I. M. (1973). *Competition and Entrepreneurship,* Chicago, IL., University of Chicago Press.

Kirzner, I. M. (1997). Entrepreneurial discovery and the competitive market process: an Austrian approach, *J. Econ. Lit.,* Vol. 35, pp. 60-85.

Klaukien, A. and Patzely, H. (2008). Entrepreneurial Passion and its Effect on Decision Making, *Frontiers of Entrepreneurial Research,* Vol. 28, No. 6.

Klein, G. (1998). *Sources of Power: How People Make Decisions,* Cambridge, MA., The MIT Press.

Klein, M. (1948). *Contributions to Psychoanalysis 1921-45,* London, Hogarth Press.

Klein, M. (1975). Envy and Gratitude and other works 1946-1963. London, Hogarth Press.

Klepper, S. and Simons, K. L. (2000). Dominance by birthrite: entry of prior radio producers and competitive ramifications in the U.S. television receiver industry, *Strategic Management Journal,* Vol. 21, pp. 997-1016.

Klepper, S. And Sleeper, S. (2001). Entry by spinoffs, Working Paper, Pittsburgh, Carnegie Mellon University.

Klevorick, A.R., Levin, R., Nelson, R, and Winter, S. (1995). On the sources of significance of inter-industry differences in technological opportunities, *Research Policy,* Vol. 24, pp. 185-205.

Koehler, D. J. (1991). Explanation, Imagination, and confidence in judgment, *Psychological Bulletin,* Vol. 110, pp. 499-519.

Kohn, M. L., Slomezynski, K. M. and Schoenbach, C. (1986). Social stratification and the transmission of values in the family: A cross-national assessment, *Sociological Forum,* Vol. 1, No. 1, pp. 73-102.

Kloosterman, R. and Rath, J. (Editors.), (2003). *Immigrant Entrepreneurs: Venturing Abroad in the Age of Globalization,* New York, Berg.

Kluckhohn, C., (1944). *Mirror for Man,* New York, Fawcett.

Kluckhohn, F.R. and Strodtbeck, F.L. (1961). *Variations in Value Orientations,* New York, Doubleday Currency.

Knight, R. M. (1987). Can Business Schools Produce Entrepreneurs? An Empirical Study, *FER,* Wellesley, MA. Babson College, pp. 603-604.

Ko, S. and Butler, J. E. (2003). *Alertness, Bisociative Thinking ability, and the discovery of Entrepreneurial Opportunities in Asian Hi-Tech Firms,* Frontiers of Entrepreneurial Research, Wellesley, MA, Babson College, *http://www.babson.edu/entrep/fer/BABSON2003/XVI/XVI-P3/xvi-p3.htm,* (Accessed 16th March 2010).

Kobak, R, (1999). The Emotional Dynamics of Disruptions in Attachment Relationships, In: Cassidy, J. and Shaver, P, (Eds.), *Handbook of Attachment,* New York, Guilford Press.

Koestler, A. (1976). *The Art of Creation,* London, Hutchinson.

Kohut, H. and Wolf, E. S. (1978). The Disorders of the Self and their Treatment: An Outline, *International Journal of Psycho-Analysis,* Vol. 59., pp. 413-425.

Kolb, D. A., Osland, J. S. and Rubin, I. M. (1995). *Organizational Behavior – An Experimental Approach, 6th Ed.,* Englewood Cliffs, Prentice-Hall.

Kotter, J. (2008). *A Sense of Urgency,* Boston, Harvard Business Press.

Korchin, S. J. (1986). Field Dependence, Personality Theory, and Clinical Research, In: Bertini, M., Pizzamiglio, L. and Wapner, S. (Eds.), *Field Dependence in Psychological Theory, Research and Application,* Hillsdale, NJ, Erbaum Associates Publishers, pp. 119-125.

Kornhaber, M. L. (2001). Howard Gardner, In: Palmer, J. A. (Ed.), *Fifty Modern Thinkers on Education. From Piaget to the present,* London, Routledge.

Kourilsky, M. (1994). Predictors of entrepreneurship in a simulated economy, *Journal of Creative Behavior,* Vol. 14, No. 3, pp. 175-198.

Kowert, P. A. (2002). Groupthink or deadlock: When do leaders learn from their advisors? Albany, Blackwell Publishing.

Kramer, R. M. (1998). Revisiting the Bay of Pigs and Vietnam decisions 25 years later: How well has the groupthink hypothesis stood the test of time?, *Organizational Behavior & Human Decision Processes,* Vol. 72, No. 2-3, pp. 236-271.

Kramer, R. M. (2003). The Harder They Fall, *Harvard Business Review,* Vol. 81, No. 10, pp. 58-66, 136.

Krueger, N. F. (1993). The impact of prior entrepreneurial exposure on perceptions of new venture feasibility and desirability, *Entrepreneurship, Theory and Practice,* Vol. 18, No. 1., pp. 5-21.

Krueger, N. F. and Carsrud, A. (1993). Entrepreneurship intentions: Applying the theory of planned behaviour, *Entrepreneurship & Regional Development,* Vol. 5, pp. 315-330.

Krueger, N. F. (2002). *Entrepreneurship: Critical perspectives on business and management, Vol. 1,* London, Routledge.

Kruglonski, A. W. (2001).Motivational Social Cognition: Enemies or a love story? *International Journal of Psychology and Psychological Therapy,* Vol. 1, No. 1., pp. 33-45.

Kruglanski, A. W. and Webster, B. M. (1991). Group member's reactions to opinion deviates and conformists at varying degrees of proximity to decision deadline and of environmental noise, *Journal of Personality and Psychology,* Vol. 61., pp. 212-225.

Kunreuther, F. (2003). The Changing of the Guard: What Generational Differences Tell us about Social-Change Organizations, *Nonprofit and Voluntary Sector Quarterly,* Vol. 32, No. 3, pp. 450-457.

Kuhn, A. (2008). Concerns Rise with Water of Three Gorges Dam, *NPR,* 2nd January, *http://www.npr.org/templates/story/story.php?storyId=17723829,* (Accessed 10th January 2010).

Kunjufu, J., (1986). *To be popular or smart: The black peer group,* Chicago, African American Images.

Ladner, L. (2005). Bringing Mindfulness to Your Practice, *Psychology Networker,* July/August, pp. 19-21.

Lahiff, S., & Hamilton, B. (2008). *MyGeneration Age of Avatars,* Sydney, Special Broadcasting Service, (Documentary).

Landau, R. (1982). The innovative milieu, In: Landstedt, S.B. & Colglarzion, E.W. Jr., (Eds.). *Managing Innovation: The social dimensions of creativity, invention, and technology,* New York, Pergamon Press.

Landry, R. R., McMillan, B. and Essiembre, C. (1992). A macroscopic model of the social and psychological determinants of entrepreneurial intent, In: Churchill, N., Birley, S., Bygrave, W., Muzyka, D., Wahlbin, C.and Wetzel, W. (Eds.). *Frontiers of Entrepreneurship Research,* Babson Park, babson College, pp. 591-605.

Lareau, A. (2002). Invisible inequality: social class and childrearing in black families and white families, *American Sociological Review,* Vol. 65, No. 5, pp. 747-776.

Larsen, R. J. and Buss, D. M. (2005). *Personality Psychology, 2nd Ed.,* New York, McGraw-Hill.

Larson, J. K. And Rogers, E. M. (1986). *Silicon Valley Fever: growth of high productivity culture,* Phoenix, Unwin Counterpoint.

Larsen, R. J. (2000). Toward a Science of Mood Regulation, *Psychological Inquiry,* Vol. 11, pp. 129-141.

Lasserre, P. and Schutte, H. (2006). *Strategies for Asia Pacific: Meeting new challenges, 3rd Edition,* Basingstoke, Hampshire and New York, Palmgrave MacMillan.

Laurie, L. and Whittaker, W. (1977). Managerial Myopia: Self-serving biases in organizational planning, *Journal of Applied Psychology,* April, pp. 194-198.

Lazarus, R. (1999). The Cognition-emotion Debate, In: Dalgleish, T. and Power, M. (Eds.). *A Handbook of Cognition and Emotion,* London, Wiley, pp. 3-20.

Lazarus, R. And Folkman, S. (1984). *Stress, Appraisal and Coping, New York, Springer-Veriag.*

Lazarus, R. S. and Cohen-Charash, Y. (2001). Discrete emotions in organizational life, In: Payne, R. L. and Cooper, C. L., (Eds.). *Emotions at Work: theory, research and applications for management,* Chichester, Sussex, John Wiley & Sons, pp. 45-81.

Le, A. (1999). Empirical Studies of Self-Employment, Journal of Economic Surveys, Vol. 13, No. 4, pp. 381-416.

Lean, G. (2006). The dead sea that sprang to life, *The Independent on Sunday: Environment,* 28th May, *http://www.independent.co.uk/environment/the-dead-sea-that-sprang-to-life-480061.html,* (accessed 10th January 2010).

Leighton, J. P. and Sternberg, R. J. (2003). Reasoning and problem solving, In: Healy, A. F. and Proctor, R. W. (Eds.), *Handbook of Psychology: Experimental Psychology, Vol. 4.,* New York, John Riley & Sons. Inc., pp. 623-648.

Leong, F.T. L. and Boyle, K. A. (1997). An individual differences and approach to midlife career adjustment: An exploratory study, In: Lachman, M. E. and James, J. B. (Eds), *Multiple Paths of Mid-Life Development,* Chicago, The University of Chicago Press, pp. 411-451.

Lerner, M., Brush, C. and Hisrich, R. (1995). Factors affecting performance of Israeli women entrepreneurs: An examination of alternative perspectives, In: Bygrave, W., Bird, B., Birley, S., Churchill, N., Hay., M., Keeley, R. and Wetzel, W., (Eds), *Frontiers of Entrepreneurial Research,* Babson Park, Babson College, pp. 308-322.

Lerner, M. and Hendeles, Y. (1993). New entrepreneurs and entrepreneurial aspirations among immigrants from the former USSR in Israel, In: Churchill, N., Birley, S., Bygrave, W., Doutriaux, J., Gatewood, E., Hoy, F. And Wetzel, W., (Eds.), *Frontiers of Entrepreneurship Research,* Babson Park, Babson College, pp. 562-575.

Lerner, M. J. and Miller, D. T. (2001). Just World Research and the Attributes Process – Looking Back and Ahead, *Psychology Bulletin,* Vol. 85., pp. 1030-1031, 1041-1042.

Leventhal, H. (1982). The integration of emotions and cognition: A view from the perceptual-motor theory of emotion, In: Clark, M. S. and Fiske, S. T. (Eds.). *Affect and Cognition: The 17th Annual Carnegie Symposium on Cognition,* Hillsdale, NJ., Eribaum.

Leventhal, H. (1984). A perceptual-motor theory of emotion, In: Berkowitz, L. (Ed.). *Advances in experimental social psychology,* New York, Academic Press, pp. 117-182.

Levison, D. (1978). *The Season's of a Man's Life,* New York, Knopf.

Levitt, J. (1960). Marketing Myopia, *Harvard Business School,* July-August, pp. 275-276.

Licht, A. N., Goldschmidt, C. and Schwartz, S. H. (2004). Culture, Law and Corporate Governance, Working paper, February 20, 2004, accessed at *http://papers.ssrn.com/sol3/papers.cfm?abstract_id=508402* (5th January 2010).

Lieberman, H. R. (2007). Cognitive methods for assessing mental energy, *Nutrition Neuroscience,* Vol. 10, No. 5-6, pp. 229-242.

Lichtenstein, P., Hershberger, S. L. and Pedersen, N. L. (1995). Dimensions of occupations; Genetic and Environmental influences, *Journal of Biosocial science,* Vol. 27, pp. 193-206.

Loasby, B., (1976). *Choice, Complexity and Ignorance,* Cambridge, Cambridge University Press.

Loasby, B. (1991). *Equilibrium and Evolution – An exploration of Connecting Principals in Economics,* Manchester, Manchester University Press.

Loftus, E. E. (1975). Leading questions and the eyewitness report, *Cognitive Psychology,* Vol. 7, pp. 560-572.

Loftus, E. F. (1993). The reality of repressed memories, *American Psychologist,* Vol. 48, pp. 518-537.

Low, A. (1976). *Zen and the Art of Creative Management,* New York, Playboy.

Lowry, A. (2009). Europe's New Lost generation, *Foreign Policy,* 13th July, *http://www.foreignpolicy.com/2009/07/13/eurpes_new_lost_generation,* (accessed 14th December 2009).

Lucan, B.C.(2008). *MyGeneration Y God,* Sydney, Special Broadcasting Service, (Documentary).

Lupton, D. (1998). *The Emotional Self: A Socio-cultural Exploration,* Thousand Oaks, Sage.

Lumsdaine, E. and Binks, M. (2003). *Keep on moving! Entrepreneurial Creativity and Effective problem Solving,* New York, McGraw-Hill.

Lumsdaine, E. and Lumsdaine, M. (1995). *Creative Problemsolving: Thinking skills for a changing world,* New York, McGraw-Hill.

Lykken, D. T. (2005). Mental Energy, *Intelligence,* Vol. 33, No. 4, pp. 321-335.

McCelland, D. C. (1968).Characteristics of successful entrepreneurs, Paper presented to the *Third Creativity, Innovation and Entrepreneurship Symposium,* Framingham, MA.

McGregor, D. M., (1960). *The Human Side of Enterprise,* New York, McGraw-Hill.

McQuial, D. (1983). *With Benefits to Hindsight: reflections on uses and Gratifications research: Critical Studies in mass Communication Theory: An Introduction,* Beverly Hills, CA, sage.

McClelland, D. C. (1961). *The achieving society,* Princeton, D. Van Nostrand.

McClelland, D. C. (1967). The Achieving Society, New York, Free Press.

McClelland, J. L. and Rumelhart, D. E. (1981). An interactive-activation model of context effects in letter perception, Part 1. An Account of Basic Findings, *Psychological Review,* Vol. 88, pp. 375-407.

McCormick, B. and Wahba, J. (2001). Overseas work experience, Savings and Entrepreneurship amongst migrants to LDCs, *Scottish Journal of political Economy,* Vol. 48, No. 2, pp. 164-178.

McDonnell, M. J. and Pickett, S. T.A. (1990). Ecosystem structure and function along urban-rural gradients: An unexploited opportunity for ecology, *Ecology,* Vol. 71, No. 4, pp. 1232-1237.

McMullan, W. E. and Long, W. A. (1987). Entrepreneurship education in the Nineties, *Journal of Business Venturing,* Vol. 2, No. 3, pp. 261-275.

McMullan, W. E., Long, W. A., Ray, D. A. and Vesper, K. H. (1988). New-Venture Development: The Calgary Experience, *JSBE,* Vol. 5, No. 4, pp. 3-11.

McWilliams, N. (1994). Psychoanalytic diagnosis: Understanding personality structure in the clinical process, New York, Guilford Press.

Maccoby, M. (2000). Narcissistic Leaders: The Incredible Pros, The Inevitable Cons, *Harvard Business Review,* Vol. 78, pp. 68-78.

Malecki, E. (1994). Entrepreneurship in regional and local development, *International Regional Science Review,* Vol. 16, No. 1 & 2, pp. 112-153.

March, J. (1996). Understanding how decisions happen in organizations, In: Shapira, Z. (Ed.), *Organizational Decision Making,* New York, Cambridge University Press, pp. 9-32.

Marcia, J. E. (2002). Identity and psychological development in adulthood, *Identity,* Vol. 2, pp. 7-28.

Markman, G. D., Balkin, D. B. and Baron, R. A. (2002). Inventors and new venture formation: The effects of general self-efficacy and regretful thinking, *Entrepreneurship: Theory & Practice,* Vol. 27, No. 2, pp. 149-165.

Markman, G. D. and Baron, R. A. (2003). Person-Entrepreneurship fit: why some people are more successful as entrepreneurs than others, *human Resource Management Review,* Vol. 13, pp. 281-301.

Marshall, J. (1994). Why women leave senior management jobs, In: Tanton, M, (Editor). *Women in Management: A developing presence,* London, Routledge, pp. 185-202.

Marshall, G. (2001). Creativity, Imagination and the World-Wide Web, *International technology and Society,* Vol. 4, No. 2.

Mason, M, Singleton, A. & Webber, R. (2008). *The Spirit Generation of Y: Young People's Spirituality in a Changing Australia,* Mulgrave, Victoria, John Garrett Publishing.

Matthews, G. B. (1969). Mental Copies, *Philosophical Review,* Vol. 78, pp. 53-73.

Matthews, C. and Moser, S., (1995). Family background and gender: Implications for interest in small firm ownership, *Entrepreneurship and Regional Development,* Vol. 7, pp. 365-377.

Mayo, E., (1945), *The Social Problems of an Industrial Civilization,* Boston, Harvard University Graduate School of Business Administration, Division of Research.

Mayo, E., (1947), *The Political Problems of an Industrial Civilization,* Boston, Harvard University Graduate School of Business Administration, Division of Research.

MCOT, (2006). Japanese firm to Assist in Setting up OTOP distribution centre in Japan, *Thai News Agency,* MCOT, Bangkok, 16th February 2006, *http://etna.mcot.net/query.php?nid=6740*

Menzies, I. E. P. (1960). A case-Study in the functioning of Social Systems as a Defence Against Anxiety: A Report on a Study of the Nursing Service of a General Hospital, *Human Relations,* Vol. 13, pp. 95-121.

Mesch, G. and Czamanski, D. (1997). Occupational closure and immigrant entrepreneurship: Russian Jews in Israel, *Journal of Socio-Economics,* Vol. 26, No. 6, pp. 597-611.

Metzner, R, (1997). The Buddhist six-worlds of consciousness and realty, *Journal of Transpersonal Psychology*, Vol. 28, No. 2., pp. 155-166.

Meyer, D. E. and Schvaneveldt, R. W. (1976). Meaning, Memory, Structure, and Mental Processes, *Science,* Vol. 192, pp. 27-33.

Meyerson, D. (1990). Uncovering socially undesirable emotions, *The American Behavioral,* Vol. 33, No. 3, pp. 296-307.

Miner, J. B. (1997). *A Psychological Typology of Successful Entrepreneurs,* Westport, CT, Quorum Books.

Miner, J.B., Smith, N. R., & Bracker, J.S. (1992). Defining the inventor-entrepreneur in the context of established typologies, *Journal of Business Venturing,* Vol. 7, No. 2, pp. 103-113.

Minniti, M. (1999). *Social environment and alternative patterns of entrepreneurial activity*, Working Paper, Babson, MA., Babson College.

Minniti, M. and Arenius, P. (2003). Women in Entrepreneurship, *The Entrepreneurial Advantage of Nations: First Annual Global Entrepreneurship Symposium,* April 29th, New York, United Nations.

Mintzberg, H. (1983). *Power In and Around Organizations,* Englewood Cliffs, Prentice-Hall.

Mirels, H. L. (1980). The avowal of responsibility for good and bad outcomes: The effects of generalized self-serving biases, *Personality and Social Psychology Bulletin,* Vol. 6, pp. 299-306.

Mirvis, P. H. and hall, D. T. (1996). Career development for the older worker, In: Hall, D. T. (Ed.), *The career is dead –long live the career,* San Francisco, Jossey-Bass, pp. 15-45.

Mitchell, R. W. (1993). Mental Models of Mirror-Self-Recognition: Two Theories, *New ideas in Psychology,* Vol. 3, pp. 295-325.

Mitchell, R. K., Smith, B., Seawright, K. W., Morse, E., (2000). Cross-Cultural Cognitions and the venture creative decisions, *Academy of management Journal,* Vol. 43, No. 5, pp. 974-993.

Mitchell, R. K, Smith, J. B, Morse, E. A, Seawright, H. W, Perero, A. M, and Mckenzie, B, (2002). Are entrepreneurial cognitions universal? Assessing entrepreneurial cognition across cultures, *Entrepreneurial Theory and Practice,* Vol. 26, No. 4, pp. 9-32.

Mitchell, R. K, Busenitz, L, Lant, J, McDougall, P. P, Morse, E. A, and Smith, B. (2004). The distinctive and inclusive domain of entrepreneurial cognition research, *Entrepreneurship, Theory and Practice,* Vol. 28, No. 6, pp. 505-518.

Mitroff, I. I. (1984). *Stakeholders of the Organizational Mind,* San Francisco, Jossey-Bass.

Mitroff, I. I. and Kilmann, R. H. (1976). Organization Stories: An Approach to the Design and Analysis of Organizations Through Myths and Stories, In: Kilmaan, R. H., Pondy, L. R. and Slevin, D. P. (Eds.), *The Management of Organization Design Strategies and Implementation,* New York, Elsevier/North Holland.

Moacanin, R. (1986). Jung's Psychology and Tibetan Buddhism: Western and Eastern Paths to the Heart, Boston, Wisdom Publications.

Moon, S. M. (2003). Personal talent, *High Ability Studies,* Vol. 14, No. 1, pp. 5-21.

Moore, T. (1992). *Care of the Soul: A Guide for Cultivating Depth and Sacredness in Everyday Life,* New York, HarperCollins.

Morales-Gualdrón, S. T. and Roig, S. (2005). The new venture decision: An analysis based on the GEM database, *International Entrepreneurship and management Journal,* Vol. 1, pp. 479-499.

Morgan, G. (2006). *Images of Organization (Updated Edition),* Thousand Oaks, California, Sage Publishing Inc.

Morgan, M. G. and Henrion, M. (1990). Uncertainty: A Guide to Dealing with Uncertainty in Quantitative Risk and Policy Analysis, Cambridge, Cambridge University Press.

Mortimer, J. T. (1974). Patterns of intergenerational occupational movements: A smallest-space analysis, *American Journal of Sociology,* Vol. 79, No. 5, pp. 1278-1299.

Mortimer, J. T. (1976). Social class, work and the family: Some implications of the father's occupation and their son's career decisions, *Journal of Marriage and the Family,* Vol. 38, No. 2, pp. 241-256.

Mueller, S. L. And Thomas, A. S. (2001). Culture and Entrepreneurial Potential: a Nine Country study of Locus of Control and Innovativeness, *Journal of Business Venturing,* Vol. 16, pp. 51-75.

Muir, D. and Bass, S. (2009). 1 in 6 Americans Live Below the Poverty Line, *abc News,* Oct. 20th, *http://abcnews.go.com/pint?id=8875374,* (accessed 21st February 2010).

Murphy, P. E. (1981). Community Attitudes to Tourism: A Comparative Analysis, *Journal of International Tourism management,* Vol. 2, No. 3, pp. 189-195.

Murray, M. (1991). *Beyond the myths and the magic of mentoring: How to facilitate an effective mentoring program,* San Francisco, Jossey-Bass.

Murray, H. A. (1938). *Explorations in Personality,* New York, Oxford University Press.

Nesher, P. (1987). Towards and instructional theory: The role of students' misconceptions, *For Learning of Mathematics,* Vol. 7, No. 3, pp. 33-40.

Nesse, R. (1991). What good is feeling bad? *The Sciences,* Nov-Dec., pp. 30-37.

Nesse, R. (1998). Emotional disorder in evolutionary perspective, *British Journal of medical Psychology,* Vol. 71, pp. 397-415.

Newell, A. and Simon, H. A. (1972). *Human Problem Solving,* Englewood Cliffs, NJ, Prentice-Hall.

Newman, B. M. and Newman, P. R. (2007). *Theories of Human Development,* Mahwah, NJ, Lawrence Erlbaum Associates Publishers.

Ng, E. G. H. and Ng, C. W. (2003). Women Micro-Entrepreneurs in Hong Kong, In: Butler, J. (Editor). *New Perspectives on Women Entrepreneurs,* Greenwich, Connecticut, Information Age Publishing, pp. 121-150.

Nicolaou, N., Shane, S., Cherkus, L., Hunkin, J., and Spector, T. D., (2008). Is there a tendency to engage in entrepreneurship genetic?, *Management Science,* Vol. 54, No. 1, pp. 167-179.

Nicolaou, N., Shane, S., Cherkus, L., and Spector, T. D., (2008). Opportunity Recognition and the tendency to be an entrepreneur: A bivariate genetics perspective, *Organization Behavior and Decision Processes,* Vol. 110, No. 2, pp. 106-117.

Niefert, M. and Tchouvakhina, M (2006). Gründungen aus der Arbeitslosigkeit – Besondere Merkmale und Unterschiede zu anderen Gründungen, *Mittelstands- und Strukturpolitik,* Vol. 35, pp. 109-123.

Norman, D. A., (1968). Toward a theory of memory and attention, *Psychological Review,* Vol. 75, pp. 522-536.

North, D. C. (1990). *Institutions, Institutional Change and Economic Performance,* Cambridge, UK, Cambridge University Press.

North, D. C. and Davis, L. (1971). *Institutional Change and American Economic Growth,* Cambridge, Cambridge University Press.

North, D. C., Davis, L. and Weingast, B. (1989). Constitutions and Commitment: The Evolution of Institutions Governing Public Choices in Eighteenth Century England, *Journal of Economic History,* Vol. 49, pp. 803-832.

Noveck, J. and Tompson, T. (2007). *Poll: Family ties to youth happiness,* http//www.Boston.com/news/education/k_12/articles/2007/08/20/pdl_family_ties_key_to _youth_happiness/, (accessed 16th December 2009).

O'Brien, G., (1986), *Psychology of Work and Unemployment,* Psychology and Productivity at Work Series, Chichester, John Wiley & Sons.

O'Conner, P. (1981). *Understanding the Mid-Life Crisis,* Sydney, Sun Australia.

O'Connor, P. J. (2006). Mental Energy: Assessing the Mood Dimension, *Nutrition Reviews,* Vol. 64, No. 7, pp. S7-S9.

Odiorne, J. (1991). Competence verses passion, *Training and Development,* Vol. 45, pp. 61-65.

Ogbu, J. U. (1991). Immigrant and Involuntary Minorities in Comparative Perspective, In: Ogbu, J. U. And Gibson, M., (Eds.), *A Comparative Study of Immigrant and Involuntary Minorities,* New York, Garland.

Orhan, M. and Scott, D. (2001). Why Women Enter into Entrepreneurship: An explanatory Model, *Women in Management Review,* Vol. 16, No. 5, pp. 232-247.

Osbourne, M. (1991). The dark side of the entrepreneur, *Long range Planning,* Vol. 24, No. 3, pp. 26-31.

Ouchi, William, G. (1981). *Theory Z: how American business can meet the Japanese challenge,* Reading, Mass., Addison-Wesley.

Ouellette, J. (2007). The Death and Life of American Imagination, *The Rake, 16th* October, *http://www.secretsofthecity.com/magazine/reporting/features/death-and-life-american-imagination,* (accessed 15th February 2010).

Pang, J. (1972). Towards a certain "contextualism" II. (Foresight vs. Hindsight) vs. Insight, *Philosophia Mathematics,* s1-9, No, 2, pp. 158-167.

Panksepp, J. (1988). Posterior pituitary hormones and separation distress in chicks, Abstracts, *Society for Neuroscience,* Vol. 14, 287.

Parker, M. (2000). *Organizational Culture and Identity,* London, Sage.

Parker, S. C. (2004). *The Economics of Self-Employment and Entrepreneurship,* Cambridge, Cambridge University Press.

Payne, J. W. (1976). Task complexity and contingent processing in decision making: An information search and protocol analysis, *Organizational Behavior and Human Performance,* Vol. 16, pp. 366-387.

Payne, J. W., Bettman, J. R. and Johnson, E. J. (1993). *The Adaptive Decision Maker,* Cambridge, Cambridge University Press.

Peay, T. R. and Dyer, W. G. Jr. (1989). Power orientations of entrepreneurs and succession planning, *Journal of Small Business Planning,* January, pp. 47-52.

Peters, T. J. and Waterman, R. H. (1982). *In Search of Excellence: Lessons from America's Best-Run Companies,* New York, Collins.

Petty, R. E. and Cacioppo, J. J. (1986). The Elaboration Likelihood Model of Persuasion, IN Berkowitz, L. (Ed.), *Advances in Experimental Social Psychology,* Vol. 19., New York, Academic Press, pp. 123-205.

Pham, M. T. (2004). The logic of feeling, *Journal of Consumer Psychology,* Vol. 14, pp. 360-369.

Pizzamiglio, L. (1974). Handedness, ear-performance and field dependence, *Perceptual and Motor Skills,* Vol. 38, pp. 700-702.

Plaschka, G. R. and Welsch, H. P. (1990). Emerging structures in entrepreneurship education: Curricular designs and strategies, *ETP,* Vol. 14, No. 3, pp. 55-71.

Plomin, R., and Daniels, D. (1987). Why are children in the same family so different from one another?, *Behavioral and Brain Sciences,* Vol. 10, pp. 1-16.

Plomin, R. and Spinath, F. M., (2004). Intelligence: Genetics, genes, and genomics, *Journal of Personality and Social Psychology,* Vol. 86, pp. 112-129.

Plomin, R., DeFries, J. C., McClearn, G. E., and McGuffin, P. (2008). *Behavioral Genetics, 5th Edition,* New York, World Publishers.

Porter, M. E. (1980). *Competitive Strategy: Techniques for Analyzing Industries and Competitors,* New York, Free Press.

Portes, A. and Min Zhou, (1992). Divergent Destinies: Immigration, Poverty, and Entrepreneurship in the United States, Unpublished Manuscript, Department of Sociology, John Hopkins University, Baltimore, MD, *http://ladark.lib.utsa.edu/6/1/ladark8.txt,* (accessed 15th February 2010).

Posner, M. I., DiGirolamo, G. J. and Fernandez-Duque, D., (1997). Brain Mechanisms of Cognitive Skills, *Consciousness and Cognition,* Vol. 6, pp. 267-290.

Praag, C. and Pohem, H. (1995). Determinants of willingness and opportunity to start as an entrepreneur, *Kyklos,* Vol. 48, No. 4, pp. 513-540.

Prahalad, C. K. and Hart, S. (2002). The Fortune at the bottom of the pyramid, *Strategy and Business,* Vol. 26, pp. 54-67.

Prahalad, C. K. (2004). *The Fortune at the Bottom of the Pyramid: Eradicating Poverty Through profit,* Upper Saddle River, NJ., Wharton School Publishing.

Pronin, E., Lin, D. Y. and Ross, L. (2002). The Bias Blind Spot: Perceptions of Bias in Self verses Others, *PSPB,* Vol. 28, No. 3, pp. 369-381.

Qalo, R. (1997). *Small business. A Study of a Fijian Family,* Suva, Fiji, Macunabitu Education trust.

Qutb, S. (1953). *Social Justice in Islam,* Translated by John B. Hardie, New York, The American Council of Learned Societies.

Rafaeli, A. (1989). When Cashiers meet Customers: An Analysis of the Role of Supermarket Cashiers, *Academy of Management Journal,* Vol. 32, pp. 245-273.

Ramírez, M., and Castañeda, A., (1974). *Cultural Democracy, Bicognitive Development and Education,* New York, Academic Press.

Rashid, N. I. (19988). Work Values of Malay and Chinese Managers: A comparative Study, *Jurnal Psikologi Malaysia,* Vol. 4, pp. 24-45.

Ratcliff, R. and McKoon, G. (1988). A retrieval theory of priming in memory, *Psychological Review,* Vol. 95, pp. 385-408.

Ray, S. and Cardozo, R. (1996). Sensitivity and creativity in entrepreneurial opportunity recognition: a framework for empirical investigation, paper presented to the 6th Global Entrepreneurship Research Conference, Imperial College London.

Reed, S. K. (2007). *Cognition: Theory and Applications 7th Edition*, Belmont, CA, Thomson-Wadsworth.

Renn, O. (2004). Public Perception of nanotechnology, In: Proceedings of *Nanotechnologies: A Preliminary Risk Analysis,* 1-2 March, Brussels, Health and Consumer Protection Directorate general of the European Commission, *http://europa.eu.int/comm/health/ph_risk_en.htm*, (accessed 12th February 2010).

Renzulli, L., Aldrich, H. E., and Moody, J. (2000). Family matters: Consequences of personal networks for business startup and survival, *Social Forces,* Vol. 79, No. 2. Pp. 523-546.

Resnick, L. B., Nesher, P., Leonard, F., Magone, M., Omanson, S. and Peled, I. (1989). Conceptual basis of arithmetic errors: The case of decimal fractions, *Journal of Research in Mathematics Education,* Vol. 20, pp. 8-27.

Ressler, K., Sullivan, S. and Buck, L. (1994). A molecular dissection of spatial patterning in the olfactory system, *Current Opinion in Neurobiology,* Vol. 4, pp. 588-596.

Reynolds, P. (1997). Who wants new firms? Preliminary explorations of firms-in-gestation, *Small Business Economics,* Vol. 9, pp. 449-462.

Reynolds, P. D., Camp, S. M., Bygrave, W. D., Autio, E., and Hay, M. (2002). *Global Entrepreneurship Monitor 2001 Executive Report,* Babson Park and London, Babson College and London Business School.

Riding, R. and Rayner, S. (1998). *Cognitive Styles and Learning Strategies,* London, David Fulton Publishers.

Rioch, M. J. (1970). The Work of Wilfred Bion on Groups, *Psychiatry,* Vol. 33, No. 1, pp. 56-66.

Riessman, F. (1962). *The Culturally Deprived Child,* New York, Harper.

Robbins, A. (2006). The overachievers: The secret lives of driven kids, New York, Hyperion.

Roberts, E. (1991). *Entrepreneurs in High Technology,* New York, Oxford University Press.

Robinson, P. and Sexton, E. (2004). The effect of education and experience on self-employment success, *Journal of Business Venturing,* Vol. 9, No. 2, pp. 141-156.

Romanelli, E. and Schoonhoven, K. (2001). The local origins of new firms, In: Schoonhoven, K. and Romanelli, E. (Editors), *The Entrepreneurial Dynamic,* Stanford, Stanford University Press, pp. 40-67.

Ronstadt, R. (1988). The corridor principal, *Journal of Business Venturing,* Vol. 1, No. 3, pp. 31-40.

Rorty, R. (1980). *Philosophy and the mirror of nature,* Oxford, Blackwell.

Rosa. P., Hamilton, D., Carter, S. and Burns, H. (1994). The impact of gender on small business management: preliminary findings of a British study, *International Small Business Journal,* Vol. 21, No. 3, pp. 25-32.

Rosa, P., Kodithuwakku, S. S. and Balunywa, W., (2008). Entrepreneurial Motivation in Developing Countries: What does 'necessity' and 'opportunity' entrepreneurship really mean?, *Babson College Entrepreneurship Research Conference (BCERC),* http:ssm,com/abstract=1310913, (accessed 14th March 2010).

Roschelle, J. and Clancey, W. J. (1992). Learning as a social and neural, *Educational Psychologist,* Vol. 27, pp. 435-453.

Rosenzweig, P. (2007), *The Halo Effect,* London, Pocket Books.

Ross, B. H. and Kennedy, P. T. (1990). Generalizing from use of earlier examples in problem solving, *Journal of experimental Psychology: Learning, memory and Cognition,* Vol. 16, pp. 42-55.

Rotter, J. B. (1966). Generalized expectancies for internal verses external control of reinforcements, *Psychological Monographs,* Vol. 80, No. 609.

Rousseau, F. L. and Vallerand, R. J. (2003). The role of passion in the subjective well-being of the elderly, *Revue Quebecoise de Psychologie,* Vol. 24, pp. 197-211.

Rumelhart, D. E., Hinton, G. E. and McCelland, J. L. (1986). A general framework for parallel distributed processing, In: Rumelhart, D. E., McCelland, J. L. and the PDP Research Group (Eds.), *Parallel distributed processing: Explorations in the microstructure of cognition, (Vol. 1),* Cambridge, MA, Bradford.

Rowe, A. J. (2004). *Creative Intelligence: discovering the innovative potential in ourselves and others,* Upper Saddle River, NJ, FT Press.

Saarilouma, P. (1992). Visuospatial and articulatory interference in chess players' information intake, *Applied Cognitive Psychology,* Vol. 6, pp. 77-89.

Sachs, J. D. (2005). *The End of Poverty: Economic Possibilities for Our Time,* New York, Penguin Books.

Sadowski, M. S., Birchman, J. A. and Abe Harris, L. V. (2006). An Assessment of Graphics Faculty and Student Learning Styles, *Engineering Design Graphics Journal,* Vol. 70, No. 2, pp. 17-22.

Safran, J. D. (2003). Psychoanalysis and Buddhism as cultural institutions, In: Safran, J. D. (Editor), *Psychoanalysis and Buddhism: An unfolding dialogue,* Boston, Wisdom Publications, pp. 1-34.

Salinger, J. D. (1951). *The Catcher on the Rye,* Boston, Little, Brown & Co.

Sarasvathy, S. D. (2003). Entrepreneurship as a science of the artificial, *Journal of Economic Psychology,* Vol. 24, pp. 203-220.

Sarasvathy, S. D. (2001). Causation and Effectuation: Towards a theoretical shift from economic inevitability to entrepreneurial contingency, *Academy of Management Review,* Vol. 26, No. 2, pp. 243-263.

Sardello, R. (1992). *Facing the World with Soul: The Reimagination of modern life,* New York, HarperPerennial.

Sathe, V. (1989). Fostering entrepreneurship in the large diversified firm, *Organizational Dynamics,* Vol. 18, No. 1, pp. 20-32.

Saxenian, A. L. (1996). Beyond Boundaries: Open Labor markets and learning at Silicon Valley, In: Arthur, M. B. and Rousseau, D. M. (Eds.), *The Boundaryless Career,* New York, Oxford University Press, pp. 23-39.

Scarr, S. and McCartney, K. (1983). How children make there own environments: A theory of genotype environment effects, *Child Development,* Vo. 54, pp. 424-435.

Scarr, S., (1985). An authors frame of mind (Review of Frames of Mind: The Theory of Multiple Intelligences), *New Ideas in Psychology,* Vol. 3, No. 1, pp. 95-100.

Scarr, S. (1992). Development Theories for 1990s: Development and Individual Differences, *Child Development,* Vol. 63, pp. 1-19.

Schank, R. and Abelson, R. (1977). Scripts, goals, and understanding, Hillsdale, NJ, Erlbaum.

Schein, E. H. (1978). *Career Dynamics,* Reading, MA., Addison-Wesley.

Schein, E. H. (1980). *Organizational Psychology, 3rd Edition,* Englewood Cliffs, NJ., Prentice-Hall.

Schein, E.H., (2005). *Organizational Culture and Leadership, 3rd Edition,* San Francisco, Jossey-Bass.

Schlee, R. (2000). Mentoring and the professional development of business students, *Journal of Management Education,* Vol. 24, No. 3, pp. 322-337.

Schmitz, T, W., De Rosa, E. and Anderson, A. K., (2009). Opposing influences of affective state valence on visual cortical encoding, *The Journal of Neuroscience,* Vol. 29, No. 22, pp. 7199-7207.

Schnall, P. L., Landsbergis, P. A., and Baker, D. (1994). Job strain and cardiovascular disease, *Annual Review of Public Health,* Vol. 15, pp. 381-411.

Schneider, B. L. and Stevenson, D. (1999). *The ambitious generation: America's teenagers, motivated but directionless,* New Haven, CT, Yale University Press.

Schoenberger, E. (1993). Corporate Strategy and Corporate Strategists: Power, Identity, and Knowledge within the Firm, *Environment and Planning A,* Vol. 26, pp. 435-451.

Schumacher, E. F. (1973). *Small is Beautiful: Economics as if People Mattered,* London, Blond and Briggs.

Schwartz, S. H. (1996). Value priorities and behavior: Applying the Theory of Integrated Value systems, In: Seligman, C., Olsen, J. M. and Zanna, M. P. (eds.), *The Psychology of values, The Ontario Symposium, Vol. 8.,* Hillsdale, NJ., Erlbaum, pp. 1-24.

Schwartz, B. (2004). *The paradox of choice: Why more is less,* New York, Harper Perennial.

Scott, M. and Twomey, D. (1988). The long-term supply of entrepreneurs: Students career aspirations in relation to entrepreneurs, *Journal of Small Business Management,* Vol. 26, No. 4, pp. 5-13.

Segal, N. L. (1999). *Entwined Lives: Twins and what they tell us about human behavior,* New York, Plume.

Seo, M., Barrett, L. F., and Bartunek, J. M. (2004). The role of affective experience in work motivation, *Academy Management Review,* Vol. 29, pp. 423-440.

Sexton, D. L. And Bowman-Upton, N. (1985). The entrepreneur: A capable executive and more, *Journal of Business venturing,* Vol. 1, pp. 129-140.

Senge, P. (2006). *The Fifth Discipline: The Art and Practice of the Learning Organization,* (Revised and Updated Edition), London, Random House.

Sewell W.H. Jr. (1992). A theory of structure: duality, agency and transformation, *American Journal of Sociology,* Vol. 98, No. 1, pp. 1-29.

Sexton, D. L. and Bowman, N. (1985). The entrepreneur: A capable executive and more, *Journal of Business Venturing,* Vol. 1, No. 1, pp. 129-140.

Sexton, D. L. and Smilor, R. W. (1986). *The Art and Science of Entrepreneurship,* Cambridge, MA, Ballinger Publishing Company.

Shanahan, M. J. And Hofer, S. M. (2005). Social context in gene-environment interactions: Retrospect and prospect, *Journal of Gerontology,* (Special issue 1), pp. 65-76.

Shane, S. (1996). Hybrid organizational arrangements and their implications for firm growth and survival: A study of new franchisors, *Academy of Management Journal,* Vol. 39, No. 1, pp. 216-234.

Shane, S. (1999). Prior knowledge and the discovery of entrepreneurial opportunities, *Organizational Science,* Vol. 11, No. 4, pp. 448-469.

Shane, S., (2000). Prior Knowledge and the Discovery of entrepreneurial opportunities, *Organizational Science,* Vol. 11, pp. 448-469.

Shane, S. (2003). *A general Theory of Entrepreneurship: The individual-Opportunity Nexus,* Cheltenham, UK, Edward Elgar.

Shane, S. and Kurana, R. (2001). Career experiences and firm foundings, Paper presented to the Academy of management Meetings.

Shanker, M. C. and Astrachan, J. H. 'Family Business' Contribution to the U.S. Economy, *Family Business Review,* Vol. 16, No. 4, pp. 235.

Shapero, A. (1975). The displaced, uncomfortable entrepreneur, *Psychology today,* Vol. 11, No. 9, pp. 83-88.

Shapero, A. and Sokol. L., (1982). The social dimensions of entrepreneurship, In: Kent, C. A., Sexton, D. L. and Vesper, K. H. (Eds.), Encyclopedia of Entrepreneurship, Englewood Cliffs, HJ, Prentice-Hall, pp. 72-90

Shaver, K. G. and Scott, L. R. (1991). Person, Process, Choice: The psychology of new venture creation, *Entrepreneurship, Theory and Practice,* Vol. 16, No. 2, pp. 23-45.

Sherman, S. J., Cialdini, R. B., Schwartzman, D. F. and Reynolds, K. D. (1985). Imagining can heighten or lower the perceived likelihood of contracting disease: the mediating effort of ease of imagery, *Personality and Social Psychology Bulletin,* Vol. 5, pp. 207-232.

Sherwood, P. M. (2005). Buddhist Psychology: Marriage of Eastern and Western Psychologies, *www.sophiacollege.com/publications/Buudd%20pschoz.pdf,* (accessed 20th October 2009).

Shepherd, D. A. (2003). Learning from business failure: Propositions of grief recovery for the self employed, *Academy of Management Review,* Vol. 282, pp. 318-329.

Shirahase, S. (2000). Women's Increased Higher Education and the Declining Fertility rate in Japan, *Review of Population and Social Policy,* No. 9, pp. 47-63.

Shuman, J., Sussman, G. and Shaw, J. (1985). Business plans and the start-up of rapid growth companies, In: Hornaday, J., Shils, E., Timmons, J. and Vesper, K. (Eds.). *Frontiers of Entrepreneurial Research,* Babson Park, Babson College.

Shwaltz, J. and Wald, M. L. (2003). Smart people working collectively can be dumber than the sum of their brains: "Groupthink" is 30 years old and still going strong. *New York Times, 3rd March.*

Skirius, J. (2003). Railroad, Oil, and Other Foreign Interest in the Mexican Revolution, 1911-1914, *Journal of Latin American Studies,* Feb., pp. 25.

Sigrist, B. (1999). Entrepreneurial opportunity recognition, presented to the *Annual UIC/AMA Symposium at Marketing/Entrepreneurship Interface,* Sofia-Antipolis, France.

Silverman, A. J., Adevai, G. and McGough, W. E., (1966). Some relationships between handedness and perception, *Journal of Psychosomatic Research,* Vol. 10, pp. 151-158.

Simon, H. A. (1957). *Models of Man,* New York, Wiley.

Simon, H. A. (1971). Human problem solving: The state of the theory in 1970, *American Psychologist,* Vol. 26, pp. 145-159.

Simon, H. A. (1997). Behavioural economics and bounded rationality, *Models of Bounded Rationality,* Vol. 3, Cambridge, MA, MIT Press, Chapter 3.

Simon, H. A. (1997a). *Administrative Behavior, 4th Edition,* New York, Free Press.

Singh, S. P. Ruthie, G. and Muhammed, S. (2001). A gender based performance analysis of micro and small enterprises in Java Indonesia, *Journal of Small Business Management,* Vol. 39, No. 2, pp. 174-182.

Sinha, Y., Jain, U. C. and Pandey, J. (1980). Attribution of Causality to Poverty, *Journal of Social and Economic Studies,* Vol. 8, pp. 349-359.

Siu, W-S. (1996). Entrepreneur Typologies: The case of the owner managers in China, *International Small Business Journal,* Vol. 14, No. 1, pp. 53-64.

Smith, R. (1984). Groupthink and the hostage rescue mission, *British Journal of Political Science,* Vol. 15, pp. 117-126.

Smith-Hunter, A., Kapp, J. and Yonkers, V. (2003). A psychological model of entrepreneurial behavior, *Journal of Academy of Business and Economics,* Vol. 2, No. 2, pp. 180-192.

Smith, C. And Lazarus, R. (1993). Appraisal Components, Core Relational Themes, and the Emotions, *Cognition and Emotion,* Vol. 7, pp. 233-269.

Smith, M. (1987). The Huemean Theory of Motivation, *Mind,* Vol. 96, No. 381, pp. 36-61

Solomon, G. T. and Winslow, E, K. (1988). Toward a descriptive profile of an entrepreneur, *Journal of Creative Behavior,* Vol. 22, No. 1., pp. 162-171.

Sorensen, J. (2006). Closure vs. Exposure: mechanisms in the intergenerational transmission of self-employment, In: Ruef, M. and Lounsbury, M. (Eds.), *Research in the Sociology of organizations,* Elsevier, JAI Press.

Stanat, M. (2006). China's Generation Y: Understanding the future leaders of the World's next superpower, Paramus, NJ, Homa and Sekey.

Stanley, R. O. and Burrows, G. D. (2001). Varieties and functions of human emotion, In: Payne, R. L. and Cooper, C. L., (Eds.). *Emotions at Work: theory, research and applications for management,* Chichester, Sussex, John Wiley & Sons, pp. 3-20.

Stangler, D. (2009). *The Coming Entrepreneurship Boom,* Ewing Marion Kauffman Foundation, June, *http://papers.ssrn.com/sol3/papers.cfm?abstract_id=1456428,* (accessed 20th January 2010).

Sternberg, R. J. (1977). Component processes in analogical reasoning, *Psychological Review,* Vol. 84, pp. 353-378.

Still, L. V. and Timms, W. (2000). "I want to make a difference": Women Small Business Owners: Their Businesses, Dreams, Lifestyles, and Measures of Success, *Proceedings of the 44th International Council of Small business World Conference, http://161.31.108.27/research/icsb/2000/pdf/077.PDF,* (accessed 8th March 2010).

Sternberg, R. J. (1983). How much Gall is too much gall? (Review of Frames of Mind: The Theory of Multiple Intelligences), *Contemporary Education Review,* Vol. 2, No. 3, pp. 215-224.

Sternberg, R. J. (1991). Death, taxes and intelligence tests, *Intelligence,* Vol. 15, No. 3, pp. 257-270.

Stone, M. H., (1993). Abnormalities of Personality: Within and Beyond the Realm of treatment, New York, W. W. Norton & Co.

Storey, D. (1994). *Entrepreneurship and the New Firm,* London, Croom Helm.

Storr, A. (1979). *The Art of Psychotherapy,* New York, Methuen.

Strauss, W. and Howe, N. (1992). *Generations: The history of America's future 1584 to 2069,* New York, Harper-Perennial.

Strauss, W. and Howe, N. (2000). *Millennials rising: The next great generation,* New York, Vintage Books.

Stuart, R. W. And Abetti, P. A. (1990). Impact of entrepreneurial and management experience on early performance, *Journal of Business Venturing,* Vol. 5, pp. 151-162.

Stuart, T., Huang, H. and Hybels, R. (1999). Interorganizational endorsements and the performance of entrepreneurial ventures, *Administrative Science Quarterly,* Vol. 44, pp. 315-349.

Stumpf, S. S., Dunbar, R. L. and Mullen, T. P. (1991). Simulations in Entrepreneurship Education: Oxymoron or Untapped Opportunity?, *FER,* Wellesley, MA, Babson College, pp. 681-694.

Super, D., Savickas, M. L. and Super, C. M. (1996). The life-span, life-space approach to careers, In: Brown, D. and Brooks, L. (Eds.), *Career Choice and Development, 3rd Edition, San Francisco,* Jossey-Bass, pp. 121-178.

Sutherland, M. B. (1971). *Everyday imagining and education,* London, Routledge and kegan Paul.

Sweeny, R. (2006). *Millennial behaviors and demographics, http://library2.njit.edu/staff-folders/sweeney/Millennials/Article-Millennials-Behaviors.doc,* (accessed 15th December 2009).

Sy, T., Cote, S., and Saaverdra, R. (2005). The Contagious Leader: Impact of the leader's mood on the mood of group members, group affect tone, and group processes, *Journal of Applied Psychology,* Vol. 90, No. 2, pp. 295-305.

Tafuna'I, A. (2002). Poverty of Opportunity, Paper presented to the *New Zealand Development Network Conference,* Massey University, Palmerston North, New Zealand.

Taleb, N. N., (2007). *The Black Swan,* New York, Random House Inc.

Tashi Tsering, Geshe (2006). *Buddhist Psychology: The Foundation of Buddhist Thought, Vol. 3,* Somerville, MA., Wisdom Publications, P. 46.

Tarvis, C. and Aronson, E., (2007). Mistakes Were Made (but not by me): Why We Justify Our Foolish Beliefs, Bad Decisions and Harmful Acts, London, Pinter and Martin.

Tawney, R. H. (1926). *Religion and the Rise of Capitalism,* New York, Harcourt, Brace.

Taylor, S. E. and Brown, J. D. (1988). Illusion and well-being: a social psychological perspective on mental health, *Psychological bulletin,* Vol. 103, pp. 193-201.

Teece, D. J., Rumelt, R., Dosi, G., and Winter S. (1994). Understanding corporate coherence: Theory and evidence, *Journal of Economic behavior & Organization,* Vol. 23, pp. 1-30.

Tellegen, A., Lykken, D. T., Bouchard, T. J., Wilcox, K., Segal, N. and Rich, S. (1988). Personality similarity in twins reared apart and together, *Journal of Personality and Social Psychology,* Vol. 54, pp. 1031-1039.

Thomas, N. J. T. (1999). Are Theories of Imagery Theories of Imagination? An Active Perception Approach to Conscious Mental Content, *Cognitive Science,* Vol. 23, No. 2, pp. 207-245.

Thorndyke, P. W. (1984). Applications of schema theory in cognitive research, In: Anderson, J. R. and Kosslyn, S. M. (Eds.), *Tutorials in Learning and Memory,* San Francisco, Freeman.

Tiger, L. and Fox, R. (1971). *The Imperial Animal,* New York, Holt, Rinehart and Winston.

Tohmatsu, D. T. (2006). *Who are the Millennials? A.K.A. Generation, http://www/deloitte.com/dttcda/doc/content/us_consulting_millennialfactsheet_080606.pdf* (accessed 17th December 2009).

Todd D. (2010). Five Spiritual trends with Staying Power: The intersection f eastern and Western Religious beliefs is no longer just a topic for individuals, *The Vancouver Sun,* 9th January, *http://www.vancouversun.com/technology/Five+spiritual+trends+with+staying+power/ 2423895/story.html*, (accessed 13th January 2010).

Tominc, P. and Rebernik, M., (2007). Growth Aspirations and Cultural Support for Entrepreneurship: A Comparison of Post Socialist Countries, *Small Business Economics,* Vol. 28, No. 2-3, pp. 239-255.

Trungpa, C. (1975). Glimpses of Abhidharma: From a Seminar on Buddhist Psychology, Boston, M.A., Shambhala Publications.

Tulving, E. and Thomson, D. M. (1973). Encoding specificity and retrieval processes in episodic memory, *Psychological Review,* Vol. 80, pp. 352-373.

Tutkimusraportteja, S. A. (2009). *Global Entrepreneurship Monitor, Finnish 2008 Report,* Global Entrepreneurship Research Association, London, Babson Park, London Business School, Babson College.

Tversky, A. and Kahneman, D. (1973). Availability: a heuristic for judging frequency and probability, *Cognitive Psychology,* Vol. 5, pp. 207-232.

Tversky, A. and Kahneman, D. (1974). Judgment under Uncertainty: Heuristics and Biases, *Science,* Vol. 185, pp. 251-284.

Tversky, A. and Kahneman, D. (1982). Judgment under Uncertainty: Heuristics and Biases, In: Kahneman, D., Slovic, P., and Tversky, A., (Eds.), *Judgment under uncertainty: Heuristics and Biases,* Cambridge, Cambridge University Press, pp. 3-20.

Twenge, J. M. (2006). Generation me: Why today's young Americans are more confident, assertive, entitled _ and more miserable than ever before, New York, Free Press.

Tyson, P. and Tyson, R. L. (1995). Development. In: Moore, B. R. and Fine B. D. (Eds.). *Psychoanalysis: The major concepts,* New Haven, Yale University Press, pp. 395-420.

Ucbasaran, D., Westhead, P. and Wright, M. (2004). Human capital based determinants of opportunity identification, In: Bygrave, W., Brush, D *et. al* (Eds.), *Frontiers of Entrepreneurship Research,* Wellesley, MA, Babson College, pp. 430-444.

Ulanov, A. B. (1999). *Religion and the Spiritual in Carl Jung,* New York, Paulist Press

Ulrich, T.A. and Cole, G. S. (1987). Toward more effective training of future entrepreneurs, *JSBM,* Vol. 25, No. 4, pp. 32-39.

Vaidya, S.and Chansky, N. M. (1980). Cognitive development and cognitive style as factors in mathematics achievement, *Journal of Education Psychology,* Vol. 72, pp. 326-330.

Vallerand, R. J. (2008). On the psychology of passion: In search of what makes people's lives most worth living, *Canadian Psychology,* Vol. 49, pp. 1-13.

Vallerand, R. J., Mageau, G. A., Ratelle, C., Leonard, M., Blancard, C., Koestner, R, and Gagne, M., (2003). Les Passion de l' Ame: On Obseessive and harmonious passion, *Journal of Personality and Social Psychology,* Vol. 85, No. 4, pp. 756-767.

Valliant, G. E. (1977). *Adaptation to Life,* Boston, Little, Brown & Co.

Vajiranana, M., (1962). *Buddhist meditation in theory and practice*, Colombo, M. D. Gunasena & Co., Ltd.

Vaughan, D. (1996). The Challenger Launch Decision: Risky technology, Culture and Deviance at NASA, Chicago, University of Chicago Press.

Venkataraman, S. and Sarasvathy, S. D. (2000). *Strategy and Entrepreneurship: Outlines of an Untold Story,* Darden Graduate School of Business Administration, University of Virginia, Working Paper No. 01-06, *http://papers.ssrn.com/paper.taf?abstract_id=275186*, (accessed 15th march 2010).

Vick, S. G. (2002). Degrees of Belief: Subjective Probability and Engineering Judgment, Reston, VA., ASCE Press.

Vinchur, A. J., Schippmann, J. S., Switzer III, F, S., and Roth, P. L. (1998). A meta-analytical view of job performance for salespeople, *Journal of Applied Psychology,* Vol. 84, No. 4., pp. 586-597.

Volkow, N. D. (2004). Mediation of saliency in health and addition, paper presented to the *157th Meeting of the American Psychiatric Association, New York.*

Von Hippel, E., (1994). "Sticky information" and the locus of problem solving: implications for innovation, *Management Science,* Vol. 40, No. 4, pp. 429-439.

Von Hippel, E. (1986). Lead users: A source of novel product concepts, *Management Science,* Vol. 32, pp. 791-805.

Vrij, A., van der Steen, J. and Koppelaar, L. (1995). The effects of street noise and field independence on police officers' shooting behavior, *Journal of Applied Social Psychology,* Vol. 82, pp. 1714-1725.

Wagner, H. E. (1991). The Open Corporation, *California Management Review,* Vol. 33. No. 4, pp. 46-60.

Walsh, J. P. and Fahey, L. (1986). The role of negotiated belief structures in strategy making, *Journal of Management,* Vol. 12, No. 3, pp. 325-338.

Warrington, E. K. and Weiskrantz, L. (1970). Amnesic syndrome: Consolidation or retrieval?, *Nature,* Vol. 228, pp. 628-630.

Watson, D. and Clark, L. A. (1984). Negative Affectivity: The disposition to experience negative emotional states, *Psychological Bulletin,* Vol. 96, pp. 465-490.

Watts, A, (1996). Buddhism the Religion of No-Religion: The edited transcripts, Boston, Turtle Publishing.

Weber, M. (1930). *The Protestant Ethic and the Spirit of Capitalism,* London, Unwin, Hyman.

Weber, M. (1978). In: Roth, G. and Wittich, C. (Eds.), *Economy and Society,* Berkeley, CA, University of California Press.

Weber, M. (1981). Bureaucracy, In: Grusky, O. and Miller, G. A. (Eds.), *The Sociology of Organizations: Basic Studies,* New York, Free Press.

Weick, K. E. (1979). *The Social Psychology of Organizing,2nd Edition.* Reading, MA, Addison-Wesley.

Weinstein, N. D. (1980). Unrealistic Optimism About Future Life Events, *Journal of Personality and Social Psychology,* Vol. 39, No. 5, pp. 806-820.

Welwood, J. (1996). Reflection and Presence: The Dialectic of Self-Knowledge, *The Journal of Transpersonal Psychology,* Vol. 28, No. 2, pp. 107-128.

Welwood, J. (2001). The unfolding of experience: Psychotherapy and beyond, In: Schneider, K. J., Bugental, J. F. T., & Pierson, J. F. (Eds.), *The Handbook of humanistic psychology: Leading edges in theory, research and practice,* London, Sage Publications.

Wertsch, J. and Kanner, B., (1992). A Socio-Cultural Approach to Intellectual Development, In: Sternberg, R. and Berg, C. A. (Eds.). *Intellectual Development,* New York, Cambridge University Press, pp. 328-349.

Whiston, S. C. and Keller, B. K. (2004). The influences of the family of origin on career development: A review and analysis, *The Counseling Psychologist,* Vol. 32, No. 4, pp. 493-568.

Whyte, G. (1998). Recasting Janis's Groupthink Model: The key role of collective efficacy in decision fiascos. *Organizational Behavior and Human Decision Processes,* Vol. 72, No. 2-3, pp. 185-209.

Wicker, A. and King, J., (1989). Employment, Ownership and Survival in Microbusiness: A studyof new retail and service establishments, *Small Business Economics,* Vol. 1, pp. 137-152.

Willerman, L. (1979). Effects of families on intellectual development, *American Psychologist,* Vol. 34, pp. 923-929.

Williamson, O. E. (2000). The New Institutional Economics: Taking Stock, Looking Ahead, *Journal of Economic Literature,* Vol. 38, pp. 595-613.

Wilson, M. and Gerber, L. E. (2008). How Generational Theory Can Improve Teaching: Strategies for Working with the "Millenials", *Currents in Teaching and Learning,* Vol. 1, No. 1, 29-42.

Wilson, T. D., Houston, C., Etling, K. M. and Brekke, N., (1996). A new look at anchoring effects: Basic anchoring and its antecedents, *Journal of Experimental Psychology: General,* Vol. 4, pp. 387-402.

Wilson, K. and martin, W. A. (1982). Ethnic Enclaves: A comparison of the Cuban and black Economies in Miami, *American Journal of Sociology.* Vol. 88, pp. 135-160.

Winn, J. (2004). Entrepreneurship: not an easy path to the top management for women, *Women in Management Review,* Vol. 19, No. 3, pp. 145-153.

Winnicott, D. W. (1965). *The maturational processes and the facilitating environment,* New York, International University Press.

Winnicott, D. W. (1971). *Mirror-role of mother and family in child development,* London, Tavistock Publications.

Winter, D. G. (1973). *The Power Motive,* New York, Free Press.

Winter, S. G. (1988). On Coarse, competence, and the corporation, *Journal of Law and Economics and Organization,* Vol. 4, pp. 163-180.

Witkin, H. A., (1977). Role of the field-dependent and field-independent cognitive styles in academic evolution: A longitudinal study, *Journal of Educational Psychology,* Vol. 69, pp. 197-211.

Witkin, H. A., Lewis, H. B., Hertzman, M., Machover, K., Meissner, P. B. and Wapner, S. (1954). *Personality Through Perception: An experimental and clinical study,* New York, Harper.

Witkin, H. A. and Goodenough, D. R. (1977). Field Dependence and Interpersonal Behavior, *Pyschological Bulletin,* Vol. 84, pp. 661-689.

Witkin, H. A., Moore, C. A., Goodenough, D. R. and Cox, P. W., (1977). Field-Dependent and Field-Independent Cognitive Styles and Their Educational Implications, *Review of Educational Research,* Vol. 47, pp. 1-64.

Witt, U. (1998). Imagination and leadership – The neglected dimension of an evolutionary theory of the firm, *Journal of Economic Behavior & Organization,* Vol. 35, pp. 161-177.

Woo, C.Y. & Cooper, A.C. (1991). The development and interpretation of entrepreneurial typologies, *Journal of Business Venturing,* Vol. 6, No. 2, pp. 93-114.

Wood, R. and Bandura, A. (1989). Social Cognitive Theory of Organizational Management, *Academy of Management Review,* Vol. 14, No. 3, pp. 361-384.

Woodman, M. and Dickson, E. (1996). *Dancing in the Flames: The dark Goddess in the transformation of Consciousness,* Boston, Shambala.

World Health Organization (2004). *The Top Ten causes of Death, http://www.who.int/mediacentre/factsheets/fs310/en/index.html,* (accessed 5th November 2009).

Wright, W. F. and Bower, G. H. (1992). Mood effects on subjective probability assessment, *Organizational Behavior and Human Decision Processes,* Vol. 52, pp. 276-291.

Wright, M., Hoskisson, R. E., Busenitiz, L. W. and Dial, J. (2000). Entrepreneurial Growth through Privatization: The Upside of Management Buyouts, *Academy of Management Review,* Vol. 25, No. 3, pp. 591-601.

Yiu, L. & Saner, R. (2007). Witkin's Cognitive Styles and Field Therapy Applied to the Study of Global managers and OD Practitioners, *Research in Organizational Change and Development,* Vol. 16, pp. 191-219.

Zabusky, S. E. and Barley, S. R. (1996). Refining success: ethnographic observations on the careers of technicians, In: Osterman, P. (Ed.), *Broken Ladders,* New York, Oxford University Press, pp. 185-214.

Zahra, S. And George, G. (2002). Absorptive capacity: A review, reconceptualization, and extension, *Academy of Management Review,* Vol. 27, No. 2, pp. 185-203.

Zimberoff, D. & Hartman, D, (2002). Attachment, detachment, nonattachment: achieving synthesis, *Journal of Heart Centered Therapies*, Vol. 5, No. 1., pp. 3-94.

Zucher, L., Darby, M. and Brewer, M. (1998). Intellectual human capital and the birth of US Biotechnology Enterprises, *American Economic review,* Vol. 88, No. 1, pp. 290-305.

Chapter 4

CREATIVITY AND MAKING CONNECTIONS: THE PATCHWORK OF OPPORTUNITY

INTRODUCTION

Creativity is an extremely important aspect of opportunity, strategy and entrepreneurship. Without creativity, very little would develop, function and contribute to the wellbeing of the enterprise. Creativity is especially important in;

- Generating new ideas,
- Developing sources of opportunities from new technological developments, competencies, resources and networks, etc.
- Combining resources, skills, competencies, networks, and strategies to create new ventures,
- Developing ideas along a vision and path of implementation (strategy),
- Managing competitive strategy,
- Developing flexibility within an enterprise,
- Managing growth, and
- Solving routine and non-routine enterprise problems.

The concept of creativity is elusive, cannot be observed directly, measured or even acknowledged until sometime after the creative act has taken place[1]. Relatively little research has been undertaken on creativity until the 1960s (Sternberg & Lubart 1996). However within the last three decades there has been a massive serge in research, new theories and the development of many creative tools.

Many creative ideas, products or processes are the result of a lifetime of work for any individual. Some may be extraordinary and rare like a painted masterpiece or theory about the *cosmos*. Some creations may answer perplexing questions and have far reaching influences, beyond the expectations of their creators. Consequently people assume that the way these creations come and the people that create them must in some ways also be extraordinary

---

[1] For example a painting or piece of art may not be recognized by the art community as being creative until many years after it has been created. This leads to the situation where many pieces of art only accumulate value after the artist has passed away and the act of creativity is only realized as such long after the event.

about the intellectual and cognitive capacities they possess. However the intellect required for creativity is not outside the norm and everybody is capable of exercising the same cognitive processes. Our thought processes are ordinary and utilize past knowledge with new information (Weisberg 1993). Within the process of creativity, there are no leaps or illuminations that come from nowhere. The Wright Brothers' invention of the airplane, Thomas Edison's development of the light globe and Picasso's development of a new style of painting were all the result of incremental advances built upon previous work. Creativity is not mysterious and can mostly be explained by computational concepts in artificial intelligence (Boden 1990).

Probably the greatest difference between highly creative and average people is that highly creative people are experts in their domain. They are also highly motivated which takes them along various paths of inquiry into matters of interest that others ignore. Highly creative people take intellectual risks and have immense perseverance that others don't have (Sternberg & Lobart 1996). Complete immersion into a subject could be an important factor in gaining creative insights, especially in fields where there is an abundance of prior knowledge and experience (Proctor 1999).

It is creativity that allows us to see things differently and this is one of the main reasons behind our continued evolution. Creativity is a natural activity and probably depends upon our ability to be imaginative, open minded, curious, intuitive, insightful and able to tolerate ambiguity (Piirto 1998). The creative person needs to be flexible to react effectively to technological, economic, social and regulatory changes, under new circumstances, where new opportunity exists.

Creativity is an ever developing ability rather than a static attribute that someone is endowed with at birth (Simonton 2000). Creativity is not the result of a comfortable environment, but rather the broad life experiences a person has lived through which can enable a person to take fresh perspectives. The ability to be creative is probably enhanced more from the experiences of challenging life experiences than a stable and secure life, which may help develop the quality of perseverance (Simonton 1994). Perseverance is vital to creativity and problem solving, which is usually associated with barriers, obstacles and difficulties before the problem can be solved.

Creativity can be viewed as a process where the cognitive system utilizes attention to draw upon relevant knowledge, restructure problem information and look for analogies, new connections or associations within prior knowledge to solve a problem (Smith 2003, Smith *et. al.* 1994). Creativity can also be viewed as a product or outcome, where the result is recognized as being creative by others. The creative end may be a new product, new process, a piece of art, a new business model or a new strategy.

There is lack of consensus about what constitutes creativity and whether emphasis should be placed on the process, or the ends, and whether it is an individual or group phenomenon. From the point of view of this book creativity is generally defined as the production of novel, useful ideas or the production of solutions to problems. Creativity thus refers to both, the generation of new ideas, problem solving, as well as the actual idea or solution (Amabile 1983, Sternberg 1988, Weisberg 1988). Creativity is also about firm innovation, which is closely related to creativity and the implementation of new ideas (Amabile *et. al.* 1996, Politis 2005) as strategy.

Creativity has a rich cultural context, as ideas and solutions take place within a cultural environment that embodies a sense of meaning to those living within it. Culture immerses individual within language, numbers and scripts, music and entertainment, a national sense of humor, a culinary style, its own rituals and taboos, laws, heroes and villains, myths and legends, values and sense of success, etc. Creativity over time changes the way things are done which affects symbols, traditions and meaning within a culture. Creativity is the means by which a culture evolves (Csikszentmihalyi 1996, P. 9). Creativity and culture cannot be separated.

Creativity is selective and not necessarily a general trait. Creativity also tends to be domain specific rather than a trait that can be applied across other domains, *i.e., a person may be a creative chef but not a creative painter or artist.* Creativity can occur within a selective discipline when a person develops knowledge of the domain and its symbols. The person must also develop a cluster of skills that are unique and relevant to the domain, *i.e., for painting, sight, strokes, spatial, etc.* In addition to specific knowledge and skills, a person must have sensibility, interest, imagination, curiosity and being willing to experiment within the domain to be creative (see Figure 4.1.).

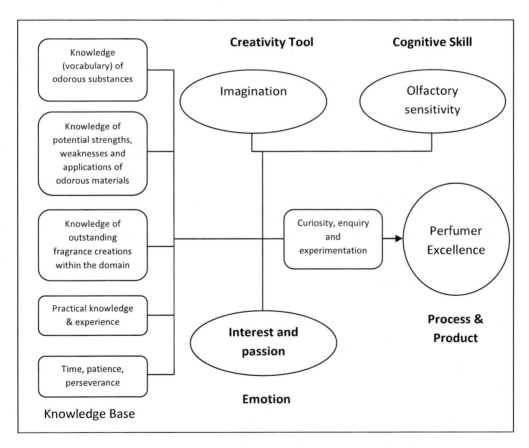

Figure 4.1. Creativity is Domain Specific: The elements of creativity for a perfumer.

As creativity can be seen as both a process and product, it becomes a concept very close to innovation. If innovation can be seen as the introduction of new things, ideas or ways of doing things[2], then innovation can be seen as the product or application of creativity. Somehow creativity occurs out of the interaction between an individual *(or group)* and the environment where it may be possible to identify something that can be acted upon *(an opportunity)*. The conclusion or decisions made are the result of complex interactions within the environment by actors, inventions and events. For example, it is decisively difficult to identify who created commercial aviation, the post office, the communications industry or the entertainment industry. Was it one person, one event or a collection of many complex interactions, inventions and innovations that created a stage for potential new opportunities to be discovered?

Who are the people that perceive and exploit opportunities? Are they people with lots of ideas or others with more experience and creative insight into how to develop successful implementation strategies? The answer to this may be seen in the time it takes many *Fortune 500* companies to turn an innovation into something that has value and provides an above industry average return (Wadhwa *et. al.* 2008). It is not an overnight occurrence. Many people may have the same idea but not all people have the same ability to implement and exploit it successfully. Creativity is a definite element in the exploitation of profitable opportunities (Shane & Venkataraman 2000).

The importance of creativity in enterprise lays in opportunity recognition, discovery and construction. Creativity is further required to develop realizable strategies by coupling resources, capabilities and networks together, and implement them and solve problems along the way. Creativity is also a path to flexibility which is needed in a dynamic environment. The ability to be flexible is also the ability to develop a competitive edge in the marketplace. Flexibility is also needed where problems have very little or no precedent (Proctor 1999), where one can break out of existing patterns and see new perspectives that may provide insight into solutions.

Certain characteristics must be present in a person and the situation must be conducive for a person to be creative. Creative thinking must be merged with logical thinking and reasoning, to solve many problems, as we will see in various problem solving processes. Our future is tied to creativity. This chapter will now look at all these issues in more detail.

THE COGNITIVE ASPECT OF CREATIVITY

As mentioned in chapter three, new methods available to monitor brain functions have greatly improved our understanding of how the brain operates in leaps and bounds. The *frontal lobes*, located in the front of the temples are very important to the function of creativity. This is the most recently developed part of the brain in our evolution and makes up approximately 30% of the *cortex's* total surface.

The *frontal lobes* are larger in humans than any other primate and posses a large number of complex and reciprocal connections with the rest of the brain (Stuss & Benson 1986). It is believed that the *frontal lobes* fulfill an executive function within the brain to aid complex behavior that requires simultaneous integration with information flow. The *frontal lobes* help us maintain attention to tasks and manage the switching over to other tasks as required (Koechlin *et. al.* 1999). The *frontal lobes* are where thought and action is initiated in response

---

[2] Oxford Dictionary definition.

to non-routine challenges. They also integrate cognition and emotion through the recall process, retrieving the memory of specific past events and the emotion attached to them. This emotion is used in imagination about similar events in the future. The *frontal lobes* allow us to move through time in a virtual manner and manipulate objects, people and events. This is important in the construction of opportunities and contemplation of implementation strategies. The *Frontal lobes* appear to be the key to our self awareness where cognition is integrated with affect and emotion (Wheeler *et. al.* 1997). The *frontal lobes* are also important to humor which as we will see uses some of the same processes that creativity uses. *The frontal lobes* are the source of our intuition or *'gut feel'*.

The neural circuits that process information for non-creative activities are the same circuits utilized for creative activities in the *frontal lobes* (Dietrich 2004). Novel combinations of information are created from information possessed in other parts of the brain. Creativity also requires control over short term memory, sustained attention, cognitive flexibility and judgment, which are also functions of the *frontal lobes.*

The right brain hemisphere also plays some role in problems that require insight and spatial perspectives and where re-arrangements are of information are required (Bowden & Beeman 1998). The functions of the left and right brain hemispheres are discussed in more detail later.

HOW WE SEE THE ENVIRONMENT THROUGH MENTAL MODELS

The environment is so rich and complex that we need methods to simplify what we see to give it meaning (O'Connor & Seymour 1995). We make these simplifications, general sense and meaning about the environment through the mental models we develop. These mental models can be defined as deeply ingrained assumptions, generalizations, and even pictures or images that influence how we see and understand the world and how we take action (Senge 2006, P. 8). Mental models are the brain processes we use to make sense of our world. They mould the thoughts we have, develop our sets of heuristics, and contain our biases, ethics and philosophies. Our mental models decide how we perceive the external environment, where our attention will be focused, and how we will respond to particular situations. Our mental models affect all aspects of our lives including, our views of the world, our career, relationships, dreams, ambitions, opinions and quality of life. Mental models exist in a hierarchy from a general overall mental model (the total set of our schemata), to our philosophical and ethical models, personal belief mental models (individual or clustered schemata), to specific task mental models (or scripts).

Our mental models begin developing at birth. Infants begin to make sense of the world from genetically inherited instructions, incoming stimuli and early experiences. The infant recognizes their mother early on as a source of food and nurturing, and their father and siblings over the first few months of their life. The infant's comprehension, and consequently ability to develop a deeper relationship with their immediate family, depends upon the development of their mental models. This continues to develop into adulthood and throughout the rest of his or her life.

As the infant continues to grow into a toddler and child, she builds upon her mental model by adding more and more information to create deeper meaning. Mental models allow a person to learn through the creation of a holistic picture of the environment, complete with feelings and emotions. Without a mental model there is no ability to learn. During the early learning periods an infant's curiosity and attitudes to learning develop. This is why infants marvel and get excited over sensing, touching and seeing new things that we take for granted.

The mind creates an internal world of its own, parallel to our external world. Our internal world is consistent and complete, unlike the external world that is complex and not totally comprehensible. Most of what we absorb through our senses about the external world is discarded, as external information is blended with relevant internal information for us to make sense and meaning of the external world (Wind & Crook 2006, P. 9). As we saw in chapter three, perception is not a linear process of information reception, processing, storage and recall, but a very complex, interactive, subjective and evocative process. Therefore how we make sense of the world is through our mind relying only on stimuli from the external world to a small extent. We believe what we see, which primarily comes from our internal world.

Our mental model is a configuration of *who we are*, our identity, which is drawn from our experiences, stories, images, relationships and learning. In this way our identity is socially constructed and immersed within our mental model. Thus our mental model controls how we react to situations and how we behave. Thus through the structure of our mental model we are trapped into the perceptions, views and behaviour that are embedded and associated with our ways of thinking and interrelationships with others and the environment.

Our views and actions are shaped by our models that govern how we act. For example, if we believe people are basically lazy and untrustworthy, we would manage a work situation under strict controls. If we believe growth is fundamental to a business, we may pursue a path of growth which would have the predictable elements of developing new products and new markets within a competitive environment. Other potential creative strategies will not be seen or be dismissed without consideration, as the views formed by our mental model would prevail, preventing learning and change. If we managed an airline, under a rigid mental model we would tend to seek growth through standard industry practices, not considering alternatives. Being an innovator and seeking entry into the developing the low cost market segment would not be an acceptable strategy, until our mental model changes and we see the benefit of doing so, through realization and learning instigated by competitive shock.

Mental models affect how we see. Two people looking at the same object or situation may see something different depending upon their mental models. This is very obvious in the political arena where different commentators based on their own political biases may interpret the same event in different ways. For example a *'left'* leaning politician may extol the need for social benefits for unemployed people, while a *'right'* leaning politician may dismiss the need for benefits for the unemployed because they are seen as being unemployed by choice and labeled as *lazy*. Essentially elections are fought on different sets of policies or mental maps. Thus vision is bounded and structured within a particular set of beliefs, focusing on different issues and policies that are important for each candidate and party. This bounding and structure prevents an individual seeing other views.

As we have seen in chapter three, it is very easy for cognitive traps and psychosis to become part of a mental model which will distort a person's perception of the environment and their reasoning.

When a person looks at the environment there is a complex number of factors that need to be perceived and understood for meaning to occur. Each individual factor has a meaning and together with other objects creates complex field of inter-meanings. Any environment has the following factors;

- A field,
- Objects within the field,
- Relationships between objects,
- Actors,
- Relationships between actors,
- Events,
- Relationships between events,
- Relationships between actors and events,
- Relationships between actors and objects,
- Relationships between actors, objects and the field,
- Relationships (or no relationships) between everything,
- The situation,
- Movements and stillness,
- motives,
- relationship between self and the actors, objects and the field, and
- Interpretations of the above.

The variables back in the opportunity gap (see figure 3.35.) can be seen in terms of the above factors to better understand their dynamics and inertia. There is the potential to discover connections between the various field elements. Where one can see interrelationships and trends, where movements and opportunities can be discovered and constructed. However when we are immersed within the system itself, it is hard to see the dynamism of the elements of the field and we act in a similar manner to others as we cannot see any change (Senge 2006, P. 42).

Our existing knowledge can constrain and keep us within our existing bounds of thought. It is only when a person can be aware of their own mental model that they can see and think beyond it. When one is free of their mental model, new connections between unrelated actors, objects, events and the field can be seen. Through imagination new potential realities can be formed internally leading to change in the existing mental models. This is the point where creativity flows and innovation may occur.

An opportunity is thus a person's unique perspective, scenario, future reality, which the person feels can be created. Potential changes that can occur like the shifting from a production to consumer perspective, going from a top down to a bottom up approach taking up internet journalism and self publishing, changing a diet, etc., are all examples of changing the arrangements between actors, objects, events and the field. As the environment continually evolves individuals seek change and others accept or reject it. Changing mental models is thus necessary for survival. Mental models both help to create and limit opportunities.

Somehow perceived opportunities must influence our sense of identity for action to occur. Without this influence any perceptions will just be passing thoughts. When we are aware of the restrictions of our mental models, imagination becomes an instrument of virtual reality. Imagination is a way to see the consequences of potential future actions, and take action upon them.

Changing mental models has been an important theme in management literature over the last three decades. Mitroff and Linstone (1993) espoused the need to challenge key assumptions and move from old thinking to *unbounded systems thinking.* Peter Senge (2006) places importance on mental models for personal and organizational learning. Russell Ackoff (1981) espouses the importance of challenging fundamental models, starting with a desired end, working backwards to the goals and objectives to reach it.

MOTIVATIONAL TRIGGER

When an individual has some form of vision, tension begins to build up within his or her psych. The gap can create positive or negative feelings. When positive, a person will feel ambitious, energetic and ready for a challenge. When negative, a person will feel powerless, distraught, think negatively and may lack self esteem. A positive effect of the gap between a person's reality and vision is the creation of a source of psychic energy that will drive an individual's creative curiosity. This is the tension needed to help drive the creative process.

A gap based on delusion or fantasy about something that cannot be realistically achieved will usually result in a person having to *self justify* their personal failings. This may manifest itself in external blame or feelings of low self esteem and self efficacy. A person with no gap between their reality and vision will not have any feeling of need to be curious about anything and will have very little urge to think about new possibilities as they accept the way they are.

Tension built up in a person because of the gap between their personal reality and vision can be released in two ways. The first way is to achieve the vision thus closing the gap being the most desired solution. This release will take a period of time to bring reality in line with vision, providing a wide range of emotions during the journey which include a sense of challenge, excitement, and passion on one side and frustration, impatience and contemplation on the other side. The second way to reduce the tension is by lowering the vision, which leads to disappointment, low self esteem, anxiety, and a feeling of powerlessness. The vision may incrementally decline to repeated poor achievement within a domain that a person has a vision. This may result in the individual slowly lowering the expectation and explaining the failing away, *i.e., coming 4th was good enough.*

Tension created by the gap can create positive energy. The vision acts as a motivator, something that creates a frame of positive feelings which creates a good environment for creativity. However, deep within our psych, people have self doubts about being able to achieve their visions. There is a dormant belief that we are unable to fulfill our desires because as children we learn our self limitations[3]. This is important to our self preservation and ultimate survival that continues into our adult life (Fritz 1989). Thus this leads to another deep unconscious assumption that we cannot always have what we want, which can create a deep inner feeling of worthlessness. So vision on one hand creating a feeling of challenge and excitement and a deep feeling of worthlessness on the other creates a paradox where our

---

[3] As a child we learn that we cannot jump off the roof and fly like a bird and cannot jump out of a moving car etc. The inner assumption of not being able to achieve our fantasies is a primal assumption designed to keep a person out of harm's way.

personal energies can be channeled in a number of ways. This paradox can lead to a loss of psychic energy where we decide to let the vision erode. Alternatively we may question whether we really want the vision and psychically manipulate ourselves into greater efforts to pursue it. Finally we may find (or sub-consciously create) obstacles as an excuse for our failure to meet the vision. Our deep assumption of self limitation may lead to a fear of failure, which in the extreme could lead to the avoidance of challenges. Alternatively this paradox may lead to total focus and dedication, where all obstacles can be overcome. Focus and lots of reserves of psychic energy can in the extreme lead to compulsive behavior, which may be good for achieving visions but have secondary costs associated with success like a neglected and failed personal life[4].

When there is a strong belief that a vision can be achieved, psychic energy will increase as clarity and success reinforces the belief in successfully achieving the vision. The strength of the belief in success has more "gravity" than the person's deeply held assumptions of worthlessness. However when things don't go well and there is personal doubt about achieving the vision, psychic energy greatly decreases and the "gravity" of the deep assumption of worthlessness is stronger than that of the vision and pulls the person towards giving up. This is depicted in Figure 4.2.

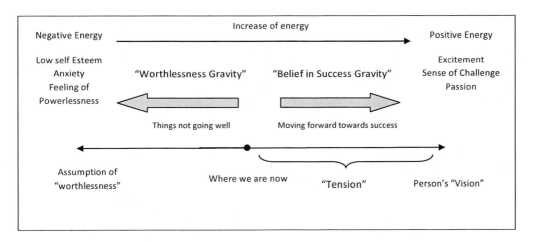

Figure 4.2. The Forces of the Motivational Trigger.

CREATIVE SENSITIVITY

The environment is full of a complexity of consistencies and inconsistencies, discontinuities and disparities concerning objects, people and events in life. Our association with the environment is also a complex one. The relationship between our self and the environment is full of peculiarities and subtleties of meaning, if we are sensitive enough to pick them up. Creative sensitivity is related to our ability to perceive and understand the complex situations we observe and are involved in. High creative sensitivity therefore implies that we are more observant and aware of the things around us and feel comfortable with the

---

[4] This is something common in many great achievers in public life.

complexity rather than trying to simplify meaning according to the perceptions we have (Hicks 2004, P. 45).

People who can perceive the richness of the environment have higher levels of creative sensitivity and should therefore be able to pick up the relevance of seemingly random facts and information. They will be better placed to make connections between them than someone who is less sensitive to the environment. Creative sensitivity is an important precondition to creativity.

In order to solve problems it is necessary to be able to perceive them. This is not a uniform characteristic across the population and some people are more endowed than others. Creative sensitivity is believed to be something people are born with (Eikleberry 2007). Creativity partly relies on external stimuli to act as cues to assist in long term memory recall. Creative sensitivity coupled with defocused or general attention to the environment will pick out subtle cues which will aid in the recall of prior knowledge, experience and information deeply locked away in the long term memory (Dewing and Battye 1971, Dykes and McGhie 1976, Mendelsohn 1976, Martingdale 1977), aiding the associative process and imagination. Therefore people with low creative sensitivity would not pick up as much stimuli from the environment as someone with high creative sensitivity, which will result in a lower number of cues to stimulate recall from the long term memory.

The characteristic of creative sensitivity gives a person some heightened sensitivity to some aspect of their life. Creative sensitivity is usually restricted to limited areas, such as, colour, pictures, sounds, music, values and ethics, human behavior, empathy, spiritual and spatial dimensions, etc[5]. People's sensitivity also ebbs and wanes during the day, month and different times in a person's life[6]. At mean levels of creative sensitivity, a person will tend to perceive more in their area of sensitivity endowment and experience subtle satisfactions or disappointments concerning certain pieces of art, music, performance, etc. Pleasant appreciations can lead to increased vigor and energy in a person's area of sensitivity. This leads a person to have good intuition in their particular areas of sensitivity. However, one may become bored or impatient with ordinary and mediocre things within their area of sensitivity. Too much creative sensitivity on the other hand can lead a person to suffer pain due to empathy, as nothing will satisfy their expectations. This can lead to deep emotions, *i.e., feeling pain for the poor,* and in the extreme, feelings of depression and lethargic states.

Creative sensitivity assists a person develop a deeper understanding of their area of sensitivity than what the average individual would. Consequently a sensitive person becomes aware and concerned about what is wrong within their area of sensitivity. This is where creativity begins, with the finding of a problem. Only after sensing that there is a problem can a person put their attention to solving the problem. Creative people focus on what is wrong, out of place, missing, not complete, lacking something, knowing that something needs to be changed for the better. Problem solving is not the centre of creativity and not the process that actually creates the opportunity. It is the finding of the problem and the way a person mentally structures it that creates the birth of a potential opportunity.

---

[5] To find out what aspect your creative sensitivity exists, think about what issues your find repulsive, irritating and distressful.

[6] For example, a person may be spiritually sensitive and as a consequence become devoted to a particular religion or philosophy. One will have changing levels of commitment to their spirituality as life progresses and certain events happen.

FOCUS AND ATTENTION

Another important prerequisite to creativity is focus and attention. Focus is important for the selection of what information coming in from our senses we concentrate on, *i.e.,* what cues we select for attention. Attention determines our concentration on what information we decide to put our mental effort upon to process and understand. We are continually bombarded with so many different kinds of perceptual stimuli, where we must decide what to take notice of and what to ignore. Our attention to selective information is the way we allocate our cognitive processing effort to information we perceive. Focus and concentration are very important characteristics to prevent the overloading of our limited cognitive processes.

A key characteristic of attention is that it is limited and we are simply unable to process all incoming information at once. In chapter three we discussed the bottleneck where only some stimuli/information is allowed through into our conscious awareness at a time. To recall this, take for example looking at a street scene. You will see the whole picture, but not be focused everywhere at once. Our mode of sight is like at spotlight on the middle of the picture (Posner 1980) and anything we see around the periphery gets much less attention. This is termed spatial attention. If we are looking at the scene and a neon light starts flashing, it will involuntarily capture our attention. This is called attentional capture, where a person's attention is involuntarily drawn by some stimulus. This is perhaps a leftover from our primal programming to ensure that we can spot any immediate danger quickly. As we look at a general scene our head may remain stationary but our eyes will move more and focus on different objects for short periods of time (<1/10 *sec.*). This is called object-based attention (Cave & Bichot 1999). We can give attention to objects in either of these attentional modes (Soto & Blanco 2004).

Attention is also important with auditory stimuli where we are only able to focus upon one message at a time. There will be little awareness of the content of any other messages, however we will be aware of some of the message characteristics such as pitch, but not content (Moray 1959). This phenomenon can be experienced at a party where many conversations are going on at the same time, but an individual has trouble focusing on anymore than one conversation at a time, just hearing pitching and droning in the background. This is an example of selective attention, as the other conversations are not processed for meaning.

However some studies mid last century showed that individuals can be distracted by cues that divert their attention from one piece of information to another. Treisman's (1960) research supports this postulation, where subjects were asked to wear a headphone where two separate mixed up messages were spoken through each side of the headphone. Many subjects switched their attention halfway through the messages from one ear to the other and were able to recite a meaningful message, made up of the two mixed messages. This infers that our attention is also influenced by cues, which can displace attention.

Attention is also the device through which we commit our mental effort necessary to initiate cognitive processing. Attention is manipulated to assist us consider, examine, and respond to outside stimuli in an appropriate manner necessary for a person to carry out daily activities. Attention allows us to allocate our short term working memory time between the various tasks we undertake. We have a certain amount of choice in this matter through deciding on what we want to perceive. This partly regulates what we identify and interpret for given meaning to through cognitive processing.

In daily life we are engaged in multiple tasks like walking, talking, reading, eating, writing, playing, and watching TV, etc. Doing some of these tasks concurrently requires giving them divided attention. This requires multiple focuses which will lead to the decline in individual task performance. Research into multitasking activities such as driving a car and talking on a mobile phone at the same time, shows that driving response times are substantially longer than if a person was just driving a car (Beede & kass 2006). This occurs due to the bottleneck theory and limited short term memory capacity, discussed in the section on cognition in part II of the previous chapter.

As we have a limited attention capacity and use it to undertake all the various tasks we need to do, there will be no surplus capacity left for undertaking other cognitive tasks. Creativity relies on having surplus attention available. People occupied with busy jobs would tend to have less capacity than those with idle cognitive time that can be utilized for creative tasks. However, when tasks become automatically processed, *i.e., without the need for conscious awareness,* the mental effort required to undertake these tasks diminishes (Borgh & Chartrand 1999). This frees up cognitive resources and allows concentration for other tasks. This can be understood best through the example of learning to ride a bicycle. When learning to ride, initially a person's full concentration is required. However once one has practiced, has some experience and developed riding skills, less concentration is needed. Under such conditions mental effort can be put into other tasks like the incubation of ideas, where insights can occur, discussed later on in the creativity process.

Attention is an important mechanism in the creativity process and is influenced by situational and other factors. Our existing patterning processes and routines tend to control our attention and thus suppress potential insights into new ideas. The patterns we use become polarized and therefore self perpetuating, where other stimuli is ignored, as our attention is focused on existing patterns.

Generally speaking the capacity for attention, particularly multitasking declines with age (Hartley 1992, Kramer & Larish 1996). However older adults who have strong skills and experience in a particular area will be still able to multitask, regardless of their age (Jennings & Jacoby 1993). For example older people tend to perform better than younger less experienced drivers in talking and driving simultaneously (Strayer & Drews 2004).

In regards to environment, rigid, tradition based, authoritarian and collective cultural environments tend to suppress the development of insightful ideas, as these types of societies do not welcome them. This leaves little incentive for people to give attention to new connections and ways of doing things. Thus creativity within oppressive cultural situations requires enormous amounts of attention to be able to break out of traditional patterns and develop new insights (Csikszentmihalyi 1996, P. 9). This also occurs in organizations that are bureaucratic and follow rigid procedures (Leonard 1998).

ATTENUATION

Treisman (1960) postulated that unattended acoustic information is not completely blocked from our filtering and patterning during the attention phase. These stimuli are weak, but nevertheless make it into our cognitive system, where it is enough to trigger recognition and maybe stored in the long term memory. Other theories like Deutsch and Deutsch's (1963) late-selection theory postulates that all incoming information is identified, but only the selected piece of information emerges into phenomenal consciousness.

Although these theories are related to acoustic attention, it could be surmised that more information than we realize flows into our long term memory, which can potentially be utilized in the sub-conscious incubation process discussed later within the creativity process.

IMAGINATION

Imagination is the ability to form a mental image of something that is not perceived through our senses. As we examined in chapter three, imagination is the ability of the mind to build mental scenes, objects, or events that do not exist, or are not present or happened in the past. As we have seen, memory is a manifestation of imagination and we use imagination in almost everything we do. Imagination is a useful planning tool where we envisage the conduct of future meetings and events. Although imagination builds upon our knowledge, knowledge alone cannot create imagination. Imagination is a product of our creative intelligence, and as such, a powerful tool to visualize and understand potential scenarios that we may plan for the future. In this way visualization or mental imagery is something similar to intuition or insight and is vital to the creativity process.

Imagination is also a tool for the development of determination and courage to follow through on visions through repeated mental rehearsal in our minds. As mentioned again in chapter three, an athlete will go over a race time and time again to mentally prepare him or herself for the mental and physical effort they need to put in and predetermine all the potential dangers that may prevent him or her from achieving their goal. Imagination enables the athlete to recognize difficulties and develop enough resourcefulness to solve any potential and expected problems before they occur. Imagination also boosts a person's desire by helping a person experience what it would feel like to succeed.

Any consideration a person makes about something requiring a solution requires imagination to manipulate memory. Imagination is a process that can combine past experiences, knowledge and feeling into new images and concepts. In this way new connections made between bits of knowledge and past experience create novel concepts. Imagination is not totally a conscious process. It may also incubate sub-consciously when a person has surplus attention to focus on recombining memory and external stimuli into new mental images. Imagination plays a major role in the creation of new ideas.

Imagination is not only a contributor to the process of creativity it is also a manifestation of creativity. We use imagination whenever we are designing something like a dress or a building, developing a new product or landscaping a front yard of a house. Imagination links with many other creative aspects such as humor, metaphor and analogy, vision, memory, developing understanding, learning and empathy. Imagination is the tool we use to extrapolate concepts into ideas and opportunities into strategies.

Imagination does not generate completely novel and new to the world concepts. As Einstein once said, *"the secret of creativity is knowing how to hide your sources"*. Anything novel we come up with through our imagination and insight is based upon our prior knowledge and past experiences. Thus inadvertently much of the novelty we create in anything is likely to be based upon something that existed previously, be it in another domain or field that an individual has exposure to. This is what Marsh and bower (1993) call *inadvertent plagiarism*. Therefore it's likely in most cases that novel creations are inspired by something in the past, although through imagery, the concepts may have been given new types of manifestations. However through the imagery of analogies, many breakthroughs in science have been achieved (Shepard 1988). For example, Einstein developed his insight for the theory of relativity through imagining what would happen if he travelled at the speed of light, Faraday claimed to have visualized force lines from electric and magnetic fields giving insight into the theory of electromagnetic fields and kekulé reported that he discovered the concept of the molecule after he imagined a snake coiled up in a circle.

CURIOSITY

Curiosity is an emotion we share with many animals. Curiosity sparks inquisitive behavior and is another important aspect of the creativity process and is also an important part of our learning. Curiosity is a trigger and a drive that leads to the development of an interest, love or passion for doing, investigating or exploring something.

Curiosity begins at the moment of birth where we start to explore the world as we know it. Our curiosity fuels our ability to learn and develop as human beings in a social environment. Curiosity continues through our infancy, adolescence, teenage and into our adulthood driving us to seek new knowledge and understanding about our surroundings, and relationships, etc. In our early life we begin to understand basic concepts through our exploration and discovery, where we begin to find domains that we have interest in. For example as children we play with insects, dig tunnels, fly kites and build model planes, where one or more of these interests may continue into our adult life. Many things we learn such as the lifecycle of insects and through analogy, enables individuals to understand that all living things have limited lifecycles. Through continuous discovery during our early years individuals learn about life, science and society.

Certain activities we undertake will create a certain level of excitement and an individual will spend more time within the domains they are excited about. Strong curiosity leads the development of new skills in the domain of interest. Through repeated use of these skills an individual begins to develop mastery within a domain, a common trait among many notable public figures who have made breakthroughs in their domains of interest (Gardner 1993). It is mastery that develops potential in individuals. Mastery separates great individuals from the rest, where those who have mastered their domain have the potential to make great insights about their field of interest. Personal mastery usually contains personal vision, a much stronger dedication than others in their field of interest, a passion for more knowledge and a deep love for what they are doing (Senge 1990). Mastery brings spiritual development to a person where they become self assured, confident, secure, with a deep sense of purpose about themselves. This is all driven by a person's passion for the domain.

Figure 4.3. True personal mastery is rare in people.

Curiosity consists of two separate elements which are paradoxical. On one side curiosity brings openness and willingness to learn, but on the other side it brings obsessive persistence. Both these elements are important if we want to master a domain, to question things and develop new ideas. The elements of curiosity promote an active cognitive system which through this paradox is able to look for connections of different information within the domain. Curiosity maintains an active cognitive system which becomes more proficient in seeking connections through learning as time and dedication goes on. The ability to gain insight takes time as it is not a short term or immediate activity. Mastery is a necessary ingredient which takes time to develop. The cycle that curiosity sparks in creativity is depicted in figure 4.4.

Without curiosity people will lack the passion needed to engage domains, seek further knowledge and wisdom. They will become apathetic and settle for an incomplete understanding of things. Lack of curiosity will lead us to missing information in the environment which will hinder our ability to develop new ideas, *i.e., suppress our ability to be imaginative.*

When curiosity develops a high spiritual level within us, we will start pondering upon the complex questions of our existence such as; *'Where do we come from?'* *'Is there life after death?'* *'Is there a supreme-being, force or god?'* and *'What exists in the universe besides us?'* This role that curiosity plays in our spiritual life through our imagination and fantasy leads us to new possibilities, excitements and sense of spiritual purpose.

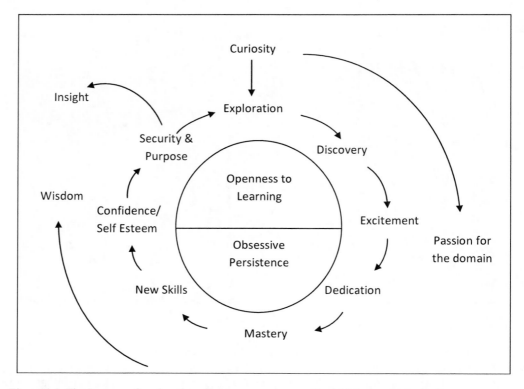

Figure 4.4. The Process of exploration, discovery, mastery and insight that curiosity ignites.

PRIOR KNOWLEDGE

As we saw in chapter three, prior knowledge is knowledge that accumulates in our memory from previous experiences. As our memory builds up this knowledge our capacity to learn and generate new ideas increases. Prior knowledge influences our modes of perception[7], focus of attention, modes of reasoning and beliefs about knowledge. Much of these influences are socially or culturally biased within the domain and field we operate within (Latour 1987, Knorr 1981). We think in the metaphors and analogies that are based in our socially impregnated prior knowledge (Einstein 1950). Most of our ideas are based on everyday knowledge of our domains and fields that we are surrounded in (Wertheimer 1982, Miller 1986).

We construct our ideas and meanings from incoming perceptions and the images and metaphors of our prior knowledge (Lightman 1989, Miller 1986). Piaget's theory postulates that new knowledge is the result of combining of new experiences with our prior schemata (Inhelder & Piaget 1958). In this way new knowledge doesn't replace prior knowledge, it

---

[7] For example, when people try to explain the throwing of a ball straight up in the air, the motion may be described as the ball having an initial upwards force which slowly dies out until it is balanced by gravity at the top of trajectory. In contrast a physicist may explain the ball throw in terms of gravity exerting a single constant force, which gradually changes the momentum of the ball, i.e., going up with a declining positive momentum, at the top with a zero momentum and going down where the momentum is increasingly negative (DiSessa 1993).

reuses and refines it, restructuring it into something different[8]. Conceptual change only occurs slowly where prior knowledge is restructured to encompass new ideas (Toulmin 1972), that are really variations upon an interrelated system of knowledge. Our schemata start developing from childhood and continue to develop throughout life, slowly developing conceptual change to the ideas we have (Piaget 1970). As we mature our ability to make sense of the knowledge we have improves with the enhanced reasoning tools and capacities we develop (Corsini 1994). Thus prior knowledge is paramount in how we make sense of our interactive experiences. So our knowledge grows with the assimilation of new perceptions with prior knowledge in our existing schemata.

For the reasons above, prior knowledge is important in problem solving as it influences our search procedures and heuristics to guide the search (Newell & Simon 1972), as we look for analogies and similarities with what we already know. Prior knowledge also assists in comprehending a story through construction with information and ideas we already have. Prior knowledge thus acts as a filter as to how we see things, interpreting our perceptions according to what we tend to believe. Research has shown that jurors' decisions are often based on how information is presented to them. When information tends to be consistent to what they believe through their prior knowledge, they will tend to make their judgments on prior knowledge rather than new facts (Carlson & Russo 2001). Prior knowledge will influence people to stereotype objects, people and events. For example, African Americans tend to believe in stories of police misconduct and bigotry, because of their backgrounds, than White Americans (Hastie & Pennington 2000). In fact our prior knowledge is made up of both fact and belief.

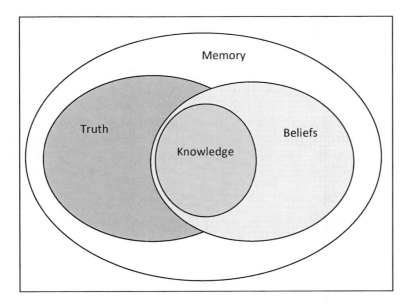

Figure 4.5. Our Prior knowledge is made up of both truth and beliefs.

---

[8] This is perhaps why innovation is only incremental on the whole. To develop completely new innovations, where paradigms are shifted requires thinking beyond the base of domain prior knowledge (Kuhn 1970). When an individual utilizes some unrelated prior knowledge to the domain that one is working within, then transformations rather than incremental changes can occur.

We develop two forms of knowledge that are important for the creativity process. The first is domain knowledge, which relates to a discipline like mathematics, astronomy, cooking, music or poetry, etc. Each domain is clearly defined with its unique sets of rules, syntax and symbols. It is domain knowledge that helps an individual develop mastery within a discipline. Without in-depth domain knowledge it is very difficult for a person to develop insights in that particular discipline. Mastery of one domain enables an individual to extend into adjacent domains. For example, a scientist with knowledge in pharmacy may be able to make contributions in the domain of biochemistry or biotechnology. Creative insights can come from emerging from one domain to another. Experts within domains have a larger knowledge base from which to work that enhances their chances of being creative, relative to novices in the domain. However, although domain knowledge is very important to creativity, narrow focus within a single domain can create tunnel vision and hinder creativity. The second area of knowledge is the field, which can be as large as society itself, or as small as a few people or corporations[9]. The field requires a certain amount of social capital to be accepted and recognized within[10]. The sum of domain knowledge determines what can or cannot be done in the field, as innovation within the field will come from a specific domain. Fields have profound effect upon creativity. A field may be reactive or proactive in the pursuit of new knowledge and differ in attitude towards novelty.

Through prior knowledge we tend to be a product of the various influences upon our lives. Our thoughts tend to reflect this in some way, where ideas, information and knowledge from the society we are immersed within has a strong influence upon us. From this point of view prior knowledge is culturally and domain biased. Our ideas are based on familiar knowledge that through syntheses creates something unfamiliar and seen as novel by our society. Margaret Boden (2004) in her book *The Creative Mind* describes how even the most creative people have adapted ideas from the works of others through some form of syntheses[11].

Prior knowledge is very important in the creativity process, although it may have a positive or negative impact. Specialized domain knowledge is very important in both the creativity and the opportunity discovery process. It enhances the chances of finding new associations and connections. However the rigid patterning that develops from prior knowledge can restrict both the way we perceive the environment and way we look at information and problems, thus restricting our capability to make associations between unrelated pieces of information.

EMOTION, AFFECT AND CREATIVITY

Our emotions and feelings to some extent influence our thinking and behavior. For example if we are excited about undertaking a new course of study, we will look forward to

---

[9] For example the field for a consumer product manufacturer will be all of the consumers, competitors, suppliers and regulators regarding the markets the company serves. The field for a nuclear scientist will be limited to a few thousand scientists, selected institutions and regulatory bodies, etc.

[10] Refer to Pierre Bourdieu's concepts of habitus, field and capital in chapter three.

[11] Margaret Boden gives the examples that Darwin's grandfather had similar ideas of evolution, Shakespeare was influenced by plots from Plutarch, Bach was influenced by themes from Vivaldi and Picasso was influenced by pictures by Velasquez.

going to class, undertake our study and do our assignments with enthusiasm because we may believe that this course of action is good for us. Likewise many of us fear going to the dentist and will be inclined to try to put visits off unless it is absolutely necessary. Our emotions and feelings play a role in our decisions and subsequent behaviors. In fact a great deal of our behavior is based on irrationality such as getting into fights, bad moods, getting angry with people, stereotyping people and disliking certain events and things. These behaviors can make us inconsistent, ignore relevant information, deceive ourselves and jump to conclusions, etc. This influence is stronger when we are not aware of our emotions. When emotions exist sub-consciously, they may exert much greater influence and even rule our decisions and behaviors (this issue is discussed in more detail in the section on psychotic states in chapter three). Our emotions and how we feel about things affect decisions we make, our ability to recognize opportunities and our energy levels to commit and do things.

Emotion influences how we rate the importance or intensity of various events in our life. This is terms affect intensity. People with high affect intensity see events more intensely than those people with low affect intensity. For example, where an event is rated as *moderately good* by an average person, a person with high affect intensity would rate the event as *extremely good*. Likewise where an event would be rated as moderately bad by an average person, a person with high affect intensity would rate the event as *extremely bad*. Individuals with high affect intensity are more reactive to emotion producing events in their lives, whether they are good or bad.

Although mood change is a normal aspect in life, high affect intensity individuals would tend to exhibit more mood variation than other people (Larsen 1987). Mood change influences personality, sociability and arousal to environmental stimuli. High affect intensity individuals tend to have vigorous and energetic lives, tend to be more outgoing and sociable and tend to seek out more stimulating and arousing things around their lives. They shun boredom and will look for things to do even if what they do is antisocial (Larsen & Buss 2005, P. 441). Extreme affect intensity can be seen as neurotic extraversion (Cooper & McConville 1993).

The relationship between affect intensity and creativity is inconsistent and probably depends upon the type of emotions and situation. However in general positive affective states can enhance creativity where negative affective states can inhibit creativity. There is much anecdotal evidence to show that positive emotions do assist in the creativity process. The mathematician Henri Poincare is reported to have experienced creative breakthroughs while on vacations and Mozart claimed that pleasant moods were the most conductive to his creativity (Vernon 1970).

Affect-laden thoughts may enhance the ability of the cognitive retrieval processes to recall affect-laden information from the long term memory. This may emerge during our thought process, fantasy or imagination (Russ 1993, P. 12). Affect may assist in focusing an individual to affect states, *i.e., areas that are intensely important to the individual* (Russ 1993, P. 13). Affect may also manifest pleasure to the individual engaged in the challenge of discovering problems, working on solutions, gaining insights and seeing them develop into opportunities in their domains and fields of expertise. This intense pleasure could be described as passion. Fredrickson (1998, 2001) postulated that positive emotions such as joy and love broaden a person's repertoire of behavioral scripts, enabling them to pursue novel and creative paths of action. This is supported by empirical evidence of a number of studies that show that positive affect can induce changes in cognitive processing that facilitate creative processes in individuals (Amabile *et. al.* 2005).

Other studies have shown that negative affect can also lead to greater creativity in some areas. Ludwig (1992) found in a study of 1,000 prominent individuals from almost 50 different professions that there was some evidence of a correlation between depression and the level of creative achievement. Other studies have shown that many highly creative individuals had affective disorders, primarily bipolar illness and depression (Feist 1998)[12]. Negative affect can also be a signal that something is amiss and motivate an individual to work hard to find a solution (George & Zhou 2002)[13].

Another possible outcome from high affect, either positive or negative, is that these strong emotions take control of attention and absorb available psychic energy. People in a high affect state may tend to be controlled by this state. People become preoccupied with their emotions and their behavior will be aimed at dealing with their emotion (Weiss & Cropanzano 1996). Excessive emotions, positive or negative can distract from creativity and task performance.

From the cognitive point of view Martindale (1999) suggests that attention becomes focused on arousal inducing situations when strong arousal states exist, leaving no cognitive capacity to focus on making associative connections necessary for novel ideas. However the simultaneous experiencing of positive and negative emotions may stimulate creativity by increasing the breath of cognitive information available, where a given complex mood may active numerous memory modes. Mixed emotions may develop crossovers of memory modes which bring new associations and novel ideas (Rothenberg 1990, Richards 1994). Other studies found it was not the moods, but the mood swings that gave contrasts where contradictory moods gave rise to different perceptions and observations of the environment (Jamison 1993), thus increasing the variety and breath of potential associations as input for the creative process.

Positive Affect and creativity may also co-exist as positive experiences may be associated with the task of creativity itself. Creative behavior according to Csikszentmihalyi (1975, 1996) is actually a "flow state", a merging of individual and the creative process into the one activity, which creates feelings of enjoyment and enthusiasm. Affect in itself may be a form of intrinsic motivation for creativity (Amabile 1996).

THE ROLE OF THE EGO CONCEPT IN CREATIVITY

If we combine the concepts of Jung's *ego/consciousness*, Freud's *ego, id and superego* with Bourdieu's concept of *habitus*, we have a central '*mind sponge*' that absorbs external stimuli and blends them with our internal knowledge, beliefs, feelings and emotions to form a singular spatial concept/image we call our self[14]. The structure of our ego concept has influence over our thoughts, feelings and emotions that govern our sense of reality, view of

---

[12] Feist also pointed out that the relationship between affective illness and high levels of creative accomplishment applied mainly to artistic and not scientific creativity.

[13] This study also found that when there is positive affect may signal that the affected state is well, they may have achieved their creative goal and there is no need to do anything. As a consequence positive affect may dampen creativity.

[14] In this section the author uses the term 'ego concept' as a composite.

the world, inner drives, motivation and attention. As a consequence, our ego concept also has a great bearing upon our cognitive functioning and behavior. Although the ego concept is not directly involved in the creativity process, it exerts many indirect influences that are of an important nature.

The ego concept both makes up many personality traits and is also influenced by personality traits. Likewise both the ego concept and personality is influenced by our situational conditioning and life experience as well as our inheritance. The ego concept is the frame of reference that comprises both our personal possibilities as well as our personal constraints. The ego concept is the bridge between the external and internal, acting as both a gatekeeper and the creator and interpreter of our personal meaning. At one extreme our ego concept protects our self image by interpreting the world in a way that provides for security, but at the other extreme our ego concept seeks challenge and adventure. These interpretations and constructions made by the ego concept act as a driver for the individual. The intervention of the ego concept into our cognition is necessary for a person to carry out a normal life.

The role of the ego concept in everyday life is to provide enough motivation, ambition, self confidence, attention, dedication and morality to undertake important tasks. Without the attention and drive from the ego, a person will not look after their own survival and that of their family. The ego concept contains the inner programming to survive and provides strategies for achieving this. The ego concept provides an aggressive-destructive or a sensitive-appreciative drive to a person when facing challenging life situations. It also determines whether a person will attempt to dominate others or be dominated by others as a means to providing oneself with what they need to survive. The ego concept will determine whether a person is ego-centric or altruistic towards others. These may not be absolute and rigid strategies, maintaining fluidity for various situational encounters a person experiences.

Through these embedded assumptions and beliefs within the ego concept, incoming information is judged as to its significance to survival and self image. The ego concept defends against any threatening realities manifesting themselves through panic, rage, anger, hate, or guilt, etc, in response to any situation that is challenging and cannot master (Hart 1950). Within the realms of normality, threats will lead to thoughts, feelings and emotions and then judgments, but if the ego concept overwhelms the psych with emotion, then there are risks that the ego concept becomes unbalanced and dysfunctional leading to psychosis, as discussed back in chapter three. Balance of the ego concept is important to a person's libidinal love for what is outside. Psychotic unbalance will turn a person inward into their internal world, taking over all the limited attention a person has for other activities. This may lead to a decline in curiosity because of the attention to selfish goals (Csikszentmihalyi 1997, P. 345).

The functions of the ego concept are very important in providing some of the positive psychic positions needed for creativity. The ego concept provides strong motivation and sense of achievement that enables people to undertake challenges where creativity is needed (Aguilar-Alonso 1996). This allows a person to challenge existing realities, where they are not satisfied with *'what is'*. From Bourdieu's point of view, entrepreneurs are not in a state of *doxa*, and consequently don't accept the realities of the *field*, thus the *habitus* and the *field* are out of alignment. This unstable subject-object relationship requires some form of creativity and innovation to bring some new form of alignment. This motivates or drives a person to desire and seek new realities, rejecting the *status quo* of today.

From the point of view of psychoanalysis, the insight needed in creativity is intuitive perception that is the result of unconscious synthesis (Hart 1950, P. 14). We are inclined to overestimate the conscious aspects of creativity. Therefore much of the creativity process occurs within the unconscious and what we perceive unconsciously vastly outweighs what we perceive consciously. Through the interchange of conscious and unconscious perception we develop either original creation or psychosis depending upon the balance of our ego.

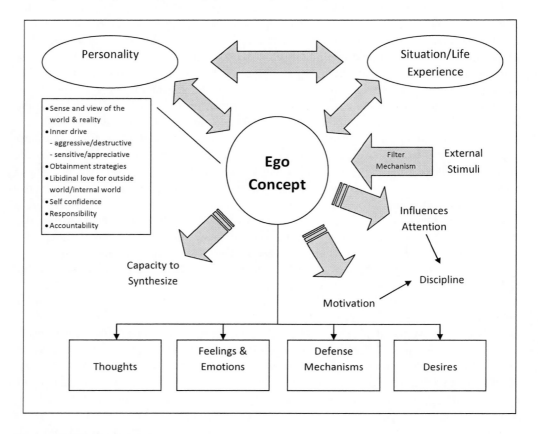

Figure 4.6. The ego concept.

An unbalanced ego concept can destroy the potential for creativity and insight in a number of ways. Our basic aggressive-destructive programming leaves little room for creativity, if this is a dominant instinctual way of thinking. A person who is submissive to others for survival will usually suffer from the repression of any creativity, as he or she must accept the will of others (Paul & Elder 2002, P. 177)[15]. Although a certain amount of *Ego-centricity* leads to confidence, it also creates a belief that '*one is the centre of life*' and '*they know how things really are*'. This lowers curiosity where one follows their own intuition without ever challenging it. *Ego-centricity* filters information in a way that is stereotyped and '*self justifying*'. It leads to self centered interests and objectives leaving little room for open

---

[15] This was seen in the hierarchy of totalitarian regimes over the centuries, and can be seen in marriages where one partner dominates the other.

mindedness. *Ego-centricity* leads to lack of empathy and an inability to see other viewpoints. This destroys any potential for insightful thinking, where in extreme cases the destructive forces of social prejudice, conflict, anger, anger and depression may occur. Extreme *social ego-centricity* prevented humankind understanding the universe for many centuries, insisting that the Earth was the centre of the universe.

HUMOUR AND CREATIVITY

The cognitive processes behind humor are very similar to those behind creativity. Therefore having a brief look at the concept of humor will help us understand more about how we build up tension, make associations and develop insight, all ingredients necessary for creativity. Humor is both cognitive and emotive. Humor is created from an incongruency between what a person expects and what actually happens, which creates an element of shock and surprise, *i.e., an emotional response.*

Take for example the situation where a migrant just arriving in a city who doesn't speak English well, asks for a job at a fruit stall. He gets the job and asks the owner what to say if somebody comes and asks for some fruit. The owner responds by telling him if the person asks *"how much are the oranges?"* to tell them *"60 cents"*. The owner continues and says if the person asks *"are they good or bad?"* to tell them *"some are good and some are bad"*. Then the owner said if the customer asks *"do you think I buy them?"* to answer *"if you don't somebody else will"*.

On the migrant's first day on the job, a lady walks up and asks *"how much are the oranges?"* The migrant answers "60 cents". The lady asks *"are they good or bad?"* and the migrant replies *"some are good and some are bad"*. The lady asks *"do you think I should buy them?"* and the migrant answers *"if you don't somebody else will?"*

A little later a man walks up and asks *"how much are the oranges?"* The migrant answers "60 cents". The man asks *"are they good or bad?"* and the migrant replies *"some are good and some are bad"*. The man asks *"do you think I should buy them?"* and the migrant answers *"if you don't somebody else will?"*

Then another lady comes and asks *"how much are the oranges?"* The migrant answers "60 cents". The lady asks *"are they good or bad?"* and the migrant replies *"some are good and some are bad"*. The lady asks *"do you think I should buy them?"* and the migrant answers *"if you don't somebody else will?"*

At 6 o'clock that night just as the migrant was closing the store a man walked up and asked *"what is the time please?"* The migrant answered "60 cents". The man replied *"stop joking will you"* and the migrant replied *"some are good and some are bad"*. Then the man getting a little angry said *"do you want a punch in the nose?"* and the migrant replied *"if you don't somebody else will?"*

A joke sets up a situation which has some imaginative scenario within it that enables us to create a certain set of images and vision within our mind. We have expectations that the story should play out in a certain way, but tension builds up. The story is heading towards an incongruency, something that is going to shock and surprise us. The rhythm and tension of the story builds up, as this is important to the shock, surprise and emotions generated. This is important to the humorous element as we are waiting for something, in the case of a joke the incongruence to manifest itself. The punch line is where the listener should develop insight followed by an emotive moment, just like in the process of creativity.

It is difficult without telling the whole joke to understand why it is humorous. The joke must be explained in full detail. We cannot point out exactly why it was funny. For a joke like the one above to be humorous to the individual, they must see the association between the punch line and their expectations. The incongruent transformation must transvaluate our values in a certain way or else it won't be humorous. It is this transvaluation that the incongruence taking an unexpected path away from our expected outcome that made the humor. We recognize the incongruence, the link between the story and the punch line, which are unrelated until we make the association. A humorous story or event challenges our expectations in the way things are (our patterns), turning expectations upside down, where we make new connections, enabling us to see the funny side. This is the same way we make creative connections. Like creativity, humor uses knowledge through creating different patterns to create new meanings.

Without the tension building up about what we expect to happen and what may shock us there can be no humor. Just like creativity we also need to perceive and understand the situation from both the cultural and experiential aspects (prior knowledge), otherwise we will not understand the various elements of the joke (Clouse 1993).

THE CREATIVITY PROCESS

There are vast differences in the way people reach a creative solution, develop a new idea, conceptual process or product which reflects the various differences in creative sensitivity, focus and attention, energy, imagination, curiosity, ego, empathy, confidence, discipline, experience, patience, persistence, prior knowledge, level of comfort and the environment they are surrounded in. There are also just as many theories about the process of creativity, which was pioneered by Graham Wallas (1926) in his book the *Art of Thought*. Wallas outlined a four staged sequential model of the creativity, depicting it as an evolutionary process of thinking. Since Wallas's model many enhancements, modifications and variations have been proposed along this evolutionary theme. The general steps as mentioned in several theories of the evolutionary creativity model are outlined as follows.

THE ENGAGEMENT PERIOD

The creative process begins with some form of puzzling situation, curiosity, questioning of something given or problem. With the correct motivation our attention and psychic energy is deployed towards contemplation of this issue. This must be triggered by some sort of personal experience, interaction with another person, feel of a need to be satisfied or some form of challenge or conflict between a personal and perceived reality. A combination of the factors discussed earlier in this part of the book influence whether or not the person will engage upon a quest for clarity and understanding and pursue a solution to the issue, down the path or process which we call creativity.

Engagement is the first step. Not all people are looking to engage in all quests and pursuits for answers to puzzles, problems and issues due to lack of need or low levels of curiosity. Not all people for the reasons that we have discussed can see the same things in the environment. Not all people can see an issue or problem to be curious about. People have different levels of sensitivity to the environment and different motivations to engage. Busy people with hectic schedules will be less likely to pick up stimulus from the environment than those with more time on their hands and greater creative sensitivity. No engagement, no creativity process.

THE PREPARATION PERIOD

Before a problem can be solved a certain amount of cognitive preparation must be undertaken. The preparation stage is where a person has made the realization that something is not right, does not fit, can be done better, or can be done differently. In this stage the scope, direction and depth of the problem is more or less defined in a preliminary form, for later refinement. Potential methods of solution or patterns are selected as ways to solve the problem. Potentially relevant prior knowledge and experience is also selected for recall along with the collection of new information for cognitive matching.

Once a person becomes focused and curious about the particular problem they have identified, the creativity process begins in earnest. Different types of problems take different lengths of time to solve, ranging from a very short time to many years. Different problems also require different thinking strategies and styles to solve them. Thinking about what to whip up for lunch from leftovers in the refrigerator takes up a different time frame and thinking style to a person constructing a scientific hypothesis. Some problems may be very rigid with only a limited number of potential solutions while other problems maybe open ended requiring the construction of something novel and unique to the field it concerns, such as a new product concept.

The preparation process is a period of discovery about what the problem really is, possible ways in how it can be solved and what information is relevant to the solution.

THE FRUSTRATION PERIOD

Sometimes a period during the creative process occurs where all exploration leads to dead-ends and frustration. This may especially be the case when a few attempts have been made to solve the problem. The problem may not be as simple as it first appeared and deeper implications may emerge making the solution much more complex. This is often the case in very complex problems like hypothesis building by a scientist or developing a conceptual case for a new product. Frustration may lead to a person *'back to the drawing board'* because of the utilization of thinking strategies that did not make any headway in solving the problem. Alternately a person may abandon the problem metaphorically putting it into the *'too hard basket'* because *'they bit off more than they can chew'*. However abandonment of the problem may not necessarily mean an end to the creativity process. Mentally retreating from the problem for either the purpose of finding another way to solve it or the wish to abandon it, leads onto another process that acts within our sub-conscious levels, the process of incubation.

THE INCUBATION OR SUB-CONSCIOUS CONTEMPLATION PERIOD

When one has become frustrated and/or feels the problem is not worth pursuing any further, the person stops putting in his or her psychic energy into the problem thereby releasing the mental tension they have been putting themselves under. Taking a rest allows the creativity process to become sublimed within the sub-conscious. During the process of sublimation all the bits of information are digested in the mind within a set of processes that appraise, rearrange and seek to reorganize connections between the pieces of information and the problem. The sublimation of the mental processes may allow the mind some freedom from the patterning of our conscious thinking. This may be the case that some misleading information we rely upon during our conscious reckoning of the problem is dropped (Smith & Blankenship 1991)[16], some form of block is removed (Smith 1995), pieces of other information are applied to the problem which were not consciously considered, or some untried thinking strategies are utilized. This process will not begin until the conscious process stops.

The incubation or sub-conscious contemplation period is perhaps the most significant aspect of the creation process where different thought strategies occur without the explicit awareness of the person. We are not sure exactly what these processes are but we know the brain is very active during this period and strong anecdotal evidence exists where many scientists, engineers, artists, and writers often arrive at some form of realization after this process of incubation or subconscious contemplation (Wallas 1926)[17]. For this reason these processes remain somewhat mysterious to us. There may be a process of combining random or seemingly unrelated strings of information that may assimilate to some forms of connections found in prior knowledge[18]. For example, folklore states that Isaac Newton only developed an insight about the force of gravity after witnessing an apple fall from a tree he was sitting under. Incubation may allow dominant left hemisphere serial thinking to give way to right hemisphere holistic thinking processes thus allowing the problem to be seen differently. Conceptual generations from holistic thinking may ordinarily be rejected during conscious thinking because we are trying to think in a rational and logic manner. The incubation process seems to work best when a person is immersed in a different environment than usual (Smith 1995). The environment should be relaxed, out of routine and without outside stimulation like meetings, radio or television in order to allow the mind to give attention to sub-conscious processing. One situation is sleep where the brain is still very active and empirical evidence seems to support anecdotal evidence that sleep assists the creativity process (Wagner *et. al.* 2004). This long relaxed period may allow information

---

[16] Misleading information cues can be forgotten as time elapses can also partly explain why a problem may be solved after a period of time.

[17] It must also be mentioned that there is skepticism about the effects of a sub-conscious incubation period (Dominowski and Jenrick (1972), Olton (1979), Olton and Johnson (1976).

[18] One must have sufficient domain and field knowledge to draw upon, even at the sub-conscious level. Sub-conscious processing must still remain within the bounded patterns of knowledge within the domain and the field. Knowledge is also necessary to be able to reject some parts of accepted domain knowledge in favor of new theorem and hypothesis, where new advances in knowledge are made.

situated deep in the long term memory be recalled and applied to the problem. The incubation or sub-conscious contemplation period can go on from a couple of hours to a period of months or even longer in some cases.

One way to demonstrate frustration and incubation is to look at a gestalt illustration. Figure 4.7. depicts an ambiguous picture. You may be able to see at once a young woman in the left three-quarter view. However you may be the one person in five that can see an old woman facing to the left. You may be blocked from seeing one of the figures, as you need to re-arrange and use the parts the picture to make a new picture. By sitting and looking at the picture forcing yourself to see the other perspective, you may start to become impatient and frustrated. This frustration will tend to take-over from your curiosity and if you cannot see the other perspective, stress may even be evoked within you. If you do not see the picture at this sitting, put the book down and return to the picture at a later time and the other perspective may come to you when you look at it afresh.

Figure 4.7. An Ambiguous Gestalt Picture.

Recent research has shown when individuals are left undisturbed the brain is not idle, where there is actually increased activity, localized in the pre-frontal cortex (Ingvar 1974). The brain during any resting period is actually quite vigorous, where without any stimulation the mind freely wanders through past recollections, envisioning future plans, and other thoughts and experiences (Andreasen et. al. 1995, Buckner & Carroll 2007). This phenomenon was termed the 'default network' to describe the brain activity at rest (Gusnard et. al. 2001, Gusnard & Raichle 2001). The significance of the 'default network' to creativity is that continued underlying processes still occur that are unrelated to conscious thought occur, something described in the incubation process mode of the creativity process (Buckner *et. al.* 2008). Research has shown that mindfulness can activate the 'default network' (Jang *et. al.* 2011). The 'default network' deactivates is active when an individual is at rest and shuts down when an individual becomes active and is focused on the outside world.

THE CREATIVE INSIGHT

When a sub-conscious connection between two bits of information fit a problem, a realization that brings a feeling of insight occurs. This illumination is often described as the *'aha'* or the *'eureka'* moment. This insight may not bring the whole solution of the problem but perhaps provide a key piece of information that enables the problem to be restructured, reorganized, reframed, reconstructed or reconsidered in some now light, where a solution comes forward with relative ease.

In hindsight the solution will normally be a simplistic and logical one, ironic given the difficulty in arriving at the insight. A simple block or misplaced assumption that was removed during the incubation and sub-conscious contemplation process made way for the insight to occur (Robertson-Riegler & Robertson-Riegler 2008, pp. 472-3). Accepted prior knowledge of a domain and field can sometimes block an insight, especially where knowledge is accepted as a given and not previously questioned.

Acceptance of the IATA[19] regime that regulates airlines within the airline industry could be seen as an example of a block of innovative insight, if it was taken as a field given that could not be challenged. IATA develops and governs voluntary codes of in-flight service, fare regimes, and baggage allowances, etc. Breaking out of these industry assumptions allowed Singapore Airlines in the late 1970s provide a superior quality of in-flight service with lots of complementary items like free drinks that helped to propel the airline into one of the best in the world at the time. Similarly, the advent of low cost airline services beginning with Laker Airways in the 1970s developing low-cost charter services utilizing novel flight practices and secondary airports at the time created a new concept of airline. Around the same time Southwest Airlines began in Texas, which has been followed by Virgin and more recently Air Asia, among many others utilizing this low cost business model.

Insight is the example of a product produced through our brain's self organizing system which begins to associate external information from the environment, our domain and field knowledge and our prior experience held in the long term memory. This may operate in a similar manner to the way we combine words into phrases, phrases into sentences and sentences into ideas and stories to create meaning. Imagination may also play some role in creating vision and imagery and assisting in drawing analogies during this process. The insight is the product of the connection between these bits of information in some sort of semantic, conceptual or visual form, which assists the advancement of the problem solving process. Any meaningful connection of ideas will immediately flash into our conscious

---

[19] The International Air Transport Association (IATA) is an international airline industry group of airlines with the objective of representing the interests of the airline industry. One of IATA's main functions is to set international airfares through bilateral government agreements rather than market mechanisms. This was a powerful mechanism until the deregulation of the airline industry around the world began in the early 1990s. This has brought many criticisms of IATA as a cartel and as a consequence many airlines, especially low-cost airlines have opted to stay outside the IATA framework.

memory as an insight previously not considered in regards to the problem. The mind as a self organizing system during the incubation and insight processes is illustrated below in Figure 4.8.

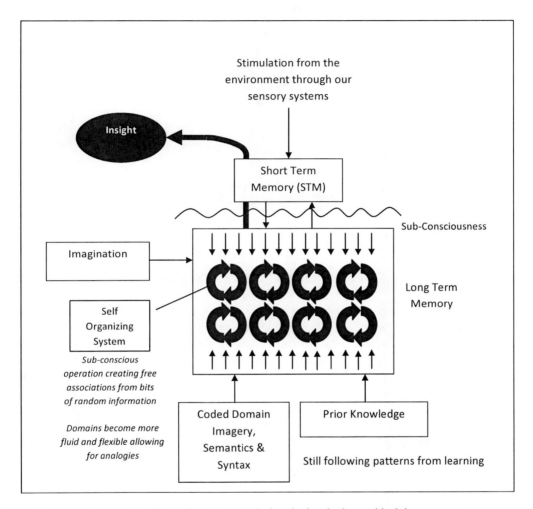

Figure 4.8. The mind as a self organizing system during the incubation and insight processes.

One way to demonstrate insight is to show an illustrative visual example taken from Gestalt psychology. Figure 4.9. shows a figure-ground phenomenon which can be seen as a black chalice on a white background. If however you change perspective and look at the white figures on a black background you will see two heads in profile silhouette. When the perspective is changed, there is some surprise when a completely different perspective is seen. This is insight, the *'aha'*, the *'eureka'* moment of discovering something new.

Figure 4.9. The Gestalt figure-ground phenomenon.

THE VERIFICATION PERIOD

When an insight occurs, the person who had the insight must verify that the illumination can solve the problem, become a key in solving the problem or highlight a concept that has potential as an idea and opportunity. The product of the new insight in the form of a solution or concept must be compatible with the domain and field it will be applied to. It doesn't matter if the solution or concept shifts paradigms or challenges existing knowledge, what counts is viability. If the insight is found to be flawed, then the person will return to the preparation, frustration or incubation stage. Too much frustration may even return the person to the pre-engagement stage again, as there may be a re-contemplation of continual engagement. If the insight is found to be flawless, then the routine work of elaborating on the concept may begin to turn the insight solution or concept into an idea and eventually a potential opportunity.

THE ELABORATION PERIOD

A concept that has emerged through insight must be elaborated upon to turn it into an idea and a plausible opportunity that is capable of being exploited. This process needs to be undertaken with an open mind or logic and rationality may destroy it before it can be sketched out into a full idea. The process begins with generating as many characteristics about the concept as possible until a full idea emerges (Parnes 1972). This requires developing narrative and imagery about the concept so that detail emerges, giving it fullness. This process may require further creative association to develop the conceptual characteristics of product, manufacturing, marketing and how it relates to the supply and value chains. This will involve asking and seeking solutions to questions like, *How will the product work? How will the product look? How will the product be manufactured? What materials need to go into the product? Where can these materials be sourced and acquired? How will the product reach consumers?* etc. Answering these types of questions requires the creativity process to develop a series of innovations that go behind the future product strategy and make the whole idea work.

A full concept is an idea which can be evaluated in terms of opportunity potential. First the idea must be consistent with the goals and aspirations of the person who developed it. The idea must also meet the person's moral, financial, competency, resource, technical and business acumen criteria. Then if the idea is still suitable, it can be analyzed, evaluated, and further refined until a working opportunity scenario exists. The elaborative process therefore requires both creative thinking to fill out the concept into a full idea, create the innovations that will enable the idea to be considered an opportunity, and an analytical or reasoning process to evaluative the concept and determine whether a potential opportunity exists. The whole creativity process is shown in Figure 4.10.

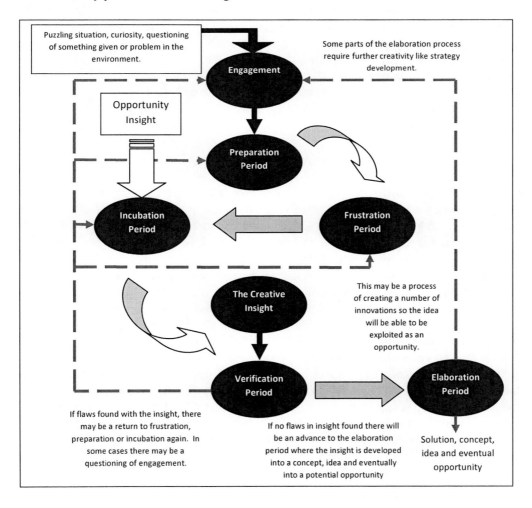

Figure 4.10. The Creativity Process.

Many experienced people in specific domains and fields may appear to see opportunity in an instantaneous manner, as if creativity is instantly intuitive. People with vast knowledge and experience may be able to survey the environment and pass through the engagement, preparation and frustration stages, directly into a very brief period of incubation before gaining some form of insight. This type of intuitive insight is sometime called *'gut feeling'* and is very common in many entrepreneurs. This however does not mean that these intuitive insights do not need verification and elaboration. It just means that some people may be skilled at seeing gaps in the market where potential opportunities may exist quickly, based on their long experience within a domain and field.

The creativity process requires hard and sometimes painstaking work. Many concepts and problems may require months or even years of careful trial and error before a hypothesis is developed or something works. This can occur throughout the preparation, frustration, verification and elaboration processes. Thomas A. Edison, the inventor of the telegraph, phonograph and motion pictures was quoted as saying *"Genius is one percent inspiration and ninety-nine percent perspiration",* inferring that creativity is not about insight but dedicated work and perseverance. Oscar Wilde describes the tedious part of creativity by saying *"I was working on the proof of one of my poems all the morning, and took out a comma. In the afternoon I put it in again."* Great authors like Ernest Hemingway and James Michener wrote as many as 25 drafts of the books they produced. A scientist may undertake the same experiment changing a single parameter hundreds of times before achieving any success. Creativity requires total emersion, patience, persistence and finally enjoyment.

APPROACHES TO CREATIVITY WHOLE BRAIN THINKING

There are many different types of thinking that aid the creativity and problem solving processes. Intuition, imagination and transformation are important methods of developing new ideas, while logic and reasoning may be important methods of thinking for certain types of solving problems and decision making. Strategy development tends to come from abductive rather than deductive thinking.

Bowden *et. al.* (2005) found that insightful problem solving stimulated parts of the right side of the brain[20], while non insightful problem solving did not. This tends to confirm some of the different operations of the left and right sides of the brain. The Nobel laureate Roger Wolcott Sperry in his split brain research found that the left half of the brain tends to function by processing information in an analytical, sequential and logical manner, which has been labeled by others as serial or convergent thinking and the right hand half of the brain tends to function through recognizing relationships and synthesizing information, which has been labeled by others as divergent, lateral or holistic thinking (Evarts 1990). Although we label the left hand side of the brain as serial and the right hand side of the brain as holistic, this is an over simplification (Robertson-Riegler & Robertson-Riegler 2008, P. 481). The general functions and approaches used by the left and right side of the brain are shown in figure 4.11.

---

[20] Anterior superior temporal gyres

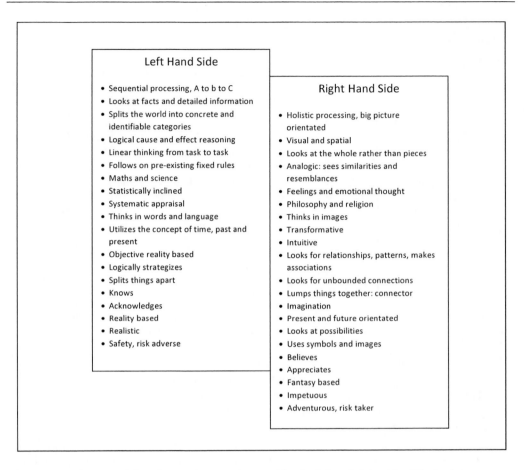

Figure 4.11. The general functions and approaches used by the left and right side of the brain.

Consequently, left hand hemisphere thinking is selective and goes through logical steps to derive a definite answer or logical conclusion. Serial thinking will discard irrelevant information and utilize fixed classifications or categories when using information. Right hand hemisphere thinking looks for associations with all information at hand and make up new categories and classifications, if necessary. Holistic thinking will restructure information to create new concepts or alternatives. Within the concept of creative thinking, holistic thinking will develop new alternatives while serial thinking screens the generated alternatives, makes judgments, develops concepts towards the objectives of the problem, or creates detail to an idea (Isaksen & Treffinger 1985). Creativity requires both serial and holistic thinking to develop and complete the detail for useable concepts.

Michael Kirton (1994) postulated that individuals adopt a particular cognitive style of creativity and problem solving. Kirton believed that an individual's thinking style will be somewhere along an adaptor-innovator continuum, depending upon how much structure they prefer when solving problems (Kirton 1994a). Adaptors have a preference for doing things better, while innovators trade immediate efficiency in pursuit of doing something conceptually better (Kirton 1994b). The characteristics of adaptors and innovators are listed in Table 4.1.

Table 4.1. Some characteristics of adaptors and innovators.

Adaptors	Innovators
<ul><li>Like to be precise, reliable, efficient, disciplined.</li><li>Concerned with solving residual problems within the current industry paradigm.</li><li>Seeks solutions within the frame of existing technologies, products and business models.</li><li>Tends to be focused on means.</li><li>Able to concentrate for long periods of time.</li><li>Is an authority within a given domain.</li></ul>	<ul><li>Tends to be undisciplined, approaching tasks from unusual angles.</li><li>Tends to search for problems and alternative avenues of solution.</li><li>Challenges existing assumptions.</li><li>Can go through strict routines for only short periods of time.</li><li>Tends to dominate in unstructured situations.</li></ul>

Kitron (1994a, P. 28) found that adaptors are more left brain dominated, being reflective and sequential, whereas innovators are more holistic thinking, active and hands on in their approach.

The two approaches to problem solving can lead to different types of innovation. Adaptors employ a disciplined methodological approach to problem solving which tends to be orientated within the existing technology, business and product models, upon the existing industry plain. This results in incremental improvement moving along the industry innovation curves, shown in figure 4.12. This may be an improvement of technology or a way of doing things within an existing industry better. An innovator on the other hand looks at problems from unique or novel angles and discovers new solutions, bypassing existing industry assumptions. The innovator's approach is ends rather than process based that the adaptor employs, and bypasses existing industry knowledge, products and business models, leading to something completely new, as a new technology, a new to the world product or a new business model. The innovation has used ideas from outside the industry that bring breakthroughs, rather than the incremental improvements that the adaptor usually develops[21].

Kirton (1994a, P. 28) provides us with some indication of habitual adaptor and innovator characteristics which may give some clue to their entrepreneurial style and preferred business strategies. Habitual adaptors may tend to have a low self esteem and sense of self efficacy. They tend to be introverts, conscientious, controlled, subdued, process orientated and emotionally naive. The habitual innovator is almost the opposite, tending to be unstructured, non-conforming, self confident, somewhat ostentatious, risk taking, and task orientated person. However Isaksen and Puccio (1988) state that the relationship between a person's characteristics according to their creative style are not as straight forward as Kirton suggests,

---

[21] One must mention here that being an innovator does not necessary imply more success than an adaptor. Innovators have the challenge of convincing potential customers that their breakthrough has benefits and advantages over what is already available on the market. In contrast the adaptor is raising the level of the market to a new point of competitive advantage favoring the adaptor over other competitors.

as there are numerous creative styles and characteristics as creativity is a complex issue. The rest of this chapter looks at different creative styles and strategies.

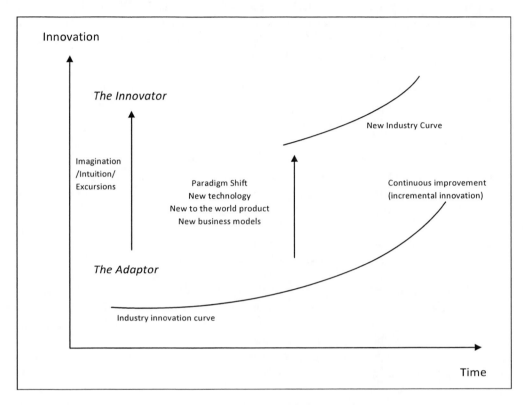

Figure 4.12. Adaptor/Innovator innovation affect on an industry.

MULTIPLE INTELLIGENCE AND THE METAPHORICAL CONCEPT OF "CREATIVE INTELLIGENCE"

In chapter three we looked at the concept of multiple intelligences. As we saw, Gardner's work widened the narrow concept of a general intelligence to the broader concept where individuals can exhibit different types of intelligent behavior. Gardner initially listed seven types of intelligence, *body-kinesthetic, verbal-linguistic, logical-mathematical, visual-spatial, musical, interpersonal and intrapersonal intelligence.* Gardner also affirmed that our separate types of intelligences may not just be limited to the seven above and that others may also exist. The multiple intelligences theory recognizes that broad mental abilities are needed in society and that every person has a unique blend of different intelligences. There is no agreement on whether the theory of multiple intelligences is valid, however metaphorically this is a very good way to look at an individual's cognitive abilities.

Therefore, our creative style has little to do with our general intelligence (Kirton 1994). Our creativity has more to do with particular characteristics, thinking styles and processes than the nature of intelligence. A couple of other intelligence theories may assist in developing our understanding of some of the characteristics of creativity and place it in a social context. Expanding upon Gardner's concept of interpersonal intelligence is the concept of emotional intelligence (EQ), which has become very popular over the last two decades. Emotional intelligence places emphasis on a number of characteristics that are important for creativity within a group or social setting. Some of these characteristics include;

- Knowing oneself in terms of emotions and the ability to recognize emerging feelings,
- Being able to handle these emerging feelings when appropriate,
- Being self motivated and being able to delay self gratification,
- Having empathy with others,
- Being able to handle relationships and social settings,
- Being open minded, able to speak one's own mind, and an attentive listener, and
- Having a personal style to manage stress, take responsibility and be in self control (Dulewicz & Higgs 1998).

Consequently emotional intelligence emphasizes the social domain of creativity, which is important in some of the group creativity tools discussed later on.

Gardner also speculated at the possibility of spiritual intelligence. Zohar and Marshall (2000) postulated that we have a spiritual intelligence which has a moral base enabling us to question the issues of *'what'* and *'why'* about things, and whether we should or shouldn't be involved in particular things. Unlike general intelligence which is logical and rational, spiritual intelligence enables us to question, which is central to the concept of creativity.

Therefore to be creative in the social arena, a person should have a high level of emotional and spiritual intelligence (Hicks 2004, P. 337), of which the characteristics are important aspects related to the development of creative thinking. Sternberg (2002) mentioned the concept of practical intelligence which is necessary for a person to adapt, shape and make selections in everyday life in order to be successful. Practical intelligence is thus a measure of tacit knowledge, where tacit knowledge is what is needed to be successful in a given environment[22].

In the same article Sternberg mentions the concept of creative intelligence. The concept of creative intelligence is also mentioned by a number of authors, although the term is used broadly and there is little consensus upon what it really constitutes. Creative intelligence is a term grouping together the cognitive and non-cognitive aspects of creative generation like intense interest, motivation and other social influences (Cropley 1994), or a term that refers more to styles of creative thinking (Khandwalla 2004, Rowe 2004).

So both concepts of creative intelligence widen the concept of creativity by placing importance on the contextual and environmental variables on one hand and on thinking processes, applications, or styles on the other. Rowe (2004, P. 3) outlines four styles of creative intelligence;

- Intuition which is based on past experience to guide action,
- Innovation which concentrates on systematic and data orientated problem solving,

---

[22] Tacit knowledge is generally acquired on one's own, usually unspoken and implicit, procedural in natural, not readily articulated and directly related to practical goals that people value (Sternberg 2002, P. 11).

- Imagination which uses visualization to create opportunities, and
- Inspiration, which emotionally focuses on the changing of something.

Khandwalla (2004, P. 213) focuses on a number of personal characteristics like sensitivity, problem restructuring ability, fluency, flexibility, guessing ability, originality and elaboration and the uses of various thinking processes that support them, *e.g., convergent thinking, problem restructuring, and elaboration, etc.* These approaches show that creativity is both influenced by the environment and thinking processes employed.

In such a context creativity can be broadly considered an ability or intelligence in itself. A metaphorical construct of creative intelligence would look something like Figure 4.13. A person is surrounded by their social environment. The social environment stimulates an individual's perceptions, socializes beliefs and makes judgments upon creative efforts. The family, domicile outlook, generational influence, age, education, work and life experiences, etc, all have some influence, discussed in detail back in chapter three. Also within the environment is the domain the person is interested in and passionate about, *e.g. art, teaching, engineering, science, home duties, sports, etc.* The environment is completed by the field which ultimately makes social decisions about what is creative and what is not. For example the art community decides what art is outstanding and what art is mediocre. These judgments may only occur years after the object of art was created, as it may take an artist years to become recognized. Likewise, peers in each science through journals and conferences decide what new information to the domain is acceptable or unacceptable. A new fad product may be considered something creative during *'the fad period'*, where afterwards the product's creative edge disappears.

Four types of situations require creative intelligence. These are the quest for new ideas, the search for as yet unknown opportunities, the development of strategies to exploit potential opportunities and solving a multitude of problems that face individuals through life. Our perception of the outside world is greatly dependent upon our patterning, heuristics, other biases, and prior knowledge. What we notice or don't notice depends upon our creative sensitivity, focus and attention. What we are interested in, have passion for and confidence in, all influence our perception of people, objects and events. Our perception and reaction to external stimuli and how our cognitive system will process incoming data depends upon the existing tension within our motivational trigger. If there is tension between *'where we are'* and *'what we envisage, desire or aspire'*, attention and energy will be drawn into the following cognitive processes.

Our thinking processes will normally follow our existing patterning. Patterned thinking is usually controlled through heuristics that are based upon our beliefs and experience stored within our prior knowledge. Tacit knowledge also exists and can assist in opportunity discovery and problem solving. Imagination and fantasy can emerge and manifest as visions, ideas, new connections, or potential solutions to problems.

Emotion is another factor that influences our cognitive processing. When emotion is dominant or within our sub-conscious, it will to some extent control our thinking patterns, particularly if we are unaware of the emotion.

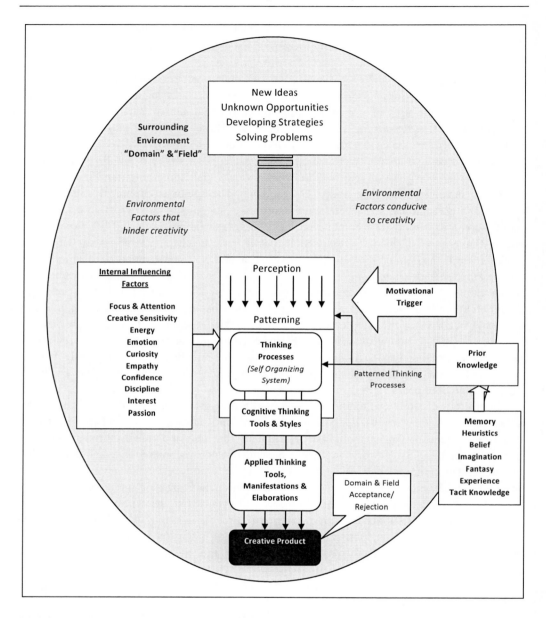

Figure 4.13. A Metaphoric Construct of "Creative Intelligence".

Our thinking processes are extremely complex. We still do not completely understand how these processes occur today in much detail. Our cognitive operations are independent from the external environment and our consciousness. All cognitive processes are the result of changing neural and receptor interactions that occur within different parts of the brain. Our perceptions, reasoning, concept of self are not concentrated on one part of the brain as they are distributed. There is no centre of convergence and connections between the different parts of the brain functions. Cognitive processes are not serial, but operate in parallel, reciprocal and distributed interaction (Singer 2009). For example when we see an object and touch it, our sight and tactile preceptors make independent contributions to the identification of the object. There is thus no single locus or point for the identification of objects. The representations of objects are made up of spatial-temporal patterns of distributed neural activity (Singer 2009, P. 325).

From the information processing point of view, the brain is highly distributed rather than centralized, which relies upon a self organizing system to coordinate and function as there is no single convergence centre. Therefore the brain is a decentralized system that utilizes information in different locations to produce our perceptions, thoughts, reasoning and intuition. Information within the brain is distributed in a decentralized configuration, functioning as a whole through a strategy called *assembly coding* (Singer 2009, P. 326). This is a very flexible coding strategy as it can reorganize and recombine information in a numerous number of ways. Through this mechanism we are able to continually make perceptions in an ever changing world[23].

The way information is organized is of paramount importance to how we see things and in solving a problem. As the brain processes in parallel and can recombine information in numerous ways, this assists an individual develop new thoughts, new ideas and to solve problems. Making analogies is a matter of comparing two different concepts that share some similarity in parallel. The creative process goes through a number of steps, which relies on the mind as a *self organizing system* to make new associations and enable problems to be solved. This usually occurs during a period of incubation which because of the need to reorganize information could be one of the most important aspects of seeing new associations and finding solutions to problems.

Rather than rely on our raw natural thinking processes, we can utilize disciplined and controlled thinking styles and tools that change our thinking patterns for enhancing creative thought. These are discussed later on in this chapter. These tools can assist us to look at situations and problems in different ways so we can see new associations and linkages which may lead to new ideas or solutions to problems. Special applied tools of thinking can also be utilized for applied business tasks, like reengineering and radical transactiveness.

There are a number of factors that are conducive to or hinder creativity. The environment can either be inspiring and conducive to creativity or hinder creativity. Emotions like fear, complacency, organizational politics or a conservative society that frowns on novelty can stifle creativity of both individuals and groups. These will be discussed in much more detail at the end of this chapter.

So broadly speaking a metaphoric concept of creative intelligence is made up of our environment, the factors and variables that influence our perceptions and cognitive thinking processes, a motivational trigger, our prior knowledge, our thinking styles, tools that we can employ to enhance creativity, and the product of the process itself, which will be accepted or rejected as being something creative. If this model is representative of what creative intelligence is, then by manipulating the environmental parameters, being aware of our

---

[23] An example of how assembly coding enables the identification of novel objects through flexible recombination can be understood by seeing how a small child may identify a cow for the first time, if they have no previous experience or understanding of what a cow is. The child upon seeing the cow at the zoo identifies the cow (a novel object) as a large version of the dog, he or she has at home. It is only after the parents explain that a cow is a different animal to a dog, that the child can refine his or her identification of the cow as a separate animal to a dog. Reading is another activity that shows how the brain can understand the recombination of letters making up different words, sentences and paragraphs into unique meaning.

emotions and other influences upon our perception and thinking, and by developing new thinking styles through the use of thinking tools we can enhance our creative ability.

CREATIVE PROBLEM SOLVING PROCESSES (CPS)

Finding novel connections and solving problems often requires new ways of looking at things, which often has to be forced through, breaking away from logical and serial thinking to holistic or lateral thinking. Many creative problem solving (CPS) techniques have been developed which are generally based and extended upon Alex Osborne's Brainstorming processes, discussed in this section, William Gordon's Synectics techniques, discussed under metaphors and analogies or Edward De Bono's creativity tools discussed under frames of thinking. Brainstorming originated from a marketing environment, Synectics from a research and development environment and De Bono's techniques from a psychology background.

Each method has its similarities and differences and strengths and weaknesses. Brainstorming and some of De Bono's methods are very good for generating very quick new ideas, while the more sophisticated Synectics is much more focused on provoking idea generation through specific techniques. De Bono's *'Six thinking hats'* is very good for making selections and weighing up various issues.

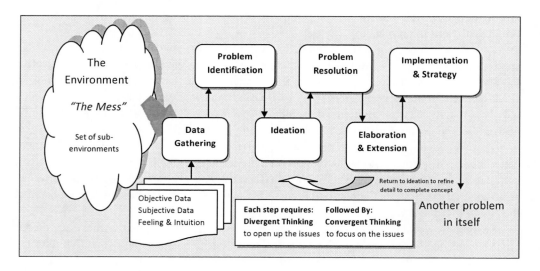

Figure 4.14. The Generic Steps of the Problem Solving Process.

The problem solving process goes through a number of stages. All models in existence acknowledge this and have specific and particular steps. The model presented in Figure 4.14. is a generic schematic of the problem solving process, showing all the common steps that would be undertaken in solving common problems.

The Environment

Within the general environment that we are personally emerged within, there will always be issues, problems and unknown opportunities in existence. The general environment also consists of smaller but just as complex sub-environments that can be defined in numerous ways[24]. The environment is not always as we would wish and there is sometimes an urge to change things. Within pockets of sub-environments there will be *'a mess'* that a person or group may become concerned about, begin give attention to and focus as an issue, problem, or potential opportunity[25]. It takes tension and motivation to focus upon and think about any particular aspect of the environment.

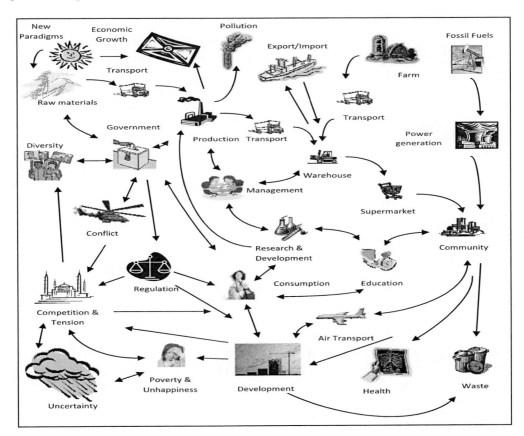

Figure 4.15. A Simplified View of an Environment.

---

[24] Sub-environments can be made up of a domain or field, an industry, a community, a region, an infrastructural service like education or the court system, a family, or an organization, etc.

[25] A 'mess' is a complex issue which does not have any well defined structure, making it difficult to define the actual problem. Complex issues usually have many factors involved, of which many cannot be quantified. In problem solving these problems must be considered as a whole because many factors are interrelated in ways we are not sure. In contrast, problems have much more defined structures, of which we have more understanding. There are usually a number of alternative solutions, depending upon resources at hand and the value systems used for decision making. See Ackoff (1974).

The wish to impose some future condition upon the environment means that an issue or problem must be solved or an opportunity observed, discovered or constructed from the perceived 'mess'. Real world situations may appear extremely complex at the beginning with the feeling of 'where do I start ?'' Through just casual observation it is very difficult to see changes in demographics, industry changes, emerging technologies that will have impact upon industries, regulatory changes, the effects of the economy and incongruities. But through consistent observation and some historical understanding, one will begin to notice "patterns" and "relationships" existing. We need methods that simplify what we see, so some meaning can be extracted from the environment, in order to progress. We must also be aware of the effects our emotions and other cognitive biases have on our perceptions. Figure 4.15. shows a simplified diagram of an environment.

In the divergent phase of looking at the 'mess', the use of a simple systems diagrams, mind maps, or other forms of illustration that can portray some order, may be helpful. This assists in isolating factors and relationships from the 'mess' so some sense can be made. Convergent thinking can be used to prioritize the factors, issues and relationships through guided questions like 'how do things work here?', 'what is the flow of things?', 'what are the stages things go through?', 'what influences what?', and 'what changes are taking place?', etc. One can then look at the diagrams, maps or illustrations ask 'where are the areas that they have influence over?', 'How much influence can be exerted?', 'who else has influence?', and 'what other things influence the things we want to influence?' Imagination can then be utilized to visualize potential desired futures and compare them with the power to act[26].

Data Gathering

What type of data should be collected will depend upon the type of the problem being considered and the type of approach being used. It is very important to know precisely what questions are intended to be answered and what data and information will assist in answering these predetermined questions.

Interviews and observations can provide views on what people actually do, and perhaps give some indications as to why. Questionnaires can provide statistical data that shows the percentages of people or things that are in common and different. Different types of information collected, different methods of collection, and different people collecting the information will greatly influence the data collected. Hard data is very important in looking at cyclic, automated and machine type problems. Soft data is useful more at human related issues[27]. The types of information that can be collected are listed in Table 4.2.

---

[26] The power to act will depend upon, skills, competencies and capabilities, resources, networks, an competition, etc.

[27] Hard data can be classified as any quantitative data, data collected from flows, organizational data from reporting channels, products and the organizational structure. Soft data would include hunches, guesses, intuitions, perceptions of the people involved I the problematic situation, judgments about skills, competencies, efficiencies perceived status, attitudes, motivated needs and individuals (Checkland 1981).

Table 4.2. Types of Information that can be collected.

Information	Knowledge, facts, intelligence, recollections – what is known and can be perceived, calculated, verified, discovered or inferred. Information can usually be verified from other sources.
Tacit information	The unwritten rules of the game, informal ways things are done.
Structural	The structure of domains fields, industries, markets, organizations and consumers.
'The flow of things'	How things flow within a domain, field, industry, market and organization.
'What'	What is the *'mess'* doing? What are the unmet objectives that are not satisfied? What resources, skills, competencies and capabilities are used?
'Where'	Where are the important locations, positions, focal points, concentrations, centralizations and decentralizations. Is it concentrated or fragmented?
'When'	When are the important times, intervals, deadlines, schedules, cycles, beginnings and endings?
'Why'	The reasons, meanings, goals, objectives, aims, intentions of the areas of focus?
'How'	How do things happen?
Stakeholders	Who are the stakeholders of the domain, field, industry, market and organization.
Impressions	Images, visualizations, and other artefacts retained from experience. Hunches, intuitive guesses, speculations, etc.
Beliefs	Assumptions, beliefs and values that people and organizations operate from.
Observations	Perceptions, comments.
Feelings	Desires, aspirations, emotions, sentiments, empathy, etc.
Questions	Curiosity when have lack of information.

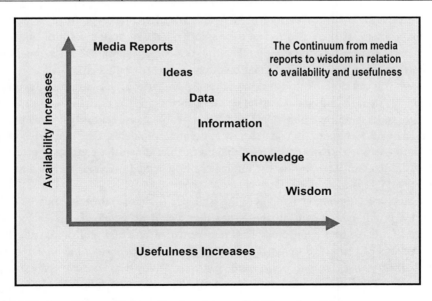

Figure 4.16. The Continuum of information based on availability and usefulness.

One must be aware of the different types of information and its usefulness. There are many sources of information that will vary in validity. Information comes in a continuum beginning from third party opinions and media reports, which may or may not be informed, across to one's own wisdom in perceiving and reading the situation. Figure 4.16. shows the *'trade off'* between the availability of information and its usefulness (Hunter 2009, P. 216).

Using the above sources of information one can take stock of the situation by determining what is really known and what is not known. Looking at the system and asking the above questions can assist in breaking out of patterned or habitual thinking and look beyond stereotyping. One should now be able to break away pieces of the *'mess'* that were obscured, overlooked, or gone unnoticed and find hidden patterns and interrelationships among parts of the environment.

Now, one should be able to see *'who has special strengths, resources and networks that make them able to solve the problem situation?', 'how are they solving the problem situation?', and 'what influence can I have over people, resources, networks, places, channels and the problem situation?'*

The data gathering process should begin to challenge our previous ideas, where attention now wonders to questions and areas of concern. This process should have already brought our thinking beyond the usual contemplations, where learning is occurring. Focus on these areas may have brought some insight into what the problem really is or already generated some ideas[28].

Problem Identification

The process of reaching the problem identification stage and making and articulate definition and description of the problem is central to the problem solving process. Rushing to define a problem can often lead to the loss of great time, energy and resources in going in the wrong direction. In many cases, the correct identification of the problem is half way to solving the problem, as there is often an easy solution. Getting to the point of understanding the real problem, rather than the symptoms within the *'mess'* within the environment is a real achievement, as there is a glut of information often leading to confusion.

Although it is not possible to list down all cause and effect relationships, attempts should be made to begin isolating and identifying these factors. So in defining any problem it is necessary to understand the subsystems and the probable cause and effect dynamics. There are numerous CPS techniques in use to assist in defining problems. One method to define the problem is to use an Ishikawa (fishbone) diagram to list down the cause and effect. Figure 4.17. shows a diagram intending to list the factors influencing essential oil yield and quality (Hunter 2009, P. 319).

A pre-step or an alternative method to the Ishikawa (fishbone) diagram may be utilizing a cognitive (or mind) map where all the issues that would appear to be associated with the problem can be listed and connected. This may assist in ordering and organizing thinking. Sets of questions can be asked to assist such as *'What is the purpose of the object, process or function?' 'What is necessary to perform the function?'* and *'What are the side effects of the function?' etc.* These conceptual problem definition and description processes will be influenced by our beliefs, attitudes, own hypothesis, prejudices, expectations, values and objectives. A cognitive (or mind) map showing the major issues causing changes in essential

---

[28] However if early ideas or potential opportunities are already perceived, the process should not be stopped. Going through the other stages may help generate other alternatives which may also warrant consideration.

oil yield and constituents and another map breaking down the climate factor is illustrated in figure 4.18. below.

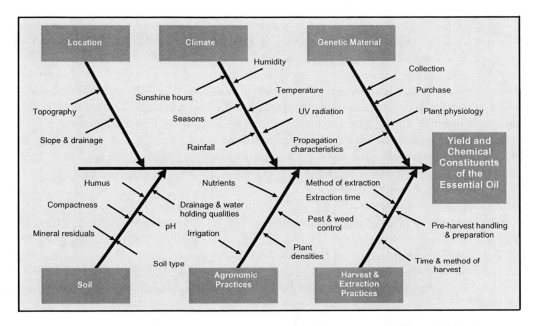

Figure 4.17. Factors Influencing Essential Oil Yield and Constituents on an Ishikawa (fishbone) Diagram.

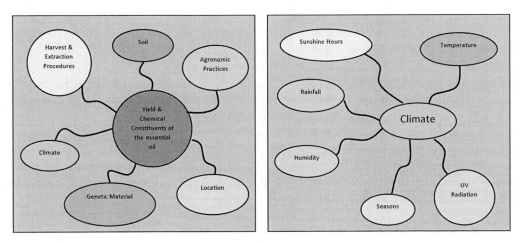

Figure 4.18. A cognitive (or mind) map showing the major causes of essential oil yield and chemical constituent variances (left) and another map breaking down the climate variable (right).

Many people believe that taking time to define and map the problem is a retrograde step and wasting time. One of the major mistakes made in problem solving is jumping to conclusions and assuming we know what the problem is and the underlying causes. This step allows a person to step outside their own frames of thinking and get new perspectives on the problem.

Ideation

The ideation stage is similar to the ideation stage in the new product development process (Hunter 2009, P. 560). In this stage it is necessary to be able to look at the problem from different vantage points. In this stage, each idea should be accepted without judgment, or criticism, just noted for later evaluation.

If a problem has a number of known potential solutions, then logical and convergent thinking processes like evaluating the strengths and weaknesses, benefits and undesirable side effects can be utilized to determine the acceptability of each option. The problem can be solved through direct evaluation and the divergent ideation process is not required.

There are hundreds of different techniques used by consultants for idea generation in the problem solving process. However most methods can be classified within seven basic categories listed below (Van Gundy 1988);

Attribute Listing

Attribute listing is a tool that can be used for breaking down an object, system or problem into its many parts or attributes. This would include problems such as identifying the attributes of a system *i.e., the factors causing variance in the yield and quality of an essential oil,* finding alternative uses for products, breaking a product into its individual parts to evaluate where they can be improved, or breaking down the emotional state of a person into attributes, etc. This allows a group to concentrate on a single attribute at a time in understanding the issues and coming up with a solution or ideas for improvement. This technique may include simple brainstorming to come up with the attributes and systematically looking for improvements in each attributes.

Attribute listing has many applications including the areas of engineering, quality, marketing and systems analysis. For example, in engineering a product can be conceptually decomposed to learn how it was manufactured *(see reengineering).* A machine can be broken down into parts to examine issues like fatigue and wear. In quality a product, service or process can be broken down to find out which aspects are poor or undesirable, needing improvement, etc. This could be used to analyze a product, a customer service program, or a production process. In marketing, attribute listing can be used to discover what necessary attributes are desirable to develop product specifications. The method can also be used to develop the marketing and promotional mixes for products and promotional campaigns, etc. In systems analysis, attribute listing can be used to develop the needed characteristics of a new computer program or application or the analysis of attributes of employee satisfaction/dissatisfaction in the workplace.

Absurd Solutions (Wishful Thinking)

Coming up with absurd solutions is a way of creating divergent thinking in coming up with any idea, however extreme to find a new vector in solving a problem. Van Gundy (1988) called this wishful thinking where anything is possible as a potential solution to a problem. Once an absurd solution has been identified, the gist or essence of the idea may have some merit. For example, *'eliminate the opposition',* can be worked back through stages until a practical solution is found (Proctor 1999, P. 164), such as *'inviting the opposition to sit on the committee'* or *'make some contribution to the processes'* where they cannot later dissent from what they agreed upon. In this way an extreme and apparently irrelevant solution can form the basis for a practical solution. Absurd solutions are more common in our thinking processes than we realize. For example, as a solution to the problem of Indian students being bashed and robbed in Melbourne, Victoria, Australia, Simon Overland, the Victorian Police Commissioner suggested that *"Indians should not look rich to avoid being targeted"*, which was considered absurd by many commentators[29].

Brainstorming

Brainstorming was developed by Alex Osborn in the early 1950's as a tool in advertising for groups to generate a large number of ideas without consideration for their merits. Osborn describes brainstorming as the brain storming over creative problems in a commando fashion which each *'stormer'* attacking the same objective through their imagination (Osborn 1953). To develop maximum creativity from the group, four rules must be strictly enforced and followed by all;

1. Critical judgment is not allowed,
2. Complete freedom is welcomed,
3. Quantity over quality is wanted, and
4. Combination and improvement are sought.

Other specific aspects that will enhance effectiveness are a) sessions should be limited to around one hour, b) the problem shouldn't be revealed before the session, c) the problem should be clearly stated and not too broad, and d) if a product is being discussed actual samples should be present (Whiting 1955). *Brainstorming* assists decision makers think of unexpected and potentially useful strategies for settling a problem. Brainstorming relies on unaided thinking and can consequently produce a number of shallow ideas, but it can also increase the overall creativity of a group. Brainstorming is used as part of almost every other problem solving technique.

As mentioned, *Brainstorming* spread from advertising to all types of management decision making, however it is extremely limited for specific technical problems (Adams 1986), and best for finding new markets for existing products, *i.e., 'are there any opportunities that are being missed?'*, new uses for products, *'what are the potential other uses for this product?'*, product names or just to encourage creativity within a group.

There are many enhancements and variations upon brainstorming. The use of checklists can add direction to a session and as a regenerative method to move along stalling groups. Brainwriting requires the group to put their ideas in writing, rather than verbally, where ideas can be circulated anonymously for enhancement. Recently *brainstorming* software has been developed (Gaynier 1999) to assist groups and some companies like *Australia Post* have developed brainstorming labs where employees can hold sessions using the walls to scribble upon.

Forced Relationships (or Analogies)

Forced relationships or analogies are another way of generating ideas by comparing two unrelated object and looking for things they have in common for new insights. Relationships

---

[29] See: Look poor to avoid attacks: Oz top cop to Indian students, NDTV, 7th February 2010, http://www.ndtv.com/news/world/look_poor_to_avoid_attacks_oz_top_cop_to_indian_students.php

can be forced between almost any two objects. This is usually done through giving a group a random word or a card with a word or image on it, to commence idea generation. An example of a relationship between seemingly two unrelated objects is a bicycle wheel and a theme park. Walt Disney designed Disneyland with a meeting place in the middle with various theme radiating out from the meeting place, *i.e., Fantasyland, Tomorrowland, Frontierland* and *Adventureland, etc.*

This type of problem solving process would begin with the question *'how is this problem like a (inserted word)?'* Brainstorming or brainwriting techniques can be used to generate analogies. Then the group would go on and consider *'how could this problem be solved with a (inserted word)?'* This can be supplemented with questions like *'If our organization was like (inserted word), what would it be like?'* Similarities between the two objects can be considered and characteristics from one object superimposed on the other. For example, a leopard is quick and aggressive like a company marketing campaign, etc. This technique can bring new vectors of thought into a group and assist in developing product and branding attributes and strategy development, etc.

Checklists

Another technique to generate new ideas and solve problems is through checklists. Framed checklists contain many questions to prompt ideas, stimulate imagination, and evaluate ideas. Checklists assist people look at problems from different perspectives. Specific checklists can be developed for particular applications such as developing a new product, finding a new use for a material, how to deal with waste products, how improve customer services and evaluate competition, etc. A concept generation checklist for consumer products is shown in Table 4.3. (Hunter 2009, P. 581).

Excursions

An excursion is a method used to find new possibilities through imagination, analogies and metaphor. It is used as part of the synectics framework, which is discussed in the next section on metaphors and the use of analogies in creativity.

Morphological Analysis

Morphological analysis (MA) is a method used to undertake the systematic analysis of complex systems. It is useful in the search for new products, making national policies, stakeholder analysis, developing new types of systems, and other types of non-quantified modeling. Morphological systems are useful where there are a large set of factors to consider which cannot be easily quantified, are in uncertain conditions, and the situation cannot be causally modeled.

Morphological analysis was developed to work at the level of *'messes'* where variables are unstructured and not easily defined. Morphological analysis puts structure into the problem. As the different aspects of the *'mess'* interrelate to each other in yet unknown ways, one of the mistakes that can be made in solving these types of problems is to break them up into smaller parts (Pidd 2003). This mistake is regularly made as humans find it difficult to work in high levels of complexity. Morphological analysis examines the whole mess first, establishing the boundaries so that internal relationships can be analyzed before going on to generate alternative solutions and solve the problem like a puzzle.

Table 4.3. A concept generation checklist for consumer products.

1. Review existing products in the market *a) What benefits they offer to consumers? (Is this a major issue?)* *b) appearance, efficacy, odour, colour, etc.* *c) branding, image and theme* This study will assist in determining what benefits of the new product should be highlighted in the marketing campaign.
2. Is the product concept compatible with the branding? *Must ensure the finished product formulation reinforces the brand image the company wishes to show consumers – i.e., colour, odour, softness, efficacy, appearance, use of particular materials.*
3. What distribution channels do competitors utilize? Can I break in? What are the barriers to entry? Are there alternative channels?
4. Is the proposed formulation compatible with the proposed packaging? *a) Is the nature of the product consistent with the proposed packaging?* *b) What product bulk densities will be required?* *c) Can the product be filled efficiently during the production process?* *d) Will the proposed packaging affect product stability?*
5. What logistic considerations may require special packaging? *a) required storage times* *b) Heat, especially harsh temperature variations* *c) Exposure to light* *d) Transport* *e) Product/supply chain integrity (Halal, Kosher, organic)* *f) Product/supply chain audit trails*
6. Can the product meet organizational expectations? *a) If not, what compromises are required?* *b) What is realistic?* *c) Can the product objectives be achieved within company unit cost expectations? – i.e.,* *products active levels, functional ingredients can become ascetic ingredients, fragrance* *Is the most expensive material? Can vary dosage or quality?*
7. Where can I source raw materials? *a) What type of product formulation system is best?* *b) What alternative materials can be used? If not available look for another system.* *c) Can I get good technical support?*
8. Does the product have to be pre-registered before launch? If so, how long does this process take and what information is required? *a) What standards need to be met?* *b) Is any efficacy testing required?*

Morphological analysis uses grids to facilitate a systematic and logical search for ideas. The simplest of typologies[30] is a two-dimensional table allows two variables or attributes to be examined. Using a third attribute turns the model into three dimensions. This will create a grid or matrix or grid with clearly defined cells (see Figure 4.19.). Through this grid one can hypothesize relationships and generate theory. Morphological analysis can go up to around a four-dimensional limit before it becomes too hard to handle graphically, but many more attributes can be handled using specialized computer programs.

---

[30] A typology is a simple model based on the possible combinations obtained between two or more variables with each variable containing a (finite) range of discrete values or conditions.

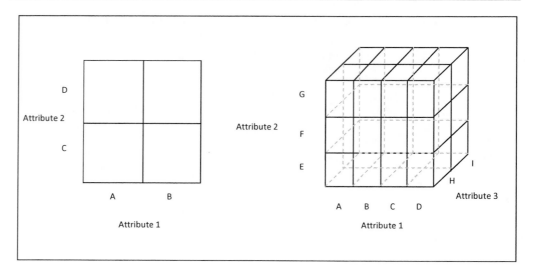

Figure 4.19. Two-dimension and three-dimension grids or matrixes.

A morphological analysis goes through a number of steps where a group undertakes an analysis-synthesis cycle. The time needed to undertake an analysis depends upon the complexity of the mess, the number of attributes used, and the depth of each attribute variation. It is not possible in any study to cover all variables, so decisions have to initially be made during the first step as to which attributes to include in the analysis. The more variables selected, the more comprehensive will be the analysis. For example in developing a new shampoo, we may decide that the main attributes will be a single shampoo for all hair conditions, different variants for different hair conditions and a shampoo/conditioner (2 in 1) configuration. This attribute will assist in selecting the market segment that the company desires to compete within.

The second step is then to provide a spectrum of value or conditions for each attribute. In the case of the shampoo, this may be something to do with formulations, such as low active concentration, medium active concentration, and high active concentration. This attributes indirectly selects the level of the market, *i.e., lower, middle, or upper,* that the company wishes to compete within.

The third step would be to decide up the third set of attributes which may include, organically produced, or highly fragranced. This attribute represents the basic product/market strategy the company desires to implement.

The totality of the parameters and their respective values is the morphological field. This represents the decision making universe. In this example there are 3 X 3 X 2 attributes = 18 potential configurations, as shown in Figure 4.20. below.

Out of the 18 possible configurations, these can be reduced through eliminating any illogical or unviable options until a feasible set is left to make decisions upon. The morphological analysis can assist in determining the attributes of a new product and the potential elements of strategy for the product under consideration. In the shampoo example, one product for all hair conditions, or a specialized product for each specific hair condition, or a shampoo/conditioner (2 in 1) configuration could be developed for one of those market segments. This decision can be made on the basis of the market segment size, or the level of competition, etc. Secondly the company can produce a low active, medium active or high active concentration product. There are now nine potential combinations of product attribute/strategy scenarios and some will be more feasible than others. The selections will be based on factors such as competition in each segment, potential volume/profitability, etc. Finally there is a decision concerning positioning the shampoo as an organic or *highly fragranced* product, that would leave a fragrance residual all day[31].

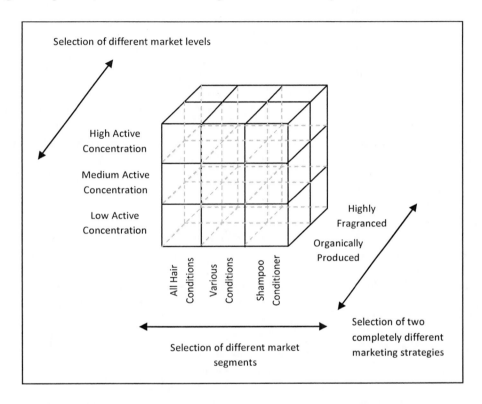

Figure 4.20. A Tri-axis Morphological Model Showing the Potential Field for a Conceptual Shampoo.

This analytical tool can be made more complex through increasing the number of attributes for consideration. Alternatively a conceptual project can be analyzed a number of times looking at different aspects of a product, such as product attributes, strategies, promotional concepts, etc, through a number of sequential analyses. This method is able to generate numerous combinations of variable for consideration. However care must be made in the initial stages of analysis to select the most relevant attributes for analysis to make the data generated applicable to the problem. Adaptations of morphological analysis have been used in the areas of marketing and corporate strategy disciplines for many decades[32].

---

[31] This emulates the strategy of the Andrew Jergens (now called kao Brands) shampoo Gee Your Hair Smells Terrific in the mid 1970s. The product was boosted with a perfume that left a long residual odour on a person's hair during the day. The advertising campaign used this benefit to highlight the product and it became a very successful product within the teenage category for a number of years during that period.

[32] The Boston Consulting Group matrix can be considered a simple morphological typology. Igor Ansoff (1965) also used adaptations of simple morphological typologies in his seminal book "Corporate Strategy".

Problem Resolution

The problem resolution stage is where generated ideas are evaluated and those that show a good fit in solving the defined problem are developed, so as to become a possible solution. This can range from, a very straight forward process of deciding which is the best solution, to the necessity to undertake an analysis of each idea by using a set of criteria to select the best fitting ideas as problem solutions.

If set criteria for selection of a problem are already known, then a rational decision making technique like Kepner-Tregoe's Decision-Making Analysis can be used to determine the best ideas as the solution. If the decision making criteria is very *'vague'* or not yet known then more work must be undertaken to select the solution. A third alternative exists to utilize components of various ideas generated into some form of composite solution to the problem.

Good rational decisions depend upon a precise definition of the specific factors (criteria/objectives) that need to be met by the chosen solution, the relative evaluations of the other alternatives, and our understanding of the consequences of these alternatives (Kepner-Tregoe 1981). Before decisions are made on a day to day basis, options are subjectively evaluated to develop a number of options and select the best solution. What constitutes the best option in each case is not easy to define as each individual will weigh up the criteria they make selections on, according to their own set of circumstances. The Kepner-Tregoe Decision-Making Analysis assumes the most rational decision based on the cumulated benefits of the criteria considered in each decision made. The way decisions are made within this process is very similar to *additive strategies* discussed in *Problem Solving and Decision Making* in chapter three.

The decision analysis process involves four basic steps of which two can be considered problem solving stages. These steps may not necessarily be undertaken in sequence but are nevertheless required in effective decision making.

1. A decision statement is an intention about what action is wanted and what result is hoped for. For example, this could be about the naming of a new brand, deciding about entry into a new market, or whether a new retail outlet should be opened. Some limitations should be imposed upon the extent of potential alternatives in regards to budgets and resources required, etc.

2. The selection and classification of objectives involves selecting the criteria that will be used to compare and evaluate alternatives. The criteria should be classified into MUSTS and WANTS, where those alternatives not satisfying musts will be immediately rejected and WANTS are criteria we would like for each alternative. The relative importance of the WANTS can be prioritized and weighted in the evaluation.

3. Evaluating alternatives can begin once all assessment criteria have been finalized. Each alternative is compared against MUSTS and WANTS, rejected if they don't meet with a MUST and scored against the WANTS. Any score for a WANT is multiplied by the weight that it has been given. After this process all scores are tallied.

   It is important to be aware of scores that are either too high or too low. This may indicate that unrealistic expectations exist and for low scores, the criteria of measurement selected are not appropriate.

4. Comparing and choosing the best alternative involves putting each alternative under scrutiny for potential risks and potential negative or adverse occurrences. The probability of these occurrences happening should be estimated. Kepner and Tregoe (1981, P. 100) recommend asking the following questions for each alternative;

- What is required to succeed?
- What factors could hinder implementation?
- What kind of environmental or organizational changes could harm long-term success? and
- What issues may cause problems in implementing this kind of decision?

Are a number of arguments that groups tend to make inferior decisions to individuals because of the need to find compromise and agree on a consensus solution (Hicks 2004, P. 179). However William Ouchi (1981) in his seminal book *Theory Z* argues *that it is better to make a poor decision and everybody support it, than to make a good decision and nobody support it.*

Some other methods used to evaluate ideas and decisions, especially where there is little objective or quantifiable data to work on, includes the use of checklists, comparisons, and grids. Checklists can consist of generic type questions relating to costs, resources required, acceptability, time, space and usefulness. Each criterion can be equal or weighted according to priority and importance. The *Paired Comparison Analysis* enables the ranking of ideas and options according to their usefulness, according to predetermined criterion. This method is useful when selections have to be made between resource competing proposals that may not be similar. Reverse Brainstorming is a method where each option is considered through *'a devil's advocate'* frame to find options with the least wrong with them. The *grid evaluation method* allows the rating of ideas as *very good, good, average* and *poor,* as a means to make a final selection. Criteria used for specific problems should be relevant, concise, consistent, and clear (Isaksen & Treffinger 1985).

There are basically two types of decisions that need to be taken during the problem resolution process. The first type is a problem that has a number of potential solutions and it is a matter of selecting the best decision according to the criteria selected. The final selection of any option will depend upon the decision criteria. Thus the selection of the relevant criteria is crucial to the ability of the process to generate the optimal and rational solution, according to the initial desired outcomes[33]. The second type of problem is where there is only one solution that requires deep consideration concerning the characteristics of the solution. The process here is more about refinement through the selection of what solution characteristics are needed and desired, which may require selection through developing MUSTS and WANTS criteria and prioritizing, etc.

---

[33] However very often in complex problem solving the original objectives themselves may change during the process.

Elaboration and Extension

The elaboration and extension stage in the problem solving process is very similar to the elaboration period in the creativity process. Like the elaboration period in the creativity process, problem elaboration involves completing the details of the solution until a fully viable concept is developed, that can be considered ready for implementation. Every solution to a problem has a set of characteristics or attributes, which are essentially the strategy module that encases the solution. A solution without a set of characteristics cannot be implemented, be used to exploit an opportunity, or repair a deficient situation requiring remedy. Figure 4.21. shows the previous shampoo example developed in the morphological analysis, into a strategy that can be implemented.

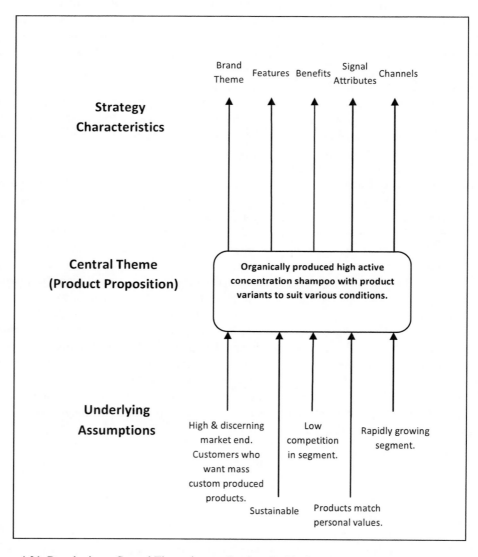

Figure 4.21. Developing a Central Theme into an Implementable Strategy.

The elaboration and extension process begins with the process of generating as many potential characteristics about the solution as possible through techniques like Brainstorming. The desired characteristics must then be selected, refined and integrated with the solution theme under development until it is considered feasible for implementation. This process may require a return to the ideation and problem resolution processes to generate and evaluate potential solution characteristics. Selected characteristics must match and integrate with the primary solution theme, match the organization's objectives, goals, processes and flow, or the organization must change to integrate, transform or evolve itself to match the envisaged solution.

Once the characteristics have been developed elaborate and extend the solution into a potential strategy, the solution with its characteristics can once again be reappraised through the problem appraisal process to reaffirm its viability.

Implementation and Strategy

Although the problem solving process may have generated an *optimal* and *rational* solution, whether it can be successfully implemented will depend upon the cultural beliefs and values of the organization and stakeholders. *Is the solution culturally acceptable and are all stakeholder going to agree with the solution?* One can see conflict generated in organizations and societies because company or government decisions are not compatible with underlying cultural norms and values and against sectional stakeholder interests.

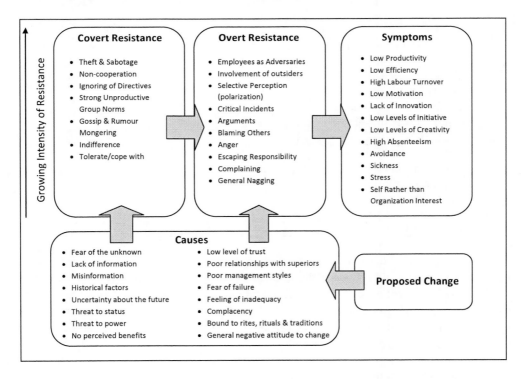

Figure 4.22. The causes of covert and overt resistance to change and the corresponding symptoms.

Another barrier to implementing solutions is the inertia groups and organizations have towards change, opting in preference to the unambiguous and stable *status quo*. Most often change is feared due to the ambiguity and uncertainty it brings to people both on an individual and group basis. The fear generated by change is often resisted through our defence mechanisms externalizing the anxiety through either overt or covert group resistance. The stresses and emotions change brings to the individual and group will eventually create a number of symptoms within the organization that will hinder any potential change. In solving problems and developing creative strategies within organizations, these issues must be considered in the implementation stage. A schematic showing the causes of covert and overt resistance to change and the manifesting symptoms is illustrated in Figure 4.22.

Putting the above issues aside, any solution being implemented can go wrong. There are potential barriers and foreseeable events which may block its execution and lead to failure. These could involve matters of planning, internal causes or external events as listed in Table 4.4. below

Table 4.4. Things that can go wrong during problem implementation.

Matters of Planning
• Wrong assumptions made in critical areas
• Under-estimate of resources required
• Strategy not properly matched with competencies and skills required
• Deadlines to tight with little leeway
• Market too far away to effectively service it well *(i.e., interstate or overseas market)*
• Generally poor planning under estimating the degree of difficulty

Internal Causes
• Unable to gain distribution
• Not enough resources
• Production problems
• Product quality problems
• Human resource problems
• Mismatch with organizational procedures, flow, culture, etc

External Events
• Customers dislike the product
• Competitor comes in with a similar product
• Not enough customers
• Legal problem
• Forced product recall
• Acts of God

Before going into the implementation stage, it is important to look for what potential mishaps could occur and influence the implementation of the solution. Kepner and Tregoe (1981) advocate a process called *Potential Problem Analysis (PPA)* that involves trying to determine what might go conceivably go wrong, what can be done to prevent the mishap occurring and what type of contingency can be put in place in case the mishap occurs. This process can be broken up into four stages.

1. Identify the vulnerable areas.

This requires identifying any potential weak and vulnerable areas, using experience and knowledge from past similar situations and commonsense. This process can be undertaken through Brainstorming. A second method is to go through each step of the plan carefully in chronological order and assessing the weak areas, where contingencies may be needed.

2.   Identify specific problems which are serious enough to require action now.

Each identified problem can then be prioritized as to the potential of the mishap occurring, ranking at the top what is most likely to occur, down to what is least likely to occur.

3.   Identify the likely causes of each potential problem and any preventative action that can be taken.

The likely causes of each potential event should be identified and then a group can make decisions about what can be done about them.

4.   Identify any contingent actions that can be taken as preventative action or as a contingency action, in case the predicted mishap occurs.

Preventative and contingency strategies can be developed for each identified potential mishap. Trivial problems may be ignored for the more critical ones identified. Action may also be taken for those that can easily be prevented. If a potential problem cannot be prevented, then a contingency should be drawn up to counter its effects should it occur.

The *Potential Problem Analysis* should result in an action plan to improve the strategy implementation phase and make ready any potential contingencies required for what are perceived critical potential problems. An alternative method to evaluate an implementation plan for potential mishaps is to use a checklist to go through each part of the plan. Unfortunately many people and organizations fail to undertake a *Potential Problem Analysis* or check their plan off against a checklist and are either less effective or fail due to not anticipating potential problems before they act.

METAPHOR AND THE USE OF ANALOGIES IN CREATIVITY

In essence this book is essentially a group of meta-metaphors attempting to provide a vector of understanding of the issues that the author is trying to put across to the reader. Metaphors are primarily a conceptual construction linking our meaning with something familiar so that we can perceive some of the qualities of the familiar into the conceptual meaning of the unfamiliar. These are usually abstract meanings from familiar things which we implant into the person, object or event we are describing, in the abstract but not literal sense. For example *"He has a heart of gold", "Time is money", "Shooting from the hip"* and *"running on borrowed time", etc.* Consequently metaphors evolve from our collective *(social)* imagination that is required to make the associations[34]. Metaphorization sometimes carries over emotions with the abstractions it creates. For example *"I'm so hungry I can eat a horse", "I am dazzled by the lights",* or *"He was drinking like a camel".* Metaphors pervade all aspects of our lives and can be verbal, non-verbal, body language or grunts and sighs, physical things or symbolistic and imaginative (Lawley & Tompkins 2000).

Metaphors assist us develop our conceptual thought and ideas. According to Lakoff and Johnson (1980), the conceptual system of how we think is primarily metaphorical in nature. It is very hard to avoid metaphorical thinking and communication. For example, most management, marketing and strategic theory is metaphorical in nature, e.g., *"Blue Ocean Strategy", "Guerilla Marketing", "Scientific Management", "Quality Circles", "Just in Time", "Market Penetration", "Strategic Thrusts", "Defensive Strategies"* and *"Six Thinking Hats", etc.* Metaphors help to structure what we see through symbolic models which make our understanding easier. Metaphors show how we reason and go about conducting inquiry into solving problems, how we evaluate issues, how we should act, and provide some understanding of ourselves and others in society (Lakoff & Johnson 1980). Therefore if our cognitive conceptual development is largely symbolic, and we also perceive things through symbolism, then the concept of metaphor is a very important to creativity.

Metaphors assist a person carry over knowledge from one domain to another to help improve perception and understanding. This can assist in making new associations and creating new constructs of knowledge. For example, to explain how a hydrogen atom might be structured, Lord Rutherford used the solar system as a metaphor to represent its structure. Almost all our mental construction is abstract and relies on developing and explaining concepts in terms of other familiar concepts. We use spatial relationships to explain abstract topics such as science, warfare, economics, business, sports, economics or morality, etc. This has entered into our everyday language where spatial relationships figure in our expressions, *i.e., 'you blasted him away with your argument', 'your argument is indefensible',* and *'we were just wiped out', etc.* Our cognitive system cannot process information unless it symbolized and metaphor creates most of our symbols we need to think. Our reasoning depends upon our bodily sensations, environment and what we sense to symbolize as meaning, so reasoning is mostly unconscious, metaphorical, imaginative, and emotionally engaged (Lakoff & Johnson 1999).

The use of analogies is an important technique used in stimulating imaginative and creative thinking, especially in the solving of problems. An analogy is a relationship, parallel or similarity between two situations, problems or concepts. It relates an unfamiliar task to a familiar task that can be useful in solving many types of problems. Analogies require holistic or divergent thinking to find similarities with other situations. Narrative about the similar situation can be developed and then reapplied back to the original situation. For example, Alfred Wagner saw the ice breaking off the glaziers in Iceland and postulated the concept of *continental drift.* Understanding an analogy helps to put two situations into the same conceptual alignment so the analogized situation can be understood better.

The objective of using an analogy is to get some leverage to solve a problem at hand. However sometimes it is difficult to spontaneously find any analogies that link with the problem (Gick & Holyoak 1980). But it is not always important that the analogy fits

---

[34] Metaphors require a social imagination so that everyone understands the symbolism of the metaphoric suggestions.

completely, providing it can illuminate a new way of looking at a problem (De Bono 1970, P. 149). Seeing both the similarities and differences can play a role in better understanding of a problem (Genter & Markman 1997). For example, an analogy between undoing knots and traffic snarls shows some insight, but doesn't show how to solve the traffic snarls. The analogy just provides a way to look at the situation.

Synectics

William Gordon utilized analogies and metaphors into a creativity problem solving (CPS) tool that assists in the idea generation process, called *Synectics.* Synectics is based on the assumption that creativity can be both described and taught to individuals and groups (Gordon 1961). The aim of Synectics is to get the mind away from the problem, thus enabling a person to make new connections and generate new ideas. Synectics forces a conscious effort to look at the problem from a completely different viewpoint. This is achieved through excursions, which aim to make the group forget the immediate problem, so they can generate some irrelevant material to relate back to the problem, in order to generate new ideas.

The basic *Synectics* process is shown in figure 4.23. The *Synectics* process begins by laying out the problem statement to the group. This may be from the problem owner's point of view or may be presented from a number of points of view. In the analysis stage, background information is presented about the problem, not from the point of view of understanding it but to trigger potential directions, thoughts and reactions to the issues.

The goal orientation stage is where the group tries to see the problem in a number of ways, so as to look for potential directions to go. Speculation and wishing for desirable outcomes is encouraged as a method to set goals. Through suggesting unrelated words or phrases to the group, the prompting they may give can act as springboards to assist the group develop alternative angles or frames about the problem. Brainstorming is also used to develop new ideas about the problem. The outcome of the goal orientation stage is to select a defined problem with a desirable wished outcome in mind. The goal orientation process is a safe way of airing differences in opinion between group members, as disagreements can be redefined as potential directions for possible solutions.

Now the group moves into the ideation stage where excursions are used to generate and explore new ideas. The method selected will depend upon the novel needed in the new idea. Four types of analogy are used to stimulate creativity: *personal, direct, symbolic* and *fantasy.* With personal analogy we imagine what it would be like to *'be'* the object of our interest and use the experience to help resolve the problem. With direct analogy a straightforward analogy between the object and something similar from a different environment is made. In symbolic analogy, the essence of the problem is summed up in some metaphorical way. In fantasy analogy, the problem is projected into some form of fantasy. These are considered the tools to initiate and sustain the creative processes. Very many different formats for excursions are used, such as relying on word lists, the development of mental images by the group, line and picture drawing, sculpturing, and story writing as springboards into new ideas. An example of the effectiveness of this method is the solution found for underwater construction by drawing analogies to shipworms, where they tunnel into wood and create a watertight compartment for themselves.

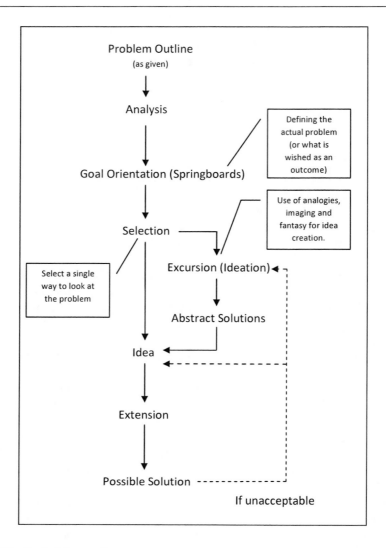

Figure 4.23. The Basic *Synectics* Process.

The problem owner is asked after the abstract solution stage which possible solutions he or she likes and then they are paraphrased. At this stage is important to look at the positive and practical aspects of ideas, rather than any negativity. These concepts are then extended into full ideas by the group, from where they can be appraised for feasibility in solving the defined problem.

Synectics is more suitable in looking at complex problems than Brainstorming (Newman *et. al.* 1972), although Brainstorming is used throughout the *Synectics* process. *Synectics* is not as well known as brainstorming but it has potentially greater application in decision making, especially where risk and uncertainty exists.

Metaphors and analogies are useful heuristics for solving problems and developing insights in a large number of situations. Many important scientific ideas, breakthroughs and solutions have come from metaphors and analogies, *i.e., neural-transmitters fit into neural receptors like a key fits into a lock* (Genter & Markman 1997). However, the usefulness of analogical reasoning in problem solving will depend upon; 1. Problem similarity, where there must be a reasonable degree of similarity between the already understood situation and the metaphor or analogy, 2. There must be a parallel structure between the source and target problems, so that elements and relationships can be translated to the problem, and, 3. The goals of the target and source problems must be the same (Holyoak & Thagard 1997).

FRAMES OF THINKING

Our view of the objective environment is very subjective. We are socially conditioned to think rationally and logically and accept existing social structures and processes. Our view of the world is also biased by our patterning and emotions, so we have little chance of seeing anything truly objectively. This implies that our perceptions and interpretations are limited and consequently we miss much detail and meaning that exists in the environment. From the opportunity point of view, this suggests that the majority of people see similar meaning in the environment and subjected to a singular sense of meaning. This hinders our ability to see new perspectives and make new connections to form new meanings.

We generally see through a single perspective which can be illusionary and if we change our perspective perception of an object[35], a whole new meaning can be discovered. Therefore we are most often unaware of the multiple perspectives and meanings that can be sensed in our environment as we are locked into a single frame of thinking. For everything we see there are alternative views and meaning. The ability to see the environment's multiple perspectives and meaning should have some advantage in opportunity discovery.

We usually have blocks that prevent us from seeing other perspectives as we have habitually looked at things from a single frame. Cognitively this assists in cutting down on the high amount of environmental information so we are able to manage our cognitive processes without overloading them. However this also prevents us from reorganizing information and hinders the creativity process. Our preference for logic and rationality blocks our ability to arrive at new insights (De Bono 1969).

To be creative we must break out of the singular frame thinking we are used to. Through our education, professions and professional experiences we are often restricted in the use of creativity because of the tendency to conform to the accepted ways of domain thinking and how things are done (De Bono 1976). We must develop skills that allow us to look at an object from different frames or perspectives without allowing our emotions and existing thought patterns interfere with what we are seeing. This requires changing our thinking processes so we can look through new patterns that allows us to go beyond domain rules and use intuition, utilize our sub-conscious thought processes and break free of the semantic logics that we are used too (Koestler 1975). Figure 4.24. shows a metaphorical diagram of this objective.

A number of thinking tools have been created for assisting people change their patterns or frames of thinking. Mezirow (1981) developed a model which inserted reflective thinking as a means to gain insights. Kolb's (1984) model of experimental learning and Gibbs (1988) model of reflective thinking also utilized reflection as a means of insight and learning. Johns

---

[35] This can mean object, person or event.

(1994, 1995) looked at the nursing profession and developed specific frames to assist as cues from which nurses can use to reflect upon different perspectives within occupational situations nurses experience[36]. However Johns frames were perceived as complex and difficult to use due to the number of cues that need to be worked through (Kenny 2003).

A number of conceptual and structured models have been developed to assist in sorting and categorizing information so problems can be looked at from different perspectives. One tool uses hexagons as a flexible mapping tool to rearrange thoughts into models and classifying issues into different frames via the use of colour coding (Hodgson 1992). De Bono (1986) developed the six thinking hats game to assist people think across patterns and look at an issue from multiple perspectives in a structured way.

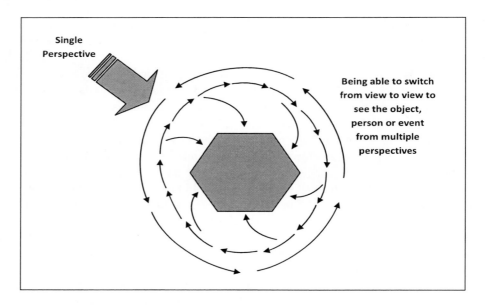

Figure 4.24. A metaphorical diagram showing single and multiple perspectives of an object.

De Bono's *Six Thinking Hats* creative tool colors each hat to represent a different way of thinking. De Bono suggests that the six hats represent the main basic types or domains of thinking (De Bono 1995). The thinking domain that each hat represents and value in looking at problems are summarized as follows;

- **The white hat:** is concerned about information and takes the metaphorical white colour of paper. The white hat is concerned about what information a person has and what information is missing to make informed decisions. As facts are not opinions, information cannot be challenged. However opinions that are not based on fact can

---

[36] Johns (1994) included reflective practice cues like: Aesthetics, What was I trying to achieve? Why did I respond as I did? What are the consequences for others?, Personal, How did I feel in this situation? What internal factors were influencing me?, Ethics, How did my actions match with my beliefs? What factors made me act in incongruent ways? And Empirics, What knowledge did or should have informed me? How does this connect with previous experience? Could I handle this better in similar circumstances?

be easily exposed. The white hat thinking domain is useful for challenging assumptions and separating the truth from fiction.

- *The red hat:* is metaphoric for fire or warmth and is concerned with emotions, feelings and intuition. It allows a person to explore their own feelings and the feelings of others. The red hat domain helps a person acknowledge difficult feelings that may block or prevent paths of action or things from happening.
- *The black hat:* is suggestive of judicial robes and represents caution, danger, legality, codes of conduct and ethics. It is the basis of critical thinking and tends to look at things along our existing patterns of doing things highlighting something different from what we are used to. The black hat domain is useful for looking at risk, danger, legality, process and ethical aspects of a problem or situation.
- *The yellow hat:* represents sunshine and optimism. It is also logical and practical. It seeks out the advantages and benefits of things. By seeking the constructive and positive aspects of something its potential benefits to the problem or situation can be determined. The yellow hat is useful in opportunity seeking.
- *The green hat:* metaphorically resembles vegetation and is associated with growth, energy, vitality and life. The green hat is directly concerned with creativity. It looks for new beginnings, alternatives, change and going beyond existing situations. The aim of the green hat is to take a person out of their existing patterns of thinking.
- *The blue hat*: is about reflection and reflexivity to assess what has been achieved so far. The blue hat can set goals and objectives and guide the rest of the hats in a focused direction. Blue hat thinking is responsible for summarizing the process and keeping it going. It can be used for interjections and challenging the other hats.

The six hats process facilitates parallel thinking where a person is able to understand each perspective of a situation. This according to De Bono (De Bono 1986, P. 4) allows a subject to be explored thoroughly, getting out of the bounds of restriction that adversarial and confrontational thinking brings.

De Bono's thinking tools have been used for a number of years by educational, business and governmental groups to develop creative thinking skills. There have been criticisms of these *'pragmatic'* approaches to creative thinking on the basis of these tools not being scientifically developed upon our understanding of the thinking processes and therefore may lack validity and efficacy (Sternberg & Lubart 1999, Moseley *et. al.* 2005).

EMPATHY

Empathy is a capacity we have to connect to others and feel what they are feeling. Empathy helps a person know emotionally what others are experiencing from that person's frame of reference (Berger 1987). Empathy allows our mind *'to detach itself from one's self'* and see the reality of the world from someone else's, feelings, emotions, pain and reasoning (Lampert 2005). Empathy is an imaginative process. It is primarily an intrinsic trait many people have, but the sensitivity needed to be empathetic can be learned. Through our sensitivity we pick up other people's body movements, facial expressions, tone of voice and narrative, as a means to sense their feelings, emotions and beliefs (Meltzoff & Decety 2003). In this way we reduce interpersonal ambiguity.

However we must be very careful to the differences within the various signs we read and pick up from others. For example a parent may have an aspiration about further education for their children, but what are the sub-conscious reasons behind their aspirations? This is not necessarily easy (even for trained psychologists) to determine without time to compare narratives and other signs given at other time by the parents. The potential motivations for a parent's aspiration for their child's higher education are shown in Figure 4.25. The reality could be any one or combination of these reasons.

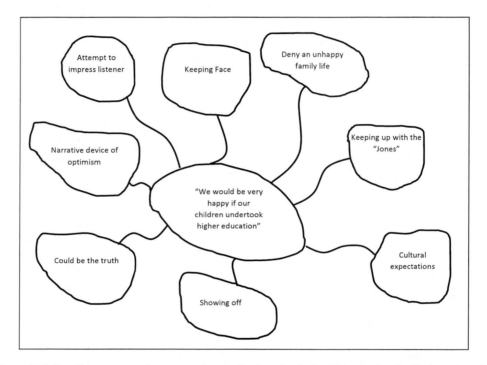

Figure 4.25. Possible reasons why a parent has aspirations for their child to undertake further education.

Empathy is an emotion that is very different from the emotions of pity, sympathy and compassion, although empathy can on some occasions lead to those emotions in the observer. In the context of this section, empathy is a means of directly experiencing the emotions of others, even though the observer may not necessarily agree with the other person's point of view. Consequently empathic understanding is an important characteristic in psychoanalysis where a *client-centered* therapist attempts to understand the feelings of others as if they their own (Rogers 1975)[37]. Through *client-centered* therapy, the therapist uses empathy to feel the patient's feelings and emotions. Through introspection, the client's thoughts and feelings are mirrored back to the client to seek confirmation that the therapist understands his or her point

---

[37] Client-centered therapy developed by Carl Rogers in the 1940s and 50s is a non-directive method of therapy using the technique of active listening. Active listening involves reframing and rephrasing what the client said to confirm understanding. This technique is intended to be unobtrusive to the client.

of view (Kohut 1959). Through what the therapist learns through empathy enables him or her to intervene into the client's view of reality.

There is empirical evidence of a correlation between empathy and creativity (Parson 1993, Carlozzi *et. al.* 1995). Creativity is especially important in interpersonal and inter-social interactions (Legrenzi 2005), which is a prerequisite for group creativity in organizations. Empathy enables insight into other ideas and points of view. Openness and tolerance to new ideas is extremely important to the ability to be creative. Research has shown that the more tolerant a society is to diversity, the more creative and innovative is that society (Florida 2002). Societies that are intolerant to the differences of others and have strict adherence to existing social customs and manners, tend not to be receptive to new ideas[38]. At the opposite of the continuum to creativity is *intellectual self centeredness*. This is a barrier to creativity. When we think from a self centered perspective, we are unable to understand other peoples thoughts, emotions and feelings and thus unable to see other points of view to their own. *Intellectual self centeredness* focuses attention[39] inward towards our own ideas, our own problems and our own pain (Paul & Elder 2002). We are unable to consider the problems and viewpoints of others that differ from our own.

Within a group perspective, empathy is very important in preventing conflicts. Creativity in organizations is very much a group process and empathy contributes to building the trust that is needed so members of the group feel safe to contribute new ideas. Without empathy, the group could very quickly develop mistrust between members and behave according to organizational hierarchical rigidity[40] which would prevent constructive discussion, exchange of views, decision making and problem solving (Leonard & Swap 1999).

Empathy is used as a creative tool in everyday life. Creativity is very much a social phenomenon and we are dependent upon creativity to develop our relationships. For example, if we lose somebody in a crowded place, we begin to try and imagine where that person may be, based on their past habits. We try to predict the person's movements so that we can find them. If we want to give someone a gift, we try to think of what they would like and be surprised with. In preparing for presentations at meetings we try and anticipate what questions and objections people would come up with. Likewise a lawyer defending a client in a courtroom will try and understand what the members of the jury are feeling, in order to try to influence them. Empathy is also important in games like chess, where an opponent will try to anticipate the other person's next move and strategy[41].

Empathy is a very important tool in competitive strategy. Strategy crafting is often based on what we think our competitors will do, how our competitors will react to our moves, and what do our competitors think we will do, etc. Managers who have a deep understanding of their competitors are in a good position to anticipate their potential moves, and consequently will be able to sense potential opportunities and gain competitive advantage with the right

---

[38] Richard Florida (2002) believes that the two major ingredients required for innovation are talent and tolerance. Therefore high-tech industries will develop in some regions faster than other regions because they are open to new ideas by not being judgmental upon other points of view. Consequently Florida said that the gay index is an excellent measure for potential innovation, not because innovative people are gay, but it is a revealing indicator of mental openness and tolerance, necessary in creativity.

[39] As we have limited cognitive attention available intellectual self centeredness tends to monopolize this resource leaving little, if none available for creative processes.

[40] Extreme cases of hierarchical rigidity can exist where those a hierarchy are expected to give absolute obedience to their superior without any question and those above have absolute authority over those below them.

[41] However one must remember in complex game theory many outcomes may end up relying on chance due to the multiplicity of factors involved.

decisions. This is a key quality many entrepreneurs exhibit in the marketplace by being able to develop niche positioning without direct competition.

Empathy in this application is a form of insight and very important in marketing and competitive strategy. Branding is also another form of empathy. Brands are developed in a manner to try to capture empathy with potential customers, by appealing to their self views and aspirations.

Empathy is an important element in moving creativity from an individual pursuit to a group process. The collective mind of a group with empathy present should be able to generate more connections and ideas than any individual. This requires developing an environment where ideas from outside can move into a group without being filtered by the *'group boundary'* which may prevent external concepts being accepted. This requires a highly developed empathy that is stronger than forces within the ego that may suppress empathy. When this highly developed empathy can operate freely, creativity can become infused with outside ideas and also diffuse innovative concepts[42].

It is generally believed that females tend to be more empathetic than males, as empathy is often classified as a right hemisphere female trait. However many studies indicate that empathy tends to be equally divided between males and females. One of the keys to empathy is motivational differences (Ickes 1997, Klein & Hodges 2001).

COMPETITIVE IMAGINATION

Competitive imagination is concerned about gaining insights into problems that a firm has previously not known to have existed prior to looking at the fringes of their stakeholder environments. The term was first used by Stuart Hart and Sanjay Sharma (2004) in their article *Engaging fringe Stakeholders for Competitive Imagination*. Hart and Sharma foresaw that competitive imagination can occur through two processes that can challenge existing business models and frames of reference, leading to new bases of competitive advantage.

The first process called *radical transactiveness* involves systematically identifying, exploring and integrating the views of fringe stakeholders to the firm to devise strategies that would create disruptive change or creative destruction by developing imagination about a future novel and competitive business model (Hart & Sharma 2004, P. 7). *Radical transactiveness* seeks to look at the periphery of the fringe poor, weak, isolated or disadvantaged people and acquire and combine knowledge gained from these groups to develop new opportunities and business models. These are the segments where future competitive advantage and even survival will come from (Hamel & Prahalad 1994, Hart & Milstein 1999). *Radical transactiveness* seeks to engage management in a two-way dialogue with fringe stakeholders so that each is influenced and influences the other. This is where learning is believed to exist and the example of Hindustan Lever Limited in India, requiring their managers spend six weeks a year in the villages to learn consumer needs and habits is espoused by Hart and Co. It is believed in this way, yet unmet needs and yet to be served

---

[42] The research and development laboratory at 3M was trying to develop a more effective glue, but they were unsuccessful. The new material did not harden and always remained sticky. As the story goes one of the secretaries of another department learned about this material and started using it for sticking small memo notes to the surfaces of her workstation. All the other secretaries followed and the concept of the product Post-it emerged. So a use was found for a material that was first thought to be useless and a failure.

markets can be identified and understood. Great emphasis is put on the skill of empathy as a means of understanding different perspectives, needs and thereby being able to see future opportunities.

Many examples of success from companies which have expanded their boundaries into the fringes of the market are given as evidence of the potential of using *radical transactiveness* as a tool for insight. The examples of Hindustan Lever providing product sizes that can be purchased and consumed on a daily basis through *'moms and pops'* stores within these fringe communities, the CEMEX *'Patrimonio Hoy'* program where savings clubs were encouraged to help poor Mexican families buy materials to build home extensions and Grameen Bank's micro-credit scheme in Bangladesh are cited as success stories. Hart and Sharma used the example of Nike to show that failure to use *radical transactiveness* can lead to disappointing results within potential fringe stakeholder markets. Nike's low priced *'World Shoe'* was cited as a failure because of the company overlooking the need for a dialogue with the fringe groups that they sought to reach and using their existing sales channels in China alongside their premium products, rather than build new channels that can better reach them.

The second process is *radical transparency* which means going further than statutory disclosure requirements in the full and open disclosure of all the firm's activities, strategies and impacts (Hart and Sharma 2004, P. 17). *Radical transparency* targets core stakeholder who can directly affect the business. Radical transparency promotes the concept of a firm operating by the mandate of its stakeholders, especially to avoid stakeholder rage which can challenge the power, legitimacy and survival of the company. The Shell UK experience with their Brent Spar North Sea oil storage and tanker loading bouy in the Brent oilfield demonstrates the concept of *radical transparency*. In the Brent Spar case, the building of an oil pipeline from Sullom Voe in Shetland led to the redundancy of the facility as an oil storage depot. Shell planned to dump Brent Spar in deep Atlantic waters with British Government support. However this led to a worldwide media campaign against Shell and where Greenpeace occupied the Brent Spar for a number of weeks. In the face of public opposition and a consumer boycott in Europe, Shell abandoned its plans. Shell's Brent Spar experience shows how much damage can be done when a company loses sight of what their stakeholders want. Shell's behavior showed lack of empathy with its stakeholders as it was dominated by its engineering culture and did not back down initially as they could not understand the symbolic effects of dumping the Brent Spar in deep water. The effects of the Brent Spar issue have driven home many corporate lessons about the need for gaining different perspectives and reputation management (Fombrun & Rindova 2000, Hooghiemstra 2004).

The steps recommended by Hart and Sharma (2004) within a transnational corporate context to generate competitive imagination are described in table 4.5. below.

Radical transactiveness helps a firm widen its possibilities by including fringe stakeholders in the lower socio-economic groups as a means of generating competitive imagination to come up with potential future products, services, markets and business models. It drives approaches to marketing, management, production and research and development. Ideas about escaping direct competition by reconstructing market boundaries to gain new market space like those espoused in *Blue Ocean Strategy* (Chan Kim & Mauborgne 2005) and the tools presented like the *four actions framework* and *strategy canvas* require a form of competitive imagination to make the framework work successfully. *Blue Ocean Strategy* appears very insightful in retrospect but requires competitive imagination to use it into the future. Competitive imagination is still a relatively new concept which will in the near future be expanded as a concept with a much broader definition and supported with more elaborate working models that will be based on further research into the area of future modeling.

Table 4.5. The steps involved in implementing competitive imagination within a transnational corporate context

Step	Description/Process	Costs/Benefits
1. Identification of periphery stakeholders and understand their concerns.	Look at all potential fringe stakeholders, their concerns, influence of firms operations upon these groups, develop communications with these groups for the purpose of addressing their concerns before these groups connect to media, NGOs or political parties, etc. See what actions the firm can take to better interconnect with these groups in terms of products, wastage, improvements in the way the company deals with them.	Benefits: Developing good corporate reputations, better legitimacy and a mandate from stakeholders, more operating freedom, fast tracking rather than delays on implementing projects. Costs: Management training, managerial time, travel and other activities unrelated to present general operational functioning.
2. Identify any business contexts that are the reverse of the way the company currently operates the business. Seek to generate imagination and create ideas about potential new product and business innovations related to the identified fringe stakeholder groups.	Consider issues of social equity, biodiversity, ecosystem preservation, human rights, human dignity, indigenous rights, climate change, etc to identify stakeholder concerns that are contrary to what the firm is doing now. This could focus on regions and communities that have been heavily affected by globalization, industrialization, exploding populations, migration, urban/rural drift, lack of education, basic infrastructure, etc. Look for previously unvoiced groups to invite concerns and reactions. Create a list of potential areas where learning can take place so that new products and business models can be generated.	Benefits: Creating radical new ideas for products, services and business models. Costs: Training, time, travel, and attention away from existing operations.
3. Develop interaction with fringe stakeholders to generate new product ideas and business innovations and bring potential tacit operating knowledge to the firm.	Develop cultural sensitivity through management training. Put management into the targeted regions to learn about the region, market and people the firm has identified to serve. Explore stakeholder needs and new approaches for meeting their needs in an innovative manner.	Benefits: Generating competitive imagination for future products and business models that will achieve future growth for the firm. Costs: Training, time, travel, and attention away from existing operations.
4. Incubate, operationalize and implement the radical innovations and business models developed.	Develop new organizational informational flows. Setting up of task groups to develop new products and business models. Test and refine ideas through continual communication with stakeholders.	Benefits: Generating disruptive innovations in products, services and/or business models and addressing ethical, social and environmental issues and concerns of stakeholders and preventing the creation of adversarial resistance to the firm. Costs: Expenditure of organizational resources.

VISUALIZATION OF THE FUTURE – LOOKING AT TRENDS

The overall desire of an individual or enterprise is to be in a position to understand how the future will be shaped and determine how they can benefit. Stating this in a slightly more confident manner could be rephrased as *'how can the individual or enterprise through its plans and actions influence and shape the future (market) where they can benefit?'* Success in enterprise depends on thinking and acting upon a *'more or less'* correctly imagined future situation.

Predicting the future accurately is impossibility. This is because future events have not yet happened. Therefore we cannot know for sure that any event will happen. However what we do know is the present and we also know the past from our own personal perspectives, so that we have some idea about the probability of something occurring like a scheduled meeting or TV program, etc. More generally what we know from the immediate past and the present gives us a strong indication about what is most likely to happen in the immediate future, excepting unexpected events and disasters. Through our constructs we basically make predictions from observing the development and momentum of trends in the past and present and assume that they will continue into the future Kelly (1955).

This is how John Naisbitt (1982) wrote *"Megatrends"* through astutely picking up on emerging trends and extrapolating them until they have a *futuristic* major effect upon our lives. Insignificant events can build to a critical mass, from where something new emerges in a significant way (Gladwell 2000). Most management theories are developed from past events and history where the theory fits the facts and is able to explain the past very well. However when orientating these theories towards the future they become less than accurate. This may be partly explained by the ever changing factors (social, economic, technological or regulatory), either subtly or significantly thereby creating new conditions which the original theories were not designed to account for.

The popularized Nostradamus himself also seemed to rely on the past to predict the future when writing the *quatrains* of *Les Propheties*. Nostradamus assumed that many central historical themes would always repeat themselves from century to century regardless of our learning and considered advancement. Moreover it strongly appears that Nostradamus was influenced by and borrowed from the work of past and contemporary writers of his time (Lemesurier 2003). This should not be of any great shock to anyone, as the bulk of ideas and new products appearing onto a market, usually bare great resemblance to other ideas and products already existing in the market. Pure originality and novel innovation is actually a rare commodity[43].

With inside industry and market knowledge a person develops an understanding about how a field operates in terms of; *who are the players?, how do consumers behave?, are they generally satisfied with what is on offer to them?, who are the suppliers?, how important are they?, which stakeholders seem to have strong influence?, what important skills and capabilities are necessary to succeed?, who is strong and weak in them?, what resources are needed?, where can these resources be obtained?, who do you need to now in this field to get*

---

[43] The technology to develop the jet engine and some advanced aerodynamic designing came from Scientists in Nazi Germany who defected to Britain, the United States and Soviet Union after the war. The same goes for the rocket engine, where after being developed in Nazi Germany, technology and personnel continued their work in both the Soviet Union and the United States leading to the space race and development of the intercontinental ballistic missile.

things done?, where does the research and innovation come from?, and very importantly, *what direction is the industry going?* A person with industry and market knowledge will understand the implications of and relationships between these questions. An insider has opinions, intuition, ideas, and hypotheses about how things work and why they might influence the future. When a person makes predictions and they are validated through becoming reality, a person's confidence in their own *'hypotheses'* can make a person feel confident[44], maybe confident enough to do something that may have some impact on shaping the future.

A person *'emotionally embedded'* within the industry will feel how things work, how the supply chain is interrelated, where it is strong and where it is weak. He or she knows the players, their competencies, their weaknesses, their triumphs and their failures. He or she will know how reactive multinationals are to the local market and how local companies are experts of developing small niches that maintain their place in the market. Knowing how reactive or proactive a multinational company is in the marketplace is one of the bits of information that may have great significance in the concept of opportunity. This may go completely unnoticed to an industry outsider.

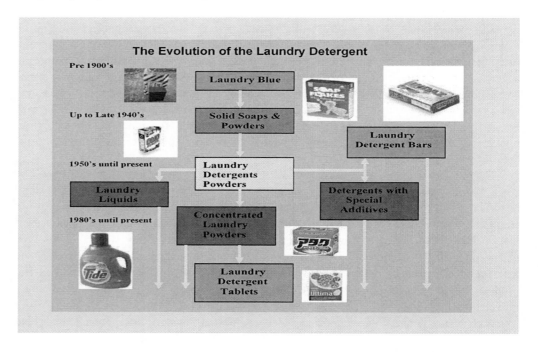

Figure 4.26. The Evolution (Family Tree) of Laundry Detergent over the last 100 years (Hunter 2009, P. 563).

When a person sees the industry evolving and the small steps of incremental evolution within it, they will normally be in a good position to anticipate the future of the industry based on their own specific prior knowledge. This is the potential platform for insight that

----

[44] In contrast, an outsider unless having some specialized skill important in the field, may struggle to develop the intricate understanding that an insider has.

only insiders have. One can see product evolution like one sees a family tree emerge over a few generations. The products in the market have profound meaning to the insider, who knows what has been and is excited about what will be. This is the point where an insider can visualize the future. To the outsider, *'raw information'* without rich background knowledge is nothing without knowing the background. Background knowledge is necessary to make order out of the chaos that others see.

Through experiencing the industry and being aware of change, a person develops their unique mental map or *'self hypothesis'* of meaning about what, how, why and where the industry is going. A sensitive person will see changes in the factors that influence the industry over time; one day about consumer sentiments, another day about technology, yet another about government intervention and regulation, another about competitor actions, and emerging technologies and their significance. This all digests, is simplified as it incubates, cooks up, is twisted and turned until, *'bingo'*, an opportunity lies there starring the person in the face, which no one else or not many people have seen. This is the moment when you have put all your money on the number 16 on the roulette table and the number comes up. Excitement and passion emerges. It is not about the money but about doing something successful that no one else has done, climbing the Mount Everest of the field.

Through being exposed to the field day in, day out, our cognitive processes can create associations that we don't normally consider, think of consciously or connect together. This may happen when we drive to work, drive home from work, have dinner, go for a walk, or have a shower. Everything from the environment we experience is felt with emotion. These complex factors spanning the group of factors that cause opportunity gaps are simplified into new concepts. This happens when we are away from the work environment that allows repressed material to emerge and be reorganized into new associations. All the information about the environment has worked itself up from the basic into new insights and concepts.

Table 4.6. The factors that make up the opportunity gap and stimulate associations.

Social	Economic	Technology	Government
Social and cultural trends as drivers Reviving historical trends Influence of international trends Changing demographics Styles fashions & fads	Stage of economic development State of the economy Level of disposable income Macroeconomic, general industry conditions, financial and geographic environment	Current state of the art and emerging technology Re-evaluating and utilizing existing technology in new areas New knowledge Invention	Government needs and priorities Restrictions by Government New laws and regulations & impact on product markets and supply chains Trade liberalization
Market Themes			
Market Channels			
Competition			
Randomness & Unexpectedness			

The insights about new ideas, potential opportunities and strategies are not the product of any rational thought processes or CPS tools. They are totally intuitive, or *'gut feel'*, which through retrospective logic cay be rationalized as a *'good idea'*, *'something sensible'* and *'something worth going after'*. The many potential combinations of the four major opportunity gap drivers (social, economic, technology and government), mixed with market themes, market channels, and competition, with something random or unexpected lead to an infinite number of potential combinations, of which only a few are sound opportunities. What is important is whether the identified, discovered or constructed opportunity can influence the future, even if at the time of contemplating the opportunity, we are not sure what the actual future will be. This is the foresight that some people have that can change the direction of the future?

Through connecting a trend to a current product, one can see potential new value, if consumers also perceive it. If the innovation is radical and new to the world, a breakthrough may occur, and once again if accepted by the consumer, a new industry may be born. Seeing social trends into the future will help one imagine new ideas about products and new products as well. Changing economic conditions can quickly change consumer habits and reading this correctly can lead to new forms of existing products and new products where incongruities exist. Modified, borrowed or new technology can change the way things are done and lead to leaps and bounds in product and market evolution. Government regulation can end a product and give birth to a new product, and dictate where and how things can be sold. Constantly evolving market themes and channels, and the effects of competition change the vector of the metaphorical line we travel along. Without change, this line extends the past and present into the future without deviation. However with any change of the opportunity gap drivers, the line will deviate upwards or downwards depending upon the scope of the change. Incremental changes will develop new market segments like new types of shampoo like 2 in 1 or sugarless carbonated drinks. A major technological breakthrough may create a totally new industry like the home computer industry in the 1970s or the mobile phone industry in the 1980s. Where we can go from the present to the future is pictorially portrayed is a matter of how we construct the new opportunity and its leveraging in the field as shown in Figure 4.27.

The opportunity actualization process requires sub-conscious incubation something similar to the process of meditation that Shapiro describes (1984). During meditation a person sees the whole field through *'wide-angle-lens"* with attention focusing on a broad range of ideas and elements of the environment. This allows various elements to be opened up for further observation and sub-conscious contemplation. Then the mind switches to a *'zoom lens'* attention on certain aspects of the field in a concentrative way. There is a shift between these two strategies until some elements can be seen both through concentration and holistic mindfulness, which takes a person above the patterning their mind is used to (Abdullah & Schuchman 1976). A person starts to recognize recurrent themes and repetitions that can be extended into the future. This enables a person to extend their own existing constructions to see things in new ways where their construct or own view of reality is altered, through making new associations of knowledge to create a new construct or hypothesis about the future (Kelly 1955). As each person constructs the world differently, a person's observations and hypothesis about the future is likely to be relatively unique[45].

---

[45] A person's construct depends upon their experience of events and people and their emotions about their experiences. A person's construct will also depend upon their own motivations and situation.

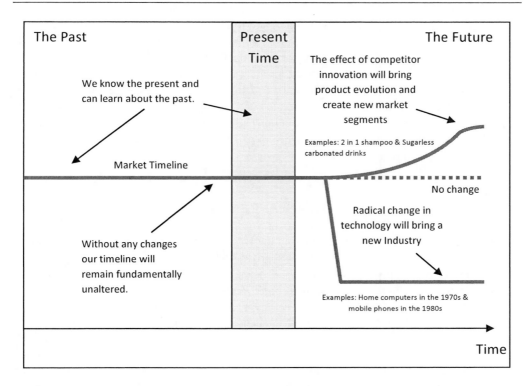

Figure 4.27. Where we can go in the future with changes in the opportunity gap factors.

To see opportunities within an industry requires domain knowledge. However domain knowledge through the rigid patterning it can create can also *'lock'* a person into the way the domain thinks. The person has to be able to break out of these patterns to be able to see things in fresh ways. In hindsight new ideas and concepts that have changed a market or changed an industry will appear very simple and extremely logical. However the process of discovering these opportunities is far from a logical process. It has required novel and divergent thinking away from the existing industry patterns. In essence a new opportunity is in fact a new construct about the realities they experience in the field.

This process of foresight that assists in discovering new opportunities within an industry is based on a mix of insight, imagination, analysis and action. This is a four stage creativity process where a person through environmental data, clarifies the problems, and then develops his or her own ideas. These are developed and refined until a stage comes for taking action upon them. According to Puccio (2002) some people at better than others at each stage of this process. Puccio (2002) has developed a creativity style assessment tool to determine people's strengths and weaknesses in this process by giving four individual scores. Basically *'clarifiers'* are focused, orderly, serious, methodical and deliberate, *'ideators'* are playful, social, flexible, independent, imaginative, adaptable and adventurous, *'developers'* are reflective, pragmatic, cautious and structured, and *'implementers'* are persistent, determined, action orientated, decisive and assertive (Puccio 2002, pp. 8-11). Some people may be a high *'clarifier'*, while others may be a high *'developer'*, *'implementer'* and *'finisher'*.

Another way of developing new product and market combinations is through the use of morphological diagrams discussed previously in this chapter. One can plot potential new combinations along the axis and look for new combinations of a product and how new strategic directions could be taken for the product could be put together. This can develop quite a large number of potential new product and strategy ideas. The key to this exercise is to find new degrees of freedom for a product and strategy that hasn't been used in the marketplace where competitive differentiation can be achieved. As mentioned previously anything new in the world is usually made up of known elements recombined in different ways, which leads onto the next method of reengineering.

REENGINEERING

Michael Hammer published an article in the Harvard Business Review in 1990 proposing a radical rethink and redesign of business processes to achieve radical improvements in performance, cost, quality, service and speed. Hammer expanded upon this philosophy with James Champy in 1993 with their seminal book *Reengineering the Corporation,* advocating the complete analysis of all business processes in a company and redesigning them in the most efficient way possible to eliminate all wastage. This was based on the premise that when companies grow, they develop processes in *ad hoc* ways which develop complacency and inefficiency as the firm becomes set in the ways it does things. Moreover the processes and company goals are based on assumptions about technologies, people and processes that are no longer valid. The tool that Hammer and Champy (1993) proposed to radically change the nature of the enterprise was *business process reengineering (BPR).*

Rohit Talwar (1993) defined reengineering in a much broader sense. Talwar, like Hammer and Champy proposed starting from a clean slate, where the company would be completely redefined with long terms goals, its competencies and competitive strategy to create maximum value to customers and shareholders. Cross *et. al.* (1994) saw that traditional business models were being challenged and there was a need for companies to go beyond continuous improvement and quality programs where old assumptions about technology, people and organizations goals could be changed in favor of relevant ones. They quoted the cases of the US Post office ignoring the growth of Federal Express, US car manufacturers ignoring the advent of Japanese luxury cars, Sears building a tower, while Wal-Mart opened new outlets, the decline of research libraries as electronic journals came online, CNN using one person crews reporting through the internet, while other networks saw this as insignificant, IBM's malaise about Apple in the 1980s and Microsoft in the 1990s, and the decline of Wang Computer and Digital Equipment due to failure to see market shifts, as examples where irrelevancy set in. Reengineering has facilitated the rise of new business models to deliver products and services like Dell and Amazon books, online auctions at eBay, the way the Toyota Scion is at Gen Y consumers, through custom design and ordering, and low cost airlines, etc.

Certainly creativity has not been associated with reengineering. However reengineering as a broad conceptual approach has the potential to realign and reorganize a firm so that it aligned to new and emerging opportunities, thus leaving declining or closing opportunity windows the firm has been servicing. In the light that firms have limited lifecycles, reengineering is the tool that maintains a firm's relevance to the opportunity environment. It is the major creativity tool a firm could use to maintain its survival. Reengineering is important for a firm in the growth and maturity stages, where processes developed soon after start-up, are found not to be as efficient as they could be. Efficiency is important to competitiveness and profitability. Without an overhaul of the business, there is risk that newer companies will become more competitive, leaving the original firm at disadvantage.

A firm must reengineer itself[46], every time it reassesses its opportunities and aligns its objectives and strategies towards the shifting opportunity landscape. The business model must be reconstructed to maximize the effectiveness and efficiency of the planned strategies. The pursuit of new opportunities requires a complete reassessment of goals, objectives, strategies, processes, structure, competencies, resources, and networks to succeed. Today the difference between survival and success is little. To survive a firm must be successful, anything less will be unsustainable in some aspect. Therefore the change in pursuit of opportunities must also bring transformation within the organization; otherwise any new opportunity will not be exploited effectively. Reengineering is the tool of organizational realignment.

Reengineering is not a new tool; it is what an organization needs to do to survive. As Foster and Kaplan (2001) showed in their study, the turnover rate of S&P companies is nearly 10% where a firm may survive in the S&P 500 list for no more than 10 years. Therefore by 2020 around 75% of companies on the S&P list will consist of companies we don't know today. These will be new companies that have aligned themselves with newly discovered opportunities. Thus competitive advantage in an industry will depend upon how well a company's goals, strategies, networks, organization and business models, skills, competencies and technologies and resources are aligned with the identified opportunity. Older companies formed around an opportunity identified in the past will tend to be aligned with that past opportunity. But the opportunity itself slowly drifts as consumer tastes evolve, demographics change, and technologies evolve, etc. From the competitive side, disruptive innovation, creative destruction and competitive imagination move opportunity (March 1991, Hamel 2000).

This is why sometimes a new company can create a value chain that is more aligned with the opportunity at hand, with great advantages over existing companies that are aligned against opportunities that were identified in the past. The new company is more up to date with its goals, networks, strategies, skills, competencies and technologies, and resources than existing companies in the industry that have not realigned their companies with the new characteristics of shifting opportunity. The newcomer to the market isn't burdened by the need to adapt and realign itself to the shifting opportunity and is freer to be creative and innovate. This is why some new firms quickly disrupt markets and take the initiative away from the incumbent companies in the market. Figure 4.28. shows how a firm must be continually reengineered to maintain its relevance to the opportunity landscape.

The position of opportunity[47] and the theoretically best corresponding value chain configuration to exploit it is made up of how a firm sets goals, crafts strategies, supports strategy with a an organizational structure and business model, skills, competences and

---

[46] This term could just as easily be reconstruct, recombine, regenerate, or transform.

[47] The position of opportunity refers to the characteristics of an opportunity based on demographics, technologies, regulation, economic conditions, etc. Opportunity slowly changes where demand patterns very slowly or rapidly change depending upon the industry.

technologies utilized allocated resources and supporting networks of stakeholders. This configuration must be continually monitored to maintain the maximum configuration effectiveness as the opportunity landscape is continually changing. The configuration is manifested by the level of competitiveness it generates relative to any competitors.

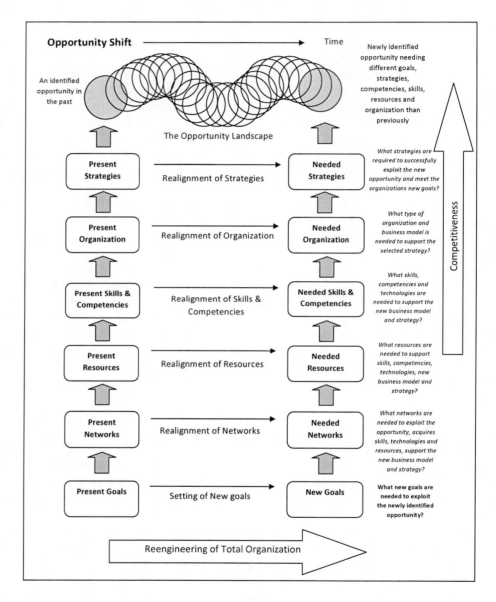

Figure 4.28. How a firm must be continually reengineered to maintain its relevance to the opportunity landscape.

Reengineering became a new *'buzzword'* in the mid 1990s. However many critics saw reengineering as a return to the days of *Taylorism* and *Scientific Management*[48], while others criticized it as a lean excuse for redundancies, which were being forced upon many corporations due to the advent of information technology that was reducing the need for employees. One of the greatest problems with the philosophy was that executives were only too willing to cut down aspects of the organization that didn't personally affect them, but were loathed to do anything that would affect their own livelihoods. As Hammer himself said that executives were the ones themselves that undermined the very structure of their rebuilt enterprises (Champy 1995). Consequently reengineering became another management *"catch cry"* bringing in large revenues for CSC Management Consultancy, which James Champy was principal[49]. Companies like Hallmark Cards and Kodak in the US successfully applied reengineering with very positive results, *BPR* became so much associated with redundancies, and it forced a change of name to *Business Process Improvement (BPI)*.

Although Reengineering became a *'distrusted'* word in business, the dogmatic *'self proclaimed manifesto' Reengineering the Corporation* highlighted that corporations need to change and transform themselves to survive. For change and transformation to occur people need to support it. One would expect that in the near future broader and more subtle concepts or *reengineering,* under a different name will emerge.

A second common form of reengineering is product reengineering. Product reengineering involves the examination, inspection and breaking down the physical parts of an existing product in the market to determine what it is made of and how it was manufactured. In reality, the majority of *new to the world products*[50] launched into the marketplace each year is only

---

[48] At the turn of the 20th Century, the business community was primarily concerned with manufacturing and assembly. There were no guide books or management manuals to assist managers at the time and management thought had been guided by historical antidote. Frederick Taylor was an engineer who carried out time and motion experiments on the workforce at the two steel mills he worked at. Taylor came up with a set of principals in what became known as scientific management. Taylor believed that the principal objective of management was to secure the maximum output per worker, taking all thinking away from the shop-floor. He laid down a set of guidelines for managers to determine the single best way of doing things, eliminating all useless movements. Workers would be set targets and quotas with incentives and penalties. Management would walk around the shop-floor timing workers performance and measuring it against standards. Management would be able to find the best person to perform each action, thus leading to optimum efficiency.

    The concept of scientific management sweep through corporate America. It was seen as a solution to poor worker motivation, which was considered a major problem at the time. Scientific management had its critics then and now, been seen as dehumanizing. It was also criticized for focusing on quantity and ignoring quality. However, scientific management was the first set of management principals that could be put into effect by managers at the time. In fact, there are still thousands upon thousands of factories around the world today that utilize this philosophy, without managers even knowing it is scientific management. Ninety years later elements of Taylor's principals have re-emerged in Hammer and Champy's concept of re-engineering.

[49] Reengineering as practiced relied on outside consultants who diagnosed the problems and specified remedies with little involvement of internal employees. This approach tended to ignore the 'cultural' and 'historical' aspects of a company, which are very important to meaning for those within the organization. Meaning implies motivation for a person to be in the organization and support its goals and objectives. When this aspect is ignored, employee motivation is likely to drop dramatically. This has occurred in many organizations utilizing reengineering.

[50] Here we mean 'new to the world products' as the first of their kind in the market. They are usually something invented or enhanced by a significant change or advance in technology, such as a new discovery or different method utilizing modified processes, materials or methods in producing a product. These products would revolutionize the market segment or even create a new market, which may require significant consumer learning to become familiar with the new product. Examples of this would include the progression from land line based telephones to mobile phones and now hand phones, the progression from typewriters to electric typewriters to word processors and personal computers, the change from wood, to gas to electric and microwave cooking and the advent of the Sony walkman and Ipods. New to the world products make up only a small proportion of new products and they are perceived as the riskiest types of new products to launch as manufacturers have to deal

about 10% of the total number new products. Therefore 90% of all products launched into the marketplace resemble existing products already in existence (Kleinschmidt & Cooper 1991)[51]. Therefore in some form or another, the majority of new product development is benchmarked on existing products in the marketplace. A firm will work backwards to learn how to produce a variation of that product, with or without enhancements. Through product reengineering, post World War II Japanese industry learnt how to manufacture numerous different types of products, which they eventually enhanced into products of superior quality to their Western competitors (Kotler *et. al.* 1985).

The product reengineering process begins with a full examination of existing products in the market. The functions and benefits to consumers are fully appraised. Products are also tested for their efficacy, performance and durability in product trials while other samples are slowly deconstructed to determine the materials used in their production and how they were manufactured. All characteristics of the products including what consumer benefits are used to develop a set of specifications for the new product to be developed. At this point, the most probable production methods are appraised and deductions made on probable processes from initial product examinations, as guidelines.

The full product technical and market specifications developed act as a roadmap for the following product development task[52]. Based on examination of existing products, the development team will have some fairly good ideas about what types of materials to use, how to develop the manufacturing processes and what marketing features they want. At this stage the team may or may not decide to develop an enhanced product by adding new features or design improvements over what already exists in the marketplace. An example of the market and technical specifications required for the product development process is listed in *a concept generation checklist* in shown back in Table 4.3. (Hunter 2009). Patents and other intellectual property issues are also examined both as a guide to the development process[53] and a check to ensure the company does not breach any 'intellectual rights' attributable to any other companies.

Once the concept generation list is completed, trial formulations, trial production processes and prototype products can be developed, tested and reassessed. Prototype products can be trialed in real conditions either by company staff or through consumer focus group tests. This is a period of trial and error where learning comes from results, providing some insights so modifications to be made to materials and production processes. Product issues that require further improvement will undergo further formulation and/or process development. Eventually when all the faults are eliminated from product prototypes and

---

with consumers inexperience with the new concepts and incompatibilities with their prior consuming experiences, which act as barriers to consumer adoption.

[51] About 10% of new products launched are new to the world products, which increases to around 18% in moderate to high tech industries. New product lines (which are new products for a firm) are about 26% of new products, but much higher at 37.6% in moderate to high tech industries. Additions to existing product lines are around 26%, but dropping to 18% in high tech industries. Product changes and improvements are around 26% of new products, 19.8% in moderate to high tech industries and product re-positioning are 7%, but almost non existent in moderate to high tech industries. Thus, the majority of new products are developments and variations based on existing products.

[52] In the case of new to the world products, the technical and market specifications would have to be developed without direct referral to other products, completely through expanding upon a new idea.

[53] Examining patents can provide a deep understanding of how a product is manufactured. Skilled professionals can 'work around' intellectual property, i.e., find new chemical synthesis routes, assembly processes or utilize alternative materials to those mentioned in existing patents.

production processes are effective and efficient, the product will be ready for a launch into the market. This whole product reengineering process is shown in Figure 4.29.

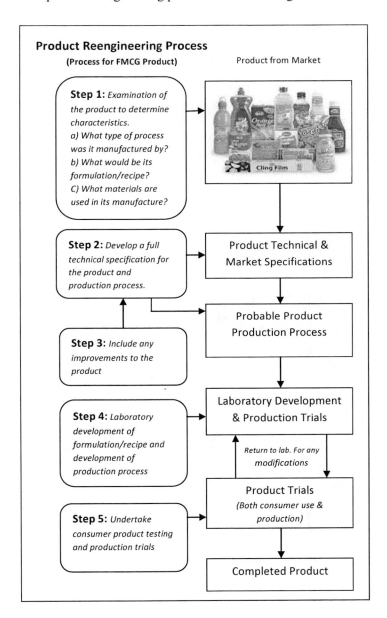

Figure 4.29. The whole product reengineering process.

Another creativity tool related to reengineering is W. Kim Chan and Renée Mauborgne's (2005) strategy canvass. The strategy canvass acts as a means to examine competitors product attributes or principals *(as the authors call them)*, such as price, image, consumer awareness[54], etc, so that a new product's attributes and product strategy can be developed. The product attributes make up the total product proposition that are points of competition across the market. A line drawn across the product attributes becomes what is known as the value curve, a graphic depiction of a product's value position. Once this benchmark is determined, it can be analyzed using a framework of questions *(four actions framework)* to create other important attributes that a new product will make its proposed value proposition upon. As the *strategy canvass* technique breaks up products into their individual product attributes to facilitate the building of a product with a new set of attributes as a benchmark, this technique can also be considered a form of product reengineering based on breaking down the product value components.

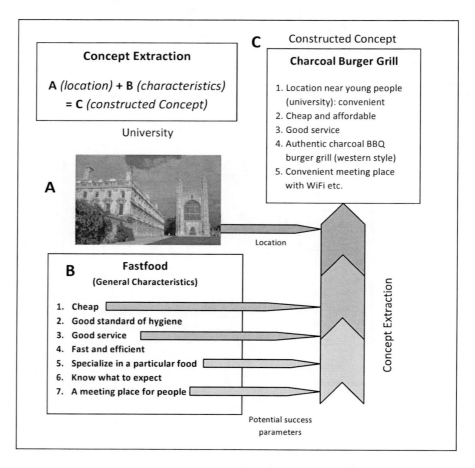

Figure 4.30. A constructed conceptual concept of a charcoal BBQ Burger Grill.

Concepts can be extracted and synergized from unrelated locations, objects and other business models. For example, a person may secure a particular location and wish to create some form of business model that would serve potential customers within that location. Potential young customers around the precinct of a university like to gather at near campus

---

[54] It is necessary to select which product attributes (or principals) are important in the product mapping stage.

restaurants or coffee lounges for snacks and social gatherings. The general characteristics of a generic fast-food business is that it is cheap, has a good standard of hygiene, good service, fast and efficient, specializing in a particular food, people know what to expect and a meeting place for people. After study of the situation some of the characteristics of a generic fast-food business can be extracted according to what the potential entrepreneur feels are most important to the potential clientele of the potential location and a new concept constructed. A hypothetical result might be a charcoal BBQ Burger Grill which is conveniently located, cheap and affordable, has good service, a unique and tasty charcoal grill, and is a convenient meeting place with WiFi, etc. This is called concept extraction where the potentially successful elements of a concept are synergized together to create a new idea. This is shown pictorially in Figure 4.30.

THE BARRIERS TO CREATIVITY

As we have seen, creativity comprises of a combination of expertise, motivation and our creative thinking skills. Expertise includes all our knowledge and experience, including technical, practical, and tacit knowledge. There are various forms of motivation, but it is the implicit forms that are most influential in driving our will to be creative. Our creative skills and ways we think are important tools to produce a new idea or solution to a problem. Our creativity also depends upon our sensitivity, focus, attention, curiosity, imagination, energy and our ego.

However just as some factors promote the ability to be creative, creativity can be blocked and a person prevented from seeing new associations and solutions to problems. This can happen both to the individual, and at the social and organizational levels. This rest of this section will outline some of the individual and organizational blocks to creativity.

Early Creativity and Social Blocks

During our early years we tend to be uninhibited in what we do. Our drawings, acting (or mimicking) and views of the world may be naive, but uninhibited. We are imaginative and fantasize much more easily than when we are adults. In the pre-computer, TV and multi-media world, it was often our own imagination that kept us entertained building sandcastles, mud houses, cubby houses, doll enactments and plays, etc, imitating the world we know[55]. Our creative tools also helped us to make sense of the world we were growing up in through wishing, rearranging, structuring, and imagining. These tools are vital parts of the learning process.

As we get older and go to school we learn our logical sides and slowly drop the artistic and creative sides in favour of 'life skills'. The memory retention orientation of our early education systems (and those still in Asia and Africa today) very quickly diminish our

---

[55] The children of the Millennial generation are now going to school. They are much more impatient than previous generation and don't have the same discipline, although they are experts with new technologies. They have been brought up with more gadgets and money than previous generations and their play has been almost entirely with today's technology. Millennials have a strong desire to succeed and do things their own way (Carlson 2005), but how creative this generation is still up to debate.

creative tendencies. Parent and society expectation put high value on professions like law, medicine, engineering, science and business. Art, acting, sculpturing, painting, writing and dramatic careers tend to be gauged as fantasy occupations that are not for the rational to pursue. The steering of career orientation and rejections, criticisms and humiliations during the early stages of our learning affect our views and can dampen any natural creative tendencies (Prince *et. al.* 2000). We are very sensitive to criticism, rejection and humiliation and in most cases usually willing to change our behaviour to maintain acceptance from others. We start to lose our creative skills like fantasy, imagination, wishing, transforming and comparing, replacing them with psychological blocks that in extreme form resemble various forms of psychosis.

Mental Models and Mental Blocks

Mental models are articulated concepts of how we manage our relationships, our interactions with the environment and our general view of the world. Our mental model is the sum of all our schemata and scripts, our total knowledge. Mental models act as templates to provide meaning to what we see in the world.

But just as mental models guide us, mental models tend to be relatively rigid and can also blind us to other potential possibilities. Our psych has a vested interest in rigidity because if our mental models are challenged by what we see, they can break down and lead to uncertainty and ambiguity where stress and anxiety will develop.

Conceptual blocks stop thinking processes through unconscious mental blocks. Mental blocks affect us in different ways, where various filters or patterning upon our perceptions or prevent us from letting ideas emerge from our sub-conscious (Prince 1998). Our senses are optimized for our everyday survival. For example, if we live in an area well known for snakes running across housing estates, we will tend to be alert for this type of danger. Many dangers to us are more subtle than that and our mind utilizes various strategies to protect the person.

James Adams (1979) compiled a list of conceptual blocks, classifying them as perceptual blocks, which confuse data coming from our senses and disrupt the way our mind manages that data, emotional blocks where our emotions and desires interfere with our ability to form thoughts, cultural blocks that place acceptability limitations on what we think and do, environmental blocks where we incur physical distractions, and intellectual and expressive blocks which deal with problem solving strategies. Many blocks also have undesirable side effects because we utilize them as long term strategies rather than short term tactics when prehistoric humankind had to utilize fight/flight responses to mortal dangers. A summary of some of the different types of conceptual blocks are listed in table 4.7.

Some of the heuristics listed above assist an individual on an everyday basis to solve problems. They are short cuts in judgments that are convenient and save time by cutting down on the complexity. However the above listed heuristics can also prove to be great flaws in our perception and reasoning as they produce misconceptions[56].

---

[56] For example a pilot in night flight may have great difficulty in judging the distances of objects from the aircraft and personal orientation to the horizon. In this situation the pilot's senses are confused and therefore must rely upon flight instruments rather than senses for information.

Table 4.7. List of Some Different types of Conceptual Blocks[57]

Conceptual Blocks	Stereotyping Halo Effect Self-fulfilling Prophecy Preconceptions (prevents and inventor see new directions) Wrong polarity in perception (i.e., Field dependence/independence) Overwhelming data – Confusion Tunnel Vision Lack of Focus Inability to perceive a problem from different viewpoints Failure to utilize all senses correctly.
Emotional Blocks	Obsessive desire for security and order Fear of making a mistake Lack of motivation Inability to reflect on ideas Trying to solves problems too quickly A tendency to make prejudgments Lack of imagination or imaginative control
Cultural Blocks	Time restraints on problem solving Daydreaming and reflection Preference of logic Taboos and tradition Lack of social support
Environment Blocks	Distractions Monotony Physical and mental discomfort Lack of communication
Intellectual and Expressive Blocks	Incorrect choice of problem solving method Inflexible or inadequate use of problem solving skills or strategies Lack of correct information Incorrect or inadequate means of expression Unable to define problem

Limited Domain Knowledge

Quite often our mental models are flawed, which often lead to individuals using the wrong analogies and therefore missing meaning (Kempton 1986). We often misunderstand how things really work and make decisions based on our misconceptions. Limited domain knowledge can handicap a person in being able to frame a problem (Proffitt *et. al.* 1990). Even if a problem can be framed, we may use the appropriate information, may use it inappropriately or fail to use the information at all to solve the problem. Instruction, training and knowledge in a domain assists our ability to reason within it. However that training within a discipline may not always eliminate misbeliefs (Kozhevnikov & Hegarty 2001).

As technology becomes more advanced and problems require a multi-disciplined view to develop a comprehensive understanding, any single individual may lack the knowledge required to deal with the issues involved. Therefore greater reliance on teams that can look at

---

[57] Most of these are discussed in detail in Chapter three.

issues from multiple disciplines is desirable. Professionals entering the workforce in the future are likely to have some background in more than one discipline. An example where multiple disciplines are needed is in the case of the analysis of essential oils from plants. Essential oils are natural aromatic substances derived from plants through distillation that exhibit a usually complex odour. To be able to analyze an essential oil, a person needs to understand the domains of chemistry, biochemistry, botany, thermodynamics, and analytical chemistry (Hunter 1994). The analytical equipment used in the analysis of the essential oil, a Gas Chromatograph Mass-Spectrometer may identify compound X as present. However our botany and biochemistry knowledge enables us to understand whether it is possible for compound X to exist, due to the way the plant synthesizes its metabolites. Consequently another compound with a similar structure may be present in compound X's place, leading to the identification of a different compound (Hunter 2009, P. 160). Figure 4.31. shows the merging of domains that is required to analyze essential oils within plants. Many tasks are now extremely complex and require synergized views of problems to solve them.

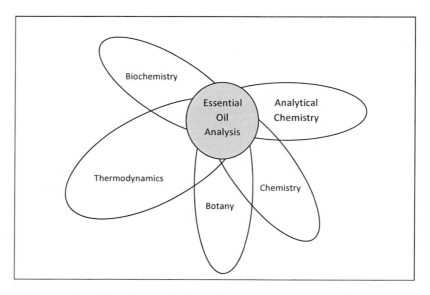

Figure 4.31. The merging of domains required to carry out an essential oil analysis.

Organizational Barriers

About half of new companies close their doors within the first five years of operations. Out of the five remaining, four will survive into their tenth year and three into their fifteenth year of operation (Birch 1987). Among the large corporations listed in the *Fortune 500* between 1970 and 1986, almost one third vanished completely (de Geus 1988). Historically company *excellence* only lasts a short time, where the average life-cycle of a company is around 40 years (Collins 2001). Peter Drucker espoused that companies are only entrepreneurial in the early stages of their life, where after establishment they slip into the guise of being an *ordinarily* managed company (Drucker 1986).

A company's decline does not usually occur from the lack of resources, information, knowledge or finance. The company's decline occurs because of a changing environment that is not detected. To sustain a company new ideas are needed to exploit evolving and transforming opportunities, as well as develop the strategies required to achieve successful exploitation. This requires creativity.

Any opportunity has a limited lifecycle. As the opportunity drifts, companies require new technologies, new products and/or new ways in delivering products and services to maintain their relevance in the market. A company can only survive as long as an opportunity remains viable and the company is aligned with it. This may mean that new ideas and strategies based on new technologies, the development of products (and the cessation of old products), the entry into new markets or the development of new ways of doing business is needed to maintain that alignment.

Companies over time can become rigid and develop an egocentric manner. The management sees the company as the centre of the field, the market or industry leader where nothing can harm them. A number of conditions develop within organizations that make management within them lose their sense of adventure, entrepreneurship, and creativity. These conditions will be discussed in the following sections.

Compartmentalized Thinking

One of the characteristics of a maturing company is its division into compartments or departments which tend to influence how people within the organization look at the environment. People tend to take the points of view of their specialized departments. The fun that was shared through formation and early growth is switched for the more formal functional processes of production, procurement, administration, sales, marketing and finance, etc. Departmentalization discourages an environmental wide view of things, in favour of narrower departmental and disciplinary approaches.

Although specialization has always been assumed to bring efficiency, this is sometimes questionable from the organizational point of view. The potential efficiencies that can be gained from increased specialization can lead to the loss of interdisciplinary thinking within the organization, as people tend to look only from their departmental points of view. The disadvantages of departmentalization can be seen in the example of cars built in Detroit during the 1960's and 1970's where different sized bolts where used in different parts of the car, leading to increased costs and the need for more inventory items, just because the car was designed from different functional perspectives. This was in stark contrast to the Japanese cars that were manufactured with common bolts to streamline the production and procurement processes. Departmentalization can hinder company integration where departments become egocentrically concerned with their 'turf' and position, often leading to conflicts and power struggles within interdepartmental relationships. This diverts energy, focus and attention away from creativity towards maintaining the interdepartmental *status quo* within the organization.

Hierarchy

Hierarchy automatically builds in assumptions about how information flows, the nature of connections between the different components of the organization and outside stakeholders, and how power and influence operates. Organizations will also have a desired level of diversity within it, either by deliberate design, policy, or through the influence informal conformity to norms by those responsible for selecting new personnel[58]. An organization will also tend to have entropy towards the maintaining the *status quo* or being amicable towards continuous change.

According to Stacey (1996) how organizations tackle these organizational dimensions will have enormous influence over the level of creativity and innovation. Information flows within a traditional hierarchy where authority is important will be on a strictly need to know basis. Information will be a protected commodity accessed only by those in authority. Ideas will flow from the top down the hierarchy, where the lower levels are only responsible for implementation under supervision. There will be no room within an authoritative hierarchy where power-distance is high for ideas to flow from the bottom up. In those types of organizations people are not expected to think outside established rules and processes. In fact thinking outside established rules and procedures would land a person into trouble.

In highly controlled organizations, communication up and down the various tiers is controlled and rigid. It is the prerogative of superiors to make any decisions that established rules and procedures do not settle. There is no room for alternative ideas or perspectives and anybody exhibiting alternative opinions would go against the norms of the prevailing conservative culture within the organization. Those with actual power are cautious in their decision making and people would be fearful of expressing alternative ideas in public. Consequently such organizations would create high levels of stress and anxiety for those employed within it. Such organizations would be very rigid and not know how to handle information that differs from what those within the organization are used to. This would just add to stress and anxiety rather than a cue for needed analysis and change. Subsequently any forms of creativity, except for dysfunctional behaviour would not occur within these types of organizations.

Creativity is best served by an organization that has unhindered flows of ordered information that can be accessed by all relevant people. Power is best based on knowledge and expertise rather than position or political positioning. Interdisciplinary groups of diverse people are encouraged to take a holistic view of problems and opportunities. Finally the organizational leadership would be open to new ideas from all parts of the organization and see change as a necessity for organizational survival.

However too much freedom at the other end of the continuum may allow too much unfocused creativity, where an organization would also be paralyzed through indecisiveness. In such an environment there would be information overload where it would be too confusing to determine what information is important and what should be disregarded. Alternative opinions are canvassed to the point that no decisions or commitments can be made. Groups within the organization may be so diverse that little common ground, that there may be little

---

[58] For example, domineering leaders may tend to select people who will follow passively and are of the same social background, while high-tech start-up companies in Silicon Valley may select people based on knowledge and ability, regardless of social background.

sense of common mission. Such an organization seeks change without having commitment and agreement about what change should occur. Although being a creative organization, none of its creativity results in any form of innovation because of lack of focus, discipline and formal decision making processes.

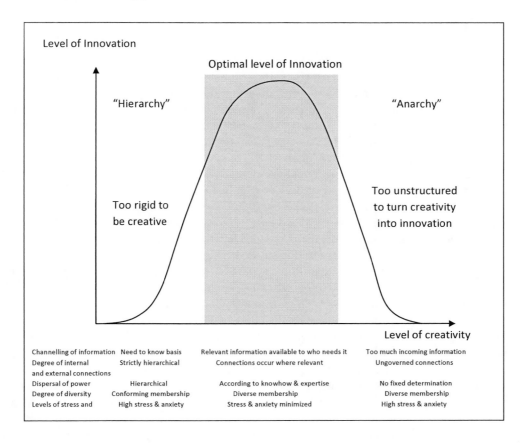

Figure 4.32. Continuum of hierarchy to anarchy.

A graphical view of the continuum of hierarchy to anarchy within an organization is depicted in figure 4.32. On the left side formalized and authoritative hierarchies allow little room for creativity and innovation. These would include very production orientated organizations and companies that still subscribe to the concepts of *scientific management*. These may also include organizations dominated by a founder who wishes to make all decisions within the organization. At the other extreme is an organization in chaos where there may be great creative potential but no mechanisms to channel and focus creativity into innovation. Groups run into conflict over differing ideas where frustration develops. Many examples of this form of organization may be early start-ups made up of groups who find it difficult to make decisions. These organizations start moving once they are able to define how to channel and develop decision making procedures. The middle of the continuum is where organizations can be creative through allowing information flow, diverse groups to work on problems and authority based on knowledge and expertise. This is where innovation will be at the maximum because of focus and sense of mission within the organization. There will never be two organizations adopting exactly the same mix of organizational parameters. Each company will find from experience what works best for them.

Rigidity

Rigidity is a product of hierarchical organizations that are traditionally locked into operating through strict rules and procedures. Although rigidity has some advantages in sustaining individuals in times of stress and anxiety, rigidity is the true antithesis of creativity within an organization. Rigidity within an organization can come in many forms. Rigidity is caused from over-learning, where the same generalizations are applied to every problem facing the organization, with an intense attachment to rules, procedures and beliefs within an organization, especially conservative ones.

Organizations that don't interact with the environment to protect themselves and rely on rules and procedures to operate regardless of what happens in the outside, tend to develop strong dogma as a unifying force (Rokeach 1960). Each member is expected to hold the shared set of beliefs that may be considered fanatical to outsiders. Only incoming information that supports the organizational dogma is acceptable where all other information is part of a conspiracy to undermine the organization or leadership. Within such an organization one would regularly hear comments like *"this is the (name of the organization) way of doing things"*, *"around here we must do things like this"*, or *"outsiders don't understand us and try to undermine what we stand for"*. Organizations wrapped in dogma may border on the psychotic and there is some chance that members of the leadership are psychotic to some degree. Creativity within these organizations is seen as a threat to stability and is generally suppressed.

Rigid organizations may look at issues and people through stereotyped vision. Generalizations are made about the classes of people without evidence about their attributes or qualities. This leads to distorted views of the world like *"all Muslims are terrorists"*, *"all Americans are anti Muslim"*, *"all Germans are Nazis"*, and *"all Australians are anti-Asian"*, *etc.* Stereotyping helps to make the unfamiliar look familiar but suppresses our curiosity and ability to question about what we see. In the mild state, stereotyping is narrow mindedness, but in the extreme stereotyping is a symptom of psychotic behaviour. Adorno *et. al.* (1950) espoused that those harshly treated by someone in their childhood years may grow to adulthood with extreme hate for certain stereotyped groups of people. This can lead to the type of dogmatism discussed above.

Over-learning can cause functional fixedness, a state where a person can only see one conventional function or use for particular objects. Functional fixedness can often occur within professions where people will tend to rely on the training of their respective disciplines to solve problems. For example, a marketing person would look for a market solution, where a legal person may want to consider a legal solution. This form of rigidity prevents individuals from using objects and concepts in new ways, as he or she is locked into one specific use for the items or concepts in question. Thus individuals will respond to a problem in a fixed way rather than look at new possibilities. This prevents a person from seeing new connections and associations which blocks creativity. Functional fixedness is very common and requires a conscious attempt to break out of this type of thinking through CPS techniques discussed previously.

Fear and Conformity

If we sufficiently fear something, our capacity to be creative is greatly diminished. There are a number of sources of fear that take away our focus, energy and attention, dampening our curiosity.

One of our most common fears in organizations is that of uncertainty, the unknown and the ambiguous. Ambiguity, uncertainty and complexity discomforts most people who are unable to cope and develop stress and anxiety. Most people actually have a need for customs, procedures, rituals, routines, and traditions, etc., for security and stability. Even though this may cost many opportunities for personal growth the benefits of comfort and security are worth it in most people's view. The roots of conformity go deep from the time of being reared as a child to what is socially right and wrong behaviour. Children are also taught the social severity of deviation. This is why conformity is difficult to let go easily where a person needs to question traditions, structures and be exposed to other dynamic cultures.

Fear is also a group phenomenon where the group develops beliefs, norms and values that bind people together. Breaking the group's beliefs, norms and values will lead to sanctions from the rest of the group. Conformity is another form of organizational rigidity which hinders creativity (Parnes & Meadow 1963).

Another form of fear is the fear of failure. In a mild form the fear of failure is a strong motivation to maintain sharpness, focus on doing a better job that creates some competitiveness in a person or group. However in the extreme form it may prevent a person take any risks and play things safe by not taking on any activities that may appear risky to a person's self image, should they fail at the activity. For example, a bad review for an artist may turn him or her off doing anymore works. Therefore people with a fear of failure will stick to undertaking tasks that avoid competition and there is certainty that they will win. People with a fear of failure will look for excuses of why they would fail and go into excessive fright and nervousness when there is some form of test situation. A fear of failure can retard divergent thinking and discourage people from undertaking new activities (Khandwalla 2004, P. 293).

People also fear criticism and humiliation. In the mild forms, some level of criticism can be motivational. Criticism or humiliation can have the effect of bringing groups into more cohesion *(i.e., to defend against a common enemy)*. Other effects of criticism and humiliation create touchiness and resistance to innovative ideas. An organization that has an atmosphere of negative criticism will destroy employees' intrinsic motivation to the point they will fear to present any new ideas (Amabile 1998, P. 83).

Defensive Routines

Defensive routines are actions or policies that protect us from fear or embarrassment of exposing our thinking to others. Defensive routines form a protective shell around a group or organization that shields any scrutiny or attack upon its general assumptions that may produce pain or anxiety. Defensive routines can prevent people in organizations from seeing things, solving problems and learning. For example, management may focus on making short term profits by cutting down on costs, even if this may threaten longer term profitability. The 'O'-rings on the space shuttle Challenger were numerous times by the engineers who did nothing about them because it may threaten the program schedule, thus preventing any dealing with the matter before the tragedy occurred. When sales fall, managers responsible may jump in and develop a program of discounts and sales promotions, without looking for any reasons why sales are falling, thus failing to learn the fundamental reasons behind the sales downturn. All these events hide the reality and truth of the situation. Things are hidden because there is a fear that errors will be found by others.

Chris Argyris (1990) proposed that most behaviour in organizations is shaped by a set of 'governing variables'. This means that people will strive to avoid embarrassment and threats by advocating views without encouraging inquiry, undertake actions that save face or are defensive, design and manage situations in order to maintain control, evaluate the thoughts and actions of others in ways that don't encourage the testing of the validity of the evaluation itself, attribute causes for things without really validating them and encourage defensive actions like blaming, stereotyping, and intellectualizing to suppress anxieties.

These 'governing variables' don't necessary match the values that people espouse, so there ends up being an espoused theory of action and an actual theory of action (Argyris & Schön 1974). The behaviour contradicts with what is espoused. The actions taken are based on stress and mistrust as an attempt to escape exposure for something wrong. This type of behaviour prevents learning, creativity and the development of innovative solutions to problems facing the organization.

Complacency

Complacency was discussed in chapter three in relation to the concept of opportunity. But complacency also has an effect on creativity. When a company is immersed within the same environment on an everyday basis, this brings familiarity, where familiarity brings insensitivity to detecting any small or modest change. This is very important to seeing new opportunities. One of the best examples of blindness caused by complacency was the US car industry which didn't take much notice of the Japanese car makers when they came to the US in the 1960s. It was only when the Japanese car makers gained more than 20% market share in the 1980s, the US car makers woke up to the threat and changing opportunities. The US car makers were hesitant to move into the new market segments created by the Japanese car makers, and became unable to innovate. Blindness due to complacency develops a lethargic attitude towards the need to be creative and innovative. Complacency is a primary reason why companies decline and completely disappear from the market place.

Time and Resources

Organizations most often operate according to schedules. Work hours are scheduled, breaks are scheduled, projects run according to timetables and product launches are timed. Schedules have advantages in that they create some pressure on an individual's performance, something like when swatting for an upcoming examination at school, where there is a deadline to be met. If there was no deadline, most probably there would be little pressure to study. The effect of competitive and time pressure was partly responsible for the breakthrough in World War II, the arms and space race between the US and USSR during the 1960s. However continuous tight deadlines can turn into mistrust, where employees feel over controlled and eventually burnout.

However creativity requires time and tight deadlines can kill creativity. Many problems are only solved after a period of intense work without making any progress, where insight will come after a person has stopped thinking about the problem. Unfortunately the timing of insight cannot be controlled to conform to schedules. For serious creativity to occur time is needed for exploration and incubation. The pressure to solve problems quickly is a major obstacle in solving problems as they require insight to solve them. Tight schedules also undermine technology or new product breakthroughs that need to occur from continuous experimentation and trial and error.

The correct resources are also needed to develop creativity. Work groups should have the right diversity and backgrounds within them with an interdisciplinary scattering so there can be a diversity of perspectives. Homogeneous teams may tend to reach compromise solutions avoiding intergroup conflict. There must also be the resources necessary, *i.e., labs, office space, funding and time, etc.* for the group to do their job. This includes the right physical space so work can be undertaken efficiently. However too many resources and facilities can also hinder creativity by developing an *isolated comfort zone.* Many breakthroughs have come from individual inventors with very limited resources, rather than large corporate R&D labs.

Organizational Culture and Management Style

The prevailing organizational culture and management style of a company has a major impact upon the creativity of the organization. The general beliefs and values within the organization are greatly influenced by the management style practiced within the organization. Management style may either encourage or hinder creativity. Teresa Amabile (1998) proposed that management style influences employees' sense of challenge, freedom, availability of resources, work group composition, supervisory encouragement and organizational support for creativity.

Teresa Amabile believes that managers don't always match the most suitable people to an assignment to optimize creativity. Often people with the wrong expertise and motivation are given jobs that are not suitable for them. Once people have been allocated a task they should be given the maximum freedom to undertake the job, *i.e., authority and responsibility.* This allows employees to work on the problem with their own expertise and creative skills and develop intrinsic motivation along the way, where they can gain a sense of ownership. Managers often fail to define clear objectives and give true autonomy to a job, thus hindering creativity.

The amount of resources allocated to a project can support or kill potential creativity. The assembly of problem solving or idea generating groups is very important where a diversity of views and perspectives can be gained. This requires putting people together that have different intellectual bases and creative styles. Amabile (1998, P. 83) considered it very important the group members share excitement, help their teammates during difficult periods and also recognize the unique knowledge and perspectives of the other members. To be able to assemble such groups managers must have a deep understanding of their employees. Selecting a homogenous group will tend not to be as creative as a diverse and motivated group, which can be very powerful if differences don't turn into conflict. The best atmosphere to provide for this group is one of supervisory support that underlines to the group that their work is important to the organization. Managers will quickly kill creativity if they criticize new ideas, give across the attitude of skepticism, or take a long period of time to respond. Finally, creativity is enhanced when a whole organization is supportive of it. Organizations that make creative people the heroes will put a positive emphasis on creative behaviour. Very few organizations actually have this positive attitude towards creativity. This is particularly the case where many people see giving criticism to others is a way to look intelligent to the boss. Problems then start becoming considered in the light of political gamesmanship. These organizational dysfunctions take attention away from work and clutter up open communication with gossip and games, destroying the potential for positive collaboration.

Other Blocks to Organizational Creativity

There are a number of other potential blocks to organizational creativity, some of which were discussed at length in chapter three. Leaps of abstraction are very quick generalizations made about situations. These generalizations impede an objective view of the environment and situations that may occur within it. Groupthink and collective thinking, especially within homogeneous groups often lead to the suppression of ideas and information people for particular reasons don't want to hear. This leads to failure for the group to canvass the important issues and less than optimal decision making. The benefit of collective thinking in many cases may be a fallacy according to De Bono (2002), where a person working on their own may produce a lot more new ideas than those working in a group.

To build a creative organization actually requires an understanding of what management factors foster creativity and what impedes creativity. Creativity within an organization needs;

- Expertise and interdisciplinary knowledge – technical, procedural, formal, informal, practical experience, and intellectual thinking. There must be interaction with other professionals to develop interdisciplinary approaches to generating ideas and solving problems.
- Motivation – inner passion to find and solve problems, where this motivation should be intrinsic rather than extrinsic.
- Time to enable incubation of ideas or undertake exploration through trial and error, and
- Creative thinking skills to enable flexibility and various methods to look at and solve problems as well as generate new ideas.

To be creative in the organizational sense, the idea or solution must be appropriate, useful and achievable. It must influence the way business is done, improve productivity, or show a new way of doing something.

CONCLUSION

In this chapter, the author has argued that the process of creativity depends upon a number of elements. The raw material for idea generation and problem solving comes from knowledge. A person cannot move forward in a field unless they have knowledge. Knowledge comes from many sources, has various accuracies, reliabilities and truths. The different levels of knowledge were shown back in figure 4.16., which affects the quality of decision making.

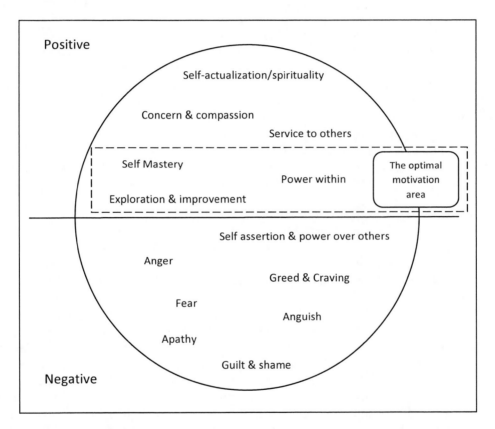

Figure 4.33. The Hierarchy of Motivations for Creativity.

Different forms of knowledge have different benefits to the creativity process. Expertise is the sum of all the other forms of knowledge and can be applied directly to problems and the creative process. Technical and intellectual knowledge are two forms of explicit knowledge which can be expressed in words, numbers, data and other forms of information. Practical knowledge and experience is tacit, based on personal knowledge, hunches, insights and intuitions. Tacit knowledge is deeply rooted in an individual's modes of actions, ideals, values and emotion, a person embraces (Edvinsson & Malone 1997). All these forms of knowledge create a person's cognitive dimension, consisting of beliefs, perceptions, ideals, values, emotions, and ingrained mental models, which gives a person a sense of personal mastery and wisdom in a particular domain. However it must be remembered that knowledge can both enhance and hinder creativity.

Intrinsic motivators are essential to creativity. There are both positive and negative intrinsic motivators, which are based upon our basic primal and social emotions under ego influence and control. The lower negative intrinsic emotions are usually overpowering on a person. This is related to our *'leftover'* primitive survival instincts. Conversely, our higher positive intrinsic motivators tend to be related to our sense of social altruism and self actualization or spirituality. These various forms of motivators influence our creativity and decision making processes. For example, a person motivated by greed and anger will be driven by blame and retribution, whereas a person motivated by self actualization will be driven by their desire for spirituality. Different motivations will result in a person seeing the world very differently. The hierarchy of creativity motivations is shown in Figure 4.33.

According to Amabile (1983) people do not really undertake creative work within a field unless they truly love what they are doing and focus on the work rather than the potential rewards. This infers the optimal types of motivation for creativity are positive intrinsic motivators, self mastery, the power within and exploration and improvement.

It is also very important to have thinking styles that allow one to think in different ways. Different forms of creativity depend upon the style of thinking used. The various creative thinking tools discussed within this part utilize one or more forms of these thinking styles. Miller *et. al.* (1996) described four different styles of creative thinking as;

- Modifying where facts and figures are used to develop new actions that improve upon what already exists. This is a problem solving style of creativity where facts and figures are used in various methods of decision making that have worked in the past. This is a means of improving efficiency and making incremental improvements within a stable environment. Persons using this style tend to maintain their original assumptions and be comfortable with using facts and figures and dislike working within an ambiguous environment. This approach would be very useful for product, process and business improvement within the same product/market/industry set.

- Exploring uses insights, finding ways to perceive new connections and metaphors that yield new perspectives. This is achieved through amassing lots of information in the hope that it will lead to new insights. Exploring allows assumptions to be challenged. Through insight we can develop new ideas that tend to be novel approaches to what is already done. This approach would be very useful in finding new products and opportunities to develop. This approach is used in some parts of Synectics.

- Experimentation uses facts and observations to find new ways to develop a concept or solve an existing problem. Experimenting is based on a cyclic trial and error process that will expose problems with a variable that can tend be changed or modified. This approach is the most disciplined of all the styles and often requires great perseverance. Experimentation is very good for developing a new product or process, improving it, or refining a design, etc. This form of creativity style is excellent for refining concepts into ideas and exploitable opportunities. This style is sometimes used in reengineering.

- Visioning or imagining the future looks for foresight that will create a desired future situation to take action upon. Visioning is a very instinctive, intuitive or even fanciful style of creative thinking which can emerge with novel concepts, ideas and potential opportunities. This style is sometimes used in Brainstorming, Synectics and competitive imagination.

However these styles of creativity must be accompanied with intellectual skills, a) to see problems in new ways and escape the bounds of conventional thinking, b) the skill to recognize which ideas are worth pursuing, and c) to know how to persuade others as to the value of the idea (Sternberg 1985).

Another factor important to creativity is our perception of the environment. As we have seen, perception is subjective rather than objective, being heavily influenced by our mental models. Our sensitivity, curiosity and attention are all influenced by a complex group of factors which have been explained within their respective sections. Triggers act upon the interface of the environment and our sense of self, and influence our motivation, energy and curiosity. Finally our unconscious cognitive processes within our sub-conscious re-organize information in ways that may provide insights into new perspectives upon problems or potential opportunity concepts. This is especially evident during the incubation period of the creativity process. A overview of the factors that influence the creativity process is shown in Figure 4.34.

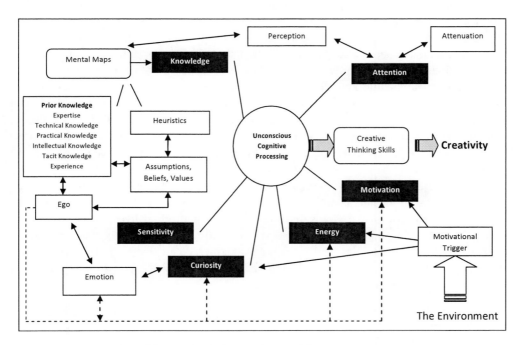

Figure 4.34. An overview of factors that influence the creativity process.

Stories of entrepreneurial successes show that the road to lucrative exploitation of opportunities has various routes and methods. The ways to success are as diverse as success itself. There are the stories of serendipity where things were discovered by accident. The game of rugby, x-rays, penicillin and Teflon were all discoveries made by accident. However it is not the discovery that makes success, it's was the hard work afterwards. Some may explain Bill Gates success as knowing where there is a willing buyer and seller at the right time. Is this vision, hustling, shrewdness or ruthlessness? Ray Kroc saw a model, but it took action upon his part to make it happen. Did he discover opportunity or was he an opportunist? Tony Fernandes, the founder of Air Asia followed a business model clearly established by others in different continents. Is he a visionary or is he a copycat?

Forget about the semantics above, the important point here is that creativity and the corresponding innovation is easy to pass judgment upon in retrospect, but was no doubt a challenge to each of them before their respective successes, requiring both insight and foresight. Creativity is wide and varied and innovation is subjective. There are too many possible variables in the model to prescribe successful strategies. Each success in a way is unique, based on the various factors and situations. It is not always a case of incremental or radical innovation, as a new opportunity may require a number of innovations patched together in order to be exploited successfully, as we will see in chapter one of volume two.

Every individual has a different set of traits in relation to the factors that influence creativity. These include different levels and types of intelligence, energy, laziness, boredom, troubles at home, within society or work, etc. One will also be influenced by different emotions and aspirations. Thus creativity is not evenly distributed around individuals and to some degree creativity can be considered a scarce resource. In addition creativity is often latent and underdeveloped in people. Creativity is important in start-ups, when product lifecycles are coming to an end, industry structures and supply chains are changing, technologies are converging and being improved both incrementally and drastically, regulation is changing and global influence is strengthening. It is through creativity that firms compete with each other within and across industries. Behind the concept of entrepreneurial management and marketing lays the concept of creativity. Creativity is what assists in the opportunity identification process and strategy crafting, thus creativity is an intangible asset that differentiates companies. Creativity is what blends together resources, skills, capabilities, technologies, products and networks within some form of blend that is unique and may have advantage over others. Creativity is the tool that helps a firm respond to unfamiliar situations by modifying existing routines (Jones & Craven 2001).

Creativity is evolutionary and social. It is influenced and influences our social evolution, and it is a manifest of the human mind. This is supported by our growth of knowledge and the behavior of other people. Creativity is thus the generative part of our lives, the economy, and our social and cultural systems. The second volume will look at the sources of opportunity, resources, skills and capabilities, and networks as the ingredients that make up opportunities and strategies to generate the continued birth and rebirth of novelty, growth, prosperity and the future images of our society.

REFERENCES

Abdullah, S. and Schuchman, H. (1976). Cerebral leteralisation, bimodal consciousness and related developments in psychiatry, *Research and Communications in Psychology, Psychiatry and behavior,* Vol. 1, pp. 671-679.

Ackoff, R. (1974). *Redesigning the Future,* London, Oxford University Press.

Ackoff, R. L. (1981). *Changing the corporate future: Plan or be planned for,* New York, Wiley.

Adams, J. L. (1979). *Conceptual Blockbusting: A guide to better ideas, 2nd Edition,* New York, W. W. Norton.

Adams, J., L, (1986), *The care and feeding of ideas: a guide to encouraging creativity,* Reading, Mass., Addison-Wesley.

Adorno, T. W., Frankel-Brunswik, E., Levinson, D. J. And Sanford, R. N. (1950). *The Authoritarian Personality,* New York, Harper.

Aguilar-Alonso, A. (1996). Personality and Creativity, *Person. Individ. Diff.,*Vol. 21, No. 6, pp. 959-969.

Amabile, T. M. (1983). *The Social Psychology of Creativity,* New York, Springer-Verlag.

Amabile, T. M. (1996). Creativity in context; Update to the social psychology of creativity, Boulder, CO, Westview Press.

Amabile, T. M. (1998). How to Kill Creativity, *Harvard Business Review,* September-October, pp. 77-87.

Amabile, T. M., Conti, R., Lazenby, H. J., and Herron, M. (1996). Assessing the work environment for creativity, *Academy of Management Journal,* Vol. 39, No. 2, pp. 54-84.

Amabile, T. M., Barsade, S. G., Mueller, J. S., and Staw, B. M. (2005). Affect and Creativity at Work, *Administrative Science Quarterly,* Vol. 50, pp. 367-403.

Andreasan, N.C, O'Leary, D.S., Cizacho, T., Arndt, S., Rezai, K. (1995). Remembering the past: two facets of episodic memory explored with position emission tomography, *American Journal of Psychiatry,* Vol. 152, pp. 1575-1585.

Ansoff, I. H. (1965). *Corporate Strategy,* New York, McGraw-Hill.

Argyris, C. (1990). *Overcoming Organisational Defences: Facilitating Organisational Learning,* Needham Heights, MA, Allyn & Bacon.

Argyris, C. and Schön, D. (1974). *Organisational Learning: A theory of action perspective,* Reading, Mass. Addison Wesley.

Beede, K. E. and kass, S. J. (2006). Engrossed in conversation: the impact of cell phones on simulated driving performance, *Accident Analysis & Prevention,* Vol. 38, pp. 415-421.

Berger, D. M. (1987). *Clinical Empathy,* Northvale, Jason Aronson, Inc.

Birch, D. (1987). *Job Creation,* New York, Free Press.

Boden, M. A. (1990). *The creative mind: Myths and mechanisms,* London, Weidenfeld and Nicolson.

Boden, M. A. (2004). *The Creative Mind: Myths and mechanisms, 2nd Edition,* London, Routledge.

Bowden, E. M. and Beeman, M. J., (1998). Getting the right idea: Semantic activation in the right hemisphere may help solve insight problems, *Psychological Science,* Vol. 9, pp. 435-440.

Bowden, E. M., Jung-Beeman, M., Fleck, J., and Kounios, J. (2005). New Approaches to demystifying insight, *Trends in Cognitive Science,* Vol. 9, pp. 322-328.

Buckner, R. & Carroll, D.C. (2007). Self-projection and the brain, *Trends Cogn. Sci.,* Vol. 11, pp. 49-57.

Buckner, R.L., Andrews-Hanna, J.R., & Schacter, D.L., (2008). The brains default network: Anatomy, Function, and Relevance to Disease, *Annals of the New York Academy of Science,* Vol. 1114, pp. 1-38.

Carlozzi, A. F., Bill, K. S., Eells, G. T. and Hurlburt, J. D. (1995). Empathy as related to creativity, dogmatism and expressiveness, *Journal of Psychology,* Vol. 129, pp. 365-373.

Carlson, K.A. and Russo, J. E. (2001). Biased interpretation of evidence by mock jurors, *Journal of Cognitive Neuroscience,* Vol. 10, pp. 1-34.

Carlson, S. (2005). The Net generation Goes to College, *The Chronicle of Higher Education,* Vol. 52, No. 7, accessed at *http://www.msnc.la.edu/include/learning_resources/todays_ learner/The_Net_ Generation.pdf,* (accessed on 15th May 2010).

Cave, K. E. and Bichot, N. P. (1999). Visualspatial attention: Beyond a spotlight model, *Psychonomic Bulletin & Review,* Vol. 6, pp. 204-223.

Champy, J. (1995). *Re-engineering Management: The Mandate for New Leadership,* New York, Harper Business

Chan Kim, W. and Mauborgne, R. (2005). *Blue Ocean Strategy: How to create uncontested market space and make the competition irrelevant,* Boston, Harvard University Press.

Checkland, P. B. (1981). *Systems Thinking, Systems Practice,* Chichester, John Wiley.

Clouse, R.W. (1993). Humor: It's impact on school culture, Paper presented to the *11th International Conference on Humor and Laughter,* The international Society for Humor Studies, Dulibois European Centre, Miami University, Centre Universitaire De Luxemburg, Lyeu De Garcons De Luxembourg.

Collins, J. (2001). *Good to Great: Why some companies make the leap...and others don't,* New York, HarperCollins.

Cooper, C. and McConville. C. (1993). Affect Intensity: Factor or Artifact?, *Personality and Individual Differences,* Vol. 14, No. 1, pp. 135-143.

Corsini, R. J. (1994). *Encyclopedia of Psychology, 2nd Edition,* New York, John Wiley, pp. 85-89.

Cropley, A. J. (1994). Creative Intelligence: A Concept of True Giftedness, *High Ability Studies,* Vol. 5, No. 1, pp. 6-23.

Cross, K. F., Feather, J. J., and Lynch, R. L. (1994). *Corporate Renaissance: the art of reengineering,* Malden, MA., Blackwell Publishers.

Csikszentmihalyi, M. (1975). *Beyond boredom and anxiety,* San Francisco, Jossey-Bass.

Csikszentmihalyi, M. (1996). *Creativity: Flow and the Psychology of Discovery and Invention,* New York, Harper-Collins.

De Bono, E, (1969). *The Mechanism of Mind,* Middlesex, Penguin Books.

De Bono, E. (1970). *Lateral Thinking,* London, Penguin Books.

De Bono, E. (1976). *Practical Thinking,* Middlesex, Penguin Books.

De Bono, E. (1986). *Six Thinking Hats,* New York, Viking Books.

De Bono, E. (1995). *Edward de Bono's Mind Pack,* London, Dorling Kindersley.

De Geus, A. (1988). Planning as Learning, *Harvard Business Review,* March/April, pp. 70-74.

Deutsch, J. A. and Deutsch, D. (1963). Attention: Some theoretical considerations, *Psychological Review,* Vol. 70, pp. 80-90.

Dewing, K. and battye, G. (1971). Attentional deployment and non-verbal fluency, *Journal of personality and Social Psychology,* Vol. 17, pp. 214-218.

Dietrich, A. (2004). The cognitive neuroscience of creativity, *Psychonomic Bulletin and Review,* Vol. 11, pp. 1011-1026.

DiSessa, A, A, (1993). Towards an epistemology of physics, *Cognition and Instruction,* Vol. 10, No. 2 & 3, pp. 105-125.

Dominowski, R., L. and Jenrick, R. (1972). Effects of hints and interpolated activity on solution of an insight problem, *Pyschonomic Science,* Vol. 26, pp. 335-338.

Drucker, P. F. (1986). *Entrepreneurship and Innovation: Practices and Principals,* New York, HarperCollins.

Dulewicz, V. and Higgs, M. (1998). *Emotional Intelligence: Management fad or valid construct,* Working Paper 9813, Oxford, Henley Management College.

Dykes, M. and McGhie, a. (1976). A comparative study of attentional strategies in schizophrenics and highly creative normal subjects, *British Journal of Psychiatry,* Vol. 128, pp. 50-56.

Edvinsson, L. and Malone, M. S. (1997). *Intellectual Capital: Realizing Your Company's True value by Finding Its Hidden Brainpower,* New York, Harper business.

Eikleberry, C. (2007). *The career guide for the creative and unconventional people,* Berkley, California, Ten Speed press.

Einstein, A. (1950). *Out of my later years,* New York, Philosophical library.

Evarts, E. V. (1990). Foreword: Coordination of movement as a key to higher brain function: Roger W. Sperry's contributions from 1939 to 1952, In: Trevarthen, C. (editor). *Brain Circuits and Functions of the Mind: Essays in Honor of Roger W. Sperry,* Cambridge, Cambridge University Press, pp. xiii-xvii.

Feist, G. J. (1998). A meta-analysis of personality in scientific and artistic creativity, *Personality and social Psychology Review,* Vol. 2, pp. 290-309.

Florida, R. (2002). *The Rise of the Creative Class: And how its transforming Work, Leisure, Community and Everyday Life,* New York, Basic Books.

Fombrum, C. J. and Rindova, V. P. (2000). The road to transparency: Reputation Management at Royal Dutch/Shell, In: Schultz, M., Hatch, M. J. and Larsen, M. H., *The Expressive Organization: Linking Identity, Reputation and the Corporate Brand,* Oxford, Oxford University Press, pp. 77-98.

Foster, R. and Kaplan, S. (2001). *Creative Destruction,* New York, Currency.

Frederickson, B. L. 91998). What good are positive emotions?, *review of General Psychology,* Vol. 2, pp. 300-319.

Frederickson, B. L. (2001). The role of positive emotions in positive psychology, *American Psychologist,* Vol. 56, pp. 218-226.

Fritz, R. (1989). *The path of best resistance: Learning to be creative in your own life,* New York, Fawcett Boulder.

Gaynier, T., (1999), 'Problem Solving Software Delivers WOW! Solutions', *Machine Design,* Vol. 71, No. 19, P. 164.

Gardner, H. (1993). *Creating Minds,* New York, Basic books.

Genter, D. and Markman, A, B. (1997). Structure mapping in analogy and similarity, *American Psychologist,* Vol. 52, pp. 45-56.

George, J. M. and Zhou, J. (2002). Understanding when bad moods foster creativity and good moods don't: The role of context and clarity of feelings, *Journal of Applied Psychology,* Vol. 87, pp. 567-697.

Gibbs, G. (1988). *Learning by Doing: A Guide to Teaching and learning Methods,* Oxford, Oxford Further Education Unit.

Gick, M. L. and Holyoak, K. J. (1980). Analogical problem solving, *Cognitive Psychology,* Vol. 12, pp. 306-355.

Gladwell, M. (2000). *The Tipping Point: How Little Things Can Make a Big Difference,* New York, Little, Brown.

Gordon, W., J., J., (1961), *Synetics,* London, Collier-Macmillan Ltd.

Gusnard, D.A. & Raichie, M.E. (2001). Searching for a baseline: Functional imaging and the resting human brain, *Nat. Rev. Neuosci,* Vol. 2, pp. 685-694.

Gusnard, D.A., Akbudak, E., Shulman, G.L., & Raichle, M.E. (2001). Medial prefrontal cortex and self-referential mental activity relation to a default mode of brain function, *Proc. Natl. Acad. Sci. U.S.A.,* Vol. 98, pp. 4259-4264.

Hamel, G. (2000), *Leading the Revolution,* Boston, Harvard Business School Press.

Hamel, G. and Prahalad, C. K. (1994). *Competing for the Future,* Boston, Harvard Business School Press.

Hammer, M., (1990), 'Re-engineering Work: Don't Automate, Obliterate', *Harvard Business Review,* July-August.

Hammer, M., and Champy, J. (1993) *Re-engineering the Corporation,* New York, Harper Business.

Hart, H. (1950). The integrative function in Creativity, *Psychiatric Quarterly,* Vol. 24, No. 1, pp. 1-16.

Hart, S. and Milstein, M. (1999). Global sustainability and the creative destruction of industries, *Sloan Management Review,* Vol. 41, No. 1, pp. 23-33.

Hart, S. L. and Sharma, S. (2004). Engaging fringe stakeholders for competitive imagination, *Academy of management Executive,* Vol. 18, No. 1, pp. 7-18.

Hartley, A. A. (1992). Attention, In: Craik, F. I. M. and Salthouse, T. A. (Eds.). *The handbook of ageing and cognition,* Hillsdale, NJ., Erlbaum, pp. 3-49.

Hastie, R. and Pennington, N. (2000). Explanation based decision making, In: Connolly, T., Arkes, H. R. and Hammond, K. R. (Eds.). *Judgment and decision making: An interdisciplinary reader, 2nd Edition,* Cambridge, Cambridge University Press, pp. 212-228.

Hicks, M. J. (2004). *Problem Solving and Decision Making: Hard, soft and creative approaches,* London, Thomson learning.

Hodgson, A. M. (1992). Hexagons for systems thinking, *European Journal of Operational Research,* Vol. 59, No. 1, pp. 220-230.

Holyoak, K. J. and Thagard, P. (1997), The analogical mind, *American Psychologist,* Vol. 52, pp. 35-44.

Hooghiemstra, R. (2004). Corporate communication and Impression management – New perspectives on why companies engage in corporate social reporting, *Journal of Business Ethics,* Vol. 27, No. 1-2, pp. 55-68.

Hunter, M. (1994). The need of a multidisciplinary approach to the development of essential oils in Malaysia, paper presented to *8th Asian Symposium on Medicinal Plants, Spices and Other Natural products (ASOMPS VIII)*, Melaka, Malaysia, 12-16th June.

Hunter, M. (2009). *Essential Oils: Art, Science, Agriculture, Industry & Entrepreneurship: A Focus on the Asia-Pacific Region,* New York, Nova.

Inhelder, B. and Piaget, J (1958). *The growth of logical thinking from childhood to adolescence: An essay on the construction of formal operational structures,* London, Routledge.

Isaksen, S. G. and Treffinger, D. J. (1985). *Creative Problem Solving: The Basic Course,* Buffalo, NY, Bearly Ltd.

Isaksen, S. G. and Puccio, G. J. (1988). Adaption-Innovation and the Torrance tests of creative thinking: The level-style issue revisited, *Psychological Reports,* Vol. 63, pp. 659-670.

Ickes, W. (1997). *Empathic Accuracy,* New York, The Guilford Press.

Ingvar, G.H. (1974). Patterns of brain activity revealed by measurements of regional cerebral blood flow, *Alfred Benzon Symposium VIII, Copenhagen.*

Jamison, K. R. (1993). Touched with fire: manic depressive illness and the artistic temperament, New York, Free Press.

Jang, J.H., Jung, W.H., Kang, D-H, Byun, M.S., Kwan, D-H, Choi, C-H, & Kwan, J.S. (2011). Increased default mode network connectivity associated with meditation, *Neuroscience Letters,* Vol. 487, No. 3, pp. 358-362.

Jennings, J. M. and Jacoby, L. L. (1993). Automatic verses intentional uses of memory, aging, attention, and control, *Psychology and Aging,* Vol. 8, pp. 283-293.

Johns, C. C. (1994). Guided reflection, In: Palmer, A., Burns, S. and Bulman, C. (Eds.). *Reflective Practice in Nursing: the Growth of the Professional Practitioner,* Oxford, Blackwell Science.

Johns, C. C, (1995). Framing learning through reflection within Carper's fundamental ways of knowing, *Journal of Advanced Nursing,* Vol. 22, pp. 226-234.

Jones, O. and craven, M. (2001). Expanding capabilities in a mature manufacturing firm: absorptive capacity and the TCS, *International Small Business Journal,* Vol. 19, No. 3, pp. 39-55.

Kelly, G. (1955). *The Psychology of Personal Constructs,* New York, W. W. Norton & Company, Inc.

Kempton, W. (1986). Two theories of home heat control, *Cognitive Science,* Vol. 10, pp. 75-90.

Kenny, L. J. (2003).Using Edward de Bono's six hats game to aid critical thinking and reflection in palliative care, *International Journal of Palliative Nursing,* Vol. 9, No. 3., pp. 105-112.

Kepner, C. H. And Tregoe, B. B. (1981), *The New Rational Manager,* London, John Martin Publishing.

Khandwalla, P. N. (2004). *Lifelong Creativity: An Unending Quest,* New Delhi, Tata McGraw-Hill.

Kirton, M. J. (1994). Five years on, Preface to the second edition, In: Kirton, M. J. (Ed.), *Adaptors and Innovators: Styles of creativity and problem solving, 2nd edition,* London, Routledge, pp. 1-33.

Kirton, M. J. (1994a). A theory of cognitive style, in Kirton, M. J. (Editor). *Adaptors and Innovators: Styles of Creativity and Problem Solving, 2nd edition,* London, Routledge, pp. 1-33.

Kirton, M. J. (1994b). A theory explored, preface to first edition, In: Kirton, M. J. *Adaptors and Innovators: Styles of Creativity and Problem Solving, 1ˢᵗ edition,* London, Routledge, pp.x-xiii.

Klein, K. and Hodges, S. (2001). Gender differences, motivation and empathic accuracy: when it pays to understand, *Personality and Social psychology Bulletin,* Vol. 27, No. 6, pp. 720-730.

Kleinschmidt, E., J. and Cooper, R., G., (1991), 'The Impact of Product Innovativeness on Performance', *Journal of Product Innovation Management, Vol.*8, pp. 240-251.

Knorr, K. (1981). *The manufacture of Knowledge: An essay on the constructivist and contextual nature of science,* Oxford, Pergammon Press.

Koechlin, E., Basso, G., Pietrini, P. panzer, S. and Grafman, J. (1999). The role of the anterior prefrontal cortex in human cognition, *Nature,* Vol. 399, No. 6733, pp. 148-151.

Koestler, A. (1975). *The Art of Creation,* London, Pan Books.

Kohut, S. (1959). Introspection, empathy, and psychoanalysis, *Journal of the American Psychoanalytic Association,* Vol. 7, pp. 459-483.

Kolb, D. (1984). *Experimental Learning: Experience as the Source of Learning,* New Jersey, Prentice Hall.

Kotler, P., Fahey, L., and Jatusripitak, S. (1985). *The New Competition: Meeting the Marketing Challenge from the Far East,* Englewood Cliffs, Prentice-Hall.

Kozhevnikov, M. and Hegarty, M. (2001). Impetus beliefs as default heuristics: Dissociations between explicit and implicit knowledge, *Psychodynamic Bulletin & Review,* Vol. 8, pp. 439-453.

Kramer, A. F. and Larish, J. L. (1996). Aging and dual-task performance, In: Rogers, W. A., Fisk, A. D. and Walker, N. (Eds.). *Aging and skilled performance,* Hillsdale, NJ., Erlbaum, pp. 83-112.

Kuhn, T. (1970). *The structure of scientific revolutions,* Chicago, University of Chicago Press.

Lakoff, G. P. and Johnson, M. (1980). *Metaphors We Live By,* Chicago, University of Chicago Press.

Lakoff, G. P. and Johnson, M. (1999). *Philosophy of the Flesh: The Embodied Mind and its Challenge to Western thought,* Chicago, University of Chicago Press.

Lampert, K. (2005). *Traditions of Compassion: From Religious Duty to Social Activism,* New York, Palgrave-Macmillan.

Larsen, R. J. (1987). The stability of mood variability: A special analytic approach to daily mood assessments, *Journal of Personality and Social Psychology,* Vol. 52, pp. 119-1204.

Larsen, R. J. and Buss, D. M. (2005). *Personality Psychology, 2ⁿᵈ Edition,* New York, McGraw-Hill Higher Education.

Latour, B. (1987). *Science in Action,* Cambridge, MA, Harvard University Press.

Lawley, J. and Tompkins, P. (2000). *Metaphors in Mind: Transformation through symbolic modeling,* London, The Developing Company Press.

Legrenzi, P. (2005). *Creativitá e Innovazione,* Bologna, Italia, II Mulino.

Lemesurier, P. (2003). *The Unknown Nostradamus: 500 year biography,* Ropley, Hampshire, O Books.

Leonard, D. (1998). *Wellsprings of knowledge: building and sustaining the sources of innovation,* Boston, Harvard Business School Press.

Leonard, D. A. and Swap, W. C. (1999). *When the Sparks Fly: Igniting creativity within groups,* Boston, Harvard University Press.

Lightman, A. P. (1989). Magic on the Mind: Physicist's use of metaphor, *The American Scholar,* Winter Issue, pp. 97-101.

Ludwig, A. m. (1992). Creative achievement and psychopathology: a comparison among professions, *American Journal of Psychotherapy,* Vol. 46, pp. 330-356.

March, J. (1991). Exploration and exploitation in organizational learning, *Organization Science,* Vol. 2, No. 1, pp. 71-87.

Marsh, R. L. and Bower, G. H. (1993). Eliciting cryptomnesia: Unconscious plagiarism in a puzzle task, *Journal of Experimental Psychology: learning, memory and Cognition,* Vol. 24, pp. 673-688.

Martindale, C. (1977). Creativity, consciousness, and cortical arousal, *Journal of Altered States of Consciousness,* Vol. 3, pp. 69-87.

Martindale, C. (1999). Biological basis of creativity, In: Sternberg, R. J. (Ed.). *Handbook of creativity,* Cambridge, Cambridge University Press, pp. 137-152.

Meltzoff, A. N. and Decety, J. (2003). What imitation tells us about social cognition: A rapprochement between developmental psychology and cognitive neuroscience, *Philosophical Transactions of the Royal Society London,* Vol. 358, pp. 491-500.

Mendelsohn, G. A. (1976). Associative and attentional processes in creative performance, *Journal of Personality,* Vol. 44, pp. 341-369.

Mezirow, J. (181). A critical theory of adult learning and education, *Adult Education,* Vol. 32, No. 1, pp. 3-24.

Miller, A. I. (1986). *Imagery and Scientific Thought,* Cambridge, MA, MIT Press.

Miller, W. C., Couger, J. D. and Higgins, L. F. (1998). Innovation Styles of IS Personnel vs. Other Occupations, *Creativity and Innovation Management,* Vol. 5, No. 4, pp. 226-233.

Mitroff, I. I. and Linstone, H. A. (1993). *The Unbounded Mind: breaking the chains of traditional business thinking,* New York, Oxford University Press.

Moray, N. (1959). Attention in dichotic listening: Affective cues and the influence of instructions, *Quarterly Journal of Experimental Psychology,* Vol. 11, pp. 56-60.

Moseley, D., Baumfield, V., Elliot, J., Gregson, M. Higgins, S., Miller, J., and Newton, D. (2005). De Bono's lateral and parallel thinking tools, In: Moseley, D. (Ed.). *Frameworks for Thinking,* Cambridge, Cambridge University Press.

Naisbitt, J. (1982). *Megatrends: Ten New Directions Transforming Our lives,* New York, Warner.

Newell, A. and Simon, H. A. (1972). *Human Problem Solving,* Englewood Cliffs, NJ, Prentice-Hall.

Newman, W., H., Summer, C., E. and Warren, K., E., (1972), *The Process of Management, 3rd. Ed.,* Englewood Cliffs, Prentice-Hall.

O'Connor, J. and Seymour, J. (1995). *Introducing NLP: Psychological Skills for understanding and influencing people,* London, Thorsons

Olton, R., M., (1979). Experimental studies of incubation: searching for the elusive, *Journal of Creative Behavior,* Vol. 13, pp. 9-22.

Olton, R., M. and Johnson, D. M. (1976). Mechanisms of incubation in creative problem solving, *American Journal of Psychology,* Vol. 89, pp. 617-630.

Osborn, A., F., (1953), *Applied Imagination,* New York, Charles Scribner's Sons.

Ouchi, W. G. (1981). *Theory Z: How American Business can meet the Japanese Challenge,* Reading, Mass, Addison-Wesley.

Parnes, S. J. P. (1972). Programming creative behavior, In: Taylor, C. W. (Ed.), *Climate for Creativity,* New York, Pergamon, pp. 198-221.

Parnes, S. J. and Meadow, A. (1963). Development of individual creative talent, In: Taylor, C. W. And Barron, F. (eds.). *Scientific Creativity,* New York, Wiley.

Parson, E. R. (1993). Ethnotherapeutic Empathy (EthE)- Part 1: Definition, Theory, and Practice, *Journal of Contemporary Psychotherapy,* Vol. 23, No. 1, pp. 5-18.

Paul, R. W. and Elder, L. (2002). *Critical Thinking: Tools for taking charge of your professional and personal life,* Upper Saddle River, Financial Times-Prentice Hall.

Piaget, J. (1970). *The child's conception of movement and speed,* New York, Basic Books.

Pidd, M. (2003) *Tools for Thinking,* Chichester, Wiley.

Piirto, J. (1998). *Understanding those who create,* Scottsdale, Arizona, Gufted Psychology Press, Inc.

Politis, J. D. (2005). Dispersed leadership predictor of the work environment for creativity and productivity, *European Journal of Innovation Management,* Vol. 8, No. 2, pp. 182-204.

Posner, M. I. (1980). Orienting of attention, *Quarterly Journal Experimental Psychology,* Vol. 32, pp. 3-25.

Prince, G. M, (1998). *Mind Spring,* London, Changemaker Publications.

Prince, G. M., Weaver, W. T. And Logan-Prince, K. (2000). Liberating creativity and learning Part 1: Understanding the inhibitors of good thinking, In: Nolan, V. (Ed.). *Creative Education: Educating a nation of innovators,* Stoke, Manderville, Bucks, Synectics Education Initiative.

Proctor, T. (1999). *Creative Problem Solving for Managers,* London, Routledge.

Proffitt, D. R., Kaiser, M. K. and Whelan, S. M. (1990). Understanding wheel dynamics, *Cognitive Science,* Vol. 22, pp. 342-373.

Puccio, G. J. (2002). Foursight Overview& rationale for creation, *Foursight Technical Manual, http://www.foursightonline.com/dojo/4/manual.pdf,* (accessed 7th April 2010).

Richards, R. (1994). Creativity and bipolar mood swings: Why the association? In Shaw, M. P. and Runco, A. (Eds.), *Creativity and Affect,* Norwood, NJ, Ablex, pp. 127-146.

Robertson-Riegler, G., and Robertson-Riegler, B. (2008). *Cognitive Psychology: Applying the Science of the Mind, 2nd Edition,* Boston, Pearson Education, Inc.

Rogers, C. R. (1975). Empathic: An unappreciated way of being, *The Counseling Psychologist,* Vol. 5, pp. 2-10.

Rokeach, M. (1960). *The Open and Closed Mind: Investigations into the nature of belief systems and personality systems,* New York, Basic Books.

Rothenberg, A. (1990). *Creativity and madness: New findings and old stereotypes*, Baltimore, MD., John Hopkins University Press.

Rowe, A. J. (2004). *Creative Intelligence: Discovering the Innovative Potential in Ourselves and Others,* Upper Saddle River, Pearson Education.

Russ, S. W. (1993). *Affect & Creativity: The role of affect and play in the creative process,* Hillsdale, NJ., Lawrence Erlbaum associates, Inc.

Senge, P. M. (2006). *The Fifth Discipline: The art and practice of the learning organization, (revised and updated edition),* London, Random House.

Shane, S. and Venkataraman, S. (2000). The promise of entrepreneurship as a field of research, *Academy of Management Review,* Vol. 25, pp. 217-226.

Shapiro, S. (1984). Classic perspectives in meditation: toward an empirical understanding of mediatation as an altered state of consciousness, In: Shapiro, D. and Walsch, R. (Eds.), *Meditation: classic and Contemporary Perspectives,* New York, Aldine Publishing Company.

Shepard, R. N. (1988). The imagination of a scientists, In: Egan, K. and Nadaner, D., (Eds.). *Imagination and Education,* New York, Teachers College Press, pp. 153-183.

Simonton, D. K. (1994). *Greatness,* New York, Guilford.

Simonton, D. K. (2000). Creativity: Cognitive, Personal, Developmental, and Social Aspects, *American Psychologist,* Vol. 55, No. 1, pp. 151-158.

Singer, W. (2009). The Brain, a Complex Self-Organizing System, *European Review,* Vol. 17, No. 2, pp. 321-329.

Smith, S. M. (1995). Getting into and out of mental ruts: a theory of fixation, incubation and insight, In: Sternberg, R. J. and Davidson, J. E. (Eds.), *The nature of insight,* Cambridge, MA., MIT Press.

Smith, S. M. and Blankenship, S. E. (1991). Incubation effects, *Bulletin of the Psychonomic Society,* Vol. 27, pp. 311-314.

Smith, S. M. (2003). The constraining effects of initial ideas, In: Paulus, P. B. and Nijstad, B. A, (Eds.). *Group creativity: Innovation through collaboration,* New York, Oxford University Press, pp. 15-31.

Smith, S, M., Ward, T. B., and Finke, R. A. (1994). *The Creative Cognition Approach,* Cambridge, MA, MIT Press.

Soto, D., and Blanco, M. J. (2004). Spatial attention and object-based attention: A comparison within a single task, *Vision Research,* Vol. 44, pp. 69-81.

Stacey, R. (1996). *Complexity and Creativity in Organizations,* San Francisco, Barren-Koehler Publications.

Sternberg, R. J. (1985). *Beyond IQ: A triarchic theory of human intelligence,* New York, Cambridge University Press.

Sternberg, R. J. and Lubart, T. L. (1999). The concept of creativity, In: Sternberg, R. J. (Ed.). *Handbook of Creativity,* Cambridge, Cambridge University Press.

Sternberg, R. J. and Lubart, T. I. (1996). Investing in Creativity, *American Psychologist,* Vol. 51, No. 7, pp. 677-688.

Sternberg, R. J. (2002). Successful Intelligence: A New Approach to leadership, In: Riggio, R. E., Murphy, S. E, and Pirozzolo, F. J. (Eds.). *Multiple Intelligences and Leadership,* Mahwah, NJ., Lawrence Erlbaum Associates, Inc., pp. 9-28.

Sternberg, R. J. (1988). *The nature of creativity: Contemporary Psychological Perspectives,* Cambridge, Cambridge University Press.

Strayer, D. L. and Drews, F. A. (2004). Profiles in driver distraction: Effects of cell phone conversations on younger and older drivers, *Human Factors,* Vol. 46, pp. 640-649.

Stuss, D. and benson, D. F. (1986). *The Frontal Lobes,* New York, Raven Press.

Talwar, R. (1993). Business re-engineering – a strategy driven approach, *Long range Planning,* Vol. 26, No. 6, pp. 22-40.

Toulmin, S. (1972). *Human Understanding,* Princeton, NJ, Princeton.

Triesman, A. (1960). Contextual cues in selective listening, *Quarterly Journal of Experimental Psychology,* Vol. 12, pp. 242-248.

Van Gundy, A. B. (1988). *Techniques of structured problem solving, 2nd Edition,* New York, Van Nostrand Reinhold.

Vernon, P. E. (1970). *Creativity,* Middlesex, UK, Penguin Books.

Wadhwa, V., Freeman, R. and Rising, B. (2008). *Education and tech Entrepreneurship,* Ewing Marion Kauffman Foundation, *http://www.kauffman.org/uploadedfiles/Education_Tech_Ent_061108.pdf,* (accessed 15th May 2009).

Wagner, U., Gais, S., Haider, H., Verleger, R. and Born, J. (2004). Sleep inspires insight, *Nature,* Vol. 427, pp. 352-355.

Wallas, G. (1926). *The Art of Thought,* London, J. Cape.

Weisberg, R. W. (1988). Problem solving and creativity, In: Sternberg, R. J. (Ed.). *The nature of Creativity: Contemporary Psychological Perspectives,* Cambridge. Cambridge University Press, pp. 148-176.

Weiss, H. M. and Cropanzano, R. (1996). Affective events theory: A theoretical discussion of the structure, causes and consequences of affective experiences at work, In: Staw, B. M. and Cummings, L. L. (Eds.), *Research in Organizational Behavior,* Greenwich, CT, JAI Press.

Wertheimer, M. (1982). *Productive Thinking,* Chicago, University of Chicago Press.

Wheeler, M., Stuss, D., and Tulving, E. (1997). Toward a theory of episodic memory: The frontal lobes and autonoetic consciousness, *Psychological Bulletin,* Vol. 121, No. 3, pp. 331-354.

Whiting, C., S., (1955), 'Operational Techniques of Creative Thinking', *Advanced Management,* October.

Wind, Y (J), and Crook, C. (2006). *The Power of Impossible thinking: transform the business of your life and the life of your business,* Upper Saddle River, NJ, Wharton School publishing.

Zohor, D. and Marshall, I. (2000). *Spiritual Intelligence: The ultimate intelligence,* London, Bloomsburg Publishing.

INDEX

B

C

F

H

I

U

V

Z